# Lecture Notes in Computer Science    1603

Edited by G. Goos, J. Hartmanis and J. van Leeuwen

**Springer**

*Berlin*
*Heidelberg*
*New York*
*Barcelona*
*Hong Kong*
*London*
*Milan*
*Paris*
*Singapore*
*Tokyo*

Jan Vitek   Christian D. Jensen (Eds.)

# Secure Internet Programming

## Security Issues
## for Mobile and Distributed Objects

Springer

Series Editors

Gerhard Goos, Karlsruhe University, Germany
Juris Hartmanis, Cornell University, NY, USA
Jan van Leeuwen, Utrecht University, The Netherlands


Volume Editors

Jan Vitek
University of Geneva, Object Systems Group
CH-1211 Geneva 4, Switzerland
E-mail: Jan.Vitek@cui.unige.ch

Christian D. Jensen
Trinity College Dublin, Department of Computer Science
O'Reilly Institute, Dublin 2, Ireland
E-mail: Christian.Jensen@cs.tcd.ie


Cataloging-in-Publication data applied for


Die Deutsche Bibliothek - CIP-Einheitsaufnahme

Secure Internet programming : security issues for mobile and distributed
objects / Jan Vitek ; Christian D. Jensen (ed.). - Berlin ; Heidelberg ; New
York ; Barcelona ; Hong Kong ; London ; Milan ; Paris ; Singapore ; Tokyo
: Springer, 1999
  (Lecture notes in computer science ; Vol. 1603)
  ISBN 3-540-66130-1


CR Subject Classification (1998): C.2, D.1.3, D.1.5, D.2.4, H.4.3, I.2, K.4.4,
K.5.1, K.6.5

ISSN 0302-9743
ISBN 3-540-66130-1 Springer-Verlag Berlin Heidelberg New York

© Springer-Verlag Berlin Heidelberg 1999
Printed in Germany

Typesetting: Camera-ready by author
SPIN: 10704834    06/3142 – 5 4 3 2 1 0    Printed on acid-free paper

# Preface

This book is a collection of articles on security in large–scale open distributed systems and, in particular, issues pertaining to distributed and mobile object technologies. The role of open systems is to provide an infrastructure for assembling global applications out of software and hardware components coming from multiple sources. Open systems rely on publicly available standards to permit heterogeneous components to interact. The Internet is the archetype of an open distributed system. Standards such as HTTP, HTML, and XML together with the widespread adoption of the Java language are the cornerstones of many distributed systems. Distributed object technologies such as RMI, CORBA, and DCOM, as well as more ambitious mobile technologies (mobile agents, ambients, etc.) offer a large palette of approaches to building those systems.

While the benefits of these technological solutions are undeniable, they raise legitimate security questions. What kind of trust can we have in a system composed of components belonging to different organisations and used by users from all corners of the world? Open systems lack a common trusted computing base, and often have minimal authentication and authorisation frameworks. The possibility of moving code from site to site raises the stakes even higher. We must be able to establish trust among users and programs, and to specify policies that will regulate the use of resources and the spread of information. We must find ways to integrate untrusted downloaded programs with audited local code so that security remains meaningful. We must investigate means to systematically enforce security properties in programming languages for those systems. And, if everything else fails, we must be able to diagnose when policies have been breached and pinpoint the guilty party.

These are a few of the challenges facing us today. The papers in this collection are a snapshot of this very active research area.

The idea for this book arose from a number of discussions and presentations given at two workshops: the *ECOOP Workshop on Distributed Object Security* (EWDOS) and the *Mobile Object Systems: Secure Internet Mobile Computations* (MOS98) workshop held in June 1998 in conjunction with the European Conference on Object–Oriented Programming in Brussels. Both workshops were reviewed and the authors of the best papers of each invited to contribute to this volume. In addition to these core papers, a small number of classic papers in the field were reprinted. The outcome is a well balanced collection of papers that explore many of the essential questions outlined above.

## Overview

The book is organised in three parts: (I) Foundations, (II) Concepts, and (III) Implementation, followed by an appendix.

Part I of the book contains chapters giving background and dealing with fundamental issues in trust, programming, and mobile computations in large scale open distributed systems. The paper by Swarup and Fábrega is a comprehensive study of trust in open distributed systems. The paper by Abadi discusses abstractions for protection and

VI

the correctness of their implementation. The paper by Ancona et al. analyses the use of reflection to integrate authorisation mechanisms into an object–oriented system. The paper by Cardelli discusses the difficulties of computing with mobility and proposes a unified framework to overcome these difficulties based on mobile computational ambients. The paper by Hennesy and Riely studies the type safety properties of mobile code in an open distributed system. The paper by De Nicola et al. describes the security mechanisms of the programming language KLAIM, that is used to program mobile agents. The paper by Leroy and Rouaix formulates and proves security properties that well–typed applets possess and identifies sufficient conditions for the execution environment to be safe.

Part II contains descriptions of general concepts in security in open distributed systems. The paper by Blaze et al. describes the use of trust management engines to avoid the need to resolve "identities" in an authorisation decision. The paper by Aura discusses the advantages and limitations of delegation certificates in access control mechanisms. The paper by Brose proposes a new fine grained access control model for CORBA based on views. The paper by Tschudin introduces the concept of apoptosis (programmed death) in mobile code based services. The paper by Yee discusses the problem of ensuring confidentiality and integrity for mobile agents. The paper by Roth describes how two co–operating agents, executing on different machines, can be used to protect the confidentiality and integrity of the individual agent against tampering.

Part III contains papers detailing implementations of security concepts in open distributed systems. Most of the papers in this part also introduce new security concepts, but devote a large portion to a particular implementation of these concepts. The paper by Jaeger describes the use of role based access control policies in configurable systems and its implementation in the Lava Security Architecture. The paper by Grimm and Bershad discusses secure execution of possibly untrusted extensions in the SPIN extensible operating system. The paper by Jones describes a simple and efficient way of interposing code between user programs and the underlying system's interface. The paper by von Eicken et al. discusses the inadequacy of object references for access control and describes an implementation of capabilities in the J–Kernel. The paper by van Doorn et al. describes the implementation of secure network objects, which is an extension of Modula–3 network objects. The paper by Edjlali et al. describes an access control mechanism in which access is granted based on the history of interactions with the requesting principal. The paper by Alexander et al. discusses security issues in active networks, and the solutions that have been implemented in the Secure Active Network Environment. The paper by Hulaas et al. discusses the problem of mobile agent interactions in an open environment. The paper by Wilhelm et al. describes how trusted tamper resistant devices can be used to ensure the integrity of mobile agents.

**Acknowledgements**

We would like to thank the members of the programme committees of the two workshops. For EWDOS, they were: George Coulouris, Leendert van Doorn, Li Gong, Daniel Hagimont, Trent Jaeger. For MOS98, the committee included: Martín Abadi, Brian Bershad, Ciarán Bryce, Luca Cardelli, Giuseppe Castagna, Robert Gray, Leila

Ismail, Dag Johansen, Eric Jul, Doug Lea, Christian Tschudin, Dennis Volpano. Furthermore, we wish to thank: Vinny Cahill, Daniel LeMetayer, Tommy Thorn, Hitesh Tewari, and Mary Ellen Zurko for additional reviewing, and Alfred Hofmann from Springer–Verlag for his support in getting the volume published.

February 1999                                                    J. Vitek and C. D. Jensen

# Table of Contents

---

**III Implementations**

---

---

**IV Appendix**

---

# Part I

# Foundations

# Trust: Benefits, Models, and Mechanisms

Vipin Swarup and Javier Thayer Fábrega

**Abstract.** Trust provides many practical benefits in open distributed systems. It enables cooperation between pairs of entities, provides a safe and inexpensive basis for lowering access barriers to secured resources, and facilitates complex transactions among multiple entities. In this paper, we describe a wide range of notions and aspects of trust in open systems, with particular focus on trust between autonomous entities. We argue for computational models and mechanisms that enable trust between entities to be produced, manipulated and degraded and we summarize the state-of-the-art from this perspective.

## 1 Introduction

Trust is a fundamental concept in computer security. However, while many central concepts in computer security such as privacy and integrity now have commonly accepted definitions, trust remains an ambiguous term. There are numerous notions of trust in the computer security literature, including trust as assurance in the correct and secure functioning of software, computer systems, and legal systems; trust as belief in the benevolent, honest, competent, and predictable behavior of autonomous agents (human or software); and trust as a tendency to depend on others. Different kinds of trust often satisfy different properties; for instance, some kinds of trust are transitive (e.g., trust in the context of network administration tools such as SATAN [11]) while others are not (e.g., trust in the context of name-key binding mechanisms such as PGP).

Trust-based security architectures are widely deployed. For instance, in network administration, trust is a relationship that exists between an entity managing local resources and a remote client, whenever that client can access local resources without local authentication or authorization (e.g., .rhost files in Unix) [11]. In network security, a prevalent paradigm is to partition the network into regions and to use firewalls to filter network packets between regions; the filtering policies implemented by the firewalls are based on the trust relationships between regions [16]. In distributed system security, participants use identity certificates to identify each other; they need to trust other participants to issue good certificates and to recommend reliable third parties for accomplishing specific tasks, including signing certificates [14, 9]. In mobile agent security, a mobile agent may be given access to resources at a host based on the host's level of trust in the agent; this trust can depend on many factors including the endorser of the agent, the hosts that the agent has visited in the past [12, 2], and the access requests that the agent has made in the past [8].

Trust is important due to the many practical benefits it provides. For instance, trust serves many important roles in agent societies: it is central to agents engaging in cooperative activities; it provides an inexpensive (though often imprecise) basis for lowering expensive access barriers between agents; and it enables agents to form clusters within which complex transactions have a high likelihood of success. We need computational models of trust that describe how trust between autonomous agents can be produced, manipulated, and degraded. Agents can develop trust in each other by using mechanisms that implement those models [21, 27]. This will enable software agents to trade in unfamiliar environments with unfamiliar trading partners by relying on trust that is built remotely across computer networks and appears essential for agents to play an important role in distributed electronic commerce.

In this paper, we elaborate on the various distinctions on trust that are mentioned above, drawing from a vast literature on trust in the social sciences and in computer security. In Section 2, we present a classification of the various meanings of trust. Although we consider the full range of meanings of trust, our focus is on trust between agents and not on system trust or dispositional trust. In Section 3, we motivate the importance of trust by describing its central role in three significant areas: cooperation, lowering of access barriers, and clustering. In Section 4, we describe how trust can be produced, manipulated, and degraded. In Section 5, we summarize graph models of trust propagation that have been proposed in the literature. Section 6 concludes this paper.

## 2   Classification

Trust is not a well-defined concept – numerous definitions of trust can be found in the literature. McKnight and Chervany [23] have proposed a classification system that distinguishes between several kinds of trust. Although this classification is not comprehensive, it does cover some of the more important forms of trust and is useful in describing different aspects of a computational trust model. We summarize their classification scheme below; we have grouped their trust classes into three broad categories: system trust, entity trust, and dispositional trust.

**System Trust:** "The extent to which an entity believes that proper system structures are in place to enable it to anticipate a successful future endeavor." [23] Safeguards such as regulations, guarantees, and security mechanisms reduce the potential negative consequences of trusting behavior. Stabilizing intermediaries (e.g., insurance companies) reduce uncertainty and risk (e.g., financial risk). Most work in information systems security is aimed at managing risk, thus increasing system trust and enabling entities to feel more secure in trusting others.

**Entity Trust:** Entity trust includes all trust relationships between two or more entities. These relationships can be further categorized as follows:

**Trusting Belief:** "The extent to which an entity believes that another entity is willing and able to act in the former's best interests." [23] The belief can be based on a variety of attributes including the other's benevolence, honesty, competence, and predictability. Assessing these attributes directly is an inherently subjective process and is typically handled by procedural mechanisms.

As an example, consider public key certification schemes (e.g., PGP and X.509) that use identify certificates to bind keys to names. The schemes include computational trust models [14, 10] that enable the holder of a set of certificates to decide whether to believe a particular name-key binding. This decision may be based on the holder's belief in the trustworthiness of the issuers of the certificates. We will examine several such models in Section 5.

**Trusting Intention:** "The extent to which an entity is willing to depend on another entity in a given situation with a feeling of relative security, even though negative consequences are possible." [23] For instance, if a trust metric for the PGP trust model yields some trust value for the issuer of an identity certificate, the holder of the certificate must decide whether the trust value is sufficient for it to believe the name-key binding stated in the certificate. This decision function represents the trusting intention of the holder.

**Trusting Behavior:** "The extent to which an entity depends on another entity in a given situation with a feeling of relative security, even though negative consequences are possible." [23]. For instance, a .rhost file on a Unix host represents unconditional trusting behavior. If a user joe on host orion creates a .rhost file that contains the name of host pluto, then any user authenticated as joe on pluto can access joe's account on orion without further authentication. Thus joe must trust pluto to enforce appropriate security safeguards to protect joe's account on orion.

Trusting belief, intention, and behavior are described as relations between two entities. However, these same notions can describe trust relationships between multiple entities. McKnight and Chervany [23] identify the following kind of multi-entity trust as important and prevalent:

**Situational Decision to Trust:** "The extent to which an entity intends to depend on other entities in a given situation." [23] For instance, a user may intend to depend on the system administrators (to recover her files) in the event that her files get corrupted.

**Dispositional Trust:** "The extent to which an entity has a consistent tendency to trust across a broad spectrum of situations and entities." [23] This kind of trust may be viewed as a policy or strategy which produces trusting intentions. It could arise because the entity believes others to be trustworthy in general, or because it expects to obtain better outcomes by trusting others irrespective of whether they are trustworthy. In computational trust models, dispositional trust is manifested by threshold values. For instance, an entity may enter a dependency relationship with another entity if its trusting belief expectation in that entity exceeds its dispositional trust threshold.

In the remainder of this paper, we explore different aspects of entity trust between two or more autonomous agents. Although we do not consider the subcategories of entity trust in this paper, a real-world computational model of entity trust must account for these distinctions.

# 3 Benefits

System trust plays an important role in enabling and sustaining cooperation between agents. Entity trust between two agents reduces the costs of identification and access control between the agents, while entity trust among multiple agents reduces the costs of complex multi-agent transactions. These benefits underscore the importance of trust in distributed agent systems.

## 3.1 Enabling Cooperation

Agents will be willing to cooperate (e.g., engage in e-commerce transactions) only if they trust that the system satisfies certain properties (e.g., their credit card numbers are protected). Williams [32] defines cooperation as follows: "Two agents *cooperate* when they engage in a joint venture for the outcome of which the actions of each are necessary, and where a necessary action by at least one of them is not under the immediate control of the other". Under this definition, if two agents cooperate, then at least one of them depends on the other. For instance, in an e-commerce transaction, the buyer of a product depends on the seller to dispatch the product, while the seller depends on the buyer to dispatch payment; in this situation, the buyer and seller depend on each other.

Williams [32] asserts that cooperation can arise only in the presence of two motivations (in the same society, not necessarily in the same agent): agents must be motivated to enter into dependent positions, and agents must be motivated not to defect if they are in a non-dependent position. Dependent agents need some degree of assurance that non-dependent agents will not defect, and cooperation will happen only if this assurance is to some extent well based. System trust plays an important role in providing this assurance, thus enabling and sustaining cooperation among agents.

## 3.2 Lowering Access Barriers

A major goal of security is the protection of resources from undesired access. In practice, this is achieved by creating barriers around resources. A barrier may constrain every access to a resource, or it may constrain access into a domain from which a number of resources may be accessed without further constraints. In the physical world, permission to traverse a barrier may depend on the identity of the requestor and perhaps other considerations such as payment of a fee. The identity of the requestor is determined by a picture ID such as a license or a passport and the adequacy of the fee is determined by characteristics of the paper used for payment such as treasury watermarks and the denomination of the bill.

Traversing access barriers can be tedious, consume time and resources, and discourage commerce and productive behavior. For example, Fukuyama [13] mentions the possibility of patrons sneaking out of restaurants without paying (and thus having illegal access to food). To prevent this, owners could require cash deposits before seating patrons. Conversely, patrons who fear being cheated could demand certificates of competence before entering restaurants. The resulting war of mistrust would likely lead to restaurants going out of business and the public losing the pleasures of dining out.

Similarly, U.S. stores consider a current driver's license from any U.S. state as valid identification for cashing checks, thus trusting the states' ability to issue valid name-picture certificates. The cost to the stores and the inconvenience to shoppers would be too great if each store had to issue its own identity certificates.

As another example, consider a person who wishes to purchase a round-the-world air ticket at a low price. She locates a travel agent who can provide her with a ticket at a substantially lower price than the airline's lowest published fare. The travel agent obtains the ticket from a consolidator who purchases blocks of unsold seats from the airline at discount prices. This is a complex transaction involving four agents and multiple trust relationships. The prospective traveler must trust the travel agent to provide her with a valid ticket, the consolidator to pay the airline before the flight, and the airline to provide her with transportation. The travel agent must trust the consolidator to obtain seats. These trust relationships reduce the need for safeguards (such as legal contracts) that would increase the cost of the transaction.

These examples provide analogies to why trust is needed in computer security. In particular, trust reduces the cost of access control. It is a basis for granting privilege by lowering access barriers selectively [5]. Further, trust reduces the cost of identification. It provides an identification infrastructure which decentralizes the creation of identity certificates [4].

## 3.3 Creating Communities

Dual to the notion of trust as a means of reducing the cost of access barriers between individuals is that of trust as an indication of the willingness of individuals to associate. Fukuyama [13] defines sociability as a measure of the propensity to form associations (independent of the efficacy of those associations). Human associations can be classified by the nature of their origins, for instance, those that originate from family relationships or those that are created by the initiative of some authority such as the state. Spontaneous sociability, that is propensity to form associations derived from sources other than kinship or the state, is a prerequisite for the formation of a large class of organizations. One of Fukuyama's main theses is that spontaneous sociability is a cultural characteristic directly related to the levels of trust in a society.

These concepts are useful in understanding how culture affects economic institutions, particularly cooperative behavior in organizations and the structure of business ownership. For instance, a large organization may require processes that involve many employees and have no central point of control. For these processes to succeed, employees must be motivated to initiate and participate in activities which might fail if other employees in the workflow do not perform competently. This motivation requires trust in the capabilities and motivations of other employees in the organization. This trust goes beyond system trust or pairwise trust.

However, these concepts also provide a framework for understanding associations in any community, including software agents. In order for this approach to be useful in explaining the growth and dynamics of associations, there has to be some account of counterbalancing forces, such as diminishing economies of scale, which limit the size of associations.

At a more abstract level, the propensity to form associations within some set of individuals is a measure of the capacity for clustering. There are many examples of clustering in physics, for instance, Ising models to explain spontaneous ferromagnetism. To produce an economic model along similar lines, note that a successful business must be very effective in performing tasks that require many transactions. This suggests a transaction model for certain kinds of social activities. In this model, we associate a transaction $T(k_1, k_2, \alpha)$ with individuals $k_1, k_2$ and activities $\alpha$. The transaction $T(k_1, k_2, \alpha)$ may succeed or fail. A *cluster* is a set of individuals in which suites of transactions between individuals in the set are likely to succeed.

## 3.4 Example: Mobile Computations

Mobile computations offer a paradigm for computing in the presence of network access barriers. For instance, consider two agents that are separated by a firewall and that wish to communicate using a custom protocol that is blocked by the firewall. One common solution to this problem is for the agents to tunnel through the firewall—the agents encapsulate their communications as data within a protocol that the firewall accepts, thus bypassing the filtering constraints of the firewall. Mobile computations offer another solution whereby an agent migrates across the firewall. The firewall may enforce a filtering policy on agent migration; thereafter, the agents may communicate without restriction.

However, when mobile computations cross the security domain boundaries guarded by firewalls, they may cause trust relationships to change in complex ways [2, 12]. For instance, a host's trust in a software agent may vary depending on whether the agent has migrated through other potentially hostile hosts. As another example, a system may no longer assume that all hosts within a security domain are trusted equally (since hosts may be mobile), or that all code installed in a domain is trusted (since code may be mobile).

Further, mobile agent systems involve complex trust relationships among hosts, program code, agents, and users. For instance, agent routing policies may prevent agents from migrating to untrusted servers. However, since agents are routed and executed by servers, the agents must trust some servers to enforce their routing policies. The servers, in turn, may have to trust incoming agents to respect their security policies.

The problems are exacerbated in wide-area networks where entities have no knowledge of most other entities or of their trust relationships. Traditional static assumptions about trust are inappropriate—these systems need trust models that enable complex trust decision rules to be established dynamically. As described earlier, this dynamically determined trust can play an important role in enabling cooperation between agents, lowering access barriers between agents and hosts, and supporting the clustering of agents into communities.

# 4 Operations

Entity trust between autonomous agents can be produced by operations such as multiple successful interactions, manipulated by operations such as propagation and substitution, and degraded by operations such as natural decay and malicious attacks.

## 4.1 Production

Trust can be established *directly* between two or more agents in a variety of ways [24, 18].

**Swift trust** is based on a series of hedges in which agents behave in a trusting manner but also hedge to reduce the risks of betrayal. *Blind trust* is an extreme case of this where an agent trusts without hedges because that is the best choice in its situation.

**Deterrence-based trust** is based on a credible threat of punishment for cheating or failing to cooperate. For instance, when there are repeated interactions, cheaters are deterred by the possibility of being punished in the future. Audit and audit reduction mechanisms are examples of this, where the mechanisms raise a credible threat of being detected and punished for circumventing the security policy of a system.

**Knowledge-based trust** is based on sufficient knowledge of other agents' dispositions so that their behavior can be predicted reliably. For instance, in history-based access control models [8], an agent's access rights depend on the access requests made by the agent in the past. In some probabilistic models [22], an agent's trust in another agent depends on the number of successful interactions the former has had with the latter.

**Identification-based trust** is based on common preferences where agents have taken on the needs and desires of others as personal goals and act in ways that consider joint gains. For instance, a firewall establishes a trust domain within which all agents trust each other based on some common identification such as being agents of employees of the same company.

**Social trust** is based on social relationships between people, for instance, neutrality and social status. Social interactions help define the identities and social worth of people, and these in turn influence social relationships. Social trust is based on emotions in contrast with the previous operations which are based on rational thought. In agent systems, social trust appears in models where one's trust in an agent is based on one's social trust in the principals that have signed (and hence endorsed) the agent.

Current computational trust models assume that direct trust valuations are given as input and they describe how to compute indirect trust (see Section 4.2). Establishing and assessing direct trust is considered to be subjective and is outside the scope of these models. By contrast, agent-based systems cannot rely on manual trust valuations and need technical mechanisms for producing trust directly.

## 4.2 Manipulation

An agent may not be able to establish trust in another agent directly. The agent can then use mechanisms that obviate the need to establish the trust [26], or mechanisms to establish trust indirectly (that is, involving other "third-party" agents).

**Trust substitution** mechanisms alter the trust relationships that would otherwise be required between agents. These include technical solutions that eliminate one's need to trust an agent, substituting it with trust in a third party instead. For instance, in the physical world, the trustworthiness of a tamper-resistant smartcard depends on the manufacturer of the card and is independent of the entity that physically hosts the card. If the card is used for electronic commerce, then participants in transactions need only trust the manufacturer of the card and not necessarily its owner. Mobile cryptography [30] provides similar functionality for software agents.

**Trust propagation** mechanisms propagate trust from one principal to another. This kind of trust is known as *indirect trust*. For instance, professional organizations and recommendation services impart trust by virtue of their reputations, and insurance companies impart trust by increasing the (financial) predictability of outcomes. In all these cases, trust flows from reputable institutions to other principals.

Propagation mechanisms typically combine different trust valuations from different principals into new trust valuations. Certain kinds of trust are transitive while others are not. Trusting behavior (see Section 2) is often transitive. For instance, if a UNIX host venus has a trusting relationship with host pluto via a .rhost file, and pluto has a similar relationship with host orion, then venus also has a trusting behavior relationship with orion. Trusting beliefs are often not transitive. For instance, if Nisha trusts Ignacio to make good recommendations, and Ignacio trusts William to make good recommendations, then Nisha does not necessarily trust William. Most work on formal computational trust models deals with non-transitive propagation trust; the aim of these models is to address the name-key binding problem of identification and authentication. Section 5 presents a summary of such models.

## 4.3 Degradation

Trust is time dependent. In fact, without reinforcing interactions, trust may decay naturally over time. Trust may also degrade during propagation. Further, trust is subject to attack in that principals may subvert some of the elements that support a network of trust. For instance, a human principal can be physically attacked and its keying material stolen.

Trust can also be destroyed by systematic operations and techniques, usually in situations where compromise is suspected. This may protect honest agents from making decisions on biased trust data. Key revocation schemes are an example of this—a key revocation certificate is issued when a key may be compromised; the certificate destroys other agents' trust in the revoked key.

## 5 Models

The social science literature contains numerous models of trust production while the computer security literature contains numerous models of trust propagation. Trust production is a subjective process for which adequate computational models have yet to be developed. Thus, in this section, we examine formal models of trust propagation only and we describe some of their limitations. The axiomatic (or mathematical) models of trust discussed here are graph models in the sense that the mathematical structure used to model trust is a finite directed graph; we do not consider models based on belief logics [25, 7, 1, 19].

In graph models, the nodes of a graph represent principals and the directed edges of a graph represent trust relationships between principals. There may be additional structure associated with a graph, such as labels on the nodes and edges. The graphs are used to propagate beliefs about statements (e.g., "the key P belongs to Nisha"). The trust graphs are extended with nodes that represent statements and with edges from principal nodes to statement nodes that represent certificates (i.e., signed statements). These axiomatic models are useful to the extent they allow deduction and calculation using unambiguous rules. A given axiomatic model still needs justification to determine whether it says anything useful about the real world.

## 5.1 Simple Graph Models

The simplest kind of graph model is given as follows:

1. The graph consists of two disjoint sets of nodes: A set of principals (keys) and a set of statements (e.g., name-key bindings).
2. Directed edges are of two kinds:
   - An arrow $k \to k'$ means $k$ signs a certificate saying "$k$ trusts $k'$ to issue certificates with valid statements only". The trust represented by this edge has been referred to in the literature as *recommendation trust* ([3]). There is a similar concept in [20] referred to as delegation.

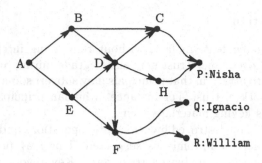

**Fig. 1.** Simple trust graph

- An arrow $k \rightsquigarrow s$ means $k$ signs a certificate saying $s$. Again there is a similar notion in [20].

Figure 1 contains a simple trust graph in which there are seven principals $A, B, C, D, E, F, H$ and three statements P:Nisha, Q:Ignacio, R:William. The statement P:Nisha asserts that the key $P$ belongs to Nisha. The edge $C \rightsquigarrow$ P:Nisha represents a certificate issued by $C$ that says P:Nisha. The edge $B \rightarrow C$ represents a certificate issued by $B$ that says "$B$ trusts $C$ to issue certificates with valid statements only".

## 5.2 Trust Decisions

A graph model provides a graphical picture of the keys, statements, certificates, and trust relationships in a community at a particular moment. It is important to note that the trust graph by itself provides no information about which are the valid statements nor does it indicate whether a principal should believe a statement. The model must contend with the fact that trust can be unfounded since, in the real world, there are principals who issue false certificates for fun and profit.

**Definition 1.** *A state of a trust graph is a subset $G_v$ of the set of statements, intended to denote the set of valid statements. A principal $k$ is* fraudulent *with respect to $G_v$ if there is an edge $k \rightsquigarrow s \notin G_v$.*

Figure 2 illustrates a state of a trust graph in which there are two valid statements P:Nisha, Q:Ignacio and a fraudulent principal $F$ which certifies the invalid statement R:William.

**Definition 2.** *Let $\mathcal{G}$ be the set of trust graphs. A trust decision rule $\beta$ associated to $\mathcal{G}$ is a boolean function $(G, k, s) \mapsto \beta(G, k, s)$ defined whenever $G$ is a graph in $\mathcal{G}$, $k$ is a key in $G$, and $s$ is a statement in $G$.*

Figure 3 illustrates a trust decision rule in which the rule is $\beta(G, k, s) = \text{true}$ only when there are two independent corroborating trust paths from $k$ to the

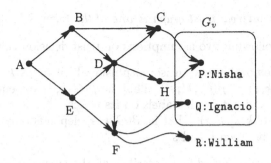

**Fig. 2.** State of a trust graph

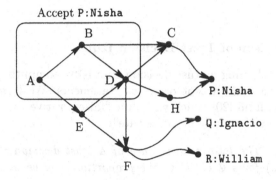

**Fig. 3.** Example of a trust decision rule

statement $s$. Thus, according to this rule, the keys $A, B, D$ are the only ones to accept the statement P:Nisha. Moreover this rule rejects all other statements. Notice that under this trust decision rule, nodes $C, F, H$ in the example should not accept any statements, including the statements they certify; these nodes may accept statements based on other models of trust such as a model of direct trust. The literature describes several trust decision rules including rules where $\beta(G, k, s) = \mathbf{true}$ only when there is a path from $k$ to $s$ whose length is smaller than some threshold [33, 14], or when the number of bounded node-disjoint paths from $k$ to $s$ exceeds some threshold [28].

Notice that a trust decision rule depends only on the graph and is independent of the trust state. Moreover, as defined above, the value of $\beta(G, k, s)$ may depend on the structure of the entire graph, including parts of the graph preceding the node $k$ along an oriented path. However, a key $k$ should decide trust not on who trusts $k$ but on whom $k$ trusts. To make this notion precise we define a trust "interval": Given a statement node $s$ and a key node $k$ of $G$, $G[k, s]$ is the set of nodes that lie on some oriented path starting at $k$ and ending at $s$. Notice that $k$, $s$ are both nodes in $G[k, s]$. Moreover, $s$ is the only statement node in $G[k, s]$.

**Definition 3.** *An interval trust graph is one of the form* $G[k, s]$.

We make the following two assumptions on trust decision rules:

1. If $G, G'$ are isomorphic via an isomorphism which maps $k \mapsto k'$ and $s \mapsto s'$, then $\beta(G, k, s) = \beta(G', k', s')$. That is, $\beta(G, k, s)$ depends only on the structure of $G$ and not on the labels on its nodes.
2. $\beta(G, k, s) = \beta(G[k, s], k, s)$. That is, $\beta(G, k, s)$ depends only on the interval structure of $G$ between $k$ and $s$

The following easily proved fact describes all the trust decision rules:

Any boolean function $\phi$ on interval graphs defines a trust decision rule by $\beta_\phi(G, k, s) = \phi(G[k, s])$. Moreover, any trust decision rule is of this form.

## 5.3 Comparison of Trust Decision Rules

One way of evaluating a trust decision rule is by computing the proportion of keys that erroneously accept or reject statements. We formalize this concept using a notion from [20] which we call a "false positive rate" and we define its dual which we call a "false negative rate".

**Definition 4.** *The false positive rate of a trust decision rule $\beta$ associates to each $(G, G_v, s)$ for $s \notin G_v \subseteq G$ the proportion of keys that accept the invalid statement $s$:*

$$\frac{number\ of\ keys\ k\ such\ that\ \beta(G, k, s) = \texttt{true}}{number\ of\ keys\ k\ in\ G}$$

**Definition 5.** *The false negative rate of a trust decision rule $\beta$ associates to each $(G, G_v, s)$ for $s \in G_v \subseteq G$ the proportion of keys that reject the valid statement $s$:*

$$\frac{number\ of\ keys\ k\ such\ that\ \beta(G, k, s) = \texttt{false}}{number\ of\ keys\ k\ in\ G}$$

In the example of Figures 2 and 3, the trust decision rule has no false positives. On the other hand, the valid statement Q:Ignacio is rejected by all keys; the trust decision rule thus has a false negative rate of 1 for that statement.

Positive results in this direction attempt to establish "stability" of trust decision rules [20] under degradation or attacks. Figure 4 illustrates the effect of attacking a trust graph by modification of a single direct trust edge from $H \rightsquigarrow$ P:Nisha to $H \rightsquigarrow$ R:William.

## 5.4 Valued Graph Models

Thus far, we have considered simple graph models in which edges are unlabeled. Some models [34, 15] refine these simple graph models by placing constraints on the trust relationships represented by edges. For instance, $E$ may trust $F$ to issue

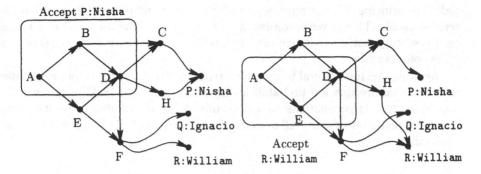

**Fig. 4.** Attack on a trust graph

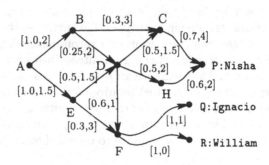

**Fig. 5.** Valued trust graph

valid certificates but not to make good recommendations. Some models assign values to trust relationships based on various presumed properties of trust such as likelihood of failure (of trusting behavior), cost of failure, and an aggregation from assessments of third parties. The notions of trust state, trust decision rule, trust attack, and false positive rate apply to these valued graph models as well and we consider them below.

**Network Flow Models.** Figure 5 contains a valued trust graph in which each edge is labeled by a pair of numbers that represents the flow capacity and the cost of the edge. Trust decision rules include rules where $\beta(G, k, s) = \texttt{true}$ only when the cost per unit flow from $k$ to $s$ is smaller than some threshold, or when the maximum network flow from $k$ to $s$ exceeds some threshold [20]. Note that with unit costs and capacities, these metrics reduce to shortest path and edge-disjoint path metrics for simple trust graphs.

**Probabilistic Models.** Some categories of trust (see Section 2) are based on expectations that certain events will occur. For these kinds of trust, $P$ trusts $Q$ means $P$ expects occurrences of certain events under the control (at least partially) of principal $Q$. For purposes of discussion let us refer to these events as *trusted events*. These events consist of a set of possible outcomes. For instance, see [3] where trusted events consist of those outcomes in which $Q$ reliably provides some service.

Accordingly, it is natural to construct trust models in which values associated to trust relationships are probabilities of events [22, 31]. In [3], [6] the value associated to a trust relationship is determined by the number of positive trial outcomes relative to the overall number of trials, while in [17] it is a second order probability estimate.

**Economic Models.** Measurement of trust can be regarded as obtaining quantitative bounds on risk. This is based on the view that higher levels of trust correspond to lower levels of risk. Insurance is usually regarded as a means of transfering financial risk among principals. For instance, the model described in the paper [29] assigns monetary values to recommendation relationships. The trust assigned to an assertion is the guaranteed insurance award if the assertion proves to be false. The insurance approach to trust valuation is a promising direction especially in regard to trust required for commercial electronic transactions where losses attributed to authentication failures can be assessed. However, this approach only addresses reparable losses (e.g., financial losses); it does not address irreparable losses such as damage to personal relationships or reputation.

# 6 Conclusion

Trust plays a critical role in several aspects of agent societies. First, cooperation between agents depends on their trust in the underlying computer systems and software. Second, cooperative transactions can incur substantial costs due to access barriers between agents; trust between agents enables them to lower these access barriers thus reducing transaction costs. Finally, trust can lead to the clustering of agents into communities within which complex multi-agent transactions have a high likelihood of success.

Trust is an overloaded term with numerous meanings, each with distinct properties. It can be established directly between two or more agents in a variety of ways. It can be propagated among a network of agents, and one form of trust can be substituted by other forms. Finally, it can be degraded in several ways. This paper illustrates the complex nature of trust and the numerous problems that remain to be solved before software agents can employ computational trust models.

*Acknowledgements.* We thank Joshua Guttman, Marion Michaud, and John Vasak for comments which led to improvements in the presentation of this paper. This work was supported by MITRE's Information Assurance Technical Operations Program.

# References

[1] M. Abadi, M. Burrows, B. Lampson, and G. Plotkin. A calculus for access control in distributed systems. *ACM Transactions on Programming Languages and Systems*, 15(4):706–734, October 1993.

[2] S. Berkovits, J. D. Guttman, and V. Swarup. Authentication for mobile agents. Lecture Notes in Computer Science 1419, Special issue on Mobile Agents and Security, 1998.

[3] T. Beth, M. Borcherding, and B. Klein. Valuation of trust in open networks. In D. Gollman, editor, *Proceedings of the European Symposium on Research in Computer Security (ESORICS)*, LNCS 875, pages 3–18. Springer Verlag, 1994.

[4] A. Birrell, B. Lampson, R. Needham, and M. Shroeder. A global authentication service without global trust. In *Proceedings of the IEEE Symposium on Security and Privacy*, pages 223–230, 1986.

[5] M. Blaze, J. Feigenbaum, and J. Lacy. Decentralized trust management. In *Proceedings of the IEEE Symposium on Security and Privacy*, pages 164–173, 1996.

[6] B. Borcherding and M. Borcherding. Covered trust values in distributed systems. In *Proceedings of the Working Conference on Multimedia and Communication Security*, pages 24–31. Chapman & Hall, 1995.

[7] Michael Burrows, Martín Abadi, and Roger Needham. A logic of authentication. *Proceedings of the Royal Society*, Series A, 426(1871):233–271, December 1989. Also appeared as SRC Research Report 39 and, in a shortened form, in ACM Transactions on Computer Systems 8, 1 (February 1990), 18-36.

[8] G. Edjlali, A. Acharya, and V. Chaudhary. History-based access control for mobile code. In *Proceedings of the ACM Conference on Computer and Communications Security*, 1998.

[9] C. M. Ellison, B. Frantz, B. Lampson, R. Rivest, B. M. Thomas, and T. Ylonen. Simple public key certificate. Internet Draft (Work in Progress), November 1998.

[10] C. M. Ellison, B. Frantz, B. Lampson, R. Rivest, B. M. Thomas, and T. Ylonen. SPKI certificate theory. Internet Draft (Work in Progress), November 1998.

[11] D. Farmer and W. Venema. *SATAN Overview*, 1995. http://www.fish.com/.

[12] W. M. Farmer, J. D. Guttman, and V. Swarup. Security for mobile agents: Authentication and state appraisal. In *Proceedings of the European Symposium on Research in Computer Security (ESORICS)*, LNCS 1146, pages 118–130, 1996.

[13] F. Fukuyama. *Trust : The Social Virtues and the Creation of Prosperity*. Free Press, June 1996.

[14] S. Garfinkel. *PGP: Pretty Good Privacy*. O'Reilly and Associates, 1994.

[15] E. Gerck. *Towards a real-world model of trust: reliance on received information*. MCG, 1998. http://www.mcg.org.br/trustdef.htm.

[16] J. D. Guttman. Filtering postures: Local enforcement for global policies. In *Proceedings of the IEEE Symposium on Security and Privacy*, 1997.

[17] A. Josang. A model for trust in security systems. In *Proceedings of the Second Nordic Workshop on Secure Computer Systems*, 1997.

[18] R. M. Kramer and T. R. Tyler, editors. *Trust in Organizations : Frontiers of Theory and Research*. Sage Publications, February 1996.

[19] B. Lampson, M. Abadi, M. Burrows, and E. Wobber. Authentication in distributed systems: Theory and practice. *ACM Transactions on Computer Systems*, 10(4):265–310, November 1992.

[20] R. Levien and A. Aiken. Attack-resistant trust metrics for public key certification. In *Proceedings of the 7th USENIX Security Symposium*, 1998.

[21] S.P. Marsh. *Formalising Trust as a Computational Concept*. PhD thesis, Department of Computer Science and Mathematics, University of Sterling, April 1994.

[22] U. Maurer. Modeling a public-key infrastructure. In *Proceedings of the European Symposium on Research in Computer Security (ESORICS)*, LNCS 1146, pages 118–130. Springer Verlag, 1996.

[23] D.H. McKnight and N.L. Chervany. The meanings of trust. Working paper, Carlson School of Management, University of Minnesota, 1996. `http://www.misrc.umn.edu/wpaper/wp96-04.htm`.

[24] B. A. Misztal. *Trust in Modern Societies : The Search for the Bases of Social Order*. Polity Press, December 1995.

[25] P. Venkat Rangan. An axiomatic basis of trust in distributed systems. In *Proceedings of the IEEE Symposium on Security and Privacy*, pages 204–210, 1988.

[26] J.M. Reagle. Trust in a cryptographic economy and digital security deposits: Protocols and policies. Master's thesis, Technology and Policy Program, Massachusetts Institute of Technology, May 1996.

[27] J.M. Reagle. Trust in electronic markets: The convergence of cryptographers and economists. *First Monday*, 1(2), August 1996. `http://www.firstmonday.dk/issues/issue2/markets/index.html`.

[28] M. K. Reiter and S. G. Stubblebine. Path independence for authentication in large-scale systems. In *Proceedings of the 4th ACM Conference on Computer and Communications Security*, pages 57–66, 1997.

[29] M. K. Reiter and S. G. Stubblebine. Toward acceptable metrics of authentication. In *Proceedings of the IEEE Symposium on Security and Privacy*, pages 3–18, 1997.

[30] T. Sander and C. Tschudin. Towards mobile cryptography. In *Proceedings of the IEEE Symposium on Security and Privacy*, 1998.

[31] A. Tarah and C. Huitema. Associating metrics to certification paths. In *Proceedings of the European Symposium on Research in Computer Security (ESORICS)*, LNCS 648, pages 175–189. Springer Verlag, 1992.

[32] Bernard Williams. Formal structures and social reality. In D. Gambetta, editor, *Trust: Making and Breaking Cooperative Relations*, pages 3–13. Basil Blackwell, 1988.

[33] R. Yahalom, B. Klein, and Th. Beth. Trust relationships in secure systems – a distributed authentication perspective. In *Proceedings of the IEEE Symposium on Security and Privacy*, 1993.

[34] R. Yahalom, B. Klein, and Th. Beth. Trust-based navigation in distributed systems. *Computing Systems*, 7(1):45–73, 1994.

# Protection in
# Programming-Language Translations*

Martín Abadi

**Abstract.** We discuss abstractions for protection and the correctness of their implementations. Relying on the concept of full abstraction, we consider two examples: (1) the translation of Java classes to an intermediate bytecode language, and (2) in the setting of the pi calculus, the implementation of private channels in terms of cryptographic operations.

## 1 Introduction

Tangible crimes and measures against those crimes are sometimes explained through abstract models—with mixed results, as the detective Erik Lönnrot discovered [9]. Protection in computer systems relies on abstractions too. For example, an access matrix is a high-level specification that describes the allowed accesses of subjects to objects in a computer system; the system may rely on mechanisms such as access lists and capabilities for implementing an access matrix [22].

Abstractions are often embodied in programming-language constructs. Recent work on Java [17] has popularized the idea that languages are relevant to security, but the relation between languages and security is much older. In particular, objects and types have long been used for protection against incompetence and malice, at least since the 1970s [36, 24, 20]. In the realm of distributed systems, programming languages (or their libraries) have sometimes provided abstractions for communication on secure channels of the kind implemented with cryptography [7, 49, 47, 50, 46].

Security depends not only on the design of clear and expressive abstractions but also on the correctness of their implementations. Unfortunately, the criteria for correctness are rarely stated precisely—and presumably they are rarely met. These criteria seem particularly delicate when a principal relies on those abstractions but interacts with other principals at a lower level. For example, the principal may express its programs and policies in terms of objects and remote method invocations, but may send and receive bit strings. Moreover, the bit strings that it receives may not have been the output of software trusted to respect the abstractions. Such situations seem to be more common now than in the 1970s.

One of the difficulties in the correct implementation of secure systems is that the standard notion of refinement (e.g., [19, 21]) does not preserve security

---

* This is a slightly revised version of a paper that appeared in *Automata, Languages and Programming: 25th International Colloquium, ICALP'98*, Springer-Verlag, July 1998.

properties. Ordinarily, the non-determinism of a specification may be intended to allow a variety of implementations. In security, the non-determinism may also serve for hiding sensitive data. As an example, let us consider a specification that describes a computer that displays an arbitrary but fixed string in a corner of a screen. A proposed implementation might always display a user's password as that string. Although this implementation may be functionally correct, we may consider it incorrect for security purposes, because it leaks more information than the specification seems to allow. Security properties are thus different from other common properties; in fact, it has been argued that security properties do not conform to the usual definition of properties as predicates on behaviors [6, 21, 28].

Reexamining this example, let us write $P$ for the user's password, $I(P)$ for the proposed implementation, and $S(P)$ for the specification. Since the set of behaviors allowed by the specification does not depend on $P$, clearly $S(P)$ is equivalent to $S(P')$ for any other password $P'$. On the other hand, $I(P)$ and $I(P')$ are not equivalent, since an observer can distinguish them. Since the mapping from specification to implementation does not preserve equivalence, we may say that it is not fully abstract [30, 40]. We may explain the perceived weakness of the proposed implementation by this failure of full abstraction.

This paper suggests that, more generally, the concept of full abstraction is a useful tool for understanding the problem of implementing secure systems. Full abstraction seems particularly pertinent in systems that rely on translations between languages—for example, higher-level languages with objects and secure channels, lower-level languages with memory addresses and cryptographic keys.

We consider two examples of rather different natures and review some standard security concerns, relating these concerns to the pursuit of full abstraction. The first example arises in the context of Java (section 2). The second one concerns the implementation of secure channels, and relies on the pi calculus as formal framework (section 3). The thesis of this paper about full abstraction is in part a device for discussing these two examples.

This paper is rather informal and partly tutorial; its contributions are a perspective on some security problems and some examples, not new theorems. Related results appear in more technical papers [44, 2].

## Full abstraction, revisited

We say that two expressions are equivalent in a given language if they yield the same observable results in all contexts of the language. A translation from a language $L_1$ to a language $L_2$ is equationally fully abstract if (1) it maps equivalent $L_1$ expressions to equivalent $L_2$ expressions, and (2) conversely, it maps nonequivalent $L_1$ expressions to nonequivalent $L_2$ expressions [30, 40, 43, 35, 42]. We may think of the context of an expression as an attacker that interacts with the expression, perhaps trying to learn some sensitive information (e.g., [3]). With this view, condition (1) means that the translation does not introduce information leaks. Since equations may express not only secrecy properties but also some integrity properties, the translation must preserve those properties as well. Because of these consequences of condition (1), we focus on it; we mostly ignore condition (2), although it can be useful too, in particular for excluding trivial translations.

Closely related to equational full abstraction is logical full abstraction [27]. A translation from a language $L_1$ to a language $L_2$ is logically fully abstract if it preserves logical properties of the expressions being translated. Longley and Plotkin have identified conditions under which equational and logical full abstraction are equivalent. Since we use the concept of full abstraction loosely, we do not distinguish its nuances.

An expression of the source language $L_1$ may be written in a silly, incompetent, or even malicious way. For example, the expression may be a program that broadcasts some sensitive information—so this expression is insecure on its own, even before any translation to $L_2$. Thus, full abstraction is clearly not sufficient for security; however, as we discuss in this paper, it is often relevant.

## 2 Objects and Mobile Code

The Java programming language is typically compiled to an intermediate language, which we call JVML and which is implemented by the Java Virtual Machine [17, 26]. JVML programs are often communicated across networks, for example from Web servers to their clients. A client may run a JVML program in a Java Virtual Machine embedded in a Web browser. The Java Virtual Machine helps protect local resources from mobile JVML programs while allowing those programs to interact with local class libraries. Some of these local class libraries perform essential functions (for example, input and output), so they are often viewed as part of the Java Virtual Machine.

### 2.1 Translating Java to JVML

As a first example we consider the following trivial Java class:

```
class C {
    private int x;
    public void set_x(int v) {
      this.x = v;
    };
}
```

This class describes objects with a field x and a method set_x. The method set_x takes an integer argument v and updates the field x to v. The keyword **this** represents the self of an object; the keyword **public** indicates that any client or subclass can access set_x directly; the keyword **private** disallows a similar direct access to x from outside the class. Therefore, the field x can be written but never read.

The result of compiling this class to JVML may be expressed roughly as follows. (Here we do not use the official, concrete syntax of JVML, which is not designed for human understanding.)

```
class C {
    private int x;
    public void set_x(int) {
        .framelimits locals = 2, stack = 2;
        aload_0;      // load this
        iload_1;      // load v
        putfield x;   // set x
    };
}
```

As this example indicates, JVML is a fairly high-level language, and in particular it features object-oriented constructs such as classes, methods, and self. It differs from Java in that methods manipulate local variables, a stack, and a heap using low-level load and store operations. The details of those operations are not important for our purposes. Each method body declares how many local variables and stack slots its activation may require. The Java Virtual Machine includes a bytecode verifier, which checks that those declarations are conservative (for instance, that the stack will not overflow). If undetected, dynamic errors such as stack overflow could lead to unpredictable behavior and to security breaches.

The writer of a Java program may have some security-related expectations about the program. In our simple example, the field x cannot be read from outside the class, so it may be used for storing sensitive information. Our example is so trivial that this information cannot be exploited in any way, but there are more substantial and interesting examples that permit controlled access to fields with the qualifier **private** and similar qualifiers. For instance, a Java class for random-number generation (like java.util.Random) may store seeds in private fields. In these examples, a security property of a Java class may be deduced— or presumed—by considering all possible Java contexts in which the class can be used. Because those contexts must obey the type rules of Java, they cannot access private fields of the class.

When a Java class is translated to JVML, one would like the resulting JVML code to have the security properties that were expected at the Java level. However, the JVML code interacts with a JVML context, not with a Java context. If the translation from Java to JVML is fully abstract, then matters are considerably simplified—in that case, JVML contexts have no more power than Java contexts. Unfortunately, as we point out below, the current translation is not fully abstract (at least not in a straightforward sense). Nevertheless, the translation approximates full abstraction:

– In our example, the translation retains the qualifier **private** for x. The occurrence of this qualifier at the JVML level may not be surprising, but it cannot be taken for granted. (At the JVML level, the qualifier does not have the benefit of helping programmers adhere to sound software-engineering practices, since programmers hardly ever write JVML, so the qualifier might have been omitted from JVML.)

- Furthermore, the bytecode verifier can perform standard typechecking, guaranteeing in particular that a JVML class does not refer to a private field of another JVML class.
- The bytecode verifier can also check that dynamic errors such as stack overflow will not occur. Therefore, the behavior of JVML classes should conform to the intended JVML semantics; JVML code cannot get around the JVML type system for accessing a private field inappropriately.

Thus, the bytecode verifier restricts the set of JVML contexts, and in effect makes them resemble Java contexts (cf. [17, p. 220]). As the set of JVML contexts decreases, the set of equivalences satisfied by JVML programs increases, so the translation from Java to JVML gets closer to full abstraction. Therefore, we might even view full abstraction as the goal of bytecode verification.

Recently, there have been several rigorous studies of the Java Virtual Machine, and in particular of the bytecode verifier [10, 44, 41, 16]. These studies focus on the type-safety of the JVML programs accepted by the bytecode verifier. As has long been believed, and as Leroy and Rouaix have recently proved in a somewhat different context [25], strong typing yields some basic but important security guarantees. However, those guarantees do not concern language translations. By themselves, those guarantees do not imply that libraries written in a high-level language have expected security properties when they interact with lower-level mobile code.

## 2.2   Obstacles to full abstraction

As noted, the current translation of Java to JVML is not fully abstract. The following variant of our first example illustrates the failure of full abstraction. We have no reason to believe that it illustrates the only reason for the failure of full abstraction, or the most worrisome one; Dean, Felten, Wallach, and Balfanz have discovered several significant discrepancies between the semantics of Java and that of JVML [12].

```
class D {
    class E {
        private int y = x;
    };
    private int x;
    public void set_x(int v) {
        this.x = v;
    };
}
```

The class E is an inner class [45]. To each instance of an inner class such as E corresponds an instance of its outer class, D in this example. The inner class may legally refer to the private fields of the outer class.

Unlike Java, JVML does not include an inner-class construct. Therefore, compilers "flatten" inner classes while adding accessor methods. Basically, as far as compilation is concerned, we may as well have written the following classes instead of D:

```
class D {
    private int x;
    public void set_x(int v) {
        this.x = v;
    };
    static int get_x(D d) {
        return d.x;
    };
}

class E {
    ... get_x ...
}
```

Here E is moved to the top level. A method get_x is added to D and used in E for reading x; the details of E do not matter for our purposes. The method get_x can be used not just in E, however—any other class within the same package may refer to get_x.

When the classes D and E are compiled to JVML, therefore, a JVML context may be able to read x in a way that was not possible at the Java level. This possibility results in the loss of full abstraction, since there is a JVML context that distinguishes objects that could not be distinguished by any Java context. More precisely, a JVML context that runs get_x and returns the result distinguishes instances of D with different values for x.

This loss of full abstraction may result in the leak of some sensitive information, if any was stored in the field x. The leak of the contents of a private component of an object can be a concern when the object is part of the Java Virtual Machine, or when it is trusted by the Java Virtual Machine (for example, because a trusted principal digitally signed the object's class). On the other hand, when the object is part of an applet, this leak should not be surprising: applets cannot usually be protected from their execution environments.

For better or for worse, the Java security story is more complicated and dynamic than the discussion above might suggest. In addition to protection by the qualifier **private**, Java has a default mode of protection that protects classes in one package against classes in other packages. At the language level, this mode of protection is void—any class can claim to belong to any package. However, Java class loaders can treat certain packages in special ways, guaranteeing that only trusted classes belong to them. Our example with inner classes does not pose a security problem as long as D and E are in one of those packages.

In hindsight, it is not clear whether one should base any security expectations on qualifiers like **private**, and more generally on other Java constructs. As Dean et al. have argued [12], the definition of Java is weaker than it should be from a security viewpoint. Although it would be prudent to strengthen that definition, a full-blown requirement of full abstraction may not be a necessary addition. More modest additions may suffice. Section 4 discusses this subject further.

# 3 Channels for Distributed Communication

In this section, we consider the problem of implementing secure channels in distributed systems. As mentioned in the introduction, some systems for distributed programming offer abstractions for creating and using secure channels. The implementations of those channels typically rely on cryptography for ensuring the privacy and the integrity of network communication. The relation between the abstractions and their implementations is usually explained only informally. Moreover, the abstractions are seldom explained in a self-contained manner that would permit reasoning about them without considering their implementations at least occasionally.

The concept of full abstraction can serve as a guide in understanding secure channels. When trying to approximate full abstraction, we rediscover common attacks and countermeasures. Most importantly, the pursuit of full abstraction entails a healthy attention to the connections between an implementation and higher-level programs that use the implementation, beyond the intrinsic properties of the implementation.

## 3.1 Translating the pi calculus to the spi calculus

The formal setting for this section is the pi calculus [32, 34, 33], which serves as a core calculus with primitives for creating and using channels. By applying the pi calculus restriction operator, these channels can be made private. We discuss the problem of mapping the pi calculus to a lower-level calculus, the spi calculus [4, 5, 3], implementing communication on private channels by encrypted communication on public channels. Several low-level attacks can be cast as counterexamples to the full abstraction of this mapping. Some of the attacks can be thwarted through techniques common in the literature on protocol design [29]. Some other attacks suggest fundamental difficulties in achieving full abstraction for the pi calculus.

First we briefly review the spi calculus. In the variant that we consider here, the syntax of this calculus assumes an infinite set of names and an infinite set of variables. We let $c$, $d$, $m$, $n$, and $p$ range over names, and let $w$, $x$, $y$, and $z$ range over variables. We usually assume that all these names and variables are different (for example, that $m$ and $n$ are different names). The set of terms of the spi calculus is defined by the following grammar:

| $L, M, N ::=$ | | terms |
| --- | --- | --- |
| | $n$ | name |
| | $x$ | variable |
| | $\{M_1, \ldots, M_k\}_N$ | encryption ($k \geq 0$) |

Intuitively, $\{M_1, \ldots, M_k\}_N$ represents the ciphertext obtained by encrypting the terms $M_1, \ldots, M_k$ under the key $N$ (using a symmetric cryptosystem such as DES or RC5 [29]). The set of processes of the spi calculus is defined by the following grammar:

| $P, Q ::=$ | processes |
| --- | --- |
| $\overline{M}\langle N_1, \ldots, N_k \rangle$ | output $(k \geq 0)$ |
| $M(x_1, \ldots, x_k).P$ | input $(k \geq 0)$ |
| $\mathbf{0}$ | nil |
| $P \mid Q$ | composition |
| $!P$ | replication |
| $(\nu n)P$ | restriction |
| $[M \text{ is } N]\, P$ | match |
| $case\ L\ of\ \{x_1, \ldots, x_k\}_N\ in\ P$ | decryption $(k \geq 0)$ |

An output process $\overline{M}\langle N_1, \ldots, N_k \rangle$ sends the tuple $N_1, \ldots, N_k$ on $M$. An input process $M(x_1, \ldots, x_k).Q$ is ready to input $k$ terms $N_1, \ldots, N_k$ on $M$, and then to behave as $Q[N_1/x_1, \ldots, N_k/x_k]$. Here we write $Q[N_1/x_1, \ldots, N_k/x_k]$ for the result of replacing each free occurrence of $x_i$ in $Q$ with $N_i$, for $i \in 1..k$. Both $M(x_1, \ldots, x_k).Q$ and $case\ L\ of\ \{x_1, \ldots, x_k\}_N\ in\ P$ (explained below) bind the variables $x_1, \ldots, x_k$. The nil process $\mathbf{0}$ does nothing. A composition $P \mid Q$ behaves as $P$ and $Q$ running in parallel. A replication $!P$ behaves as infinitely many copies of $P$ running in parallel. A restriction $(\nu n)P$ makes a new name $n$ and then behaves as $P$; it binds the name $n$. A match process $[M \text{ is } N]\, P$ behaves as $P$ if $M$ and $N$ are equal; otherwise it does nothing. A decryption process $case\ L\ of\ \{x_1, \ldots, x_k\}_N\ in\ P$ attempts to decrypt $L$ with the key $N$; if $L$ has the form $\{M_1, \ldots, M_k\}_N$, then the process behaves as $P[M_1/x_1, \ldots, M_k/x_k]$; otherwise it does nothing.

By omitting the constructs $\{M_1, \ldots, M_k\}_N$ and $case\ L\ of\ \{x_1, \ldots, x_k\}_N\ in\ P$ from these grammars, we obtain the syntax of the pi calculus (more precisely, of a polyadic, asynchronous version of the pi calculus).

As a first example, we consider the trivial pi calculus process:

$$(\nu n)(\overline{n}\langle m \rangle \mid n(x).\mathbf{0})$$

This is a process that creates a channel $n$, then uses it for transmitting the name $m$, with no further consequence. Communication on $n$ is secure in the sense that no context can discover $m$ by interacting with this process, and no context can cause a different message to be sent on $n$; these are typical secrecy and integrity properties. Such properties can be expressed as equivalences (in particular, as testing equivalences [11, 8, 3]). For example, we may express the secrecy of $m$ as the equivalence between $(\nu n)(\overline{n}\langle m \rangle \mid n(x).\mathbf{0})$ and $(\nu n)(\overline{n}\langle m' \rangle \mid n(x).\mathbf{0})$, for any names $m$ and $m'$.

Intuitively, the subprocesses $\overline{n}\langle m \rangle$ and $n(x).\mathbf{0}$ may execute on different machines; the network between these machines may not be physically secure. Therefore, we would like to explicate a channel like $n$ in lower-level terms, mapping it to some sort of encrypted connection multiplexed on a public channel. For example, we might translate our first process, $(\nu n)(\overline{n}\langle m\rangle \mid n(x).0)$, into the following spi calculus process:

$$(\nu n)(\overline{c}\langle\{m\}_n\rangle \mid c(y).case\ y\ of\ \{x\}_n\ in\ 0)$$

Here $c$ is a distinguished, free name, intuitively the name of a well-known public channel. The name $n$ still appears, with a restriction, but it is used for a key rather than for a channel. The sender encrypts $m$ using $n$; the recipient tries to decrypt a ciphertext $y$ that it receives on $c$ using $n$; if the decryption succeeds, the recipient obtains a cleartext $x$ (hopefully $m$).

This translation strategy may seem promising. However, it has numerous weaknesses; we describe several of those weaknesses in what follows. The weaknesses represent obstacles to full abstraction and are also significant in practical terms.

## 3.2 Obstacles to full abstraction

**Leak of traffic patterns** In the pi calculus, $(\nu n)(\overline{n}\langle m\rangle \mid n(x).0)$ is simply equivalent to $0$, because the internal communication on $n$ cannot be observed. On the other hand, in the spi calculus, $(\nu n)(\overline{c}\langle\{m\}_n\rangle \mid c(y).case\ y\ of\ \{x\}_n\ in\ 0)$ is not equivalent to the obvious implementation of $0$, namely $0$. A spi calculus process that interacts with $(\nu n)(\overline{c}\langle\{m\}_n\rangle \mid c(y).case\ y\ of\ \{x\}_n\ in\ 0)$ can detect traffic on $c$, even if it cannot decrypt that traffic.

The obvious way to protect against this leak is to add noise to communication lines. In the context of the spi calculus, we may for example compose all our implementations with the noise process $!(\nu p)\overline{c}\langle\{\}_p\rangle$. This process continually generates keys and uses those keys for producing encrypted traffic on the public channel $c$.

In practice, since noise is rather wasteful of communication resources, and since a certain amount of noise might be assumed to exist on communication lines as a matter of course, noise is not always added in implementations. Without noise, full abstraction fails.

**Trivial denial-of-service vulnerability** Consider the pi calculus process

$$(\nu n)(\overline{n}\langle m\rangle \mid n(x).\overline{x}\langle\rangle)$$

which is a small variant of the first example where, after its receipt, the message $m$ is used for sending an empty message. This process preserves the integrity of $m$, in the sense that no other name can be received and used instead of $m$; therefore, this process is equivalent to $\overline{m}\langle\rangle$.

The obvious spi calculus implementations of $(\nu n)(\overline{n}\langle m\rangle \mid n(x).\overline{x}\langle\rangle)$ and $\overline{m}\langle\rangle$ are respectively

$$(\nu n)(\overline{c}\langle\{m\}_n\rangle \mid c(y).case\ y\ of\ \{x\}_n\ in\ \overline{c}\langle\{\}_x\rangle)$$

and $\bar{c}\langle\{\}_m\rangle$. These implementations can be distinguished not only by traffic analysis but also in other trivial ways. For example, the former implementation may become stuck when it interacts with $\bar{c}\langle p\rangle$, because the decryption *case y of* $\{x\}_n$ *in* $\bar{c}\langle\{\}_x\rangle$ fails when $y$ is $p$ rather than a ciphertext. In contrast, the latter implementation does not suffer from this problem.

Informally, we may say that the process $\bar{c}\langle p\rangle$ mounts a denial-of-service attack. Formally, such attacks can sometimes be ignored by focusing on process equivalences that capture only safety properties, and not liveness properties. In addition, the implementations may be strengthened, as is commonly done in practical systems. For example, as a first improvement, we may add some replication to $(\nu n)(\bar{c}\langle\{m\}_n\rangle \mid c(y).case\ y\ of\ \{x\}_n\ in\ \bar{c}\langle\{\}_x\rangle)$, obtaining:

$$(\nu n)(\bar{c}\langle\{m\}_n\rangle \mid !c(y).case\ y\ of\ \{x\}_n\ in\ \bar{c}\langle\{\}_x\rangle)$$

This use of replication protects against $\bar{c}\langle p\rangle$.

**Exposure to replay attacks** Another shortcoming of our implementation strategy is exposure to replay attacks. As an example, we consider the pi calculus process:

$$(\nu n)(\bar{n}\langle m_1\rangle \mid \bar{n}\langle m_2\rangle \mid n(x).\bar{x}\langle\rangle \mid n(x).\bar{x}\langle\rangle)$$

which differs from the previous example only in that two names $m_1$ and $m_2$ are transmitted on $n$, asynchronously. In the pi calculus, this process is equivalent to $\overline{m_1}\langle\rangle \mid \overline{m_2}\langle\rangle$: it is guaranteed that both $m_1$ and $m_2$ go from sender to receiver exactly once.

This guarantee is not shared by the spi calculus implementation

$$(\nu n)\begin{pmatrix} \bar{c}\langle\{m_1\}_n\rangle \mid \bar{c}\langle\{m_2\}_n\rangle \mid \\ c(y).case\ y\ of\ \{x\}_n\ in\ \bar{c}\langle\{\}_x\rangle \mid \\ c(y).case\ y\ of\ \{x\}_n\ in\ \bar{c}\langle\{\}_x\rangle \end{pmatrix}$$

independently of any denial-of-service attacks. When this implementation is combined with the spi calculus process $c(y).(\bar{c}\langle y\rangle \mid \bar{c}\langle y\rangle)$, which duplicates a message on $c$, two identical messages may result, either $\bar{c}\langle\{\}_{m_1}\rangle \mid \bar{c}\langle\{\}_{m_1}\rangle$ or $\bar{c}\langle\{\}_{m_2}\rangle \mid \bar{c}\langle\{\}_{m_2}\rangle$.

Informally, we may say that the process $c(y).(\bar{c}\langle y\rangle \mid \bar{c}\langle y\rangle)$ mounts a replay attack. Standard countermeasures apply: timestamps, sequence numbers, and challenge-response protocols. In this example, the addition of a minimal challenge-response protocol leads to the following spi calculus process:

$$(\nu n)\begin{pmatrix} c(z_1).\bar{c}\langle\{m_1, z_1\}_n\rangle \mid c(z_2).\bar{c}\langle\{m_2, z_2\}_n\rangle \mid \\ (\nu p_1)(\bar{c}\langle p_1\rangle \mid c(y).case\ y\ of\ \{x, z_1\}_n\ in\ [z_1\ is\ p_1]\ \bar{c}\langle\{\}_x\rangle) \mid \\ (\nu p_2)(\bar{c}\langle p_2\rangle \mid c(y).case\ y\ of\ \{x, z_2\}_n\ in\ [z_2\ is\ p_2]\ \bar{c}\langle\{\}_x\rangle) \end{pmatrix}$$

The names $p_1$ and $p_2$ serve as challenges; they are sent by the subprocesses that are meant to receive $m_1$ and $m_2$, received by the subprocesses that send $m_1$ and $m_2$, and included along with $m_1$ and $m_2$ under $n$. This challenge-response protocol is rather simplistic in that the challenges may get "crossed" and then neither $m_1$ nor $m_2$ would be transmitted successfully; it is a simple matter of programming to protect against this confusion. In any case, for each challenge, at most one message is accepted under $n$. This use of challenges thwarts replay attacks.

**Leak of message equalities** In the pi calculus, the identity of messages sent on private channels is concealed. For example, an observer of the process

$$(\nu n)(\overline{n}\langle m_1 \rangle \mid \overline{n}\langle m_2 \rangle \mid n(x).0 \mid n(x).0)$$

will not even discover whether $m_1 = m_2$. (For this example, we drop the implicit assumption that $m_1$ and $m_2$ are different names.) On the other hand, suppose that we translate this process to:

$$(\nu n)\begin{pmatrix} \overline{c}\langle \{m_1\}_n \rangle \mid \overline{c}\langle \{m_2\}_n \rangle \mid \\ c(y).case\ y\ of\ \{x\}_n\ in\ 0 \mid \\ c(y).case\ y\ of\ \{x\}_n\ in\ 0 \end{pmatrix}$$

An observer of this process can tell whether $m_1 = m_2$, even without knowing $m_1$ or $m_2$ (or $n$). In particular, the observer may execute:

$$c(x).c(y).([x\ is\ y]\ \overline{d}\langle\rangle \mid \overline{c}\langle x \rangle \mid \overline{c}\langle y \rangle)$$

This process reads and relays two messages on the channel $c$, and emits a message on the channel $d$ if the two messages are equal. It therefore distinguishes whether $m_1 = m_2$. The importance of this sort of leak depends on circumstances. In an extreme case, one cleartext may have been guessed (for example, the cleartext "attack at dawn"); knowing that another message contains the same cleartext may then be significant.

A simple countermeasure consists in including a different confounder component in each encrypted message. In this example, the implementation would become:

$$(\nu n)\begin{pmatrix} (\nu p_1)\overline{c}\langle \{m_1, p_1\}_n \rangle \mid (\nu p_2)\overline{c}\langle \{m_2, p_2\}_n \rangle \mid \\ c(y).case\ y\ of\ \{x, z_1\}_n\ in\ 0 \mid \\ c(y).case\ y\ of\ \{x, z_2\}_n\ in\ 0 \end{pmatrix}$$

The names $p_1$ and $p_2$ are used only to differentiate the two messages being transmitted. Their inclusion in those messages ensures that a comparison on ciphertexts does not reveal an equality of cleartexts.

**Lack of forward secrecy** As a final example, we consider the pi calculus process:

$$(\nu n)(\overline{n}\langle m \rangle \mid n(x).\overline{p}\langle n \rangle)$$

This process transmits the name $m$ on the channel $n$, which is private until this point. Then it releases $n$ by sending it on the public channel $p$. Other processes may use $n$ afterwards, but cannot recover the contents of the first message sent on $n$. Therefore, this process is equivalent to

$$(\nu n)(\overline{n}\langle m'\rangle \mid n(x).\overline{p}\langle n\rangle)$$

for any $m'$. Interestingly, this example relies crucially on scope extrusion, a feature of the pi calculus not present in simpler calculi such as CCS [31].

A spi calculus implementation of $(\nu n)(\overline{n}\langle m\rangle \mid n(x).\overline{p}\langle n\rangle)$ might be:

$$(\nu n)(\overline{c}\langle\{m\}_n\rangle \mid c(y).case\ y\ of\ \{x\}_n\ in\ \overline{c}\langle\{n\}_p\rangle)$$

However, this implementation lacks the forward-secrecy property [14]: the disclosure of the key $n$ compromises all data previously sent under $n$. More precisely, a process may read messages on $c$ and remember them, obtain $n$ by decrypting $\{n\}_p$, then use $n$ for decrypting older messages on $c$. In particular, the spi calculus process

$$c(x).(\overline{c}\langle x\rangle \mid c(y).case\ y\ of\ \{z\}_p\ in\ case\ x\ of\ \{w\}_z\ in\ \overline{d}\langle w\rangle)$$

may read and relay $\{m\}_n$, read and decrypt $\{n\}_p$, then go back to obtain $m$ from $\{m\}_n$, and finally release $m$ on the public channel $d$.

Full abstraction is lost, as with the other attacks; in this case, however, it seems much harder to recover. Several solutions may be considered.

- We may restrict the pi calculus somehow, ruling out troublesome cases of scope extrusion. It is not immediately clear whether enough expressiveness for practical programming can be retained.
- We may add some constructs to the pi calculus, for example a construct that given the name $n$ of a channel will yield all previous messages sent on the channel $n$. The addition of this construct will destroy the source-language equivalence that was not preserved by the translation. On the other hand, this construct seems fairly artificial.
- We may somehow indicate that source-language equivalences should not be taken too seriously. In particular, we may reveal some aspects of the implementation, warning that forward secrecy may not hold. We may also specify which source-language properties are maintained in the implementation. This solution is perhaps the most realistic one, although we do not yet know how to write the necessary specifications in a precise and manageable form.
- Finally, we may try to strengthen the implementation. For example, we may vary the key that corresponds to a pi calculus channel by, at each instant, computing a new key by hashing the previous one. This approach is fairly elaborate and expensive.

The problem of forward secrecy may be neatly avoided by shifting from the pi calculus to the join calculus [15]. The join calculus separates the capabilities for sending and receiving on a channel, and forbids the communication of the latter capability. Because of this asymmetry, the join calculus is somewhat easier to map to a lower-level calculus with cryptographic constructs. This mapping is the subject of current work [2]; although still impractical, the translation obtained is fully abstract.

# 4 Full Abstraction in Context

With progress on security infrastructures and techniques, it may become less important for translations to approximate full abstraction. Instead, we may rely on the intrinsic security properties of target-language code and on digital signatures on this code. We may also rely on the security properties of source-language code, but only when a precise specification asserts that translation preserves those properties. Unfortunately, several caveats apply.

- The intrinsic security properties of target-language code may be extremely hard to discover a posteriori. Languages such as JVML are not designed for ease of reading. Furthermore, the proof of those properties may require the analysis of delicate and complex cryptographic protocols. Certifying compilers [39, 37] may alleviate these problems but may not fully solve them.
- Digital signatures complement static analyses but do not obviate them. In particular, digital signatures cannot protect against incompetence or against misplaced trust. Moreover, digital signatures do not seem applicable in all settings. For example, digital signatures on spi calculus processes would be of little use, since these processes never migrate from one machine to another.
- Finally, we still have only a limited understanding of how to specify and prove that a translation preserves particular security properties. This question deserves further attention. It may be worthwhile to address it first in special cases, for example for information-flow properties [13] as captured in type systems [48, 1, 38, 18].

The judicious use of abstractions can contribute to simplicity, and thus to security. On the other hand, abstractions and their translations can give rise to complications, subtleties, and ultimately to security flaws. As Lampson wrote [23], "neither abstraction nor simplicity is a substitute for getting it right". Concepts such as full abstraction should help in getting it right.

## Acknowledgements

Most of the observations of this paper were made during joint work with Cédric Fournet, Georges Gonthier, Andy Gordon, and Raymie Stata. Drew Dean, Mark Lillibridge, and Dan Wallach helped by explaining various Java subtleties. Mike Burrows, Cédric Fournet, Mark Lillibridge, John Mitchell, and Dan Wallach suggested improvements to a draft. The title is derived from that of a paper by Jim Morris [36].

# References

1. Martín Abadi. Secrecy by typing in security protocols. In *Theoretical Aspects of Computer Software*, volume 1281 of *Lecture Notes in Computer Science*, pages 611–638. Springer-Verlag, 1997.

2. Martín Abadi, Cédric Fournet, and Georges Gonthier. Secure implementation of channel abstractions. In *Proceedings of the Thirteenth Annual IEEE Symposium on Logic in Computer Science*, pages 105–116, June 1998.
3. Martín Abadi and Andrew D. Gordon. A calculus for cryptographic protocols: The spi calculus. Technical Report 414, University of Cambridge Computer Laboratory, January 1997. Extended version of both [4] and [5]. A revised version appeared as Digital Equipment Corporation Systems Research Center report No. 149, January 1998, and an abridged version will appear in *Information and Computation*.
4. Martín Abadi and Andrew D. Gordon. A calculus for cryptographic protocols: The spi calculus. In *Proceedings of the Fourth ACM Conference on Computer and Communications Security*, pages 36–47, 1997.
5. Martín Abadi and Andrew D. Gordon. Reasoning about cryptographic protocols in the spi calculus. In *Proceedings of the 8th International Conference on Concurrency Theory*, volume 1243 of *Lecture Notes in Computer Science*, pages 59–73. Springer-Verlag, July 1997.
6. Bowen Alpern and Fred B. Schneider. Defining liveness. *Information Processing Letters*, 21(4):181–185, October 1985.
7. Andrew D. Birrell. Secure communication using remote procedure calls. *ACM Transactions on Computer Systems*, 3(1):1–14, February 1985.
8. Michele Boreale and Rocco De Nicola. Testing equivalence for mobile processes. *Information and Computation*, 120(2):279–303, August 1995.
9. Jorge Luis Borges. La muerte y la brújula. In *Obras completas 1923–1972*, pages 499–507. Emecé Editores, Buenos Aires, 1974. Titled "Death and the compass" in English translations.
10. Richard M. Cohen. Defensive Java Virtual Machine version 0.5 alpha release. Web pages at http://www.cli.com/, May 1997.
11. Rocco De Nicola and Matthew C. B. Hennessy. Testing equivalences for processes. *Theoretical Computer Science*, 34:83–133, 1984.
12. Drew Dean, Edward W. Felten, Dan S. Wallach, and Dirk Balfanz. Java security: Web browsers and beyond. In Dorothy E. Denning and Peter J. Denning, editors, *Internet besieged: countering cyberspace scofflaws*, pages 241–269. ACM Press, 1998.
13. Dorothy E. Denning. *Cryptography and Data Security*. Addison-Wesley, Reading, Mass., 1982.
14. Whitfield Diffie, Paul C. van Oorschot, and Michael J. Wiener. Authentication and authenticated key exchanges. *Designs, Codes and Cryptography*, 2:107–125, 1992.
15. Cédric Fournet and Georges Gonthier. The reflexive chemical abstract machine and the join-calculus. In *Proceedings of the 23rd ACM Symposium on Principles of Programming Languages*, pages 372–385, January 1996.
16. Stephen N. Freund and John C. Mitchell. A type system for object initialization in the Java bytecode language. In *OOPSLA '98 Conference Proceedings: Object-Oriented Programming, Systems, Languages, and Applications*, pages 310–327, 1998.
17. James Gosling, Bill Joy, and Guy L. Steele. *The Java Language Specification*. Addison-Wesley, 1996.
18. Nevin Heintze and Jon G. Riecke. The SLam calculus: programming with secrecy and integrity. In *Proceedings of the 25th ACM Symposium on Principles of Programming Languages*, pages 365–377, 1998.
19. C. A. R. Hoare. Proof of correctness of data representations. *Acta Informatica*, 1:271–281, 1972.

20. Anita K. Jones and Barbara H. Liskov. A language extension for expressing constraints on data access. *Communications of the ACM*, 21(5):358–367, May 1978.
21. Leslie Lamport. A simple approach to specifying concurrent systems. *Communications of the ACM*, 32(1):32–45, January 1989.
22. Butler W. Lampson. Protection. In *Proceedings of the 5th Princeton Conference on Information Sciences and Systems*, pages 437–443, 1971.
23. Butler W. Lampson. Hints for computer system design. *Operating Systems Review*, 17(5):33–48, October 1983. Proceedings of the Ninth ACM Symposium on Operating System Principles.
24. Butler W. Lampson and Howard E. Sturgis. Reflections on an operating system design. *Communications of the ACM*, 19(5):251–265, May 1976.
25. Xavier Leroy and François Rouaix. Security properties of typed applets. In *Proceedings of the 25th ACM Symposium on Principles of Programming Languages*, pages 391–403, 1998.
26. Tim Lindholm and Frank Yellin. *The Java Virtual Machine Specification*. Addison-Wesley, 1996.
27. John Longley and Gordon Plotkin. Logical full abstraction and PCF. In Jonathan Ginzburg, Zurab Khasidashvili, Carl Vogel, Jean-Jacques Lévy, and Enric Vallduví, editors, *The Tbilisi Symposium on Logic, Language and Computation: Selected Papers*, pages 333–352. CSLI Publications and FoLLI, 1998.
28. John McLean. A general theory of composition for a class of "possibilistic" properties. *IEEE Transactions on Software Engineering*, 22(1):53–66, January 1996.
29. Alfred J. Menezes, Paul C. van Oorschot, and Scott A. Vanstone. *Handbook of Applied Cryptography*. CRC Press, 1996.
30. Robin Milner. Fully abstract models of typed $\lambda$-calculi. *Theoretical Computer Science*, 4:1–22, 1977.
31. Robin Milner. *Communication and Concurrency*. Prentice-Hall International, 1989.
32. Robin Milner. Functions as processes. *Mathematical Structures in Computer Science*, 2:119–141, 1992.
33. Robin Milner. The polyadic $\pi$-calculus: a tutorial. In Bauer, Brauer, and Schwichtenberg, editors, *Logic and Algebra of Specification*. Springer-Verlag, 1993.
34. Robin Milner, Joachim Parrow, and David Walker. A calculus of mobile processes, parts I and II. *Information and Computation*, 100:1–40 and 41–77, September 1992.
35. John C. Mitchell. On abstraction and the expressive power of programming languages. *Science of Computer Programming*, 21(2):141–163, October 1993.
36. James H. Morris, Jr. Protection in programming languages. *Communications of the ACM*, 16(1):15–21, January 1973.
37. Greg Morrisett, David Walker, Karl Crary, and Neal Glew. From System F to Typed Assembly Language. In *Proceedings of the 25th ACM Symposium on Principles of Programming Languages*, pages 85–97, 1998.
38. Andrew C. Myers and Barbara Liskov. A decentralized model for information flow control. In *Proceedings of the 16th ACM Symposium on Operating System Principles*, pages 129–142, 1997.
39. George C. Necula and Peter Lee. The design and implementation of a certifying compiler. In *Proceedings of the ACM SIGPLAN'98 Conference on Programming Language Design and Implementation (PLDI)*, pages 333–344, 1998.
40. Gordon Plotkin. LCF considered as a programming language. *Theoretical Computer Science*, 5:223–256, 1977.

41. Zhenyu Qian. A formal specification of Java Virtual Machine instructions for objects, methods and subroutines. In Jim Alves-Foss, editor, *Formal Syntax and Semantics of Java™*. Springer-Verlag, 1998. To appear.

42. Jon G. Riecke. Fully abstract translations between functional languages. *Mathematical Structures in Computer Science*, 3(4):387–415, December 1993.

43. Ehud Shapiro. Separating concurrent languages with categories of language embeddings. In *Proceedings of the Twenty Third Annual ACM Symposium on the Theory of Computing*, pages 198–208, 1991.

44. Raymie Stata and Martín Abadi. A type system for Java bytecode subroutines. In *Proceedings of the 25th ACM Symposium on Principles of Programming Languages*, pages 149–160, January 1998.

45. Sun Microsystems, Inc. Inner classes specification. Web pages at `http://java.sun.com/products/jdk/1.1/docs/guide/innerclasses/`, 1997.

46. Sun Microsystems, Inc. RMI enhancements. Web pages at `http://java.sun.com/products/jdk/1.2/docs/guide/rmi/index.html`, 1997.

47. Leendert van Doorn, Martín Abadi, Mike Burrows, and Edward Wobber. Secure network objects. In *Proceedings 1996 IEEE Symposium on Security and Privacy*, pages 211–221, May 1996.

48. Dennis Volpano, Cynthia Irvine, and Geoffrey Smith. A sound type system for secure flow analysis. *Journal of Computer Security*, 4:167–187, 1996.

49. Edward Wobber, Martín Abadi, Michael Burrows, and Butler Lampson. Authentication in the Taos operating system. *ACM Transactions on Computer Systems*, 12(1):3–32, February 1994.

50. Ann Wollrath, Roger Riggs, and Jim Waldo. A distributed object model for the Java system. *Computing Systems*, 9(4):265–290, Fall 1996.

# Reflective Authorization Systems: Possibilities, Benefits, and Drawbacks

Massimo Ancona, Walter Cazzola, and Eduardo B. Fernandez

**Abstract.** We analyze how to use the reflective approach to integrate an authorization system into a distributed object-oriented framework. The expected benefits from the reflective approach are: more stability of the security layer (i.e., with a more limited number of hidden bugs), better software and development modularity, more reusability, and the possibility to adapt the security module with at most a few changes to other applications. Our analysis is supported by simple and illustrative examples written in Java.

Keywords: Authorization, Distributed Objects, Object Orientation, Reflection, Security.

## 1 Introduction

Security implies not only protection from external intrusions but also controlling the actions of internally-executing entities and the operations of the whole software system. In this case, the interleaving between operations and data protection may become very complicated and often intractable. For this reason, security must be specified and designed in a system from its early design steps [11]. From another point of view

- it is very important that the security mechanisms of the application be correct and stable;
- the security code should not be mixed with the application code, otherwise it should be very hard to reuse well-proven implementations of the security model.

If this is not done, when a new secure application is developed the designer|implementer wastes time to re-implement and to test the security modules of the application. Moreover, security is related to: "who is allowed to do what, where and when"; so security is not functionally part of the solution of the application problem, but an added feature defining constraints on object interactions. From this last remark we can think of security as a feature operating at a different computational level and we can separate its implementation from the application implementation.

In our opinion it is possible to exploit some typical reflection features, like *separation of concerns* and *transparency*, to split a secure system into two levels: at the first level there are (distributed) objects cooperating to solve the system application; at the second one, rights and authorizations for such entities are identified, specified and mapped onto reflective entities which transparently monitor the objects of the first level and authorize the allowed access to other objects, services, or information.

Working in this way it is possible to develop stable and reliable entities for handling security. It is also possible to reuse them during system development, thus reducing development time and costs, and increasing application level assurance. In most systems, authorization is defined with respect to persistent data and enforced by the DBMS and|or operating system. Object-oriented systems define everything as an object, some persistent some temporary, where this separation is not visible at the application level. In these systems authorization must be defined at the application level to take advantage of the semantic restrictions of the information [10]. An early system (not object-oriented) (see [11], page 195), attempted this kind of control by defining programs that had predefined and preauthorized accesses. Reflection appears as a good possibility for this type of control because it does not separate persistent from temporary entities. The Birlix operating system [18] used reflection to adapt its nonfunctional properties (including security) to different execution and application environments (for more details on how satisfy nonfunctional requirements using reflection, see [21]). In this paper we examine how to use a reflective architecture, such as those described above, to manage the authorization aspects of an application and the advantages and drawbacks of using such an approach.

## 2 Background on Reflection and Security

### 2.1 Reflection

Computational reflection or just reflection is defined as the activity performed by an agent when doing computations about itself [15]. Behavioral and structural reflection are special cases which involve, respectively, agent computation and structure (for more details see [8]).

A reflective system is logically structured in two or more levels, constituting a *reflective tower*. Entities working in the base level, called base-entities or reflective entities, define the system basic behavior. Entities in the other levels (meta-levels), called meta-entities, perform the reflective actions and define further characteristics beyond the application dependent system behavior.

Each level is causally connected to adjacent levels, i.e., entities belonging to a level maintain data structures representing (or, in reflection parlance, *reifying*) the states and the structures of the entities in the level below. Any change in the state or structure of an entity is reflected in the data structures reifying it, and any modification to such data structures affects the entity's state, structure and behavior.

Computational reflection allows properties and functionalities to be added to the application system in a manner that is transparent to the system itself (separation of concerns) [20]. To this respect, it is useful to consider also *reflection granularity* [6], that is, the minimal entity in a software system for which a reflective model defines a different meta-behavior. A finer granularity allows more

flexibility and modularity in the software system at the cost of meta-entity proliferation. The reflective models considered here are: *meta-object*, and *channel reification*.

**Meta-Object Model.** In the meta-object model, meta-entities (called *meta-objects*) are objects, instances of a proper class. Each base-entity, called also *referent*, can be bound to a meta-object. Such a meta-object supervises the work of the linked referent. The meta-object model is well known in literature, more on it can be found in [15].

**Channel Reification Model.** In the channel reification model [1, 2], one or more objects, called *channels* are established between two interacting objects. Each channel is characterized by a triple composed by the objects it connects and by the *kind* of the meta-computation it performs.

$$\text{channel} \equiv (\text{client, server, channel\_kind})$$

A *channel kind* identifies the meta-behavior provided by the channel. The kind is used to distinguish the reflective activity to be performed: several channels (distinguishable by the kind) can be established between the same pair of objects at the same moment.

Each channel persists after each meta-computation, and is reused when a communication characterized by the same triple is generated. The features of the model are: method-level granularity, information continuity, channel lazy creation, and global view[1]. Each service request of a specific kind is trapped (shift-up action) by the channel of the corresponding kind connecting client and server objects, if it exists. Otherwise, such a channel is created; in either case, it then performs its meta-computation and transmits the service request to the supplier. The server's answer is collected and returned to the requesting object (shift-down action).

## 2.2 Security: Authorization Systems

An authorization system plays a monitoring role, judging if the requests sent by an object to another object are permissible requests. The judgment is based on security information related to *objects* and *subjects*; where a subject represents an entity performing or requesting an activity (i.e., an active object playing the client role), while an object is a passive entity supplying a service (i.e., a passive object or an active object playing the role of server). One way to model such authorizations is the access matrix model (see [14]). In this model the authorization rules are described by a bidimensional matrix indexed on subject and objects and access to an object o is allowed to a subject s when the item $\langle s,o \rangle$ of

---

[1] The global view concept is defined in [6] as the situation in which the meta-computation can involve all base-entities and aspects involved in the computation on which it reifies.

the matrix contains the permitted access type. Such a model can be realized by *capability lists, access control lists*, or combinations of these. Formally, an authorization right R for a subject s to access an object o, through message (method) m can be written R(s)=(m,o). Here m usually represents a high-level access type, e.g., hire an employee.

A Role-Based Access Control (RBAC) model is particularly suitable for object-oriented systems [17], because accesses can be defined as operations defined in the objects according to the need-to-know of the roles [9]. Because reflection supports a fine granularity of access, its combination with RBAC can be quite effective.

## 3  How We Model Security With Reflection

A computational system answers questions and supports actions in some applicative *domain*. Following P. Maes [15] we can say that:

> "A system is *causally connected* with its domain if the internal structures and the domain they represent are linked in such a way that if one of them changes, this leads to a corresponding effect upon the other."

For example a *control software* is causally connected with the controlled process if changes of the state of the physical process are reflected by changes of the control software state and vice versa. For this purpose a control software system incorporates structures representing the state of the controlled process. If we consider authorization rights added to a critical control system we note an *indirect* causal connection of authorization with the application domain. Authorization (and more generally security) defines capabilities related to human and/or mechanical agents concerned with the responsibility of performing tasks that are considered critical for the controlled system behavior. Thus, an authorization validation mechanism is a *nonfunctional* feature causally connected with software agents and objects performing control tasks. This is our motivation for adopting a reflective architecture for implementing authorization schemes. In other words, security specifications correspond to nonfunctional specifications [9] and should be implemented into a meta-level.

Using computational reflection we can separate the authorization control mechanism from the application. Moreover, the meta-level should be protected from malicious intrusions and attacks from the base-level or from other processes. A solution could consist in executing the meta-level in a different address space as an independent process, communicating with the base-level via a mechanism similar to the *local procedure calls* (LPC) of Windows NT [7]. LPC is a locally optimized form of the well known mechanism of *remote procedure call* (RPC) of Unix and other systems: LPC is a message-passing mechanism through which clients make requests to servers and used for the server's reply. The main necessary feature of the LPC mechanism is the protection domain installed around an LPC call.

## 3.1 Illustrative Scenario

We illustrate our ideas by using the following scenario: the system is composed of several objects interacting in a client-server manner. For security reasons the services supplied by a server and its data are protected and prohibited to some subjects. To support our presentation we use some stubs of Java code. The code is tailored to the case of three clients and one server supplying two methods, one reading the server state and the other modifying it. Each client has different rights on the two supplied services. Java [3] is not a reflective language, for our purposes we realize the reflection in a naive way by emulating it with inheritance. Of course in this way transparency and efficiency are compromised. However, we chose this approach for simplicity and because it permits to point out the advantages and the weak points of the reflective approach. In particular, it shows the necessity to implement the context switch in a secure way. The complete code can be downloaded from http://www.disi.unige.it/person/CazzolaW/OORSecurity.html.

In the next section, in order to avoid confusion with objects in object-oriented systems, we use the term *base-objects* to refer either to subjects and objects of the authorization terminology. Moreover, we call *service request* (or method call) every access performed by a subject on an object. There are several reflective architectures suitable for applying authorization rules, we consider only two of them: the *meta-object model* and the *channel reification model*. Each of them

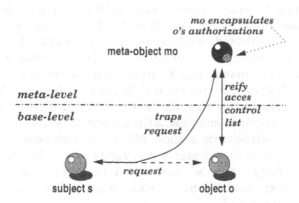

**Fig. 1. Meta-object model for security**

provides features suitable to handle different security aspects.

## 3.2 Meta-Object Approach

In the meta-object model a meta-object is associated with each object (as shown in Fig. 1); this meta-object encapsulates the related access control list of the

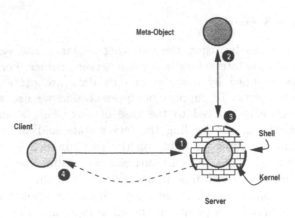

**Fig. 2.** Meta-object approach: the Java structure

referred object. Each request performed by a subject s to an object o is trapped by the related meta-object mo, which evaluates the authorization request. Then, it either rejects the request by rising an exception, or it delivers the request to the original destination s.

The Java architecture in shown in Fig. 2. In this case the reflective approach is handled by the server part of the application. The client is directed to talk only to the server. To make this approach to work, we have wrapped the server code (the kernel of Fig. 2) into a shell which receives all client requests and performs the shift-up action by forwarding each request to its own meta-object. Thus, a server is composed of two parts: a kernel and a shell, related by the inheritance link.    As it can be deducted by inspecting the code (Listing 1), the shell waits for a client request and forwards it to the meta-object by calling the meta-object **metaBehavior** method (rows ⑤ and ⑩) to check if the request is authorized or should be rejected. Then, if the request is authorized by the meta-object, the shell proceeds to the execution by calling the corresponding method of the kernel (rows ⑥ and ❶). The meta-object implements the authorization policy. All the work is performed by the **metaBehavior** method. Method **metaBehavior**, when activated for the first time, reads the referent access rights from a file and encapsulates the referent capability list. In all other activations, method **metaBehavior** uses the capability list encapsulated by the meta-object to check if the request has to be authorized or rejected.

When a client issues the following call:

$$permission = server.methodRead();$$

a request for the execution of **methodRead** is trapped by the shell (step ❶ in Fig. 2) which calls the meta-object for obtaining the authorization (step ❷ in Fig. 2). The meta-object replies to the shell (step ❸ in Fig. 2) and if authorized, allows the kernel to return the reply to the request. Otherwise, the shell notifies the client that a violation occurred by sending it an error message (step ❹ in Fig. 2).

---

**Listing 1 Java code for the server shell**

```
①  public class TheServer extends RServer {
②    String REF2;
③    InterSMO rem_obj2;   // declaration of an SMO remote object

④    public boolean methodRead(int IDClient) {
⑤      boolean access = rem_obj2.metaBehavior(METHOD_READ, IDClient);
⑥      if (access) return super.methodRead(1);
⑦      else return false;
⑧    }

⑨    public boolean methodWrite(int IDClient) {
⑩      boolean access = rem_obj2.metaBehavior(METHOD_WRITE, IDClient);
⓫      if (access) return super.methodWrite(1);
⓬      else return false;
⓭    }

⓮    public static void main(String args[]) {
⓯      System.setSecurityManager(new RMISecurityManager());  // RMI Registration

         // Client declaration of the TheServer+SMO client-serving, in which we look
         // up and fetch the remote object SMO.

⓰      rem_obj2 = (InterSMO) Naming.lookup("//SMO"+IDServer);
⓱      REF = "//CS";

         // Creation of one instance of the remote object TheServer

⓲      TheServer rem_obj  = new TheServer();
⓳      Naming.rebind(REF, rem_obj);
⓴      System.out.println("Waiting for some client request...");
①    }

②  }
```

---

This model is suitable for implementing highly specialized role rights (specialized per object, per subject or per service request). Moreover, each meta-object may hold the methods necessary to modify authorization rules of the base-objects [12], which can be called for modifying active authorizations. In this way, the developer of base-objects does not need to worry about validity of authorization updates, which are encapsulated into the meta-object behavior. Obviously our example suffers of efficiency penalties due to the reflective implementation in Java.

## 3.3 Channel Reification Approach

As we can see by inspecting the meta-object code of the previous section, the meta-object reifies many pieces of information, and when the authorization mechanisms become more complex, the metaBehavior code grows in complexity and size, thus making the code error prone. In our example relative to the meta-object, we use two simple access modes: *allowed to read*, and *allowed to write*, both managed by a single meta-object. The example is quite simple but sufficiently complex to show the increase in complexity of the code necessary to handle all cases.

---

## Listing 2 Java code for the server kernel

```java
public class RServer {

public boolean methodRead(int i) {
    System.out.println("sending methodRead");
    return true;
}

public boolean methodWrite(int i) {
    System.out.println("sending methodWrite");
    return true;
}

}
```

---

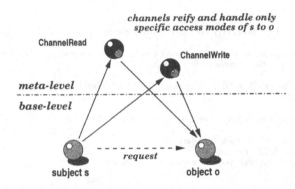

**Fig. 3. Channel to model access mode authorization**

Another approach consists of using a reflective model with a finer granularity than that of the meta-object model, by entrusting each access mode into a different reflective entity. By using the channel reification model [2] we can define a channel kind for each existing access mode. Each element of the access matrix is encapsulated by one or more channels (one for each value assigned to the matrix item). For example, when a request is sent by s to o, with access mode **write**, the request is trapped by the channel of kind *write* (ChannelWrite), established between s and o, which validates it (see Fig. 3). In this way the authorization validation process is simplified: each channel checks few authorizations and there exists reflective entities only for base-entities requiring an authorization validation protocol. Obviously, the main drawback of this approach with respect to the meta-object approach is a higher number of reflective entities created, however it is possible to limit this number by merging together meta-entities showing a similar behavior.

Due to the *global view* property (see [6]) of the channel reification model, each reflective action starts from the client and involves the client, the server, and a channel in its execution. The reflective behavior is achieved by overriding the normal behavior of the binding|look-up between the client and the server, and

## Listing 3 Java code for the security meta-object

```java
public class SMO {
    static String REF2;

    int idserver; // referents id

    boolean[] caplist_read = null;
    boolean[] caplist_write = null;

    public boolean metaBehavior(char MethodType, int ClientName) {
        if (caplist_read == null) {
            FileInputStream rights = new FileInputStream("rights");
            int clients, servers;
            servers = rights.read();
            caplist_read = new boolean [clients = rights.read()];
            caplist_write = new boolean [clients];
            rights.skip(idserver*(2*clients+1));
            for (int i=0; i<clients;i++) {
                caplist_read[i] = ((rights.read() == "R")?true:false);
                caplist_write[i] = ((rights.read() == "W")?true:false);
            }
        }
        return ((method_type == "R")?caplist_read[ClientName]:caplist_write[ClientName]);
    }

    public static void main(String args[]) {
        idserver = args[0];
        System.setSecurityManager(new RMISecurityManager());
        REF2 = "//SMO";
        SMO rem_obj2 = new SMO();
        Naming.rebind(REF2, rem_obj2);
        System.out.println("Security meta-object waits for some request.. ");
    }
}
```

the remote method invocation in order to divert the request from the server to the channel. The client is composed of three layers (see Fig. 4). The inner layer supplies the operations necessary to communicate with the server. The central layer encapsulates all operations of the inner layer and uses them to communicate with the right channel. The outer layer defines the behavior of the client. The server code corresponds exactly to the kernel code of the previous approach. There is no need to wrap it because the server receives requests that have been previously filtered by the channels, it cannot be accessed directly by the clients.

The above splitting of responsibility of the validation mechanism, makes the code of a channel simpler and more modular than that of the meta-object. Operations channelRead and channelWrite are very similar, they differ only in the encapsulated information and the use they make of it. In our example channels and meta-objects are similar because the validation phase is simple; however, it should be noted that the amount of information encapsulated and managed by a single channel has decreased.

When a client issues the call (see Fig. 4):

$$permission = server.methodRead();$$

## Listing 4 Java code for the inner layer

```java
public class operations {
    int IDClient;

    public static Object rem_server;

    // Here the remote channel object is bound to the URL

    public Object Binding(String str) {
        return Naming.lookup("//" + str);
    }

    // This function invokes the remote methods in TheServer

    public Object rmi(int method, int ClientName) {
        if (method == 0) return ((InterCS)rem_server).Method_Read(ClientName);
        else return ((InterCS)rem_server).Method_Write(ClientName);
    }

}
```

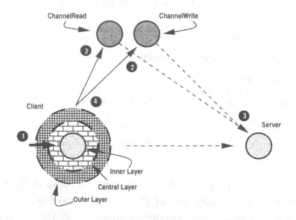

**Fig. 4. Java structure for the channel reification approach**

the control is dispatched to the central layer of the client (step ❶ in Fig. 4) which determines the right channel to be invoked on the basis of the request kind. The request is then forwarded to the channel while the client idles until a reply is sent back to it (step ❷ in Fig. 4). The channel validates the request and, if legal, forwards it to the server (step ❸ in Fig. 4). When the channel receives the reply from the server, it forwards it back to the client (step ❹ in Fig. 4). The server is unaware of the validation process: it executes only filtered requests. Thus a good *separation of concerns* and implementation modularity is achieved.

Security models based on communication flow [5] can be easily modeled by the channel reification model: in particular, models based on the concept of *flow* such as those of Escort of Scout [19] and Corps [16]. A path is a first class object encapsulating data flowing through a set of modules. A path is a logical channel

## Listing 5 Java code for the central layer

```java
public class reflectiveLayer extends operations {

    Boolean Right;

    private InterCCRead rem_chr;
    private InterCCWrite rem_chw;

    // Here the remote channel object is prepared to bind the URL
    // (see the Operations class for the actual binding )

    public Object Binding(String str) {
        rem_chr = (InterCCRead) super.Binding("CCR"+IDClient+"-"+IDServer);
        rem_chw = (InterCCWrite) super.Binding("CCW"+IDClient+"-"+IDServer);
        return null;
    }

    // Here the rmi method invokes the metaBehavior function in the Channel
    // classes, where the checking about client permissions is performed

    public Object rmi(int method) {
        if (method==0) Right = rem_chr.metaBehavior(method);
        if (method==1) Right = rem_chw.metaBehavior(method);
        return Right;
    }

}
```

made up of data flow connecting several modules. Other two security mechanisms adopted in Escort are *filters* and *protection domains*. A filter restricts the interface between two adjacent modules. However, filters include no mechanism to ensure that a module does not bypass the interface by directly accessing the memory of the other module. A protection domain is a boundary drawn between a pair of modules to ensure that the mutual access is performed only through the defined interface. Filters and protection domains may be modeled respectively by standard reflective channels and *protected* channels, i.e., channels executing in a different address space. The concept of path is more complex and requires an extension of the channel reification mechanism. A channel controlling a path may be obtained by piping or composing the channels controlling the sequence of modules forming a path or by defining a complex channel successively controlling the interface of a sequence of modules in a path. Another approach could be based on a three-level reflective tower, but this approach increases the system complexity without significant advantages.

## 4  Evaluation

Using computational reflection to include an authorization mechanism into a software system offers many advantages during software development. We can specify, develop, implement and test the modules which implement authorization mechanisms separately from the rest of the application. In this way we encourage reuse and improve software stability. Moreover, the authorization process is hid-

## Listing 6 Java channel code

```java
public class channelRead {
  int IDClient, IDServer; Boolean result = null; String REF; InterCS rem_objS;

  // Method Constructor with two parameters used to identify channel's client and server
  public channelRead(int c, int s) {
    IDClient = c; IDServer = s;
  }

  public Boolean metaBehavior(int MethodType) {
    if (result == null) {    // we have to read access matrix in order to initialize channel
      ...
    }
    if (cell == 34) {              // 34 is the int code for "R"
      System.out.println("\nYou have the READ permission !");
      return rem_objS.Method_Read();
    else {
      System.out.println("\nYou don't have the READ permission !!");
      return Boolean.FALSE;
    }
  }
}

  public static void main(String args[]) {
    channelRead rem_obj;

    // creation and installation of the security manager
    System.setSecurityManager( new RMISecurityManager());

    // Here the remote TheServer object is bound to the URL
    rem_objS = ( InterCS ) Naming.lookup("//CS");

    // this is the server set-up for TheClient-channelRead system
    REF = "//CCR"+args[0]+args[1];

    // creation of an instance of the remote class
    rem_obj = new channelRead(Integer.parseInt(args[0]), Integer.parseInt(args[1]));

    // creation of the registry-remote object binding
    Naming.rebind(REF, rem_obj);
    System.out.println("Reading channel["+args[0]+","+args[1]+"] waits for some requests");
  }

}
```

den to the application entities, thus the code of such entities is simplified. While this can be accomplished by current DBMS authorization systems, we are now controlling access to all executing entities, not just the application's persistent data.

The advantages from the security point of view are that only the entities performing the validation of the authorizations of an object know its authorizations constraints. In this way authorization leaking is minimized.

A first drawback is that flexibility has a cost in terms of efficiency due to repeated method activation. The Achille's heel of using reflection to realize security could be its implementation mechanism. In fact, as it is stressed by our examples, each reflective approach has a mechanism, which permits to forward each request to meta-entities. These trap actions (shift-up and shift-down) are critical actions. It is possible for a malicious user to intercept the trap and to hijack the request to another entity bypassing the authorization system and illegally authorizing each request. For this reason it is important to protect the meta-level and the access to it and for the same reason it is important to limit the meta-entities communication and, thus, using a reflective model having the global view feature. One way to avoid this attack consists of implementing the whole meta-computation, and in particular the trap actions, as protected routines. From another point of view this drawback can be converted into an advantage of the model with respect to standard authorization models, because it minimizes the vulnerable points to known system locations that can be more efficiently protected. The possibility of using different address spaces (e.g., different processes) to implement the two reflective layers with kernel system intervention for exchanging information represents an improvement to the security of the complete system.

Some recent proposals to control actions of Java applets have similar purposes to our proposal. In those systems, e.g., in [13], execution domains are created and enforced for specific applications using downloaded content. However, the objective of these approaches is to control access to operating system resources, e.g., files, memory spaces, ..., not to control high-level actions between objects.

## 5 Conclusions

Reflection offers several advantages when used to model authorization mechanisms. Its main advantages are separation of concerns and modularity. Authorization mechanisms can be designed within the application from early development stages, but, at the same time, they can be maintained separate both from the logical and implementative point of view. This fact improves reusability of both functional and authorization software and supports an independent testing of both. More important, it controls access to all executing entities, not just to persistent data.

Another advantage is the ability of implementing a protection layer around the authorization software, thus making the system more robust to unauthorized attempts to change role rights. Obviously, there are also drawbacks: the first is a reduced execution efficiency; flexibility costs in efficiency. The second problem could be presented by the protection mechanism around the authorization layer (meta-level). Running it in a different address space may make programs too inefficient for most applications. Thus, more efficient protection mechanisms, not performing a complete context switching, should be designed. Hardware capability systems appear promising for this purpose.

Moreover, the existence of such a protection makes more *understandable*, to malicious users, *where to address attacks to the fortress* and easier to discover Achilles' heels.

Future developments are represented by complete workflow authorizations combining specific sequences of service requests: they require that the meta-entities controlling the activated server objects, interact with each other for discriminating legal sequences from illegal ones. More complex authorization schemes may require the introduction of meta-meta-levels, i.e., to raise the reflective tower and the system complexity.

Finally, some prototyping of the proposed architecture and practical experiments will improve the understanding of the role played by reflection in the implementation of authorization systems of high assurance. In particular, its possible use to control the actions of downloaded content would be of high practical interest. Another possible use is for the control of information flow in object-oriented systems as proposed in [4].

## Acknowledgments

A preliminary version of this work appears in the proceedings of the $1^{st}$ ECOOP Workshop on Distributed Object Security, pages 35-39, Belgium, July 1998.

## References

[1] Massimo Ancona, Walter Cazzola, Gabriella Dodero, and Vittoria Gianuzzi. Channel Reification: a Reflective Approach to Fault-Tolerant Software Development. In *OOPSLA'95 (poster section)*, page 137, Austin, Texas, USA, on 15th-19th October 1995. ACM. Available at http://www.disi.unige.it/person/CazzolaW/references.html.

[2] Massimo Ancona, Walter Cazzola, Gabriella Dodero, and Vittoria Gianuzzi. Channel Reification: A Reflective Model for Distributed Computation. In *proceedings of IEEE International Performance Computing, and Communication Conference (IPCCC'98)*, 98CH36191, pages 32-36, Phoenix, Arizona, USA, on 16th-18th February 1998. IEEE.

[3] Ken Arnold and James Gosling. *The Java Programming Language*. The Java Series ... from the Source. Addison-Wesley, Reading, Massachussetts, second edition, December 1997.

[4] Elisa Bertino, Sabrina De Capitani di Vimercati, Elena Ferrari, and Pierangela Samarati. Exception-Based Information Flow Control in Object-Oriented Systems. *ACM Transactions on Information and System Security (TISSEC)*, 1(1), November 1998.

[5] W. E. Boebert and R. Y. Kain. A Pratical Alternative to Hierarchical Integrity Policies. In *proceedings of 8th National Computing Security Conference*, Gaithersburg, October 1985.

[6] Walter Cazzola. Evaluation of Object-Oriented Reflective Models. In *proceedings of ECOOP Workshop on Reflective Object-Oriented Programming and Systems (EWROOPS'98)*, in 12th European Conference on Object-Oriented Programming (ECOOP'98), Brussels, Belgium, on 20th-24th July 1998. Available at http://www.disi.unige.it/person/CazzolaW/references.html.

[7] Helen Custer. *Inside Windows NT*. Microsoft Press, Redmond, WA, 1993.

[8] François-Nicola Demers and Jacques Malenfant. Reflection in Logic, Functional and Object-Oriented Programming: a Short Comparative Study. In *proceedings of the workshop section*, in IJCAI'95 (International Join Conference on AI), Montréal, Canada, August 1995.

[9] Eduardo B. Fernandez and J. C. Hawkins. Determining Role Rights from Use Cases. In *proceedings of the 2nd ACM Workshop on Role Based Access Control (RBAC'97)*, pages 121-125, November 1997.

[10] Eduardo B. Fernandez, Maria M. Larrondo-Petrie, and Ehud Gudes. A Method-Based Authorization Model for Object-Oriented Databases. In *proceedings of the OOPSLA'93 Workshop on Security in Object-Oriented Systems*, pages 70–79. ACM, 1993.

[11] Eduardo B. Fernandez, Rita C. Summers, and Christopher Wood. *Database Security and Integrity*. Addison-Wesley, Reading, Massachusetts, 1981.

[12] Michael A. Harrison, Walter L. Ruzzo, and Jeffrey D. Ullman. Protection in Operating Systems. *Communication of the ACM*, 19(8):461–471, August 1976.

[13] Trent Jaeger, Nayeen Islam, Rangachari Anand, Atul Prakash, and Jochen Liedtke. Flexible Control of Downloaded Executable Content. http://www.ibm.com/Java/education/flexcontrol, 1997.

[14] Butler W. Lampson. Protection. *Operating System Review*, 8(1):18–34, January 1974. Reprint.

[15] Pattie Maes. Concepts and Experiments in Computational Reflection. In *proceedings of OOPSLA'87*, volume 22 of *Sigplan Notices*, pages 147–156. ACM, October 1987.

[16] Edwin Menze, F. Reynolds, and F. Travostino. Programming with System Resources in Support of Real-Time Distributed Applications. In *proceedings of the 1996 IEEE Workshop on Object-Oriented Real-Time Dependable Systems*, pages 36–45, Laguna Beach, Ca, February 1996. IEEE.

[17] Ravi Sandhu, Edward J. Coyne, Hal L. Feinstein, and Charles E. Youman. Role-Based Access Control Models. *Computer*, 29(2):38–47, February 1996.

[18] Susann Sonntag, Hermann Härtig, Oliver Kowalski, Winfried Kühnhauser, and Wolfang Lux. Adaptability Using Reflection. In *proceedings of the 27th Annual Hawaii International Conference on System Sciences*, pages 383–392, 1994.

[19] Oliver Spatscheck and Larry L. Peterson. Escort: A Path-Based OS Security Architecture. Technical Report TR-97-17, Department of Computer Science, The University of Arizona, Tucson, AZ 85721, November 1997.

[20] Robert J. Stroud. Transparency and Reflection in Distributed Systems. *ACM Operating System Review*, 22:99–103, April 1992.

[21] Robert J. Stroud and Zhixue Wu. Using Metaobject Protocols to Satisfy Non-Functional Requirements. In Chris Zimmerman, editor, *Advances in Object-Oriented Metalevel Architectures and Reflection*, chapter 3, pages 31–52. CRC Press, Inc., 2000 Corporate Blvd.,N.W., Boca Raton, Florida 33431, 1996.

# Abstractions for Mobile Computation

Luca Cardelli

**Abstract.** We discuss the difficulties caused by mobile computing and mobile computation over wide-area networks. We propose a unified framework for overcoming such difficulties.

## 1 Introduction

The Internet and the World-Wide-Web provide a computational infrastructure that spans the planet. It is appealing to imagine writing programs that exploit this global infrastructure. Unfortunately, the Web violates many familiar assumptions about the behavior of distributed systems, and demands novel and specialized programming techniques. In particular, three phenomena that remain largely hidden in local-area network architectures become readily observable on the Web:

- *(A) Virtual locations*. Barriers are erected between mutually distrustful administrative domains. Therefore, a program must be aware of where it is, and of how to move or communicate between different domains. The existence of separate administrative domains induces a notion of virtual locations and of virtual distance between locations.

- *(B) Physical locations*. On a planet-size structure, the speed of light becomes tangible. For example, a procedure call to the antipodes requires at least 1/10 of a second, independently of future improvements in networking technology. This absolute lower bound to latency induces a notion of physical locations and physical distance between locations.

- *(C) Bandwidth fluctuations*. A global network is susceptible to unpredictable congestion and partitioning, which results in fluctuations or temporary interruptions of bandwidth. Moreover, mobile devices may perceive bandwidth changes as a consequence of physical movement. Programs need to be able to observe and react to these fluctuations.

These features may interact among themselves. For example, bandwidth fluctuations may be related to physical location because of different patterns of day and night network utilization, and to virtual location because of authentication and encryption across domain boundaries. Virtual and physical locations are often related, but need not coincide.

In addition, another phenomenon becomes unobservable on the Web:

- *(D) Failures*. On the Web, there is no practical upper bound to communication delays. In particular, failures become indistinguishable from long delays, and thus undetectable. Failure recovery becomes indistinguishable from intermittent connectivity. Furthermore, delays (and, implicitly, failures) are frequent and unpredictable.

These four phenomena determine the set of *observables* of the Web: the events or states that can be in principle detected. Observables, in turn, influence the basic building blocks of computation. In moving from local-area networks to wide-area networks, the set of observables changes, and so does the computational model, the programming constructs, and the kind of programs one can write. The question of how to "program the Web" reduces to the question of how to program with the new set of observables provided by the Web.

At least one general technique has emerged to cope with the observables characteristic of a wide-area network such as the Web. *Mobile computation* is the notion that running programs need not be forever tied to a single network node. Mobile computation can deal in original ways with the following phenomena:

- *(A) Virtual locations*. Given adequate trust mechanisms, mobile computations can cross barriers and move between virtual locations. Barriers are designed to impede access, but when code is allowed to cross them, it can access local resources without the impediment of the barrier.

- *(B) Physical locations*. Mobile computations can move between physical locations, turning remote calls into local calls, and thus avoiding the latency limit.

- *(C) Bandwidth fluctuations*. Mobile computations can react to bandwidth fluctuations, either by moving to a better-placed location, or by transferring code that establishes a customized protocol over a connection.

- *(D) Failures*. Mobile computations can run away from anticipated failures, and can move around presumed failures.

Mobile computation is also strongly related to recent hardware advances, since computations move implicitly when carried on portable devices. In this sense, we cannot avoid the issues raised by mobile computation: more than an avant-garde software technique, it is an existing hardware reality.

In this paper, we discuss mobile computation at an entirely informal level; formal accounts of our framework can be found in [13]. In Section 2 we describe the basic characteristics of our existing computational infrastructure, and the difficulties that must be overcome to use it effectively. In Section 3 we review existing ways of modeling distribution and mobility. In Section 4 we introduce an abstract model, the *ambient calculus*, that attempts to capture fundamental features of distribution and mobility in a simple framework. In Section 5, we discuss applications of this model to programming issues, including a detailed example and a programming challenge.

## 2 Three Mental Images

We begin by comparing and contrasting three *mental images*; that is, three abstracted views of distributed computation. From the differences between these mental images we derive the need for new approaches to global computation.

## 2.1 Local Area Networks

The first mental image corresponds to the now standard, and quickly becoming obsolete, model of computation over local area networks.

When workstations and PCs started replacing mainframes, local networks were invented to connect autonomous computers for the purpose of resource sharing. A typical local area network consists of a collection of computers of about the same power (within a couple of hardware generations) and of network links of about the same bandwidth and latency. This environment is not always completely uniform: specialized machines may operate as servers or as engineering workstations, and specialized subnetworks may offer optimized services. Still, by and large, the structure of a LAN can be depicted as the uniform network of nodes (computers) and links (connections) in Mental Image 1:

Administrative Domain

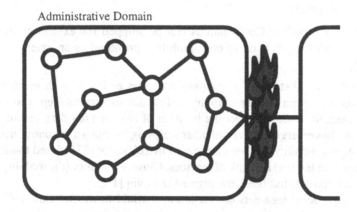

**Mental Image 1: Local Area Network**

A main property of such a network is its predictability. Communication delays are bounded, and processor response times can be estimated. Therefore, link and process failures can be detected by time-outs and by "pinging" nodes.

Another important property of local area networks is that they are usually well-administered and, in recent times, protected against attack. Network administrators have the task of keeping the network running and protect it against infiltration. In the picture, the boundary line represents an *administration domain*, and the flames represent the protection provided by a *firewall*. Protection is necessary because local area networks are rarely completely disconnected: they usually have slower links to the outside world, which are however enough to make administrators nervous about infiltration.

The architecture of local area networks is very different from the older, highly centralized, mainframe architecture. This difference, and the difficulties implied by it, resulted in the emergence of novel distributed computing techniques, such as remote-procedure-call, client-server architecture, and distributed object-oriented programming. The combined aim and effect of these techniques is to make the programming and application environment stable and uniform (as in mainframes). In particular, the network topology is carefully hidden so that any two computers can be considered as lying one logical step apart. Moreover, computers can be considered immobile; for example, they usually preserve their network address when physically moved.

Even in this relatively static environment, the notion of mobility has gradually acquired prominence, in a variety of forms. For example:

- **Control mobility**. During an RPC (Remote Procedure Call) or RMI (Remote Method Invocation) call, a thread of control is thought of as moving from one machine to another and back.

- **Data mobility**. In RPC/RMI, data is linearized, transported, and reconstructed across machines.

- **Link mobility**. The end-points of network channels, or remote object proxies, can be transmitted.

- **Object mobility**. For load balancing purposes, objects can be moved between different servers.

- **Remote Execution**. Computations can be shipped for execution on a server. (This is an early version of code mobility, proposed as an extension of RPC. [35])

In recent years, distributed computing has been endowed with greater mobility properties and easier network programming. Techniques such as Object Request Brokers have emerged to abstract over the location of objects providing certain services. Code mobility has emerged in Tcl and other scripting languages to control network applications. Agent mobility has been pioneered in Telescript [37], aimed towards a uniform (although wide-area) network of services. Closure mobility (the mobility of active and connected entities) has been investigated in Obliq [11].

In due time, local-area-network techniques would have smoothly and gradually evolved towards deployment on wide-area networks, e.g. as was explicitly attempted by the CORBA effort. But, suddenly, a particular wide-area network came along that radically changed the fundamental assumptions of distributed computing and its pace of progress: the Web.

## 2.2 Wide Area Networks

Global computing evolved over the span of a few decades in the form of the Internet. But it was not until the emergence of the Web that the peculiar characteristics of the Internet were exposed in a way that anybody could verify with just a few mouse clicks. For clarity and simplicity we will refer to the Web as the primary global information infrastructure, although it was certainly not the first one.

We should remember that the notions of a *global address space* and of a *global file system* have been popular at times as an extension of mainframe architecture to wide-area networks. The first obvious feature of the Web is that, although it forms a global computational resource, it is nothing like a global mainframe. The Web has no single reliable component, but it also has no single failure point; it is definitely not the centralized all-powerful mainframe of 1950's science fiction novels that could be shut off by attacking its single "brain"[1]. Fortunately, the fact that the Web is not a mainframe is not a big concern; we have already successfully tackled distributed computing based on LANs.

More distressing is the fact that the Web does not behave like a LAN either. Many proposals have emerged along the lines of extending LAN concepts to a global environment; that is, in turning the Internet into a *distributed address space*, or a *distributed file system*. However, since the global environment does not have the stability properties of a LAN, this can be achieved only by introducing redundancy (for reliability), replication (for quality of service), and scalability (for management) at many different levels. Things might have evolved in this direction, but this is not the way the Web came to be. The Web is, almost by definition, unreliable, unpredictable, and unmanageable as a whole, and was not designed with LAN-like guarantees of service.

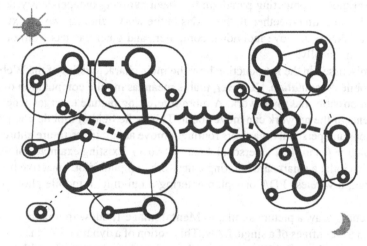

**Mental Image 2: Wide Area Network (for example, the Web)**

Therefore, the main problem with the Web is that it is not just a big LAN, otherwise, modulo issues of scale, we would already know how to deal with it. There are several ways in which the Web is not a big LAN, and we will describe them shortly. But the fundamental reason is that, unlike a LAN, the Web is not centrally administered. Instead, it is a dynamic collection of countless independent administrative domains, all widely different and mutually distrustful. This is represented in Mental Image 2.

In that picture, computers differ greatly in power and availability, while network links differ greatly in capacity and reliability. Large physical distances have visible effects, and so do time zones. The architecture of a wide-area network is yet again fundamentally different from that of a local area network. Most prominently, the network topology is dynamic and non-trivial. Computers become intrinsically mobile: they require different addressing when physically moved across administrative boundaries. Techniques based on mobility become more important and sometimes essential. For ex-

---

[1] Still, a single faulty routing configuration file spread over the Internet in July 1997, causing the disappearance of a large number of Internet domains. In this case, the vulnerable "brain" was the collection of Internet routers.

ample, mobile Java applets provided the first disciplined mechanism for running code able to (and allowed to) systematically penetrate other people's firewalls. Countless projects have emerged in the last few years with the aim of supporting mobile computation over wide areas, and are beginning to be consolidated.

At this point, our architectural goal might be to devise techniques for managing computation over an unreliable collection of far-flung computers. However, this is not yet the full picture. Not only are network links and nodes widely dispersed and unreliable; they are not even liable to stay put, as we discuss next.

## 2.3 Mobile Computing

A different global computing paradigm has been evolving independently of the Web. Instead of connecting together all the LANs in the world, another way of extending the reach of a LAN is to move individual computers and other gadgets from one LAN to another, dynamically.

We discussed in the Introduction how the main characteristics of the Web point towards mobile comput*ation*. However, that is meant as mobile computation over a fixed (although possibly flaky) network. A more interesting picture emerges when the very components of the network can move about. This is the field of mobile comput*ing*. Today, laptops and personal organizers routinely move about; in the future entire networks will go mobile (as in IBM's Personal Area Network). Existing examples of this kind of mobility include: a smart card entering a network computer slot; an active badge entering a room; a wireless PDA or laptop entering a building; a mobile phone entering a phone cell.

We could draw a picture similar to Mental Image 1, but with mobile devices moving within the confines of a single LAN. This notion of a dynamic LAN is a fairly minor extension of the basic LAN concepts, and presents few conceptual problems (wireless LANs are already common). A much more interesting picture emerges when we think of mobile gadgets over a WAN, because administrative boundaries and multiple access pathways then interact in complex ways, as anybody who travels with a laptop knows all too well.

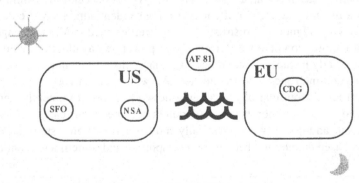

**Mental Image 3: Mobile Computing**

Mental Image 3 focuses on two domains: the United States and the European Union, each enclosed by a political boundary that regulates the movement of people and computers. Within a political boundary, private companies and public agencies may further regulate the flow of people and devices across their doors. Over the Atlantic we see a third domain, representing Air France flight 81 travelling from San Francisco to Paris. AF81 is a very active mobile computational environment: it is full of people working with their laptops and possibly connecting to the Internet through airphones. (Not to mention the hundreds of computers that control the airplane and let it communicate with ground stations.)

Abstracting a bit from people and computation devices, we see here a hierarchy of boundaries that enforce controls and require permissions for crossing. Passports are required to cross political boundaries, reservations are required for restaurants, tickets are required for airplanes, and special clearances are required to enter (and exit!) agencies such as the NSA. Sometimes, whole mobile boundaries cross in and out of other boundaries and similarly need permissions, as the mobile environment of AF81 needs permission to enter an airspace. On the other hand, once an entity has been allowed across a boundary, it is fairly free to roam within the confines of the boundary, until another boundary needs to be crossed.

## 2.4 General Mobility

We have described two different notions of mobility. The first, *mobile computation*, has to do with virtual mobility (mobile software). The second, *mobile computing*, has to do with physical mobility (mobile hardware). These two fields are today almost disconnected, the first dominated by a software community, and the second dominated by a hardware community. However, the borders between virtual and physical mobility are fuzzy, and eventually we will have to treat all kinds of mobility in a uniform way. Here are two examples where the different forms of mobility interact.

The first example is one of virtual mobility achieved by physical means. Consider a software agent in a laptop. The agent can move by propagating over the network, but can also move by being physically transported with the laptop from one location to another. In the first case, the agent may have to undergo security checks when it crosses administration domains. In the second case the agent may have to undergo security checks (e.g. virus detection) when the laptop is physically allowed inside a new administrative domain. Do we need two completely separate security infrastructures for these two cases, or can we somehow find a common principle? A plausible security policy for a given domain would be that a physical barrier (a building door) should provide the same security guarantees as a virtual barrier (a firewall).

The second example is one of physical mobility achieved by virtual means. Software exists that allows remote control of a computer, by bringing the screen of a remote computer on a local screen. The providers of such software may claim that this is just as good as moving the computer physically, e.g. to access its local data. Moreover, if the remote computer has a network connection, this is also equivalent to "stringing wire" from the remote location, since the remote network is now locally accessible. For example, using remote control over a phone line to connect from home to work where a high-bandwidth Internet connection is available, is almost as good as having a high-bandwidth Internet connection brought into the home.

The other side of the coin of being mobile is of becoming disconnected or intermittently connected. Even barring flaky networks, intermittent connectivity can be caused by physical movement, for example when a wireless user moves into some form of Faraday cage. More interestingly, intermittent connectivity may be caused by virtual movement, for example when an agent moves in and out of an administrative domain that does not allow communication. Neither case is really a failure of the infrastructure; in both cases, lack of connectivity may in fact be a desirable security feature. Therefore, we have to assume that intermittent connectivity, caused equivalently by physical or virtual means, is an essential feature of mobility.

In the future we should be prepared to see increased interactions between virtual and physical mobility, and we should develop frameworks where we can discuss and manipulate these interactions.

## 2.5 Barriers and Action-at-a-Distance

The unifying difficulty in both mobile computing and mobile computation is the proliferation of barriers, and the problems involved in crossing them. This central difficulty implies that we must regard barriers as fundamental features of our computational models. This seems contrary to the usual trend.

Access barriers have arisen many times in the history of computing, and one of the main tasks of computer science has been to "abstract them away", often by the proverbial extra level of indirection. For example, physical memory boundaries are circumvented by virtual memory; address space boundaries are circumvented by network proxies; firewall boundaries are circumvented by secure tunnels and agent sandboxing. Unfortunately, when barriers are not purely technological it is not possible to completely abstract them away. The crossing of administrative barriers must be performed by explicit bureaucratic operations, such as exhibiting equipment removal passes and export licences.

Therefore, administrative barriers constitute a nasty fundamental change in the way we compute. Let's review some historical examples.

In the early days of the Internet, any computer could talk to any other computer by knowing its IP number. We can now forget about flat IP addressing and transparent routing: routers and firewalls effectively hide certain IP addresses from view and make them unreachable by direct means.

In the early days of programming languages, people envisioned a universal address space in which all programs would live and share data, possibly with world-wide garbage-collection, and possibly with strong typing to guarantee the integrity of the pointers. We can now forget about universal addressing: although pointers are allowed across machines on a LAN (by network proxies), they are generally disallowed across firewalls. Similarly, we can forget about transparent distributed object systems: some network objects will be kept well hidden within certain domains, and reaching them will require effort.

In the early days of mobile agents, people envisioned agents moving freely across the network on behalf of their owners. We can now forget about free-roaming: if sites do not trust agents they will not allow them in. If agents do not trust sites to execute them fairly, they will not want to visit them.

In general, we can forget about the notion of *action-at-a-distance computing*: the idea that resources are available transparently at any time, no matter how far away. Instead, we have to get used to the notion that movement and communication are step-by-step activities, and that they are visibly so: the multiple steps involved cannot be hidden, collapsed, or rendered atomic.

The action-at-a-distance paradigm is still prevalent within LANs, and this is another reason why LANs are different from WANs, where such an assumption cannot hold.

## 2.6 Why a WAN is not a big LAN

We have already discussed in the Introduction how a WAN exhibits a different set of observable than a LAN. But could one emulate a LAN on top of a WAN, restoring a more familiar set of observables, and therefore a more familiar set of programming techniques? If this were possible, we could then go on and program the Internet just like we now program a LAN.

To turn a WAN into a LAN we would have to hide the new observables that a WAN introduces, and we would have to reveal the observables that a WAN hides. These tasks ranges from difficult, to intolerable, to impossible. Referring to the classification in the Introduction, we would have to achieve the following.

*(A) Hiding virtual locations*. We would have to devise a security infrastructure that makes navigation across multiple administration domains painless and transparent (when legitimate). Although a great deal of cryptographic technology is available, there may be impossibility results lurking in some corners. For example, it is far from clear whether one can in principle guarantee the integrity of mobile computations against hostile or unfair servers [33]. (This can be solved on a LAN by having all computers under physical supervision.)

*(B) Hiding physical locations*. One cannot "hide" the speed of light; techniques such as caching and replication may help, but they cannot fool processes that attempt to perform long-distance real-time control and interaction. In principle, one could make all delays uniform, so that programs would not behave differently in different places. Ultimately this can be achieved only by slowing down the entire infrastructure, by embedding the maximal propagation delay in all communications. (This would be about 1/10 of a second on the surface, but would grow dramatically as the Web is extended to satellite communication, orbital stations, and further away.)

*(C) Hiding bandwidth fluctuations*. It is possible to introduce service guarantees in the networking infrastructure, and therefore eliminate bandwidth fluctuations, or reduce them below certain thresholds. However, in overload situations this has the only effect of turning network congestion into access failures, which brings us to the next point.

*(D) Revealing failures*. We would have to make failures as observable as on a LAN. This is where we run into fundamental trouble. A basic result in distributed systems states that we cannot achieve distributed consensus (such as agreeing on which nodes have failed) in a system consisting of a collection of asynchronous processes [19]. The Web is such a system: we can make no assumption about the relative speed of processors (they may be overloaded, or temporarily disconnected), about the speed of communication (the network may be congested or partitioned), about the order of arrival of messages, or even about the number of processes involved in a computation. In

these circumstances, it is impossible to detect the failure of processors or of network nodes or links; any consensus algorithm can be delayed indefinitely. The common partial solutions for this unsolvable problem are to dictate some degree of synchrony and failure detection. These solutions work well on a LAN, but they seem unlikely to apply to WANs simply because individual users may arbitrarily decide to turn off their processors without warning, or take them into unreachable places. Other partial solutions involve multiple-round broadcast-based probabilistic algorithms [9] which might be expensive on a WAN in terms of communication load, and would be subject to light-speed delays. Moreover, it is difficult to talk about the failure of processors that are invisible because they are hidden behind firewalls, and yet take part in computations. Therefore, it seems unlikely that techniques developed to deal with asynchrony in operating systems and LANs can be successfully applied to a WAN such as the Web in full generality. The Web is an inherently asynchronous system, and the impossibility result of [19] applies with full force.

In summary: task (A) may be unsolvable for mobile code; in any case, a non-zero amount of bureaucracy will always be required; task (B) is only solvable (in full) by introducing unacceptable delays; task (C) can be solved in a way that reduces it to (D); task (D) is unsolvable in principle, while probabilistic solutions run into task (B).

## 2.7 WAN Postulates

We summarize this section by a collection of postulates that capture the main properties of the reality we are interested in modeling:

- 1) Separate locations exist.
- 2) Since different locations have different properties, both people and programs will want to move between them.
- 3) Barriers to mobility will be erected to preserve certain properties of certain locations.
- 4) Some people and some programs will still need to cross those barriers.

The point of these postulates is to stress that mobility and barrier crossing are inevitable requirements of our current and future computing infrastructure.

The observables that are characteristic of wide-area networks have the following implications:

- Distinct virtual locations:
  - Are observed because of the existence of distinct administrative domains, which are produced by the inevitable existence of attackers.
  - Preclude the unfettered execution of actions across domains. Preclude continuous connectivity.
  - Require a security model.
- Distinct physical locations:
  - Are observed, over large distances, because of the inevitable latency limit given by the speed of light.

- Preclude instantaneous action at a distance.
- Require a mobility model.
- Bandwidth fluctuations (including hidden failures):
  - Are observed because of the inevitable exercise of free will by network users, both in terms of communication and movement.
  - Preclude reliance on response time.
  - Require an asynchronous communication model.

# 3 Modeling Mobility

Section 2 was dedicated to showing that the reality of mobile computation over a WAN does not fall into familiar categories. Therefore, we need to invent a new paradigm, or model, that can help us in understanding and eventually in taking advantage of this reality.

Since the Web is, after all, a distributed system, it is worth reviewing the existing literature on models of distributed systems to see if there is something there that we can already use. Readers who are not interested or experienced in models of concurrency, may skip ahead to Section 4.

## 3.1 Formalisms for Concurrency, Distribution, and Security

The π-calculus [30], along with its variations, is a prominent model of concurrency, and is the starting point for our work. It is based on the notion of processes communicating over channels, with the ability to create new channels and to exchange channels over channels.

We spend some time discussing why some of the basic assumptions of the π-calculus and of other concurrent formalisms do not satisfy our particular needs.

### Static Connectivity

Some early paradigms for concurrency, such as Actors [3], allowed highly dynamic systems. However, the main formalized descriptions of concurrency began by considering only static connectivity. This is the case for Petri Nets [10], for Hoare's Communicating Sequential Processes (CSP) [24], and for Milner's Calculus of Communicating Systems (CCS) [28]. In CCS, in particular, the set of communication channels that a processes has available does not change during execution. In some versions of CSP (and in Occam [26]) the set of processes cannot change either.

These models are insufficient for modeling mobility in a general sense. Instead, they best characterize the situation in Mental Image 1, where the only form of mobility is the mobility of data over communication channels.

### Dynamic Connectivity

The π-calculus is an extension of CCS where channels can be transmitted over other channels, so that a process can dynamically acquire new channels. Channel transmission (also called channel mobility) is a powerful extension of the basic communication model. The transmission of a channel over another channel gives the recipient the ability to communicate on that channel. It is perhaps best to think that a channel end-point has been transmitted.

Let us consider a channel end-point that is transmitted across a domain boundary over another channel that already crosses the boundary. If the transmitted end-point remains functional, it provides a dynamically-established connection between the two sides of the boundary. This is the kind of connection that firewalls typically forbid: opening arbitrary network connections or allowing network-object proxy requests is not allowed without further checks. The new channel that crosses the firewall could be seen as an implicit firewall tunnel, but the establishment of trusted tunnels involves more than simply passing a channel over another one, otherwise the firewall would loose all control of security.

A firewall must watch the communication traffic over each channel that crosses it; that is, it must act as an intermediary and forwarder of messages between the outside and the inside of a domain. If a channel end-point is seen passing through, the firewall must decide whether to allow communication on that channel, and if so it must create a forwarder for it. So, a channel through a firewall must really be handled as two channels connected by a filter [20].

Therefore, ability to communicate on a channel depends not only on possessing the end-point of a channel, but also on where the other end-point of the channel is, and how it got there. If the other end-point was sent through a firewall, then the ability to effectively communicate on that channel depends on the attitude of the firewall.

Our approach: We provide a framework where processes exist in multiple disjoint locations, and such that the location of a process influences its ability to communicate with other processes. Dynamic connectivity is achieved by movement, but movement does not guarantee continued connectivity.

### Distribution

The π-calculus has no inherent notion of distribution. Processes exist in a single contiguous location, by default, because there is no built-in notion of distinct locations and their effects on processes. Interaction between processes is achieved by global, shared names (the channel names); therefore every process is assumed to be within earshot of every other process. Incidentally, this makes distributed implementation of the original π-calculus (and of CCS) quite hard, requiring some form of distributed consensus.

Various proposals have emerged to make the π-calculus suitable for distributed implementation, and to extend it with location-awareness. The asynchronous π-calculus [25] is obtained by a simple weakening of the π-calculus synchronization primitives. Asynchronous messages simplify the requirements for distributed synchronization [32], but they still do not localize the management of communication decisions. The join-calculus [20] approaches this problem by rooting each channel at a particular process; this provides a single place where synchronization is resolved. LLinda [18] is a formalization of Linda [15] using process calculi techniques; as in distributed versions of Linda, LLinda has multiple distributed tuple spaces, each with its local synchronization manager.

Our approach: We restrict communication to happen within a single location, so that communication can be locally managed. In particular, interaction is by shared location, not by shared names. Remote communication is modeled by a combination of mobility and local communication.

## Locality

By locality we mean here distribution-awareness: a process has some notion of the location it occupies, in an absolute or relative sense.

A growing body of literature is concentrating on the idea of adding discrete locations to a process calculus and considering failure of those locations [4, 21]. A notion of locations alone is not sufficient, since locations could all really be in the "same place". However, in presence of failures one could observe that certain locations have failed and others have not, and deduce that those locations are truly in different places, otherwise they would all have failed at the same time. The distributed join-calculus [21], for example, adds a notion of named locations, and a notion of distributed failure; locations form a tree, and subtrees can migrate from one part of the tree to another, therefore becoming subject to different failure patterns.

This failure-based approach aims to model traditional distributed environments, and traditional algorithms that tolerate node failures. However, on the Internet, node failure is almost irrelevant compared with inability to reach nodes. Web servers do not often fail forever, but they frequently disappear from sight because of network or node overload, and then they come back. Sometimes they come back in a different place, for example, when a Web site changes its Internet Service Provider. Moreover, inability to reach a Web site only implies that a certain path is unavailable; it implies neither failure of that site nor global unreachability. In this sense, a perceived node failure cannot simply be associated with the node itself, but instead is a property of the whole network, a property that changes over time.

Our approach: The notion of locality is induced not by failures, but by the need to cross barriers. Barriers produce a non-trivial and dynamic topology of locations. Locations are observably distinct because it takes effort to move between them, and because some locations may be "absent" and are distinguishable from locations that are "present". Failure is only represented, in a weak but realistic sense, as becoming forever unreachable.

## Mobility

There are different senses in which people talk about "process mobility"; we try to distinguish between them.

A $\pi$-calculus channel is mobile in the sense that it can be transmitted over another channel. Let's imagine a process as having a mass, and its channels as springs connecting it to other processes. When springs are added and removed by communication, the process mass is pulled in different directions. Therefore, the set of channels of a process influences its location, and a change of channels causes the process to change location. This is particularly clear if a process has a single active channel at any time, because a single spring will strongly influence a process location. By this analogy, channel mobility can be interpreted as causing process mobility.

However, our desired notion of process mobility is tied to the idea of crossing domain barriers. This is a very discrete, on-off, kind of mobility: either a process is inside a domain, or it is not. Representing this kind of mobility by adding and removing channels is not immediate. For example, if a $\pi$-calculus channel crosses a barrier (that is, if it is communicated to a process meant to represent a barrier), there is still no clear sense in which the process has also crossed the barrier. In fact, the same channel may cross several disjoint domain barriers, but a process should not exist in all those domains at once. Therefore, a $\pi$-calculus process can be made to span several domains, which is something we would like to rule out from the start.

Our notion of process mobility is tied to the notion of nested domains. It still remains to be seen how simple hierarchies, such as the ones we have emphasized in our mental images, can capture the sometimes complex relationships between administrative domains. Still, some notion of domain nesting seems natural, and this is difficult to represent adequately in process calculi like the $\pi$-calculus that are based on "flat" sets of processes.

Another, more direct, form of process mobility has been proposed: a process may move by being transmitted over a channel to another process. This mechanism is not present in the basic $\pi$-calculus, but is present in so-called higher-order $\pi$-calculi[2]. This is certainly a form of process mobility of the kind found in mobile agent systems, where "whole" and "alive" agents are transmitted over communication channels. However, there are a couple of details that should raise some concern, again having to do with domain boundaries.

First, transmitting a process through a firewall over a channel relies on the existence of a channel that already crosses a firewall. That is, we still have to separately model the establishment of firewall tunnels.

Second, if a process has connections before the move, does it maintain them on the other side of the firewall? If the answer is "yes", then arbitrary channels can be made to penetrate a firewall from the existence of a single channel. If the answer is "not necessarily", why and how do those other channels break? If the firewall acts as a filter, then it has to analyze the processes that are passing though and their communication capabilities; this may be considerably more complex than analyzing simple messages.

Third, transmitting a process over a channel is a *copy* rather than *move* operation. Nothing prevents the original process from continuing, and nothing prevents the transmitted process from being further replicated. That is, the idea that *the same process* moved from here to there seems to be lost.

Our approach: mobility is not represented by passing channels over channels, nor by passing processes over channels. It is represented by processes jumping across boundaries. The identity of the moving process is preserved because a process that crosses a boundary disappears from its previous location.

## Security

It is possible to extend a concurrent calculus with cryptographic primitives, as in the spi calculus extension of the $\pi$-calculus [2]. Much fundamental progress is being made in this direction.

In our approach, security is not tied to cryptographic primitives, but on the ability or inability to cross barriers, which is conferred by capabilities. Given the mechanisms

---

[2] The fact that the latter can be formally reduced to the former [34] is best ignored for this discussion.

already required to handle boundaries, the need for cryptographic extensions does not arise immediately. For example, a boundary enclosing a piece of text can be seen as an encryption of the text, in the sense that a capability, the cryptokey, is needed to cross the boundary and read the text. There is an unexpected similarity between a firewall surrounding a major company and the encryption of a piece of data, both being barrier-based security mechanisms at vastly different scales.

## 3.2 Formalisms for Reactivity

An important part of interacting and computing on the Web is being able to react to bandwidth fluctuations in real time. We will not talk about this subject further, preferring to concentrate on the other computational observables discussed in the Introduction. We just note that the vast literature on real-time reactive systems should be relevant in this context (e.g., see [6]), and that some Web-related work in this area has been carried out [12] and has found applications [27].

# 4 Ambients

We have now sufficiently discussed our design constraints and the deficiencies of existing solutions, and we are finally ready to explain our own proposal in detail. We want to capture in an abstract way, notions of locality, of mobility, and of ability to cross barriers. To this end, we focus on *mobile computational ambients*; that is, places where computation happens and that are themselves mobile.

## 4.1 Overview

Briefly, an *ambient*, in the sense in which we are going to use this word, is a place that is delimited by a boundary and where computation happens. Each ambient has a *name*, a collection of local *processes*, and a collection of *subambients*. Ambients can move in and out of other ambients, subject to *capabilities* that are associated with ambient names. Ambient names are unforgeable, this fact being the most basic security property.

In further detail, an ambient has the following main characteristics.

- An ambient is a *bounded* place where computation happens.

  If we want to move computations easily we must be able to determine what parts should move. A boundary determines what is inside and what is outside an ambient, and therefore determines what moves. Examples of ambients, in this sense, are: a web page (bounded by a file), a virtual address space (bounded by an addressing range), a Unix file system (bounded within a physical volume), a single data object (bounded by "self") and a laptop (bounded by its case and data ports). Non-examples are: threads (where the boundary of what is "reachable" is difficult to determine) and logically related collections of objects. We can already see that a boundary implies some flexible addressing scheme that can denote entities across the boundary; examples are symbolic links, URLs (Uniform Resource Locators) and Remote Procedure Call proxies. Flexible addressing is what enables, or at least facilitates, mobility. It is also, of course, a cause of problems when the addressing links are "broken".

- Ambients can be nested within other ambients, forming a tree structure.

  As we discussed, administrative domains are (often) organized hierarchically. Mobility is represented as navigation across a hierarchy of ambients. For example, if we want to move a running application from work to home, the application must be removed from an enclosing (work) ambient and inserted in a different enclosing (home) ambient.

- Each ambient has a collection of local running processes.

  A local process of an ambient is one that is contained in the ambient but not in any of its subambients. These "top level" local processes have direct control of the ambient, and in particular they can instruct the ambient to move. In contrast, the local processes of a subambient have no direct control on the parent ambient: this helps guaranteeing the integrity of the parent.

- Each ambient moves as a whole with all its subcomponents.

  The activity of a single local process may, by causing movement of its parent, influence the location, and therefore the activity, of other local processes and subambients. For example, if we move a laptop and reconnect it to a different network, then all the threads, address spaces, and file systems within it move accordingly and automatically, and have to cope with their new surrounding. Agent mobility is a special case of ambient mobility, since agents are usually single-threaded. Agents, like ambients, automatically carry with them a collection of private data as they move.

- Each ambient has a name.

  The name of an ambient is used to control access (entry, exit, communication, etc.). In a realistic situation the true name of an ambient would be guarded very closely, and only specific capabilities based on the name would be handed out. In our examples we are usually more liberal in the handling of names, for the sake of simplicity.

We have developed and are still studying a formal calculus of ambients [13]. In this paper we stay away from formalism; the essential features of the ambient calculus will be conveyed by (fairly precise) metaphors.

As a first metaphor, already partially outlined, we can consider a foreign travel scenario. A country with border guards can be seen as an example of a static ambient. Local officers (privileged processes) govern movement across the border and communication within the border. Entry and exit capabilities (passports and visas) moderate mobility across the border. Officers may decide who may join them as new officers.

As an example of a mobile ambient we may consider a tourist traveling to such a country. The tourist travels by being transported by another mobile ambient: a train, or airplane. The tourist's visas are checked on entry and exit. The tourist may be imprisoned within the country (by withholding the exit capability) or, if not careful, even killed. On the other hand, the tourist may be allowed to become a local officer (be naturalized), and in such a function may act as a spy or a saboteur, sending out encrypted messages or disabling subsystems.

In the following section we discuss a more abstract metaphor that is easy to describe and has an intuitive graphical presentation. It corresponds faithfully to the full, formal, ambient calculus.

## 4.2 The Folder Calculus: Mobility

In this office-style metaphor we represent an ambient as a folder. A folder confines its contents: something is either inside or outside any given folder. Each folder has a name that is written on the folder tag. Folders are naturally nested, and can be moved from place to place.

The computational aspect of the calculus is represented by assuming that folders are active. In addition to subfolders, folders may contain *gremlins* that cause the folder to move around, and are moved together with their folder.

A folder with label *n* and contents *P*

We now describe the *reductions* (atomic computation steps) that can arise in the folder calculus. Each reduction can happen at the "top level" of the computation (say, "on the desktop") or inside a folder. That is, the folder hierarchy is active at every level, with some caveats noted below.

### *The Enter Reduction*

Our first reduction causes a folder to enter another folder. On the left of the arrow, in the figure below, the folder labeled *n* contains a gremlin that is ready to execute the instruction *in m* (meaning: "let the surrounding folder enter a folder labeled *m*"), and then continue with *P*. (The partial occlusion of *P* in the figure is meant to indicate that the instruction *in m* must execute before *P* can be activated.) The collection of other gremlins and subfolders that may be contained in *n* is represented by the letter *Q*, and similarly by *R* within *m*. A folder labeled *m* happens to exist near the folder *n*, where "near" means "within the same surrounding folder, or on the desktop".

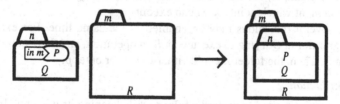

Enter reduction

In this situation the operation *in m* can execute, resulting in the configuration to the right of the arrow. The result of the operation is that the folder *n* becomes a subfolder of the folder *m*, and the gremlin who executed the instruction is ready to continue with *P*. The instruction *in m* has been consumed. Any other gremlins or subfolders in *Q* and *R* are unchanged.

A reduction can happen only if the conditions on the left of the arrow are satisfied. That is, *in m* executes only if there is a sibling folder labeled *m*. Otherwise, the operation remains blocked until a sibling folder labeled *m* appears nearby. Such a folder may appear, for example, because it moves near *n*, or because some of the gremlins in *Q* cause *n* to move near it.

Many reductions can be simultaneously enabled, in which case one is chosen non-deterministically. For example, there could be two distinct folders labeled $m$ near $n$, in which case $n$ could enter either one. Also, there could be another gremlin, as part of $Q$, trying to execute an *in m* operation, in which case exactly one of the gremlins would succeed. Moreover, there could be another gremlin in $Q$ trying to execute an *in p* operation, and there could be another folder labeled $p$ near $n$, in which case the $n$ folder could enter either $m$ or $p$.

### The Exit Reduction

Our second reduction is essentially the inverse of the previous one: two nested folders become siblings. On the left of the arrow, the folder labeled $n$ contains a gremlin that is ready to execute the instruction *out m* (meaning: "let the surrounding folder exit its parent labeled $m$"), and then continue with $P$. The parent folder is in fact labeled $m$.

In this situation the operation *out m* can execute, resulting in the configuration to the right of the arrow. The result of the operation is that the folder $n$ becomes a sibling of the folder $m$, and the gremlin who executed the instruction is ready to continue with $P$. The instruction *out m* has been consumed. Any other gremlins or subfolders in $Q$ and $R$ are unchanged.

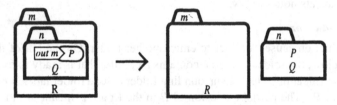

**Exit reduction**

The operation *out m* executes only if the parent folder is labeled $m$. Otherwise, the operation remains blocked until a parent folder labeled $m$ materializes. The parent may become $m$, for example, because some of the gremlins in $Q$ cause $n$ to move inside a folder labeled $m$, at which point *out m* can execute.

Again, several reductions may be enabled at the same time. For example, there could be a gremlin in $Q$ trying to execute an *in p* operation, and there could be a folder labeled $p$ in $R$. Then, the folder $n$ could either exit $m$ or enter $p$.

### The Open Reduction

Our third reduction is used to discard a folder while keeping its contents. In the picture it is helpful to imagine that there is a folder surrounding the entities on the left of the arrow, so that *open n* followed by $P$ is a gremlin of that folder, and $n$ is one of its subfolders. The gremlin is ready to execute the instruction *open n* (meaning: "let a nearby folder labeled $n$ be opened"), and then continue with $P$. A folder labeled $n$ happens to exist nearby.

In this situation the operation *open n* can execute, resulting in the configuration to the right of the arrow. The result of the operation is that the folder $n$ is discarded, but its contents $Q$ are spilled in the place where the folder $n$ used to be. The instruction *open n* has been consumed, and the gremlin is ready to continue with $P$.

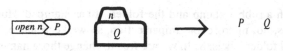

**Open reduction**

As before, the operation *open n* is blocked if there are no folders labeled *n* nearby. If there are several ones, any one of them may be opened.

### The Copy Reduction

Our fourth reduction is used to replicate folders and all their contents. On the left of the arrow, a copy machine is ready to make copies of a folder *P* (actually, *P* could also be a gremlin or any collection of folders and gremlins). We should imagine that the original *P* is firmly placed under the cover of the copy machine, and is compressed into immobility: none of the gremlins or folders of *P* can operate or move around (otherwise the copy might be "blurred"). However, as soon as a copy of *P* is made, that copy is free to execute.

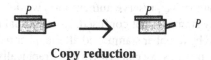

**Copy reduction**

The copy machine can produce a new copy of *P* and of all its contents at will (nobody needs to push the copy button). After that, the copy machine can operate again, indefinitely. So, on the right of the arrow we have the same configuration as on the left, plus a fresh copy of *P*. We could think that copies of *P* are made on demand, whenever needed, rather than being continuously produced.

### Name Creation

The handling of names is a delicate and fundamental part of our calculus. Fortunately, it is very well understood: it comes directly from the π-calculus.

Name creation is an implicit operation, in the sense that there are no reductions associated with it. It is represented below as the creation of a rubber stamp for a name *n*, which can be used to stamp folder labels. Any number of folders can be stamped with the same rubber stamp.

A rubber stamp is used not as much to give a name, as to give *authenticity* to a folder. There are several components to this notion, and we need to stretch our office metaphor a bit to make it fit with the intended semantics.

At a microscopic scale, each rubber stamp has slight imperfections that can be used to tell which rubber stamp was used to stamp each particular folder. Therefore, the particular name chosen for a rubber stamp is irrelevant: what is really important is the relationship between a rubber stamp and the folders it has stamped. Humans, however, like to read names, not microscopic imperfection, so we keep names associated with rubber stamps and folder labels. Still, we are free to change those names at any time, as long as this is done consistently for a rubber stamp, all its related folders, and all the other uses of the name on the rubber stamp. This consistent renaming could be considered as a reduction, but it is simple enough to be considered as a basic equivalence between configurations of folders, expressing the fact that superficial names are not really important.

In our metaphor, a copy machine can be used to copy anything contained in a folder, including rubber stamps. Therefore, even if we started with all the rubber stamps having different names, eventually there might be multiple rubber stamps carrying the same name. To make authenticity work, we have to assume that copy machines cannot copy rubber stamps perfectly at the microscopic level: when a rubber stamp is replicated, a different set of microscopic imperfections is generated. That is, rubber stamps are unforgeable by assumption.

For all these reasons, two rubber stamps carrying the same name $n$ are really two different rubber stamps. To preserve authenticity, we do not want these rubber stamps, and the folders they stamp, to get confused. In our visual representation, we collect all the folders stamped by a rubber stamp, and all the other occurrences of its name, within a dashed boundary: this way we can always tell, graphically, which folders were authenticated by a rubber stamp, even when different rubber stamps have the same name.

This dashed border is a flexible boundary and can move about fairly freely (it is just a bookkeeping device). We have three main invariants for where a dashed border can be placed. First it must always be connected with its original rubber stamp. Second, it must always enclose all the folders that have ever been stamped with its particular stamp and all other occurrences of the name (e.g. within gremlin code); if a folder moves away, the dashed boundary may have to be enlarged. Third, dashed boundaries for two rubber stamps with the same name must not intersect; if we should ever need to do so we shall first systematically rename one of the two rubber stamps and the related names, so that there is no confusion. The dashed boundaries for rubber stamps with different names can freely intersect.

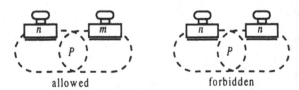

allowed     forbidden

It is allowable to nest dashed boundaries for rubber stamps with the same name: an occurrence of that name will refer to the closest enclosing rubber stamp, in standard block scoping style.

### Leaves of the Syntax

At the bottom of our syntax there is the inactive gremlin, which can be represented as an empty border. The inactive gremlin has no reductions.

Inactive gremlin

Inactive gremlins are often simply discarded or omitted. For example, multiple inactive gremlins can be collapsed into one inactive gremlin, and a folder containing only one inactive gremlin is usually represented as an empty folder.

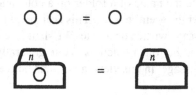

Programs in the folder calculus are built from these foundations, by assembling collections of gremlins, folders, rubber stamps, and copy machines, and possibly placing them inside other folders.

### The Theoretical Power of Mobility

Before moving on to our next and final reduction, we pause and consider the operations we have introduced so far. These operations are purely combinatorial, that is, they introduce no notion of parameter passing, or message exchange. Also, they deal purely with mobility, not with communication or computation of any familiar kind. Yet, they are computationally complete: Turing machines can be encoded in a fairly direct way (see [13]).

Moreover, very informally, it is possible to see an analogy between the Enter reduction and increment, the Exit reduction and decrement, the Open reduction and test, and the Copy reduction and iteration. Therefore all the ingredients for performing arithmetic are present, and it is in fact possible to represent numbers as towers of nested folders, with appropriate operations.

Data structures such as records and trees can be represented easily, by nested folders; folder names represent pointers into such data structures. Storage cells can be represented as folders whose contents change in response interactions with other folders; in this case a folder name represents the address of a cell.

In summary, the mobility part of the Folder Calculus already has the full power of any computationally complete language. In principle, one could use it as a graphical scripting language for the office/desktop metaphor.

### 4.3 The Folder Calculus: Communication

Mobility is by itself a computationally complete paradigm. Still, we want to talk about communication in a direct way; for example, gremlins may want to exchange names of folders to visit. Representing communication within the existing set of mobility primitives is theoretically possible, but unbearably clumsy. So, our next task is to introduce communication primitives that do not invalidate the principles described in Section 3, and that do not spoil the folder metaphor. The primitives we introduce next are probably

the simplest imaginable. In particular, they do not conflict with the notion of strict folder containment, and do not duplicate mobility functionality.

### The Read Reduction

We begin by introducing a new entity that can sit inside a folder: a message. To remain
within the office metaphor, we imagine writing messages onto throw-away Post-it notes
that are attached to the inside of folders.

A gremlin can write the name of a folder on a note, and can attach the note to the
current folder (the folder the gremlin is in). This is an output operation, and is represented graphically by a message written on a note. We shall discuss shortly what are the particular messages used in the folder calculus. More generally, we may imagine writing
any kind of data as a message; in this view, a note can be seen as nameless data file that
is kept within a folder.

**Output**

Conversely, a gremlin can grab any note attached to the current folder, read its message, discard the note, and proceed with the knowledge of the message. This is an input
operation, and is represented graphically by a process $P$ with occurrences of the variable
$x$ (written $P\{x\}$) that is waiting for a note with a message to be bound to x.

**Input**

The Read reduction is the interaction between input and output operations or,
equivalently, between message notes and input operations. In a situation where an input
and an output are present, the Read reduction can execute, resulting in the configuration
on the right of the arrow, which is simply $P\{M\}$: the residual gremlin $P$ that has read $M$
into $x$. The note that appears on the left of the arrow is discarded: it is consumed by reading and does not appear on the right. (If the note needs to persist, it can be replicated by
a copy machine.)

**Read reduction**

An input operation blocks if there are no available messages. Several input operations may contend for the same message and only one of them will obtain it and be able
to proceed. An output operation, however, never blocks (it is *asynchronous*); it simply
drops a message in the current folder and has no continuation.

Inputs and outputs usually happen within a folder (although the reduction above allows them to happen on the desktop). Within such a folder, the identity of the input or output gremlins are not important: anybody can talk to anybody else, in the style of a chat room. In practice, different folders will be dedicated to different kinds of conversation, so one can make assumptions about what should be said and what can be heard in a given folder. This idea gives rise to a type system for the folder calculus [14].

### Messages and Capabilities

We can imagine many kinds of messages that can be written on Post-it notes. Here we focus on messages that are *capabilities*: they allow the reader of a message to perform privileged actions. There are two kinds of capabilities, used in different contexts: *naming capabilities* and *navigation capabilities*.

Naming capabilities are simply ambient names used as messages. A name $n$ can be seen as a capability to construct (and rubber-stamp) a folder named $n$.

We have already seen the main navigation capabilities, implicitly. We have presented the operations *in n*, *out n* and *open n* as three distinct operations followed by a continuation $P$. In fact, they are special cases of a single operation $M.P$, where $M$ is a navigation capability and $P$ is the continuation after navigation. Given a name $n$, *in n* is the capability to enter an ambient named $n$, *out n* is the capability to exit an ambient named $n$, and *open n* is the capability to open an ambient named $n$. Navigation capabilities are extracted from naming capabilities, meaning that knowing $n$ implies the ability to construct, for example, *in n*, but knowing *in n* does not imply knowing $n$.

Navigation capabilities can be composed into navigation paths. For example, *in n. out m. open p. out q* is a path capability that can be written in a single message, read into an input variable $x$, and executed in its entirety by $x.P$ (assuming, of course, that the path can be followed). It useful to have an empty navigation path, written *here*, such that *here.P* has no effect and continues with $P$, and $M.here = here.M = M$.

### Example

This is an artificial example that uses each of the five folder reductions once. We use a single dashed line for multiple rubber stamps when the order of nesting of dashed lines does not matter. We remove rubber stamps when they are no longer needed.

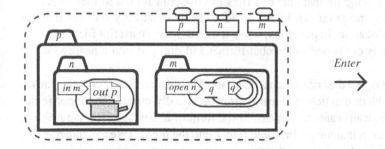

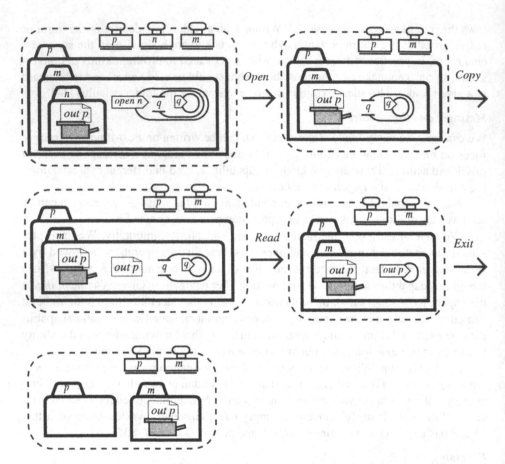

The reader is encouraged to follow the reductions, comparing them with their definitions.

### Example: Adobe Distiller

Adobe Distiller is a program that converts files in Postscript format to files in Adobe Acrobat format. The program can be set up to work automatically on files that are placed in a special location. In particular, when a user drops a Postscript file into an *inbox* folder, the file is converted to Acrobat format and dropped into a nearby *outbox* folder.

The following figure describes such a behavior. The *distiller* folder contains the *inbox* and *outbox* folders mentioned above; *outbox* is initially empty. The *input* folder contains the file the user wants to convert, in the form of a message. The input folder contains also a gremlin that moves the *input* folder into the *inbox*. (We can imagine that this piece of gremlin code is generated automatically as a result of the user dragging the *input* folder into the *inbox* folder.)

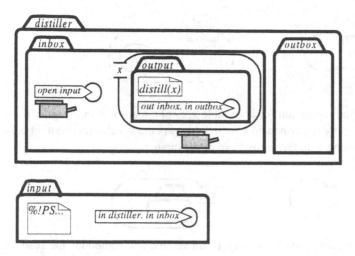

The *inbox* contains the program necessary to do the format conversion and drop the result into the *outbox*. First, any *input* folder arriving into the *inbox* must be opened to reveal the Postscript file; this is done by the copy machine on the left. Then, any such file is read; this is done by the copy machine on the right. As a result of each read, an *output* folder is created to contain a result. Inside each *output* folder, a file is distilled (by the external operation *distill(x)*) and left there as an output. The output folder is moved into the *outbox* folder.

It should be noted that the program above represents highly concurrent behavior, according to the reduction semantics of the folder calculus. Multiple files can be dropped into the *inbox* and can be processed concurrently. The opening of the *input* folders and the reading of their contents is done in a producer-consumer style. Moreover, each distilling process may be executing while its *output* folder is traveling to the *outbox*. Representing this behavior in an ordinary concurrent language would not be entirely trivial; here we have been able to express it without cumbersome locking and synchronization instructions.

### Example: Synchronous Output

It is sometimes useful to know that a message has been read by somebody before proceeding. Synchronous output is an output operation with a continuation that is triggered only after the output message has been read.

Synchronous output is expressible within the folder calculus, if we assume that the calculus has been extended to allow the exchange of pairs of values (this extension can in fact be encoded within the calculus). Together with synchronous output, we need to define a matching input operation. These new operations are depicted with additional striped borders in the figures.

The synchronous output of a message $M$ is obtained by creating a fresh name, $k$, outputting (asynchronously) the pair $M,k$, and waiting for the appearance of a folder named $k$ before proceeding.

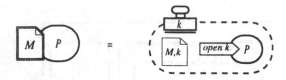

The corresponding input operation for a variable $x$, is obtained by expecting an input pair $x,k$, creating an empty folder named $k$ (which triggers the synchronous output continuation), and continuing with the normal use of the input $x$.

Therefore, when the process $P$ starts running, it can assume that somebody has read the message $M$.

## 4.4 Security

The folder calculus has built-in features that allow it to represent security and encryption situations rather directly; that is, without extending the calculus with ad-hoc primitives for encryption and decryption. In this section, we discuss a number of examples based on simple security protocols.

We should make clear here what we mean by security for the folder calculus. Security problems arise at every level of a software system, not just at the cryptographic level. Given any set of security primitives, and any system written with those primitives, one can ask whether the system can be attached at the "low-level", by attacking weaknesses in the implementation of the primitives, or at the "high-level", by attaching weaknesses in how the primitives are used. Efforts are underway to study the security of high-level abstractions under low-level attacks [1], but here we are only concerned with high-level attacks. That is, we assume that an attacker has at its disposal only the primitives of the folder calculus. This is the kind of attack that a malicious party could mount against honest folders interacting within a trusted server or over a trusted network. For example, even within a perfectly trusted server, if a folder gives away its name $a$, it could be killed by an attacker performing *open a*.

### *Authentication*

In this example, a *home* folder is willing to let any folder in, but is willing to open only those folders that are recognized as having originally come from *home*. Opening a folder implies conferring top-level execution privilege to its gremlins, and this privilege should not be given to just anybody. A particular *home* gremlin that has execution privilege wants to leave *home* and then wants to come back *home* and be given the same execution privilege it enjoyed before.

The mechanism the *home* folder uses to recognize the gremlin is a pass: a use-once authentication token. Passes are generated in the left-hand side of the figure below, where a copy machine produces fresh configurations, each consisting of a new rubber stamp, a single message (the pass) stamped by the rubber stamp, and a single open capability for the name on the rubber stamp.

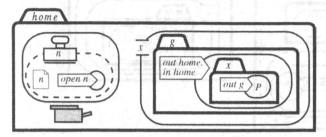

The traveling gremlin is on the right-hand side of the figure. It inputs a pass $n$ by reading a message into a variable $x$, and it eventually uses the pass to label a folder. The gremlin, in the form of the folder $g$, takes a short walk outside and comes back. Then it exposes a folder named $n$, which is opened by the corresponding *open n* capability that was left behind. The gremlin $P$ can then continue execution at the top level of *home*; for example, it may read another pass and leave again.

Since the scope of each pass $n$ is restricted by a locally-generated rubber stamp, the capability *open n* is not at risk of ever opening some foreign folder. There are actually two underlying security assumptions here. The first is that nobody can accidentally or maliciously create a pass that matches $n$: this can be guaranteed in practice with arbitrarily high probability. The other assumption is that nobody can steal the name $n$ from the traveling gremlin. This seems very hard or impossible to guarantee in general, particularly if the gremlin visits a hostile location that disassembles the gremlin by low-level mechanisms (below the abstraction level of the folder calculus). However, if the gremlin visits only trusted locations through trusted networks (ones that preserve the abstractions of the folder calculus), then no interaction can cause the gremlin to be unwillingly deprived of its pass.

### Nonces

A nonce is a use-once token that can be used to ensure the freshness of a message. In the example below, a nonce is represented by a fresh name $n$. The folder $a$ sends the nonce to the folder $b$, where the nonce is paired with a message $M$ and sent back.

The folder $a$ then checks that the nonce returned by $b$ is the same one that was sent to $b$. This is achieved by creating an empty folder named by the returned nonce, and trying to open that folder with the original nonce. If the test is successful, then $a$ knows that the message $M$ is fresh: it was generated after the creation of $n$.

If *nonce* and *msg* are public names, then an attacker could disrupt this protocol by destroying the message folders in transit. Even worse, an attacker could inject *nonce* and *msg* folders into $a$ or $b$ containing misleading information or damaging code. If $a$ and $b$ have already established shared keys, they can avoid these problems by exchanging and opening only messages encrypted under the keys (this is discussed shortly).

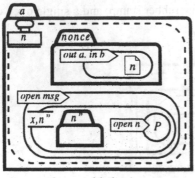
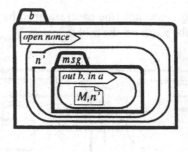

An attacker could also impersonate *a* or *b* by creating folders with those names, and could then intercept messages. However, the names of principals like *a* and *b* will normally be closely guarded secrets, so that impersonation cannot happen. In contrast, capabilities like *in a* will be given out freely, since the act of entering a folder cannot by itself cause damage to the folder, even if who enters is malicious.

### Shared Keys

A name can be used as a shared key, as long as it is kept secret and shared only by certain parties. A shared key can be reused multiple times, e.g., to encrypt a stream of messages.

A message encrypted under a key *k* can be represented as a folder that contains the message and whose label is *k*. We call such a folder a *k*-envelope for the message. Knowledge of *k* (or, at least, of the capability *open k*) is required to open the folder and read the message.

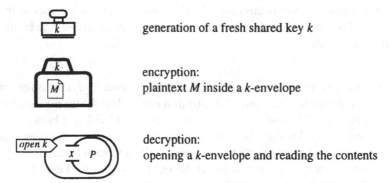

generation of a fresh shared key *k*

encryption:
plaintext *M* inside a *k*-envelope

decryption:
opening a *k*-envelope and reading the contents

To continue the Authentication example, a traveling gremlin could carry a shared key *k*, generated inside the *home* folder, and send messages back *home* inside *k*-envelopes. The *home* folder could decrypt those messages by using the shared key. If the shared key is unique to a particular gremlin, this has the effect of authenticating the source of the messages.

In many classical distributed protocols, shared keys are assume to be distributed by unspecified covert means, separately from ordinary communication on public channels. The principals are assumed to have already established shared keys before they begin interacting. The key distribution problems is left as a separate problem.

In our framework, which includes mobility, some aspects of key distribution can be modeled explicitly. For example, a key can become shared between distant principals because they generate the key when they are in the same location, and then move apart. Or, a courier folder can transport a key from a principal to another over a trusted network, and then the principals can use the key to communicate over an untrusted network.

## 4.5 Textual Syntax

So far we have been relying on a visual syntax, but we are going to need some textual syntax for writing further examples. The following table summarizes the folder calculus visual syntax, and introduces the corresponding textual syntax. There is a one-to-one correspondence between textual syntax and visual syntax; therefore, it is possible to freely mix them, if desired, nesting either one inside the other.

### Correspondence Between Textual and Visual Syntax

We use $P,Q,R$ to range over ambient and process expressions, and $M,N$ to range over message expressions. As shown in the table, the creation of a new name is written $(\nu n)P$ where the Greek letter $\nu$ (nu) binds the name $n$ within the scope $P$. An ambient is written $n[P]$ where $n$ is the ambient name, where the brackets denote the ambient boundary, and where $P$ is the contents of the ambient.

Processes P,Q,R

| Textual Syntax | Visual Syntax | Comments |
|---|---|---|
| $(\nu n)P$ | | New name $n$ in a scope $P$. |
| $n[P]$ | | Folder (ambient) of name $n$ and contents $P$. |
| $M.P$ | | Action $M$ followed by $P$. |
| $P \mid Q$ | $P \quad Q$ | Two processes in parallel. (Visually: contiguously placed in 2D.) |
| $0$ | | Inactive process (often omitted). |
| $!P$ | | Replication of $P$. |

| | | |
|---|---|---|
| (M) | M | Output M. |
| (n).P | n P | Input n followed by P. |
| (P) | P | Grouping. |

*Messages M,N*

| | |
|---|---|
| n | A name |
| in n | An entry capability |
| out n | An exit capability |
| open n | An open capability |
| here | The empty path of capabilities |
| M.N | The concatenation of two paths |

The textual syntax for the folder calculus is in fact the full syntax of the ambient calculus we were alluding to previously. Therefore, our folder calculus metaphor is quite exact: the syntax and semantics of our formal ambient calculus [13] has now been completely explained through the metaphor.

### Example: Adobe Distiller

This is the textual representation of the example in Section 4.3.

```
distiller[
    inbox[
        !open input |
        !(x) output[⟨distill(x)⟩ | out inbox. in outbox]] |
    outbox[]]
|
input[⟨"%!PS..."⟩ | in distiller. in inbox]
```

## 5 Ideas for Wide-Area Languages

The ambient calculus is a minimal formalism designed for theoretical study. Our final goal, though, is to program the Internet; for this we are certainly going to need something more elaborate and convenient than a formal calculus. Still, the basic constructs of the ambient calculus represent our understanding of the fundamental properties of mobile computation over wide-area networks. Therefore, we aim to find programming constructs that are semantically compatible with the principles of the ambient calculus, and consequently of wide-area-networks.

These principles include (A) *WAN-soundness*: a wide-area network language cannot adopt primitives that entail action-at-a-distance, continued connectivity, or security bypasses, and (B) *WAN-completeness*: a wide area network language must be able to express the behavior of web surfers and of mobile agents and users.

## 5.1 Related Languages

Many software systems have explored and are exploring notions of mobility and wide-area computation. Among these are:

- Obliq [11]. The Obliq language attacks the problems of remote execution and mobility for distributed computing. It was designed in the context of local area networks. Within its scope, Obliq works quite well, but is not really suitable for computation and mobility over the Web, just like most other distributed paradigms developed in pre-Web days.

- Telescript [37]. Our ambient model is partially inspired by Telescript, but is almost dual to it. In Telescript, agents move whereas places stay put. Ambients, instead, move whereas processes are confined to ambients. A Telescript agent, however, is itself a little ambient, since it contains a "suitcase" of data. Some nesting of places is allowed in Telescript.

- Java [23]. Java provides a working paradigm for mobile computation, as well as a huge amount of available and expected infrastructure on which to base more ambitious mobility efforts. The original Java mobility model, however was based on mobility of code, not mobility of data or active computations. Data mobility has now been achieved by the Java RMI extension, but computation mobility (e.g. for threads or live objects) is still problematic.

- Linda [15]. Linda is a "coordination language" where multiple processes interact in a common space (called a tuple space) by dropping and picking up tokens asynchronously. Distributed versions of Linda exist that use multiple tuple spaces and allow remote operations over those. A dialect of Linda [16] allows nested tuple spaces, but not mobility of the tuple spaces.

- The Join Calculus Language [22] is an implementation of the distributed Join Calculus. The plain Join Calculus introduced an original and elegant synchronization mechanism, where a procedure invocation may be triggered by the join of multiple partial invocations originating from different processes. The Distributed Join Calculus extends the Join Calculus with an explicit hierarchy of locations. As we already mentioned, the nature of this calculus makes distributed implementation relatively easy. Migration of locations is allowed within the hierarchy. Behavior of the system under a failure model is being investigated.

- WebL [27] is a language that specializes on fetching and processing Web pages. It uses service combinators [12] to retrieve streams of data from unreliable servers, and it uses a sophisticated pattern matching sublanguage for analyzing structured (but highly variable) data and reassembling it.

## 5.2 Wide-Area Languages

We do not have a full-blown language or library to propose yet; what is more important here is the general flavor of such a language or library. In this section we discuss programming constructs that are directly inspired by the ambient calculus and that are not usually found in standard programming environments. In the remaining sections we show a detailed example involving some of these constructs, and we speculate on a specific wide-area application that could hopefully be better written using a wide-area language.

### Ambients as a Programming Abstraction

Our basic abstraction is that of mobile computational ambients. The ambient calculus brings this abstraction to an extreme, by representing *everything* in terms of ambients at a very fine grain. In practice, to be useful as a programming abstraction, ambients would have to be medium or large-grained entities. Ambient contents should include standard programming subsystems such as modules, classes, objects, and threads.

In that sense, ambients could be used simply as wrappers of ordinary software subsystems, for the purpose of rendering those subsystems mobile. An ambient library could include mechanisms for creating empty ambients, adding threads, objects, and subambients to them, allowing threads to communicate with other ambients, and, of course, allowing ambients to move around.

We should notice that the ability to smoothly move a collection of running threads is almost unheard of in current software infrastructures. In this sense, ambients would be a novel and non-trivial addition to our collection of programming abstractions.

### Names vs. Pointers

The only way to use an ambient is by its name. No matter how we organize our hierarchies of ambients, the only way to manipulate the resulting structure is by using ambient names. These names are detached from their corresponding ambients; one may possess a name without having immediate access to any ambient of that name.

Therefore, names are like pointers, providing access to structures, but are only "symbolic pointers": more like file names and URLs than memory addresses. Like file names, these pointers need not always denote the same structure: they denote any ambient of the corresponding name, and this may change over time. When these pointers denote no ambient, they are not "broken" (like dangling pointers, or illegal file names) but rather "blocked" until a suitable ambient becomes available. Of course, one might feel nervous about the possibility of blocking whenever one tries to use a name. On the other hand, a blocked computation can be unblocked by providing an appropriate ambient, thus modeling both dynamic linking and the installation of plug-ins.

In an ambient-based language, every pointer to a data structure or other resource outside of a given ambient should behave like a name. This is necessary to allow ambients to move around freely without being restrained by immobile ties.

### Locations

Ambients can be used to model both physical and virtual locations. Some physical locations are mobile (such as airplanes) while others are immobile (such as buildings). Similarly, some virtual locations are mobile (such as agents) while others are immobile (such as mainframe computers). These mobility distinctions are not reflected in the semantics of ambients, but can be added as a refinement of the basic model, or embedded in type systems that restrict the mobility of certain ambients.

## Migration and Transportation

Each ambient is completely self-contained, and can be moved at any time with all its running computations. If an ambient encloses a whole application, then the whole running application can be moved without need to restart it or reinitialize it. In practice, an application will have ties to the local window system, the local file system, etc. These ties, however, should only be via ambient names. When moving the applications, the old window system ambient, say, becomes unavailable, and eventually the new window system ambient becomes available. Therefore, the whole application can smoothly move and reconnect its bindings to the new local environment. Some care will still be needed to restart in a good state (say, to refresh the application window), but this is a minor adjustment compared to what one would have to do if hard connections existed between the application and the environment [5].

## Communication

The basic communication primitives of the ambient calculus are based on the asynchronous model and do not support global consensus or failure detection. These properties should be preserved by any higher-level communication primitives that may be added to the basic model, so that the intended semantics of communication over a wide-area networks is preserved.

The ambient calculus directly supports only local communication within an ambient. Remote communication (for example, RPC) can be interpreted as mobile output packets that transport and deposit messages to remote locations, wait for local input, and then come back. The originator of an RPC call may block for the answer to come back before proceeding, in the style of a synchronous call. In this interpretation, the outgoing and incoming packets may get stuck for an arbitrary amount of time, or get lost. There may be no indication that the communication has failed, and therefore the invoking process may block forever without receiving a communication exception. This is as it should be, since arbitrary delays are indistinguishable from failures. (Note, though, that a time-out mechanism is easily implemented, by placing a remote invocation in parallel with another activity that waits a certain time and, if the invocation has not completed, cause something else to happen.)

Other examples of derived communication mechanisms include parent-child communication, and communication between siblings (perhaps aided by the common parent). All these appear quite useful, and will likely need to be included in any convenient language.

## Data Structures

Basic data structures, such as booleans and integers, can be encoded in terms of ambients, but the encodings are not practical. Therefore, basic types should be taken as primitive, as usual.

Ambients can directly express hierarchies, so it should not be surprising that they can easily represent structured data types. For example, a record structure of the form

$\{l_1=e_1, ..., l_n=e_n\}$ can be represented as:

$$r[l_1[!(\langle e_1\rangle|open\ accessor)] \mid ... \mid l_n[!(\langle e_n\rangle|open\ accessor)]]$$

where the name $r$ is the address of the record, and the record fields $l_i=e_i$ are represented by subambients of the record ambient. The values $e_i$ are placed into the subambients as outputs, waiting for an accessor ambient to go inside and read them.

The ambient semantics, though, is a bit richer than the minimum required for data structures. For example, we would not normally want to allow the fields of a record to take off and leave. Some possibilities supported by the ambient semantics are intriguing but probably not worth the trouble, such as the ability to concatenate records by opening them inside a new record.

Therefore, it would be prudent to build-in ordinary data structures, without relying too much on the possibilities provided by the ambient semantics. Still, for ambients to work at all we need these data structures to be mobile. Therefore, the "address" of a data structure should be a proper ambient name, in the sense that it should provide blocking behavior on access if needed.

### Recursion

Many behaviors are naturally defined recursively. It is convenient to use a recursion construct of the form, for example, $rec\ X.\ P$, representing a recursively defined process $P$ where any occurrence of $X$ again denotes $P$. More generally, one can introduce mutually recursive definitions, as done below when discussing resources.

The ambient calculus embeds what is essentially an iteration construct, $!P$. In terms of theoretical power, this is sufficient to encode recursion. As a programming construct, though, it is inconvenient, and is also hard to implement because of its flavor of unbounded generation. So, for programming practice $!P$ should be removed in favor of recursion facilities.

### Synchronization

Synchronization primitives are needed to coordinate the activities of multiple processes within an ambient. In the ambient calculus, it is easy to represent basic synchronization constructs, such as mutexes:

| | |
|---|---|
| $release\ n;\ P\ \triangleq\ n[]\mid P$ | release a mutex called $n$, and do $P$ |
| $acquire\ n;\ P\ \triangleq\ open\ n.\ P$ | acquire a mutex called $n$, then do $P$ |

where the *open* instruction blocks until a mutex is released, and consumes the mutex.

A useful technique is to synchronize on the change of name of an ambient. That is, a process may wait for an ambient to change its name to a given name, and another process may perform the change to trigger the first process. Name change can be represented in the ambient calculus, but not in a way that is atomic with respect to arbitrary actions (particularly, movement) performed by other processes. A proper solution would require all the processes in an ambient to synchronize on a mutex before any movement or name change. This is a bit laborious; therefore it is convenient to introduce name change as a primitive with the following atomic reduction:

$$n[be\ m.P \mid Q] \;\rightarrow\; m[P \mid Q]$$

## Static and Dynamic Binding

Wide-area systems are outside the control of any single administrator, and therefore their maintenance cannot rely entirely on static configurations. In programming language terms, they cannot rely completely on static binding of variables. A programer who needs to change a static binding can usually change it, recompile the program, and restart it. But one cannot easily restart the Internet, or any large system deployed across it. Therefore some form of dynamic binding is necessary.

The names of the ambient calculus represent an unusual combination of static and dynamic binding. Formally, the names obey the classical rules of static scoping, including consistent renaming, capture-avoidance, and block nesting. However, the navigation primitives behave by dynamically binding a name to any ambient that has the right name. The connection between a name and an ambient of that name is fully dynamic, much like in dynamic linking.

The basic ambient calculus does not have any definitional facilities, but these are clearly needed when building any large-scale systems, or even medium scale examples. We are going to need definitional facilities for both static and dynamic binding, corresponding to the underlying semantic features.

Statically-bound definitions can be represented by fairly normal *let* constructions. A process-producing definition can be written:

$$let\ f(x_1...x_n) = P;\ P' \qquad (let\ f(x_1...x_n)\ be\ P\ within\ the\ scope\ P')$$

with a standard expansion semantics within the scope $P'$. For call-by-value parameter passing, assuming that $V_1...V_n$ are fully-evaluated messages, we have:

$$f(V_1...V_n) \triangleq P\{x_1{\leftarrow}V_1...x_n{\leftarrow}V_n\}$$

Dynamically bound definitions are much less routine, and more closely tied to the ambient semantics; we discuss them next.

## Resources

In the mobile agent paradigm, sites differ from each other by the collection of resources that they provide to visiting agents. Agents bind dynamically to these resources as they enter the ambient. Similarly, it is natural to think of each ambient as providing a collection of local resources, which could be seen as forming the interface, namespace, environment, method suite, etc., of the ambient.

To this end, we introduce a mechanism of local resource definitions that is compatible with the general ambient semantics, and can be easily explained in terms of the primitives of Section 4. These resource definitions may occur only at the top level of an ambient, and have the following form:

$$def\ f(x_1...x_n) = P; \qquad (bind\ the\ resource\ f(x_1...x_n)\ to\ P\ within\ the\ ambient)$$

Note that the name $f$ is not bound by this definition; it must be bound by a ν binder at some sufficiently global level. This way, different resources named $f$ can be provided in different ambients, and each use of the resource $f$ will be relative to a given ambient. A typical such resource could be the local window-system library.

A resource $f$ can be invoked as follows, within an ambient where it is defined:

$$f(V_1...V_n)/here \triangleq P\{x_1 \leftarrow V_1...x_n \leftarrow V_n\}$$

where the suffix "/here" indicates that a definition of $f$ has to be found in the ambient where $f$ is invoked. In general, a path may be used in place of *here*, in which case the definition of the resource is retrieved from the ambient obtained by following the path, and the invocation is executed there. In other words, the effect of $f(V_1...V_n)/p$ is to transport the invocation $f(V_1...V_n)$ along the path $p$, and then to invoke it within the target ambient. This can be expressed by two rules that each transport an invocation one step further:

$$f(V_1...V_n)/in\ n.p \mid n[Q] \triangleq n[Q \mid f(V_1...V_n)/p]$$
$$n[f(V_1...V_n)/out\ n.p \mid Q] \triangleq f(V_1...V_n)/p \mid n[Q]$$

For example, we could have an expression such as the following:

$n[def\ x() = \langle 1 \rangle;$
$\quad def\ f(y) = x()/here \mid (x'). \langle x'+y \rangle]$
$\mid f(3)/in\ n$

producing, after the invocation $f(3)/in\ n$:

$n[def\ x() = \langle 1 \rangle;$
$\quad def\ f(y) = x()/here \mid (x'). \langle x'+y \rangle;$
$\quad \langle 4 \rangle]$

The definition and invocation of resources can be encoded in the pure ambient calculus; this way, resources automatically acquire an ambient-like flavor. In particular, if an ambient has no definition for an invocation, the invocation blocks until the definition becomes available in the designated place. If an ambient has multiple definitions for an invocation, any one of them may be used. If an ambient containing definitions is opened, its definitions become definitions of its parent.

### Modularization

An ambient $P$ that includes a collection of local definitions can be seen as a module, or a class. More precisely, $!P$ can be seen as a module or a class (since $P$ there is inactive), while any active $P$ generated from it can be seen as a module instance or an object.

The action of performing an *open* on such an ambient can be seen as importing from a module or inheriting from a class, since ambient definitions are transplanted from one ambient to another. Moreover, one can regard the notation $f(M)/p$ either in module-oriented style as $p.f(M)$ (the invocation of $f(M)$ from the module at $p$), or in object-oriented style as *delegation* [36] of $f(M)$ to the object found at $p$.

When seen as modules or components, ambients have several interesting and unusual properties.

First, ambients are *first class modules*, in the sense that one can choose at run time which particular instance of a module to use.

Second, ambients support *dynamic linking*: missing subsystems can be added to a running system simply by placing them in the right spot.

Third, ambients support *dynamic reconfiguration*. In most module and class systems, the identity of individual modules is lost immediately after static or dynamic linking. Ambients, though, maintain their identity at run time. As a consequence, a system composed of ambients can be reconfigured by dynamically replacing an ambient with another one. The blocking semantics of ambient interactions allows the system to smoothly suspend during a configuration transition. Moreover, the hierarchical nature of ambients allows the modular reconfiguration of entire subsystem, not just of individual modules. Dynamic reconfiguration is particularly valuable in long-running and widely-deployed systems that cannot be easily stopped (for example, in telephone switches); it is certainly no accident that thinking about the Internet led us to this property.

Therefore, ambients can be seen as proper *software components*, according to a paradigm often advocated in software engineering, where the components are not only replaceable but also mobile.

## Security

Ambient security is based on capabilities and on the notion that security checks are performed at ambient boundaries, after which processes are free to execute until they need to cross another boundary. This is a capability-based model of security, as opposed to a cryptography-based model, or an access-control based model.

These three models are all interdefinable. In our case, access control is obtained by using ambients to implement RPC-like invocations that have to cross boundaries and authenticate every time. The cryptographic model is obtained by interpreting encryption keys as ambient names, which are by assumption unforgeable. Then, encryption is given by wrapping some content in an ambient of a given name, and decryption is obtained by either entering or opening such an ambient given an appropriate capability (the decryption key).

## Summary

We believe we have sufficiently illustrated how the ambient semantics naturally induces unusual programming constructs that are well-suited for wide-area computation. The combination of mobility, security, communication, and dynamic binding issues has not been widely explored yet at the language-design level, and certainly not within a unifying semantic paradigm. We hope our unifying foundation will facilitate the design of such new languages.

## 5.3 Example: Public Transportation

We now show an example of a program written in ambient notation. Some additional constructs used here have been introduced in the previous section.

This example emphasizes the mobility aspects of ambients, and the fact that an ambient may be transported from one place to another without having to know the exact route to be followed. A passenger on a train, for example, only needs to know the destination station, and need not be concerned with the intermediate stations a train may or may not stop at.

In this example, there are three train stations, represented by ambients: *stationA*, *stationB* and *stationC* (of course, these particular ambients will never move). There are three trains, also represented by ambients: a train from *stationA* to *stationB* originating at *stationA*, and two trains between *stationB* and *stationC*, one originating at each end. There are two passengers, again represented by ambients; *joe* and *nancy*. Joe wants to go from *stationA* to *stationC* by changing trains at *stationB*; *nancy* wants to go the other way.

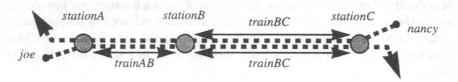

We begin by defining a parametric process that can be instantiated to trains going between different stations at different speeds. The parameters are: *stationX*: the origin station; *stationY*: the destination station; *XYatX*, the tag that the train between *X* and *Y* displays when stationed at *X*; *XYatY*, the tag that the train between *X* and *Y* displays when stationed at *Y*; *tripTime*, the time a train takes to travel between origin and destination.

```
let train(stationX stationY XYatX XYatY tripTime) =
    (ν moving)                    // assumes the train originates inside stationX
        moving[rec T.
            be XYatX. wait 2.0.
            be moving. out stationX. wait tripTime. in stationY.
            be XYatY. wait 2.0.
            be moving. out stationY. wait tripTime. in stationX.
            T];
```

The definition of a train begins with the creation of a new name, *moving*, that is intermittently used as the name of the train. While the train is *moving*, passengers should not be allowed to (dis)embark; this is achieved by keeping *moving* a secret name. The train begins as an ambient with name *moving*, and contains a single recursive thread that shuttles the train back and forth between two stations. Initially, the train declares itself to be a train between *X* and *Y* stationed at *X*, and waits some time for passengers to enter and exit. Then it becomes *moving*, so passengers can no longer (dis)embark. It exits the origin station, travels for the *tripTime*, enters the destination station, and declares itself to be the train between *X* and *Y* at *Y*. Again, passengers can (dis)embark during the wait time at the station. Then the train becomes *moving* again, goes back the other way, and then repeats the whole process.

Next we have the configuration of stations and trains. We create fresh names for the three stations and for the train tags. Then we construct three ambients for the three stations, each containing an appropriately instantiated train.

```
(ν stationA stationB stationC ABatA ABatB BCatB BCatC)
    stationA[train(stationA stationB ABatA ABatB 10.0)] |
    stationB[train(stationB stationC BCatB BCatC 20.0)] |
    stationC[train(stationC stationB BCatC BCatB 30.0)] |
```

Finally, we have the code for the passengers. *Joe*'s itinerary is to enter *stationA*, wait to enter the train from *A* to *B* when it is stationed at *A*, exit at *B*, wait for the train from *B* to *C* when it is stationed at *B*, exit at *C* and finally exit *stationC*. During the time that *joe* is waiting to exit a train, he is blocked waiting for the train to acquire the appropriate tag. The train could change tags at intermediate stations, but this would not affect *joe*, who is waiting to exit at a particular station. When that station is reached, and the train assumes the right tag, *joe* will attempt to exit. However, there is no guarantee that he will succeed. For example, *joe* may have fallen asleep, or there may be such a rush that *joe* does not manage to exit the train in time. In that case, *joe* keeps shuttling back and forth between two stations until he is able to exit at the right station.

> (ν *joe*)
>> *joe*[
>>> *in stationA*.
>>> *in ABatA*. *out ABatB*.
>>> *in BCatB*. *out BCatC*.
>>> *out stationC*] |

The code for *nancy* is similar, except that she goes in the other direction. Given the timing of the trains, it is very likely that *nancy* will meet *joe* on the platform at *stationB*.

> (ν *nancy*)
>> *nancy*[
>>> *in stationC*.
>>> *in BCatC*. *out BCatB*.
>>> *in ABatB*. *out ABatA*.
>>> *out stationA*]

In all this, *joe* and *nancy* are active ambients that are being transported by other ambients. Sometimes they move of their own initiative, while at other times they move because their context moves. Note that there are two trains between *stationB* and *stationC*, which assume the same names when stopped at a station. *Joe* and *nancy* do not care which of these two train they travel on; all they need to know is the correct train tag for their itinerary, not the "serial number" of the train that carries them. Therefore, having multiple ambients with the same name simplifies matters.

When all these definitions are put together and activated, we obtain a real-time simulation of the system of stations, trains, and passengers. A partial trace looks like this:

| | |
|---|---|
| *nancy*: | moved in *stationC* |
| *nancy*: | moved in *BCatC* |
| *joe*: | moved in *stationA* |
| *joe*: | moved in *ABatA* |
| *joe*: | moved out *ABatB* |
| *nancy*: | moved out *BCatB* |
| *joe*: | moved in *BCatB* |
| *nancy*: | moved in *ABatB* |

*nancy*:   moved out *ABatA*
*nancy*:   moved out *stationA*
*joe*:     moved out *BCatC*
*joe*:     moved out *stationC*

## 5.4 Challenge: A Conference Reviewing System

We conclude with the outline of an ambitious wide-area application. The application described here does not fit well with simple-minded Web-based technology because of the complex flow of active code and stateful information between different sites, and because of an essential requirement for disconnected operation. The application fits well within the agent paradigm, but also involves the traversal of multiple administrative domains, and has security and confidentiality requirements.

This is meant both as an example of an application that could be programmed in a wide-area language, and as a challenge for any such language to demonstrate its usability. We hope that a language based on ambients or similar notions would cope well with this kind of situation.

### Description of the problem

The problem consists in managing a virtual program committee meeting for a conference. The basic architecture was suggested to me by comments by Richard Connors, as well as by my own experience with organizing program committee meetings and with using Web-based reviewing software developed for ECOOP and other conferences.

In the following scenario, the first occurrence of each of the principals involved is shown in boldface.

### Announcement

A **conference** is announced, and an electronic **submission form**, signed by the **conference chair**, is publicized.

### Submission

Each **author** fetches the submission form, checks the signature of the conference chair, and activates the form. Once activated, the form actively guides most of the reviewing process. Each author fills an instance of the form and attaches a **paper**. The form checks that none of the required fields are left blank, electronically signs the paper with a signature key provided by the author, encrypts the attached paper, and finds its way to the **program chair**. The program chair collects the submissions forms, and gives them a decryption key so that they can decrypt the attached papers and verify the signatures of the authors. (All following communications are signed and encrypted; we omit most of these details from now on.)

### Assignment

The program chair then assigns the submissions to the **committee members**, by instructing each submission form to generate a **review forms** for each assigned member. The review forms incorporate the paper (this time signed by the program chair) and find their way to the appropriate committee members.

*Review*

Each committee member is a **reviewer**, and may decide to review the paper directly, or to send it to another reviewer. The review form keeps tracks of the chain of reviewers so that it can find its way back when either completed or refused, and so that each reviewer can check the work of the subreviewers. Eventually a review is filled. The form performs various consistency checks, such as verifying that the assigned scores are in range and that no required fields are left blank. Then it finds its way back to the program chair.

*Report generation*

Once the review forms reach the program chair, they become **report forms**. The various report forms for each paper merge with each other incrementally to form a single report form that accumulates the scores and the reviews. The program chair monitors the report form for each paper. If the reviews are in agreement, the program chair declares the form an **accepted paper report form**, or a **rejected paper review form**.

*Conflict resolution*

If the reports are in disagreement, the program chair declares the form an **unresolved review form**. An unresolved review form circulates between the reviewers and the program chair, accumulating further comments, until the program chair declares the paper accepted or rejected.

*Notification*

The report form for an accepted or rejected paper finds its way back to the author (minus the confidential comments), with appropriate congratulations or regrets.

*Final versions*

Once it reaches the author, an accepted paper report form spawns a **final submission form**. In due time, the author attaches to it the final version of the paper and signs the copyright release notice. The completed final submissions form finds its way back to the program chair.

*Proceedings*

The final submission forms, upon reaching the program chair, merge themselves into the **proceedings**. The program chair checks that all the final versions have arrived, sorts them into a conference schedule, attaches a preface, and lets the proceedings find their way to the conference chair.

*Publication*

The conference chair files the copyright release forms, signs the proceedings, and posts them to public sites.

*Comments*

A few critical features characterize this application as particularly well-suited for experimenting with wide-area languages.

First, it is a requirement of this application that most interactions happen in absence of connectivity. Virtual committee meetings occur over the span of one month of reviewing and one or two weeks of discussion. It is highly unlikely that all the committee members will be continuously near their main workstation, or any workstation, during such a span of time. Yet, progress cannot be interrupted by the temporary absence of any one member. Furthermore, progress cannot be interrupted by the absence of connectivity for any one member: paper reviews are commonly done on airplanes, in doctors waiting rooms, in lines at the Post Office, in cafe's, etc. While a laptop or personal organizer can be easily carried in those environments, continuous connectivity is far from easy to achieve. This is to be contrasted with current web-based review systems, which require reviewers to sit at a connected workstation while filling the review forms.

Second, form-filling requires semantic checking, which is best done while the form is being filled. Therefore, active forms are required even during off-line operation. This is to be contrasted with the filling of on-line Web-based review forms which require, in practice, preparing reviews off-line on paper or in ASCII, and later typing them or pasting them laboriously into on-line forms in order to obtain the semantic checking. Alternatively, if the review is simply e-mailed in ASCII, then the program chair has the considerable burden of performing the parsing and semantic checking.

Third, unattended operations is highly desirable also for the program chair. The program chair may go in vacation after the assignment phase and come back to find all the report forms already merged, thanks to the use of active forms.

Fourth, the system must handle multiple administrative domains. Committee members are intentionally selected to belong to widely diverse and dispersed institutions, many of which are protected by firewalls. In this respect, this situation is different from classical office workflow on a local area network, although it shares many fundamental features with it.

Fifth, all the forms are active. This relieves various principals from the tedious and error-prone task of collecting, checking, and collating pieces of information, and distributing them to the correct sets of other principals.

In summary, in this example, interactions between various parts of the system happen over a wide-area network. The people involved may be physically moving during or between interaction. As they move, they may transport without warning active parts of the system. At other times, active parts of the system move by their own initiative and must find a route to the appropriate principals wherever they are.

## 6 Conclusions

The global computational infrastructure has evolved in fundamental ways beyond standard notions of sequential, concurrent, and distributed computational models. *Mobile ambients* capture the structure and properties of wide-area networks, of mobile computing, and of mobile computation. The ambient calculus [13] formalizes these notions simply and powerfully. It supports reasoning about mobility and security, and has an intuitive presentation in terms of the folder calculus. On this basis, we can envision new programming methodologies, libraries and languages for global computation.

# 7 Acknowledgments

The ideas presented in this paper originated in the heated atmosphere of Silicon Valley during the Web explosion, and were annealed by the cool and reflective environment of Cambridge UK. I am deeply indebted to people in both locations, particularly to Andrew Gordon, who is also a coauthor of related papers. In addition, Martín Abadi and Cédric Fournet made comments and suggestions on recent drafts.

# References

[1]  Abadi, M., Fournet, C., Gonthier, G.: Secure Implementation of Channel Abstractions. Proc. of the Thirteenth Annual IEEE Symposium on Logic in Computer Science (1998) 105-116.

[2]  Abadi, M., Gordon, A.D.: A Calculus for Cryptographic Protocols: the Spi Calculus. Proc. of the Fourth ACM Conference on Computer and Communications Security (1997) 36-47.

[3]  Agha, G.A.: Actors: A Model of Concurrent Computing in Distributed Systems. MIT Press (1986).

[4]  Amadio, R.M.: An Asynchronous Model of Locality, Failure, and Process Mobility. Proc. COORDINATION 97, Lecture Notes in Computer Science 1282, Springer Verlag (1997).

[5]  Bharat, K., Cardelli, L.: Migratory Applications. Proc. of the ACM Symposium on User Interface Software and Technology '95 (1995) 133-142.

[6]  Berry, G.: The Foundations of Esterel. In: Plotkin, G., Stirling C., Tofte, M. (eds.): Proof, Language and Interaction: Essays in Honour of Robin Milner. MIT Press (1998).

[7]  Berry, G., Boudol, G.: The Chemical Abstract Machine. Theoretical Computer Science 96(1) (1992) 217-248.

[8]  Boudol, G.: Asynchrony and the π-calculus. Technical Report 1702, INRIA, Sophia-Antipolis (1992).

[9]  Bracha, G., Toueg, S.: Asynchronous Consensus and Broadcast Protocols. J.ACM 32(4) (1985) 824-840.

[10] Brauer, W. (ed.): Net Theory and Applications. Proc. of the Advanced Course on General Net Theory of Processes and Systems, Hamburg, 1979. Lecture Notes in Computer Science 84. Springer-Verlag (1980).

[11] Cardelli, L.: A Language with Distributed Scope. Computing Systems, 8(1), MIT Press (1995) 27-59.

[12] Cardelli, L., Davies, R.: Service Combinators for Web Computing. Proc. of the First Usenix Conference on Domain Specific Languages, Santa Barbara (1997).

[13] Cardelli, L., Gordon, A.D.: Mobile Ambients. In: Nivat, M. (ed.): Foundations of Software Science and Computational Structures, Lecture Notes in Computer Science 1378, Springer (1998) 140-155.

[14] Cardelli, L., Gordon, A.D.: Types for Mobile Ambients. Proc. of the 26th ACM Symposium on Principles of Programming Languages (1999) 79-92.

[15] Carriero, N., Gelernter, D.: Linda in Context. Communications of the ACM, 32(4) (1989) 444-458.

[16] Carriero, N., Gelernter, D., Zuck, L.: Bauhaus Linda. In: Ciancarini, P., Nierstrasz., O., Yonezawa, A. (eds.): Object-Based Models and Languages for Concurrent Systems. Lecture Notes in Computer Science 924, Springer Verlag (1995) 66-76.

[17] Chandra, T.D., Toueg, S.: Unreliable Failure Detectors for Asynchronous Systems. ACM Symposium on Principles of Distributed Computing (1991) 325-340.

[18] De Nicola, R., Ferrari, G.-L., Pugliese, R.: Locality Based Linda: Programming with Explicit Localities. Proc. TAPSOFT'97. Lecture Notes in Computer Science 1214, Springer Verlag (1997) 712-726.

[19] Fischer, M.J., Lynch, N.A., Paterson, M.S.: Impossibility of Distributed Consensus with One Faulty Process. J.ACM 32(2) (1985) 374-382.

[20] Fournet, C., Gonthier, G.: The Reflexive CHAM and the Join-Calculus. Proc. 23rd Annual ACM Symposium on Principles of Programming Languages (1996) 372-385.

[21] Fournet, C., Gonthier, G., Lévy, J.-J., Maranget, L., Rémy, D.: A Calculus of Mobile Agents. Proc. 7th International Conference on Concurrency Theory (CONCUR'96) (1996) 406-421.

[22] Fournet, C., Maranget, L.: The Join-Calculus Language - Documentation and User's Guide. <http://pauillac.inria.fr/join/> (1997).

[23] Gosling, J., Joy, B., Steele, G.: The Java Language Specification. Addison-Wesley (1996).

[24] Hoare, C.A.R., Communicating Sequential Processes. Communications of the ACM 21(8) (1978) 666-678.

[25] Honda., K., Tokoro, M.: An Object Calculus for Asynchronous Communication. Proc. ECOOP'91, Lecture Notes in Computer Science 521, Springer Verlag (1991) 133-147.

[26] INMOS Ltd.: occam programming manual. Prentice Hall (1984).

[27] Kistler, T., Marais, J.: WebL - A Programming Language for the Web. In Computer Networks and ISDN Systems, 30. Elsevier (1998) 259-270.

[28] Milner, R.: A Calculus of Communicating Systems. Lecture Notes in Computer Science 92. Springer Verlag (1980).

[29] Milner, R.: Functions as Processes. Mathematical Structures in Computer Science 2 (1992) 119-141.

[30] Milner, R., Parrow, J., Walker, D.: A Calculus of Mobile Processes, Parts 1-2. Information and Computation, 100(1) (1992) 1-77.

[31] Morris, J.H.: Lambda-Calculus Models of Programming Languages. Ph.D. Thesis, MIT (Dec 1968).

[32] Palamidessi, C.: Comparing the Expressive Power of the Synchronous and the Asynchronous Pi-calculus. Proc. 24th ACM Symposium on Principles of Programming Languages (1997) 256-265.

[33] Sander, A., Tschudin, C.F.: Towards Mobile Cryptography. ICSI technical report 97-049, November 1997. Proc. IEEE Symposium on Security and Privacy (1998).

[34] Sangiorgi, D.: From $\pi$-calculus to Higher-Order $\pi$-calculus - and Back. Proc. TAPSOFT '93., Lecture Notes in Computer Science 668, Springer Verlag (1992).

[35] Stamos, J.W., Gifford, D.K.: Remote Evaluation. ACM Transactions on Programming Languages and Systems 12(4) (1990) 537-565.

[36] Stein, L.A., Lieberman, H., Ungar, D.: A Shared View of Sharing: The treaty of Orlando. In: Kim, W., Lochowsky, F. (eds.): Object-Oriented Concepts, Applications, and Databases. Addison-Wesley (1988) 31-48.

[37] White, J.E.: Mobile Agents. In: Bradshaw, J. (ed.): Software Agents. AAAI Press / The MIT Press (1996).

# Type-Safe Execution of Mobile Agents in Anonymous Networks

Matthew Hennessy and James Riely

**Abstract.** We study type-safety properties of *open* distributed systems of mobile agents, where not all sites are known to be well-typed. We adopt the underlying model of an *anonymous network*, allowing that code may be corrupted on transmission and that the source of incoming code is unknowable. Nonetheless, we are able to guarantee a weak form of type-safety at "good" sites using a mix of static and dynamic typing.

## 1 Introduction

In [6] we presented a type system for controlling the use of resources in a distributed system. The type system guarantees that resource access is always *safe*, in the sense that, for example, integer channels are always used with integers and boolean channels are always used with booleans. The type system of [6], however, requires that all agents in the system be well-typed. In open systems, such as the internet, such global properties are impossible to verify. In this paper, we present a type system for *partially typed* networks, where only a subset of agents are assumed to be well typed.

This notion of partial typing is presented using the language D$\pi$, from [6]. In D$\pi$ mobile agents are modeled as *threads*, using a thread language based on the $\pi$-calculus. Threads are *located*, carrying out computations at *locations* or *sites*. Located threads, or *agents* interact using local *channels*, or *resources*.

In an open system, not all sites are necessarily benign. Some sites may harbor malicious agents that do not respect the typing rules laid down for the use of resources. For example, consider the system

$$k[\![(\nu c\mathord{:}\mathsf{chan}\langle\mathsf{int}\rangle)\ \mathsf{go}\,m.\,a!\langle k[c]\rangle]\!]$$
$$|\ m[\![a?(z[x])\ \mathsf{go}\,z.\,x!\langle\mathsf{t}\rangle]\!]$$

consisting of two sites $k$ and $m$. The first generates a new local channel $c$ for transmitting integers and makes it known to the second site $m$, by sending it along the channel $a$ local to $m$. Here, the value $k[c]$ and the pattern $z[x]$ are *dependent pairs*, where the first element represents a location and the second element represents a resource *at that location*. In a benign world $k$ could assume that any mobile agent that subsequently migrates from $m$ to $k$ would only use this new channel $c$ to transmit integers at $k$. However in an insecure world $m$ may not play according to the rules; in our example it sends an agent to $k$ which misuses the new resource by sending the boolean value t along it.

In this paper we formalize one strategy that sites can use to protect themselves from such attacks. The strategy makes no assumptions about the security of the underlying network. For example, it is not assumed that the source of a message (or agent) can be reliably determined. We refer to such networks as *anonymous networks*.

In the presence of anonymous networks a reasonable strategy for sites is based on *paranoia*. Since the source of messages cannot be determined it is impossible to distinguish messages from potentially "trusted" sites; thus no site can be trusted. To protect itself, a site must bar entry of any mobile agent that cannot be proven to use local resources as intended.

The requirement that incoming agents be checked entails that the runtime semantics is of necessity more complicated than that of [6]. Each location must retain information about its local resources against which the incoming agents are checked. This information is encapsulated as a location type, giving the names of the resources available locally, together with their types; agent checking then amounts to a form of *local runtime typechecking*.

The paper proceeds as follows. In the next section we review the language Dπ of [6] and recall its *standard* semantics. While the paper is self contained, we rely on [6] for examples and motivation for Dπ. This is followed, in Section 3, by a formal description of the modified run-time semantics, where sites retain local information against which incoming agents are checked.

In Section 4, we discuss the effectiveness of this runtime strategy; we show that *good sites* cannot be harmed by *bad* sites, in the sense that local resources can not be misused at good sites, even in systems which may contain malicious sites. This is formalized in terms of a static typing system, for which we prove Subject Reduction and Type Safety theorems. The paper ends with a critique of both the run-time strategy and the typing system.

## 2 The Language

We present the syntax and standard semantics of Dπ. For a full treatment of the language, including many examples, see [6]. The language is a simplification and refinement of that introduced in [11].

### 2.1 Syntax

The syntax is given in Table 1. We defer the discussion of types, T, to Section 2.3. The syntax is parameterized with respect to the following syntactic sets, which we assume to be disjoint:

- *Var*, of *variables*, ranged over by $x$-$z$,
- *Name*, of *names*, ranged over by $a$-$m$,
- *Int*, of *integers*, ranged over by $i$, and
- *Bool* = {t, f}, of *booleans*, ranged over by bv.

We use $u$-$w$ to range over the set of *identifiers*, $Id = Var \cup Name$. We typically use the names $a$-$d$ to refer to channels and $k$-$m$ to refer to locations, although the distinction is formally imposed by the type system. We use $e$ to refer to names that might be of either type. The main syntactic categories of the language are as follows:

- *Threads, P-R*, are (almost) terms of the ordinary polyadic π-calculus [8]. The thread language includes the static combinators for composition '|' and typed restriction

---

**Table 1** Syntax

$$Id: \quad u,v,w \ ::= \ e \mid x$$
$$Val: \quad U,V \ ::= \ i \mid bv \mid u \mid w[u_1, .., u_n] \mid (U_1, .., U_n)$$
$$Pat: \quad X,Y \ ::= \qquad x \mid z[x_1, .., x_n] \mid (X_1, .., X_n)$$

$$Thread: \ P,Q,R \ ::= \ \text{stop} \mid u!\langle V\rangle P \mid u?(X{:}T)Q \mid *P$$
$$\mid \ \text{go}\,u.P \mid \text{if } U = V \text{ then } P \text{ else } Q$$
$$\mid \ P|Q \mid (\nu e{:}T)P$$

$$System: \quad M,N \ ::= \ 0 \mid \ell[\![P]\!] \mid M|N \mid (\nu_\ell e{:}T)N$$

---

'$(\nu e{:}T)$', as well as constructs for movement '$\text{go}\,\ell.P$', output '$u!\langle V\rangle P$', typed input '$u?(X{:}T)Q$', (mis)matching 'if $U = V$ then $P$ else $Q$' and iteration '$*P$'.
- *Agents*, $\ell[\![P]\!]$, are located threads.
- *Systems*, *M-N*, are collections of agents combined using the static combinators '$|$' and '$(\nu_\ell e{:}T)$'.

The output and input constructs make use of syntactic categories for *values*, *U-V*, and *patterns*, *X-Y*, respectively. Values include variables, names, base values, and tuples of these. A value of the form $w[u_1, .., u_n]$ includes a location $w$ and a collection of channels $u_1, .., u_n$ allocated at $w$. Patterns, *X-Y*, provide destructors for each type. To be well-formed, we require that patterns be linear, *i.e.* each variable appear at most once.

As an example of a system, consider the term:

$$\ell[\![P]\!] \mid (\nu_\ell a{:}A)\,(\ell[\![Q]\!] \mid k[\![R]\!])$$

This system contains three agents, $\ell[\![P]\!]$, $\ell[\![Q]\!]$ and $k[\![R]\!]$. The first two agents are running at location $\ell$, the third at location $k$. Moreover $Q$ and $R$ share a private channel $a$ of type A, allocated at $\ell$ and unknown to $P$.

Unlike [3, 5], agents are relatively lightweight in D$\pi$. They are single-threaded and can be freely split and merged using structural rules and communication. As such, they are unnamed.

NOTATION. We adopt several notational conventions, as in [6].

- In the concrete syntax, "move" has greater binding power than composition. Thus $\text{go}\,\ell.P \mid Q$ should be read $(\text{go}\,\ell.P) \mid Q$. We adopt several standard abbreviations. For example, we routinely drop type annotations when they are not of interest. We omit trailing occurrences of **stop** and often denote tuples and other groups using a tilde. For example, we write $\tilde{a}$ instead of $(a_1, .., a_n)$ and $(\nu\tilde{e}{:}\tilde{T})P$ instead of $(\nu e_1{:}T_1)..(\nu e_n{:}T_n)P$. We also write 'if $U = V$ then $P$' instead of 'if $U = V$ then $P$ else **stop**' and 'if $U \neq V$ then $Q$' instead of 'if $U = V$ then **stop** else $Q$.'

- We assume the standard notion of *free* and *bound* occurrences of variables and names in systems and threads. The variables in the pattern $X$ are bound by the input construct $u?(X)Q$, the scope is $Q$. The name $e$ is bound by the restrictions $(\nu_\ell e{:}T)N$ and $(\nu e{:}T)P$, the scopes are $N$ and $P$, respectively. A term with no free variables is

**Table 2** Standard Reduction

Structural equivalence:

$$
\begin{array}{lll}
\text{(s-stop)} & \ell[\![\text{stop}]\!] \equiv 0 \\
\text{(s-split)} & \ell[\![P \mid Q]\!] \equiv \ell[\![P]\!] \mid \ell[\![Q]\!] \\
\text{(s-itr)} & \ell[\![*P]\!] \equiv \ell[\![P]\!] \mid \ell[\![*P]\!] \\
\text{(s-new)} & \ell[\![(\text{v}e{:}T)\,P]\!] \equiv (\text{v}_\ell e{:}T)\,\ell[\![P]\!] \\
\text{(s-extr)} & M \mid (\text{v}_\ell e{:}T)\,N \equiv (\text{v}_\ell e{:}T)\,(M \mid N) \quad \text{if } e \notin \text{fn}(M)
\end{array}
$$

Reduction:

$$
\begin{array}{ll}
\text{(r-move)} & \ell[\![\text{go}\,k.\,P]\!] \longrightarrow k[\![P]\!] \\
\text{(r-comm)} & \ell[\![a!\langle V\rangle\,P]\!] \mid \ell[\![a?(X)\,Q]\!] \longrightarrow \ell[\![P]\!] \mid \ell[\![Q\{V\!/x\}]\!] \\
\text{(r-eq}_1\text{)} & \ell[\![\text{if } U = U \text{ then } P \text{ else } Q]\!] \longrightarrow \ell[\![P]\!] \\
\text{(r-eq}_2\text{)} & \ell[\![\text{if } U = V \text{ then } P \text{ else } Q]\!] \longrightarrow \ell[\![Q]\!] \quad \text{if } U \neq V
\end{array}
$$

$$
\text{(r-new)} \quad \frac{N \longrightarrow N'}{(\text{v}_\ell e{:}T)\,N \longrightarrow (\text{v}_\ell e{:}T)\,N'}
$$

$$
\text{(r-str)} \quad \frac{N \longrightarrow N'}{M \mid N \longrightarrow M \mid N'} \qquad \frac{N \equiv M \longrightarrow M' \equiv N'}{N \longrightarrow N'}
$$

---

*closed.* The functions $\text{fn}(N)$ and $\text{fid}(N)$ return respectively the sets of free names and free identifiers occurring in $N$.

- We also assume a standard notion *substitution*, where $N\{u\!/x\}$ denotes the capture-avoiding substitution of $u$ for $x$ in $N$. The notation $N\{V\!/x\}$ generalizes this in an obvious way as a sequence of substitutions. For example, $N\{\ell[a]\!/z[x]\} = N\{a\!/z\}\{a\!/x\}$.

- In the sequel we identify terms up to renaming of bound identifiers.  ☐

## 2.2 Standard Reduction

The standard reduction semantics is given in Table 2. The structural equivalence ($N \equiv M$) and reduction relation ($N \longrightarrow N'$) both relate *closed* system terms. The structural equivalence is defined to be the least equivalence relation that is closed under composition and restriction, satisfies the monoid laws for composition,[1] and in addition satisfies the axioms given in Table 2.

The structural rules allow for agent splitting $\ell[\![P \mid Q]\!] \equiv \ell[\![P]\!] \mid \ell[\![Q]\!]$ and garbage collection $\ell[\![\text{stop}]\!] \equiv 0$. Note that when a new name is lifted out of an agent, using the structural rule (s-new), the system-level restriction records the name of the location which allocated the name $\ell[\![(\text{v}e{:}T)\,P]\!] \equiv (\text{v}_\ell e{:}T)\,\ell[\![P]\!]$; these location tags are used only for static typing.

Most of the rules of the reduction relation are taken directly from the $\pi$-calculus, with a few changes to accommodate the fact that agents are explicitly located. The main rule of interest here is (r-move),

$$
\ell[\![\text{go}\,k.\,P]\!] \longrightarrow k[\![P]\!]
$$

---

[1] The monoid laws are: $N \mid 0 \equiv N$, $N \mid M \equiv M \mid N$, and $N \mid (M \mid O) \equiv (N \mid M) \mid O$.

which states that an agent located at $\ell$ can move to $k$ using the move operator $go\,k.\,P$. This is the only rule that varies significantly between the standard semantics and the semantics for open systems defined later. Note that in (r-comm), communication is purely local:

$$\ell[\![a!\langle V\rangle\,P]\!] \mid \ell[\![a?(X)\,Q]\!] \longrightarrow \ell[\![P]\!] \mid \ell[\![Q\{^V\!/x\}]\!]$$

As an example, suppose that we wish to write a system of two agents, one at $k$ and one at $\ell$. The agent at $k$ wishes to send a fresh integer channel $a$, located at $k$, to the other agent using the channel $b$, located at $\ell$. This system could be written:

$$
\begin{aligned}
& \ell[\![b?(z[x])\,Q]\!] \mid k[\![(\nu a)\,(P \mid go\,\ell.\,b!\langle k[a]\rangle)]\!] \\
\equiv\ & \ell[\![b?(z[x])\,Q]\!] \mid (\nu_k a)\,(k[\![P]\!] \mid k[\![go\,\ell.\,b!\langle k[a]\rangle]\!]) \quad \text{(s-new)}\,,\text{(s-split)} \\
\longrightarrow\ & \ell[\![b?(z[x])\,Q]\!] \mid (\nu_k a)\,(k[\![P]\!] \mid \ell[\![b!\langle k[a]\rangle]\!]) \quad \text{(r-move)} \\
\longrightarrow\ & (\nu_k a)\,(\ell[\![Q\{^{k[a]}\!/_{z[x]}\}]\!] \mid k[\![P]\!]) \quad \text{(s-extr)}\,,\text{(r-comm)}\,,\text{(s-stop)}
\end{aligned}
$$

Beside each reduction, we have written the rules used to infer it, omitting (r-str) and (r-new), which are almost always used. Note that after arriving at $\ell$, the agent sends the value $k[a]$ rather than simply $a$. In the type system, this identifies the resource $a$ as *non-local* at $\ell$. If a simple resource value, such as $a$, had been communicated to $Q$, it would have had to have been local to $\ell$, rather than $k$. An example of a process $Q$ that uses the received value $z[x]$ is $go\,z.\,x!\langle 1\rangle$, which after the communication would become $go\,k.\,a!\langle 1\rangle$. This can move to the location $k$ and send the integer 1 on the newly received channel $a$.

## 2.3 Types and Subtyping

The purpose of the type system is to ensure proper use of base types, channels and locations. In this paper we use the simple type languages from [6, §4], extended with base types for integers and booleans. We use uppercase Roman letters to range over types, whose syntax is as follows:

$$
\begin{aligned}
TChan\text{:}\quad & \text{A},\text{B},\text{C} &&::= \text{chan}\langle\text{T}\rangle \\
TLoc\text{:}\quad & \text{K},\text{L},\text{M} &&::= \text{loc}\{a_1\text{:}A_1,\,..,\,a_n\text{:}A_n\},\ a_i \text{ distinct} \\
TVal\text{:}\quad & \text{S},\text{T} &&::= \text{bool} \mid \text{int} \mid \text{A} \mid \text{K}[B_1,\,..,\,B_h],\ \mid (T_1,\,..,\,T_n)
\end{aligned}
$$

Types are divided into the following syntactic groups:

- *TChan* of channel types, which specify the type of values communicated over a channel, $\text{chan}\langle\text{T}\rangle$.
- *TLoc* of simple location types, which specify the set of typed channels available at a location, $\text{loc}\{\widetilde{a}\text{:}\widetilde{A}\}$.
- *TVal* of value types, which include types for base values, channels, locations and tuples.

In value types, location types have the form $\text{loc}\{a_1\text{:}A_1,\,..,\,a_n\text{:}A_n\}[B_1,\,..,\,B_h]$. The extended form allows for a certain amount of first-order existential polymorphism. Informally, $\text{loc}\{\widetilde{a}\text{:}\widetilde{A}\}[\widetilde{B}]$ may be read "$\exists\widetilde{x}\text{:}\ \text{loc}\{\widetilde{a}\text{:}\widetilde{A},\widetilde{x}\text{:}\widetilde{B}\}$", *i.e.* the type of a location which has channels $\widetilde{a}$ of types $\widetilde{A}$ and some (unnamed) channels of types $\widetilde{B}$.

Location types are essentially the same as standard record types, and we identify location types up to reordering of their "fields". Thus $\mathsf{loc}\{a{:}A, b{:}B\}[C] = \mathsf{loc}\{b{:}B, a{:}A\}[C]$. But reordering is not allowed on "abstract" fields. Thus if B and C are different, then $\mathsf{loc}\{a{:}A\}[B,C] \neq \mathsf{loc}\{a{:}A\}[C,B]$.

Throughout the text, we drop empty braces when clear from context, writing 'loc' instead of 'loc{ }[]', 'K' instead of 'K[]', and '$u$' instead of '$u$[]'.

The subtyping relation $(T \leq S)$ is discussed at length in [6]. On base types and channel types there is no nontrivial subtyping; for example, $\mathsf{chan}\langle T\rangle \leq \mathsf{chan}\langle T'\rangle$ if and only if $T = T'$. On location types (both simple and "existential"), the subtyping relation is similar to that traditionally defined for record or object types:

$$\mathsf{loc}\{\widetilde{a}{:}\widetilde{A}, b{:}B\} \leq \mathsf{loc}\{\widetilde{a}{:}\widetilde{A}\}$$
$$\mathsf{loc}\{\widetilde{a}{:}\widetilde{A}, b{:}B\}[\widetilde{C}] \leq \mathsf{loc}\{\widetilde{a}{:}\widetilde{A}\}[\widetilde{C}]$$

On tuples, the definition is by homomorphic extension: $\widetilde{S} \leq \widetilde{T}$ if $\forall i{:}\ S_i \leq T_i$

Both subtyping and existential dependent types are inherited from our earlier work. Whereas subtyping is not essential to the work at hand, dependent types are, as will be seen in Section 3.1.

## 2.4 Type Environments

Location types contain the names of the channels known to be defined at a location. To present typing systems for the language in later sections, it is useful to generalize location types to allow the inclusion of *variables* as well as names. Variables are allowed at types int and bool, in addition to channel types A. The resulting types are called *v-open* location types, $\mathbb{K}$:

$$TSimple{:} \quad H, G \ ::= \ \mathsf{int} \mid \mathsf{bool} \mid A$$
$$TOpen{:} \quad \mathbb{K}, \mathbb{L}, \mathbb{M} \ ::= \ \mathsf{loc}\{\widetilde{u}{:}\widetilde{H}\}, \ u_i \ \text{distinct}$$

To be well-formed, we require that every *name* in a v-open location type be associated with a channel type.

The subtyping relation extends directly to v-open location types:

$$\mathsf{loc}\{\widetilde{u}{:}\widetilde{H}, \widetilde{v}{:}\widetilde{G}\} \leq \mathsf{loc}\{\widetilde{u}{:}\widetilde{H}\}$$

A type environment, $\Gamma$, maps identifiers to v-open location types. An example of a type environment is:

$$\Gamma = \left\{ \begin{array}{l} k : \mathsf{loc}\ \{a{:}\mathsf{chan}\langle\mathsf{int}\rangle, x{:}\mathsf{int}\} \\ z : \mathsf{loc}\left\{ \begin{array}{l} a{:}\mathsf{chan}\langle\mathsf{loc}[\mathsf{chan}\langle\mathsf{int}\rangle]\rangle \\ y{:}\mathsf{chan}\langle\mathsf{loc}[\mathsf{chan}\langle\mathsf{bool}\rangle]\rangle \end{array} \right\} \end{array} \right\}$$

Here we have two locations, $k$ and $z$. The first has an integer channel named $a$ and an integer variable $x$. The second has two channels: $a$, which communicates (potentially remote) integer channels and $y$ which communicates (potentially remote) boolean channels.

If a type environment contains no variables, we say that it is *closed*. Closed type environments map names to (closed) location types K.

In the typing system of the next section we need some notation for extending (v-open) location types and for convenience we explain this notation here. The location type $\mathbb{L}$ may be extended using the notation '$\mathbb{L}, V{:}T$', defined by induction on $V$:

$$(\mathsf{loc}\{\tilde{u}{:}\tilde{H}\}), v{:}G = \mathsf{loc}\{\tilde{u}{:}\tilde{H}, v{:}G\} \quad \text{if } \forall i{:}\ u_i \neq v$$
$$\mathbb{L}, w[\tilde{u}]{:}K[\tilde{A}] = \mathbb{L} \quad \text{if } \{w, \tilde{u}\} \text{ disjoint dom}(\mathbb{L})$$
$$\mathbb{L}, bv{:}bool = \mathbb{L}$$
$$\mathbb{L}, i{:}int = \mathbb{L}$$
$$\mathbb{L}, \tilde{U}{:}\tilde{T} = ((\dots(\mathbb{L}, U_1{:}T_1), \dots), U_n{:}T_n)$$

Therefore the extension of $\mathbb{L}$ by $V{:}T$ adds only information about *local identifiers* to $\mathbb{L}$. For example:

$$\mathsf{loc}\{d{:}D\}, (0, x, z[y]){:}(int, A, \mathsf{loc}\{c{:}C\}[B]) = \mathsf{loc}\{d{:}D, x{:}A\}$$

Note that every location type L is also a v-open location type, and thus this definition applies to "closed" location types as well. In the same way the definition applies to patterns, as well as values, since syntactically every pattern is also a value.

We use a similar notation for extending type environments: If $u$ is not in the domain of $\Gamma$ then $\Gamma, u{:}\mathbb{L}$ denotes the new type environment, which is similar to $\Gamma$ but in addition maps $u$ to type $\mathbb{L}$.

## 3  Semantics for Open Systems

As we have explained in the introduction, using the standard run-time semantics local resources may be intentionally misused by malicious sites; in the example given in the Introduction, we have seen that the local resource $a$ at location $k$ is deliberately misused by a mobile agent originating at location $m$. In this section we modify the run-time semantics in a manner which offers protection against such misuse.

We are assuming that agents are working in an anonymous network and the run-time strategy suggested in the introduction is for every site to keep a record of local resources against which all incoming agents are checked. In our formulation this distributed information is collected together as closed type environment and thus reductions of the runtime semantics take the form

$$\Delta \triangleright N \longmapsto N'$$

where $\Delta$ is a closed type environment and $N$ and $N'$ are systems.

The reduction semantics is given in Table 3. Most of the rules are simple adaptations of the corresponding rules in Table 2. For example, the rules for local communication and matching of values are essentially as before, as $\Delta$ is not consulted for these reductions. There is a minor change in the rule for the restriction operator, because $\Delta$ must be augmented to reflect the addition of the new name.

**Table 3** Reduction for Open Systems

| | | |
|---|---|---|
| (r-move) | $\Delta \triangleright \ell[\![\text{go}\,k.\,P]\!] \longrightarrow k[\![P]\!]$ | if $\Delta(k) \vdash P$ |
| (r-comm) | $\Delta \triangleright \ell[\![a!\langle V \rangle P]\!] \mid \ell[\![a?(X)\,Q]\!] \longrightarrow \ell[\![P]\!] \mid \ell[\![Q\{^V\!/x\}]\!]$ | |
| (r-eq$_1$) | $\Delta \triangleright \ell[\![\text{if } U = U \text{ then } P \text{ else } Q]\!] \longrightarrow \ell[\![P]\!]$ | |
| (r-eq$_2$) | $\Delta \triangleright \ell[\![\text{if } U = V \text{ then } P \text{ else } Q]\!] \longrightarrow \ell[\![Q]\!]$ | if $U \neq V$ |

$$\text{(r-new)} \quad \frac{\Delta, \ell{:}(\mathrm{L}, a{:}\mathrm{A}) \triangleright N \longrightarrow N'}{\Delta, \ell{:}\mathrm{L} \triangleright (\nu_\ell a{:}\mathrm{A})\,N \longrightarrow (\nu_\ell a{:}\mathrm{A})\,N'} \qquad \frac{\Delta, \ell{:}\mathrm{L}, k{:}\mathrm{K} \triangleright N \longrightarrow N'}{\Delta, \ell{:}\mathrm{L} \triangleright (\nu_\ell k{:}\mathrm{K})\,N \longrightarrow (\nu_\ell k{:}\mathrm{K})\,N'}$$

$$\text{(r-str)} \quad \frac{\Delta \triangleright N \longrightarrow N'}{\Delta \triangleright M \mid N \longrightarrow M \mid N'} \qquad \frac{N \equiv M \quad \Delta \triangleright M \longrightarrow M' \quad M' \equiv N'}{\Delta \triangleright N \longrightarrow N'}$$

The only significant change from the standard run-time semantics is in the rule for code movement:

$$\Delta \triangleright \ell[\![\text{go}\,k.\,P]\!] \longmapsto k[\![P]\!] \quad \text{if } \Delta(k) \vdash P$$

This says that the agent $P$ can move from location $\ell$ to location $k$ only if $P$ is guaranteed not to misuse the local resources of $k$, *i.e.* $\Delta(k) \vdash P$. Here $P$ is type-checked dynamically against $\Delta(k)$, which gives the names and types of the resources available at $k$.

## 3.1 Runtime Typing

The definition of this runtime local type-checking is given in Table 4. This is a *light weight* typing in that the incoming code is only checked to the extent of its references to local resources. Thus judgments are of the form

$$\mathbb{L} \vdash P$$

indicating that $P$ can safely run at a location that provides resources as defined in $\mathbb{L}$.

Perhaps the most surprising rule in this light weight type checking is (t-move), which involves no type checking whatsoever. However this is reasonable as an agent such as $\text{go}\,\ell.\,P$ running at $k$ uses no local resources; it moves immediately to the site $\ell$. As a result of this rule notice that reductions of the form

$$\Delta \triangleright m[\![\text{go}\,k.\,\text{go}\,\ell.\,P]\!] \longmapsto k[\![\text{go}\,\ell.\,P]\!]$$

are always allowed, regardless of the information in $\Delta$.

The only significant local checking is carried out by the two rules (t-r), (t-w) which we examine in some detail. The subtlety in the read rule (t-r) is to some extent hidden in the rule for updating location types and this is best explained by example. The rule dictates, for example, that the agent $a?(x{:}\text{chan}\langle T \rangle)\,Q$ can migrate to a location with local resources $\mathbb{L}$ provided:

- $a$ is a local channel of the appropriate type, in this case a channel for communicating values of type chan$\langle T \rangle$
- $Q$ is locally well-typed with respect to an augmented set of resources, $\mathbb{L}, x{:}\text{chan}\langle T \rangle$.

---

**Table 4** Typing for Values and Threads

Values:

$$(\text{t-sit}) \quad \frac{\mathbb{L} \le \text{loc}\{u:H\}}{\mathbb{L} \vdash u:H} \qquad\qquad (\text{t-base}) \quad \frac{}{\mathbb{L} \vdash n:\text{int, } bv:\text{bool}}$$

$$(\text{t-loc}) \quad \frac{}{\mathbb{L} \vdash u[v_1, .., v_n]:K[A_1, .., A_n]} \qquad (\text{t-tup}) \quad \frac{\forall i:\ \mathbb{L} \vdash U_i:T_i}{\mathbb{L} \vdash (U_1, .., U_n):(T_1, .., T_n)}$$

Threads:

$$(\text{t-move}) \quad \frac{}{\mathbb{L} \vdash \text{go}\,u.\,P} \qquad\qquad (\text{t-newl}) \quad \frac{\mathbb{L} \vdash P}{\mathbb{L} \vdash (vk{:}K)\,P}$$

$$(\text{t-r}) \quad \frac{\mathbb{L} \vdash u:\text{chan}\langle T\rangle \quad \mathbb{L},\, X{:}T \vdash Q}{\mathbb{L} \vdash u?(X{:}T)\,Q} \qquad (\text{t-newc}) \quad \frac{\mathbb{L},\, a{:}A \vdash P}{\mathbb{L} \vdash (va{:}A)\,P}$$

$$(\text{t-w}) \quad \frac{\mathbb{L} \vdash u:\text{chan}\langle T\rangle,\, V{:}T,\, P}{\mathbb{L} \vdash u!\langle V\rangle\,P} \qquad (\text{t-str}) \quad \frac{\mathbb{L} \vdash P,\, Q}{\mathbb{L} \vdash \text{stop}, *P, P\,|\,Q}$$

$$(\text{t-eq}) \quad \frac{\mathbb{L} \vdash U{:}T,\, V{:}T,\, P,\, Q}{\mathbb{L} \vdash \text{if } U = V \text{ then } P \text{ else } Q}$$

---

However suppose the channel $a$ communicates non-local information; *e.g.* when is $a?(z[x]{:}K[A])\,Q$ locally well-typed? The rule (t-r) simply demands that, in addition to $a$ having the appropriate local type, $Q$ is well-typed with respect to the same set of local resources $\mathbb{L}$. Formally this is because according to the definitions given in Section 2.4 $\mathbb{L}, z[x]{:}K[A]$ is simply $\mathbb{L}$. Intuitively this is reasonable since any non-local information received on $a$ will not be used locally and thus it may be ignored.

The rule (t-w) states that agent $a!\langle V\rangle\,P$ is locally well-typed provided

- the continuation $P$ is locally well-typed
- the channel $a$ has an appropriate local type, say $\text{chan}\langle T\rangle$
- the value to be transmitted $V$ is locally well-typed to be transmitted on $a$, $\mathbb{L} \vdash V{:}T$; this means that it must be possible to assign to $V$ the local object type of the channel $a$, namely T.

Once more there is a subtlety, this time in the local type checking of values. If the value $V$ to be transmitted is a local resource, say a channel name $b$, then according to the rule (t-sit) $b$ must have the local type T. If, on the other hand, $V$ is a non-local value, say $k[b]$, then locally this is of no interest; according to (t-loc) $k[b]$ can be assigned *any* location type which in effect means that when it is transmitted locally on $a$ its validity is not checked.

This ends our discussion of runtime local type checking, and of the runtime semantics.

## 3.2 An Example

As an example consider a system of three locations, $k$, $\ell$ and $m$, with the following distributed type environment, $\Delta$.

$$\Delta = \left\{ \begin{array}{l} k : \mathsf{loc}\{a:\mathsf{chan}\langle\mathsf{int}\rangle\} \\ \ell : \mathsf{loc}\{b:\mathsf{chan}\langle\mathsf{loc}[\mathsf{chan}\langle\mathsf{bool}\rangle])\rangle\} \\ m : \mathsf{loc}\{d:\mathsf{chan}\langle\mathsf{loc}[\mathsf{chan}\langle\mathsf{bool}\rangle])\rangle\} \end{array} \right\}.$$

Let $N$ be the following system:

$$k[\![\mathsf{go}\,m.\,d!\langle k[a]\rangle]\!]$$
$$|\ m[\![d?(z[x])\ \mathsf{go}\,\ell.\,b!\langle z[x]\rangle]\!]$$
$$|\ \ell[\![b?(z[x])\ \mathsf{go}\,z.\,x!\langle\mathsf{t}\rangle]\!]$$

Here $k$ communicates the name of its integer channel $a$ to $m$, using the channel $d$ local to $m$. Then $m$ misinforms $\ell$ about the type of $a$ at $k$: the communication along $b$ fools $\ell$ into believing that $a$ is a boolean channel. Subsequently $\ell$ attempts to send an agent to $k$ that violates the type of local resource $a$, by sending a boolean value where an integer is expected.

The reader can check that according to our runtime semantics the first code movement between $k$ and $m$ is allowed:

$$\Delta \triangleright k[\![\mathsf{go}\,m.\,d!\langle k[a]\rangle]\!] \longmapsto m[\![d!\langle k[a]\rangle]\!]$$

as local type checking of the migrating agent succeeds, $\Delta(m) \vdash d!\langle k[a]\rangle$. The local channel $d$ is used correctly and since the value transmitted, $k[a]$, is non-local it is essentially not examined (only the number of names is checked, not their types).

The local communication at $m$ on channel $d$ now occurs and the second code movement between $m$ and $\ell$ is also allowed,

$$\Delta \triangleright m[\![d!\langle k[a]\rangle]\!]\ |\ m[\![d?(z[x])\ \mathsf{go}\,\ell.\,b!\langle z[x]\rangle]\!] \longmapsto \cdot \longmapsto \ell[\![b!\langle k[a]\rangle]\!]$$

because the migrating thread, $b!\langle k[a]\rangle$, is also successful in its type check against local resources, $\Delta(\ell)$. The local communication along $b$ now occurs

$$\Delta \triangleright \ell[\![b!\langle k[a]\rangle]\!]\ |\ \ell[\![b?(z[x])\ \mathsf{go}\,z.\,x!\langle\mathsf{t}\rangle]\!] \longmapsto \ell[\![\mathsf{go}\,k.\,a!\langle\mathsf{t}\rangle]\!]$$

However the next potential move, the migration of the thread $a!\langle\mathsf{t}\rangle$ from $\ell$ to $k$, is disallowed by the rule (r-move); the thread is locally type checked against the resources at $k$, where $a$ is known to be an integer channel, and its potential misuse is discovered.

## 4  Static typing

In the runtime semantics misuse of local resources can certainly occur, since there is no requirement that values have the object type specified by the transmitting channel. For example the reduction

$$\Delta \triangleright k[\![a!\langle\mathsf{t}\rangle]\!]\ |\ k[\![a?(x)\ Q]\!] \longmapsto k[\![\mathsf{stop}]\!]\ |\ k[\![Q\{\mathsf{t}\!/\!x\}]\!]$$

---

**Table 5** Static Typing

Values and threads: As in Table 4

Systems:

$$\text{(t-rung)} \quad \frac{\mathbb{L} \vdash P}{\Gamma, \ell{:}\mathbb{L} \vdash \ell[\![P]\!]} \qquad\qquad \text{(t-runb)} \quad \frac{\ell \notin \text{dom}(\Gamma)}{\Gamma \vdash \ell[\![P]\!]}$$

$$\text{(t-newcg)} \quad \frac{\Gamma, \ell{:}(\mathbb{L}, a{:}A) \vdash N}{\Gamma, \ell{:}\mathbb{L} \vdash (\nu_\ell a{:}A) N} \qquad \text{(t-newcb)} \quad \frac{\ell \notin \text{dom}(\Gamma) \quad \Gamma \vdash N}{\Gamma \vdash (\nu_\ell a{:}A) N}$$

$$\text{(t-newlg)} \quad \frac{\Gamma, \ell{:}\mathbb{L}, k{:}K \vdash N}{\Gamma, \ell{:}\mathbb{L} \vdash (\nu_\ell k{:}K) N} \qquad \text{(t-newlb)} \quad \frac{\ell \notin \text{dom}(\Gamma) \quad \Gamma \vdash N}{\Gamma \vdash (\nu_\ell k{:}K) N}$$

$$\text{(t-str)} \quad \frac{\Gamma \vdash M, N}{\Gamma \vdash 0, M \mid N}$$

Configurations:

$$\text{(t-config)} \quad \frac{\Gamma \vdash N}{\Gamma \vdash \Delta \triangleright N} \quad \forall \ell \in \text{dom}(\Gamma) : \Gamma(\ell) \leq \Delta(k)$$

---

is allowed even if the object type of the channel $a$ at $k$ is int, *i.e.* $\Delta(k) \leq \text{loc}\{a{:}\text{chan}\langle\text{int}\rangle\}$.

We do not assume that all sites respect the typing constraints on their channels. For convenience let us call sites that violate the typing constraints *bad* sites, as they do not play according to the rules. A typical example is the site $m$, described at the end of the previous section; it receives an integer channel $a$ from $k$ but then attempts to use $a$ to send a boolean value. In contrast a *good* site is one where typing constraints are enforced.

In this section we present a static type system that guarantees that:

> *good* sites cannot be harmed by *bad* sites.

That is, local resources at a good site cannot be misused despite the existence of, and interaction with, bad sites. We prove Subject Reduction and Type Safety theorems for the type system. Intuitively, Subject Reduction can be interpreted as saying that the integrity of good sites is maintained as computation proceeds, while Type Safety demonstrates that local resources at good sites cannot be misused.

The static typing relation for anonymous networks is defined in Table 5. Judgments are of the form

$$\Gamma \vdash N$$

where $\Gamma$ is a (ν-open) type environment and $N$ a system. The type environment only records the types of good locations; thus $k \in \text{dom}(\Gamma)$ is to be read "$k$ is good" and $m \notin \text{dom}(\Gamma)$ may be read as "$m$ is bad." If $\Gamma \vdash N$, then those agents in $N$ that are located at sites in the domain of $\Gamma$ are guaranteed to be "well behaved".

For threads and values, the static typing relation is the same as runtime typing relation given in Table 4. The typing of a located agent $\ell[\![P]\!]$ depends on whether $\ell$ is good, *i.e.* $\ell \in \text{dom}(\Gamma)$. If $\ell$ is good, then according to (t-rung), to infer $\Gamma \vdash \ell[\![P]\!]$ we need to establish that the $P$ is well-typed to run at $\ell$, $\Gamma(\ell) \vdash P$. But if $\ell$ is not good, then it doesn't matter whether $P$ is well-typed; thus (t-runb) says that if $\ell \notin \text{dom}(\Gamma)$, then $\ell[\![P]\!]$ is well-typed for any thread $P$.

The typing of new resources at the systems level also depends on whether they are introduced at a good site. For example to infer $\Gamma, \ell{:}\mathbb{L} \vdash (\nu_\ell a{:}A)N$, where because of the notation we know $\ell$ is a good site, (t-newcg) says that we need to establish $\Gamma, \ell{:}(\mathbb{L}, a{:}A) \vdash N$, *i.e.* that $N$ is well-typed under the assumption that there is a new resource $a$ at site $\ell$. This is in contrast to the case when $\ell$ is not good, $\ell \notin \text{dom}(\Gamma)$, where according to (t-newcb) it is sufficient to establish that the system $N$ is well-typed relative to the same typing environment. Note that implicit in these two rules is the assumption that new good sites can only be generated by good sites.

Intuitively $\Gamma \vdash N$ means that in $N$ the good sites, those in the domain of $\Gamma$ use their local resources in accordance with $\Gamma$, whereas the behavior of bad sites are unconstrained. As an example consider the configuration $\Delta \triangleright N$ from Section 3.2. If we let $\Gamma$ be the typing environment defined by:

$$\Gamma = \left\{ \begin{array}{l} k : \text{loc}\{a{:}\text{chan}\langle\text{int}\rangle\} \\ \ell : \text{loc}\{b{:}\text{chan}\langle\text{loc}[\text{chan}\langle\text{bool}\rangle]\rangle\} \end{array} \right\} \tag{*}$$

Then one can easily check that $\Gamma \vdash \Delta \triangleright N$, that is $\Delta$ is consistent with $\Gamma$ and $\Gamma \vdash N$. Intuitively here we are saying that $k$ and $\ell$ are good sites which use their local resources correctly whereas no guarantee is made about the local behavior at $m$. Note, however, that if one considers static typing under $\Delta$, which includes $m$, then $\Delta$ does not type $N$.

The static typing system satisfies several important properties, such as type specialization and narrowing, which are stated and proved in Appendix A. These properties are used to establish the following result, which states that well-typing at good sites is preserved by reduction.

THEOREM 1 (SUBJECT REDUCTION).
  *If* $\Gamma \vdash \Delta \triangleright N$ *and* $\Delta \triangleright N \longmapsto N'$ *then* $\Gamma \vdash \Delta \triangleright N'$.

*Proof.* See Appendix A. □

We now discuss the extent to which in the type system precludes the misuse of local resources at good sites. This can be formalized using a notion of runtime error. In this paper, we confine our attention to runtime errors based on arity mismatching. Intuitively, an arity mismatch occurs when the value sent on a channel does not match the type that the recipient expects, or when two structurally dissimilar values are compared using the match construct. To formalize this notion, we define a compatibility relation $U \asymp T$ between (closed) values and types, and a compatibility relation $U \asymp V$ between (closed) values.

The definitions of compatibility and of runtime error are given in Table 6. Runtime error is defined as a predicate $N \xrightarrow{\text{err}_\ell}$, indicating that $N$ is capable of a runtime error at location $\ell$. Essentially an error occurs at location $\ell$ if either two incompatible values are compared at $\ell$ or an attempt is made to communicate a value along a local channel which is incompatible with the type of the channel. The only non-trivial rule is (e-new) which

---

**Table 6** Compatibility and Runtime Error

Compatibility:

$$i \asymp \text{int} \qquad\qquad i \asymp i'$$
$$\text{bv} \asymp \text{bool} \qquad\qquad \text{bv} \asymp \text{bv}'$$
$$e \asymp A \qquad\qquad e \asymp e'$$
$$e[d_1, .., d_n] \asymp K[A_1, .., A_n] \qquad\qquad e[d_1, .., d_n] \asymp e'[d'_1, .., d'_n]$$
$$(V_1, .., V_n) \asymp (T_1, .., T_n) \qquad\qquad (V_1, .., V_n) \asymp (V'_1, .., V'_n)$$
$$\text{if } \forall i: V_i \asymp T_i \qquad\qquad\qquad \text{if } \forall i: V_i \asymp V'_i$$

Runtime error:

$$\text{(e-comm)} \quad \ell[\![a!\langle V\rangle P]\!] \mid \ell[\![a?(X{:}T)Q]\!] \xrightarrow{err\ell} \quad \text{if } V \not\asymp T$$
$$\text{(e-eq)} \quad \ell[\![\text{if } U = V \text{ then } P \text{ else } Q]\!] \xrightarrow{err\ell} \quad \text{if } U \not\asymp V$$

$$\text{(e-new)} \quad \dfrac{N \xrightarrow{err k}}{(v_\ell e{:}E)N \xrightarrow{err k\{\ell/k\}}} \qquad \text{(e-str)} \quad \dfrac{N \xrightarrow{err k}}{M \mid N \xrightarrow{err k}} \quad \dfrac{N \equiv M \quad M \xrightarrow{err k}}{N \xrightarrow{err k}}$$

---

may effect a change in the name of the location where the error occurs. For example it will report an error at $\ell$ in $(v_\ell k{:}K)N$ if there is a runtime error in $N$ at location $k$.

We should point out that this definition of run-time error is considerably weaker than that employed in [6]; in that paper, the notion of run-time error took into account not only to arity mismatches but also *access violations*.

THEOREM 2 (TYPE SAFETY). *If $\Gamma \vdash N$ and $\ell \in \text{dom}(\Gamma)$ then $N \not\mapsto^{err\ell}$.*
*Proof.* See Appendix A. □

This theorem, together with Subject Reduction, can be interpreted informally as saying that as reductions proceed local resources cannot be locally misused at good sites, even in systems where not all sites which are necessarily well-behaved.

## 5 Discussion

Here we make three points which demonstrate the limitations of both the runtime strategy and the typing system.

First the static typing is very weak as it is designed only to eliminate *local* misuse of *local* resources. Let

$$\Gamma = \left\{ \begin{array}{l} \ell{:}\text{loc}\left\{ \begin{array}{l} b{:}\text{chan}\langle\text{loc}\{d{:}\text{chan}\langle\text{bool}\rangle\}\rangle \\ c{:}\text{chan}\langle\text{loc}\{d{:}\text{chan}\langle\text{int}\rangle\}\rangle \end{array} \right\} \\ k{:}\text{loc}\{d{:}\text{chan}\langle\text{int}\rangle\} \end{array} \right\}$$

Then $\Gamma \vdash \ell[\![c?(z[x])\,b!(z[x])]\!]$ although obviously here there is, at least informally, a misuse of local channels. However formally the values exchanged on $c$ and $b$ are *potentially remote* and therefore these values are not considered local. For example, consider a companion site $k$ which has one local channel $d$ of type $\text{chan}\langle\text{int}\rangle$. Then no runtime error occurs in the system

$$\Gamma \triangleright \left( \begin{array}{l} \ell[\![c?(z{:}\text{loc}\{d{:}\text{chan}\langle\text{int}\rangle\})\,b!\langle z\rangle]\!] \\ \mid k[\![\text{go}\,\ell.\,(c!\langle k\rangle\,b?(z)\,\text{go}\,z.\,d!\langle t\rangle)]\!] \end{array} \right)$$

although one could argue that at location $\ell$ there is a misuse of the channel $b$. A runtime error is avoided by the dynamic type-checking; after the communications on $c$ and $b$ the potential move

$$\ell[\![\text{go}\,k.\,d!\langle t\rangle]\!] \longmapsto k[\![d!\langle t\rangle]\!]$$

is blocked because the agent attempting to move to $k$, $d!\langle t\rangle$ does not type check against the local resources at $k$.

Second, the requirement to dynamically type-check *all* incoming threads is very inefficient; however, the weak typing system makes it is essential. Purely local type-checking makes it very difficult to introduce *trust* into the system. A site cannot even trust itself! For example suppose we revised the reduction rule (r-move) to read as follows:

$$\Delta \rhd \ell[\![\text{go}\,k.\,P]\!] \longmapsto \Delta \rhd k[\![P]\!] \quad \text{if } k = \ell \text{ or } \Delta(k) \vdash P$$

Here the site $k$ trusts itself and therefore does not type check the thread $P$. However this rule is not safe; Subject Reduction fails and runtime errors may be introduced. As an example, consider the following configuration, which uses the typing environment $\Gamma$ given at the beginning of this section:

$$\Gamma \rhd \ell[\![c?(z)\,\text{go}\,z.\,c!\langle t\rangle]\!] \mid \ell[\![c!\langle \ell\rangle]\!]$$

The configuration can be typed with respect to $\Gamma$ itself, but after the communication the result is $\Gamma \rhd \ell[\![c!\langle t\rangle]\!]$, which fails to type under $\Gamma$. Moreover $\Gamma \rhd \ell[\![c!\langle t\rangle]\!]$ induces a runtime error due to the potential misuse of channel $c$. A related phenomenon is the potential misuse of channel names as locations; *e.g.* the thread '$(\nu a{:}\text{chan}\langle\text{int}\rangle)\,\text{go}\,a.\,P$' is typable in our system.

Third, the system relies heavily on dynamic type-checking to avoid misuse of resources. This can be highlighted by considering another desirable property of a runtime semantics for open systems:

> Movement between good sites should always be allowed, even in the presence of badly behaved sites.

It is obvious from the example discussed in Section 3.2 that our run-time semantics does not satisfy this property. If we use the static environment $\Gamma$ defined in (*) (Section 4) then $k$ and $\ell$ are *good* sites. But as we have seen in Section 3.2 the intervention of $m$ eventually prevents a movement from $k$ and $\ell$.

In a companion paper [12] we address these issues by strengthening the typing system. The second concern raised here (the inability to trust oneself or to ensure that channels are not used as locations) can be addressed by reformalizing the typing system while retaining its basic "local" character; such a reformalization is given in the appendix of [12].

In [12], we go further, however, extending the notion of *trust* to arbitrary collections of sites. Dynamic typechecking is strengthened by making a site record information about all sites in the system, not only itself. While typechecking in this system is computationally more expensive, not all incoming threads need be checked; those originating at trusted sites are allowed through unchecked. This new semantics addresses the first two of the above concerns fully, and the third partially: a stronger notion of type safety is guaranteed, some incoming threads are not typechecked, and movement between mutually trusted sites is always allowed, although movement between good sites may not be.

## 6 Related Work

In this paper we have outlined a strategy for ensuring that the integrity of well-behaved sites is not compromised by the presence of potentially malicious mobile agents. Moreover we have formalized the correctness of this strategy in terms of Subject Reduction and Type Safety theorems for a *partial* type system.

In this study we used the language $D\pi$ [6], one of a number of distributed versions of the $\pi$-calculus [8]. For other variations see [5, 13]. The languages in [3, 4] are thematically similar although based on somewhat different principles. We have taken advantage of a rich type system for $D\pi$, originally presented in [6], where not only do channels have the types originally proposed in [10] for the $\pi$-calculus, but locations have types broadly similar to those of objects. An even richer type system is also proposed in [6] in which types correspond to *capabilities*, as in [4], and an interesting topic for future research would be the extension of partial typing to these richer types.

Our research is related to proposals for *proof-carrying code* outlined in [9]: code consumers, which in our case are locations, demand of code producers, in our case incoming threads, that their code is accompanied by a proof of correctness. This proof is checked by the consumer before the code is allowed to execute. The correctness is expressed in terms of a public safety policy announced by the consumer and the producer must provide code along with a proof that it satisfies this policy. In our case this safety policy is determined by the location type which records the types of the consumer's resources, and proof checking corresponds to type checking the incoming code against this record. Our work is different in that the correctness proof can be reconstructed efficiently, and therefore the producer need not supply an explicit proof.

For other examples of related work within this framework see [7, 14]. For example the former contains a number of schemes for typechecking incoming code for access violations to local private resources. However the language is very different from ours, namely a sequential higher-order functional language, and there is no direct formalization of the fact that distributed systems which employ these schemes are well-behaved.

A very different approach to system security is based on the use of cryptography and signatures. For example [1] presents a $\pi$-calculus based language which contain cryptographic constructs which ensure the exchange of data between trusted agents, while [2] contains a description of the application of this approach in a practical setting.

## A Proofs

### A.1 Properties of the static type system

First we prove two important properties of type systems with subtyping: Type Specialization and Weakening.

PROPOSITION 3 (TYPE SPECIALIZATION). *If* $\mathbb{L} \vdash V:T$ *and* $T \leq S$ *then* $\mathbb{L} \vdash V:S$.

*Proof.* By induction on the judgment $\mathbb{L} \vdash V{:}T$. If $V{:}T$ takes the form $V{:}H$ then S must coincide with H, since there is no non-trivial subtyping on channel types or base types. If $V{:}T$ has the form $w[\tilde{u}]{:}\mathbb{L}[\tilde{A}]$ then the result is trivial, using (t-loc). Finally, the case for tuples follows by induction. $\qquad\square$

### PROPOSITION 4 (WEAKENING).

– *If* $\mathbb{L} \vdash V{:}T$ *and* $\mathbb{K} \leq \mathbb{L}$ *then* $\mathbb{K} \vdash V{:}T$
– *If* $\mathbb{L} \vdash P$ *and* $\mathbb{K} \leq \mathbb{L}$ *then* $\mathbb{K} \vdash P$
– *If* $\Gamma, w{:}\mathbb{L} \vdash N$ *and* $\mathbb{K} \leq \mathbb{L}$ *then* $\Gamma, w{:}\mathbb{K} \vdash N$

*Proof.* In each case the proof is by induction on the type inference. We examine two examples of proof on threads:

(t-r). Here $\mathbb{L} \vdash u?(X{:}T)Q$ because $\mathbb{L} \vdash u{:}\text{chan}\langle T\rangle$ and $\mathbb{L}, X{:}T \vdash Q$. We can apply the first statement in the proposition to the former, to obtain $\mathbb{K} \vdash u{:}\text{chan}\langle T\rangle$, while induction to the latter gives $\mathbb{K}, X{:}T \vdash Q$. An application of (t-r) now gives the required $\mathbb{K} \vdash u?(X{:}T)Q$.

(t-newc). Here $\mathbb{L} \vdash (\nu a{:}A)P$ because $\mathbb{L}, a{:}A \vdash P$. By $\alpha$-conversion we can choose $a$ so that it does not appear in $\mathbb{K}$ and therefore by induction we have $\mathbb{K}, a{:}A \vdash P$. Now an application of (t-newc) gives the required $\mathbb{K} \vdash (\nu a{:}A)P$.

We present four cases for the proof on systems.

(t-rung). Here $\Gamma, w{:}\mathbb{L} \vdash m[\![P]\!]$ because $\mathbb{M} \vdash P$, where $\mathbb{M} \stackrel{def}{=} (\Gamma, w{:}\mathbb{L})(m)$. If $m$ and $w$ are different then we also have $\mathbb{M} = (\Gamma, w{:}\mathbb{K})(m)$ and therefore an application of (t-rung) gives the required $\Gamma, w{:}\mathbb{K} \vdash m[\![P]\!]$. On the other hand if $m$ is the same as $w$ then $\mathbb{M} = \mathbb{L}$. So we can apply the second part of the proposition to $\mathbb{M}$, obtaining $\mathbb{K} \vdash P$. Now (t-rung) also gives the required $\Gamma, w{:}\mathbb{K} \vdash m[\![P]\!]$.

(t-runb). This case is trivial.

(t-newlg). Here $\Gamma, w{:}\mathbb{L} \vdash (\nu_\ell m{:}\mathbb{M})N$ because $\ell \in \text{dom}(\Gamma, w{:}\mathbb{L})$ and $\Gamma, w{:}\mathbb{L}, m{:}\mathbb{M} \vdash N$. Applying induction we obtain $\Gamma, w{:}\mathbb{K}, m{:}\mathbb{M} \vdash N$. Now (t-newlg) can be applied since $\ell \in \text{dom}(\Gamma, w{:}\mathbb{K})$, to obtain the required $\Gamma, w{:}\mathbb{K} \vdash (\nu_\ell m{:}\mathbb{M})N$.

(t-newcb). Here $\Gamma, w{:}\mathbb{L} \vdash (\nu_\ell a{:}A)N$ because $\ell \notin \text{dom}(\Gamma, w{:}\mathbb{L})$ and $\Gamma, w{:}\mathbb{L} \vdash N$. However we also have $\ell \notin \text{dom}(\Gamma, w{:}\mathbb{K})$ and therefore (t-newcb) can also be applied to obtain the required $\Gamma, w{:}\mathbb{K} \vdash (\nu_\ell a{:}A)N$. $\qquad\square$

The following Restriction Lemma states that if $\Gamma \vdash N$ and some identifier $u$ does not occur free in $N$ then $N$ can also be typed in an environment obtained from $\Gamma$ by removing all occurrences of $u$. For any identifier $u$ let $\Gamma \backslash u$ denote the result of removing all occurrences of $u$ from $\Gamma$. For example $(\Gamma, u{:}\mathbb{L}) \backslash u$ denotes $\Gamma$ while $(\Gamma, w{:}(\mathbb{L}, u{:}A)) \backslash u$ is the same as $(\Gamma \backslash u), w{:}\mathbb{L}$.

### LEMMA 5 (RESTRICTION).

– *If* $\mathbb{L}, v{:}H \vdash U{:}T$ *and* $v \notin \text{fid}(U)$ *then* $\mathbb{L} \vdash U{:}T$
– *If* $\mathbb{L}, v{:}H \vdash P$ *and* $v \notin \text{fid}(P)$ *then* $\mathbb{L} \vdash P$
– *If* $\Gamma \vdash N$ *and* $v \notin \text{fid}(N)$ *then* $\Gamma \backslash v \vdash N$.

*Proof.* By induction on the proof of the typing judgment. $\qquad\square$

The following corollary follows by an easy induction on $V$.

COROLLARY 6.

- *If* $L, V{:}S \vdash U{:}T$ *and* $\mathrm{fid}(V)$ disjoint $\mathrm{fid}(U)$ *then* $L \vdash U{:}T$
- *If* $L, V{:}S \vdash P$ *and* $\mathrm{fid}(V)$ disjoint $\mathrm{fid}(P)$ *then* $L \vdash P$ □

## A.2 Subject Reduction

We first show that typing is preserved by the structural equivalence. The most complicated case is already covered by the Restriction proposition.

LEMMA 7 (SCOPE EXTRUSION).

*If* $e \notin \mathrm{fn}(M)$ *then* $\Gamma \vdash M \mid (\nu_\ell e{:}T)$ *if and only if* $\Gamma \vdash (\nu_\ell e{:}T)(M \mid N)$

*Proof.* There are two cases. If $\ell \notin \mathrm{dom}(\Gamma)$, then we can reason as follows:

$$\Gamma \vdash (\nu_\ell e{:}T)(M \mid N) \iff \Gamma \vdash N \text{ and } \Gamma \vdash M$$
$$\iff \Gamma \vdash N \mid (\nu_\ell e{:}T) M$$

In the case that $\ell \in \mathrm{dom}(\Gamma)$, the argument is slightly different depending on whether $e$ is a channel or a location. As an example we consider the former, and we assume $\Gamma$ has the form $\Delta, \ell{:}L$.

$$\Gamma \vdash (\nu_\ell a{:}A)(M \mid N) \iff \Delta, \ell{:}(L, a{:}A) \vdash (M \mid N)$$
$$\iff \Delta, \ell{:}(L, a{:}A) \vdash M \text{ and } \Delta, \ell{:}(L, a{:}A) \vdash N$$
$$\iff \Delta, \ell{:}L \vdash M \text{ and } \Delta, \ell{:}(L, a{:}A) \vdash N \text{ by Restriction}$$
$$\iff \Gamma \vdash M \text{ and } \Gamma \vdash (\nu_\ell a{:}A) N$$
$$\iff \Gamma \vdash M \mid (\nu_\ell a{:}A) N \qquad \square$$

PROPOSITION 8. *If* $N \equiv M$ *then* $\Gamma \vdash N$ *implies* $\Gamma \vdash M$

*Proof.* By induction on the proof that $N \equiv M$. All of the rules and most of the axioms are very easy to handle; the most difficult case is (s-extr), which follows by the previous lemma. As an example, we consider the rule (s-new): $\ell[\![(\nu e{:}T) P]\!] \equiv (\nu_\ell e{:}T) \ell[\![P]\!]$.

If $\ell \notin \mathrm{dom}(\Gamma)$ then it is immediate as both sides trivially type with respect to $\Gamma$. So suppose $\ell \in \mathrm{dom}(\Gamma)$, and, as an example, that $e{:}T$ is $a{:}A$. Let $\Gamma$ have the form $\Delta, \ell{:}L$. Then $\Gamma \vdash \ell[\![(\nu a{:}A) P]\!]$ if and only if $L, a{:}A \vdash P$ while

$$\Gamma \vdash (\nu_\ell a{:}A) \ell[\![P]\!] \iff \Delta, \ell{:}(L, a{:}A) \vdash \ell[\![P]\!]$$
$$\iff L, a{:}A \vdash P \qquad \square$$

As is normally the case the proof of Subject Reduction depends on the fact that, in some sense, typing is preserved by substitution. To prove this fact the following lemma will be useful:

LEMMA 9. *If* $L \vdash V{:}S$ *and* $L, X{:}S \vdash U{:}T$ *then* $L \vdash U\{\!|^V/x|\!\}{:}T$.

*Proof.* By induction on the structure of $X$.

Suppose $X$ is a variable, *i.e.* $X = x$ for some $x$. We then proceed by induction on $U$. If $U$ is a base value or has the form $u[\tilde{v}]$, then the result is trivial. If $U$ is a tuple we can apply the inner induction hypothesis. If $U$ is $x$, then $U\{\!\{^V\!/x\}\!\} = V$ and, by the typing rules, $S \leq T$; using type specialization, we can therefore conclude $\mathbb{L} \vdash U\{\!\{^V\!/x\}\!\}:T$, as required. If $U$ is an identifier $u$ that is different from $x$ then $x \notin \text{fid}(U)$ and $U\{\!\{^V\!/x\}\!\} = U$; therefore by the Restriction Lemma $\mathbb{L} \vdash U\{\!\{^V\!/x\}\!\}:T$, as required.

Suppose $X$ has the form $z[\tilde{x}]$, so $\mathbb{L}, X{:}S = \mathbb{L}$ and $\text{fid}(X)$ disjoint $\text{dom}(\mathbb{L})$ and therefore $U\{\!\{^V\!/x\}\!\} = U$. By Corollary 6, $\mathbb{L} \vdash U{:}T$.

If $X$ is a tuple, the result follows by induction. $\qquad\square$

PROPOSITION 10 (SUBSTITUTION). *If* $\mathbb{L} \vdash V{:}T$ *and* $\mathbb{L}, X{:}T \vdash P$ *then* $\mathbb{L} \vdash P\{\!\{^V\!/x\}\!\}$.

*Proof.* For convenience we use $P'$ to denote $P\{\!\{^V\!/x\}\!\}$ (and employ similar notation for other syntactic categories).

As before, the proof is by induction on the structure of $X$. The cases for tuples $\tilde{Y}$ and structured values $z[\tilde{x}]$ are as before. We present the case where $X = x$, for some variable $x$. In this case we proceed by a second induction on the inference $\mathbb{L}, x{:}T \vdash P$. We present the cases that involve binders.

(t-r). Here $\mathbb{L}, x{:}T \vdash u?(Y{:}S)\,Q$ because $\mathbb{L}, x{:}T \vdash u{:}\text{chan}\langle T\rangle$ and $\mathbb{L}, x{:}T, Y{:}S \vdash Q$. Applying the previous lemma to $\mathbb{L}, x{:}T \vdash u{:}\text{chan}\langle T\rangle$, we obtain $\mathbb{L} \vdash u'{:}\text{chan}\langle T\rangle$. In addition, $\mathbb{L}, x{:}T, Y{:}S \vdash Q$ can be rewritten as $\mathbb{L}, Y{:}S, x{:}T \vdash Q$. By the internal induction, we obtain $\mathbb{L}, Y{:}S \vdash Q'$. Now (t-r) gives the required $\mathbb{L} \vdash u'?(Y{:}S)\,Q'$.

(t-newc). Here $\mathbb{L}, x{:}T \vdash (va{:}A)\,P$ because $\mathbb{L}, x{:}T, a{:}A \vdash P$. The environment can be rewritten as $\mathbb{L}, a{:}A, x{:}T$, and therefore induction can be applied to obtain $\mathbb{L}, a{:} \vdash P'$. The result follows by an application of (t-newc). $\qquad\square$

THEOREM (1, SUBJECT REDUCTION).

*If* $\Gamma \vdash \Delta \triangleright N$ *and* $\Delta \triangleright N \longmapsto N'$ *then* $\Gamma \vdash \Delta \triangleright N'$.

*Proof.* From the hypothesis $\Gamma \vdash \Delta \triangleright N$ we know that $\Gamma \vdash N$ and $\Gamma(\ell) \leq \Delta(\ell)$ for every $\ell$ in $\text{dom}(\Gamma)$. So it is sufficient to show $\Gamma \vdash N'$, which we do by induction on the derivation of $\Delta \triangleright N \longmapsto N'$. We present a number of representative cases.

(r-move). Here we have $\Delta \triangleright \ell[\![\text{go}\,k.\,P]\!] \longrightarrow k[\![P]\!]$ and $\Delta(k) \vdash P$. If $k \notin \text{dom}(\Gamma)$ then the required $\Gamma \vdash k[\![P]\!]$ follows trivially from (t-runb). If $k \in \text{dom}(\Gamma)$ then we know that $\Gamma(k) \leq \Delta(k)$ and therefore, by Weakening, $\Gamma(k) \vdash P$. Now (t-rung) can be applied to obtain $\Gamma \vdash k[\![P]\!]$.

(r-comm). Here we have

$$\Delta \triangleright \ell[\![a!\langle V\rangle P]\!] \mid \ell[\![a?(X{:}T)\,Q]\!] \longrightarrow \ell[\![P]\!] \mid \ell[\![Q\{\!\{^V\!/x\}\!\}]\!]$$

If $\ell \notin \text{dom}(\Gamma)$ then the result is trivial from (t-runb). Otherwise $\ell \in \text{dom}(\Gamma)$. From $\Gamma \vdash \ell[\![a!\langle V\rangle P]\!] \mid \ell[\![a?(X)\,Q]\!]$ we know $\Gamma \vdash \ell[\![a!\langle V\rangle P]\!]$ and therefore $\Gamma(\ell) \vdash P$. It follows that $\Gamma \vdash \ell[\![P]\!]$.

It remains to show that $\Gamma \vdash \ell[\![Q\{\!\{^V\!/x\}\!\}]\!]$, that is $\Gamma(\ell) \vdash Q\{\!\{^V\!/x\}\!\}$. Again from the hypothesis we know $\Gamma \vdash \ell[\![a?(X{:}T)\,Q]\!]$ from which we can conclude that $\Gamma(\ell) \vdash u{:}\text{chan}\langle T\rangle$ and $\mathbb{L}, X{:}T \vdash Q$. From $\Gamma \vdash \ell[\![a!\langle V\rangle P]\!]$ we know that $\Gamma(\ell) \vdash V{:}S$ for some S for which we also have $\Gamma(\ell) \vdash u{:}\mathsf{chan}\langle S\rangle$. In our typing system this must mean that S and T coincide. We may therefore apply the Substitution lemma to obtain the required $\Gamma(\ell) \vdash Q\{^V/x\}$.

(r-new). We consider the case:

$$\Delta, \ell{:}L \rhd (\nu_\ell a{:}A)N \longrightarrow (\nu_\ell a{:}A)N' \quad \text{because} \quad \Delta, \ell{:}(L, a{:}A) \rhd N \longrightarrow N'$$

First suppose $\ell \in \mathsf{dom}(\Gamma)$. Since $\Gamma \vdash \Delta, \ell{:}L \rhd (\nu_\ell a{:}A)N$ we know $\Gamma$ can be written as $\Gamma', \ell{:}L'$, where $L' \leq L$ and therefore $\Gamma', \ell{:}(L', a{:}A) \vdash N$. We can now apply induction to obtain $\Gamma', \ell{:}(L', a{:}A) \vdash N'$, to which (t-newcg) can be applied to obtain the required $\Gamma \vdash (\nu_\ell a{:}A)N'$.

If $\ell \notin \mathsf{dom}(\Gamma)$ then by (t-newcb) it is sufficient to prove $\Gamma \vdash N'$. In this case $\Gamma \vdash \Delta, \ell{:}L \rhd (\nu_\ell a{:}A)N$ yields $\Gamma \vdash \Delta, \ell{:}(L, a{:}A) \rhd N$ to which induction can be applied to give the required $\Gamma \vdash N'$.

(r-str). This case follows using induction and Proposition 8. □

## A.3 Type Safety

We first show that the typing system is "compatible" with the compatibility relation $\asymp$.

LEMMA 11.
- $\mathbb{L} \vdash V{:}T$ implies $V \asymp T$
- $\mathbb{L} \vdash V{:}T$ and $\mathbb{L} \vdash U{:}T$ implies $V \asymp U$

*Proof.* A straightforward inductive argument, in the first case on the derivation of $\mathbb{L} \vdash V{:}T$ and in the second on the structure of the type T. □

THEOREM (2, TYPE SAFETY). *If* $\Gamma \vdash N$ *and* $\ell \in \mathsf{dom}(\Gamma)$ *then* $N \overset{err\ell}{\longmapsto}\!\!\!\!/\,$.

*Proof.* By induction on the proof that $N \overset{err\ell}{\longmapsto}$, we show that if $\ell \in \mathsf{dom}(\Gamma)$ and $N \overset{err\ell}{\longmapsto}$ then $\Gamma \nvdash N$, which is sufficient to establish the theorem. Let $\mathbb{L}$ denote $\Gamma(\ell)$.

(e-comm). In this case we have $\ell[\![a!\langle V\rangle P]\!] \mid \ell[\![a?(X{:}T)Q]\!] \overset{err\ell}{\longmapsto}$ because $V \nasymp T$. Now suppose, for a contradiction, that $\Gamma \vdash \ell[\![a!\langle V\rangle P]\!] \mid \ell[\![a?(X{:}T)Q]\!]$. Because there is no subtyping on channel types we know $\mathbb{L} \vdash \mathsf{chan}\langle T\rangle$ and $\mathbb{L} \vdash \mathsf{chan}\langle S\rangle$ implies $T = S$. From the alleged typing we can therefore conclude that $\mathbb{L} \vdash V{:}T$. By the first part of Lemma 11, we have $V \asymp T$ which contradictions $V \nasymp T$.

(e-eq). Here we have $\ell[\![\text{if } U = V \text{ then } P \text{ else } Q]\!] \overset{err\ell}{\longmapsto}$ because $U \nasymp V$. If we assume $\Gamma \vdash \ell[\![\text{if } U = V \text{ then } P \text{ else } Q]\!]$ then we must have $\Gamma \vdash U{:}T$ and $\Gamma \vdash V{:}T$ for some T. Now applying the second part of Lemma 11 we obtain a contradiction to $U \nasymp V$.

(e-new). First suppose that $(\nu_k e{:}E)N \overset{err\ell}{\longmapsto}$ because $N \overset{err\ell}{\longmapsto}$ and $e \neq \ell$. If $k \notin \mathsf{dom}(\Gamma)$ then by induction we have $\Gamma \nvdash N$ and by either (t-newcb) or (t-newlb) we can conclude $\Gamma \nvdash (\nu_k e{:}E)N$.

So suppose $k \in \mathsf{dom}(\Gamma)$. As an example suppose $e{:}E$ is a location; the case when it is a channel is similar. Applying induction we have $\Gamma, e{:}E \nvdash N$ and therefore by (t-newlg) we can conclude $\Gamma \nvdash (\nu_k e{:}E)N$.

Finally suppose $(\nu_\ell k{:}E)N \overset{err\ell}{\longmapsto}$ because $N \overset{err k}{\longmapsto}$. By $\alpha$-conversion we can assume that $k$ does not appear in $\Gamma$ and so we can apply induction to obtain $\Gamma, k{:}E \nvdash N$. We know that $\ell \in \mathsf{dom}(\Gamma)$ and therefore by (t-newlg) we can conclude $\Gamma \nvdash (\nu_\ell k{:}E)N$.

(e-str). Straightforward, using induction and Proposition 8. □

## Acknowledgements

We thank the referees for several comments that sharpened the presentation. Matthew Hennessy funded by CONFER II and EPSRC project GR/K60701. James Riely funded by NSF grant EIA-9805604.

## References

[1] M. Abadi and A.D. Gordon. A calculus for cryptographic protocols: The spi calculus. *Information and Computation*, To appear. Available as Compaq SRC Research Report 149 (1998).

[2] B. Bershad, B. Savage, P. Pardyak, E. Sirer, D. Becker, M. Fiuczynski, C. Chambers, and S. Eggers. Extensibility, safety and performance in the SPIN operating system. In *Symposium on Operating Systems Principles*, pages 267–284, 1997.

[3] L. Cardelli and A.D. Gordon. Mobile ambients. In *Foundations of Software Science and Computational Structures*, volume 1378 of *Lecture Notes in Computer Science*, pages 140–155. Berlin: Springer-Verlag, 1998.

[4] R. DeNicola, G. Ferrari, and R. Pugliese. Types as specifications of access policies. In J. Vitek and C. Jensen, editors, *Secure Internet Programming: Security Issues for Distributed and Mobile Objects*, Lecture Notes in Computer Science. Springer-Verlag, 1999.

[5] C. Fournet, G. Gonthier, J.J. Levy, L. Marganget, and D. Remy. A calculus of mobile agents. In U. Montanari and V. Sassone, editors, *CONCUR: Proceedings of the International Conference on Concurrency Theory*, volume 1119 of *Lecture Notes in Computer Science*, pages 406–421, Pisa, August 1996. Berlin: Springer-Verlag.

[6] M. Hennessy and J. Riely. Resource access control in systems of mobile agents. In U. Nestmann and B. Pierce, editors, *3rd International Workshop on High-Level Concurrent Languages (HLCL'98)*, volume 16(3) of *Electronic Notes in Theoretical Computer Science*, Nice, September 1998. Elsevier. Available from http://www.elsevier.nl/locate/entcs. Full version available as Sussex CSTR 98/02, 1998. Available from http://www.cogs.susx.ac.uk/.

[7] X. Leroy and F. Rouaix. Security properties of typed applets. In *Conference Record of the ACM Symposium on Principles of Programming Languages*, San Diego, January 1998. ACM Press.

[8] R. Milner. The polyadic $\pi$-calculus: a tutorial. Technical Report ECS-LFCS-91-180, Laboratory for Foundations of Computer Science, Department of Computer Science, University of Edinburgh, UK, October 1991. Also in *Logic and Algebra of Specification*, ed. F. L. Bauer, W. Brauer and H. Schwichtenberg, Springer-Verlag, 1993.

[9] G. Necula. Proof-carrying code. In *Conference Record of the ACM Symposium on Principles of Programming Languages*, Paris, January 1997. ACM Press.

[10] B. Pierce and D. Sangiorgi. Typing and subtyping for mobile processes. *Mathematical Structures in Computer Science*, 6(5):409–454, 1996. Extended abstract in LICS '93.

[11] J. Riely and M. Hennessy. A typed language for distributed mobile processes. In *Conference Record of the 25th ACM SIGPLAN-SIGACT Symposium on Principles of Programming Languages*, San Diego, January 1998. ACM Press.

[12] J. Riely and M. Hennessy. Trust and partial typing in open systems of mobile agents. In *Conference Record of the 26th ACM SIGPLAN-SIGACT Symposium on Principles of Programming Languages*, San Antonio, January 1999. ACM Press. Full version available as Sussex CSTR 98/04, 1998. Available from http://www.cogs.susx.ac.uk/.

[13] P. Sewell. Global/local subtyping and capability inference for a distributed π-calculus. In *Proceedings of the International Colloquium on Automata, Languages and Programming*, volume 1433 of *Lecture Notes in Computer Science*. Berlin: Springer-Verlag, July 1998.

[14] R. Stata and M. Abadi. A type system for java bytecode subroutines. In *Conference Record of the ACM Symposium on Principles of Programming Languages*, San Diego, January 1998. ACM Press.

# Types as Specifications of Access Policies

Rocco De Nicola, GianLuigi Ferrari, and Rosario Pugliese

**Abstract.** Mobility is a key concept for network programming; it has stimulated much research about new programming languages and paradigms. In the design of programming languages for mobile agents, i.e. processes which can migrate and execute on new hosts, the integration of security mechanisms is a major challenge. This paper presents the security mechanisms of the programming language KLAIM (a Kernel Language for Agents Interaction and Mobility). The language, by making use of a capability–based type system, provides direct support for expressing and enforcing policies that control access to resources and data.

## 1 Introduction

Most of the difficult issues to face when developing mobile applications running over a network are related to security. A typical example of security property is the requirement that only legitimate mobile agents can be granted access to specific resources, or to specific services. A common solution to this problem is to provide *secure communication channels* by means of cryptographic protocols. These protocols (e.g. SSL, S–HTTP) are designed to provide authentication facilities of both servers and agents. Another common approach relies on *security architectures* which monitor the execution of mobile agents to protect a host from external attacks to private information.

Recently several researchers have explored the possibility of considering security issues at the level of language design aiming at embedding protection mechanisms in the languages. For instance the language Java [4] exploits type information as a foundation of its security: well–typed Java programs (and the corresponding verified bytecode) will never compromise the integrity of certain data.

This idea dates back in time; type systems have been successfully used to ensure *type safety* of programs since a long time. Type safety means that every data will be used consistently with its declaration. However, there has been little work on exploring and designing type systems for security.

In this paper we discuss the design of the type system for KLAIM (*a Kernel Language for Agents Interaction and Mobility*) [14], an experimental programming language specifically designed for programming mobile agents. KLAIM provides direct support for expressing and enforcing security policies that control access to resources and data. In particular, the language uses types to protect resources and data and to establish policies for access control.

The main guidelines for the design of KLAIM and of its type system are:
– KLAIM processes and types are *network* aware;

- networks and processes are different entities;
- access control policies are network coordination policies.

KLAIM consists of core Linda [17, 16, 11] with multiple located tuple spaces. A KLAIM program, called a net, is structured as a collection of nodes. Each node has a name and consists of a process component and a tuple space component. Sites are the *concrete* names of the nodes and are the main linguistic constructs for providing references to nodes of a net.

Processes may access tuple spaces through explicit naming: operations over tuple spaces are indexed with their *locality*. Localities are the *symbolic* names of nodes and programmers are not required to know the concrete network references, i.e. the precise mapping of localities into sites.

The net primitives are designed to handle all issues related to physical distribution, scoping and mobility of processes: the visibility of localities, the allocation policies of tuple spaces, the scoping disciplines of mobile agents, etc..

KLAIM types are used to protect resources and data and to establish policies for access control. Types are abstractions of process behaviours and provide information about the *capabilities of processes*, namely the operations processes intend to perform at a specific locality (downloading/consuming a tuple, producing a tuple, activating a process, and creating a new node).

KLAIM capability–based type system encompasses both subtyping and recursively defined types. Subtyping naturally emerges when considering *hierarchies* of access rights. Recursive types are used to deal with mobile recursive agents.

The development of KLAIM applications proceed in two phases. In the first phase, processes are programmed while ignoring the precise physical allocations of tuple spaces and the access rights of processes. An inference system assigns types to processes, and checks whether processes behave in accordance with their declared intentions. All rules of the inference system are syntax driven and such that any process has a minimal type smaller than all its deducible types.

In the second phase, processes are allocated over the nodes of the net. It is in this phase that access control policies are set up as a result of a coordination activity among the nodes of the net.

By a mix of both static and dynamic typing KLAIM type system guarantees that only processes with intentions that match the access rights as granted by the net coordinators are allowed to proceed.

This paper is a tutorial presentation of the KLAIM approach to mobile agent security. Its main original contributions are a perspective on types for access control, some natural extensions of the KLAIM type system and several concrete programming examples. The interested reader can find additional material in other publications of our group. The language and the design philosophy underlying KLAIM are presented in [14]. The mathematical foundations (decidability and soundness) of the KLAIM type system can be found in [15] (a preliminary presentation appeared in [13]). The prototype implementation of the language is described in [5].

The rest of the paper proceeds as follows. Section 2 illustrates, via simple programming examples, the basic ideas of the language and of its type system. Section 3 presents the syntax of processes, types and nets, and outlines the operational semantics. Sections 4 presents several programming examples and paradigms that exhibit the flexibility and the expressive power of the language. The (static) type system which infers types of processes and the network type checking are formally presented in Section 5. Finally, Section 6 concludes the paper with a brief discussion of other works and possible extensions. The formal operational semantics of processes and nets is illustrated in the Appendix.

## 2  The KLAIM programming model

We begin this section by summarizing the Linda programming model. Then, we introduce the main features of KLAIM by means of simple examples.

Linda is a coordination language that relies on an asynchronous and associative communication mechanism based on a shared global environment called Tuple Space (TS). A tuple space is a multiset of tuples, that are sequences of actual fields (expressions or values) and formal fields (variables). *Pattern–matching* is used to select tuples in a TS. Linda provides four main primitives for handling tuples: two (non–blocking) operations add tuples to a TS, two (possibly blocking) operations read/withdraw tuples from the TS. The Linda asynchronous communication model allows programmers to explicitly control interactions among processes via shared data and to use the same set of primitives both for data manipulation and for process synchronization.

### 2.1  Nets and Processes

We now introduce the KLAIM primitives without considering typing issues. KLAIM programs are structured around the notions of *localities*, *tuples*, *tuple spaces*, *nets* and *processes*.

*Localities* can be thought of as the symbolic names for sites. Sites are the addresses (network references) of nodes. The bindings between localities and sites are stored in the *allocation environment* of each node of the net. Existence of a distinguished locality self is assumed that is used by processes to refer to their current execution site.

*Tuples* contain information items; their fields can be actual fields (i.e. expressions, localities, processes) and formal fields (i.e. variables). Syntactically, a formal field takes the form "!*ide*", where *ide* is an identifier. For instance, the sequence $("foo", 25, !u)$ is a tuple with three fields. The first two fields are basic values (a string value and an integer value) while the third field is a variable. Similarly, $(Agent(Itinerary, RetLloc), !List, Site)$ is a tuple whose first field is a process (with two parameters).

*Tuple spaces* are collections (multisets) of tuples. *Pattern–matching* is used to select elements from a tuple space. Two tuples match if they have the same number of fields and corresponding fields have matching values or variables. Variables match any value of the same type, and two values match only if they are identical.

*Nets* are sets of nodes; each node consists of a site $s$, an allocation environment $\rho$, a set of running processes $P$ and a tuple space $T$. We formally model $T$ as a special kind of process. The allocation environment $\rho$ constraints network connectivity in that a node will be able to communicate only with the subset of the nodes of the network determined by $\rho$. Hereafter, we will use

$$s_1 ::_{\rho_1} P_1 \mid T_1 \parallel \ldots \parallel s_n ::_{\rho_n} P_n \mid T_n$$

to denote a net with $n$ nodes.

*Processes* are the active computational units and may be executed concurrently either at the same site or at different sites. Processes can perform five different basic operations, called *actions*, that permit reading (writing) from (in) a tuple space, activating new threads of execution and creating new nodes.

The operation for retrieving information from a node has two variants: **in**$(t)$@$l$ and **read**$(t)$@$l$. Action **in**$(t)$@$l$ evaluates the tuple $t$ and looks for a matching tuple $t'$ in the tuple space located at $l$ ($l$ gives the logical address of the tuple space). Whenever the matching tuple $t'$ is found, it is removed from the tuple space. The corresponding values of $t'$ are assigned to the variables in the formal fields of $t$ and the operation terminates; the new bindings are used by the continuation of the process that has executed **in**$(t)$@$l$. If no matching tuple is found, the operation is suspended until one becomes available. Action **read**$(t)$@$l$ differs from **in**$(t)$@$l$ because the tuple $t'$ selected by pattern–matching is not removed from the tuple space.

The operation for placing information on a node has, again, two variants: **out**$(t)$@$l$ and **eval**$(P)$@$l$. The operation **out**$(t)$@$l$ adds the tuple resulting from the evaluation of $t$ to the tuple space located at $l$. The operation **eval**$(P)$@$l$ spawns a process (whose code is given by $P$) at the node located at $l$.

The operation for creating new nodes is **newloc**$(u_1, \ldots, u_n)$. It dynamically creates a set of $n$ different new sites that can only be accessed via locality variables $u_1, \ldots, u_n$.

We now provide some simple examples of KLAIM programs; more advanced programming examples will be presented later. Hereafter, we assume that the basic values are `integer` and `strings`.

Our first example illustrates a process that moves along the nodes of a net with a fixed binding of localities to sites (this somehow corresponds to *static scoping*). We consider a net consisting of two sites $s_1$ and $s_2$. A client process $C$ is allocated at site $s_1$ and a server process $S$ is allocated at site $s_2$. The server $S$ can accept clients for execution. The client process sends process $Q$ to the server. This is modelled by the following KLAIM code:

$$C \stackrel{def}{=} \textbf{out}(Q)@l_1.\textbf{nil}$$
$$Q \stackrel{def}{=} \textbf{in}("foo", !x)@\texttt{self}.\textbf{out}("foo", x+1)@\texttt{self}.\textbf{nil}$$
$$S \stackrel{def}{=} \textbf{in}(!X)@\texttt{self}.X$$

The behaviour of the processes above depends on the meaning of $l_1$ and `self`. It is the allocation environment that establishes the links between localities and sites. Here, we assume that the allocation environment of site $s_1$, $\rho_1$, maps `self` into $s_1$ and $l_1$ into $s_2$, while the allocation environment of site $s_2$, $\rho_2$, maps **self** into $s_2$. Finally, we assume that the tuple spaces located at $s_1$ and $s_2$ both contain the tuple $("foo", 1)$. The following KLAIM program represents the net discussed above:

$$s_1 ::_{\rho_1} C|\mathbf{out}("foo", 1) \| s_2 ::_{\rho_2} S|\mathbf{out}("foo", 1).$$

The client process $C$ sends process $Q$ for execution at the server node (locality $l_1$ is bound to $s_2$ in $\rho_1$). After the execution of $\mathbf{out}(Q)@l_1$, the tuple space at site $s_2$ contains a tuple where the code of process $Q$ is stored. Indeed, it is

$$Q' \stackrel{def}{=} \mathbf{in}("foo", !x)@s_1.\mathbf{out}("foo", x + 1)@s_1.\mathbf{nil}$$

the process stored in the tuple, as the localities occurring in $Q$ are evaluated using the environment at site $s_1$ where the action **out** has been executed. Hence, when executed at the server's site the mobile process $Q$ increases tuple $"foo"$ at the client's site. Fig. 1 gives a pictorial representation of this example.

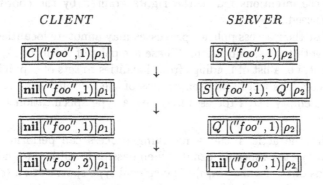

**Fig. 1.** Agent Mobility: Static Scoping

Our second example illustrates how mobile agents migrate with a *dynamic scoping* strategy. In this case the client process $C$ is $\mathbf{eval}(Q)@l_1.\mathbf{nil}$. When $\mathbf{eval}(Q)@l_1$ is executed, the process $Q$ is spawned at the remote node *without* evaluating its localities according to the allocation environment $\rho_1$. Thus, the execution of $Q$ will depend only on the allocation environment $\rho_2$ and $Q$ will increase tuple $"foo"$ at the server's site. Fig. 2 illustrates this example.

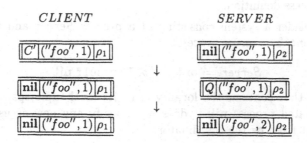

**Fig. 2.** Agent Mobility: Dynamic Scoping

## 2.2 Types for Access Control

KLAIM types provide information about the intentions of processes: downloading/consuming tuples, producing tuples, activating processes, and creating new nodes. We use $\{r, i, o, e, n\}$ to indicate the set of capabilities, where each symbol stands for the operation whose name begins with it; $r$ denotes the capability of executing a **read** action, $i$ stands for **in**, $o$ for **out**, $e$ for **eval**, and $n$ for **newloc**. Semantically, types are functions mapping localities (and locality variables) into functions from sets of capabilities to types.

Capabilities are used differently by processes and net coordinators. The capabilities of a locality $l$, within a process type, carry information about the operations the process intends to perform at $l$. The capabilities specified by a net coordinator determine the access policy of each site of a net in terms of access rights and execution privileges. Type checking will guarantee that only processes whose intentions match the rights granted by the coordinators are allowed to proceed.

To manifest their access policies processes may annotate localities and locality variables with type specifications. These are pairs of the form $\langle \lambda, \delta \rangle$, where $\lambda$ is an access list, i.e. a list of bindings from localities to sets of capabilities, and $\delta$ is a type. Access lists will be written as lists of the form $[l_1 \mapsto \pi_1, \ldots, l_n \mapsto \pi_n]$; $\phi$ denotes the empty list. Processes may use a type specification $\langle \lambda, \delta \rangle$ in four different ways.

- To restrict the actions that a receiving process can perform at (the site corresponding to) a specific locality when passing localities around via output tuple fields of the form $l : \langle \lambda, \delta \rangle$. The special type specification $\langle \phi, \top \rangle$ can be used to state that no further restriction on the access to $l$ is imposed.
- To specify the actions the rest of a reading process intends to perform at the received site when reading sites via input tuple fields of the form $!\, u : \langle \lambda, \delta \rangle$.
- To specify the access rights of the nodes of the net with respect to newly created nodes, and the vice versa, when creating new nodes by means of $\mathbf{newloc}(\tilde{u} : \langle \lambda, \delta \rangle)$. The special type specification $\langle \phi, \top \rangle$ can be used for stating that a new node inherits the access rights of the creating one.
- To specify, via formal arguments of the form $u : \langle \lambda, \delta \rangle$, the actions that a process intends to perform at the site denoted by a specific formal argument of the process definition.

Let us consider a system consisting of a process *Server* and two identical processes *Client*. The server process

$$Server \stackrel{def}{=} \mathbf{out}(l : \langle \phi, \top \rangle)@\mathbf{self}.\mathbf{nil}$$

adds a tuple, that contains the locality $l$, to its local tuple space and evolves to the terminated process **nil**; it does not specify any new access policy and maintains that fixed by the coordinator.

The client process

$$Client \stackrel{def}{=} \mathbf{read}(!\, u : \langle [\mathbf{self} \mapsto \{e\}], \delta_P \rangle)@l_S.\mathbf{eval}(P)@u.\mathbf{nil}$$

first accesses the tuple space located at $l_S$ to read an address and to assign it to the locality variable $u$, then sends process $P$ for execution at $u$. The type specification $\langle[\mathtt{self} \mapsto \{e\}], \delta_P\rangle$ expresses that $Client$ is looking for a locality where it is possible to send for execution a process with type $\delta_P$ from the site where $Client$ is running.

Let us now consider a net where $Server$ is allocated at site $s$ and the two, identical, processes $Client$ are at sites $s_1$ and $s_2$, where $l_S$ is bound to $s$ to allow clients to interact with the server.

Process $Client$ has type

$$\delta_c = l_S \mapsto \{r\} \mapsto \bot.$$

This type states that $Client$ intends to perform a **read** operation at locality $l_S$. If the net coordinator grants the following access rights to the sites $s_1$ and $s_2$ where $Client$ is willing to execute,

$$\delta_{s_1} = s \mapsto \{r\} \mapsto \bot \qquad\qquad \delta_{s_2} = s \mapsto \{o\} \mapsto \bot$$

then, after evaluating the localities that appear in $\delta_c$ according to the allocation environment of the site where $Client$ is placed, we can see that only the $Client$ at $s_1$ has the right of reading tuples at the server's site and, consequently, of sending processes for execution at $l$.

The previous example focused on using types as mechanisms for providing access control policies of sites. The next example, instead, shows how users can program their own access control policies. Consider the user process

$$P \stackrel{def}{=} \mathbf{newloc}(!u_1 : \langle\lambda_1, \delta_1\rangle, !u_2 : \langle\lambda_2, \delta_2\rangle, !u_F : \langle\phi, \top\rangle).Q$$

where, for $i \in \{1, 2\}$, $\lambda_i = [u_F \mapsto \pi_i]$. The access lists associated to $u_1$ and $u_2$ mean that all connections to the sites (denoted by) $u_1$ and $u_2$ have to pass through the site (denoted by) $u_F$, which is the only site of the net that has the rights to perform actions at $u_1$ and $u_2$. The site denoted by $u_F$, instead, is accessible by all the sites that have access to the site where $P$ is running. In other words, site $u_F$ is the *firewall* of the subnet consisting of $u_1$ and $u_2$; process $P$ can program its own firewall policy by sending in execution at $u_F$ a suitable firewall manager. External processes will be able to access the firewall only if its access path is transmitted to them. This can be done by $Q$ above either via $\mathbf{out}(u_F : \langle\phi, \top\rangle)@l$, that allows the receiving process to use $u_F$ without any additional type restriction than that fixed at the time $u_F$ was created, or via $\mathbf{out}(u_F : \langle[l_1 \mapsto \{o\}, l_2 \mapsto \{o\}], \top\rangle)@l$, that only allows processes running at (the sites corresponding to) $l_1$ and $l_2$ to send tuples to $u_F$, i.e. to submit service requests.

## 3 A Kernel Language for Agents Interaction and Mobility

This section reviews the syntax and the operational semantics of KLAIM. It may be skipped by readers interested mainly in the programming issues.

## 3.1 Processes

The syntax of KLAIM *terms* is given in Table 1; there, $P$ ranges over process terms, $a$ over actions, $t$ over tuples, $f$ over tuple fields, $e$ over value expressions, and $\ell$ over localities and locality variables. Process and locality variables are typed whenever they are bound; value variables are kept untyped. We use $\tilde{\ }$ to denote a sequence of objects and $\{\tilde{\ }\}$ to denote the set of objects in $\tilde{\ }$. Tuples are sequences of fields, hence, for a tuple $t$, $\{t\}$ will denote the set of fields of $t$. Pairs of the form $\langle \lambda, \delta \rangle$ consisting of access lists $\lambda$ and types $\delta$ will be called *type specifications*. Their precise syntax will be introduced in the next section.

| | | |
|---|---|---|
| $P ::= \mathbf{nil}$ | (null process) | |
| $\mid \quad a.P$ | (action prefixing) | |
| $\mid \quad P_1 \mid P_2$ | (parallel composition) | |
| $\mid \quad X$ | (process variable) | |
| $\mid \quad A\langle \widetilde{P}, \widetilde{\ell}, \widetilde{e} \rangle$ | (process invocation) | |
| $a ::= \mathbf{out}(t)@\ell \mid \mathbf{in}(t)@\ell \mid \mathbf{read}(t)@\ell \mid \mathbf{eval}(P)@\ell \mid \mathbf{newloc}(\widetilde{u : \langle \lambda, \delta \rangle})$ | | |
| $t ::= f \mid f,t$ | | |
| $f ::= e \mid P \mid \ell : \langle \lambda, \delta \rangle \mid !x \mid !X : \delta \mid !u : \langle \lambda, \delta \rangle$ | | |

**Table 1.** Process Syntax

Actions have been described in Section 2.1. Here we only want to add a few comments on the action $\mathbf{newloc}(\widetilde{u : \langle \lambda, \delta \rangle})$, that dynamically creates a set of "fresh" nodes together with their access paths $\widetilde{u}$. It is the only action not indexed with a locality; it is always executed at the current node. For each $u_i \in \widetilde{u}$, $\lambda_i$ specifies the access rights of the nodes of the net with respect to the new node $u_i$, symmetrically for $\delta_i$. The simultaneous creation of a set of new nodes allows writing mutually recursive type specifications for these nodes.

Variables occurring in KLAIM terms can be bound by prefixes and process definitions. More precisely, prefixes $\mathbf{in}(t)@\ell.\_$ and $\mathbf{read}(t)@\ell.\_$ act as binders for variables in the formal fields of $t$. Prefix $\mathbf{newloc}(\widetilde{u : \langle \lambda, \delta \rangle}).\_$ binds the locality variables $\widetilde{u}$. Definition $A(\widetilde{X} : \widetilde{\delta}, \widetilde{u} : \widetilde{\langle \lambda, \delta \rangle}, \widetilde{x}) \stackrel{def}{=} P$ is a binder for the variables $\{\widetilde{X}, \widetilde{u}, \widetilde{x}\}$. Hereafter, we shall assume that all bound names in processes are distinct and shall require that the arguments of **eval** operations do not contain free process variables.

We will use the standard notation $P[e/x]$ to indicate the substitution of the value expression $e$ for the free occurrences of the variable $x$ in $P$; $P[\widetilde{e}/\widetilde{x}]$ will denote the simultaneous substitution of any free occurrence of $x \in \{\widetilde{x}\}$ with the corresponding $e \in \{\widetilde{e}\}$ in $P$. When substitutions involve locality variables, e.g. like in $P[\ell/u]$, they have to be applied also to the type specifications therein. Notation $P[\widetilde{P}/\widetilde{X}, \widetilde{\ell}/\widetilde{u}, \widetilde{e}/\widetilde{x}]$ has the expected meaning.

It is assumed that each process identifier $A$ has a *single* defining equation $A(\widetilde{X} : \widetilde{\delta}, \widetilde{u} : \langle \widetilde{\lambda, \delta} \rangle, \widetilde{x}) \overset{def}{=} P$, where process and locality parameters are explicitly typed. All free (value, process and locality) variables of $P$ are contained in $\{\widetilde{X}, \widetilde{u}, \widetilde{x}\}$ and, to guarantee uniqueness of solution of recursive process definitions, all its process variables and identifiers are *guarded*, i.e. they occur within the scope of a **in/read** prefix.

A *process* is a term without free variables; localities occurring in processes are considered as constants. In Section 3.3, we will see that they are names whose meaning is defined (i.e. mapped onto sites) by coordinators.

## 3.2 Types

*Capabilities* are elements of $\{r, i, o, e, n\}$, where each symbol stands for the operation whose name begins with it; $r$ denotes the capability of executing a **read** operation, $i$ the capability of executing an **in** operation, and so on. We use $\Pi$, ranged over by $\pi$, to denote the set of non–empty subsets of $\{r, i, o, e, n\}$.

*Access lists*, ranged over by $\lambda$, are lists $[\ell_i \mapsto \pi_i]_{i=1,\ldots,n}$, where $\ell_i$ are all distinct. Semantically, access lists $\lambda$ are partial functions from localities and locality variables to sets of capabilities (i.e. $\lambda(\ell_i) = \pi_i$). The access list of $\ell$, $[\ell_i \mapsto \pi_i]_{i=1,\ldots,n}$, specifies the capabilities of $\ell_i$ ($i = 1, \ldots, n$) relatively to $\ell$.

| | |
|---|---|
| $\delta ::= \bot$ | (empty type) |
| $\mid \top$ | (universal type) |
| $\mid \ell \mapsto \pi \mapsto \delta$ | (arrow type) |
| $\mid \delta_1, \delta_2$ | (union type) |
| $\mid \nu$ | (type variable) |
| $\mid \mu\nu.\delta$ | (recursive type) |

**Table 2.** Type Syntax

The syntax of KLAIM *types* is given in Table 2; there $\nu$ ranges over type variables and $\mu$ denotes the recursive operator. Hereafter, the following notational convention will be used: "$\mapsto$" binds stronger than "$\mu$", that binds stronger than ",". variables. The type $\bot$ denotes "void", i.e. no intention is declared by the process, and, semantically, corresponds to the smallest type. Conversely, the type $\top$ denotes the intention of performing any kind of operations and is the greatest type. A type of the form $\ell \mapsto \pi \mapsto \delta$ describes the intention of performing at $\ell$ those actions allowed by $\pi$, moreover it imposes constraint $\delta$ on the processes that could possibly be executed at $\ell$ (if $e \notin \pi$ then $\delta$ is $\bot$). The type $\delta_1, \delta_2$ is the union of types $\delta_1$ and $\delta_2$; semantically, it is their *least upper bound*. Recursive types are used for typing migrating recursive processes.

A type $\delta$ generated from the grammar in Table 2 is such that any recursive type $\mu\nu.\delta'$ occurring in $\delta$ does not contain $\nu$ on the left of $\mapsto$. A consequence of the requirement that each process variable/identifier in process definitions be guarded is the fact that we only use recursive types $\mu\nu.\delta$ whose body $\delta$ can be written as $\delta_1, \ldots, \delta_n$ and at least one of the $\delta_i$ has the form $\ell \mapsto \pi \mapsto \delta'$ (for some $\ell$, $\pi$ and $\delta'$ such that $\{r, i\} \cap \pi \neq \emptyset$). In the following, we will only consider types that satisfy this condition; they will be called *legal* types.

Systems of mutually recursive type equations will be used to define $n$–tuples of type. The solution of a system of typed equations is obtained by a standard iterative technique.

An important feature of KLAIM types is the notion of subtyping. The underlying idea is that if a process $P$ has type $\delta_1$ and $\delta_1 \preceq \delta_2$ then $P$ could be considered as having type $\delta_2$ too. The subtyping relation between $\delta_1$ and $\delta_2$ allow us to say that $P_1$ with type $\delta_1$ can be safely used in place of $P_2$ with type $\delta_2$; but not the vice versa. Subtyping rules and the type inference system will be presented in Section 5.

## 3.3  Nets

KLAIM nets are collections of nodes where processes and tuple spaces can be allocated. A *node* is a 4–tuple $(s, P_s, \delta_s, \rho_s)$ where $s$ is a site, $P_s$ is the process located at $s$, $\delta_s$ is the type of $s$ specifying the access control policy of $s$, and $\rho_s$ is the *allocation environment* of $s$, i.e. a (partial) function from localities to sites. We write $s ::_{\rho_s}^{\delta_s} P_s$ to denote the node $(s, P_s, \delta_s, \rho_s)$.

Hereafter, $\mathcal{E}$ will denote the set of environments, $\phi$ the empty environment, and $\{s/l\}$ the environment that maps the locality $l$ on the site $s$. We will use $\ell\{\rho\}$ to denote $\rho(\ell)$, if $\rho(\ell)$ is defined, and $\ell$, otherwise; moreover, $\rho[s/\ell]$ will denote the environment $\rho'$ such that $\rho'(\ell) = s$ and $\rho'(\ell') = \rho(\ell')$ for $\ell' \neq \ell$.

To specify the mutual access policies of a set of nodes, hence to consistently assign types to sites/nodes, we make use of a partial function $\Lambda$ that, for each site $s$, describes the access rights of $s$ on the other sites. Types of nodes have the same syntax of types of processes. However, strictly speaking, the formers cannot be generated by the grammar given in Table 2, since we required $\ell$ to stand for localities and locality variables. For types of nodes, we let $\ell$ range over sites.

**Definition 1.** A KLAIM *net* is a pair $N_S : \Lambda$ where $N_S$ is a finite multiset of nodes over the set of sites $S$, and $\Lambda : S \rightharpoonup (S \rightharpoonup \Pi)$ is a partial function. Function $\Lambda$ induces a system of $n$ type equations in the variables $\{\nu_{s_i} \mid s_i \in S\}$ where, if $\{s_1^i, \ldots, s_k^i\} = dom(\Lambda(s_i))$, the equation of site $s_i$ is

$$\nu_{s_i} = s_1^i \mapsto \Lambda(s_i)(s_1^i) \mapsto \nu_{s_1^i}, \cdots, s_k^i \mapsto \Lambda(s_i)(s_k^i) \mapsto \nu_{s_k^i},$$

and the following conditions hold:

1. for any node $s ::_{\rho_s}^{\delta_s} P$, $\rho_s(\texttt{self}) = s$, $image(\rho_s) \subseteq S$ and $\delta_s$ is the component of the solution of the system of type equations induced by $\Lambda$ corresponding to $s$;
2. for any pair of nodes $s ::_{\rho_s}^{\delta_s} P$ and $s' ::_{\rho_{s'}}^{\delta_{s'}} P'$, $s = s'$ implies $\rho_s = \rho_{s'}$ and $\delta_s = \delta_{s'}$.

Condition 1. expresses that the local allocation environment of a node maps localities on the sites of the net; in particular, self is mapped on the name (site) of the node. Moreover, the type of the node is determined by the function $\Lambda$ associated to the net. The idea underlying condition 2. is that the nodes of a net over the same site do have the same allocation environment and type as well.

Nets will also be written according to the syntax given in Table 3.

$$
\begin{aligned}
N ::=\ & s ::_\rho^\delta P & \text{(node)} \\
| \ & N_1 \parallel N_2 & \text{(net composition)}
\end{aligned}
$$

**Table 3.** Net Syntax

When developing KLAIM applications, type checking (that shall be presented in Section 5) will be used to guarantee that the types of the processes in the net agree with the access rights of the sites where they are located. More specifically, types of processes are checked against those fixed for the nodes of the net by the net coordinator, while taking into account where each process has been located. To compare process types, that are functions mapping localities into functions from sets of capabilities to process types, with node types, that are functions mapping sites into functions from sets of capabilities to node types, localities have to be mapped into sites by using site allocation environments, i.e. localities must be *interpreted*.

**Definition 2.** The *type interpretation function* associated to a net $N_S$, $\Theta_{N_S}$ : $S \longrightarrow \mathcal{E}$ is defined as follows: for all $s \in S$, $\Theta_{N_S}(s) = \rho_s$ if $s ::_{\rho_s}^{\delta_s} P \in N_S$, for some $\delta_s$ and $P$.

The type interpretation function is well–defined because $N_S$ enjoys conditions 1. and 2. of Definition 1.

## 3.4 Operational Semantics

We describe the operational behaviour of nets using a reduction semantics. A reduction semantics is centered around the notions of structural congruence and reduction relation. They are formally presented in the Appendix, here we provide some comments to enable the reader to understand the examples.

The structural congruence provides a convenient way of rearranging nodes. The structural laws express that $\parallel$ is commutative and associative, and that it is always possible to distribute the processes located onto the same node over clones of that node.

The reduction relation specifies the basic computational steps. The execution of an **out** operation adds a tuple to a tuple space. The local allocation environment is used both to determine the site where the tuple must be placed and to evaluate the tuple. If the tuple contains a field with a process, the corresponding field of the evaluated tuple contains the process resulting from the evaluation of the used localities by using the local allocation environment. The fact that processes in tuples are transmitted after the interpretation of their localities corresponds to having a *static scoping* discipline for the generation of tuples.

A *dynamic scoping* strategy is adopted for the **eval** operation. In this case the localities of the spawned process are not interpreted using the local allocation environment. Processes not closures are transmitted and their execution can be influenced by the remote allocation environment.

A process can perform an **in** action by synchronizing with (a process representing) a matching tuple *et*. To match the two candidate tuples one has to consider the site where the operation is executed and the type interpretation function of the net. The result of the execution of an **in** action is that tuple *et* is withdrawn and its values are used to determine the values of the variables in the input tuple to be used by the continuation. Action **read** behaves similarly to **in** but leaves the matched tuple *et* in the tuple space.

The use of **newloc** leads to the creation of new nodes and modifies the topology and the types of the net. The allocation environment of the new nodes is derived from that of the creating node with the obvious update for the **self** locality. The type specifications are exploited to generate the new types. The types of the nodes of the net are "extended" by adding the rights of the existing nodes over the new ones and the rights of the new nodes over the existing ones. Access lists are used to enrich the rights of the existing nodes, while types are used to determine the rights of the new ones.

Pattern–matching is extensively used in the reduction semantics. To select (from a tuple space) a tuple containing actual fields with processes inside the pattern–matching operation checks the types of processes to ensure that they satisfy the type constraints specified by the programmer. Hence, process codes are checked before being downloaded. In other words, the pattern–matching operation performs a *run–time* type checking of incoming codes.

## 4 Examples and Programming Paradigms

In this section we show how to program in KLAIM by means of some examples. We illustrate a mobile agent for information retrieval, some basic paradigms for mobile code applications and the implementation of a few access restrictions over nets.

### 4.1 Distributed Information Retrieval

Distributed information retrieval applications gather information from a set of sources distributed over a network; the nodes to be visited may be determined either statically or dynamically. Here, we present a KLAIM solution of a distributed information retrieval problem and discuss some of the access control issues there involved.

Consider a user process that needs information about a data of which he only has a key represented, say, by "*item*", to be used for searching in a database distributed over the network. In our solution, the distributed database is modelled by located tuple spaces and it is assumed that each local database (a tuple space) reachable from $l_{item}$ (the starting point of the search which is known by the user process) contains either a tuple of the form ("*item*", $v$) with the required information $v$, or a tuple of the form ("*item*", $s_{next}$), with the site of the next node to visit.

The *user process* $UP$ asks for the execution at $l_{item}$ of the mobile *gatherer* agent, $G$, and then retrieves the result of the search at the (new) node $u_R$[1]

$$UP \stackrel{def}{=} \mathbf{newloc}(u_R : \langle[\mathbf{self} \mapsto \{i\}, l_{item} \mapsto \{o\}, l_1 \mapsto \{o\}, l_2 \mapsto \{o\}], \bot\rangle).$$

Agent $G$ travels across the nodes looking for tuples containing information associated to the search key that is passed to it as parameter. $G$ is programmed in KLAIM as follows

$$G(x, u : \langle[\mathbf{self} \mapsto \{o\}], \bot\rangle) \stackrel{def}{=} \mathbf{read}(x, !y)@\mathbf{self}.\mathbf{out}(y)@u.\mathbf{nil}$$
$$\mid \mathbf{read}(x, !u' : \langle[\mathbf{self} \mapsto \{e\}], \delta'\rangle)@\mathbf{self}.\mathbf{eval}(G\langle x, u\rangle)@u'.\mathbf{nil}.$$

Assume that $P$ has type $\delta_P$ in a context that binds all free variables in $P$. Then the types of $UP$ and $G(x, u : \langle[\mathbf{self} \mapsto \{o\}], \bot\rangle)$ are:

$$\delta_{UP} = \delta_P, \mathbf{self} \mapsto \{n\} \mapsto \bot, l_{item} \mapsto \{e\} \mapsto l_{item} \mapsto \{r\} \mapsto \bot$$
$$\delta_G = \mathbf{self} \mapsto \{r\} \mapsto \bot, u \mapsto \{o\} \mapsto \bot.$$

Notice that the type of a closed process does not contain locality variables. The operations the process intends to perform at addresses denoted by locality variables are checked against the type specifications for those variables during the inference and are not reported in the type of the process.

As an example of type constraint checked in the type inference, we have that type $\delta'$, that we deliberately have not specified, must be greater than $\delta_G$, i.e. at least all the needed rights must be asked for.

Let us now see how types can be used to enforce access control policies by considering a net with three sites $s$, $s_1$ and $s_2$, with types $\delta_s$, $\delta_{s_1}$ and $\delta_{s_2}$. Assume that $s_1$ contains the tuple ("*item*", $s_2$), $s_2$ contains the tuple ("*item*", $v$), $UP$ is allocated at site $s$, $\rho_s(l_{item}) = s_1$, $\rho_s(l_1) = s_1$ and $\rho_s(l_2) = s_2$. The KLAIM code of the net is:

$$s ::^{\delta_s}_{\rho_s} UP \parallel s_1 ::^{\delta_{s_1}}_{\rho_{s_1}} \mathbf{out}("item", s_2) \parallel s_2 ::^{\delta_{s_2}}_{\rho_{s_2}} \mathbf{out}("item", v).$$

Checking whether the net is well–typed requires determining the interpretation of $\delta_{UP}$ with respect to the allocation environments and comparing the resulting type with the access control policy given by $\delta_s$. The interpretation of $\delta_{UP}$ is

---

[1] Here, localities $l_1$ and $l_2$ are used to represent the addresses of two nodes different from the node where user process is allocated. Processes located at these nodes are allowed to perform only output actions at the node named by $u_R$. The use of $l_1$ and $l_2$ could be avoided by introducing in the type specifications a distinguished locality **others** to denote any node other than those explicitly mentioned.

$$[\delta_P], s \mapsto \{n\} \mapsto \bot, s_1 \mapsto \{e\} \mapsto s_1 \mapsto \{r\} \mapsto \bot$$

where $[\delta_P]$ denotes the interpretation of $\delta_P$. To ensure well–typedness, we should have that $[\delta_{UP}] \preceq \delta_s$ which asks for:

$$[\delta_P] \preceq \delta_s, \ s \mapsto \{n\} \mapsto \bot \preceq \delta_s \text{ and } s_1 \mapsto \{e\} \mapsto (s_1 \mapsto \{r\} \mapsto \bot) \preceq \delta_s.$$

The type $\delta'$ of the variable $u'$ (used by the agent $G$ when reading continuation sites) is used statically (by the type inference system) to check whether $\delta_G \preceq \delta'$, and dynamically (by the pattern–matching mechanism) to select the appropriate tuple. For instance, the gatherer agent $G$ can travel from $s_1$ to $s_2$ only if the tuple ($"item"$, $s_2$) can be selected. This amounts to requiring that the interpretation of $\delta'$ should not be greater than $\delta_{s_2}$.

## 4.2 Code Mobility

*Mobile Code Applications* are applications running over a network whose distinctive feature is the exploitation of forms of "mobility". According to the classification proposed in [12], we can single out three paradigms that, together the traditional *client–server* paradigm, are largely used to build mobile code applications. These paradigms are:

- *Code–On–Demand*;
- *Remote Evaluation*;
- *Mobile Agent*.

*Code–on–Demand* A component of an application running over a network on a given node, can dynamically download some code from a remote node and link it to perform a given task.

To download code that respects certain type constraints $\delta$ and is stored in a tuple at a remote tuple space $l$, action $\mathbf{read}(!X : \delta)@l.X$ can be used. The downloaded code is checked for access violations at run–time by the pattern–matching mechanism. The typing rules for **read** and **in** are designed in such a way that any downloaded code whose type is a subtype of $\delta$ will not violate type correctness.

*Remote Evaluation* Any component of a networking application can invoke services from other components by transmitting both the data needed to perform the service and the code that describes how to perform the service.

To transmit both code $P$ and data $v$ at the locality $l$ of the server, action $\mathbf{out}(\mathbf{in}(!y)@l.A\langle y\rangle, v)@l$, where $A(x) \overset{def}{=} P$, can be used. Here, we assume that the server adopts the following (code–on–demand) protocol

$$\mathbf{in}(!X : \delta, !x)@\mathtt{self}.\mathbf{out}(x)@\mathtt{self}.X.$$

To prevent "damages" from $P$, the server may mount and execute code $P$ only if $[\delta_P]$, the type of the code $P$ when interpreted at the server's site, is such that $[\delta_P] \preceq [\delta]$, where $[\delta]$ is the interpretation of $\delta$ at the server's site.

Type $\delta$ may give only minimal access permissions on the server's site, for instance, only the capability of reading some resources and giving back the results of the execution. In this case, $[\delta]$ is of the form

$$s \mapsto \{r\} \mapsto \bot, s_0 \mapsto \{o\} \mapsto \bot, s_1 \mapsto \{o\} \mapsto \bot, \ldots s_n \mapsto \{o\} \mapsto \bot,$$

where $s_i$, $i = 0, \ldots, n$ are the sites with the rights of invoking server's facilities, and $s$ is the server's site.

Notice, however, that this does not prevent $P$ from visiting other sites. In particular, agent $P$ may be programmed in such a way that after having performed the required elaboration, it transmits code $Q$ at the locality $l_i$ (the logical name of site $s_i$):

$$P \stackrel{def}{=} \mathbf{read}(!x)@l.\mathbf{out}(op(x,y))@\mathbf{self}.\mathbf{out}(Q)@l_i.\mathbf{nil}.$$

It is immediate to see that, if we assume that the client is allocated at site $s_0$ and that $P$ has type $\delta_P = l \mapsto \{r\} \mapsto \bot, \mathbf{self} \mapsto \{o\} \mapsto \bot, l_i \mapsto \{o\} \mapsto \bot$, then $[\delta_P] = s \mapsto \{r\} \mapsto \bot, s_0 \mapsto \{o\} \mapsto \bot, s_i \mapsto \{o\} \mapsto \bot$. Hence, $[\delta_P] \preceq [\delta]$ However, code $Q$ is only stored in the tuple space at $s_i$: no new thread of execution is activated at site $s_i$. Before being executed code $Q$ must be read and verified (dynamic type checking). Therefore, process $P$ cannot activate a *Trojan horse* at the remote site $s_i$.

*Mobile Agents* A process (i.e. a program and an associated state of execution) on a given node of a network can migrate to a different node where it continues its execution from the current state.

If we want to adopt a dynamic scoping discipline for a mobile agent $A$ that migrates to locality $l$ for execution, the paradigm can be programmed using action $\mathbf{eval}(A)@l$. If a static scoping discipline is preferred, then action $\mathbf{out}(A)@l$ can be used instead (of course a code–on–demand protocol is assumed to pick up and execute $A$).

With dynamic scoping, the access rights of the mobile agent $A$ are controlled *statically* when the code of action $\mathbf{eval}(A)@l$ is encountered. With static scoping, access rights of $A$ are controlled *dynamically* by the pattern–matching when the tuple containing the code of agent $A$ is picked up from the tuple space.

## 4.3 Protecting the net

We now show how types can be used at the level of net coordinators to control accesses. In other words, we show how types can be used to set up the security architecture of KLAIM nets.

*Restricting Interactions* KLAIM action primitives operate on the whole net: operations on tuple spaces are not forced to happen locally at their current site. From the point of view of access control policies, communications among different sites of the net (i.e. remote communications) could be controlled and regulated.

To force a process running on a certain site $s$ to access only local tuples it suffices to constrain the type $\delta_s$ of the site in such a way that for no $s' \neq s$ it holds that $s' \mapsto \{r\} \mapsto \bot \preceq \delta_s$. Hence, a process $P$ allocated on $s$ performing remote **read/in** operations violate the access rights. To access tuples at a remote tuple space, a well–typed process must first move (if it has the required rights) to the remote site. Also output actions can be forced to be local; it suffices requiring that for no $s' \neq s$ it holds that $s' \mapsto \{o\} \mapsto \bot \preceq \delta_s$.

*Firewall* We now show how to specify a firewall by means of suitable typing. The idea is that the type of the site where the firewall is allocated specifies the access policy of network services. Assume that the firewall is set up at site $s$ to protect sites $s_1, \ldots, s_m$ from sites $s'_1, \ldots, s'_n$.

A first requirement is that processes located at site $s'_j$ cannot directly interact and ask for services at any site $s_i$. To this purpose we impose that for each site $s'_j$, for no $\pi$ it holds that $s_i \mapsto \pi \mapsto \bot \preceq \delta_{s'_j}$. Instead, type $\delta_{s'_j}$ may have subtypes of the form $s \mapsto \{o\} \mapsto \bot$. This means that each site $s'_j$ may only send service requests to the firewall (here we assume that the service request is stored in a tuple). In other words all connections from sites $s'_1, \ldots, s'_n$ to sites $s_1, \ldots, s_m$ have to pass through site $s$, the firewall.

For instance, process $P_1 \stackrel{def}{=} \textbf{out}(\textbf{eval}(Q)@l_{s_i})@l_s.\textbf{nil}$ complies with the access rights of a site $s'_k$, while process $P_2 \stackrel{def}{=} \textbf{eval}(Q)@l_{s_i}.\textbf{nil}$ violates the access rights of site $s'_k$.

The firewall can be programmed to handle the requests according to certain policies. Typically, the firewall handles a service request by a process of the form

$$\textbf{read}(!Request : \delta).\langle\texttt{RequestHandler}\rangle$$

where type $\delta$ specifies the access policy that the service request must satisfy. For instance, if

$$\delta = s_1 \mapsto \{i\} \mapsto \bot, s_2 \mapsto \{e\} \mapsto (s_2 \mapsto \{r\} \mapsto \bot, s'_k \mapsto \{o\} \mapsto \bot),$$

then the service requests $\textbf{eval}(\textbf{read}(!x)@\textbf{self}.\textbf{out}(op(x))@l_{s'_k}.\textbf{nil})@l_{s_2}.\textbf{nil}$ and $\textbf{read}(!x)@l_{s_1}.\textbf{nil}$ both satisfy the type requirements and will be accepted. The request $\textbf{read}(!x)@l_{s_1}.\textbf{out}(op(x))@l_{s'_k}.\textbf{nil}$ violates the type constraints and will be rejected.

One can easily see that, by adding standard types for tuples (basically record types), it is possible to specify more refined policies to handle service requests. For instance, one can fix a policy where the read operations are constrained to get from the tuple space only 'plain' data tuples, without localities or process codes.

As we outlined in Section 2.2, a user can program its own firewall. Let us consider, for instance, the following user process:

$$P \stackrel{def}{=} \textbf{newloc}(!u_1 : \langle\lambda_1, \delta_1\rangle, !u_2 : \langle\lambda_2, \delta_2\rangle, \ldots !u_n : \langle\lambda_n, \delta_n\rangle, !u_F : \langle\lambda_F, \delta_F\rangle).Q,$$

where, for all $i \in \{1, \ldots, n\}$, $\lambda_i = [u_F \mapsto \pi_i]$. Process $P$ creates a subnet whose sites are associated to locality variables $u_1, \ldots, u_n$; the type specifications $\langle\lambda_i, \delta_i\rangle$ ensures that the subnet can be reached only through site $u_F$ (the firewall). The user process can specify in the type specification $\langle\lambda_F, \delta_F\rangle$ the access policy to the firewall. For instance, setting $\lambda_F = \textbf{self} \mapsto \pi$ means that the firewall site can be accessed only from the site where the user process is running.

*Fares and Tickets* A primary access control policy consists of controlling the route of a mobile agent traveling in the net. For instance, if one has to configure a set of sites with new software, a mobile agent can be programmed to travel among the sites to install the new release of the software.

If the starting site of the trip is site $s_0$ and sites $s_1, s_2, \ldots, s_n$ are visited before coming back to the starting site, then the following equalities specify the type $\delta_T$ (the access rights) of the trip:

$$\delta_0 = s_1 \mapsto \{e\} \mapsto \delta_1, \delta$$
$$\delta_1 = s_2 \mapsto \{e\} \mapsto \delta_2, \delta$$
$$\vdots$$
$$\delta_{n-1} = s_n \mapsto \{e\} \mapsto \delta', \delta$$
$$\delta' = s_0 \mapsto \{o\} \mapsto \bot$$

The idea is that at each site type $\delta$ specifies the allowed operations (e.g. installing the new release of a software package); the remaining type information specifies the structure of the trip (which is the next site of the trip). At the last site of the trip the agent has the rights of returning to the original site the results of the trip (e.g. the notification that the installation was successful).

The type discussed above can be properly interpreted as the *fare* of the trip: an agent $A$ can perform the trip provided that its type $\delta_A$ matches the fare: formally, $\delta_A$ when interpreted at site $s_0$ is a subtype of $\delta_T$. In this case the agent $A$ has the *ticket* for the trip. Notice that this ensures that a malicious agent cannot modify the itinerary of the trip to visit other sites different from those listed in its ticket.

## 5 A Capability–Based Type System

This section formally presents the KLAIM type system that generalizes the one of [15] and differs from it in three respects. Here, in addition to types, type specifications are used. Moreover, type inference is parameterized by the locality where the process is supposed to be located. Finally, derived types are completely independent of the names of the locality variables occurring in processes.

**Definition 3.** A ·type is in *canonical form* if it is generated by the following grammar

$$\delta ::= \bot \mid \top \mid \phi_1, \ldots, \phi_n \mid \mu\nu.(\phi_1, \ldots, \phi_n) \qquad (n \geq 1)$$

$$\phi ::= \nu \mid \ell \mapsto \pi \mapsto \delta$$

where $\phi_1, \ldots, \phi_n$ and $\delta$ satisfy the following constraints:

- all bound type variables are distinct;
- all union types $\phi_1, \ldots, \phi_k$ are such that, for all $i, j$ $(1 \leq i, j \leq k$ and $i \neq j)$, if $\phi_i$ and $\phi_j$ are variables then $\phi_i \neq \phi_j$, otherwise $L(\phi_i) \cap L(\phi_j) = \emptyset$, where $L(\delta)$, the set of *shallow localities* of $\delta$, is defined inductively on the syntax of $\delta$ as follows:

$$L(\bot) = L(\top) = L(\nu) = \emptyset \qquad L(\ell \mapsto \pi \mapsto \delta) = \{\ell\}$$
$$L(\delta_1, \delta_2) = L(\delta_1) \cup L(\delta_2) \qquad L(\mu\nu.\delta) = L(\delta);$$

– all $\mu$–types $\mu\nu.\delta'$ are such that $\nu$ occurs in $\delta'$ and it is always "guarded", i.e. on the right of an even number of $\mapsto$'s; moreover, if $\delta' = \phi_1, \ldots, \phi_n$ then $\phi_i \neq \nu$ for all $i$ $(1 \leq i \leq k)$.

Roughly speaking, in a canonical form $\phi_1, \ldots, \phi_n$ $(n \geq 1)$ each component $\phi_i$ $(1 \leq i \leq n)$ is either a variable or an arrow type, with the additional constraint that all shallow localities be different. The condition about shallow localities allows us to determine the capability and the type associated to a given locality within a canonical form.

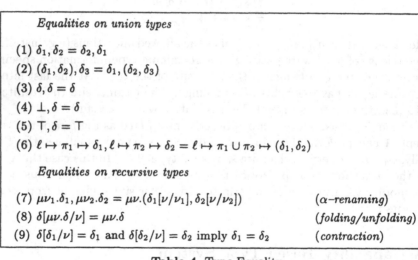

**Table 4.** Type Equality

In [15] an algorithm is given for reducing (legal) types to canonical forms. The algorithm relies on the *type equality* relation, $\cong$, the least congruence that satisfies the rules in Table 4. Rule (9) holds only when $\delta$ is *contractive* in $\nu$, that is when $\nu$ occurs in $\delta$ only under $\mapsto$. Decidability of $\cong$ has been proved in [15]. From now onward we will only consider types in canonical forms (and their unfoldings). With abuse of notation, we will continue using $\delta$ also to refer to canonical forms.

To define the subtyping relation, $\preceq$, we start by introducing an ordering between capabilities, namely a hierarchy over access rights. The chosen ordering relies on the assumptions that if a process is able to perform an **in** operation then it is also able to perform a **read** and that if a process has a set of capabilities $\pi$ then it posses any subset of $\pi$. Hence, equality of capabilities must be intended as standard set–equality but $\{i, r\} = \{i\}$.

**Definition 4.** The ordering relation on capabilities, $\sqsubseteq_\pi$, is the least reflexive and transitive relation induced by the rules in Table 5.

$$\{i\} \sqsubseteq_\Pi \{r\} \qquad \frac{\pi_1 \subseteq \pi_2}{\pi_2 \sqsubseteq_\Pi \pi_1} \qquad \frac{\pi_1 \sqsubseteq_\Pi \pi_1' \quad \pi_2 \sqsubseteq_\Pi \pi_2'}{(\pi_1 \cup \pi_2) \sqsubseteq_\Pi (\pi_1' \cup \pi_2')}$$

**Table 5.** Capability Ordering Rules

Capabilities only consider the intentions of processes relatively to fixed localities, while types consider also the intentions after migration. The subtype relation introduces a hierarchy over intentions.

$$\bot \preceq \delta \qquad\qquad\qquad\qquad\qquad\qquad\qquad\qquad (\text{ax}\bot)$$

$$\delta \preceq \top \qquad\qquad\qquad\qquad\qquad\qquad\qquad\qquad (\text{ax}\top)$$

$$\frac{\delta \cong \delta'}{\delta \preceq \delta'} \qquad\qquad\qquad\qquad\qquad\qquad\qquad (\text{eq})$$

$$\frac{\delta_i \preceq \delta_1' \text{ or } \ldots \text{ or } \delta_i \preceq \delta_k' \quad \text{for all } 1 \leq i \leq n}{\delta_1, \ldots, \delta_n \preceq \delta_1', \ldots, \delta_k'} \quad (\text{u/u})$$

$$\frac{\pi_2 \sqsubseteq_\Pi \pi_1, \quad \delta_1 \preceq \delta_2}{\ell \mapsto \pi_1 \mapsto \delta_1 \preceq \ell \mapsto \pi_2 \mapsto \delta_2} \qquad (\mapsto / \mapsto)$$

$$\frac{\ell \mapsto \pi \mapsto \delta \preceq \delta'[\mu\nu.\delta'/\nu]}{\ell \mapsto \pi \mapsto \delta \preceq \mu\nu.\delta'} \qquad (\mapsto /\mu)$$

$$\frac{\delta'[\mu\nu.\delta'/\nu] \preceq \ell \mapsto \pi \mapsto \delta}{\mu\nu.\delta' \preceq \ell \mapsto \pi \mapsto \delta} \qquad (\mu/ \mapsto)$$

$$\frac{\delta_1[\nu/\nu_1] \preceq \delta_2[\nu/\nu_2]}{\mu\nu_1.\delta_1 \preceq \mu\nu_2.\delta_2} \quad \text{where } \nu \text{ is a fresh variable } (\mu/\mu)$$

**Table 6.** Subtyping Rules

**Definition 5.** The *subtyping* relation over canonical forms and unfoldings of canonical forms, $\preceq$, is the least relation closed under the rules in Table 6.

Decidability of subtyping has been proved in [15].

## 5.1 Typing Processes

*Type contexts*, $\Gamma$ are functions mapping process variables and identifiers into types, and locality variables into type specifications. Type contexts are written as sequences of assignments $X_1 : \delta_1, \ldots, X_n : \delta_n, u_1 : \langle \lambda_1, \delta_1' \rangle, \ldots, u_m : \langle \lambda_m, \delta_m' \rangle$. The special symbol $\phi$ is used to denote the empty context.

Before presenting the judgments of the type inference system we introduce some useful notations.

First, we equip type specifications with the (postfixed) projection operations $\downarrow_1$ and $\downarrow_2$ defined as follows: $\langle\lambda,\delta\rangle\downarrow_1 = \lambda$ and $\langle\lambda,\delta\rangle\downarrow_2 = \delta$.

Notation $\delta@\ell$, defined below by induction on the syntax of $\delta$, denotes the partial evaluation of type $\delta$ which replaces $\mathtt{self}$ with the locality $\ell$.

- $\bot@\ell = \bot$, $\top@\ell = \top$, $\nu@\ell = \nu$;
- $(\ell' \mapsto \pi \mapsto \delta')@\ell = \begin{cases} \ell \mapsto \pi \mapsto (\delta'@\ell) & \text{if } \ell' = \mathtt{self} \\ \ell' \mapsto \pi \mapsto (\delta'@\ell') & \text{otherwise;} \end{cases}$
- $(\delta_1,\delta_2)@\ell = (\delta_1@\ell),(\delta_2@\ell)$;
- $(\mu\nu.\delta')@\ell = \mu\nu.(\delta'@\ell)$.

Hereafter, we write $\widetilde{\delta@\ell}$ to denote a canonical form of type $\delta@\ell$. We also write $\ell'@\ell$ to denote $\ell$ if $\ell' = \mathtt{self}$, $\ell'$ otherwise.

Given a type context $\Gamma$, we write $\Gamma[\delta/X]$ to denote either the extension of $\Gamma$ with the assignment $X : \delta$ (when $X$ is unbound in $\Gamma$), or the updating of $\Gamma$ that binds $X$ to $\delta$ ($\Gamma[\langle\lambda,\delta\rangle/u]$ has a similar meaning). The auxiliary function $update_\ell$, indexed by the locality $\ell$ where a process is located when the function is invoked, behaves like the identity function for all fields but $!\,X : \delta$ and $!\,u : \langle\lambda,\delta\rangle$. In the former case, the behaviour of the function is obvious. In the latter case, the type specification assigned to $u$ is obtained by replacing $\mathtt{self}$ with $\ell$ in $\lambda$ and by partial evaluating $\delta$ at $u$. Formally, it is defined by:

$$update_\ell(\Gamma,t) = \begin{cases} update_\ell(update_\ell(\Gamma,f),t) & \text{if } t = f,t, \\ \Gamma[\delta/X] & \text{if } t = !\,X : \delta, \\ \Gamma[\langle\lambda[\ell/\mathtt{self}],\delta@u\rangle/u] & \text{if } t = !\,u : \langle\lambda,\delta\rangle, \\ \Gamma & \text{otherwise.} \end{cases}$$

To check that the type specifications occurring in a tuple $t$ are all consistent at $\ell$, we require that, for each $u : \langle\lambda_u,\delta_u\rangle \in \{t\}$, $update_\ell(\phi,t)\!\mid\!\overline{\phantom{x}}_\ell\,\delta_u$ holds, where $\Gamma\!\mid\!\overline{\phantom{x}}_\ell\,\delta$ is the least predicate closed under the following rules:

$$\Gamma\!\mid\!\overline{\phantom{x}}_\ell\,\bot \qquad\qquad \Gamma\!\mid\!\overline{\phantom{x}}_\ell\,\top \qquad\qquad \Gamma\!\mid\!\overline{\phantom{x}}_\ell\,\nu$$

$$\frac{\ell' \in dom(\Gamma) \quad (\Gamma(\ell')\!\downarrow_1)(\ell) \sqsubseteq_\Pi \pi \quad \delta' \preceq \Gamma(\ell')\!\downarrow_2}{\Gamma\!\mid\!\overline{\phantom{x}}_\ell\,\ell' \mapsto \pi \mapsto \delta'} \qquad\qquad \frac{\ell' \notin dom(\Gamma) \quad \Gamma\!\mid\!\overline{\phantom{x}}_{\ell'}\,\delta'}{\Gamma\!\mid\!\overline{\phantom{x}}_\ell\,\ell' \mapsto \pi \mapsto \delta'}$$

$$\frac{\Gamma\!\mid\!\overline{\phantom{x}}_\ell\,\delta_1 \quad \Gamma\!\mid\!\overline{\phantom{x}}_\ell\,\delta_2}{\Gamma\!\mid\!\overline{\phantom{x}}_\ell\,\delta_1,\delta_2} \qquad\qquad \frac{\Gamma\!\mid\!\overline{\phantom{x}}_\ell\,\delta}{\Gamma\!\mid\!\overline{\phantom{x}}_\ell\,\mu\nu.\delta}$$

We will always assume that $update_\ell(\Gamma,t)$ is defined only if for each $u : \langle\lambda_u,\delta_u\rangle \in \{t\}$, $update_\ell(\phi,t)\!\mid\!\overline{\phantom{x}}_\ell\,\delta_u$ holds.

Notation $update_\ell(\Gamma,\widetilde{u} : \langle\widetilde{\lambda,\delta_u}\rangle)$ has the expected meaning, and is defined only if the type specifications there involved are all consistent. This amounts to saying that, for each $u \in \{\widetilde{u}\}$, $update_\ell(\phi,\widetilde{u} : \langle\widetilde{\lambda,\delta_u}\rangle)\!\mid\!\overline{\phantom{x}}_\ell\,\delta_u$ holds.

Given a type context $\Gamma$, a locality $\ell$, a set of locality variables $U$ such that $dom(\Gamma) \subseteq U$ and a type $\delta$, we write $\Gamma\!\mid\!\overline{\phantom{x}}_\ell\,\delta\searrow_U$ to denote the type obtained by deleting in $\delta$ the subterms relative to the variables in $U$ while checking that $\delta$ satisfies the corresponding type specifications stored in $\Gamma$. Formally, $\Gamma\!\mid\!\overline{\phantom{x}}_\ell\,\delta\searrow_U$ is defined by induction on the syntax of $\delta$ by the following rules:

$$\Gamma \vdash_{\ell} \bot \searrow_U = \bot \qquad \Gamma \vdash_{\ell} \top \searrow_U = \top \qquad \Gamma \vdash_{\ell} \nu \searrow_U = \nu$$

$$\frac{\ell' \in U \quad (\Gamma(\ell')\!\downarrow_1)(\ell) \sqsubseteq_{\Pi} \pi \quad \delta \preceq \Gamma(\ell')\!\downarrow_2}{\Gamma \vdash_{\ell} (\ell' \mapsto \pi \mapsto \delta)\searrow_U = \bot} \qquad \frac{\ell' \notin U \quad \Gamma \vdash_{\ell'} \delta\searrow_U = \delta'}{\Gamma \vdash_{\ell} (\ell' \mapsto \pi \mapsto \delta)\searrow_U = \ell' \mapsto \pi \mapsto \delta'}$$

$$\frac{\Gamma \vdash_{\ell} \delta_1 \searrow_U = \delta'_1 \qquad \Gamma \vdash_{\ell} \delta_2 \searrow_U = \delta'_2}{\Gamma \vdash_{\ell} (\delta_1,\delta_2)\searrow_U = \delta'_1,\delta'_2} \qquad \frac{\Gamma \vdash_{\ell} \delta\searrow_U = \delta'}{\Gamma \vdash_{\ell} (\mu\nu.\delta)\searrow_U = \mu\nu.\delta'}$$

The type judgments for processes take the form $\Gamma \vdash_{\ell} P : \delta$ where $\Gamma$ is a type context providing the type of free locality and process variables and that of process identifiers in $P$. The judgment $\Gamma \vdash_{\ell} P : \delta$ asserts that, within the context $\Gamma$, the intentions of $P$ when located at $\ell$ are those specified in $\delta$.

Type judgments are inferred by using the rules in Table 7. There, given a tuple $t$, we write $lv(t)$ to denote the set of locality variables occurring in $t$, i.e. the set $\{u \mid \exists \lambda, \delta : u : \langle \lambda, \delta \rangle \in \{t\}\}$. Moreover, in the conclusion of the inference rules, we shall write $(\delta_1, \delta_2)$ to denote the canonical form of the type $(\delta_1, \delta_2)$ obtained by applying the rules in Table 4. For instance, we shall write that from $\Gamma \vdash_{\ell} P : \ell' \mapsto \pi \mapsto \delta$ we derive $\Gamma \vdash_{\ell} \mathbf{out}(t)@\ell'.P : \ell' \mapsto \pi \mapsto \delta, \ell' \mapsto \{o\} \mapsto \bot$ but actually we mean $\Gamma \vdash_{\ell} \mathbf{out}(t)@\ell'.P : \ell' \mapsto \pi \cup \{o\} \mapsto \delta$. We now comment on the inference rules.

The simplest process (the null process **nil**) has no intentions at all. The type of a process variable (or identifier) is completely determined by the type context, $\Gamma$, and by the locality, $\ell$, where the process is supposed to be at. Definedness of $\Gamma(X)$ is guaranteed by the fact that processes are closed terms.

The typing rule for **out** states that the type of $\mathbf{out}(t)@\ell'.P$ extends the capabilities of $P$ at $\ell'@\ell$ with $o$. Since **out** is not a binder, $P$ is typed within the same context as $\mathbf{out}(t)@\ell'.P$.

The typing rule for **read** first derives the type $\delta$ of $P$ in a context updated with the type assignments for the process and the locality variables bound by **read**. Then it removes from $\delta$ the subterms relative to the locality variables that are in $update_t(\Gamma, t)$ and not in $\Gamma$ while checking that $\delta$ satisfies the type specifications that correspond to these variables. Finally, it extends the obtained type at $\ell'@\ell$ with capability $r$. The typing rule for **in** behaves similarly.

The typing rule for **eval** extends the type of $P$ at $\ell'@\ell$ with $e$ and records that the operations of $P$ at $\ell'@\ell$ have to be extended with those (given by $\delta'$) of the spawned process $Q$ at $\ell'@\ell$.

The typing rule for **newloc** first derives the type $\delta$ of $P$ in a context updated with the assignments of the type specifications declared for the locality variables. Then, it discharges the type information associated to the locality variables and checks that $\delta$ satisfies the type specifications that correspond to these variables. Finally, it extends the obtained type at $\ell$ with capability $n$.

The typing rule for parallel composition states that the intentions of the composed process are the union of those of the components, while the binding context is left unchanged.

The typing rule for process definition updates the type context with the types declared for the process variables occurring as parameters in the definition

$$\Gamma \vdash_{\overline{\ell}} \mathbf{nil} : \bot$$

$$\Gamma \vdash_{\overline{\ell}} X : \Gamma(X)@\ell \qquad\qquad \Gamma \vdash_{\overline{\ell}} A : \Gamma(A)@\ell$$

$$\frac{\Gamma \vdash_{\overline{\ell}} P : \delta}{\Gamma \vdash_{\overline{\ell}} \mathbf{out}(t)@\ell'.P : (\delta, (\ell'@\ell) \mapsto \{o\} \mapsto \bot)}$$

$$\frac{update_{\ell}(\Gamma, t) \vdash_{\overline{\ell}} P : \delta \qquad update_{\ell}(\Gamma, t) \vdash_{\overline{\ell}} \delta \searrow_{lv(t)} = \delta'}{\Gamma \vdash_{\overline{\ell}} \mathbf{read}(t)@\ell'.P : (\delta', (\ell'@\ell) \mapsto \{r\} \mapsto \bot)}$$

$$\frac{update_{\ell}(\Gamma, t) \vdash_{\overline{\ell}} P : \delta \qquad update_{\ell}(\Gamma, t) \vdash_{\overline{\ell}} \delta \searrow_{lv(t)} = \delta'}{\Gamma \vdash_{\overline{\ell}} \mathbf{in}(t)@\ell'.P : (\delta', (\ell'@\ell) \mapsto \{i\} \mapsto \bot)}$$

$$\frac{\Gamma \vdash_{\overline{\ell}} P : \delta \qquad \Gamma \vdash_{\overline{\ell'@\ell}} Q : \delta'}{\Gamma \vdash_{\overline{\ell}} \mathbf{eval}(Q)@\ell'.P : (\delta, (\ell'@\ell) \mapsto \{e\} \mapsto \delta')}$$

$$\frac{update_{\ell}(\Gamma, \widetilde{u} : \langle \widetilde{\lambda, \delta_u} \rangle) \vdash_{\overline{\ell}} P : \delta \qquad update_{\ell}(\Gamma, \widetilde{u} : \langle \widetilde{\lambda, \delta_u} \rangle) \vdash_{\overline{\ell}} \delta \searrow_{\{\widetilde{u}\}} = \delta'}{\Gamma \vdash_{\overline{\ell}} \mathbf{newloc}(\widetilde{u} : \langle \widetilde{\lambda, \delta_u} \rangle).P : (\delta', \ell \mapsto \{n\} \mapsto \bot)}$$

$$\frac{\Gamma \vdash_{\overline{\ell}} P : \delta_1 \qquad \Gamma \vdash_{\overline{\ell}} Q : \delta_2}{\Gamma \vdash_{\overline{\ell}} P \mid Q : (\delta_1, \delta_2)}$$

$$\frac{\Gamma[\widetilde{X} : \widetilde{\delta_X}][A : \delta] \vdash_{\overline{self}} P : \delta' \qquad \delta \cong \delta' \qquad update_{self}(\phi, \widetilde{u} : \langle \widetilde{\lambda, \delta_u} \rangle) \vdash_{\overline{self}} \delta' \searrow_{\{\widetilde{u}\}} = \delta''}{\Gamma \vdash_{\overline{self}} A : \delta}$$

$$\frac{\Gamma \vdash_{\overline{self}} A : \delta \qquad \Gamma \vdash_{\overline{\ell}} P_i : \delta_i \text{ and } \delta_i \preceq (\delta_{X_i}@\ell) \text{ for all } P_i \in \{\widetilde{P}\}}{\Gamma \vdash_{\overline{\ell}} A\langle \widetilde{P}, \widetilde{\ell}, \widetilde{e} \rangle : (\delta@\ell)[\widetilde{\ell}/\widetilde{u}]}$$

**Table 7.** KLAIM Type Inference Rules (we assume that $A(\widetilde{X} : \widetilde{\delta_X}, \widetilde{u} : \langle \widetilde{\lambda, \delta_u} \rangle, \widetilde{x}) \stackrel{def}{=} P$)

and with the binding between the process identifier $A$ and a (possibly recursive) candidate type $\delta$. The resulting context is exploited to infer (up to type equality) the type $\delta$ for $P$. A second type inference is triggered by the rule, starting from a type context that additionally contains the bindings for the locality variables occurring as parameters in the process definition. This last inference checks whether the intentions of process $P$ comply with the type specifications of its locality variables. To make types of process identifiers independent of the localities where the identifiers are invoked, it is assumed that the latters are always invoked at self.

The last typing rule is the rule for process invocation. First, it determines the type of the process identifier and those of the process arguments. Then, it checks whether the type inferred for any process argument agrees with that obtained by partially evaluating at $\ell$ the type of the corresponding formal parameter. No requirement is imposed on the other arguments. The inferred type states that, once we interpret the type of $A$ starting from $\ell$ (the actual locality where the invocation takes place), $A\langle \widetilde{P}, \widetilde{\ell}, \widetilde{e} \rangle$ intends to perform at $\widetilde{\ell}$ the same operations of $A$ at $\widetilde{u}$. Indeed, the locality variables occurring as parameters in the definition of the process may occur in the type inferred for the process identifier. Soundness of the application of $[\tilde{\ell}/\tilde{u}]$ to $\delta$ follows from the assumption that all bound names in the definition of $A$ are distinct.

In [15], it is proved decidability and derivability of a *minimal* type for any typable process. The type is called minimal because all the other deducible types are greater than it. The main impact of the existence of a minimal type is that the type inference system is decidable. The same results holds for the type system presented in this paper.

**Theorem 1.** If $\Gamma \vdash_{\ell} P : \delta'$ then there exists a minimal type $\delta$ such that $\Gamma \vdash_{\ell} P : \delta$ and $\delta \preceq \delta''$ for all $\delta''$ such that $\Gamma \vdash_{\ell} P : \delta''$.

**Corollary 1.** For any process $P$, the existence of a type $\delta$ such that $\phi \vdash_{\ell} P : \delta$ is decidable.

## 5.2 Typing Nets

In this section, we introduce the notion of well–typed net of processes.

**Definition 6.** Given a type interpretation function $\Theta_{N_S}$, a node $s \in S$ and a type $\delta$, then the *interpretation* $\delta\{\Theta_{N_S}\}_s$ of $\delta$ in $s$ is a canonical form of the type defined inductively as follows:

- $\perp\{\Theta_{N_S}\}_s = \perp$, $\top\{\Theta_{N_S}\}_s = \top$, $\nu\{\Theta_{N_S}\}_s = \nu$;
- $(\ell \mapsto \pi \mapsto \delta')\{\Theta_{N_S}\}_s = \begin{cases} \ell\{\rho_s\} \mapsto \pi \mapsto \delta'\{\Theta_{N_S}\}_{\ell\{\rho_s\}} & \text{if } \ell\{\rho_s\} \in S \\ \ell \mapsto \pi \mapsto \delta' & \text{otherwise}; \end{cases}$
- $(\delta_1, \delta_2)\{\Theta_{N_S}\}_s = \delta_1\{\Theta_{N_S}\}_s, \delta_2\{\Theta_{N_S}\}_s$;
- $(\mu\nu.\delta')\{\Theta_{N_S}\}_s = \mu\nu.\delta'\{\Theta_{N_S}\}_s$.

Hence, localities that cannot be mapped to sites of the net are left unchanged.

**Definition 7.** A net $N_S$ is *well–typed* if for any node $s ::^{\delta_s}_{\rho_s} P$, there exists $\delta'$ such that $\phi \vdash_s P : \delta'$ and if $\delta$ is a minimal type for $P$ then $\delta\{\Theta_{N_S}\}_s \preceq \delta_s$.

The well–typedness condition requires that processes cannot use a locality if this is not known in the allocation environment of the node.

The KLAIM type system enjoys two key properties: *subject reduction* and *type safety*. The former property guarantees that well–typedness is an invariant of the operational semantics. The latter guarantees that well–typed nets are free from run–time errors. Such errors are generated when processes attempt to execute actions that are not allowed by the capabilities they own. The two properties together amount to saying that well–typed nets never encounter run–time errors due to misuse of access rights. In other words, the errors that the KLAIM type system precludes are those due to access right violations. We refer to [15] for the statements and the proofs of the two properties.

# 6 Concluding Remarks

We have developed a type system which formalizes access control restrictions of programs written in KLAIM. Type information is used to specify access rights and execution privileges, and to detect violations of these policies. The implementation of the type inference system for X-KLAIM (the prototype implementation of KLAIM) is in progress; it will help us also to assess our design choices.

We plan to extend the type system by introducing types for tuples (record types), notions of multi-level security (by structuring localities into levels of security) and public or shared keys to model dynamic transmission of access rights. Ideas could also be borrowed from the spi-calculus [2], a concurrent calculus obtained by adding public-key encryption primitives to the π-calculus [21], and from the SLam calculus [18], another calculus where information about direct/indirect producers and consumers are associated to data.

Another direction for future research is considering "open" systems. In fact, our type system can safely deal with new processes landing on existing nodes, but it does not consider partially specified nets. An enrichment of types is then needed to specify the permissions granted to "unspecified" sites. Then, the choice has to be faced whether this enrichment should be specified at the level of single nodes or at the level of nets. Interfacing nets would naturally fit with extensions of our framework to hierarchical nets that would be beneficial also for more structured access controls. An alternative approach to deal with open systems could also be that of relaxing the static type checking phase by not requiring well-typedness of the whole net (this corresponds to the fact that only the typed sites can be trusted) while increasing the run-time type checking phase, e.g. agents migrating from untyped (i.e. untrusted) sites must be dynamically typechecked. This is the approach followed in [24].

Type systems have been used also for other calculi of mobile processes. Among those reminiscent of ours, although not addressing security issues, we mention the work of Pierce and Sangiorgi [23]. They develop a type system for the π-calculus using channels types to specify whether channels are used to *read* or to *write*. This type system has been extended in [20] by associating *multiplicities* to types for stating the number of times each channel can be used. The type system of [23] has been also generalized by Sewell [25] to capture locality of channel names and by Boreale and Sangiorgi [7] to trimmer bisimulation proofs.

Only recently attempts have been made to characterize security properties in terms of formal type systems. A type system for the spi-calculus has been developed by Abadi [1] to guarantee secrecy of cryptographic protocols. Abadi and Stata [3] have used type rules to specify and verify correctness of Java Bytecode Verifier. Hennessy and Riely [19] have introduced a type system for the language Dπ, a distributed variant of π-calculus for controlling the use of resources in nets. This work is similar to ours (types are abstraction of process behaviours and access rights violations are type errors), but the technical developments are quite different; resources are channels and types describe permissions to use channels. Moreover, access rights are fixed irrespectively of the localities where processes themselves are executed. In [24], the type system of

[19] has been improved for considering nets where sites can also put up malicious agents that do not respect the rules on the use of resources. Cardelli and Gordon [10] have introduced a type system for mobile ambients [9] that controls the type of the values exchanged among administrative domains (ambients) so that the communication of values cannot cause run–time faults. Volpano and Smith have developed type systems to ensure secure information flow (noninterference) for both a sequential procedural language [27] and for a multithreaded imperative language [28]. Boudol [8] has used types to abstract from terms the possible sequences of interactions and the resources used by processes. Necula [22] has introduced an approach to ensure correctness of mobile code with respect to a fixed safety policy, where code producers provide the code with a proof of correctness that code consumers check before allowing the code to execute. Vitek and Castagna [26] have proposed a language–based approach, relying on powerful mobility and protection primitives, rather than on type systems, for secure Internet programming. Bodei, Degano, Nielson and Nielson [6] have proposed an alternative approach for the analysis of security and of information flow, that relies on static analysis techniques.

## Acknowledgments

We would like to thank Betti Venneri for her contribution to the development of the KLAIM type system. We are also grateful to Lorenzo Bettini, Michele Boreale and Michele Loreti for general discussions about KLAIM.

This work has been partially supported by Esprit Working Groups *CONFER2* and *COORDINA*, and by CNR: Progetti "Metodologie e Strumenti di Analisi, Verifica e Validazione per Sistemi Software Affidabili" e "Modelli e Metodi per la Matematica e l'Ingegneria".

## A    Operational Semantics

In this section, we coerce $\ell$ to denote localities, locality variables and sites, and assume that allocation environments are extended to sites; when applied to sites, allocation environments act as the identity function. Tuples are modelled as processes and the KLAIM syntax is extended with processes of the form $\mathbf{out}(et)$ for denoting *evaluated tuples* (referred to as *et*).

The KLAIM operational semantics uses an evaluation function for tuples, $\mathcal{T}[\![ \cdot ]\!]_\rho$, that is inductively defined over the syntax of tuples by the rules in Table 8, where we use $\mathcal{E}[\![ e ]\!]$ to denote the value of the closed expression $e$. There are only two non–trivial cases, namely $\mathcal{T}[\![ \ell : \langle \lambda, \delta \rangle ]\!]_\rho$ and $\mathcal{T}[\![ P ]\!]_\rho$. In the former case, we use the local allocation environment $\rho$ for evaluating the locality $\ell$ and the access list $\lambda$, while we leave the type $\delta$ unevaluated; it will be evaluated when the tuple is considered for a matching. If $dom(\lambda) \subseteq dom(\rho)$, we write $\lambda\{\rho\}$ to denote the access list defined by:

$$\lambda\{\rho\}(s) = \bigcup\{\lambda(\ell) \mid \ell \in dom(\lambda), \rho(\ell) = s\}, \forall s : \exists \ell \in dom(\lambda) : \rho(\ell) = s;$$

$\lambda\{\rho\}$ is not defined whenever $dom(\lambda) \not\subseteq dom(\rho)$. In the latter case, we get a *process closure* $P\{\rho\}$ that is evaluated by using the laws in Table 9. There, $\delta\{\rho\}$ is obtained from $\delta$ by using $\rho$ to interpret shallow localities of $\delta$; it can be defined inductively on the syntax of $\delta$: all its clauses are structural apart for $(\ell \mapsto \pi \mapsto \delta')\{\rho\} = \ell\{\rho\} \mapsto \pi \mapsto \delta'$.

$$
\begin{aligned}
\mathcal{T}[\![\,e\,]\!]_\rho &= \mathcal{E}[\![\,e\,]\!] & \mathcal{T}[\![\,!x\,]\!]_\rho &= \,!x \\
\mathcal{T}[\![\,P\,]\!]_\rho &= P\{\rho\} & \mathcal{T}[\![\,!X:\delta\,]\!]_\rho &= \,!X:\delta \\
\mathcal{T}[\![\,\ell:\langle\lambda,\delta\rangle\,]\!]_\rho &= \rho(\ell):\langle\lambda\{\rho\},\delta\rangle & \mathcal{T}[\![\,!u:\langle\lambda,\delta\rangle\,]\!]_\rho &= \,!u:\langle\lambda\{\rho\},\delta\rangle \\
\mathcal{T}[\![\,f,t\,]\!]_\rho &= \mathcal{T}[\![\,f\,]\!]_\rho,\mathcal{T}[\![\,t\,]\!]_\rho
\end{aligned}
$$

**Table 8.** Tuple Evaluation Function

The notion of *conservative extension* of the function used to induce the types of the nodes of a net is needed to derive the new types of the nodes of the net in case of dynamic reconfiguration. Indeed, when a set of new nodes is created, the type specifications written by the programmer have to be taken into account. In general, the types of the nodes of the net have to be "extended" by adding the rights of the existing nodes over the new ones and the rights of the new nodes over the existing ones. Access lists are used to enrich the rights of the existing nodes, while types are used to determine the rights of the new nodes. An extension is called conservative whenever the rights over the new nodes are consistent with the rights over the creating node and the types specified for the new nodes are compatible with those induced by the extension; the predicate *compat* is used to this purpose.

$$
\begin{aligned}
\mathbf{nil}\{\rho\} &= \mathbf{nil} \\
X\{\rho\} &= X \\
(\mathbf{out}(t)@\ell.P)\{\rho\} &= \mathbf{out}(t\{\rho\})@\ell\{\rho\}.P\{\rho\} \\
(\mathbf{eval}(Q)@\ell.P)\{\rho\} &= \mathbf{eval}(Q)@\ell\{\rho\}.P\{\rho\} \\
(\mathbf{in}(t)@\ell.P)\{\rho\} &= \mathbf{in}(t\{\rho\})@\ell\{\rho\}.P\{\rho\} \\
(\mathbf{read}(t)@\ell.P)\{\rho\} &= \mathbf{read}(t\{\rho\})@\ell\{\rho\}.P\{\rho\} \\
(\mathbf{newloc}(\widetilde{u}:\langle\widetilde{\lambda,\delta}\rangle).P)\{\rho\} &= \mathbf{newloc}(\widetilde{u}:\langle\widetilde{\lambda,\delta}\rangle).P\{\rho\} \\
(P_1 \mid P_2)\{\rho\} &= P_1\{\rho\} \mid P_2\{\rho\} \\
A\langle\widetilde{P},\widetilde{\ell},\widetilde{e}\rangle\{\rho\} &= P[\widetilde{P}/\widetilde{X},\widetilde{\ell}/\widetilde{u},\widetilde{e}/\widetilde{x}]\{\rho\} \quad \text{if } A(\widetilde{X}:\widetilde{\delta},\widetilde{u}:\langle\widetilde{\lambda,\delta}\rangle,\widetilde{x}) \overset{def}{=} P
\end{aligned}
$$

$$
\begin{aligned}
e\{\rho\} &= e \\
(\ell:\langle\lambda,\delta\rangle)\{\rho\} &= \ell\{\rho\}:\langle\lambda\{\rho\},\delta\rangle \\
!x\{\rho\} &= \,!x \\
(!u:\langle\lambda,\delta\rangle)\{\rho\} &= \,!u:\langle\lambda\{\rho\},\delta\rangle \\
(!X:\delta)\{\rho\} &= \,!X:\delta\{\rho\} \\
(f,t)\{\rho\} &= f\{\rho\},t\{\rho\}
\end{aligned}
$$

**Table 9.** Closure Laws

As a matter of notation, if $\delta$ is in canonical form, $\delta \downarrow_c \ell$ will denote the capability of locality $\ell$, and $\delta \downarrow_t \ell$ the type of $\ell$. Both notations can be defined inductively on the syntax of $\delta$; the more relevant clause, when $\delta = \ell' \mapsto \pi \mapsto \delta'$, is:

$$\delta \downarrow_c \ell = \begin{cases} undef & \text{if } \ell \neq \ell' \\ \pi & \text{otherwise,} \end{cases} \qquad \delta \downarrow_t \ell = \begin{cases} \bot & \text{if } \ell \neq \ell' \\ \delta' & \text{otherwise.} \end{cases}$$

**Definition 8.** The *extension* of a type interpretation function $\Theta$ for a set of sites $S' = \{s_1, \ldots, s_n\}$ such that $S' \cap dom(\Theta) = \emptyset$ and a site $s \in S$, is the type interpretation function $\Theta[(\Theta(s)[s_1/\texttt{self}])/s_1, \ldots, (\Theta(s)[s_n/\texttt{self}])/s_n]$.

The (conservative) extension of a function $\Lambda$ that induces the types of the nodes of a net shall make use of predicate *compat*, that iteratively on the syntax of types checks the compatibility of the extension with $\Lambda$ and is defined as follows:

$$compat(\delta, s, \Theta, \Lambda) \stackrel{def}{=} \forall s' \in dom(\Theta) : \delta\{\Theta\}_s \downarrow_c s' \text{ is defined, we have:}$$
$$\Lambda(s)(s') \sqsubseteq_\Pi \delta\{\Theta\}_s \downarrow_c s' \text{ and } compat(\delta\{\Theta\}_s \downarrow_t s', s', \Theta, \Lambda).$$

**Definition 9.** Let $S$ be a finite set of sites and $\Lambda : S \rightharpoonup (S \rightharpoonup \Pi)$ be a partial function. The *extension* $\Lambda' : (S \cup \{\tilde{s}\}) \rightharpoonup ((S \cup \{\tilde{s}\}) \rightharpoonup \Pi)$ of $\Lambda$ with respect to a set of sites $\{\tilde{s}\}$ such that $\{\tilde{s}\} \cap S = \emptyset$, a set of type specifications $\tilde{u} : \langle \widetilde{\lambda, \delta} \rangle$ with $cardinality(\{\tilde{u}\}) = cardinality(\{\tilde{s}\})$, a type interpretation function $\Theta$ with $dom(\Theta) = S \cup \{\tilde{s}\}$ and a site $s \in S$, is defined as follows:

- for all $s_1, s_2 \in S$, we have: $\Lambda'(s_1)(s_2) = \Lambda(s_1)(s_2)$,
- for all $s_1 \in \{\tilde{s}\}$ and $s_2 \in S \cup \{\tilde{s}\}$, we have:

$$\Lambda'(s_2)(s_1) = \begin{cases} (\lambda_{s_1}[\tilde{s}/\tilde{u}]\{\Theta(s)\})(s_2) & \text{if } \lambda_{s_1} \neq \phi \\ \Lambda(s_2)(s) & \text{otherwise,} \end{cases}$$

- for all $s_1 \in \{\tilde{s}\}$ and $s_2 \in S$, we have: $\Lambda'(s_1)(s_2) = \delta_{s_1}[\tilde{s}/\tilde{u}]\{\Theta(s_1)\} \downarrow_c s_2$,

whenever the right hand sides of the equalities are defined.
$\Lambda'$ is a *conservative* extension, if it enjoys the following properties:

- for all $s_1 \in \{\tilde{s}\}$ and $s_2 \in S$, we have: $\Lambda'(s_2)(s) \sqsubseteq_\Pi \Lambda'(s_2)(s_1)$, $\Lambda'(s)(s_2) \sqsubseteq_\Pi \Lambda'(s_1)(s_2)$;
- for all $s_1 \in \{\tilde{s}\}$, we have: $\Lambda'(s)(s) \sqsubseteq_\Pi \Lambda'(s_1)(s_1)$;
- for all $s_1 \in \{\tilde{s}\}$, we have: $compat(\delta_{s_1}[\tilde{s}/\tilde{u}], s_1, \Theta, \Lambda')$.

The structural congruence, $\equiv$, is the least congruence relation such that:

$$N_1 \parallel N_2 = N_2 \parallel N_1,$$
$$(N_1 \parallel N_2) \parallel N_3 = N_1 \parallel (N_2 \parallel N_3),$$
$$s ::_\rho^\delta P = s ::_\rho^\delta (P | \textbf{nil}),$$
$$s ::_\rho^\delta (P_1 | P_2) = s ::_\rho^\delta P_1 \parallel s ::_\rho^\delta P_2.$$

The reduction relation, $\succ\!\!\longrightarrow$, is the least relation induced by the laws in Table 10, where we use the following notations.

**Notation 1.** In Table 10 the following shorthands are adopted:

- $\Theta_{N_{S'}}$ is the type interpretation function associated to $N_{S'} : \Lambda$, the net before reduction;

- $\delta^*_{s_i}$, for $s_i \in S \cup \{s\} \cup \{\widetilde{s}\}$, are the solution of the system of type equations induced by the conservative extension of $\Lambda$ with respect to $\{\widetilde{s}\}$, $\widetilde{u} : \langle\widetilde{\lambda,\delta}\rangle$, $\Theta$ and $s$, where $\Theta$ is the extension of $\Theta_{N_{S'}}$ with respect to $\{\widetilde{s}\}$ and $s$;
- $N_S[\delta^*_{s_i}/\delta_{s_i}]_{s_i \in S}$ is the net $N_S$ where the types $\delta_{s_i}$ of the nodes are replaced by $\delta^*_{s_i}$;
- $N_{\{\widetilde{s}\}}$, if $\{\widetilde{s}\} = \{s_1,\ldots,s_n\}$, is the net $s_1 ::^{\delta^*_{s_1}}_{\rho_{s_1}}$ nil $\|\ldots\| s_n ::^{\delta^*_{s_n}}_{\rho_{s_n}}$ nil.

$$\frac{s' = \rho(\ell) \qquad et = \mathcal{T}[\![\,t\,]\!]_\rho}{N_S \| s ::^\delta_\rho \text{ out}(t)@\ell.P \| s' ::^{\delta'}_{\rho'} P' \rightarrowtail N_S \| s ::^\delta_\rho P \| s' ::^{\delta'}_{\rho'} (P' \mid \text{out}(et))}$$

$$\frac{s' = \rho(\ell)}{N_S \| s ::^\delta_\rho \text{ eval}(Q)@\ell.P \| s' ::^{\delta'}_{\rho'} P' \rightarrowtail N_S \| s ::^\delta_\rho P \| s' ::^{\delta'}_{\rho'} (P' \mid Q)}$$

$$\frac{s' = \rho(\ell) \qquad match(\mathcal{T}[\![\,t\,]\!]_\rho, et, s, \Theta_{N_{S'}})}{N_S \| s ::^\delta_\rho \text{ in}(t)@\ell.P \| s' ::^{\delta'}_{\rho'} \text{ out}(et) \rightarrowtail N_S \| s ::^\delta_\rho P[et/\mathcal{T}[\![\,t\,]\!]_\rho] \| s' ::^{\delta'}_{\rho'} \text{ nil}}$$

$$\frac{s' = \rho(\ell) \qquad match(\mathcal{T}[\![\,t\,]\!]_\rho, et, s, \Theta_{N_{S'}})}{N_S \| s ::^\delta_\rho \text{ read}(t)@\ell.P \| s' ::^{\delta'}_{\rho'} \text{ out}(et) \rightarrowtail N_S \| s ::^\delta_\rho P[et/\mathcal{T}[\![\,t\,]\!]_\rho] \| s' ::^{\delta'}_{\rho'} \text{ out}(et)}$$

$$\frac{\{\widetilde{s}\} \cap (S \cup \{s\}) = \emptyset}{N_S \| s ::^{\delta_s}_{\rho_s} \text{ newloc}(\widetilde{u} : \langle\widetilde{\lambda,\delta}\rangle).P \rightarrowtail N_S[\delta^*_{s_i}/\delta_{s_i}]_{s_i \in S} \| s ::^{\delta^*_s}_{\rho_s} P[\widetilde{s}/\widetilde{u}] \| N_{\{\widetilde{s}\}}}$$

$$\frac{N_S \| s ::^\delta_\rho P[\widetilde{P}/\widetilde{X}, \widetilde{\ell}/\widetilde{u}, \widetilde{e}/\widetilde{x}] \rightarrowtail N}{N_S \| s ::^\delta_\rho A\langle\widetilde{P}, \widetilde{\ell}, \widetilde{e}\rangle \rightarrowtail N} \quad A(\widetilde{X} : \widetilde{\delta}, \widetilde{u} : \langle\widetilde{\lambda,\delta}\rangle, \widetilde{x}) \stackrel{def}{=} P$$

$$\frac{N \equiv N_1 \qquad N_1 \rightarrowtail N_2 \qquad N_2 \equiv N'}{N \rightarrowtail N'}$$

**Table 10.** KLAIM Operational Semantics (see Notation 1)

The pattern–matching predicate used in Table 10 is defined in Table 11. The matching rules ensure that if a **read/in** operation looks for processes with type $\delta$ then only processes with type $\delta'$ such that $\delta'\{\Theta_{N_S}\}_s \preceq \delta\{\Theta_{N_S}\}_s$ are accepted.

The rules also ensure that if **read/in** looks for a site $u$ with type specification $\langle\lambda_u, \delta_u\rangle$, then for selecting a site $s'$ with type specification $\langle\lambda, \delta\rangle$ it must hold that:

- the interpretation of $\delta_u[s'/u]$ at $s'$ is a subtype of both the actual type of $s'$, $\delta_{s'}$, and of the interpretation at $s'$ of the type specified for $s'$, $\delta\{\Theta_{N_S}\}_{s'}$. In the rules, $\sqcap$ is used to denote the greatest lower bound;
- the capability of a site $s''$ as specified in the input access list, $\lambda_u(s'')$, agrees with that assigned to $s''$ from $s'$ by the coordinator, $\delta_{s''} \downarrow_c s'$. Moreover, if the output access list $\lambda$ is not empty, it also agrees with the capability of $s''$ as specified by $\lambda$, $\lambda(s'')$.

$$match(v, v, s, \Theta_{NS}) \quad match(P, P, s, \Theta_{NS}) \quad match(s' : \langle \lambda, \delta \rangle, s' : \langle \lambda, \delta \rangle, s, \Theta_{NS})$$

$$match(!\,x, v, s, \Theta_{NS}) \qquad\qquad match(v, !\,x, s, \Theta_{NS})$$

$$\frac{\phi \mid_{\overline{s}} P : \delta' \quad \delta'\{\Theta_{NS}\}_s \preceq \delta\{\Theta_{NS}\}_s}{match(!\,X : \delta, P, s, \Theta_{NS})} \qquad \frac{\phi \mid_{\overline{s}} P : \delta' \quad \delta\{\Theta_{NS}\}_s \preceq \delta'\{\Theta_{NS}\}_s}{match(P, !\,X : \delta, s, \Theta_{NS})}$$

$$\frac{\delta_u[s'/u]\{\Theta_{NS}\}_{s'} \preceq \delta_{s'} \sqcap \delta\{\Theta_{NS}\}_{s'}}{\forall s'' \in dom(\lambda_u) : (\delta_{s''} \downarrow_c s' \sqsubseteq_\Pi \lambda_u(s'')) \wedge (dom(\lambda) \neq \emptyset \implies \lambda(s'') \sqsubseteq_\Pi \lambda_u(s''))}{match(!\,u : \langle \lambda_u, \delta_u \rangle, s' : \langle \lambda, \delta \rangle, s, \Theta_{NS})}$$

$$\frac{\delta_u[s'/u]\{\Theta_{NS}\}_{s'} \preceq \delta\{\Theta_{NS}\}_{s'} \quad \forall s'' \in dom(\lambda_u) : \lambda(s'') \sqsubseteq_\Pi \lambda_u(s'')}{match(s' : \langle \lambda, \delta \rangle, !\,u : \langle \lambda_u, \delta_u \rangle, s, \Theta_{NS})}$$

$$\frac{match(f_1, f_2, s, \Theta_{NS}) \quad match(t_1, t_2, s, \Theta_{NS})}{match((f_1, t_1), (f_2, t_2), s, \Theta_{NS})}$$

**Table 11.** Matching Rules

# References

1. M. Abadi. Secrecy by Typing in Cryptographic Protocols. *Theoretical Aspects of Computer Software* (TACS'97), *Proceedings* (M. Abadi, M. Ito, Eds.), *LNCS* 1281, pp.611-638, Springer, 1997.
2. M. Abadi, A.D. Gordon. A calculus for cryptographic protocols: The spi calculus. *Proc. of the ACM Conference on Computer and Communication Security*, ACM Press, 1997.
3. M. Abadi, R. Stata. A Type System for Java Bytecode Verifier. *Proc. of the ACM Symposium on Principles of Programming Languages*, ACM Press, 1998.
4. A. Arnold, J. Gosling. The Java Programming Language. Addison Wesley, 1996.
5. L. Bettini, R. De Nicola, G. Ferrari, R. Pugliese. Interactive Mobile Agents in X-Klaim. *IEEE Seventh International Workshop on Enabling Technologies: Infrastructure for Collaborative Enterprises, Proceedings* (P. Ciancarini, R. Tolksdorf, Eds.), IEEE Computer Society Press, 1998.
6. C. Bodei, P. Degano, F. Nielson, H.R. Nielson. Control Flow Analysis for the $\pi$-calculus. *Concurrency Theory* (CONCUR'98), *Proceedings* (D. Sangiorgi, R.de Simone, Eds.), *LNCS* 1466, pp.611-638, Springer, 1998.
7. M. Boreale, D. Sangiorgi. Bisimulation in Naming-Passing Calculi without Matching. *Proc. of 13th IEEE Symposium on Logic in Computer Science* (LICS '98), IEEE Computer Society Press, 1998.
8. G. Boudol. Typing the use of resources in a Concurrent Calculus. *Advances in Computing Science* (ASIAN'97), *Proceedings* (R.K. Shyamasundar, K. Ueda, Eds.), *LNCS* 1345, pp.239-253, Springer, 1997.
9. L. Cardelli, A. Gordon, Mobile Ambients. *Foundations of Software Science and Computation Structures* (FoSSaCS'98), *Proceedings* (M. Nivat, Ed.), *LNCS* 1378, pp.140-155, Springer, 1998.

10. L. Cardelli, A. Gordon, Types for Mobile Ambients. *Proc. of the ACM Symposium on Principles of Programming Languages*, ACM Press, 1999.

11. N. Carriero, D. Gelernter. Linda in Context. *Communications of the ACM*, 32(4):444-458, 1989.

12. G. Cugola, C. Ghezzi, G.P. Picco, G. Vigna. Analyzing Mobile Code Languages. In *Mobile Object Systems Towards the Programmable Internet* (J. Vitek, C. Tschudin, Eds.), *LNCS* 1222, Springer, 1997.

13. R. De Nicola, G. Ferrari, R. Pugliese. Coordinating Mobile Agents via Blackboards and Access Rights. *Coordination Languages and Models* (COORDINATION'97), *Proceedings* (D. Garlan, D. Le Metayer, Eds.), *LNCS* 1282, pp. 220-237, Springer, 1997.

14. R. De Nicola, G. Ferrari, R. Pugliese. KLAIM: a Kernel Language for Agents Interaction and Mobility. *IEEE Transactions on Software Engineering*, Vol.24(5):315-330, IEEE Computer Society Press, 1998.

15. R. De Nicola, G. Ferrari, R. Pugliese, B. Venneri. Types for Access Control. Available at http://rap.dsi.unifi.it/papers.html. To appear in *Theoretical Computer Science*.

16. D. Gelernter. Generative Communication in Linda. *ACM Transactions on Programming Languages and Systems*, 7(1):80-112, ACM Press, 1985.

17. D. Gelernter, N. Carriero, S. Chandran, et al. Parallel Programming in Linda. *Proc. of the IEEE International Conference on Parallel Programming*, pp. 255-263, IEEE Computer Society Press, 1985.

18. N. Heintz, J.G. Riecke. The SLam calculus: Programming with secrecy and integrity. *Proc. of the ACM Symposium on Principles of Programming Languages*, ACM Press, 1998.

19. M. Hennessy, J. Riely. Resource Access Control in Systems of Mobile Agents. *Proc. Int. Workshop on High-Level Concurrent Languages*, vol. 16(3) of *Electronic Notes in Theoretical Computer Science*, Elsevier, 1998.

20. N. Kobayashi, B. Pierce, D. Turner. Linearity and the $\pi$-calculus. *Proc. of the ACM Symposium on Principles of Programming Languages*, ACM Press, 1996.

21. R. Milner, J. Parrow, D. Walker. A calculus of mobile processes, (Part I and II). *Information and Computation*, 100:1-77, 1992.

22. G. Necula. Proof-carrying code. *Proc. of the ACM Symposium on Principles of Programming Languages*, ACM Press, 1997.

23. B. Pierce and D. Sangiorgi. Typing and subtyping for mobile processes. *Mathematical Structures in Comp. Science*, 6(5):409-454, 1996.

24. J. Riely, M. Hennessy. Trust and Partial Typing in Open Systems of Mobile Agents. *Proc. of the ACM Symposium on Principles of Programming Languages*, ACM Press, 1999.

25. P. Sewell. Global/Local Subtyping and Capability Inference for a Distributed $\pi$-calculus. *International Colloquium on Automata, Languages and Programming* (ICALP'98), *Proceedings* (K.G. Larsen, S. Skyum, G. Winskel, Eds.), *LNCS* 1443, Springer, 1998.

26. J. Vitek, G. Castagna. A Calculus of Secure Mobile Computations. *Proc. of Workshop on Internet Programming Languages*, Chicago, 1998.

27. D. Volpano, G. Smith. A typed-based approach to program security. *Theory and Practice of Software Development* (TAPSOFT'97), *Proceeding* (M. Bidoit, M. Dauchet, Eds.), *LNCS* 1214, pp.607-621, Springer, 1997.

28. D. Volpano, G. Smith. Secure Information Flow in a Multi-threaded Imperative Language. *Proc. of the ACM Symposium on Principles of Programming Languages*, ACM Press, 1998.

# Security Properties of Typed Applets

Xavier Leroy and François Rouaix

**Abstract.** This paper formalizes the folklore result that strongly-typed applets are more secure than untyped ones. We formulate and prove several security properties that all well-typed applets possess, and identify sufficient conditions for the applet execution environment to be safe, such as procedural encapsulation, type abstraction, and systematic type-based placement of run-time checks. These results are a first step towards formal techniques for developing and validating safe execution environments for applets.

## 1 Introduction

What, exactly, makes strongly-typed applets more secure than untyped ones? Most frameworks proposed so far for safe local execution of foreign code rely on strong typing, either statically checked at the client side [19, 44], statically checked at the server side and cryptographically signed [35], or dynamically checked by the client [8]. However, the main property guaranteed by strong typing is type soundness: "well-typed programs do not go wrong", e.g. do not apply an integer as if it were a function. While violations of type soundness constitute real security threats (casting a well-chosen string to a function or object type allows arbitrary code to be executed), there are many more security concerns, such as integrity of the running site (an applet should not delete or modify arbitrary files) and confidentiality of user's data (an applet should not divulge personal information over the network). The corresponding security violations do not generally invalidate type soundness in the conventional sense.

If we examine the various security problems identified for Java applets [12], some of them do cause a violation of Java type soundness [21]; others correspond to malicious, but well-typed, uses of improperly protected functions from the applet's execution environment [7]. Another typical example is the ActiveX applet described in [10] that does a Trojan attack on the Quicken home-banking software: money gets transferred from the user's bank account to some offshore account, all in a perfectly type-safe way.

On these examples, it is intuitively obvious that security properties must be enforced by the applet's execution environment. It is the environment that eventually decides which computer resources the applet can access. This is the essence of the so-called "sandbox model". Strong typing comes in the picture only to guarantee that this environment is used in accordance with its publicized interface. For instance, typing prevents an applet from jumping in the middle of the code for an environment function, or scanning the whole memory space of the browser, which would allow the applet to abuse or bypass entirely the execution environment.

The purpose of this paper is to give a formal foundation to the intuition above. We formulate and prove several security properties that all well-typed applets possess. Along the way, we identify sufficient conditions for the execution environment to be safe, such as procedural encapsulation, type abstraction, and systematic type-based placement of run-time checks. These results are a first step towards formal techniques for developing and validating safe execution environments for applets.

The remainder of this paper is organized as follows. Section 2 introduces a simple language for applets and their environment, and formalizes the security policy that they must obey. Section 3 proves a security property based on the notion of lexical scoping, then extends it to take procedural abstraction into account. In section 4, we equip our language with a simple type system, which is used in section 5 to prove three type-based security properties, two relying on run-time checks and the other on a combination of run-time checks and type abstraction. After a brief parallel with object-oriented languages in section 6, section 7 outlines the security architecture for applets in the MMM Web browser and discusses the relevance of our results to this practical example. Related work is discussed in section 8, followed by concluding remarks in section 9.

## 2 The language and its security policy

### 2.1 The language

The language we consider in this paper is a simple lambda-calculus with base types (integers, strings, ...), pairs as the only data structure, and references in the style of ML. The syntax of terms, with typical element $a$, is as follows:

| Terms: | $a ::= x$ | identifiers |
|--------|-----------|-------------|
| | $\mid b$ | constant of base type (integer, ...) |
| | $\mid \lambda x.a$ | function abstraction |
| | $\mid a_1(a_2)$ | function application |
| | $\mid (a_1, a_2)$ | pair construction |
| | $\mid \mathtt{fst}(a) \mid \mathtt{snd}(a)$ | pair projections |
| | $\mid \mathtt{ref}(a)$ | reference creation |
| | $\mid !a$ | dereferencing |
| | $\mid a_1 := a_2$ | reference assignment |

References are included in the language from the beginning not only to account for imperative programming (all kinds of assignment on variables and mutable data structures such as arrays can easily be modeled with references), but also to provide easily observable criteria on which we base the security policy.

### 2.2 The security policy

The security policy we apply to applets is based on the notion of sensitive store locations: locations of references that an applet must not modify during its execution, or more generally references that can be modified during the applet execution, but whose successive contents must always satisfy some invariant, i.e. remain within a given set of permitted values.

The first motivation for this policy is to formalize the intuitive idea that an applet must not trash the memory of the computer executing it. In particular, the internal state of the browser, the operating system, and other applications running on the machine must not be adversely affected by the applet.

This security policy can also be stretched to account for input/output behavior, notably accesses to files and simple cases of network connections. A low-level, hardware-oriented view of I/O is to consider hardware devices such as the disk controller and network interface as special locations in the store; I/O is then controlled by restricting what can be written to these locations. For a higher-level view, each file or network connection can be viewed as a reference, which can then be controlled independently of others. Here, the file system, the name service and the routing tables become dictionary-like data structures mapping file names, host names, and network addresses to the references representing files and connections.

By concentrating on writes to sensitive locations, we focus on integrity properties of the system running the applet. It is also possible to control reads from sensitive locations, thus establishing simple privacy properties. We will not do it in this paper for the sake of simplicity, but the results of section 3 also extend to controlled reads. More advanced privacy properties, as provided for instance by information flow models, are well beyond our approach, however.

## 2.3 The instrumented semantics

To enforce the security policy, we give a semantics to our language that monitors reference assignments, and reports run-time errors in the case of illegal writes. We use a standard big-step operational semantics in the style of [32, 39, 25]. Source terms are mapped to values, which are terms with the following syntax:

| Values: | $v ::= b$ | values of base types |
|---|---|---|
| | $\mid \lambda x.a[e]$ | function closures |
| | $\mid (v_1, v_2)$ | pairs of values |
| | $\mid \ell$ | store locations |
| Results: | $r ::= v/s$ | normal termination |
| | $\mid \mathbf{err}$ | write violation detected |
| Environments: | $e ::= [x_1 \leftarrow v_1 \ldots, x_n \leftarrow v_n]$ | |
| Stores: | $s ::= [\ell_1 \leftarrow v_1 \ldots, \ell_n \leftarrow v_n]$ | |

The evaluation relation, defined by the inference rules in Fig. 1, is written $\varphi, e, s \vdash a \to r$, meaning that in evaluation environment $e$, initial store $s$, and store control $\varphi$, the source term $a$ evaluates to the result $r$, which is either $\mathbf{err}$ if an illegal write was detected or a pair $v/s'$ of a value $v$ for the source term and a modified store $s'$.

Normal rules:

$$\varphi, e, s \vdash x \rightarrow e(x)/s \quad (1) \qquad\qquad \varphi, e, s \vdash b \rightarrow b/s \quad (2)$$

$$\varphi, e, s \vdash \lambda x.a \rightarrow \lambda x.a[e]/s \quad (3)$$

$$\frac{\varphi, e, s \vdash a_1 \rightarrow \lambda x.a'[e']/s_1 \quad \varphi, e, s_1 \vdash a_2 \rightarrow v_2/s_2 \quad \varphi, e'\{x \leftarrow v_2\}, s_2 \vdash a' \rightarrow r}{\varphi, e, s \vdash a_1(a_2) \rightarrow r} \quad (4)$$

$$\frac{\varphi, e, s \vdash a_1 \rightarrow v_1/s_1 \quad \varphi, e, s_1 \vdash a_2 \rightarrow v_2/s_2}{\varphi, e, s \vdash (a_1, a_2) \rightarrow (v_1, v_2)/s_2} \quad (5)$$

$$\frac{\varphi, e, s \vdash a \rightarrow (v_1, v_2)/s'}{\varphi, e, s \vdash \mathbf{fst}(a) \rightarrow v_1/s'} \quad (6) \qquad\qquad \frac{\varphi, e, s \vdash a \rightarrow (v_1, v_2)/s'}{\varphi, e, s \vdash \mathbf{snd}(a) \rightarrow v_2/s'} \quad (7)$$

$$\frac{\varphi, e, s \vdash a \rightarrow v/s' \quad \ell \notin \mathrm{Dom}(s') \cup \mathrm{Dom}(\varphi)}{\varphi, e, s \vdash \mathbf{ref}(a) \rightarrow \ell/s'\{\ell \leftarrow v\}} \quad (8) \qquad \frac{\varphi, e, s \vdash a \rightarrow \ell/s'}{\varphi, e, s \vdash {!}a \rightarrow s'(\ell)/s'} \quad (9)$$

$$\frac{\varphi, e, s \vdash a_1 \rightarrow \ell/s_1 \quad \varphi, e, s_1 \vdash a_2 \rightarrow v_2/s_2 \quad \ell \notin \mathrm{Dom}(\varphi) \text{ or } v_2 \in \varphi(\ell)}{\varphi, e, s \vdash (a_1 := a_2) \rightarrow ()/s_2\{\ell \leftarrow v_2\}} \quad (10)$$

$$\frac{\varphi, e, s \vdash a_1 \rightarrow \ell/s_1 \quad \varphi, e, s_1 \vdash a_2 \rightarrow v_2/s_2 \quad \ell \in \mathrm{Dom}(\varphi) \text{ and } v_2 \notin \varphi(\ell)}{\varphi, e, s \vdash (a_1 := a_2) \rightarrow \mathbf{err}} \quad (11)$$

Error propagation rules:

$$\frac{\varphi, e, s \vdash a_1 \rightarrow \mathbf{err}}{\varphi, e, s \vdash a_1(a_2) \rightarrow \mathbf{err}} \quad (12) \qquad \frac{\varphi, e, s \vdash a_1 \rightarrow v_1/s_1 \quad \varphi, e, s_1 \vdash a_2 \rightarrow \mathbf{err}}{\varphi, e, s \vdash a_1(a_2) \rightarrow \mathbf{err}} \quad (13)$$

$$\frac{\varphi, e, s \vdash a_1 \rightarrow \mathbf{err}}{\varphi, e, s \vdash (a_1, a_2) \rightarrow \mathbf{err}} \quad (14) \qquad \frac{\varphi, e, s \vdash a_1 \rightarrow v_1/s_1 \quad \varphi, e, s_1 \vdash a_2 \rightarrow \mathbf{err}}{\varphi, e, s \vdash (a_1, a_2) \rightarrow \mathbf{err}} \quad (15)$$

$$\frac{\varphi, e, s \vdash a \rightarrow \mathbf{err}}{\varphi, e, s \vdash \mathbf{fst}(a) \rightarrow \mathbf{err}} \quad (16) \qquad \frac{\varphi, e, s \vdash a \rightarrow \mathbf{err}}{\varphi, e, s \vdash \mathbf{snd}(a) \rightarrow \mathbf{err}} \quad (17)$$

$$\frac{\varphi, e, s \vdash a \rightarrow \mathbf{err}}{\varphi, e, s \vdash \mathbf{ref}(a) \rightarrow \mathbf{err}} \quad (18) \qquad \frac{\varphi, e, s \vdash a \rightarrow \mathbf{err}}{\varphi, e, s \vdash {!}a \rightarrow \mathbf{err}} \quad (19)$$

$$\frac{\varphi, e, s \vdash a_1 \rightarrow \mathbf{err}}{\varphi, e, s \vdash (a_1 := a_2) \rightarrow \mathbf{err}} \quad (20) \qquad \frac{\varphi, e, s \vdash a_1 \rightarrow v_1/s_1 \quad \varphi, e, s_1 \vdash a_2 \rightarrow \mathbf{err}}{\varphi, e, s \vdash (a_1 := a_2) \rightarrow \mathbf{err}} \quad (21)$$

**Fig. 1.** Evaluation rules

The only unusual ingredient in this semantics is the $\varphi$ component, which maps store locations to sets of values: if $\varphi(\ell)$ is defined, values written to the location $\ell$ must belong to the set $\varphi(\ell)$, otherwise a run-time error **err** is generated; if $\varphi(\ell)$ is undefined, any value can be stored at $\ell$. (See rules 10 and 11.) For instance, taking $\varphi(\ell) = \emptyset$ prevents any assignment to $\ell$.

The rules for propagating the **err** result and aborting execution (rules 12–21) are the same rules as for propagating run-time type errors (**wrong**) in [39]; the only difference is that we have no rules to detect run-time type errors, thus making no difference between run-time type violations and non-terminating programs (no derivations exist in both cases): the standard type soundness theorems show that type violations cannot occur at run-time in well-typed source terms.

An unusual aspect of our formalism is that the store control $\varphi$ must be given at the start of the execution. The reason is that, with big-step operational semantics, it does not suffice to perform a regular evaluation $e, s \vdash a \rightarrow v/s'$ and observe the differences between $s$ and $s'$ to detect illegal writes. For one thing, we would not observe temporary assignments, where a malicious applet writes illegal values to a sensitive location, then restores the original values before terminating. Also, we could not say anything about non-terminating terms: the applet could perform illegal writes, then enter an infinite loop to avoid detection. By providing the store control $\varphi$ in advance, we ensure that the first write error will be detected immediately and reported as the **err** result.

Unfortunately, this provides no way to control stores to locations created during the evaluation (rule 8 chooses these locations outside of $\text{Dom}(\varphi)$, meaning that writes to these locations will be free): only preexisting locations can be sensitive. (This can be viewed as an inadequacy of big-step semantics, and a small-step, reduction-based semantics would fare better here. However, several semantic features that play an important role in our study are easier to express in a big-step semantics than in a reduction semantics: the clean separation between browser-supplied environment and applet-supplied source term, and the ability to interpret abstract type names by arbitrary sets of values.)

# 3 Reachability-based security

## 3.1 Simple reachability

The first security property for our calculus formalizes the idea that an applet can only write to locations that are reachable from the initial environment in which it executes, or that are created during the applet's execution. For instance, if the references representing files are not reachable from the execution environment given to applets, then no applet can write to a file.

Reachability, here, is to be understood in the garbage collection sense: a location is reachable if there exists a path in the memory graph from the initial environment to the location, following one or several pointers. More formally, we define the set $RL(v, s)$ of locations reachable from a value $v$ in a store $s$ by the following equations:

$$RL(b, s) = \emptyset$$
$$RL(\lambda x.a[e], s) = RL(e, s)$$
$$RL((v_1, v_2), s) = RL(v_1, s) \cup RL(v_2, s)$$
$$RL(\ell, s) = \{\ell\} \cup RL(s(\ell), s)$$
$$RL(e, s) = \bigcup_{x \in \mathrm{Dom}(e)} RL(e(x), s)$$

The definition above is not well-founded by induction on $v$, since in the fourth case the value $s(\ell)$ is arbitrarily large and may contain $\ell$ again. It should be viewed as a fixpoint equation $RL = F(RL)$, where $F$ is an increasing operator; $RL$ is, then, the smallest fixpoint of that operator.

If $p$ is a set of sensitive locations, we define $Prot(p)$ as the store control that maps locations $\ell \in p$ to $\emptyset$, thus disallowing all writes on $\ell$, and is undefined on locations $\ell \notin p$. We can now formulate the first security property:

**Security property 1** *Let $p$ be a set of sensitive locations. If $p \cap RL(e, s) = \emptyset$, then for all applets $a$, we have $Prot(p), e, s \vdash a \not\rightarrow$ err.*

In other words, if none of the locations in $p$ is reachable from the initial environment $e$ and store $s$, then no applet $a$ can trigger an error by writing to a location in $p$: the applet will either terminate normally or loop. The proof of this property is a simple inductive argument on the evaluation derivation, using the following lemma as the induction hypothesis:

**Lemma 1.** *If $p \cap RL(e, s) = \emptyset$ and $Prot(p), e, s \vdash a \rightarrow r$, then $r \neq$ err. Instead, $r = v/s'$ for some $v$ and $s'$. Moreover, $p \cap RL(v, s') = \emptyset$, and for all values $w$ such that $p \cap RL(w, s) = \emptyset$, we have $p \cap RL(w, s') = \emptyset$.*

It is important to remark that Property 1 holds in practice only if the evaluation of $a$ on an actual processor adheres to the rules given in Fig. 1. For instance, the rules do not allow the evaluation of $b := a$ where $b$ is an integer constant, but an untyped or weakly-typed implementation might execute $b := a$ without crashing nor reporting an error in the case where $b$ is a valid memory address; this would allow the applet to write to arbitrary locations. We rely on $a$ being evaluated by a type-safe implementation to ensure that this cannot happen: either the evaluator must perform run-time type-checking, or $a$ must be well-typed in some sound static type system (such as the one presented below in section 4).

Property 1, though simple and already well-known in the field of garbage collection [26], establishes a number of properties without which no security is possible at all. First, our language has safe pointers: locations cannot be forged by casting well-chosen integers. Second, automatic memory management (garbage collection) is feasible and does not weaken security: a location that becomes unreachable remains unreachable; moreover, newly allocated locations are always initialized; therefore, unreachable locations can be reused safely. Third, the language enforces lexical scoping: the execution of the applet depends only on the environment in which it proceeds; the applet does not have access to the full execution environment of the browser — as would be the case in a dynamically-scoped language, such as Emacs Lisp, or a language with special constructs to access the environment of the caller, such as Tcl.

## 3.2 Reachability and procedural abstraction

In defining reachable locations, we have treated closures like tuples (as garbage collectors do): the locations reachable from $\lambda x.a[e]$ are those reachable from $e(y)$ for some $y \in Dom(e)$. There is, however, a big difference between closures and tuples. Tuples are passive data structures: any piece of code that has access to the tuple can then obtain pointers to the components of the tuple. Closures are active data structures: only the code part of the closure can access directly the data part of the closure (the values of the free variables); other code fragments can only apply the closure, but not access the data part directly. In other words, the code part of a closure mediates access to the data part. This property is often referred to as procedural abstraction [34].

For instance, consider the following function, similar to many Unix system calls, where uid is a reference holding the identity of the caller (applet or browser):

> λx. if !uid = browser
>     then *do something with high privileges*
>     else *do something with low privileges*

Assume this function is part of the applet environment, but not the reference uid itself. Then, there is no way that the applet can modify the location of uid, even though that location is reachable from the environment.

A less obvious example, where the reference uid is not trivially read-only, is the following function in the style of the Unix setuid system call:

> λnewid. if !uid = browser
>       then uid := newid
>       else *raise an error*

Assuming uid is not initially browser, an applet cannot change uid by calling this function.

Procedural abstraction can be viewed as the foundation for access control lists and similar programming techniques, which systematically encapsulate resources inside functions that check the identity and credentials of the caller before granting access to the requested resources. For instance, a file opening function contains the whole data structure representing the file system in its closure, but grants access only to files with suitable permissions. Thus, while all files are reachable from the closure of the open function, only those that have suitable permissions can be modified by the caller.

To formalize these ideas, we set out to define the set of locations $ML(v, s)$ that are actually modifiable (not merely reachable) from a value $v$ and a store $s$, and show that if a location $\ell$ is not in $ML(e, s)$, then any applet evaluated in the environment $e$ does not write to $\ell$. This result is stronger than Property 1 because the location $\ell$ that is not modifiable from $e$ in $s$ can still be reachable (via closures) from $e$ in $s$.

For passive data structures (locations, tuples), modifiability coincides with reachability: a location is modifiable from $v/s$ if a sequence of fst, snd, and ! operations applied to $v$ in $s$ evaluates to that location. The difficult case is defining modifiable locations for a function closure. The idea is to consider all possible applications of the closure to an argument: a location $\ell$ is considered modifiable from the closure only if one of those applications writes to the location, or causes the location to become modifiable otherwise.

More precisely, let $e_{api}$ be the execution environment given to applets, and let $c = \lambda x.a[e]$ be one of the closures contained in $e_{api}$. A location $\ell$ is modifiable from $c$ in store $s$ if there exists a value $v$ such that the following conditions hold:

**Condition 1.** The application of the closure to $v$ causes $\ell$ to be modified, i.e. $\{\ell \mapsto \emptyset\}, e\{x \leftarrow v\}, s \vdash a \rightarrow \text{err}$.

*Example:* Let $e$ be the environment $[r \leftarrow \ell]$. Then, $\ell$ is reachable from $(\lambda x.\ r := x + 1)[e]$ in any store, since any application of the closure causes $\ell$ to be assigned.

**Condition 2.** Alternatively, the application of $c$ to $v$ does not modify $\ell$, but returns a result value and a new store from which $\ell$ is modifiable.

*Example:* With $e$ as in the previous example, $\ell$ is reachable from $(\lambda x.\ (r, 1))[e]$, since any application of that closure returns a pair with $\ell$ as first component. An applet can thus write to $\ell$ by applying the closure, extracting $\ell$ from the returned result, and assigning $\ell$ directly.

**Condition 3.** Alternatively, the application of $c$ to $v$ modifies a reference accessible to the applet in such a way that $\ell$ becomes modifiable from that reference.

*Example:* Consider $c = (\lambda p.\ p := r)[e]$, where $e = [r \leftarrow \ell]$ as usual. Applying $c$ to a location $\ell'$, we obtain a modified store $s'$ such that $s'(\ell') = \ell$, i.e. $\ell$ is modifiable from $\ell'$ in $s'$ and can be modified by the applet.

**Condition 4.** Alternatively, the application of $c$ to $v$ assigns references internal to the browser functions in such a way that $\ell$ becomes modifiable from the environment $e_{api}$ in the store $s'$ at the end of the application.

*Example:* Consider the following environment $e_{api}$:

$$e_{api}(f) = (\lambda x.\ n := !n + 1)[n \leftarrow \ell_n]$$
$$e_{api}(g) = (\lambda x.\ \text{if } !n \geq 1 \text{ then } r := 0)[n \leftarrow \ell_n; r \leftarrow \ell]$$

In a store $s$ such that $s(\ell_n) = 0$, the location $\ell$ is not modifiable from $e_{api}(g)$. However, $\ell$ is modifiable from $e_{api}(f)$ in $s$, since one application of that closure returns a store $s'$ such that $s'(\ell_n) = 1$, and in that store $s'$, $\ell$ is modifiable from $e_{api}(g)$: any application of $e_{api}(g)$ with initial store $s'$ writes to $\ell$.

**Condition 5.** In conditions 1–4 above, it must be the case that the location $\ell$ found to be modifiable from the closure $c$ is not actually modifiable from the argument $v$ passed to the closure. Otherwise, we would not know whether the location really "comes from" the closure $c$, or is merely modified by the applet-provided argument $v$.

*Example:* Consider the higher-order function $c = (\lambda f.\ f(0))[\emptyset]$. If we apply $c$ to $(\lambda n.\ r := n)[r \leftarrow \ell]$, we observe a write to location $\ell$. However, $\ell$ should not be considered as modifiable from $c$, since it is also modifiable from the argument given to $c$.

As should now be apparent from the conditions 1–5 above, the notion of modifiability raises serious problems, both practical and technical. On the practical side, the set of modifiable locations $ML(v, s)$ is not computable from $v$ and $s$: in the closure case, we must consider infinitely many possible arguments. Thus, a full mathematical proof is needed to determine $ML(v, s)$.

Moreover, modifiable locations cannot be determined locally. As condition 4 shows, the modifiable locations of a closure depend on the modifiable locations of all functions from the applet environment $e_{api}$. Thus, if we manage to determine $ML(e_{api}, s)$, then add one single function to the applet environment, we must not only determine the modifiable locations from the new function, but also reconsider all other functions in the environment to see whether their modifiable locations have changed. This is clearly impractical. Hence, the notion of modifiability is not effective and is interesting only from a semantic viewpoint and as a guide to derive decidable security criteria in the sequel.

On the technical side, the conditions 1–5 above do not lead to a well-founded definition of the sets of modifiable locations $ML(v, s)$. The problem is condition 5 (the requirement that the location must not be modifiable from the argument given to the closure): viewing conditions 1–4 as a fixpoint equation for some operator, that operator is not increasing because of the negation in condition 5.

In appendix B, we tackle this problem and show that non-modifiable locations are indeed never modified in the particular case where the applet's environment $e_{api}$ is well-typed and its type $E_{api}$ does not contain any **ref** types, so that no references are exchanged directly between the applet and its environment. In the remainder of this paper, we abandon the notion of modifiability in its full generality, and develop more effective techniques to restrict writes to reachable locations, relying on type-based instrumentation of the browser code.

## 4 The type system

We now equip our language with a simple type system. The type system is based on simply-typed $\lambda$-calculus, with the addition of named, user-defined types. Despite its simplicity, this type system does not restrict drastically the expressiveness of our language. In particular, recursive functions can still be defined using references [39]. The type algebra is:

Types:  $\tau ::= \iota$        base type (int, string, etc.)
        $\mid t$        named type
        $\mid \tau_1 \to \tau_2$    function type
        $\mid \tau_1 \times \tau_2$    product type
        $\mid \tau$ ref    reference type

Conversely, we enrich the syntax of terms with two new constructs: explicit coercions to and from named types, and run-time validation of values of named types.

Terms:  $a ::= \ldots$    (as before)
        $\mid \tau(a)$        coercion to type $\tau$
        $\mid OK_t(a)$    run-time validation at type $t$

The typing rules for the calculus are shown in Fig. 3, and the extra evaluation rules for the new constructs in Fig. 2.

$$\frac{\varphi, e, s \vdash a \to r}{\varphi, e, s \vdash \tau(a) \to r} \quad (22)$$

$$\frac{\varphi, e, s \vdash a \to v/s' \qquad t \in \mathrm{Dom}(PV) \text{ implies } v \in PV(t)}{\varphi, e, s \vdash OK_t(a) \to v/s'} \quad (23)$$

$$\frac{\varphi, e, s \vdash a \to \mathbf{err}}{\varphi, e, s \vdash OK_t(a) \to \mathbf{err}} \quad (24)$$

**Fig. 2.** Extra evaluation rules for coercions and run-time checks

## 4.1 Named types

The overall approach followed in section 5 is to identify groups of references having the same type, and apply a given security policy to all of them. However, types from the simply-typed $\lambda$-calculus are too coarse for this purpose: references of type string ref can hold many different kinds of data, such as messages, filenames, and cryptographic keys; clearly, different security restrictions must be applied to these different kinds of strings.

To this end, we introduce named types $t$, defined by a mapping $TD$ for type names to type expressions, stating that the type $t$ is interconvertible with its implementation type $TD(t)$. For instance, we could introduce a type filename, defined to be equal to string. An expression $e$ of type string cannot be used implicitly with type filename; an explicit injection into filename, written filename($e$), is required. Conversely, accessing the string underlying an expression $e'$ of type filename is achieved by string($e'$). (See rules 35 and 36.) In

$$E \vdash x : E(x) \quad (25) \qquad\qquad E \vdash b : \textit{Typeof}(b) \quad (26)$$

$$\frac{E\{x \leftarrow \tau'\} \vdash a : \tau}{E \vdash \lambda x.a : \tau' \rightarrow \tau} \quad (27) \qquad\qquad \frac{E \vdash a_1 : \tau' \rightarrow \tau \quad E \vdash a_2 : \tau'}{E \vdash a_1(a_2) : \tau} \quad (28)$$

$$\frac{E \vdash a_1 : \tau_1 \quad E \vdash a_2 : \tau_2}{E \vdash (a_1, a_2) : \tau_1 \times \tau_2} \quad (29) \qquad \frac{E \vdash a : \tau_1 \times \tau_2}{E \vdash \mathtt{fst}(a) : \tau_1} \quad (30) \qquad \frac{E \vdash a : \tau_1 \times \tau_2}{E \vdash \mathtt{snd}(a) : \tau_2} \quad (31)$$

$$\frac{E \vdash a : \tau}{E \vdash \mathtt{ref}(a) : \tau \ \mathtt{ref}} \quad (32) \qquad\qquad \frac{E \vdash a : \tau \ \mathtt{ref}}{E \vdash !a : \tau} \quad (33)$$

$$\frac{E \vdash a_1 : \tau \ \mathtt{ref} \quad E \vdash a_2 : \tau}{E \vdash (a_1 := a_2) : \mathtt{unit}} \quad (34)$$

$$\frac{E \vdash a : \tau \quad \tau = TD(t)}{E \vdash t(a) : t} \quad (35) \qquad\qquad \frac{E \vdash a : t \quad \tau = TD(t)}{E \vdash \tau(a) : \tau} \quad (36)$$

$$\frac{E \vdash a : t}{E \vdash OK_t(a) : t} \quad (37)$$

**Fig. 3.** Typing rules

this respect, our named types behave very much like the is new type definition in Ada, and unlike type abbreviations in ML. Making the coercions explicit facilitates the definition of the program transformations in section 5, ensuring in particular that each term has a unique type.

The mapping $TD$ of type definitions is essentially global: type definitions local to an expression are not supported. Still, it is possible to type-check some terms against a set of type definitions $TD'$ that is a strict subset of $TD$, thus rendering the named types not defined in $TD'$ abstract in that term. We will use this facility in section 5.2 and 5.3 to make named types abstract in the applet.

## 4.2 Run-time validation of values

The other unusual feature of our type system is the family of operators $OK_t$ (one for each named type $t$) used to perform run-time validation of their argument. For each named type $t$, we assume given a set $PV(t)$ of permitted values for type $t$. (We actually allow $PV(t)$ to be undefined for some types $t$, which we take to mean that all values of type $t$ are valid.) The expression $OK_t(e)$ checks whether the value of $e$ is in $PV(t)$; if yes, it returns the value unchanged; if no, it aborts the execution of the applet and reports an error. In the evaluation rules, the "yes" case corresponds to rule 23; there is no rule for the "no" case, meaning that no evaluation derivation exists if an $OK_t$ test fails. In effect, we do not distinguish between failure of $OK_t$ and non-termination. At any rate, we must not return the **err** result when $OK_t$ fails: no write violation has occurred yet.

By varying $PV(t)$, we can control precisely the values of type $t$ that will pass run-time validation. For instance, $PV(\texttt{filename})$ could consist of all strings referencing files under the applet's temporary directory /tmp/applet.$x$, a new directory that is created empty at the beginning of the applet's execution. Combined with the techniques described in section 5, this would ensure that only files in this temporary directory can be accessed by the applet. Similarly, the set $PV(\texttt{widget})$ could consist of all GUI widget descriptors referring to widgets that are children of the applet's top widget, thus preventing the applet from interacting with widgets belonging to the browser. Other examples of run-time validation include checking cryptographic signatures on the applet code itself or on sensitive data presented by the applet.

In practice, validation $OK_t(e)$ involves not only the value of its argument $e$, but also external information such as the identity of the principal, extra capability arguments passed to the validation functions, and possibly user replies to dialog boxes. A typical example is the Java `SecurityManager` class, which determines the identity of the principal by inspection of the call stack [43]. For simplicity, we still write $OK_t$ as a function of the value of its argument.

The evaluation rule for $OK_t$ assumes of course that membership in $PV(t)$ is decidable. This raises obvious difficulties if $t$ stands for a function type, at least if the domain type is infinite. Difficulties for defining $PV(t)$ also arise if $t$ is a reference type: checking the current contents of the references offers no guarantees with respect to future modifications; checking the locations of the references against a fixed set of locations is very restrictive. For those reasons, we restrict ourselves to types $t$ that are defined as algebraic datatypes: type expressions obtained by combining base types with datatype constructors such as `list` or tuples, but not with **ref** nor the function arrow.

### 4.3 Type soundness

To relate the typing rules to the dynamic semantics, we define a semantic typing relation $S \models v : \tau$ saying whether the value $v$ is a semantically correct value for type $\tau$. The $S$ component is a store typing, associating types to store locations. We simultaneously extend the $\models$ relation to stores and store typings ($\models s : S$), and to evaluation environments and typing environments ($S \models e : E$). The definition of $\models$ is shown below, and is completely standard [39, 23].

- $S \models b : \iota$ if $Typeof(b) = \iota$
- $S \models v : t$ if $S \models v : TD(t)$
- $S \models \lambda x.a[e] : \tau_1 \to \tau_2$ if there exists a typing environment $E$ such that $S \models e : E$ and $E \vdash \lambda x.a : \tau_1 \to \tau_2$
- $S \models (v_1, v_2) : \tau_1 \times \tau_2$ if $S \models v_1 : \tau_1$ and $S \models v_2 : \tau_2$
- $S \models \ell : \tau$ **ref** if $\tau = S(\ell)$
- $S \models e : E$ if $\text{Dom}(e) = \text{Dom}(E)$ and for all $x \in \text{Dom}(e)$, $S \models e(x) : E(x)$
- $\models s : S$ if $\text{Dom}(s) = \text{Dom}(S)$ and for all $\ell \in \text{Dom}(s)$, $S \models s(\ell) : S(\ell)$.

Using the semantic typing relations defined above, we then have the familiar strong soundness property below for the type system. We say that a store typing $S'$ extends another store typing $S$ if $\mathrm{Dom}(S') \supseteq \mathrm{Dom}(S)$, and for all $\ell \in \mathrm{Dom}(S)$, we have $S'(\ell) = S(\ell)$. Remark that semantic typing is stable under store extension: if $S \models v : \tau$ and $S'$ extends $S$, we also have $S' \models v : \tau$.

**Lemma 2 (Type soundness).** *Assume $E \vdash a : \tau$ and $\models s : S$ and $S \models e : E$. If $\varphi, e, s \vdash a \to v/s'$, then there exists a store typing $S'$ extending $S$ such that $S' \models v : \tau$ and $\models s' : S'$.*

*Proof.* The proof is a simple inductive argument on the evaluation derivation; see [23, Prop. 3.6] for details.

# 5 Type-based security properties

The type-based security properties we develop in this section are based on a common idea: assuming all sensitive references have types of the form $t$ ref, we instrument the functions composing the execution environment by inserting $OK_t$ run-time checks at certain program points, in order to prevent illegal writes to references of type $t$ ref. The applets themselves are not instrumented, of course, since their source code is generally unavailable. All we know about the applet is that it is well typed in a given typing environment and set of type definitions. It is the combination of this well-typing with the instrumented environment functions that guarantees security.

To illustrate the three instrumentation schemes proposed below, we use pictures in the style of Fig. 4 showing the flow of values between the applet and its execution environment. We focus on values of a named type $t$ whose implementation type is $\tau = TD(t)$. The goal of our instrumentation schemes is to make sure that only checked values of type $t$ (solid arrows in the pictures) can reach an assignment on a $t$ ref performed by the execution environment.

## 5.1 Instrumentation of writes and procedural abstraction

The first transformation we consider inserts an $OK_t$ check before any write to a reference of type $t$ ref with $t \in \mathrm{Dom}(PV)$. This way, we are certain that if a sensitive reference has type $t$ ref, the environment functions will always store in it values that belong to $PV(t)$. See Fig. 5 for a graphical illustration. Formally, we define the instrumentation scheme $IW$, operating on terms $a^\tau$ annotated with their type $\tau$, as follows:

$$IW((a^{t\ \mathrm{ref}} := b^t)^{\mathrm{unit}}) = IW(a^{t\ \mathrm{ref}}) := OK_t(IW(b^t)) \quad \text{if } t \in \mathrm{Dom}(PV)$$

On other kinds of terms, $IW$ is a simple morphism, e.g. $IW((\lambda x.a^\tau)^{\sigma \to \tau}) = \lambda x.IW(a^\tau)$, etc.

It is easy to show that write errors cannot happen inside instrumented terms. Given the permitted values $PV$ and a store typing $S$, we define $Prot(PV, S)$ as

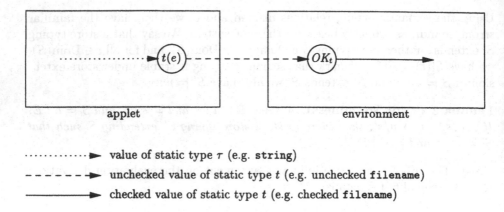

value of static type $\tau$ (e.g. **string**)

unchecked value of static type $t$ (e.g. unchecked **filename**)

checked value of static type $t$ (e.g. checked **filename**)

**Fig. 4.** Flow of values between the applet and its environment

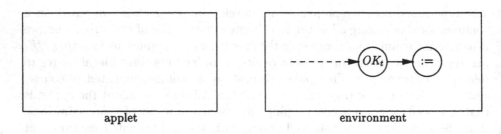

**Fig. 5.** Instrumentation of writes and procedural abstraction

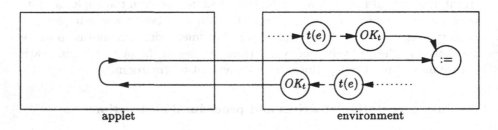

**Fig. 6.** Instrumentation of coercions and type abstraction

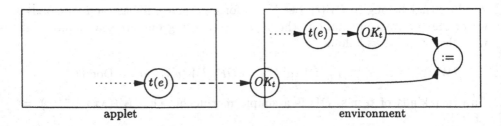

**Fig. 7.** Instrumenting coercions without type abstraction

the store control that restricts references of type $t$ ref, $t \in \text{Dom}(PV)$ to values in $PV(t)$, and allows arbitrary writes to other references: $Prot(PV,S)(\ell) = PV(t)$ if $S(\ell) = t$ and $t \in \text{Dom}(PV)$, and $Prot(PV,S)(\ell)$ is undefined otherwise.

**Lemma 3.** *Assume* $E \vdash (a^{\tau\ \text{ref}} := b^\tau) : \text{unit}$ *and* $S \models e : E$ *and* $\models s : S$. *Define* $\varphi = Prot(PV,S)$. *If* $\varphi, e, s \vdash IW(a^{\tau\ \text{ref}}) \not\to \text{err}$ *and* $\varphi, e, s \vdash IW(b^\tau) \not\to \text{err}$, *then* $\varphi, e, s \vdash IW(a^{\tau\ \text{ref}} := b^\tau) \not\to \text{err}$.

*Proof.* If $\tau = t$ for some named type $t \in \text{Dom}(PV)$, then by definition of the instrumentation scheme, the right-hand side of the assignment is of the form $OK_t(b')$ for some $b'$, which can only evaluate to an element of $PV(t)$ by rule 23. Hence, the assignment is valid with respect to $Prot(PV,S)$. If $\tau$ is not a $t$ type or is outside $\text{Dom}(PV)$, by Lemma 2, $IW(a)$ evaluates to a location $\ell$ which does not have a type of the form $t$ ref, $t \in \text{Dom}(PV)$, and therefore such that $Prot(PV,S)(\ell)$ is undefined; hence, no write error occurs either.

Lemma 3 only provides half of the security property: it shows that writes in instrumented code are safe, but only the execution environment contains instrumented code; the applet code is not instrumented and could therefore perform illegal writes to sensitive locations, if it could access those locations. In other terms, we must make sure that all sensitive locations are encapsulated inside functions, as in section 3.2. To this end, we will restrict the type $E_{api}$ of the applet's execution environment $e_{api}$ to ensure that sensitive references cannot "leak" into the applet, and be assigned illegal values there. There are several ways by which a sensitive reference of type $t$ ref could leak into an applet:

- The reference is exported directly in the environment, e.g. $E_{api}(x) = t$ ref or $E_{api}(x) = \text{int} \times (t\ \text{ref})$.
- The reference is returned by one of the functions of the environment, e.g. $E_{api}(f) = \text{int} \to t$ ref.
- The environment contains a higher-order function such as $E_{api}(h) = (t\ \text{ref} \to \text{int}) \to \text{int}$. The applet could get access to a sensitive reference if $h$ passes one to its functional argument, which can be provided by the applet.
- The environment contains a function taking as argument an applet-provided reference to a $t$ ref, e.g. $E_{api}(f) = t\ \text{ref ref} \to \text{unit}$. The environment function $f$ could then store a sensitive location into that $t$ ref ref, from which the applet can recover the sensitive location later.

We rule out all these cases by simply requiring that no type $t$ ref occurs (at any depth) in $E_{api}$. This leads to the following security property:

**Security property 2** *Assume* $S \models e_{api} : E_{api}$ *and* $\models s : S$. *Further assume that* $E_{api}$ *contains no occurrence of* $t$ ref *for any* $t$, *and that all function closures in* $e$ *and* $s$ *have been instrumented with the IW scheme (that is, $e$ and $s$ are obtained by evaluating source terms instrumented with IW). Then, for every applet $a$ well-typed in $E$, we have* $Prot(PV,S), s, e \vdash a \not\to \text{err}$.

*Proof.* We consider all assignments to references that occur in the evaluation derivation for $a$. By Lemma 3, assignments performed by environment functions cannot cause a write error, since the right-hand side has been instrumented by $IW$. For assignments performed by the applet, we use a containment lemma developed in appendix A to show that the reference being assigned cannot belong to $\text{Dom}(Prot(PV, S))$. More precisely, we apply the results of appendix A with $T$ being the set of all type expressions where $t$ ref occurs, $L_{app}$ being the set of locations with types in $T$ allocated by the applet, and $L_{env}$ being the set of locations with types in $T$ allocated by environment functions or initially present in $e_{api}$. The containment lemma (Lemma 7) then shows that the location being assigned does not belong to $L_{env}$. Moreover, by construction of $Prot$ and $L_{env}$, we have $\text{Dom}(Prot(PV, S)) \subseteq L_{env}$. Thus, assignments performed by the applet do not cause write violations either. Hence, the applet cannot evaluate to **err**.

The requirement that no $t$ ref occurs in $E_{api}$ is clearly too strong: nothing wrong could happen if, for instance, one of the environment functions has type $t$ ref $\rightarrow$ unit (the $t$ ref argument is provided by the applet). We conjecture that it suffices to require that no type $t$ ref occurs in $E_{app}$ at a positive occurrence or under a **ref** constructor. However, our proof of Property 2, and in particular the crucial containment lemma, does not extend to this weaker hypothesis.

## 5.2 Instrumentation of coercions and type abstraction

Instead of putting run-time checks on writes to references of type $t$ ref, we can ensure that all values of type $t \in \text{Dom}(PV)$ that flow through the applet's execution environment always belong to $PV(t)$. This way, values stored in a $t$ ref will automatically satisfy $PV(t)$ as well. This is achieved by adding checks to all creations of values of type $t \in \text{Dom}(PV)$ in the execution environment, i.e. to coercions of the form $t(a)$, following the instrumentation scheme $IC$ below:

$$IC(t(a)) = OK_t(t(IC(a))) \quad \text{if } t \in \text{Dom}(PV)$$

Of course, this is not enough: the applet could forge unchecked values of type $t$, by direct coercion from $t$'s implementation type, and pass them to environment functions. Hence, we also need to make the types $t \in \text{Dom}(PV)$ abstract in the applet, by type-checking it with a set of type definitions $TD'$ obtained from $TD$ by removing the definitions of the types $t \in \text{Dom}(PV)$. Then, for any $t \in \text{Dom}(PV)$, the only values of type $t$ that can be manipulated by the applet have been created and checked by the environment. This is depicted in Fig. 6.

To capture the run-time behavior of instrumented terms, we introduce a variant of the semantic typing predicate, written $PV, S \models v : \tau$, which is similar to the predicate $S \models v : \tau$ from section 4.3, with the difference that a value $v$ belongs to a named type $t$ only if $v \in PV(t)$ in addition to $v$ belonging to the definition $TD(t)$ of $t$:

- $PV, S \models b : \iota$ if $Typeof(b) = \iota$
- $PV, S \models v : t$ if $PV, S \models v : TD(t)$ and $t \in \text{Dom}(PV)$ implies $v \in PV(t)$

- $PV, S \models \lambda x.a[e] : \tau_1 \to \tau_2$ if there exists a typing environment $E$ such that $PV, S \models e : E$ and $E \vdash \lambda x.a : \tau_1 \to \tau_2$
- $PV, S \models (v_1, v_2) : \tau_1 \times \tau_2$ if $PV, S \models v_1 : \tau_1$ and $PV, S \models v_2 : \tau_2$
- $PV, S \models \ell : \tau$ **ref** if $\tau = S(\ell)$
- $PV, S \models e : E$ if $\mathrm{Dom}(e) = \mathrm{Dom}(E)$ and for all $x \in \mathrm{Dom}(e)$, $PV, S \models e(x) : E(x)$
- $PV \models s : S$ if $\mathrm{Dom}(s) = \mathrm{Dom}(S)$ and for all $\ell \in \mathrm{Dom}(s)$, $PV, S \models s(\ell) : S(\ell)$.

We then have the following characterization of the the behavior of terms instrumented with $IC$:

**Lemma 4.** *Assume $E \vdash a : \tau$ and $PV, S \models e : E$ and $PV \models s : S$. Further assume that all closures contained in $e$ and $s$ have function bodies instrumented with $IC$. If $Prot(PV, S), e, s \vdash IC(a) \to r$, then $r \neq$ err; instead, $r$ is of the form $v/s'$, and there exists a store typing $S'$ extending $S$ such that $PV, S' \models v : \tau$ and $PV \models s' : S'$.*

Compared with Lemma 2, we now use the more restrictive interpretation of named types $PV$, and require that all terms occurring in the evaluation derivation have been instrumented with $IC$. The proof is essentially identical to that of Lemma 2.

Notice that an applet $a$ well-typed within the restricted set $TD'$ of type definitions contains no coercions $t(a)$ for any $t \in \mathrm{Dom}(PV)$, hence is equal to $IC(a)$. Thus, Lemma 4 applies not only to the terms from the execution environment, but also to the applet itself. In a sense, this lemma can be viewed as a parametricity result, in that it shows soundness for arbitrary interpretations $PV$ of the types left abstract in $TD'$. From this remark, we immediately obtain the following security property:

**Security property 3** *Let $e$ be the execution environment for applets, and $s$ the initial store. Assume that all function closures in $e$ and $s$ have been instrumented with the $IC$ scheme (that is, $e$ and $s$ are obtained by evaluating source terms instrumented with $IC$). Assume $PV \models s : S$ and $PV, S \models e : E$. Then, for every applet $a$ well-typed in $E$ and in the restricted set $TD'$ of type definitions, we have $Prot(PV, S), s, e \vdash a \not\to$ err.*

Property 3 can be viewed as a formal justification for capability-based systems: by making the type of capabilities abstract to the applets, run-time security checks are necessary only at points where new capabilities are constructed and returned to the applet; capabilities presented by the applet can then be trusted without further checks.

Unlike Property 2, Property 3 does not require that types $t$ **ref** do not occur in the typing environment $E$. Indeed, once $t$ is made abstract, it is perfectly safe to make references of type $t$ **ref** accessible to the applet: the applet can then write to them, but only write safe values of type $t$. Hence, sensitive references no longer need to be systematically wrapped inside functions. As Reynolds points out [34], type abstraction and procedural abstraction are two orthogonal ways to protect data.

Another advantage of the approach described in this section over the instrumentation of writes described in section 5.1 is that it often leads to fewer run-time checks. In particular, checks at coercions can sometimes be proven redundant and therefore can be eliminated. Consider the following function that adds a .old suffix to a file name:

$$\lambda\mathtt{f}.\,OK_{\mathtt{filename}}(\mathtt{filename}(\mathtt{concat}(\mathtt{string}(\mathtt{f}),\texttt{".old"})))$$

With the definition of $PV(\mathtt{filename})$ given in section 4.2, it is easy to show that if $f$ belongs to $PV(\mathtt{filename})$, then so does the concatenation of $f$ and .old. Hence, the $OK$ test can be removed.

Of course, not all run-time tests can be removed this way: consider what happens if the suffix is given as argument:

$$\lambda\mathtt{f}.\,\lambda\mathtt{s}.\,OK_{\mathtt{filename}}(\mathtt{filename}(\mathtt{concat}(\mathtt{string}(\mathtt{f}),\mathtt{s})))$$

and the applet passes a suffix s starting with "../".

## 5.3 Instrumenting coercions without type abstraction

In some cases, the types $t \in \mathrm{Dom}(PV)$ cannot be made abstract in the applet, e.g. because it would make writing the applet too inconvenient, or entail too much run-time overhead. We can adapt the approach presented in section 5.2 to these cases, by reverting to procedural abstraction and putting checks not only at coercions, but also on all values of types $t \in \mathrm{Dom}(PV)$ that come from the applet. (This matches current practice in Unix kernels, where parameters to system calls are always checked for validity on entrance to the system call.) Figure 7 depicts this approach.

The checking of values coming from the applet is achieved by a standard wrapping scheme applied to all functions of the execution environment, inserting $OK_t$ coercions at all negative occurrences of types $t \in \mathrm{Dom}(PV)$. For instance, if the execution environment needs to export a function $f : t \to t$, it will actually export the function $\lambda x.f(OK_t(x))$, which validates its argument before passing it to the original function.

We formalize these ideas in a slightly different way, in order to build upon the results of section 5.2. Start from an applet environment defined by top-level bindings of the form

$$\mathtt{let}\ f_i : \tau_i = a_i$$

We assume given a set $TD'$ of type definitions against which the $a_i$ and the applets are type-checked, and a valuation $PV'$ assigning permitted values to named types in $TD'$.

We first associate a new named type $\hat{t}$ to each sensitive type $t \in \mathrm{Dom}(PV')$. The type $\hat{t}$ is defined as synonymous with $t$, and is intended to represent those values of type $t$ that have passed run-time validation. We define the $\hat{t}$ types by taking

$$TD = TD' \oplus [\hat{t} \mapsto t \mid t \in \text{Dom}(PV')]$$

and restrict the values they can take using the valuation $PV$ defined by $PV(\hat{t}) = PV'(t)$ and $PV$ undefined on other types.

Let $\Sigma$ be the substitution $\{t \leftarrow \hat{t} \mid t \in \text{Dom}(PV')\}$. We transform the bindings for the applet environment as follows:

$$\texttt{let } f_i : \tau_i = W^+(IC(\Sigma(a_i)) : \tau_i)$$

That is, we rewrite the terms $a_i$ to use the type $\hat{t}$ instead of $t$ for all $t \in \text{Dom}(PV')$; then apply the $IC$ instrumentation scheme to it, thus adding an $OK_{\hat{t}}$ check to each coercion $\hat{t}(a)$; finally, apply the $W^+$ wrapping scheme to the instrumented term, in order to perform both validation and coercion from $t$ to $\hat{t}$ on entrance, and the reverse coercion from $\hat{t}$ to $t$ on exit. Wrapping is directed by the expected type for its result, and is contravariant with respect to function types. We thus define both a wrapping scheme $W^+$ for positive occurrences of types and another $W^-$ for negative occurrences.

$$W^+(a : \iota) = W^-(a : \iota) = a$$
$$W^+(a : t) = t(a) \quad \text{if } t \in \text{Dom}(PV)$$
$$W^-(a : t) = OK_{\hat{t}}(\hat{t}(a)) \quad \text{if } t \in \text{Dom}(PV)$$
$$W^+(a : t) = W^-(a : t) = a \quad \text{if } t \notin \text{Dom}(PV)$$
$$W^+(a : \tau_1 \times \tau_2) = (W^+(\texttt{fst}(a) : \tau_1), W^+(\texttt{snd}(a) : \tau_2)$$
$$W^-(a : \tau_1 \times \tau_2) = (W^-(\texttt{fst}(a) : \tau_1), W^-(\texttt{snd}(a) : \tau_2)$$
$$W^+(a : \tau_1 \to \tau_2) = \lambda x.W^+(a(W^-(x : \tau_1)) : \tau_2)$$
$$W^-(a : \tau_1 \to \tau_2) = \lambda x.W^-(a(W^+(x : \tau_1)) : \tau_2)$$
$$W^+(a : \tau \texttt{ ref}) = W^-(a : \tau \texttt{ ref}) = a$$
$$\text{if no } t \in \text{Dom}(PV) \text{ occurs in } \tau$$

Wrapping is not defined on reference types containing a $t \in \text{Dom}(PV)$ because there is no way to validate these references so that they are protected against future modifications.

It is easy to see that the transformed bindings are well-typed: $\Sigma(a_i)$ has type $\Sigma(\tau_i)$; the $IC$ instrumentation preserves typing; the $W^+$ wrapping applied to a term of type $\Sigma(\tau_i)$ returns a term of type $\tau_i$, as shown by a simple induction over $\tau_i$.

Moreover, the right-hand sides of the bindings always perform an $OK_{\hat{t}}$ check before each coercion to a type $\hat{t}$: this is ensured by the $IC$ instrumentation for the coercions initially in $\Sigma(a_i)$, and by definition of the wrapping scheme for the coercions introduced by the wrapping.

Finally, the applets themselves are still type-checked in the original set $TD'$ of type definitions, in which the types $\hat{t}$ are not defined, and thus abstract for the applet.

We are therefore back to the situation studied in section 5.2: the types $\hat{t}$ are abstract in the applets and all coercions to $\hat{t}$ are instrumented in the applet environment. Thus, by Property 3, we obtain that the values of references with types $\hat{t}$ ref always remain within $PV(\hat{t}) = PV'(t)$ during the execution of any well-typed applet.

**Security property 4** *Let $e$ be the execution environment for applets and $s$ the initial store. Assume that $e$ and $s$ are obtained by evaluating a set of transformed bindings let $f_i : \tau_i = W^+(IC(\Sigma(a_i)) : \tau_i)$ as described above. Assume $PV \models s : S$ and $PV, S \models e : E$. Then, for every applet $a$ well-typed in $E$ and in the initial set $TD'$ of type definitions, we have $Prot(PV, S), s, e \vdash a \not\rightarrow$ err.*

# 6 Connections with object-oriented languages

Although the language used for this work is functional, the techniques developed here translate reasonably well to object-oriented languages. Procedural abstraction as presented in section 3.2 corresponds most closely to Smalltalk-style private instance variables: just as variables in a closure environment can only be accessed by the code associated with that closure, private instance variables of a Smalltalk object can only be accessed by the methods of that object. Java does not offer a strictly equivalent mechanism: the `private` modifier makes instance variables accessible not only to the methods of the object, but also to methods of other objects of the same class. Still, the visibility rules associated with the package mechanism and the `private` and `protected` modifiers also ensure some degree of procedural abstraction, since they restrict the set of methods that can access a given instance variable.

Similarly, type abstraction as exploited in section 5.3 corresponds most closely to `final` classes in Java. A `final` class containing only `private` fields and no default constructors offers the same level of guarantees as our abstract types: the applet cannot tamper with the fields of an existing object, nor create an object with arbitrary initial values for the fields. In non-`final` classes, the visibility rules might still ensure some degree of type abstraction, though it is unclear how much is guaranteed. Subtype polymorphism in systems such as $F_{<:}$ [11] also provide some amount of type abstraction, but this is not so in Java because the actual type of an object can be tested at run-time (downcasts).

# 7 Application: safety in the MMM browser

MMM [35] is a Web browser with applets developed by the second author. MMM ensures safe execution of applets using various techniques similar in spirit to those formulated earlier in this paper. (Essentially identical techniques are now used in the SwitchWare project at U. Penn [4,5], an active network infrastructure that allows safe downloading of applets on network routers.) Indeed, the formalization presented in this paper grew out of a desire to make more systematic and prove correct the security techniques used in MMM. This section presents the main techniques used in the MMM safe execution environment for applets, and relates them with the formal results we have obtained in this paper.

## 7.1 Type-safe dynamic linking

The MMM browser is written in Objective Caml [24] and compiled to bytecode by the Caml bytecode compiler. The bytecode is then executed by the Caml virtual machine. Applets are also compiled to Caml bytecode, then loaded in memory and linked with the browser by the Caml dynamic linker (the Dynlink library).

The dynamic linker can be configured to restrict the set of external modules and C primitives that the object file can reference. MMM uses this feature to enforce lexical scoping for applets: only the modules of MMM that comprise the applet execution environment can be referenced by the applet object code; modules internal to MMM are not made accessible to the applet.

The Caml bytecode was designed before applets were fashionable, and is therefore ill-suited to JVM-style bytecode verification. In particular, a number of low-level optimizations are performed in this bytecode (such as erasing type annotations and conflating several high-level types into the same machine-level representations) that makes type reconstruction on bytecode if not impossible, but at least very difficult.

Instead of bytecode verification, the Objective Caml dynamic linker relies on type annotations on the relocation information contained in object files to guarantee type correctness. Bytecode object files contain a list of names of external modules referenced in the file, along with the type interfaces of those modules. The object file thus records which interfaces for those external modules were used for type-checking the source code of the file. The dynamic linker, then, checks that those interfaces are identical to those of the implementations of those modules provided by the MMM browser. This ensures that the applet and the browser have been type-checked against the same type specifications for the applet-browser interface, and can therefore safely be linked together.

To keep them small, object files actually do not contain the whole Caml type interfaces for their imported modules, but only MD5 checksums of those interfaces. The dynamic linker then compares interfaces by comparing their checksums. Since MD5 is a hash function of cryptographic quality, the probability that two different interfaces have the same checksum is extremely low, and thus we can safely assume that if the checksums are equal, then so are the interfaces. However, this approach forces the two interfaces (the one expected by the object file and the one provided by the MMMimplementation) to be exactly identical, while, if we kept whole interfaces, we could use a more lenient comparison such as Caml's interface matching. The latter would allow more flexibility in evolving the applet-browser API.

Of course, comparing import interfaces at link-time guarantees type safety only if the object code contained in the object file is indeed type-correct with respect to the interfaces contained in the object file. Thus, we need to make sure that this object file has been produced by a correct Caml compiler (a compiler that performs sound static type-checking and records correctly all external modules referenced) and has not been modified afterwards (e.g. by hand-modifying some of the interfaces in the object file). This can be enforced in two ways in the context of Web applets.

The first way is to transmit applets over the network as Caml source code, which is type-checked and compiled locally (by calling the Objective Caml bytecode compiler), then dynamically linked inside the browser. Unless the local host is compromised, no tampering with the object files nor the Caml type-checker itself can happen. Unlike applet systems based on source-level interpretation, we still benefit from the efficiency of the Caml bytecode interpreter.

Transmission of applets in source form is often criticized on several grounds: the source code is larger than compiled bytecode; local compilation takes too much time; applet writers do not want to publicize their source. Our experience with Caml is that bytecode object files are about the same size as the source code (unless heavily commented); the bytecode compiler is very fast and the compilation times are small compared with Internet latencies; finally, bytecode is easy to decompile and does not offer significant protection against reverse engineering.

Another way to ensure the correctness of type annotations in bytecode object files is to rely on a cryptographic signature on the object file, which is checked locally by the MMM browser against a list of trusted signers before linking the object file in memory. Unlike Microsoft-style applet signing, this signature is not necessarily made by the author of the applet, and carries no guarantees on what the applet actually does; instead, the signature is made by the person or site who performs the compilation and type-checking of the applet, and certifies only that the applet passed type-checking by an unmodified Caml compiler and that its object file has not been tampered since.

We initially envisioned having some centralized type-checking authority: one or several reputable sites (such as INRIA) that accept source code from applet developers, type-check and compile them locally, sign the object file and return it to the applet developer. The object file can then be made available on the Web. Seeing the authority's signature, browsers can trust the type information contained in the object file and use it to validate the applet against the environment they provide. In retrospect, this approach relies too much on a centralized authority to scale up to the world-wide Web. However, it is perfectly suited to the distribution of compiled applets across a restricted network such as a corporate Intranet.

## 7.2 The execution environment for applets

The execution environment made available to applets is composed of a number of modules that provide a safe subset of the Caml standard library, as well as access to the CamlTk graphical user interface and to selected parts of the MMM browser internals. In particular, an MMM applet can not only interact graphically with the user and trigger navigation functions, like Java applets, but also extend the MMM browser itself by installing new navigation functions, menu items, viewers for new types of embedded documents, display functions for new HTML tags, and decoding functions for new "content-encoding" types.

The applet environment is derived from the OCaml standard library modules and the MMM implementation modules by two major techniques: hiding of unsafe functions via module thinning, and wrapping of unsafe functions with capability checks.

**Module thinning:** The ML module system offers the ability to take a restricted view of an existing module via a signature constraint:

```
module RestrM = (M : RestrSig)
```

Only those components of M that are mentioned in the signature RestrSig are visible in RestrM, and they have the types specified in RestrSig, which may be less precise (more abstract) than their original types in M. This module thinning mechanism thus supports both hiding components (functions, variables, types, exceptions, sub-modules) of a module and making some type components abstract. No code duplication occurs during thinning: the functions in RestrM share their code with the corresponding functions in M.

Large parts of the applet environment are obtained by thinning existing OCaml library modules. In the OCaml standard library, we hide by thinning all file input-output functions, as well as related system interface functions (such as reading environment variables and executing shell commands), and of course all type-unsafe operations (such as array accesses without bound checks and functions that operate on the low-level representation of data structures). For good measure, we also make abstract a few data types such as lexer buffers to hide their internal structure.

In the CamlTk GUI toolkit, we hide all functions that return widgets that may belong to the browser or to other applets. Such functions include finding the parent of a widget, finding a widget by its name, finding which widget owns the focus or the selection, etc. This is less restrictive than checking that widgets manipulated by the applet are children of its top-level widget: the applet can still open new windows and populate them with widgets unrelated with its initial top-level widget. Other functions that might affect browser widgets (such as binding events on all widgets of a given class or tag) are also removed.

**Capabilities:** MMM uses capabilities to control potentially harmful functionalities, such as file and network input/output, as well as extending the browser. Individual capabilities include:

- Reading files whose names match a given regular expression.
- Writing files whose names match a given regular expression.
- Accessing the contents of Web documents (e.g. the pages being displayed).
- Installing extension functions in the browser.

Applets are given an initial set of capabilities at load time, which is empty for applets loaded through the network, but allows document access and browser extension for applets loaded from the local disk. Capabilities are of course represented by an abstract data type, to prevent an applet from forging extra capabilities.

All input/output operations as well as registration of browser extensions check the capabilities presented by the applet. If the applet does not possess the capability to perform the requested operation, the browser prompts the user via a pop-up window. The user can then refuse the operation (aborting the execution of the applet), grant permission for this particular operation, or grant permission for further operations of the same kind as well. In the latter case, the browser extends in place the capabilities of the applet. To minimize the number of times the user is prompted, an applet can also request in advance the capabilities it needs later.

**Hiding capability arguments:** A well-known problem with capability-based security for applets is that all sensitive functions require an extra capability argument [42]. This clutters the source code for the applet and makes it difficult to convert a piece of stand-alone code into an applet: capability arguments must be added at many different places in the source code.

In functional languages, partial application can be used to pass the capability argument only once per sensitive function. Assume defined the functions open_in_cap : capability → string → in_channel and open_out_cap : capability → string → out_channel as capability-checking variants of the normal file opening functions open_in : string → in_channel and open_out : string → out_channel. Then, an applet can begin with the following definitions:

```
let mycapa = Capabilities.get()
let open_in = open_in_capa mycapa
let open_out = open_out_capa mycapa
... code using open_in and open_out as usual...
```

The remainder of the applet can then use the functions open_in and open_out thus obtained by partial application as if they were the normal file opening functions.

MMM makes this approach more convenient by using ML functors to perform the partial applications. Functors are parameterized modules, presented as functions from modules to modules. They provide a convenient mechanism for parameterization *en masse*: rather than partially applying $n$ functions to $m$ parameters, a structure containing the $m$ parameters is passed once to a functor that return a structure containing the $n$ functions already partially applied to the parameters. In the case of MMM, we thus have a number of functors that take the applet's capability as argument and return structures defining capability-enabled variants of the standard I/O and browser interface functions, with the same interface as for standalone programs. For instance, to perform file I/O, an MMM applet does the following:

```
module MyCapa =
struct
    let capabilities = Capabilities.get()
end
module IO = Safeio(MyCapa)
open IO
... code using open_in and other I/O operations as usual...
```

## 7.3 Assessment

The MMM security architecture relies heavily on the three basic ingredients that we considered in our formalization:

- Lexical scoping ensures that applets cannot access all the modules composing the browser and the Caml standard library, but only those "safe" modules made available to the applet during linking.
- Type abstraction prevents the applet from forging or tampering with its capability list. It also ensures that the applet cannot forge file descriptors or GUI widgets, but has to go through the safe libraries to create them.
- Procedural abstraction is used systematically to wrap sensitive functions (such as opening files or network connections, as well as installing a browser extension) with capability checks.

In particular, capability checks inside environment functions are placed essentially as suggested by the wrapping scheme $W^+$ of section 5.3. In the MMM implementation, those capability checks were placed by hand and the same type was used for checked and unchecked data, instead of exploiting two different types as in section 5.3. One of the motivations for our formalization was to systematize the placement of those capability checks, based on typing information.

Some aspects of the MMM security architecture are not accounted for by our formalism. The first one is the necessity of taking copies of mutable objects before validating them. A prime example is character strings, which, in Caml, can be modified in place like character arrays. An applet could pass a string containing a valid file name to the file opening function, then modify the string in place between the time it is validated and the time the file is actually opened. This concurrent modification can be achieved via multiple threads or via GUI callback functions.

To avoid this attack, the execution environment must first take private copies of all strings provided by the applet, then validate and utilize the private copies of those strings. Symmetrically, the execution environment must not return strings shared with its internal data structures to the applet, but copies of those strings. Inserting those string copy operations is tedious and error-prone. ¿From the standpoint of applet security, it would be much better to have immutable strings in the language. The guarantees offered by immutable strings could possibly be achieved just by removing all string modification primitives from the applet execution environment, but we have not investigated this approach yet.

Another issue not addressed by our framework is validation of functional values, such as document decoders and HTML tag handling functions installed by the applet. The main reason our framework does not handle function validation is that membership of a functional value in a set $PV(t)$ is in general undecidable. In the particular case of MMM, this problem does not arise: depending on the capabilities given to the applet, either all functions presented by the applet are rejected, or they are all accepted. For more complex situations, we could also move the validation inside the applet-provided function, by wrapping this function with checks on its inputs or outputs.

Resources that can be explicitly deallocated and reassigned later raise interesting problems. A prime example is Unix file descriptors, which are small integers. The type of file descriptors is abstract, and an applet cannot forge a file descriptor itself. However, it could open a file descriptor on a permitted file, close it immediately, keep the abstract value representing the descriptor, and wait until the browser opens a file or network connection and receives the same file descriptor in return. Then, the applet can do input/output directly on the file descriptor, thus accessing unauthorized files or network connections. This "reuse" attack is of course possible only with explicitly-deallocated resources: with implicit deallocation, the resources cannot be deallocated and reallocated as long as the applet keeps a handle on the resource. MMM addresses this problem by wrapping Unix file descriptors in an opaque data structure containing a "valid" bit that is set to false when the file descriptor is closed, and checked before every input/output operations.

The last MMM security feature not addressed by our framework is confidentiality. Our framework focuses on ensuring the integrity of the browser and of the host machine. The MMM applet environment contains security restrictions to ensure integrity (such as controlled write access to files), but also restrictions intended to protect the confidentiality of user data (such as controlled read accesses to files and restricted access to the network). Some restrictions address both integrity and confidentiality problems: for instance, a malicious document decoder could both distort the document as displayed by the browser (an integrity threat) and leak confidential information contained in the document to a third party (a confidentiality threat).

However, the confidentiality policy enforced by the MMM applet environment is simple and does not go beyond traditional access control. While the formal framework presented in this paper focuses on integrity via access control on writes, we believe that parts of this framework (procedural encapsulation and type abstraction) can be extended to deal with access control on reads, thus ensuring simple confidentiality properties adequate for MMM. More advanced confidentiality policies (such as allowing an applet to read local files or open network connections, but not both) are definitely beyond the scope of our framework, however.

# 8 Related work

## 8.1 Type systems for security

The work most closely related to ours is the recent formulations of Denning's information flow approach to security [13, 14] as non-standard type systems by Palsberg and Ørbaek [31], Volpano and Smith [41, 40], and Heintze and Riecke [20]. (Abadi *et al.* [2] reformulate some of those type systems in terms of a more basic calculus of dependency.) The main points of comparison with our work are listed below.

**Information flow vs. integrity:** The type systems developed in previous works all focus on secrecy properties, following the information flow approach. In particular, they allow high-security data to be exposed as long as no low-security code uses this data. Our work focuses on more basic integrity properties via access control. We view those integrity guarantees as a prerequisite to establishing meaningful confidentiality properties.

**Imperative vs. purely functional programs:** [31] and [20] consider purely functional languages in the style of the $\lambda$-calculus. This makes formulating the security properties delicate: [31] proves no security property properly speaking, only a subject reduction property that shows the internal consistency of the calculus, but not its relevance to security; [20] does show a non-interference property (that the value of a low-security expression is independent of the values of high-security parameters), but it is not obvious how this result applies to actual applet/browser interactions, especially input/output. Instead, we have followed [41, 40] and formulated our security policy in terms of in-place modifications on a store, which provides a simple and intuitive notion of security violation.

**Run-time validation of data:** Only [31] and our work consider the possibility of checking low-security data at run-time and promoting them to high security. In [41, 40, 20], once some data is labeled "low security", it remains so throughout the program and causes all data it comes in contact with to be marked "low security" as well. We believe that, in a typical applet/browser interaction, this policy leads to rejecting almost all applets as insecure. Run-time validation of untrusted data is essential in practice to allow a reasonable range of applets to run.

**Subtyping vs. named types and coercions:** All previous works consider type systems with subtyping, which provides a good match for the flow analysis approach they follow [30]. In contrast, we only use type synonyms with possibly checked coercions between a named type and its implementation type. However, the connections between subtyping and explicit coercions are well known [9], and we do not think this makes a major difference.

## 8.2 Security of applets

Concerning the security issues raised by applets in general, we are aware of case studies of security flaws [12], as well as informal descriptions of current and proposed security architectures for applets [16, 44, 35, 42, 18]. Our work seems to be one of the first formal studies of applet security.

On the Java side, considerable effort has been expended in proving the soundness of the Java type system [15, 37, 29] and of the JVM bytecode verifier [33, 36, 17]. Other aspects of Java that are equally important for security, such as formalizing the visibility rules and the encapsulation guarantees they provide, have only recently started to receive attention [22]. We are not aware of any formal description of security policies for Java applets.

Proof-carrying code [28, 27] provides an elegant framework to establish the safety of mobile code, but requires general proof from the applet's developer. Our approach lies at the other end of the complexity spectrum: all we require from the applet is that it is well typed in a simple, standard type system.

## 9 Concluding remarks

We have identified three basic techniques for enforcing a fairly realistic security policy for applets: lexical scoping, procedural abstraction, and type abstraction. These programming techniques are of course well known, but we believe that this work is the first to characterize precisely their implications for program security.

The techniques proposed here seem to match relatively well current practice in the area of Web applets. In particular, they account fairly well for Rouaix's implementation of safe libraries in the MMM browser.

Our techniques put almost no constraints on the applets, except being well-typed in a simple, completely standard type system. The security effort is concentrated on the execution environment provided by the browser. Typing the applets in a richer type system, such as the type systems for information flow of [31, 41, 40, 20] or the effect and region system of [38], could provide more information on the behavior of the applet and enable more flexible security policies in the execution environment. However, it is impractical to rely on rich type systems for applets, because these type systems are not likely to be widely accepted by applet developers. Whether these rich type systems can be applied to the execution environment only, while still using a standard type system for the applets, is an interesting open question.

On the technical side, the proofs of the type-based security properties are variants of usual type soundness proofs. It would be interesting to investigate the security content of other classical semantic results such as representation independence and logical relations. Given the importance of communications between the applet and its environment, it could be worthwhile to reformulate our security results for a calculus of communicating processes [6, 3, 1].

## Acknowledgements

This work has been partially supported by GIE Dyade under the "Verified Internet Protocols" project. A preliminary version of this paper appeared in the proceedings of the 25th ACM symposium on Principles of Programming Languages.

# References

1. M. Abadi. Secrecy by typing in security protocols. In *Theoretical Aspects of Computer Software '97*, volume 1281 of *Lecture Notes in Computer Science*, pages 611–638. Springer-Verlag, Sept. 1997.
2. M. Abadi, A. Banerjee, N. Heintze, and J. G. Riecke. A core calculus of dependency. In *26th symposium Principles of Programming Languages*, pages 147–160. ACM Press, 1999.
3. M. Abadi and A. D. Gordon. Reasoning about cryptographic protocols in the Spi calculus. In *CONCUR'97: Concurrency Theory*, volume 1243 of *Lecture Notes in Computer Science*, pages 59–73. Springer-Verlag, July 1997.
4. D. S. Alexander, W. A. Arbaugh, M. W. Hicks, P. Kakkar, A. D. Keromytis, J. T. Moore, C. A. Gunter, S. M. Nettles, and J. M. Smith. The SwitchWare active network architecture. *IEEE Network*, 12(3):29–36, 1998.
5. D. S. Alexander, W. A. Arbaugh, A. D. Keromytis, and J. M. Smith. Security in active networks. In J. Vitek and C. Jensen, editors, *Secure Internet Programming*, Lecture Notes in Computer Science. Springer-Verlag Inc., New York, NY, USA, 1999.
6. J.-P. Banâtre and C. Bryce. A security proof system for networks of communicating processes. Research report 2042, INRIA, Sept. 1993.
7. J.-P. Billon. Security breaches in the JDK 1.1 beta2 security API. Dyade, `http://www.dyade.fr/fr/actions/VIP/SecHole.html`, Jan. 1997.
8. N. S. Borenstein. Email with a mind of its own: the Safe-Tcl language for enabled mail. In *IFIP International Working Conference on Upper Layer Protocols, Architectures and Applications*, 1994.
9. V. Breazu-Tannen, T. Coquand, C. A. Gunter, and A. Scedrov. Inheritance as implicit coercion. *Information and Computation*, 93(1):172–221, 1991.
10. K. Brunnstein. Hostile ActiveX control demonstrated. *RISKS Forum*, 18(82), Feb. 1997.
11. L. Cardelli, S. Martini, J. C. Mitchell, and A. Scedrov. An extension of system F with subtyping. *Information and Computation*, 109(1–2):4–56, 1994.
12. D. Dean, E. W. Felten, D. S. Wallach, and D. Balfanz. Java security: Web browsers and beyond. In D. E. Denning and P. J. Denning, editors, *Internet Besieged: Countering Cyberspace Scofflaws*, pages 241–269. ACM Press, 1997.
13. D. E. Denning. A lattice model of secure information flow. *Commun. ACM*, 19(5):236–242, 1976.
14. D. E. Denning and P. J. Denning. Certification of programs for secure information flow. *Commun. ACM*, 20(7):504–513, 1977.
15. S. Drossopoulou and S. Eisenbach. Java is type safe – probably. In *Proc. 11th European Conference on Object Oriented Programming*, volume 1241 of *Lecture Notes in Computer Science*, pages 389–418. Springer-Verlag, June 1997.
16. M. Erdos, B. Hartman, and M. Mueller. Security reference model for the Java Developer's Kit 1.0.2. JavaSoft, `http://java.sun.com/security/SRM.html`, Nov. 1996.
17. S. N. Freund and J. C. Mitchell. A type system for object initialization in the Java bytecode language. In *Object-Oriented Programming Systems, Languages and Applications 1998*, pages 310–327. ACM Press, 1998.

18. L. Gong. Java security architecture (JDK1.2). JavaSoft, http://java.sun.com/products/jdk/1.2/docs/guide/security/spec/security-spec.doc.html, Oct. 1998.

19. J. Gosling and H. McGilton. The Java language environment – a white paper. JavaSoft, http://java.sun.com/docs/white/langenv, May 1996.

20. N. Heintze and J. G. Riecke. The SLam calculus: programming with secrecy and integrity. In *25th symposium Principles of Programming Languages*, pages 365–377. ACM Press, 1998.

21. D. Hopwood. Java security bug (applets can load native methods). *RISKS Forum*, 17(83), Mar. 1996.

22. T. Jensen, D. Le Métayer, and T. Thorn. Security and dynamic class loading in Java: A formalisation. In *International Conference on Computer Languages 1998*, pages 4–15. IEEE Computer Society Press, 1998.

23. X. Leroy. Polymorphic typing of an algorithmic language. Research report 1778, INRIA, 1992.

24. X. Leroy, J. Vouillon, D. Doligez, et al. The Objective Caml system. Software and documentation available on the Web, http://caml.inria.fr/ocaml/, 1996.

25. R. Milner, M. Tofte, R. Harper, and D. MacQueen. *The definition of Standard ML (revised)*. The MIT Press, 1997.

26. G. Morrisett, M. Felleisen, and R. Harper. Abstract models of memory management. In *Functional Programming Languages and Computer Architecture 1995*, pages 66–77. ACM Press, 1995.

27. G. C. Necula. Proof-carrying code. In *24th symposium Principles of Programming Languages*, pages 106–119. ACM Press, 1997.

28. G. C. Necula and P. Lee. Safe kernel extensions without run-time checking. In *Proc. Symp. Operating Systems Design and Implementation*, pages 229–243. Usenix association, 1996.

29. T. Nipkow and D. von Oheimb. JavaLight is type-safe — definitely. In *25th symposium Principles of Programming Languages*, pages 161–170. ACM Press, 1998.

30. J. Palsberg and P. O'Keefe. A type system equivalent to flow analysis. *ACM Trans. Prog. Lang. Syst.*, 17(4):576–599, 1995.

31. J. Palsberg and P. Ørbaek. Trust in the λ-calculus. *Journal of Functional Programming*, 7(6):557–591, 1997.

32. G. D. Plotkin. A structural approach to operational semantics. Technical Report DAIMI FN-19, Aarhus University, 1981.

33. Z. Qian. A formal specification of a large subset of Java Virtual Machine instructions. In J. Alves-Foss, editor, *Formal Syntax and Semantics of Java*, Lecture Notes in Computer Science. Springer-Verlag, 1998. To appear.

34. J. C. Reynolds. User-defined types and procedural data structures as complementary approaches to data abstraction. In C. Gunter and J. Mitchell, editors, *Theoretical aspects of object-oriented programming*, pages 13–23. MIT Press, 1994.

35. F. Rouaix. A Web navigator with applets in Caml. In *Proceedings of the 5th International World Wide Web Conference, Computer Networks and Telecommunications Networking*, volume 28, pages 1365–1371. Elsevier, May 1996.

36. R. Stata and M. Abadi. A type system for Java bytecode subroutines. In *25th symposium Principles of Programming Languages*, pages 149–160. ACM Press, 1998.

37. D. Syme. Proving JavaS type soundness. Technical Report 427, University of Cambridge Computer Laboratory, June 1997.

38. J.-P. Talpin and P. Jouvelot. The type and effect discipline. *Information and Computation*, 111(2):245–296, 1994.

39. M. Tofte. Type inference for polymorphic references. *Information and Computation*, 89(1), 1990.

40. D. Volpano and G. Smith. A type-based approach to program security. In *Proceedings of TAPSOFT'97, Colloquium on Formal Approaches in Software Engineering*, volume 1214 of *Lecture Notes in Computer Science*, pages 607–621. Springer-Verlag, 1997.

41. D. Volpano, G. Smith, and C. Irvine. A sound type system for secure flow analysis. *Journal of Computer Security*, 4(3):1–21, 1996.

42. D. S. Wallach, D. Balfanz, D. Dean, and E. W. Felten. Extensible security architectures for Java. Technical report 546-97, Department of Computer Science, Princeton University, Apr. 1997.

43. D. S. Wallach and E. W. Felten. Understanding Java stack inspection. In *Proceedings of the 1998 IEEE Symposium on Security and Privacy*. IEEE Computer Society Press, 1998.

44. F. Yellin. Low level security in Java. In *Proceedings of the Fourth International World Wide Web Conference*, pages 369–379. O'Reilly, 1995.

# A    Appendix: the containment lemma

In this appendix, we formalize the intuition that if the type of the applet environment does not contain certain **ref** types, then references of those types cannot be exchanged between the applet and the environment, and remain "contained" in one of them.

We annotate each source-language term $a$ as coming either from the execution environment ($a_{env}$) or from the applet ($a_{app}$). We let $m, n$ range over the two "worlds" *env* and *app*, and write $\overline{m}$ for the complement of $m$, i.e. $\overline{env} = app$ and $\overline{app} = env$.

Let $T$ be a set of type expressions satisfying the following closure property: if $\tau \in T$, then all types $\tau'$ that contain $\tau$ as a sub-term also belong to $T$. (In section 5.1, we take $T$ to be the set of all types containing an occurrence of $t$ **ref**; in appendix B, $T$ is the set of all types containing an occurrence of any **ref** type). We partition the set of locations into three countable sets:

- $L_{app}$ is the set of locations with type $\tau$ **ref** $\in T$ that have been allocated by the applet;

- $L_{env}$ is the set of locations with type $\tau$ **ref** $\in T$ that have been allocated by the environment (i.e. either initially present in the applet environment, or allocated by environment functions);

- $L_{shared}$ is the set of locations whose type $\tau$ **ref** does not belong to $T$.

To ensure that locations allocated during evaluation are drawn from the correct set, we assume all source terms $a_m^\tau$ annotated with their static type $\tau$ and their world $m$ and replace the evaluation rule for reference creation (rule 8) by the following rule:

$$\varphi, e, s \vdash a_m^\tau \rightarrow v/s' \quad \ell \notin \mathrm{Dom}(s') \cup \mathrm{Dom}(\varphi)$$
$$\ell \in L_{env} \text{ if } \tau \text{ ref} \in T \text{ and } m = env$$
$$\ell \in L_{app} \text{ if } \tau \text{ ref} \in T \text{ and } m = app \qquad (8')$$
$$\ell \in L_{shared} \text{ if } \tau \text{ ref} \notin T$$

$$\overline{\varphi, e, s \vdash \mathbf{ref}(a)_m^{\tau\ \mathbf{ref}} \rightarrow \ell/s'\{\ell \leftarrow v\}}$$

It is easy to see that the modified rule produces the same evaluation derivations as the initial rule, up to a renaming of fresh locations: if $\varphi, e, s \vdash a \rightarrow r$ with the initial rule, then $\varphi, e, s \vdash a \rightarrow r'$ with the modified rule, where $r'$ is identical to $r$ up to a renaming of locations not in $\mathrm{Dom}(s) \cup \mathrm{Dom}(\varphi)$.

We say that a value $v$ in a store $s$ is contained in world $m$, and we write $C_m(v, s)$, if any source term operating on $v$ in $s$ can directly access only locations that are in $L_m$ or $L_{shared}$, but not locations in $L_{\overline{m}}$. Formally, $C_m(v, s)$ is defined by case analysis on $v$, as follows:

- $C_m(b, s)$ is always true
- $C_m(\lambda x.a_n[e], s)$ if $C_n(e, s)$
- $C_m((v_1, v_2), s)$ if $C_m(v_1, s)$ and $C_m(v_2, s)$
- $C_m(\ell, s)$ if $l \notin L_{\overline{m}}$ and $C_m(s(\ell), s)$
- $C_m(e, s)$ if $C_m(e(x), s)$ for all $x \in \mathrm{Dom}(e)$.

Notice that for closures, it's the world $n$ of the function body $a_n$ that determines the containment of the closure environment, not the world $m$ in which the closure value is being used. The reason is that the environment values can only be accessed by the function body, not arbitrary terms of world $m$. This is characteristic of procedural abstraction in the sense of section 3.2.

As usual, the definition of $C$ above is not well-founded by induction on $v$. We view the equations above as fixpoint equations for an operator, which is increasing, and define $C$ as the greatest fixpoint of that operator. (The smallest fixpoint is always false on value/store pairs that contain a cycle, which is not what we want; it's the greatest fixpoint that gives the expected behavior for $C$. See [39] for detailed explanations.)

Here are two important lemmas on the $C$ predicate. First, assigning a value contained in world $m$ to a location which is not in $L_{\overline{m}}$ preserves the containment of all other values.

**Lemma 5.** *Assume either $\ell \in L_m$ and $C_m(v, s)$, or $\ell \in L_{shared}$ and $C_{app}(v, s)$ and $C_{env}(v, s)$. Then, for all values $w$ and worlds $n$, $C_n(w, s)$ implies $C_n(w, s\{\ell \leftarrow v\})$.*

*Proof.* The proof is a standard argument by coinduction, close to the proof of Lemma 4.6 in [39]. The only non-trival case is $w = \ell$ (the modified location). By hypothesis $C_n(w, s)$, we have $\ell \notin L_{\overline{n}}$ and $C_n(s(\ell), s)$. Write $s' = s\{\ell \leftarrow v\}$. Notice that $s'(\ell) = v$. If $n = m$, we have $C_n(v, s)$ by assumption, hence $C_n(v, s')$ by the coinduction hypothesis, from which it follows that $C_n(\ell, s')$. If $n = \overline{m}$, since $\ell \notin L_{\overline{n}}$, we have $\ell \notin L_m$ and thus it must be the case that $\ell \in L_{shared}$ and $C_{app}(v, s)$ and $C_{env}(v, s)$ to comply with the assumptions of the lemma. Thus, we have $C_n(v, s)$ and we conclude as in the previous case.

Second, values that belong to a type $\tau \notin T$ can be exchanged between the *app* and *env* worlds without breaking containment.

**Lemma 6.** *Assume* $S \models v : \tau$ *and* $\models s : S$. *If* $\tau \notin T$, *then* $C_m(v, s)$ *implies* $C_{\overline{m}}(v, s)$ *for all worlds* $m$.

*Proof.* By structural induction on $\tau$. If $\tau$ is a base type or a function type, then $v$ is a base value or a closure, and the containment of $v$ is independent of the world $m$. If $\tau$ is a product type $\tau_1 \times \tau_2$, the closure condition over $T$ guarantees that $\tau_1 \notin T$ and $\tau_2 \notin T$; the result follows from the induction hypothesis. Finally, if $\tau$ is a **ref** type, we have $v = \ell$ and $\tau = S(\ell)$ **ref**. Since $\tau \notin T$, it follows that $\ell$ belongs to $L_{shared}$, but neither to $L_{app}$ nor $L_{env}$. Hence, $l \notin L_m$. Moreover, $S(\ell) \notin T$ by the closure condition on $T$, hence $C_{\overline{m}}(s(\ell), s)$ by application of the induction hypothesis. It follows that $C_{\overline{m}}(\ell, s)$.

We can now show that containment is preserved at each evaluation step:

**Lemma 7 (Containment lemma).** *Let* $E_{api}$ *be the type of the execution environment for applets. Assume* $E_{api}(x) \notin T$ *for all* $x \in \mathrm{Dom}(E_{api})$. *Further assume* $E \vdash a_m : \tau$ *and* $S \models e : E$ *and* $\models s : S$ *and* $C_m(e, s)$. *If* $\varphi, e, s \vdash a_m \to v/s'$, *then* $C_m(v, s')$, *and for all values* $w$ *and worlds* $n$ *such that* $C_n(w, s)$, *we have* $C_n(w, s')$.

*Proof.* The proof is by induction on the evaluation derivation and case analysis on $a$. Notice that by Lemma 2, we have the additional result that there exists a store typing $S'$ extending $S$ such that $S' \models v : \tau$ and $\models s' : S'$. This makes the semantic typing hypotheses go through the induction. The interesting cases are assignment and function application; the other cases are straightforward.

*Assignment:* $a$ is $(a_1^{\sigma \text{ ref}} := a_2^\varsigma)$. We apply the induction hypothesis twice, obtaining

$$\varphi, e, s \vdash a_1 \to v_1/s_1 \qquad \varphi, e, s_1 \vdash a_2 \to v_2/s_2$$
$$C_m(v_1, s_2) \qquad C_m(v_2, s_2)$$
$$C_n(w, s) \text{ implies } C_n(w, s_2) \text{ for all } n, w$$
$$S_2 \models v_1 : \sigma \text{ ref} \qquad S_2 \models v_2 : \sigma \qquad \models s_2 : S_2.$$

Hence, $v_1$ is a location $\ell$, and since $v_1$ is contained in $m$, we have $\ell \notin L_{\overline{m}}$. Therefore, either $\ell \in L_m$ or $\ell \in L_{shared}$. But in the latter case, $\sigma \notin T$ by construction of $L_{shared}$, hence $C_m(v_2, s_2)$ implies $C_{\overline{m}}(v_2, s_2)$ as well by Lemma 6. In both cases, the hypotheses of Lemma 5 are met. Writing $s' = s_2\{\ell \leftarrow v_2\}$, we obtain the expected result: $C_n(w, s)$ implies $C_n(w, s')$ for all $n, w$. The other expected result, $C_m((), s')$, is trivial.

*Application:* $a$ is $a_1^{q \to \tau}(a_2^q)$. By applying the induction hypothesis twice, we obtain

$$\varphi, e, s \vdash a_1 \to v_1/s_1 \qquad \varphi, e, s_1 \vdash a_2 \to v_2/s_2$$
$$C_m(v_1, s_2) \qquad C_m(v_2, s_2)$$
$$C_n(w, s) \text{ implies } C_n(w, s_2) \text{ for all } n, w$$
$$S_2 \models v_1 : \sigma \to \tau \qquad S_2 \models v_2 : \sigma \qquad \models s_2 : S_2.$$

Hence, $v_1$ is a closure $\lambda x.a'_n[e']$, and the last evaluation rule used is rule 4.

If $n = m$ (intra-world call), we have $C_m(e'\{x \leftarrow v_2\}, s_2)$ as a consequence of $C_m(v_1, s_2)$ and $C_m(v_2, s_2)$, and the two conclusions follows easily from the induction hypothesis applied to the evaluation of $a'_n$.

If $n = \overline{m}$ (cross-world call), then the type $\sigma \to \tau$ of the function must occur as a sub-term of the typing environment $E_{api}$. Hence, $\sigma \notin T$ and $\tau \notin T$. Since the type of $v_2$ is not in $T$, by Lemma 6 it follows that $C_n(v_2, s_2)$. Hence, $C_n(e'\{x \leftarrow v_2\}, s_2)$, and we can apply the induction hypothesis to the evaluation of $a'_n$: $\varphi, e'\{x \leftarrow v_2\}, s_2 \vdash a'_n \to v/s'$. The resulting value $v$ is contained in world $n$ and has type $\tau$; applying again Lemma 6, we get $C_m(v, s')$, which is the expected result.

# B Appendix: modifiable locations in the case of systematic procedural encapsulation

In this appendix, we formalize the notion of modifiable locations, as introduced in section 3.2, in the particular case where the applet environment $e_{api}$ is well-typed and its type $E_{api}$ does not contain any **ref** types. This is not to say that $e_{api}$ is purely functional: the functions it provide may very well have side-effects and use references internally. Only, all those internal references must be encapsulated inside functions and never handed to the applet directly. This systematic procedural encapsulation does not reduce expressiveness in any significant way, and at any rate is a reasonable thing to do given that our goal is to characterize semantically procedural encapsulation.

From the technical side, requiring that no **ref** types occur in the applet's interface $E_{api}$ has an interesting consequence: only source terms from the browser can operate directly on locations allocated by the browser, and only terms from the applet can operate directly on locations allocated by the applet. Thus, all references are contained (in the sense of appendix A, taking $T$ to be the set of all types where the **ref** constructor occurs) either in the browser or in the applet, but never go from one world to the other.

We then rely on the notion of containment to define the set $ML(v, s)$ of locations modifiable from value $v$ in store $s$ as the smallest fixpoint of the following equations:

$$ML(b, s) = \emptyset$$
$$ML((v_1, v_2), s) = ML(v_1, s) \cup ML(v_2, s)$$

$$ML(\lambda x.a[e], s) = \{\ell \mid \text{there exists } v_1, s_1, v_2, s_2 \text{ such that}$$
$$C_{app}(v_1, s_1) \text{ and } s_1(\ell) = s(\ell) \text{ for all } \ell \in L_{env}, \text{ and either}$$
$$\{\ell \leftarrow \emptyset\}, e\{x \leftarrow v_1\}, s_1 \vdash a \rightarrow \text{err}$$
$$\text{or } \emptyset, e\{x \leftarrow v_1\}, s \vdash a \rightarrow v_2/s_2$$
$$\text{and } \ell \in ML(v_2, s_2) \cup ML(e_{api}, s_2)\}$$

$$ML(e, s) = \bigcup_{x \in \text{Dom}(e)} ML(e(x), s)$$

The case for closures follows conditions 1 and 4 in the informal discussion from section 3.2. For condition 5, we use the condition $C_{app}(v_1, s_1)$ instead of the more natural $\ell \notin ML(v_1, s_1)$, so that the equations remain increasing in $ML$ and the existence of the smallest fixpoint is guaranteed. The typing hypothesis (that $E_{api}$ contains no **ref** types) renders condition 3 vacuous, and also dispenses us with defining $ML$ over locations.

The following lemma show that modifiable locations are indeed the only locations modified during the application of a closure.

**Lemma 8.** *Let $p$ be a set of locations, with $p \subseteq L_{env}$. Let $\lambda x.a_{env}[e]$ be a closure of an environment function. Assume $p \cap ML(\lambda x.a[e], s) = \emptyset$ and $C_{app}(v, s)$. If $Prot(p), e\{x \leftarrow v\}, s \vdash a \rightarrow r$, then $r \neq$ err. Instead, $r = v'/s'$, and moreover $p \cap ML(v', s') = \emptyset$ and $p \cap ML(e_{api}, s') = \emptyset$.*

*Proof.* Assume, by way of contradiction, that $r = $ err. Given the evaluation rules, there must exist $\ell \in p$ such that $\{\ell \leftarrow \emptyset\}, e\{x \leftarrow v\}, s \vdash a \rightarrow$ err. By definition of $ML$, this means that $\ell \in ML(\lambda x.a[e], s)$. This contradicts the hypothesis $p \cap ML(\lambda x.a[e], s) = \emptyset$. Hence, $r \neq$ err. We therefore have $Prot(p), e\{x \leftarrow v\}, s \vdash a \rightarrow v'/s'$ for some $v'$ and $s'$. Given the evaluation rules, this implies that we can also derive $\emptyset, e\{x \leftarrow v\}, s \vdash a \rightarrow v'/s'$. Hence, by definition of $ML$, any $\ell$ belonging to $ML(v', s')$ or $ML(e_{api}, s')$ also belongs to $ML(\lambda x.a[e], s)$. It follows that $p \cap ML(v', s') = \emptyset$ and $p \cap ML(e_{api}, s') = \emptyset$. ∎

Using the notion of modifiable locations instead of reachable locations, we finally obtain a security property similar to Property 1: the execution of an applet cannot write to locations that are not modifiable from the initial execution environment.

**Security property 5** *Assume $S \models e_{api} : E_{api}$ and $\models s : S$. Further assume that $E_{api}$ contains no **ref** types. If $p \subseteq \text{Dom}(s)$ and $p \cap ML(e_{api}, s) = \emptyset$, then for all applets $a$, we have $Prot(p), e_{api}, s \vdash a \not\rightarrow$ err.*

The property follows from the inductive lemma below.

**Lemma 9.** *Assume $S \models e_{api} : E_{api}$ and $\models s : S$ and $E_{api}$ contains no **ref** types. Further assume $p \subseteq L_{env}$ and $p \cap ML(e_{api}, s) = \emptyset$. Assume $E \vdash a_{app} : \tau$ and $S \models e : E$ and $C_{app}(e, s)$. If $Prot(p), e, s \vdash a_{app} \rightarrow r$, then $r \neq$ err. Instead, $r = v'/s'$ and we have $p \cap ML(e_{api}, s') = \emptyset$*

*Proof.* The proof is by induction on the evaluation derivation. We rely on Lemmas 2 and 7 to ensure that the semantic typing and containment hypotheses go through the induction. The two non-obvious cases are assignment and application of a closure of a browser function. We write $\varphi = Prot(p)$.

*Assignment:* $a$ is $a_1 := a_2$. Applying the induction hypothesis twice, we obtain $\varphi, e, s \vdash a_1 \to v_1/s_1$ and $\varphi, e, s_1 \vdash a_2 \to v_2/s_2$, with $C_{app}(v_1, s_2)$ and $C_{app}(v_2, s_2)$ and $S_2 \models v_1 : \sigma \text{ ref}$ and $S_2 \models v_2 : \sigma$ and $p \cap ML(e_{api}, s_2) = \emptyset$. Hence, $v_1$ is a location $\ell$, and since $v_1$ is contained in *app*, we have $\ell \in L_{app}$. Thus, $\ell \notin p$ and the evaluation of the assignment does not result in **err**. Moreover, by definition of *ML*, we have $ML(e_{api}, s) = ML(e_{api}, s')$ if $s(\ell) = s'(l)$ for all $\ell \in L_{env}$. In the present case, the store $s'$ at the end of the evaluation is $s_2\{\ell \leftarrow v_2\}$, with $\ell \notin L_{env}$ by containment, hence $ML(e_{api}, s') = ML(e_{api}, s_2)$ and thus $p \cap ML(e_{api}, s') = \emptyset$ as expected.

*Application:* $a$ is $a_1(a_2)$. By induction hypothesis, we have $\varphi, e, s \vdash a_1 \to v_1/s_1$ and $\varphi, e, s_1 \vdash a_2 \to v_2/s_2$, with $C_{app}(v_1, s_2)$ and $C_{app}(v_2, s_2)$ and $S_2 \models v_1 : \sigma \to \tau$ and $S_2 \models v_2 : \sigma$ and $p \cap ML(e_{api}, s_2) = \emptyset$. Hence, $v_1$ is a closure $\lambda x. a'_m[e']$. If $m = app$ (the function comes from the applet), the result follows from the induction hypothesis applied to the evaluation of $a'$. If $m = env$ (the function comes from the applet environment), the closure $\lambda x. a'_m[e']$ can only be obtained by looking up a variable bound in $e_{api}$, then possibly performing some function applications or **fst** and **snd** operations. Thus, we have $ML(\lambda x. a'_m[e'], s_2) \subseteq ML(e_{api}, s_2)$, and the result follows by Lemma 8.

# Part II

# Concepts

# The Role of Trust Management in Distributed Systems Security

Matt Blaze, Joan Feigenbaum, John Ioannidis, and Angelos D. Keromytis

**Abstract.** Existing authorization mechanisms fail to provide powerful and robust tools for handling security at the scale necessary for today's Internet. These mechanisms are coming under increasing strain from the development and deployment of systems that increase the programmability of the Internet. Moreover, this "increased flexibility through programmability" trend seems to be accelerating with the advent of proposals such as Active Networking and Mobile Agents.

The *trust-management approach* to distributed-system security was developed as an answer to the inadequacy of traditional authorization mechanisms. Trust-management engines avoid the need to resolve "identities" in an authorization decision. Instead, they express privileges and restrictions in a programming language. This allows for increased flexibility and expressibility, as well as standardization of modern, scalable security mechanisms. Further advantages of the trust-management approach include proofs that requested transactions comply with local policies and system architectures that encourage developers and administrators to consider an application's security policy carefully and specify it explicitly.

In this paper, we examine existing authorization mechanisms and their inadequacies. We introduce the concept of trust management, explain its basic principles, and describe some existing trust-management engines, including *PolicyMaker* and *KeyNote*. We also report on our experience using trust-management engines in several distributed-system applications.

## 1 Introduction

With the advent of the Internet, distributed computing has become increasingly prevalent. Recent developments in programming languages, coupled with the increase in network bandwidth and end-node processing power, have made the Web a highly dynamic system. Virtually every user of the Internet is at least aware of languages such as Java [15], JavaScript, Active-X, and so on. More "futuristic" projects involve computers running almost exclusively downloaded interpreted-language applications (Network PC), or on-the-fly programmable network infrastructures (Active Networks). On a more mundane level, an increasing number of organizations use the Internet (or large Intranets) to connect their various offices, branches, databases, *etc.*

All of these emerging systems have one thing in common: the need to grant or restrict access to resources according to some security policy. There are several issues worth noting.

First, different systems and applications have different notions of what a resource is. For example, a web browser may consider CPU cycles, network bandwidth, and perhaps private information to be resources. A database server's notion of "resource" would include individual records. Similarly, a banking application would equate resources with money and accounts. While most of these resources can be viewed as combinations of more basic ones (such as CPU cycles, I/O bandwidth, and memory), it is often more convenient to refer to those combinations as single resources, abstracting from lower-level operations. Thus, a generic security mechanism should be able to handle any number and type of resources.

What should also be obvious from the few examples mentioned above is that different applications have different access-granting or -restricting policies. The criteria on which a decision is based may differ greatly among different applications (or even between different instances of the same application). The security mechanism should be able to handle those different criteria.

One security mechanism often used in operating systems is the Access Control List (ACL). Briefly, an ACL is a list describing which access rights a principal has on an object (resource). For example, an entry might read "User Foo can Read File Bar." Such a list (or table) need not physically exist in one location but may be distributed throughout the system. The $Unix^{TM}$-filesystem "permissions" mechanism is essentially an ACL.

ACLs have been used in distributed systems, because they are conceptually easy to grasp and because there is an extensive literature about them. However, there are a number of fundamental reasons that ACLs are inadequate for distributed-system security, $e.g.$,

- *Authentication:* In an operating system, the identity of a principal is well known. This is not so in a distributed system, where some form of authentication has to be performed before the decision to grant access can be made. Typically, authentication is accomplished via a username/password mechanism. Simple password-based protocols are inadequate in networked computing environments, however, even against unsophisticated adversaries; simple eavesdropping can destroy security. Other recently developed mechanisms include:
  - One-Time passwords, which do not secure the rest of the session.
  - Centralized ticket-based systems, such as Kerberos [22]. Problems with such systems include the necessity for an authentication server (and for frequent communication with it) and implicit trust assumptions.
  - Public-key based authentication protocols, which are considered the "state of the art" for scalable authentication systems.
- *Delegation* is necessary for scalability of a distributed system. It enables *decentralization* of administrative tasks. Existing distributed-system security mechanisms usually delegate directly to a "certified entity." In such systems, policy (or authorizations) may only be specified at the last step in the delegation chain (the entity enforcing policy), most commonly in the form of an ACL. The implication is that high-level administrative authorities cannot

directly specify overall security policy; rather, all they can do is "certify" lower-level authorities. This authorization structure leads easily to inconsistencies among locally-specified sub-policies.

- *Expressibility and Extensibility:* A generic security mechanism must be able to handle new and diverse conditions and restrictions. The traditional ACL approach has not provided sufficient expressibility or extensibility. Thus, many security policy elements that are not directly expressible in ACL form must be hard-coded into applications. This means that changes in security policy often require reconfiguration, rebuilding, or even rewriting of applications.

- *Local trust policy:* The number of administrative entities in a distributed system can be quite large. Each of these entities may have a different trust model for different users and other entities. For example, system A may trust system B to authenticate its users correctly, but not system C; on the other hand, system B may trust system C. It follows that the security mechanism should not enforce uniform and implicit policies and trust relations.

We believe that these points constitute a forceful argument that *Authenticode*, X.509, and, generally, the use of identity-based public-key systems in conjunction with ACLs[1] are inadequate solutions to distributed (and programmable) system-security problems. Even modern ACL-based systems like DCE fall somewhat short of satisfyingly addressing the extensibility, expressibility, and delegation issues, despite some work in these directions [10].

Furthermore, one finds insecure, inadequate, or non-scalable authentication mechanisms (such as username/password, One-Time passwords, and hardware token authentication) used in conjunction with ACLs. Finally, many policy problems are left unsolved by the "binary" authorization model employed widely in Web security (and elsewhere): access is granted on the condition that the requesting principal has a certificate by a particular Certification Authority (CA). We call this a binary authorization model because it means essentially "all-or-nothing" access. While this is sufficient in a small number of cases (*e.g.*, when read-only access to a web page is the only decision that need be made), it is obvious that this approach neither scales nor is extensible.

We believe that these unintuitive and in many ways problematic mechanisms are in use simply because of the lack of alternatives that are better suited to distributed systems. Developers have tried to adapt existing tools to their security model or *vice versa*, and neither strategy has worked particularly well. Accordingly, misconfiguration and unexpected component interactions are causing security breaches and, inevitably, loss of confidence in the security tools.

We also believe that the new Internet services now emerging as a result of increased programmability will require powerful and expressive authorization

---

[1] Sometimes the public keys are hardcoded into the application, which deprives the environment of even the limited flexibility provided by ACLs. Such an example is the under-development IEEE 1394 Digital Content Protection standard.

mechanisms without the problems present in ACL-based systems[2]. Naturally, existing services and protocols can also make good use of such mechanisms.

*Trust Management*, introduced by Blaze *et al.* [5], is a unified approach to specifying and interpreting security policies, credentials, and relationships that allows direct authorization of security-critical actions. In particular, a trust-management system combines the notion of specifying security policy with the mechanism for specifying security credentials. Credentials describe specific delegations of trust among public keys; unlike traditional certificates, which bind keys to names, trust-management credentials bind keys directly to authorizations to perform specific tasks. Trust-management systems support delegation, and policy specification and refinement at the different layers of a policy hierarchy, thus solving to a large degree the consistency and scalability problems inherent in traditional ACLs. Furthermore, trust-management systems are by design extensible and can express policies for different types of applications.

Section 2 gives an overview of Trust Management and briefly describes two tools that we have developed (*PolicyMaker* and *KeyNote*). Section 3 presents some applications of Trust Management. Finally, Section 4 discusses future work and concludes this paper.

## 2 Trust Management

This section explains the essence of the trust-management approach, describes PolicyMaker [5, 7] and KeyNote [4], and ends with a brief discussion of related trust-management work.

### 2.1 Basics

A traditional "system-security approach" to the processing of a signed request for action treats the task as a combination of *authentication* and *access control*. The receiving system first determines *who* signed the request and then queries an internal database to decide *whether* the signer should be granted access to the resources needed to perform the requested action. We believe that this is the wrong approach for today's dynamic, internetworked world. In a large, heterogeneous, distributed system, there is a huge set of people (and other entities) who may make requests, as well as a huge set of requests that may be made. These sets change often and cannot be known in advance. Even if the question "who signed this request?" could be answered reliably, it would not help in deciding whether or not to take the requested action if the requester is someone or something from whom the recipient is hearing for the first time.

The right question in a far-flung, rapidly changing network becomes "is the key that signed this request *authorized* to take this action?" Because name-key mappings and pre-computed access-control matrices are inadequate, one

---

[2] For the purposes of this discussion, we consider the traditional capability systems as ACLs, as they exhibit most of the weaknesses we mention.

needs a more flexible, more "distributed" approach to authorization. The *trust-management approach*, initiated by Blaze *et al.* [5], frames the question as follows: "Does the set $C$ of *credentials* prove that the *request r complies* with the local security *policy P*?" Each entity that receives requests must have a policy that serves as the ultimate source of authority in the local environment. The policy may directly authorize certain keys to take certain actions, but more typically it will *delegate* this responsibility to credential issuers that it trusts to have the required domain expertise as well as relationships with potential requesters. The *trust-management engine* is a separate system component that takes $(r, C, P)$ as input, outputs a decision about whether compliance with policy has been proven, and may also output some additional information about how to proceed if it hasn't.

An essential part of the trust-management approach is the use of a *general-purpose, application-independent* algorithm for checking proofs of compliance. Why is this a good idea? Since any product or service that requires some form of proof that requested transactions comply with policies could use a special-purpose algorithm implemented from scratch, what do developers, administrators, and users gain by using a general-purpose compliance checker?

The most important gain is in soundness and reliability of both the definition and the implementation of "proof of compliance." Developers who set out to implement a "simple," special-purpose compliance checker (in order to avoid what they think are the overly "complicated" syntax and semantics of a universal "meta-policy") may discover that they have underestimated their application's need for proof and expressiveness. As they discover the full extent of their requirements, they may ultimately wind up implementing a system that is as general and expressive as the "complicated" one they set out to avoid. A general-purpose compliance checker can be explained, formalized, proven correct, and implemented in a standard package, and applications that use it can be assured that the answer returned for any given input $(r, C, P)$ depends only on the input and *not* on any implicit policy decisions (or bugs) in the design or implementation of the compliance checker.

Basic questions that must be answered in the design of a trust-management engine include:

- How should "proof of compliance" be defined?
- Should policies and credentials be fully or only partially programmable? In which language or notation should they be expressed?
- How should responsibility be divided between the trust-management engine and the calling application? For example, which of these two components should perform the cryptographic signature verification? Should the application fetch all credentials needed for the compliance proof before the trust-management engine is invoked, or may the trust-management engine fetch additional credentials while it is constructing a proof?

In the rest of this section, we survey several recent and ongoing trust-management projects in which different answers to these questions are explored.

## 2.2   PolicyMaker

PolicyMaker was the first example of a "trust-management engine." That is, it was the first tool for processing signed requests that embodied the "trust-management" principles articulated in Section 2.1. It addressed the authorization problem directly, rather than handling the problem indirectly via authentication and access control, and it provided an application-independent definition of "proof of compliance" for matching up requests, credentials, and policies. PolicyMaker was introduced in the original trust-management paper by Blaze *et al.* [5], and its compliance-checking algorithm was later fleshed out in [7]. We give a high-level overview of the design decisions that went into PolicyMaker in this section and some technical details of the PolicyMaker compliance checker in Appendix A below. A full description of the system can be found in [5, 7], and experience using it in several applications is reported in [6, 18, 21].

PolicyMaker credentials and policies are fully programmable; together credentials and policies are referred to as "assertions." Roughly speaking, assertions are represented as pairs $(f, s)$, where $s$ is the *source* of authority, and $f$ is a program describing the nature of the authority being granted as well as the party or parties to whom it is being granted. In a policy assertion, the source is always the keyword **POLICY**. For the PolicyMaker trust-management engine to be able to make a decision about a requested action, the input supplied to it by the calling application must contain one or more policy assertions; these form the "trust root," *i.e.*, the ultimate source of authority for the decision about this request. In a credential assertion, the source is the public key of the issuing authority. Credentials must be signed by their issuers, and these signatures must be verified before the credentials can be used.

PolicyMaker assertions can be written in any programming language that can be "safely" interpreted by a local environment that has to import credentials from diverse (and possibly untrusted) issuing authorities. A safe version of AWK was developed for early experimental work on PolicyMaker (see Blaze *et al.* [5]), because AWK's pattern-matching constructs are a convenient way to express authorizations. For a credential assertion issued by a particular authority to be useful in a proof that a request complies with a policy, the recipient of the request must have an interpreter for the language in which the assertion is written. Thus, it would be desirable for assertion writers ultimately to converge on a small number of assertion languages so that receiving systems have to support only a small number of interpreters and so that carefully crafted credentials can be widely used. However, the question of which languages these will be was left open by the PolicyMaker project. A positive aspect of PolicyMaker's not insisting on a particular assertion language is that all of that work that has gone into designing, analyzing, and implementing the PolicyMaker compliance-checking algorithm will not have to be redone every time an assertion language is changed or a new language is introduced. The "proof of compliance" and "assertion-language design" problems are orthogonal in PolicyMaker and can be worked on independently.

One goal of the PolicyMaker project was to make the trust-management engine minimal and analyzable. Architectural boundaries were drawn so that a fair amount of responsibility was placed on the calling application rather than the trust-management engine. In particular, the calling application was made responsible for all cryptographic verification of signatures on credentials and requests. One pleasant consequence of this design decision is that the application developer's choice of signature scheme(s) can be made independently of his choice of whether or not to use PolicyMaker for compliance checking. Another important responsibility that was assigned to the calling application is credential gathering. The input $(r, C, P)$ supplied to the trust-management module is treated as a claim that credential set $C$ contains a proof that request $r$ complies with Policy $P$. The trust-management module is *not* expected to be able to discover that $C$ is missing just one credential needed to complete the proof and to go fetch that credential from *e.g.*, the corporate database, the issuer's web site, the requester himself, or elsewhere. Later trust-management engines, including KeyNote [4] and REFEREE [11] divide responsibility between the calling application and the trust-management engine differently from the way PolicyMaker divides it.

The main technical contribution of the PolicyMaker project is a notion of "proof of compliance" that is fully specified and analyzed. We give an overview of PolicyMaker's approach to compliance checking here and some details in Appendix A; a complete treatment of the compliance checker can be found in [7].

The PolicyMaker runtime system provides an environment in which the policy and credential assertions fed to it by the calling application can cooperate to produce a proof that the request complies with the policy (or can fail to produce such a proof). Among the requirements for this cooperation are a method of inter-assertion communication and a method for determining that assertions have collectively succeeded or failed to produce a proof.

Inter-assertion communication in PolicyMaker is done via a simple, write-only data structure on which all participating assertions record intermediate results. Specifically, PolicyMaker initializes the proof process by creating a "blackboard" containing only the request string $r$ and the fact that no assertions have thus far approved the request or anything else. Then PolicyMaker runs the various assertions, possibly multiple times each. When assertion $(f_i, s_i)$ is run, it reads the contents of the blackboard and then adds to the blackboard one or more *acceptance records* $(i, s_i, R_{ij})$. Here $R_{ij}$ is an application-specific action that source $s_i$ approves, based on the partial proof that has been constructed thus far. $R_{ij}$ may be the input request $r$, or it may be some related action that this application uses for inter-assertion communication. Note that the meanings of the action strings $R_{ij}$ are understood by the application-specific assertion programs $f_i$, but they are not understood by PolicyMaker. All PolicyMaker does is run the assertions and maintain the global blackboard, making sure that the assertions do not erase acceptance records previously written by other assertions, fill up the entire blackboard so that no other assertions can write, or exhibit any other non-cooperative behavior. PolicyMaker never tries to interpret the action strings $R_{ij}$.

A proof of compliance is achieved if, after PolicyMaker has finished running assertions, the blackboard contains an acceptance record indicating that a policy assertion approves the request $r$. Among the nontrivial decisions that PolicyMaker must make are (1) in what order assertions should be run, (2) how many times each assertion should be run, and (3) when an assertion should be discarded because it is behaving in a non-cooperative fashion. Blaze *et al.* [7] provide:

- A mathematically precise formulation of the PolicyMaker compliance-checking problem.
- Proof that the problem is undecidable in general and is NP-hard even in certain natural special cases.
- One special case of the problem that is polynomial-time solvable, is useful in a wide variety of applications, and is implemented in the current version of PolicyMaker.

Although the most general version of the compliance-checking problem allows assertions to be arbitrary functions, the computationally tractable version that is analyzed in [7] and implemented in PolicyMaker is guaranteed to be correct only when all assertions are monotonic. (Basically, if a monotonic assertion approves action $a$ when given evidence set $E$, then it will also approve action $a$ when given an evidence set that contains $E$; see Appendix A for a formal definition.) In particular, correctness is guaranteed only for monotonic *policy* assertions, and this excludes certain types of policies that are used in practice, most notably those that make explicit use of "negative credentials" such as revocation lists. Although it is a limitation, the monotonicity requirement has certain advantages. One of them is that, although the compliance checker may not handle all potentially desirable policies, it is at least analyzable and provably correct on a well-defined class of policies. Furthermore, the requirements of many non-monotonic policies can often be achieved by monotonic policies. For example, the effect of requiring that an entity *not* occur on a revocation list can also be achieved by requiring that it present a "certificate of non-revocation"; the choice between these two approaches involves trade-offs among the (system-wide) costs of the two kinds of credentials and the benefits of a standard compliance checker with provable properties. Finally, restriction to monotonic assertions encourages a conservative, prudent approach to security: In order to perform a potentially dangerous action, a user must present an adequate set of affirmative credentials; no potentially dangerous action is allowed "by default," simply because of the absence of negative credentials.

## 2.3 KeyNote

KeyNote [4] was designed according to the same principles as PolicyMaker, using credentials that directly authorize actions instead of dividing the authorization task into authentication and access control. Two additional design goals for KeyNote were standardization and ease of integration into applications. To address these goals, KeyNote assigns more responsibility to the trust-management engine than PolicyMaker does and less to the calling application; for example, cryptographic signature verification is done by the trust-management engine in KeyNote and by the application in PolicyMaker. KeyNote also requires that credentials and policies be written in a specific assertion language, designed to work smoothly with KeyNote's compliance checker. By fixing a specific and appropriate assertion language, KeyNote goes further than PolicyMaker toward facilitating efficiency, interoperability, and widespread use of carefully written credentials and policies.

A calling application passes to a KeyNote evaluator a list of credentials, policies, and requester public keys, and an "Action Environment." This last element consists of a list of attribute/value pairs, similar in some ways to the $Unix^{TM}$ shell environment. The action environment is constructed by the calling application and contains all information deemed relevant to the request and necessary for the trust decision. The action-environment attributes and the assignment of their values must reflect the security requirements of the application accurately. Identifying the attributes to be included in the action environment is perhaps the most important task in integrating KeyNote into new applications. The result of the evaluation is an application-defined string (perhaps with some additional information) that is passed back to the application. In the simplest case, the result is something like "authorized."

The KeyNote assertion format resembles that of e-mail headers. An example (with artificially short keys and signatures for readability) is given in Figure 1.

```
KeyNote-Version: 1
Authorizer: rsa-pkcs1-hex:"1023abcd"
Licensees: dsa-hex:"986512a1" ||
           rsa-pkcs1-hex:"19abcd02"
Comment: Authorizer delegates read
         access to either of the
         Licensees
Conditions: ($file == "/etc/passwd" &&
            $access == "read") ->
                           {return "ok"}
Signature: rsa-md5-pkcs1-hex:"f00f5673"
```

**Fig. 1.** Sample KeyNote assertion

As in PolicyMaker, policies and credentials (collectively called assertions) have the same format. The only difference between policies and credentials is that a policy (that is, an assertion with the keyword **POLICY** in the *Authorizer* field) is locally trusted (by the compliance-checker) and thus needs no signature.

KeyNote assertions are structured so that the *Licensees* field specifies explicitly the principal or principals to which authority is delegated. Syntactically, the Licensees field is a formula in which the arguments are public keys and the operations are conjunction, disjunction, and threshold. The semantics of these expressions are specified in [4].

The programs in KeyNote are encoded in the *Conditions* field and are essentially tests of the action environment variables. These tests are string comparisons, numerical operations and comparisons, and pattern-matching operations.

We chose such a simple language for KeyNote assertions for the following reasons:

- AWK, one of the first assertion languages used by PolicyMaker, was criticized as too heavyweight for most relevant applications. Because of AWK's complexity, the footprint of the interpreter is considerable, and this discourages application developers from integrating it into a trust-management component. The KeyNote assertion language is simple and has a minimal-sized interpreter.
- In languages that permit loops and recursion (including
  AWK), it is difficult to enforce resource-usage restrictions, but applications that run trust-management assertions written by unknown sources often need to limit their memory- and CPU-usage.
  We believe that for out purposes a language without loops, dynamic memory allocation, and certain other features is sufficiently powerful and expressive. The KeyNote assertion syntax is restricted so that resource usage is proportional to the program size. Similar concepts have been successfully used in other contexts [16].
- Assertions should be both understandable by human readers and easy for a tool to generate from a high-level specification. Moreover, they should be easy to analyze automatically, so that automatic verification and consistency checks can done. This is currently an area of active research.
- One of our goals is to use KeyNote as a means of exchanging policy and distributing access control information otherwise expressed in an application-native format. Thus the language should be easy to map to a number of such formats (*e.g.*, from a KeyNote assertion to packet-filtering rules).
- The language chosen was adequate for KeyNote's evaluation model.

This last point requires explanation.

In PolicyMaker, compliance proofs are constructed via repeated evaluation of assertions, along with an arbitrated "blackboard" for storage of intermediate results and inter-assertion communication.

In contrast, KeyNote uses a depth-first search (DFS) algorithm that attempts (recursively) to satisfy at least one policy assertion. Satisfying an assertion entails satisfying both the *Conditions* field and the *Licensees* key expression. Note that there is no explicit inter-assertion communication as in PolicyMaker; the *acceptance records* returned by program evaluation are used internally by the KeyNote evaluator and are never seen directly by other assertions. Because KeyNote's evaluation model is a subset of PolicyMaker's, the latter's compliance-checking guarantees are applicable to KeyNote. Whether the more restrictive nature of KeyNote allows for stronger guarantees to be made is an open question requiring further research.

Ultimately, for a request to be approved, an assertion graph must be constructed between one or more policy assertions and one or more keys that signed the request. Because of the evaluation model, an assertion located somewhere in a delegation graph can effectively only refine (or pass on) the authorizations conferred on it by the previous assertions in the graph. (This principle also holds for PolicyMaker.) For more details on the evaluation model, see [4].

It should be noted that PolicyMaker's restrictions regarding "negative credentials" also apply to KeyNote. Certificate revocation lists (CRLs) are not built into the KeyNote (or the PolicyMaker) system; these however could be provided at a higher (or lower) level, perhaps even transparently to KeyNote[3]. The problem of credential discovery is also not explicitly addressed in KeyNote. We hope that the fact that KeyNote provides an explicit, descriptive credential format will facilitate research on both credential discovery and revocation.

Finally, note that KeyNote, like other trust-management engines, does not directly *enforce* policy; it only provides advice to the applications that call it. KeyNote assumes that the application itself is trusted and that the policy assertions are correct. Nothing prevents an application from submitting misleading assertions to KeyNote or from ignoring KeyNote altogether.

## 2.4 Related Work on Trust Management

We close with a brief discussion of two general-purpose trust-management systems that share much of the basic approach initiated by PolicyMaker but depart from it in some notable ways.

The REFEREE system of Chu *et al.* [11] is like PolicyMaker in that it supports full programmability of assertions (policies and credentials). However, it differs in several important ways. It allows the trust-management engine, while evaluating a request, to fetch additional credentials and to perform cryptographic signature-verification. (Recall that PolicyMaker places the responsibility for both of these functions on the calling application and insists that they be done before the evaluation of a request begins.) Furthermore, REFEREE's notion of "proof of compliance" is more complex than PolicyMaker's; for example, it allows non-monotonic policies and credentials. The REFEREE proof system also supports a more complicated form of inter-assertion communication than PolicyMaker does. In particular, the REFEREE execution environment allows assertion programs to call each other as subroutines and to pass different arguments to different subroutines, whereas the PolicyMaker execution environment requires each assertion program to write anything it wants to communicate on a global "blackboard" that can be seen by all other assertions.

---

[3] Note that the decision to consult a CRL is (or should be) a matter of local policy.

REFEREE was designed with trust management for web browsing in mind, but it is a general-purpose language and could be used in other applications. Some of the design choices in REFEREE were influence by experience (reported in [6]) with using PolicyMaker for web-page filtering based on PICS labels [26] and users' viewing policies. It is unclear whether the cost of building and analyzing a more complex trust-management environment such as REFEREE is justified by the ability to construct more sophisticated proofs of compliance than those constructible in PolicyMaker. Assessing this tradeoff would require more experimentation with both systems, as well as a rigorous specification and analysis of the REFEREE proof system, similar to the one for PolicyMaker given in [7].

The Simple Public Key Infrastructure (SPKI) project of Ellison *et al.* [13] has proposed a standard format for authorization certificates. SPKI shares with our trust-management approach the belief that certificates can be used directly for authorization rather than simply for authentication. However, SPKI certificates are not fully programmable; they are data structures with the following five fields: "Issuer" (the source of authority), "Subject" (the entity being authorized to do something), "Delegation" (a boolean value specifying whether or not the subject is permitted to pass the authorization on to other entities), "Authorization" (a specification of the power that the issuer is conferring on the subject), and "Validity dates." The SPKI certificate format is compatible with the Simple Distributed Security Infrastructure (SDSI) local-names format proposed by Rivest and Lampson [19], and Ellison *et al.* [13] explain how to integrate the two.

The SPKI documentation [13] states that

> The processing of certificates and related objects to yield an authorization result is the province of the developer of the application or system. The processing plan presented here is an example that may be followed, but its primary purpose is to clarify the semantics of an SPKI certificate and the way it and various other kinds of certificate might be used to yield an authorization result.

Thus, strictly speaking, SPKI is not a trust-management engine according to our use of the term, because compliance checking (referred to above as "processing of certificates and related objects") may be done in an application-dependent manner. If the processing plan presented in [13] were universally adopted, then SPKI would be a trust-management engine. The resulting notion of "proof of compliance" would be considerably more restricted than PolicyMaker's; essentially, proofs would take the form of chains of certificates. On the other hand, SPKI has a standard way of handling certain types of non-monotonic policies, because validity periods and simple CRLs are part of the proposal.

# 3 Applications of Trust Management

In this section, we give a brief overview of experiences with the trust-management approach in mobile-code security, active networking, nd distributed access-control.

## 3.1 Active Networks

There has been a great deal of interest in the problem of exposing the ability to control of network infrastructure. Much of this interest has been driven by a the desire to accelerate service creation. Sometimes services can be created using features of existing systems. One of the most aggressive proposals is the notion of *programmable* network infrastructure or "active networking." In an active network, the operator or user has facilities for directly modifying the operational semantics of the network itself. Thus, the role of network and endpoint become far more malleable for the construction of new applications. This is in contrast to the "service overlay model" as employed, for example, in present-day Internet, where service introduction at the "edge" of the virtual infrastructure is very easy, but changes in the infrastructure itself have proven very difficult (*e.g.*, RSVP [8] and multicasting [12]). A number of active network architectures have been proposed and are under investigation [1, 28, 16, 27, 9, 25].

A programmable network infrastructure is potentially more vulnerable to attacks since a portion of the control plane is *intentionally* exposed, and this can lead to far more complex threats than exist with an inaccessible control plane. For example, a denial-of-service attack on the transport plane may also inhibit access to the control plane. Unauthenticated access to the control plane can have severe consequences for the security of the whole network.

It is therefore especially necessary for an active network to use a robust and powerful authorization mechanism. Because of the many interactions between network nodes and switchlets (pieces of code dynamically loaded on the switches, or code in packets that is executed on every active node they encounter), a versatile, scalable, and expressive mechanism is called for.

We have applied KeyNote [4] in one proposed active network security architecture, in the Secure Active Network Environment (SANE) [2] [3] developed at the University of Pennsylvania as part of the SwitchWare project [1].

In SANE, the principals involved in the authorization and policy decisions in the security model are users, programmers and administrators and network elements. The network elements are presumed to be under physical control of an administrator. Programmers may not have physical access to the network element, but may possess considerable access rights to resources present in the network elements. Users may have access to basic services (*e.g.*, transport), but also resources that the network elements are willing to export to all users, at an appropriate level of abstraction. Users may also be allowed to introduce their own services, or load those written by others. In such a dynamic environment, KeyNote is used to supply policy and authorization credentials for those components of the architecture that enforce resource usage and access control limits.

In particular, KeyNote policies and credentials are used to:

- Authorize principals to load code on active routers. This happens as a result of an authentication mechanism, further described in [2].
- Intimately related to the previous item, KeyNote sets resource limits (*e.g.*, memory allocated, CPU cycles consumed, memory bandwidth) that the ex-

ecution environment[4] enforces. The KeyNote evaluator is initially invoked just before a switchlet begins execution, and is provided with the switchlet owner's credentials and the node's policies. It then determines whether the switchlet is allowed to execute on the node (addressing the previous item), and what the initial resource limits are. If these are exceeded, another call to the KeyNote system is made, whereupon the decision may be to grant more resources, kill the switchlet, or raise an exception.

– Fine-grained control of what actions a switchlet may take on the active node. In our current approach, loaded code may call other loaded or resident functions (resembling inter-process communication and system call invocation respectively). Which of these calls are allowed by policy to occur is (or rather, can optionally be) controlled by KeyNote. For performance reasons, and since the switchlet language used lends itself to some degree of static analysis, this authorization step happens at link time (when a newly-loaded switchlet is dynamically linked in the runtime system). An alternative way of achieving this would be to trap into the KeyNote evaluator every time an external (to the switchlet) function was called, by generating appropriate function stubs at link time. This could lead to considerable performance problems, especially for time-critical applications (such as real-time content processing and distribution). Such functionality, however, is necessary if one needs to restrict the range of arguments that may be passed to external functions. This is currently an area of open research.

– KeyNote credentials can be used by "active firewalls" to notify nodes behind the firewall that a particular piece of active code should (or should not) be allowed to perform specific tasks [17]. In this context, KeyNote defines trust relations between active nodes (e.g., "firewall", "protected host", etc.)

Trust management for active networks is an area of continuing research.

## 3.2 Mobile Code Security

Another area of broad recent interest is the security and containment of untrusted "mobile" code. That is, executable content or mobile code is received by a host with a request to a execute it; lacking any automatic mechanisms for evaluating the security implications of executing such a piece of code, the host needs to find some other way of determining the trustworthiness of that code.

Failure to properly contain mobile code may result in serious damage or leakage or information resident on the host. Such damage can be the result of malicious intent (e.g., industrial or otherwise espionage or vandalism), or unintentional (e.g., programming failures or unexpected interactions with other system components or programs). Other consequences of failing to contain mobile code include denial-of-service attacks (the now familiar phenomenon of Java and JavaScript applets using all the system memory or CPU cycles, usually

---

[4] In the case of SANE, the execution environment is a modified and restricted runtime of the Caml [20] programming language.

because of bugs), or infiltration of a company network through a downloaded trojan horse or virus.

Of course, these threats existed long before mobile code, such as Java applets, became popular. Downloading software from a bulletin board service or through the Internet and then executing it without any form of code review or execution restrictions has almost exactly the same security implications. The problem, however, has been made more prominent because of the scale and ease with which attacks to individuals and hosts can be carried out, especially in environments where mobile code is run automatically.

As we mentioned in the introduction, various proposals exist that tie code "trustworthiness" to the existence of a digital signature or other form of authentication. Such mechanisms, however, do not address the underlying problem; a signature has value only to the extent that the verifier can evaluate the signer's trustworthiness (which may be a result of poorly-defined, or incorrectly understood, social factors, technical competence, personal knowledge, *etc.*). In that respect, signature-based mobile code schemes do not scale. Furthermore, some programs may be "safe" to run under restricted environments or a small set of platforms. Simple digital signature schemes as have been proposed cannot readily accommodate such conditions.

Trust Management has at least two different roles in mobile code security:

- Express trust relations between code-certifying entities, and the conditions under which their certification has meaning. So, for example, code-certifier *A* could state that his certification of safety of a particular piece of code is predicated by some set of conditions (presumably the conditions under which the code evaluation took place, or the assumptions made by the code that may have security implications if violated). Trust management could also be used to express the local user's (or corporate) policy on executing mobile code (*e.g.*, "must be signed by the company security officer or must be accompanied by a PCC proof" [24, 23]).
- Trust-management credentials could be used to describe the minimal set of capabilities the host environment must grant to enable the code to perform its tasks. This would then be combined with the relevant local policy[5] to restrict the system interface presented to the mobile code. This is similar in concept to the approach mentioned in Section 3.1. We are also investigating the application of this method in a traditional $Unix^{TM}$ kernel, in an environment where language-based protection is not available.

## 3.3 Access Control Distribution

An indirect, but architecturally very important, benefit of trust management involves the distribution of traditional access control list (ACL) databases. Some applications lend themselves naturally to a well-defined ACL-style interface for describing their security characteristics that do not obviously require the rich

---

[5] This would happen automatically, in the process of compliance checking.

expressiveness of a trust-management approach. For example, it may be natural to describe who is allowed to log in to a computer according to a standard list of login accounts. Even when an ACL provides sufficient expressiveness, however, it is often architecturally beneficial to implement the ACL on top of a trust-management system.

Architectures based on a trust-management system can be easily extended if, in the future, it becomes necessary to base access decisions on more complex rules than are captured by an ACL. For example, it is natural and easy to add "time-of-day" restrictions as part of a policy or individual user credentials, even if the need for such restrictions had not been anticipated at the time the system was first designed. Of course, extensibility is a general benefit of trust management that is not limited to ACL applications.

More importantly, a trust-management system decouples the specification of access control policies from the mechanism used to distribute and implement them. For example, consider a traditional access control list maintained as a simple database in a computer system. A trust-management tool could convert ACL entries into credentials automatically, with a general credential (certificate) distribution mechanism used to ensure that updated credentials are sent to the appropriate place. Distributed, reliable access control can be a very difficult problem when implemented by itself, and is greatly simplified using a credential-based trust-management scheme as a back end to a non-distributed access control database. Even if the expressive power is limited to simple ACLs, trust management allows the use of an existing credential distribution scheme to solve the most difficult aspects of the problem.

## 4    Conclusion and Future Work

In the time since "trust management" first appeared in the literature in [5], the concept has gained broad acceptance in the security research community. Trust management has a number of important advantages over traditional approaches such as distributed ACLs, hardcoded security policies, and global identity certificates. A trust-management system provides direct authorization of security-critical actions and decouples the problem of specifying policy and authorization from that of distributing credentials.

Our work on trust management has focused on designing languages and compliance checkers, identifying applications, and building practical toolkits. There are important areas that we have not yet addressed. Foremost among those is automated credential discovery; in our current systems, it is the responsibility of the requester to submit all necessary credentials, under the assumption that he holds all credentials relevant to him. Even then, however, intermediate credentials that form the necessary connections between the verifier's policy and the requester's credentials must be acquired and submitted. The various solutions to this problem range from "leave it to the application" to using distributed databases and lookup mechanisms for credential discovery. A solution along the lines of a distributed database can also assist large organizations in auditing their security and access policies.

Another area of future work is providing functionality similar to that of certificate revocation lists (CRLs), keeping in mind the constraints about "negative credentials" mentioned in Section 2.2. While adoption and deployment of a scheme similar to that of X.509 is fairly straightforward, we are still investigating the security and operational implications.

Finally, we are examining higher-level policy languages that are even more human-understandable and capable of higher levels of abstraction. Such high-level policy would be combined with network- and application-specific information and compiled into a set to trust-management credentials. Similarly, a tool for translating trust-management credentials into application-native forms would give us all the advantages of trust management (delegation, formal proof of compliance, *etc.*) while requiring minimal changes to applications.

# References

[1] D. S. Alexander, W. A. Arbaugh, M. Hicks, P. Kakkar, A. D. Keromytis, J. T. Moore, C. A. Gunter, S. M. Nettles, and J. M. Smith. The SwitchWare Active Network Architecture. *IEEE Network Magazine, special issue on Active and Programmable Networks*, 12(3):29–36, 1998.

[2] D. S. Alexander, W. A. Arbaugh, A. D. Keromytis, and J. M. Smith. A Secure Active Network Environment Architecture: Realization in SwitchWare. *IEEE Network Magazine, special issue on Active and Programmable Networks*, 12(3):37–45, 1998.

[3] D. S. Alexander, W. A. Arbaugh, A. D. Keromytis, and J. M. Smith. Security in active networks. In Jan Vitek and Christian Jensen, editors, *Secure Internet Programming*, Lecture Notes in Computer Science. Springer-Verlag Inc., New York, NY, USA, 1999.

[4] M. Blaze, J. Feigenbaum, J. Ioannidis, and A. Keromytis. The KeyNote Trust-Management System. Work in Progress, http://www.cis.upenn.edu/~angelos/keynote.html, June 1998.

[5] M. Blaze, J. Feigenbaum, and J. Lacy. Decentralized Trust Management. In *Proc. of the 17th Symposium on Security and Privacy*, pages 164–173. IEEE Computer Society Press, Los Alamitos, 1996.

[6] M. Blaze, J. Feigenbaum, P. Resnick, and M. Strauss. Managing Trust in an Information Labeling System. In *European Transactions on Telecommunications*, 8, pages 491–501, 1997.

[7] M. Blaze, J. Feigenbaum, and M. Strauss. Compliance Checking in the Policy-Maker Trust-Management System. In *Proc. of the Financial Cryptography '98, Lecture Notes in Computer Science, vol. 1465*, pages 254–274. Springer, Berlin, 1998.

[8] R. Braden, L. Zhang, S. Berson, S. Herzog, and S. Jamin. Resource ReSerVation Protocol (RSVP) – Version 1 Functional Specification. Internet RFC 2208, 1997.

[9] M. Calderon, M. Sedano, A. Azcorra, and C. Alonso. The Support of Active Networks for Fuzzy-Tolerant Multicast Applications. *IEEE Network Magazine, special issue on Active and Programmable Networks*, 12(3):20–28, 1998.

[10] J. Chinitz and S. Sonnenberg. A Transparent Security Framework For TCP/IP and Legacy Applications. Technical report, Intellisoft Corp., August 1996.

[11] Y.-H. Chu, J. Feigenbaum, B. LaMacchia, P. Resnick, and M. Strauss. REFEREE: Trust Management for Web Applications. In *World Wide Web Journal, 2*, pages 127–139, 1997.

[12] S. E. Deering. Host extensions for IP multicasting. Internet RFC 1112, 1989.

[13] C. M. Ellison, B. Frantz, R. Rivest, B. M. Thomas, and T. Ylonen. Simple Public Key Certificate. Work in Progress, http://www.pobox.com/~cme/html/spki.html, April 1997.

[14] S. Even, A. Selman, and Y. Yacobi. The Complexity of Promise Problems with Applications to Public-Key Cryptography. *Information and Control*, 61:159–174, 1984.

[15] James Gosling, Bill Joy, and Guy Steele. *The Java Language Specification*. Addison Wesley, Reading, 1996.

[16] M. Hicks, P. Kakkar, J. T. Moore, C. A. Gunter, and S. Nettles. PLAN: A Programming Language for Active Networks. Technical Report MS-CIS-98-25, Department of Computer and Information Science, University of Pennsylvania, February 1998.

[17] Angelos D. Keromytis, Matt Blaze, John Ioannidis, and Jonathan M. Smith. Firewalls in Active Networks. Technical Report MS-CIS-98-03, University of Pennsylvania, February 1998.

[18] J. Lacy, J. Snyder, and D. Maher. Music on the Internet and the Intellectual Property Protection Problem. In *Proc. of the International Symposium on Industrial Electronics*, pages SS77–83. IEEE Press, 1997.

[19] B. Lampson and R. Rivest. Cryptography and Information Security Group Research Project: A Simple Distributed Security Infrastructure. Technical report, MIT, 1997.

[20] Xavier Leroy. The Caml Special Light System (Release 1.10). http://pauillac.inria.fr/ocaml.

[21] R. Levien, L. McCarthy, and M. Blaze. Transparent Internet E-mail Security. http://www.cs.umass.edu/~lmccarth/crypto/papers/email.ps.

[22] S. P. Miller, B. C. Neuman, J. I. Schiller, and J. H. Saltzer. Kerberos authentication and authorization system. Technical report, MIT, December 1987.

[23] George C. Necula. Proof-Carrying Code. In *Proceedings of the 24th Annual ACM SIGPLAN-SIGACT Symposium on Principles of Programming Languages (POPL)*, pages 106–119. ACM Press, New York, January 1997.

[24] George C. Necula and Peter Lee. Safe Kernel Extensions Without Run-Time Checking. In *Second Symposium on Operating System Design and Implementation (OSDI)*, pages 229–243. Usenix, Seattle, 1996.

[25] C. Partridge and A. Jackson. Smart Packets. Technical report, BBN, 1996. http://www.net-tech.bbn.com-/smtpkts/smtpkts-index.html.

[26] P. Resnick and J. Miller. PICS: Internet Access Controls Without Censorship. *Communications of the ACM*, pages 87–93, October 1996.

[27] D. Wetherall, U. Legedza, and J. Guttag. Introducing New Internet Services: Why and How. *IEEE Network Magazine, special issue on Active and Programmable Networks*, 12(3):12–19, 1998.

[28] David J. Wetherall, John Guttag, and David L. Tennenhouse. Ants: A toolkit for building and dynamically deploying network protocols. In *IEEE OpenArch Proceedings*. IEEE Computer Society Press, Los Alamitos, April 1998.

# A PolicyMaker Compliance Proofs

We now give some technical details about the PolicyMaker compliance checker. This discussion is largely excerpted (with the authors' permission) from the paper of Blaze *et al.* [7].

The general problem we are concerned with is *Proof of Compliance* (POC). The question is whether a *request* $r$ complies with a *policy*. The policy is simply a function $f_0$ encoded in some well understood programming system or language and labeled by the keyword POLICY. In addition to the request and the policy, a POC instance contains a set of *credentials*, also general functions, each labeled by its source. Policies and credentials are collectively referred to as *assertions*.

Credentials are issued by *sources*. Formally, a credential is a pair $(f_i, s_i)$ of function $f_i$ and *source-ID* $s_i$, which is just a string over some appropriate alphabet. Important examples of source-IDs include public keys of credential issuers, URLs, names of people, and names of companies. With the exception of the keyword POLICY, the interpretation of source-IDs is part of the application-specific semantics of an assertion, and it is not the job of the compliance checker. From the compliance checker's point of view, the source-IDs are just strings, and the assertions encode a set of (possibly indirect and possibly conditional) trust relationships among the issuing sources. Associating each assertion with the correct source-ID is the responsibility of the calling application, as explained in Section 2.2.

The request $r$ is a string encoding an *action* for which the calling application seeks a proof of compliance. In the course of deciding whether the credentials $(f_1, s_1), \ldots, (f_{n-1}, s_{n-1})$ constitute a proof that $r$ complies with the policy $(f_0, \text{POLICY})$, the compliance checker's domain of discourse may need to include other action strings. For example, if POLICY requires that $r$ be approved by credential issuers $s_1$ and $s_2$, the credentials $(f_1, s_1)$ and $(f_2, s_2)$ may want a way to say that they approve $r$ *conditionally*, where the condition is that the other credential also approve it. A convenient way to formalize this is to use strings $R$, $R_1$, and $R_2$ over some finite alphabet $\Sigma$. The string $R$ corresponds to the requested action $r$. The strings $R_1$ and $R_2$ encode "conditional" versions of $R$ that might be approved by $s_1$ and $s_2$ as intermediate results of the compliance-checking procedure.

More generally, for each request $r$ and each assertion $(f_i, s_i)$, there is a set $\{R_{ij}\}$ of *action strings* that might arise in a compliance check. By convention, there is a distinguished string $R$ that corresponds to the input request $r$. The range of assertion $(f_i, s_i)$ is made up of *acceptance records* of the form $(i, s_i, R_{ij})$, the meaning of which is that, based on the information at its disposal, assertion number $i$, issued by source $s_i$, approves action $R_{ij}$. A set of acceptance records is referred to as an *acceptance set*. It is by maintaining acceptance sets and making them available to assertions that the PolicyMaker compliance checker manages "inter-assertion communication," giving assertions the chance to make decisions based on conditional decisions by other assertions. The compliance checker will start with *initial acceptance set* $\{(\Lambda, \Lambda, R)\}$, in which the one acceptance record means that the action string for which approval is sought is $R$ and that no assertions have yet signed off on it (or anything else). The checker will run the assertions $(f_0, \text{POLICY}), (f_1, s_1), \ldots, (f_{n-1}, s_{n-1})$ that it has received as input, not necessarily in that order and not necessarily once each, and see which acceptance records are produced. Ultimately, the compliance checker approves the request $r$ if the acceptance record $(0, \text{POLICY}, R)$, which means "policy approves the initial action string," is produced.

Thus, abstractly, an assertion is a mapping from acceptance sets to acceptance sets. Assertion $(f_i, s_i)$ looks at an acceptance set $A$ encoding the actions that have been approved so far and the numbers and sources of the assertions that approved them. Based on this information about what the sources it trusts have approved, $(f_i, s_i)$ outputs another acceptance set $A'$.

The following concrete examples show why PolicyMaker assertions are allowed to approve multiple action strings for each possible request. That is, for a given input request $r$, why do assertions need to do anything except say "I approve $r$" or refuse to say it?

First, consider the following "co-signing required" assertion $(f_0, \text{POLICY})$: "All expenditures of \$500 or more require approval by A and B." Suppose that A's policy is to approve such expenditures if and only if B approves them and that B's is to approve them if and only if A approves them. Our acceptance record structure makes such approvals straightforward. The credential $(f_1, A)$, can produce acceptance records of the form $(1, A, R)$ and $(1, A, R_B)$, where $R$ corresponds to the input request $r$; the meaning of the second is "I will approve $R$ if and only if B approves it." Similarly, the credential $(f_2, B)$, can produce records of the form $(2, B, R)$ and $(2, B, R_A)$. On input $\{(\Lambda, \Lambda, R)\}$, the sequence of acceptance records $(1, A, R_B), (2, B, R_A), (1, A, R), (2, B, R), (0, \text{POLICY}, R)$ would be produced if the assertions were run in the order $(f_1, A), (f_2, B), (f_1, A), (f_2, B), (f_0, \text{POLICY})$, and the request $r$ would be approved. If assertions could only produce binary approve/disapprove decisions, no transactions would ever be approved, unless the trust management system had some way of understanding the semantics of the assertions and knowing that it had to ask A's and B's credentials explicitly for a conditional approval. This would violate the goal of having a general-purpose, trust management system that processes requests and assertions whose semantics are only understood by the calling applications and that vary widely from application to application.

Second, consider the issue of "delegation depth." A very natural construction to use in assertion $(f_0, \text{POLICY})$ is "I delegate authority to A. Furthermore, I allow A to choose the parties to whom he will re-delegate the authority I've delegated to him. For any party B involved in the approval of a request, there must be a delegation chain of length at most two from me to B." Various "domain experts" $B_1, \ldots, B_t$ could issue credentials $(f_1, B_1), \ldots, (f_t, B_t)$ that *directly* approve actions in their areas of expertise by producing acceptance records of the form $(i, B_i, R_0^i)$. An assertion $(g_j, s_j)$ that sees such a record and explicitly trusts $B_i$ could produce an acceptance record of the form $(j, s_j, R_1^i)$, the meaning of which is that "$B_i$ approved $R^i$ directly, I trust $B_i$ directly, and so I also approve $R^i$." More generally, if an assertion $(g_l, s_l)$ trusts $s_k$ directly and sees an acceptance record of the form $(k, s_k, R_d^i)$, it can produce the acceptance record $(l, s_l, R_{d+1}^i)$. The assertion $(f_0, \text{POLICY})$ given above would approve an action $R^i$ if and only if it were run on an acceptance set that contained a record of the form $(k, A, R_1^i)$, for some $k$. Note that $(f_0, \text{POLICY})$ need not know *which* credential $(f_i, B_i)$ directly approved $R^i$ by producing $(i, B_i, R_0^i)$. All it needs to know is that it trusts $A$ and that $A$ trusts *some* $B_i$ whose credential produced such a record.

The most general version of the compliance-checking problem is:

**Proof of Compliance (POC):**

<u>Input</u> : A request $r$ and a set $\{(f_0, \text{POLICY}), (f_1, s_1), \ldots, (f_{n-1}, s_{n-1})\}$ of assertions.

<u>Question</u> : Is there a finite sequence $i_1, i_2, \ldots, i_t$ of indices such that each $i_j$ is in $\{0, 1, \ldots, n-1\}$, but the $i_j$'s are not necessarily distinct and not necessarily exhaustive of $\{0, 1, \ldots, n-1\}$ and such that

$$(0, \text{POLICY}, R) \in (f_{i_t}, s_{i_t}) \circ \cdots \circ (f_{i_1}, s_{i_1})(\{(\Lambda, \Lambda, R)\}),$$

where $R$ is the action string that corresponds to the request $r$?

This most general version of the problem is clearly undecidable. A compliance checker cannot even decide whether an arbitrary assertion $(f_i, s_i)$ halts when given an arbitrary acceptance set as input, much less whether some sequence containing $(f_i, s_i)$ produces the desired output.

When we say that "$\{(f_0, \text{POLICY}), (f_1, s_1), \ldots, (f_{n-1}, s_{n-1})\}$ contains a proof that $r$ complies with POLICY," we mean that $(r, \{(f_0, \text{POLICY}), (f_1, s_1), \ldots, (f_{n-1}, s_{n-1})\})$ is a yes-instance of this unconstrained, most general form of POC. If $F$ is a (possibly proper) subset of $\{(f_0, \text{POLICY}), (f_1, s_1), \ldots, (f_{n-1}, s_{n-1})\}$ that contains all of the assertions that actually appear in the sequence $(f_{i_t}, s_{i_t}) \circ \cdots \circ (f_{i_1}, s_{i_1})$, then we say that "$F$ contains a proof that $r$ complies with POLICY."

Restricted versions of POC are obtained by adding various pieces of information to the problem instances. Specifically, consider augmenting the instance $(r, \{(f_0, \text{POLICY}), (f_1, s_1), \ldots, (f_{n-1}, s_{n-1})\})$ in one or more of the following ways:

**Global runtime bound**: An instance may contain an integer $d$ such that a sequence of assertions $(f_{i_1}, s_{i_1}), \ldots, (f_{i_t}, s_{i_t})$ is only considered a valid proof that $r$ complies with POLICY if the total amount of time that the compliance checker needs to compute $(f_{i_t}, s_{i_t}) \circ \cdots \circ (f_{i_1}, s_{i_1})(\{(\Lambda, \Lambda, R)\})$ is $O(N^d)$. Here $N$ is the length of the original problem instance, *i.e.*, the number of bits needed to encode $r$, $(f_0, \text{POLICY}), \ldots, (f_{n-1}, s_{n-1})$, and $d$ in some standard fashion.

**Local runtime bound**: An instance may contain an integer $c$ such that $(f_{i_1}, s_{i_1}), \ldots, (f_{i_t}, s_{i_t})$ is only considered a valid proof that $r$ complies with POLICY if each $(f_{i_j}, s_{i_j})$ runs in time $O(N^c)$. Here $N$ is the length of the actual acceptance set that is input to $(f_{i_j}, s_{i_j})$ when it is run by the compliance checker. Note that the length of the input fed to an individual assertion $(f_{i_j}, s_{i_j})$ in the course of checking a proof may be considerably bigger than the length of the original problem instance $(r, \{(f_0, \text{POLICY}), (f_1, s_1), \ldots, (f_{n-1}, s_{n-1})\}, c)$, because the running of assertions $(f_{i_1}, s_{i_1}), \ldots, (f_{i_{j-1}}, s_{i_{j-1}})$ may have caused the creation of many new acceptance records.

**Bounded number of assertions in a proof**: An instance may contain an integer $l$ such that $(f_{i_1}, s_{i_1}), \ldots, (f_{i_t}, s_{i_t})$ is only considered a valid proof if $t \le l$.

**Bounded output set**: An instance may contain integers $m$ and $s$ such that an assertion $(f_i, s_i)$ can only be part of a valid proof that $r$ complies with POLICY if there is a set $O_i = \{R_{i1}, \ldots, R_{im}\}$ of $m$ action strings, such that $(f_i, s_i)(A) \subseteq O_i$ for any input set $A$, and the maximum size of an acceptance record $(i, s_i, R_{ij})$ is $s$. Intuitively, for any user-supplied request $r$, the meaningful "domain of discourse" for assertion $(f_i, s_i)$ is of size at most $m$ — there are at most $m$ actions that it would make sense for $(f_i, s_i)$ to sign off on, no matter what the other assertions in the instance say about $r$.

**Monotonicity**: Important variants of POC are obtained by restricting attention to instances in which the assertions have the following property: $(f_i, s_i)$ is *monotonic* if, for all acceptance sets $A$ and $B$, $A \subseteq B \Rightarrow (f_i, s_i)(A) \subseteq (f_i, s_i)(B)$. Thus, if $(f_i, s_i)$ approves action $R_{ij}$ when given a certain set of "evidence" that $R_{ij}$ is ok, it will also approve $R_{ij}$ when given a superset of that evidence — it does not have a notion of "negative evidence."

Any of the parameters $l$, $m$, and $s$ that are present in a particular instance should be written in unary so that they play an analogous role to $n$ (the number of assertions) in the calculation of the total size of the instance. The parameters $d$ and $c$ are exponents in a runtime bound and hence can be written in binary. Any subset of the parameters $d$, $c$, $l$, $m$, and $s$ may be present in a POC instance, and each subset defines a POC variant, some of which are more natural and interesting than others. Including a global runtime bound $d$ obviously makes the POC problem decidable, as does including parameters $c$ and $l$.

In stating and proving results about the complexity of POC, we use the notion of a *promise problem* [14]. In a standard decision problem, a language $L$ is defined by a predicate $R$ in that $x \in L \Leftrightarrow R(x)$. In a promise problem, there are two predicates, the *promise* $Q$ and the *property* $R$. A machine $M$ *solves* the promise problem $(Q, R)$ if, for all inputs $x$ for which the promise holds, the machine $M$ halts and accepts $x$ if and only if the property holds. Formally, $\forall x[Q(x) \Rightarrow [M$ halts on $x$ and $M(x)$ accepts $\Leftrightarrow R(x)]]$. Note that $M$'s behavior is unconstrained on inputs that do not satisfy the promise, and each set of choices for the behavior of $M$ on these inputs determines a different solution. Thus predicates $Q$ and $R$ define a family of languages, namely all $L$ such that $L = L(M)$ for some $M$ that solves $(Q, R)$. A promise problem is NP-hard if it has at least one solution and all of its solutions are NP-hard.

The following natural variants of POC are NP-hard. Refer to Blaze *et al.* [7] for the NP-hardness proofs.

**Locally Bounded Proof of Compliance (LBPOC):**
Input : A request $r$, a set $\{(f_0, \text{POLICY}), (f_1, s_1), \ldots, (f_{n-1}, s_{n-1})\}$ of assertions, and integers $c$, $l$, $m$, and $s$.

<u>Promise</u> : Each $(f_i, s_i)$ runs in time $O(N^c)$. On any input set that contains $(\Lambda, \Lambda, R)$, where $R$ is the action string corresponding to request $r$, for each $(f_i, s_i)$ there is a set $O_i$ of at most $m$ action strings such that $(f_i, s_i)$ only produces output from $O_i$, and $s$ is the maximum size of an acceptance record $(i, s_i, R_{ij})$, where $R_{ij} \in O_i$.

<u>Question</u> : Is there a sequence $i_1, \ldots, i_t$ of indices such that

1. Each $i_j$ is in $\{0, 1, \ldots, n-1\}$, but the $i_j$ need not be distinct or collectively exhaustive of $\{0, 1, \ldots, n-1\}$,
2. $t \le l$, and
3. $(0, \text{POLICY}, R) \in (f_{i_t}, s_{i_t}) \circ \cdots \circ (f_{i_1}, s_{i_1})(\{(\Lambda, \Lambda, R)\})$?

## Globally Bounded Proof of Compliance (GBPOC):

<u>Input</u> : A request $r$, a set $\{(f_0, \text{POLICY}), (f_1, s_1), \ldots, (f_{n-1}, s_{n-1})\}$ of assertions, and an integer $d$.

<u>Question</u> : Is there a sequence $i_1, \ldots, i_t$ of indices such that

1. Each $i_j$ is in $\{0, 1, \ldots, n-1\}$, but the $i_j$ need not be distinct or collectively exhaustive of $\{0, 1, \ldots, n-1\}$,
2. $(0, \text{POLICY}, R) \in (f_{i_t}, s_{i_t}) \circ \cdots \circ (f_{i_1}, s_{i_1})(\{(\Lambda, \Lambda, R)\})$, where $R$ is the action string corresponding to request $r$, and
3. The computation of $(f_{i_t}, s_{i_t}) \circ \cdots \circ (f_{i_1}, s_{i_1})(\{(\Lambda, \Lambda, R)\})$ runs in (total) time $O(N^d)$?

## Monotonic Proof of Compliance (MPOC):

<u>Input</u> : A request $r$, a set $\{(f_0, \text{POLICY}), (f_1, s_1), \ldots, (f_{n-1}, s_{n-1})\}$ of assertions, and integers $l$ and $c$.

<u>Promise</u> : Each assertion $(f_i, s_i)$ is monotonic and runs in time $O(N^c)$.

<u>Question</u> : Is there a sequence $i_1, \ldots, i_t$ of indices such that

1. Each $i_j$ is in $\{0, 1, \ldots, n-1\}$, but the $i_j$ need not be distinct or collectively exhaustive of $\{0, 1, \ldots, n-1\}$,
2. $t \le l$, and
3. $(0, \text{POLICY}, R) \in (f_{i_t}, s_{i_t}) \circ \cdots \circ (f_{i_1}, s_{i_1})(\{(\Lambda, \Lambda, R)\})$, where $R$ is the action string corresponding to request $r$?

Each version of POC can be defined using "agglomeration" $(f_2, s_2) \star (f_1, s_1)$ instead of composition $(f_2, s_2) \circ (f_1, s_1)$. The result of applying the sequence of assertions $(f_{i_1}, s_{i_1}), \ldots, (f_{i_t}, s_{i_t})$ agglomeratively to an acceptance set $S_0$ is defined inductively as follows: $S_1 \equiv (f_{i_1}, s_{i_1})(S_0) \cup S_0$ and, for $2 \le j \le t$, $S_j \equiv (f_{i_j}, s_{i_j})(S_{j-1}) \cup S_{j-1}$. Thus, for any acceptance set $A$, $A \subseteq (f_{i_t}, s_{i_t}) \star \cdots \star (f_{i_1}, s_{i_1})(A)$. The agglomerative versions of the decision problems are identical to the versions already given, except that the acceptance condition is "$(0, \text{POLICY}, R) \in (f_{i_t}, s_{i_t}) \star \cdots \star (f_{i_1}, s_{i_1})(\{(\Lambda, \Lambda, R)\})$?" We refer to "agglomerative POC," "agglomerative MPOC," etc., when we mean the version defined in terms of $\star$ instead of $\circ$.

A trust management system that defines "proof of compliance" in terms of agglomeration makes it impossible for an assertion to "undo" an approval that it or any other assertion has already given to an action string during the course of constructing a proof. Informally, it forces assertions to construct proofs by communicating on a "write-only blackboard." This definition of proof makes sense if it is important for the trust management system to guard against a rogue credential-issuer's ability to thwart legitimate proofs. Note that the question of whether the compliance checker combines assertions using agglomeration or composition is separate from the question of whether the assertions themselves are monotonic.

The agglomerative versions of GBPOC, LBPOC, and MPOC are also NP-hard; the NP-hardness proofs are given in [7] and are simply minor variations on the NP-hardness proofs for the composition versions.

Finally, we present the compliance-checking algorithm that is used in the current version of the PolicyMaker trust management system. The promise that defines this special case includes some conditions that we have already discussed, namely monotonicity and bounds on the runtime of assertions and on the total size of acceptance sets that assertions can produce. It also includes "authenticity," something that can be ignored when proving hardness results. An authentic assertion $(f_i, s_i)$ only produces acceptance records of the form $(i, s_i, R_{ij})$, i.e., it does not "impersonate" another assertion by producing an acceptance record of the form $(i', s_{i'}, R_{i'j})$.

PolicyMaker constructs proofs in an agglomerative fashion, and hence we use $\star$ in the following problem statement. This variant of POC could be defined using $\circ$ as well, but the algorithm given below would *not* work for the $\circ$ version.

**Locally Bounded, Monotonic, and Authentic Proof of Compliance (LBMAPOC):**

Input : A request $r$, a set $\{(f_0, \text{POLICY}), (f_1, s_1), \ldots, (f_{n-1}, s_{n-1})\}$ of assertions, and integers $c$, $m$, and $s$.

Promise : Each assertion $(f_i, s_i)$ is monotonic, authentic, and runs in time $O(N^c)$. On any input set that contains $(\Lambda, \Lambda, R)$, where $R$ is the action string corresponding to request $r$, for each $(f_i, s_i)$ there is a set $O_i$ of at most $m$ action strings, such that $(f_i, s_i)$ only produces output from $O_i$, and $s$ is the maximum size of an acceptance record $(i, s_i, R_{ij})$, such that $R_{ij} \in O_i$.

Question : Is there a sequence $i_1, \ldots, i_t$ of indices such that each $i_j$ is in $\{0, 1, \ldots, n-1\}$, but the $i_j$ need not be distinct or collectively exhaustive of $\{0, 1, \ldots, n-1\}$, and $(0, \text{POLICY}, R) \in (f_{i_t}, s_{i_t}) \star \cdots \star (f_{i_1}, s_{i_1})(\{(\Lambda, \Lambda, R)\})$.

The current algorithm is called CCA$_1$, for "compliance-checking algorithm, version 1," to allow for the evolution of PolicyMaker, and for improved algorithms CCA$_i$, $i \geq 1$.

Assertion $(f_i, s_i)$ is called "ill-formed" if it violates the promise. If CCA$_1$ discovers in the course of simulating it that $(f_i, s_i)$ is ill-formed, CCA$_1$ ignores it for the remainder of the computation. Note that an assertion $(f_i, s_i)$ may be undetectably ill-formed; for example, there may be sets $A \subseteq B$ such that $(f_i, s_i)(A) \not\subseteq (f_i, s_i)(B)$, but such that $A$ and $B$ do not arise in this run of the compliance checker. The $CCA_1$ algorithm checks for violations of the promise every time it simulates an assertion. The pseudocode for these checks is omitted from the statement of $CCA_1$ given here, because it would not illustrate the basic structure of the algorithm; the predicate $IllFormed()$ is included in the main loop to indicate that the checks are done for each simulation.

**Fig. 2.** Pseudocode for Algorithm $CCA_1$

---

```
CCA₁(r, {(f₀, POLICY), (f₁, s₁), ..., (f_{n-1}, s_{n-1})}, c, m, s):
    {
        S ← {(Λ, Λ, R)}
        I ← {}
        For j ← 1 to mn
        {
            For i ← n-1 to 0
            {
                If (fᵢ, sᵢ) ∉ I, Then S' ← (fᵢ,sᵢ)(S)
                If IllFormed((fᵢ,sᵢ)), Then I ← I ∪ {(fᵢ,sᵢ)},
                    Else S ← S ∪ S'
            }
        }
        If (0, POLICY, R) ∈ S, Then Output(Accept),
            Else Output(Reject)
    }
```

---

Note that $CCA_1$ does $mn$ iterations of the sequence $(f_{n-1}, s_{n-1}), \ldots, (f_1, s_1)$, $(f_0, \text{POLICY})$, for a total of $mn^2$ assertion-simulations. Recall that a set $F = \{(f_{j_1}, s_{j_1}), \ldots, (f_{j_t}, s_{j_t})\} \subseteq \{(f_0, \text{POLICY}), \ldots, (f_{n-1}, s_{n-1})\}$ "contains a proof that $r$ complies with POLICY" if there is some sequence $k_1, \ldots, k_u$ of the indices $j_1, \ldots, j_t$, not necessarily distinct and not necessarily exhaustive of $j_1, \ldots, j_t$, such that $(0, \text{POLICY}, R) \in (f_{k_u}, s_{k_u}) \star \cdots \star (f_{k_1}, s_{k_1})(\{(\Lambda, \Lambda, R)\})$.

The following formal claim about this algorithm is proven in [7].

**Theorem 1.** Let $(r, \{(f_0, \text{POLICY}), (f_1, s_1), \ldots, (f_{n-1}, s_{n-1})\}, c, m, s)$ be an (agglomerative) LBMAPOC instance.

(1) Suppose that $F \subseteq \{(f_0, \text{POLICY}), (f_1, s_1), \ldots, (f_{n-1}, s_{n-1})\}$ contains a proof that $r$ complies with POLICY and that every $(f_i, s_i) \in F$ satisfies the promise of LBMAPOC. Then $CCA_1$ accepts $(r, \{(f_0, \text{POLICY}), (f_1, s_1), \ldots, (f_{n-1}, s_{n-1})\}, c, m, s)$.

(2) If $\{(f_0, \text{POLICY}), (f_1, s_1), \ldots, (f_{n-1}, s_{n-1})\}$ does not contain a proof that $r$ complies with POLICY, then $CCA_1$ rejects $(r, \{(f_0, \text{POLICY}), (f_1, s_1), \ldots, (f_{n-1}, s_{n-1})\}, c, m, s)$.

(3) $CCA_1$ runs in time $O(mn^2(nms)^c)$.

Note that cases (1) and (2) do not cover all possible inputs to $CCA_1$. There may be a subset $F$ of the input assertions that does contain a proof that $r$ complies with POLICY but that contains one or more ill-formed assertions. If $CCA_1$ does not detect that any of these assertions is ill-formed, because their ill-formedness is only exhibited on acceptance sets that do not occur in this computation, then $CCA_1$ will accept the input. If it does detect ill-formedness, then, as specified here, $CCA_1$ may or may not accept the input, perhaps depending on whether the record $(0, POLICY, R)$ has already been produced at the time of detection. $CCA_1$ could be modified so that it restarts every time ill-formedness is detected, after discarding the ill-formed assertion so that it is not used in the new computation. It is not clear whether this modification would be worth the performance penalty. The point is simply that $CCA_1$ offers no guarantees about what it does when it is fed a policy that trusts, directly or indirectly, a source of ill-formed assertions, except that it will terminate in time $O(mn^2(nms)^c)$. It is the responsibility of the policy author to know which sources to trust and to modify the policy if some trusted sources are discovered to be issuing ill-formed assertions.

Finally, note that $O(mn^2(nms)^c)$ is a pessimistic upper bound on the running time of the compliance checker. It is straightforward to check (each time an assertion $(f_i, s_i)$ is run, or at some other regular interval) whether the acceptance record $(0, POLICY, R)$ has been produced and to "stop early" if it has. Thus, for many requests $R$ that do comply with policy, the algorithm $CCA_1$ will find compliance proofs in time less than $O(mn^2(nms)^c)$.

# Distributed Access-Rights Management with Delegation Certificates

Tuomas Aura

**Abstract.** New key-oriented discretionary access control systems are based on delegation of access rights with public-key certificates. This paper explains the basic idea of delegation certificates in abstract terms and discusses their advantages and limitations. We emphasize decentralization of authority and operations. The discussion is based mostly on the SPKI certificates but we avoid touching implementation details. We also describe how threshold and conditional certificates can add flexibility to the system. Examples are given of access control between intelligent networks services.

## 1 Introduction

New distributed discretionary access control mechanisms such as SPKI [14] and PolicyMaker [8, 9] aim for decentralization of authority and management operations. They do not rely on a trusted computing base (TCB) like traditional distributed access control [22]. Instead, the participants are assumed to be untrusted the way computers on open networks (e.g. Internet) are in reality.

The decentralization, however, does not mean sliding back to anarchy such as the PGP web of trust [26]. The new systems offer ways of building local relations and setting up local authorities that arise from the personal and business connections of the participants. The access control mechanisms do not mandate any hierarchical or fixed domain structure like, for example, Kerberos [18] and DSSA [16]. All entities are equally entitled to distribute rights to the services in their control and to act as an authority for those who depend on them for the services.

The main mechanism used in the new access control systems is delegation of access rights with signed certificates. The signing is done with public-key cryptography. With a certificate, one cryptographic key delegates some of its authority to another key. The certificates can form a complicated network that reflects the underlying relations between the owners of the private signature keys.

By taking the cryptographic keys as their principal entities, the systems avoid dependence on trusted name and key services such as the X.500 directory [12]. If any names are used, they are not global distinguished names but relative to the users [1, 24].

This paper explains the principles behind the delegation certificates in an abstract setting without exposing the reader to implementation details. The discussion is based primarily on the SPKI draft standard although we will not touch certificate formats. We stress distribution, scalability and locality of policy decisions. Application examples are given from the Calypso service architecture for intelligent networks [19]. The emphasis is this paper is on practical issues. More theoretical treatments of distributed access control can be found in [2, 4]. Some support from implementations is in [3, 20]. Code libraries and products using SPKI are expected to appear when the standardization work nears completion.

Sec. 2 introduces delegation certificates an explains how they aid decentralization. Sec. 3 describes two enhancements, threshold schemes and validity conditions, that add flexibility to the basic certificates. The limitations of the certificate-based approach and ways to overcome them are the topic of Sec. 4. Sec. 5 concludes the paper.

## 2 Access Control with Delegation Certificates

Sec. 2.1 introduces delegation certificates and some basic concepts. In Sec. 2.2, we describe first how access rights are distributed and verified with certificates. Then we consider redelegation and extend the verification procedure to cover chains of delegation certificates. Sec. 2.3 explains why certificates are an appealing alternative for other methods of distributed access control.

### 2.1 Basic Delegation Certificates

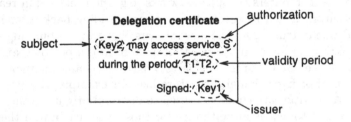

**Fig. 1.** With a delegation certificate, the issuer shares authority with the subject.

A delegation certificate (Fig. 1) is a signed message with which an entity grants access rights that it has to another entity. We are interested in systems where the certificates are signed with public-key cryptography and the entities granting and receiving access rights are, with some exceptions, cryptographic keys. A certificate has the meaning:

$$S_K(\text{During the validity period } T_1 - T_2, \text{ if I have any of the rights } R,$$
$$\text{I give them also to } K'.)$$

($S_k(\ldots)$ denotes a signed message that includes both the signature and the original message.) The key that signed the certificate ($K$) is the *issuer* and the key to whom the rights are given $(K')$ is the *subject* of the certificate, and the rights $R$ given by the certificate are the *authorization* (following the SPKI terminology). With the certificate, the issuer delegates the rights to the subject.

All delegation certificates have a *validity period* $(T_1 - T_2)$ specified on them. When the certificate expires, the subject loses the rights that the certificate may have given to it. Together with the authorization field, this parameter is used for regulating the amount of trust the issuer places on the subject. Extremely short validity periods are used to force on-line connections to the issuer. (For simplicity, we often omit the validity period in the text below.)

The authorization is usually the right to use certain services. Sometimes, it can be an attribute that the subject uses as a credential to acquire access rights. Such attributes can be interpreted as abstract rights that may not directly entitle the subject to any services but help in acquiring such rights. The syntax of the authorization is application dependent and each application must provide its own rules for comparing and combining authorizations. (See [14] Sec. Examples for some typical authorizations.)

Some characteristics of delegation certificates are that any key can issue certificates, a key may delegate rights that it does not yet have but hopes to obtain, and the issuer itself does not lose the rights it gives to the subject. In the following, we will discuss these and other properties of delegation in detail.

Our view of the world is *key-oriented.* The entities possessing, delegating and receiving access rights are cryptographic key pairs. The public key is used to identify the key pair and to verify signatures. The private key can sign messages. It is held secret by some physical entity that uses the key and the rights attributed to the key at its will. All keys are generated locally by their owners. There is no limit on the number of keys one physical entity may own. On the other hand, if a physical entity is to receive any rights from others, it must be represented by at least one key. Most public-key infrastructures (e.g. X.509) are *identity-oriented.* In them, access rights are given to names of entities and the names are separately bound to keys.

Delegation certificates also differ from traditional access control schemes in that any key may issue certificates. There is no central or trusted authority that could control the flow of access rights. All keys are free to delegate access to services in their control.

The delegation takes effect only to the extent that the issuer of a certificate itself has the authority it is trying to delegate. Nevertheless, it is perfectly legal to issue delegation certificates for rights that one does not yet have or for broader rights than one has in the hope that the issuer may later obtain these rights. Sometimes a key may delegate *all* of its rights to another key. The policy for calculating the access rights received by the the subject when the issuer itself does not possess all of the rights listed in the certificate depends on the type of authorizations in question. In this paper, we consider only *set-type* authorizations as most literature [4, 14]. The subject gets the intersection of the rights held by the issuer and the rights mentioned in the certificate. Since this limitation is true for all delegation certificates, it is usually not explicitly mentioned. If we also ignore the validity period, the certificate above can be written, in short,

$$S_K(K' \text{ has the rights } R.)$$

Since the signing of a certificate happens locally at the physical entity possessing the private issuer key, the act of signing does not invalidate any existing certificates or affect existing rights. The subject of the certificate gets new rights but the issuer does not lose any.

In this way, delegation is less powerful than transfer of rights where the originating entity loses what it gives. On the other hand, delegation is far easier to implement. The simplicity of the implementation (signing a certificate) in a distributed environment is the reason why delegation is preferable to transfer as an atomic access control primitive. (See Sec. 4.1 about implementing transfer.)

## 2.2 Certificate Chains

This section shows how the certificates are used as a proof of authority and how the rights can be passed forward through several keys and certificates.

We begin by considering the simple case of access right verification where the owner of a service has issued a certificate directly to the user of the service (like $K$ delegates to the public key $K'$ above). When the user wants to use its rights, it signs a request with its private key $(K')$ or in some other way authenticates (e.g. by establishing an authenticated session) the access request with the private key. This can be construed as redelegating the rights to the request. The user attaches the delegation certificate to the access request and sends both to the server.

Every service platform has either a single master public key that controls all access to it or access control lists (ACL) that determine the privileged public keys for each service. When the server receives an access request with an attached delegation certificate, it first verifies that the certificate is signed by a key controlling the requested service $(K)$. It then checks that the authorization in the certificate is for the service and that the key requesting the service is the same as the subject of the certificate $(K')$. In this scenario, the certificate behaves like a capability. The signature protects the capability from falsification and binds it to the subject key.

Just as a key may delegate rights to services it directly controls, it may also redelegate rights it received by delegation from other keys. In this paper we assume that redelegation is always allowed unless a certificate explicitly forbids it.

When a key delegates to another key and this key in turn redelegates to a third one, and so on, the delegation certificates form a chain. In the chain, the access rights flow from issuers through certificates to subjects. The original issuer is usually the service producer and the final subject is a client of the service.

If all the certificates in the chain delegate the same access rights and specify the same validity period, these rights are passed all the way from the first issuer to the subject of the last certificate. But it is not necessary for the certificates to have the same authorization field and validity period. We remember that the rights obtained by the subject key are the intersection of the rights possessed by the issuer and the authorization field of the certificate. Consequently, the rights passed through the chain of certificates can be computed by taking the intersection of the rights possessed by the first issuer with the authorizations on all the certificates in the chain. (Sometimes the intersection can be empty meaning that no rights are passed all the way.) Likewise, the validity period of the of the chain is the intersection of the periods specified on the individual certificates. For example, in the chain of Fig. 2, *Key4* receives the right to the web pages "http://S/file" for today only from key *Key1*.

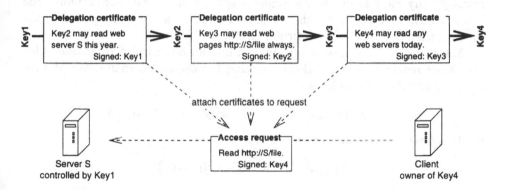

**Fig. 2.** A chain of delegation certificates

Since the certificates can be issued by anyone to anyone, they do not necessarily form simple chains. Instead, the certificates form a graph structure called *delegation network*. In the delegation network, there may be many chains of certificates between the same pair of keys. Naturally, the rights passed between two keys are the union of the rights passed by all individual chains between them. (Set-type authorizations are combined with the union operator. Other policies are possible for other types of authorizations.)

When a key requests a service and it has obtained the access rights through a chain of certificates, it attaches the entire chain to its request (Fig. 2). The server will verify that the chain originates from a key controlling access to the requested service, that it ends to the key making the request, that each certificate in the chain is signed by the subject of the previous certificate, and that each certificate in the chain authorizes the request. Several chains of certificates can be attached if the combined rights delegated by them are needed for the access.

The signing of an access request can also be thought of as redelegation to the request. Furthermore, the request may be program code. In that case, it is natural to think that the last key in a chain redelegates to the code and the code makes the actual requests. Consequently, delegation certificates should be used to express this delegation. This is done so that the last key signs a delegation certificate where the subject is not a key but a hash value of the program code. We will see an example of this in Sec. 2.4.

In a way, the delegation certificates behave like signed requests for capability propagation (see e.g [17]). The requests are honored only if the signer itself has the capability. However, it is not necessary for the server or for a trusted party to process each propagation before the next one is made, and no new capabilities need to be produced before the rights are used. Instead, the information is stored in the form of the delegation certificates.

Although the most obvious way of managing certificates is to accumulate them along the chain of delegation and to attach them to the service requests, there is no compelling reason to do this. The certificates can be stored and managed anywhere as long as the verifier gets them in the end. The accumulation is not always even possible if the certificates are not issued and renewed in the order of their positions in a particular chain.

Managing long chains of certificates can become a burden. A technique called *certificate reduction* saves work in verifying the certificate chains. We observe that two certificates forming a chain

$$S_{K_1}(K_2 \text{ has the rights } R_1.) \text{ and } S_{K_2}(K_3 \text{ has the rights } R_2.)$$

imply a direct delegation from $K_1$ to $K_3$:

$$S_{K_1}(K_3 \text{ has the rights } R_1 \cap R_2.)$$

The third certificate is redundant and signing it will have no effect of the access rights of any entity. Hence, $K_1$ can sign it after verifying the chain of signatures. Continuing the process inductively, a chain of any length can be reduced into a single certificate. If the reduced certificate is used repeatedly as a proof of access rights, savings in the verification time can be substantial. In order to compute the intersection of the authorizations, the issuer of the reduced certificate must have some understanding of the contents of the authorization fields. Other than that, the reduction is a mechanical procedure that does not involve any decision making. Certificate reduction is the main technique of certificate management in SPKI.

## 2.3 Distribution of Authority and Operations

This section explains the rationale behind delegation with certificates. We emphasize suitability for open distributed systems with no globally accepted authority. The advantages center around the high level of distribution achieved both in authority and management work load.

The first key to the distribution is that the entities are represented by their cryptographic keys instead of names. Names are a natural way of specifying entities for humans but they are less suitable for cryptographically secure authentication. Ellison [13] discusses the complicated connection between keys and identities. In a key-oriented world, we don't need trusted third parties to certify the binding between a name and a public key. Instead, the public key is used directly to specify an entity. Thus, the centralized or hierarchical certification authorities (CA) that are the heart of traditional identity-based access control lose their role in key-oriented systems. This is a major security advantage. For example in X.509, the name certificates come from a global hierarchy of officials (CAs) who must all be trusted with respect to any access control decision whose security depends on the correct mapping between a key and a name. Key-oriented access control avoids such obvious single points of failure. Fig. 3 illustrates the difference. It becomes even more obvious when we remember that, in a truly name-oriented system, the mapping from name to key must be done also for the service owner and for every key in a chain of delegation.

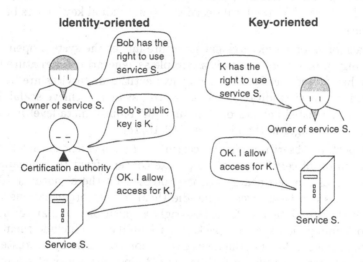

**Fig. 3.** In an identity-oriented system, security of all access control depends on trusted authorities. Key-oriented systems avoid this.

The omission of names also results in savings in communication and certificate processing. There is no need to contact a CA. The verification of the certificates in a chain is a straight-forward, mechanical procedure that involves no communication or policy decisions.

Sometimes we, nevertheless, need bindings between names and keys. This is usually because of the need to refer to legal persons or because names are a natural form of human input. In such cases, we must either trust name certificates from a some CA or, preferably, resort to SDSI-type linked name spaces [1, 24] whose relativity is explicit. But when feasible, the most robust practice is to pass the correct public key from the subject to the issuer at the time when a delegation certificate is created and to issue the certificate directly to the key.

The effect of delegation on the distribution of authority, however, is greater than only eliminating the CA. Delegation-based access control does not conceptually differentiate between keys that are allowed to grant access and ones that only use services. From technical point of view, all keys are equal regardless of the importance of rights they handle. Any key may issue certificates to others and distribute access rights to the services in its control without asking permission from any other entity.

The bottom-up formation of policy is the most distinguishing property of certificate-based access control. The certificates are issued locally by the entities that produce the services and, therefore, should be responsible for granting access to them. The certificates are formal documents of local trust relationships that arise from voluntary personal, technical and business relations between the entities possessing private keys. Nothing is mandated by global authorities. In a chain of delegation certificates, every link is a result of a local policy decision. Because of redelegation, the local decisions by individual key owners have global consequences.

The lack of enforced hierarchical structure makes the system open and scalable. Setting up new a new entity is as simple as generating a signature key. New keys may be created locally as new physical entities or services are introduced. In comparison, most traditional access control systems achieve scalability with a hierarchy of trusted entities or domains and require meta-level maintenance operations for changes in the hierarchy [12, 16, 18].

An important observation in the certificate management is that the storage and distribution of certificates is a separate concern from their meaning [8, 9]. The integrity of the certificate data is protected by the signatures. Thus, untrusted entities can be allowed to handle them. Often, organizations will want to set up certificate databases for access-right acquisition and management. Similarly, most application software packages are unlikely to include their own certificate management. Most of the tasks can be done for them by untrusted servers or helper software. Nikander and Viljanen [23] describe a way of storing certificates in the Internet domain name service and a discovery algorithm based on [3].

The certificates should be considered as sets or graphs rather than as chains. This is because the order of issuance of the certificates does not necessarily have any correlation to their order in a particular chain. The time of issuance and the validity periods depend on the local trust relations behind the certificates. These are independent of whatever chains may be formed globally. If one certificate in a chain expires, only that one needs to be refreshed immediately. The other certificates in the chain remain valid. In this way, the system is distributed not only in space but also in time. It is even possible that the private keys or the owners of the keys who issued some of the certificates have ceased to exist by the time the certificates are used as a part of a chain. This is commonly so when temporary key pairs are used for anonymity or when a old system delegates its tasks and rights to a replacing one.

Certificate reduction allows a trade-off between communication and certificate processing cost. Reduction requires one to contact the issuer of the reduced certificate. This means that the entity must be on-line at the time of the reduction and that this on-line system must be secure enough to hold the private signature key. Luckily, the reduction engine can be fairly simple to build. If all the certificates in the chain delegate the same rights or if the application has straightforward rules for computing intersections of the authorizations, the reduction is a purely syntactical transformation and it can be fully automated. The issuer of the reduced certificate does not need to fully understand the meaning of the certificates. The reduction may save significantly in the costs of certificate transfer and verification.

Unlike mandatory access control mechanisms, delegation does not have a central reference monitor to supervise access and distribution of the access rights. Neither is there a trusted computing base (TCB) to monitor the actions of the distributed entities. This is because there is no global policy to enforce on the parts of the system. In open environments like the Internet, it would not be possible to implement any global controls. Instead, the policy is determined locally by the parts.

Delegation leaves more to the discretion of the participants than many other DAC mechanisms. The system does not enforce any policies to protect users from bad decisions. All the verifier of a certificate sees is public keys and signatures. It has no way of telling if the private keys belong to legitimate entities in the system. The certificate issuer at the time of signing should, of course, have a solid reason for trusting the subject with the delegated rights. But the systems leaves it to each key owner to judge by itself who can be trusted. The issuer may or may not know the name or identity of the subject key owner. Moreover, redelegation creates a new degree of freedom. When redelegation is allowed, anyone can share his rights with others. This is equal to universal grant rights from anyone to anyone.

It may seem that redelegation should be controlled. It is, indeed, possible to add conditions on the certificates limiting redelegation. In SPKI, the choices are to allow or forbid redelegation completely. A certificate that forbids redelegation can only be the last certificate in a certificate chain.

There are, however, appealing arguments for allowing free redelegation. It may be convenient for the client to authorize someone else to use the rights on its behalf, or the client may want to redelegate the rights to one of its subsidiaries. The internal organization of the clients of a service should not be a concern to the service providers. Free redelegation makes the internals of the system parts more independent thus furthering distribution.

The key-oriented nature of the system also obscures the semantical meaning of the restrictions on redelegation. Only in special circumstances does the issuer of a certificate know that the private part of the subject key is held permanently secret by a certain physical entity. In many cases, the issuer accepts any key given by the entity that is to receive the rights. In general, there is no guarantee that the corresponding private key will not be revealed to others. Giving out the key would spread the rights as effectively as redelegation but, unlike in redelegation, the rights and their validity period could not be limited. Usually, there are also other ways to redistribute the services without the agreement of the originator, e.g. establishing proxy servers and outright duplication of the server data.

Instead of forbidding redelegation, the issuer of a certificate should consider changing the authorization and validity period. Minimizing the scope of delegated rights is the most natural way to express limited trust in the subject. The certificates make it easy to reconsider the rights and validity in each step of a delegation chain.

All in all, delegation does well the part of access control that is easy to implement: maximally discretionary distribution of access rights. Mechanisms for identity certification, limits on redistribution, rights transfer and revocation can be added where they are required. However, such features in principle require a more complex infrastructure with a TCB, tamper-resistant modules, trusted third parties or on-line communication. Therefore, the basic access control system should not require their use. We believe that there are many instances where pure delegation is a sufficient mechanism and corresponds well to the real-life access-control needs.

## 2.4 Access Control for IN Services

Delegation certificates are most suitable for use in distributed systems with no globally accepted security policy or authority and in open systems with no central registration of the servers and clients. They are unlikely to find applications in high-security environments where mandatory access control and trusted systems are a rule. Although most applications will be on the Internet, we will look at an example from the telecommunications world.

Calypso [19] is a distributed service architecture for intelligent networks (IN). It is designed for ATM access networks where a workstation running the Calypso service platform controls an ATM switch. Calypso provides flexible distribution of service and network control functions among service clients, servers and network nodes. The same architecture could also reside on top of other types of network equipment such as IP switches and firewalls.

Calypso is based on a business model where the network operator who owns the infrastructure offers network resources to service providers (SP). These resources are the lowest level of Calypso services. Service providers can either market the right to use their services to end users or they can sell them to other SPs for reselling or for use as building blocks of more sophisticated services. Complex services and their components form tree-like structures (Fig. 4).

All Calypso services are implemented as Java packages. A service may use other services by calling methods of the classes that belong to them. Hence, the network nodes must have an access control system that facilitates execution of code from mutually distrusting SPs and contracting of services between them. The Calypso security requirements and a tentative architecture for satisfying them were outlined in [6].

The IN access control mechanisms should encourage free formation of business relations between service producers and merchants distributing access rights

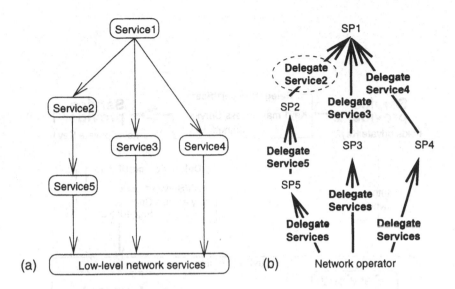

**Fig. 4.** Calypso service composition and delegation between SPs

to the services. Delegation, in a natural way, allows complex relations between the entities without forcing too much predefined structure on the service market.

Calypso uses SPKI certificates to delegate access rights between SP keys. The Calypso system differs from the standard scenario in that the last certificate in the chain always delegates the rights to (a hash value of) a Java package implementing the service that will use the access rights.

Fig. 5 shows how a service provider delegates access rights for its service to another SP that in turn delegates them to its service code. (This is the circled delegation step in Fig. 4(b).) When the code package is installed into the network nodes, it is accompanied by the certificates. In Fig. 6, the access rights are delegated through a service broker adding another link to the chain of certificates.

The delegated authorizations are always rights to access a Calypso service. Since services in the Calypso architecture are encapsulated into Java classes and packages, this gives a natural level of granularity for the access control.

Each service has exactly one key associated with it: the key of the service author or owner. This key distributes the access rights by issuing delegation certificates. The decision to delegate depends on the relations between the entities possessing the private keys. However, the service producers do not actually need to think in terms of access control policies. Instead, they sell and buy the certificates with business relations in mind.

The network operator or a service provider may want to review the client service implementation before granting access. This is because the access control mechanisms cannot effectively prevent denial of service, bad publicity and many other potential problems created by malicious or low quality services. The review

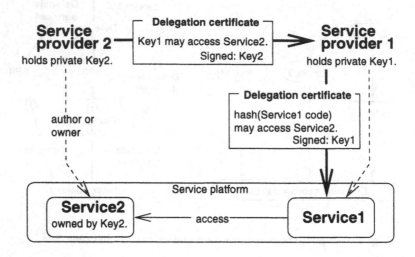

**Fig. 5.** Delegation to another service provider (SP) in Calypso

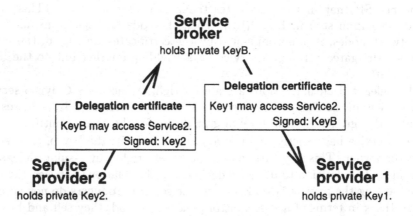

**Fig. 6.** Delegation through a service broker in Calypso

process is not easy to organize because the aim is to allow fast development of services by a large number of independent SPs. A possible solution is to use independent quality-control (QC) units that certify services if they meet some minimum quality criteria. In Fig. 7, the network operator grants access rights to SP1's code only after receiving the review results. If the QC writes a certificate to *Key1* instead, that means it has reviewed the production process of SP1 and the network operator can trust SP1 to do its own quality control.

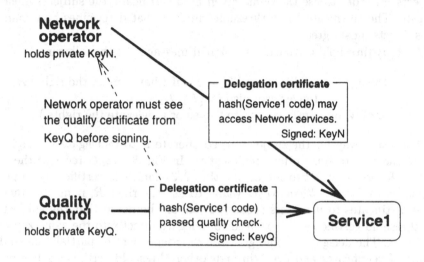

**Fig. 7.** Code quality control for IN services with basic delegation certificates

The example reveals a major limitation of the basic delegation certificates. The quality check must be passed before the network operator makes its decision. If changes are made to the code, the network operator must renew its certificate. But the network operator clearly does not make any new policy decision at that time. It only follows a fixed rule: if the quality check is ok, it will sign. In the following sections we will see how the requirement for quality check and other rules for deriving new access rights from old ones can be encoded into certificates.

## 3  Threshold and Conditional Delegation

The following sections introduce certificates with more complex structure than the ones we have seen so far. The enhancements increase significantly the flexibility of certificates as an access control tool. Threshold certificates are a means of dividing authority. Instead of giving the rights to a single subject, they are given to a group of subjects who must co-operate to use the rights. Sec. 3.1 describes the certificates and Sec. 3.2 explains how they are used. Conditional delegation is a way of expressing simple access control policy rules in certificates.

We will introduce the new type of certificates in Sec. 3.3 and look at applications in Sec. 3.4.

## 3.1 Threshold Certificates

Threshold certificates are an extension of the basic certificate structure. Instead of having only a single subject, they divide the authorization between several subjects. In order to use the rights given by a certificate, the subjects must co-operate. The certificate has a threshold number that determines how many of the subjects must agree.

A $(k, n)$-threshold certificate is a signed message like the following:

$$S_K(\text{During the validity period } T_1 - T_2, \text{ if I have any of the rights } R,$$
$$\text{I give them also to } \{K_1, K_2, ..., K_n\},$$
$$k \text{ of whom must co-operate to use or redelegate the rights.})$$

The usual way for the subjects to co-operate is to redelegate the rights to one of them or to some other single entity. In Fig. 8, $KeyC$ receives the right $R$ from $KeyS$ because two subjects of the $(2, 3)$-threshold certificate co-operate to pass it to $KeyC$. When $KeyC$ wants to use the right $R$, it must attach all three certificates to its access request. It should be noted that the subjects of the threshold certificate do not need to delegate directly to the same key as in the figure. The delegation could go through independent or partially dependent chains of certificates and even through other threshold certificates before the shares are accumulated to a single key. The general structure of such networks was studied in [4].

The threshold certificates can also be used in some situations where there is no real threshold trust scheme. An example below will show how they may improve distribution and flexibility of the system.

$(k, k)$-threshold certificates where all subjects are required to co-operate are sometimes called *joint-delegation* certificates. *Open threshold certificates* [4] are a variation of the threshold certificates where each subject is given a separate certificate and new subjects can be added later.

## 3.2 Threshold Certificates and IN Access Control

There may be intelligent network services controlled by a group of SPs so that two or more are needed to grant access to the services. Such conditions can be directly expressed with threshold certificates from the service master key to the service providers' keys. A single SP may also want to ease the burden of storing its private key securely by distributing the authority between several keys. This is exactly what is pictured in Fig. 8. The SP generates three new keys $K_1$, $K_2$ and $K_3$. It then signs a the following kind of certificate with its master key $K$.

$$S_K(\text{Any 2 of } \{K_1, K_2, K_3\} \text{ have all my rights.})$$

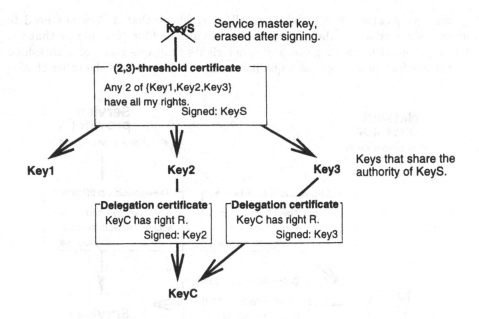

**Fig. 8.** A threshold certificate (*KeyC* gets right *R* from *KeyS*)

This certificate allows any two of the new keys to operate on behalf of the original master key. The new private keys are stored in separate places while the old private master key is destroyed or stored in a safe place and never accessed. This protects both against theft and accidental loss of the private master key. If one share is compromised, it alone is not enough to misuse the service, and if one share of the three is lost, the other two can still grant access to the service. The SP can still advertise its old public key (*K* or *KeyS*) and receive new rights delegated to that key. The threshold certificate passes all these rights to the share keys who can authorize others. This kind of protection of private keys may prove to be a much more common reason to use threshold certificates than actual threshold trust schemes between business associates.

There is another, rather unexpected, application for the threshold certificates. We will see that flexibility can be added to systems like that of Fig. 7 by encoding an implication rule in a certificate. If Fig. 9, the quality-control key (*KeyQ*) certifies the code by granting the code *all* its rights. The network operator issues a (2,2)-threshold certificate for SP1 and QC. Thus, SP1 needs the agreement of the QC before it can use the network services. The three certificates together convey the right to access Network services from *KeyN* to Service1. With these certificates, Service1 can prove its access rights when installed into a network node.

The QC key is never used for any other purpose than for certifying entities that have passed the quality check. A quality certificate can be issued to code or to service providers whose own quality control has passed an audit. In the quality certificates, the QC delegates all its rights so that it does not need to know what kind access the quality certificates are used for. This means that the QC key should never be given any other rights than one share of a threshold certificate for the purposes of a quality check on whoever gets the other share.

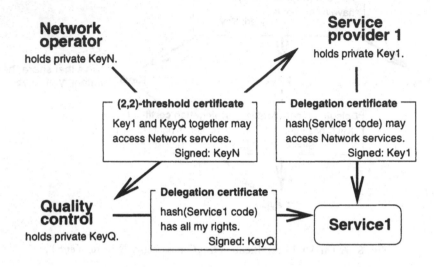

**Fig. 9.** Code quality control for IN services with threshold certificates

Compared to the use of basic delegation certificates (Fig. 7), the threshold certificate has the advantage that dependences between the quality control and the granting of access to the services have been reduced to minimum. It is not necessary to involve the network operator every time code is changed and the certificates can be signed in any order. The three certificates can be issued and renewed independently of each other.

Admittedly, this is a somewhat inelegant way to use threshold certificates. The rights delegated by the certificate are not encoded in the the authorization part ("all my rights") but in the signing key ("*KeyQ* is the quality-control key"). If there are several different authorizations (e.g. several types of quality check), the QC unit must have an equal number of signature keys. Moreover, comparing different levels of authorization becomes difficult when the authorizations are encoded in the keys. We observe that the threshold certificate in Fig. 9, in effect, carries the meaning

> "*Key1* may access the network services if it also has
> a quality certificate from *KeyQ*."

In section 3.4, we will introduce a new type of certificate that explicitly includes such conditions. The reason why we have described in length how to encode the same meaning into a threshold certificate is that only threshold delegation is currently supported by SPKI.

### 3.3 Conditional Certificates

Conditional certificates are like the basic delegation certificates except that they state additional conditions that have to be satisfied before the certificate is considered valid. A conditional certificate is a signed message with the following contents:

$$S_K(\text{During the validity period } P, \text{ if I have any of the rights } R,$$
$$\text{I give them also to } K' \text{ if it also has}$$
$$\text{the right } R_1 \text{ from } K_1, \text{ and}$$
$$\text{the right } R_2 \text{ from } K_2, \text{ and}$$
$$\text{the right } R_3 \text{ from } K_3, ...)$$

The certificate gives the rights to the subject only if all the conditions in the list are satisfied. The conditions always take the same form: they require the subject key of the certificate to have a certain authorization from a certain key. This is natural because any attribute that the subject may have can be verified only if it is expressed as an attribute certificate from a proper authority.

In order to use the certificate, the subject must provide a proof that the conditions are fulfilled. It does this by attaching appropriate certificate chains, one for each condition. The certificates in the proof of access rights form a tree (or a directed acyclic graph) rather than a chain.

When certain attributes are required before granting access to a service, a conditional certificate offers two advantages compared to the basic delegation certificates. First, the certificate is an unambiguous, standard-form statement of what kind of attribute certificates are still needed for the access. Secondly, the conditional certificate can be signed before obtaining the attribute certificates. Without conditional certificates, the client in need of access rights would first contact the issuer to find out what are the prerequisites, then try to acquire them and, in the end, return to the issuer with the collection of credentials in order to get the new certificate. When the decision rule is encoded in a certificate, the issuer needs to be contacted only once. The client may obtain the attributes before or after this contact. Thus, communication and synchronization between the entities is greatly reduced.

The conditional certificates express simple policy rules but they are, by no means, a general language for defining policies. For example, the certificates presented here cannot express symbolic rules. A more general language for expressing conditions, policies and limits on redelegation is a topic of active research.

### 3.4 Conditional Certificates and IN Access Control

Conditional certificates are just the right tool for the kind of situations where we slightly abused threshold certificates in Sec. 3.2. The code quality check for an IN service can be expressed as a condition. Fig. 10 reformulates the certificates of Fig. 9 with conditions. The result is functionally the same but the system is much more intuitive for a designer or an observer.

With the threshold certificates, the quality certificate told only indirectly what kind of authority it gives to the subject. The authorization was encoded in the signature key. In addition to being cumbersome to understand, this encoding has the disadvantage that the authorizations are not comparable. The conditional certificates, on the other hand, explicitly state the rights or attributes in the authorization field of the certificate and the authorizations can be compared. For example, we can let the IN Network operator write the required *level* of quality in the conditional certificate. If the QC issues a quality certificate with the same or higher level to Service1, the code will get the access rights.

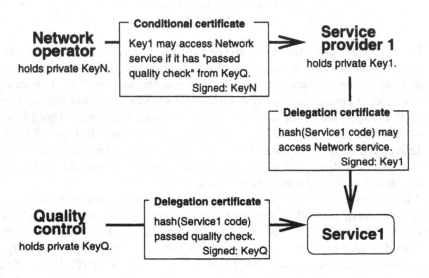

**Fig. 10.** Code quality control made simple with conditional certificates

# 4 Limitations

The flexibility of the certificates does not come completely without a price. There are many security goals that require centralized control and cannot be realized only with signed messages. We will consider such goals and see what kind of central or trusted services they imply. Sec. 4.1 discusses policies that require additional infrastructure. Sec. 4.2 brings up the issue of quantitative rights. In Sec. 4.3 we consider revocation and in Sec. 4.4 anonymity and auditing.

## 4.1 Expressive Power

The certificates are a form of discretionary access control. They cannot express mandatory policies like the Bell-LaPadula model [7] because we do not assume any mechanism for enforcing a policy globally. A mandatory policy would require all equipment on the system to be under the control of some authority so that they can be trusted to follow the policy.

Another limitation is that the certificates can only convey policies where the rights of the entities grow monotonically as they acquire new certificates. It is impossible to verify that someone does *not* have a certificate. Consequently, separation-of-duty policies like the Chinese Wall policy [11] cannot be expressed with only certificates. They need some mechanism for keeping track of the previously granted rights. Moreover, if several distributed issuers give out certificates for different conflicting rights, these issuers must share a single view of the subjects' histories. The histories must be updated in real time when new certificates are issued. An equally difficult problem is that in a key-oriented system, one physical entity might use several keys to gain conflicting rights. We must first identify the entities whose duties we want to separate and then find a way of mapping keys to unique identities. For example, a trusted official could certify the keys to be unique personal keys of the participating persons. Altogether, separation of duty appears to be one of the greatest challenges for certificate-based access control.

A related problem is the separation of access rights and grant rights. In a key-oriented architecture, someone with only grant rights could easily subvert the protection mechanism by issuing the rights to a key held by himself [15]. Therefore, every key in practice has the rights that it is allowed to delegate to others. Like the separation of duty, separate policies for granting and using rights cannot be securely implemented unless each entity has a unique identity and keys owned by the entity are bound to the identity. Consequently, key-oriented systems usually do not even try to implement pure grant rights.

An occasionally needed access control feature is a proxy that can issue certificates with longer life-times than its own existence. For example, a manager on a vacation should be able to delegate authority to a stand-in only for the time of the leave but the decisions made by the stand-in should stay valid longer than that. Unfortunately, the proxy can create valid-looking certificates even after losing its authority. He simply writes false dates on them so that they appear to be signed at the time when he was authorized. The problem can be solved with the help of a trusted time-stamping service if such a centralized authority exists. Often it is easiest to let the certificates expire when the mandate of the proxy does and have the master entity revalidate them.

The above limitations are due to fundamental properties of the access control mechanism. There are, however, some other respects in which we have deliberately satisfied us with less than the maximal expressive power. For example, symbolic expressions could be allowed in conditional certificates. The extension would make it possible to express general rules while the certificates proposed in this paper can only speak of fixed keys. The reason for presenting the less general model here is that it solves the practical problems with the basic delegation certificates that we have met in applications. Future work on symbolic conditions will determine the extent to which they are worth the increased complexity.

The question of the optimal expressive power for the certificates involves issues of computational and communication complexity and typical usage patterns in applications.

A question that we will leave open is the exact structure of the authorizations. The types of access rights and the policies for combining them depend on the application. In PolicyMaker [8,9], the authorizations are expressed as small programs of a safe programming language and certificates can communicate with each other. This maximally generic approach leads to concerns about the tractability of access control decisions [10]. But no matter how the authorizations are encoded, certificates have one general limitation in this respect: they can effectively express qualitative authorizations but not quantitative. That is the topic of the next section.

## 4.2 Accounting and Redelegation

Accounting of service usage is an essential function in many commercial applications. The delegation certificates themselves do not support accounting in any way. They are inherently reusable and can be combined with any number of access requests without losing their validity. For example, there is no use-once certificate or quota on the number of times a service can be used. Such features can, of course, be built with additional infrastructure but they cannot be encoded into certificates.

If accounting is difficult, a natural alternative is to charge a flat rate per client. But as we argued in Sec. 2.3, it is an equal challenge to keep the subjects from sharing their rights with others. By sharing their access rights, the clients can frustrate the flat rate charging policy.

The reason behind these problems is again the lack of unique identities for the individuals in the system and the lack of a global authority that could police the actions of the individuals. There are three main approaches for overcoming the problems with accounting and charging:

1. Make the charging recursive. Every reseller will be responsible for collecting payments from the clients it delegated rights to or for dividing quotas between them. Apart from physical control of the clients, there are two ways in which the reseller can divide the services and the costs between its clients.
   (a) The reseller divides the service capacity at its disposal into smaller time slots and more specific methods of access. Because the authorizations are refined to be suitable only for very narrow purposes, the clients must repeatedly request new certificates from the reseller who collects usage data.
   (b) The authorized clients may use the services at any time and the server collects usage data. The usage statistics and the certificate chains that were used as proof of access rights are propagated from the server down the tree of resellers.
2. Require the client keys in the system to be certified by a trusted entity that guarantees their payments or gives them a credit rating. The server verifies

the credit before allowing access and collects payments directly from the clients. This may not stop the sharing of access rights but it means there is someone to pay for the metered usage.

3. Require the participants to incorporate a tamper-resistant police module on their systems. Only keys on the tamper-resistant modules are allowed to participate in the distribution of the access rights. The module can do the accounting or enforce whatever limitations are wanted.

All these techniques incur a cost in that they require additional infrastructure and make parts of the system less independent. But these costs are inherent to any accounting and charging mechanism. With delegation certificates, we can decide separately for each application if such measures are needed and if their cost is acceptable.

In Calypso, we have chosen the approach 1(b) because the delegation chains between SPs are relatively short (often only one step) and the charging for component services is arranged in the same tree-like manner. Access rights and payments flow in the opposite directions in the service composition tree (Fig. 4).

A problem related to accounting is access rights *transfer* where an entity giving rights to others loses them itself. From a chain of certificates, it is not possible to see if the chain ends there or if the rights have been redelegated further. Thus, an entity that has redelegated its rights can still use them. Implementing transfer in a distributed system requires a TCB or tamper-resistant police modules. (The tamper-resistant module can, in fact, be thought of as a TCB.) One such system for the transfer of software licenses between tamper-resistant smart cards is described in [5].

## 4.3 Certificate Revocation

Sometimes an entity distributing access rights may want to reverse its decision after the rights have already been granted. The change in mind may be due to changed circumstances or more accurate information about the subject. In a certificate-based architecture, this means invalidating certificates after they have been issued but before their expiration dates. In general, any decrease in the trust placed on the subject may require the issuer to sign and new certificate and to cancel the old one.

In systems where all access is controlled by one reference monitor, access-right revocation is a simple matter. It suffices to update the access control lists or to store information on the exceptions at the place where the rights are verified.

In a distributed system, ACLs are stored and decisions to grant access are made in more than one place. It is necessary to propagate the information on revoked access rights to all these places. The communication causes unpredictable delays and, consequently, real-time revocation cannot be achieved like in a centralized system. An efficient infrastructure for propagating the revocation information is a central part of many access control systems (for example [17,21]). Some options are to broadcast revocation events or to notify only the interested parties, to immediately propagate every single revocation or to periodically update exception lists, and to transfer the information in push or pull fashion.

All the revocation methods add complexity to the access control architecture. They imply frequent communication and on-line presence of servers and clients. On open networks, it would be unreasonable to require all entities to set up the infrastructure for efficient revocation. Therefore, we prefer to avoid revocation as far as possible. Instead, we suggest limiting the validity time and authorization of a delegation certificate. They should reflect the level at which the subject can be trusted not to misuse the rights. If revocation is needed frequently, it may be just as feasible to require frequent refreshing of the certificates. The TAOS [25] operating system is an example of an architecture that relies completely on expiration dates instead of revocation.

If revocation is nevertheless needed, the implementation should follow two principles. First, the cost of the additional infrastructure should be paid only by the entities that want the service and only when it is strictly needed. If the issuer of a certificate wants to be able to revoke it, he should be responsible for setting up the distribution channels for the notification. This may be a simple task if the certificates for the rights in question are always verified in a fixed set of servers and extremely complex if there are unregistered off-line verifiers. Second, no system should completely abandon expiration times in favor of revocation. If expired certificates are not purged from the revocation lists, the lists can grow uncontrollably. The more frequently revocation occurs, the shorter the validity periods should be. Finding the right balance that minimizes the costs requires careful analysis of each individual system.

SPKI certificates can include instructions for downloading a lists of revoked certificates or for asking confirmation from an on-line server. If the issuer of a certificate wants to be able to revoke it, he must explicitly state this in the certificate. This way the cost of the revocation lists is paid only when it is strictly needed. Moreover, there is no centralized system for maintaining and distributing the lists. Instead, each certificate can have a reference to the particular server and the signature key that provide the lists.

With conditional certificates, the confirmation from an on-line server can be implemented in the same way as the quality check in Fig. 10. Normally the validity period of the quality certificates from the QC is long or infinite. Making it very short would be the same as asking the SP to get a frequent on-line confirmation from the QC.

## 4.4  Auditing and Anonymity

Designers of secure access control have traditionally emphasized audit capabilities. That is, every action should be traceable to an entity that can be held responsible for it. The shift from closed military networks to open commercial ones has brought a conflicting need, privacy. Although auditability and anonymity are both desirable security goals, it is not easy to achieve both simultaneously. Hence, we must try to balance the requirements according to the application.

The signature key does not directly reveal who is responsible for a signed request which makes it difficult to trace the responsible parties. For auditing, the keys must be bound to the persons or legal entities that are liable for their actions. That kind of bindings can be created by identity-escrow agents that guarantee to find a responsible person if the need should arise. The escrow agents issue certificates to the keys whose identities they have escrowed. The services that require auditing only accept clients with the escrow certificates.

The key-oriented system protects the users' privacy by not explicitly revealing their names. However, the keys are easily recognizable identifiers that can be used to combine data collected from different sources. Therefore, further measures are needed for reliable privacy protection. The certificate reduction (see Sec. 2.2) helps in some cases. A chain of certificates may reveal the identities of the intermediate entities but when the chain is reduced, that information is hidden. SPKI puts great emphasis on privacy aspects and relies mostly on the reduction.

An alternative anonymity technique is to create temporary keys that do not reveal their owner. When a subject entity wants its anonymity protected, it provides the issuer of a new certificate with a freshly generated public key. The temporary keys cannot be recognized and connected to the owner or to each other. This is often preferable to certificate reduction because the entity responsible for generating the temporary keys is the one whose anonymity is at risk. Although the generation of the temporary keys is costly, it can be done off-line in advance. With both techniques, however, the cost of privacy is an increase in communication and synchronization between entities.

## 5 Conclusion

This paper described delegation certificates and some of their applications in distributed access control. The goal was an abstract understanding of the basic ideas without implementation details. We found that the main advantages of the certificates lie in decentralization. We also introduced conditional certificates that help in further distribution of management operations in the system.

Delegation catches well the spirit of what is natural to access control of distributed digital services. Some access control policies require additional infrastructure such as a TCB or trusted servers. We feel that such costs should be avoided wherever possible. When their limitations are kept in mind, the delegation certificates can satisfy many every-day access control needs and can be used as a uniform basis for distributed discretionary access control.

## Acknowledgements

The work was funded by Helsinki Graduate School for Computer Science and Engineering (HeCSE) and Academy of Finland. In am thankful to professor Olli Martikainen and to Petteri Koponen and Juhana Räsänen for allowing the use of Calypso as a case study. Part of the work was done while the author was at UC Davis Computer Security Laboratory.

# References

1. Martín Abadi. On SDSI's linked local name spaces. In *Proc. 10th IEEE Computer Security Foundations Workshop*, pages 98–108, Rockport, MA, June 1997. IEEE Computer Society Press.

2. Martín Abadi, Michael Burrows, Butler Lampson, and Gordon Plotkin. A calculus for access control in distributed systems. *ACM Transactions on Programming Languages and Systems*, 15(4):706–734, September 1993.

3. Tuomas Aura. Fast access control decisions from delegation certificate databases. In *Proc. 3rd Australasian Conference on Information Security and Privacy ACISP '98*, volume 1438 of *LNCS*, pages 284–295, Brisbane, Australia, July 1998. Springer Verlag.

4. Tuomas Aura. On the structure of delegation networks. In *Proc. 11th IEEE Computer Security Foundations Workshop*, pages 14–26, Rockport, MA, June 1998. IEEE Computer Society Press.

5. Tuomas Aura and Dieter Gollmann. Software license management with smart cards. In *Proc. USENIX Workshop on Smartcard Technology*, Chicago, May 1999. USENIX Association.

6. Tuomas Aura, Petteri Koponen, and Juhana Räsänen. Delegation-based access control for intelligent network services. In *Proc. ECOOP Workshop on Distributed Object Security*, Brussels, Belgium, July 1998.

7. D. Elliott Bell and Leonard. J. LaPadula. Secure computer systems: Unified exposition and Multics interpretation. Technical Report ESD-TR-75-306, The Mitre Corporation, Bedford MA, USA, March 1976.

8. Matt Blaze, Joan Feigenbaum, John Ioannidis, and Angelos D. Keromytis. The role of trust management in distributed systems security. In J. Vitek and C. Jensen, editors, *Secure Internet Programming: Security Issues for Distributed and Mobile Objects*, LNCS. Springer-Verlag Inc, New York, NY, USA, 1999.

9. Matt Blaze, Joan Feigenbaum, and Jack Lacy. Decentralized trust management. In *Proc. 1996 IEEE Symposium on Security and Privacy*, pages 164–173, Oakland, CA, May 1996. IEEE Computer Society Press.

10. Matt Blaze, Joan Feigenbaum, and Martin Strauss. Compliance checking in the PolicyMaker trust management system. In *Proc. Financial Cryptography 98*, volume 1465 of *LNCS*, pages 254–271, Anguilla, February 1998. Springer.

11. David F. Brewer and Michael J. Nash. The Chinese wall security policy. In *Proc. IEEE Symposium on Research in Security and Privacy*, pages 206–214, Oakland, CA, May 1989. IEEE Computer Society Press.

12. *Recommendation X.509, The Directory - Authentication Framework*, volume VIII of *CCITT Blue Book*, pages 48–81. CCITT, 1988.

13. Carl M. Ellison. Establishing identity without certification authorities. In *Proc. 6th USENIX Security Symposium*, pages 67–76, San Jose, CA, July 1996. USENIX Association.

14. Carl M. Ellison, Bill Franz, Butler Lampson, Ron Rivest, Brian M. Thomas, and Tatu Ylönen. SPKI certificate theory, Simple public key certificate, SPKI examples. Internet draft, IETF SPKI Working Group, November 1997.

15. Carl M. Ellison, Bill Franz, Butler Lampson, Ron Rivest, Brian M. Thomas, and Tatu Ylönen. SPKI certificate theory. Internet draft, IETF SPKI Working Group, October 1998.

16. M. Gasser, A. Goldstein, C. Kaufman, and B. Lampson. The digital distributed system security architecture. In *Proc. National computer security conference*, pages 305–319, Baltimore, MD, USA, October 1989.

17. Li Gong. A secure identity-based capability system. In *Proc. 1989 IEEE Symposium on Research in Security and Privacy*, pages 56–63, Oakland, CA, May 1989. IEEE, IEEE Computer Society Press.
18. J. Kohl and C. Neuman. The Kerberos network authentication service (V5). RFC 1510, IETF Network Working Group, September 1993.
19. Petteri Koponen, Juhana Räsänen, and Olli Martikainen. Calypso service architecture for broadband networks. In *Proc. IFIP TC6 WG6.7 International Conference on Intelligent Networks and Intelligence in Networks*. Chapman & Hall, September 1997.
20. Ilari Lehti and Pekka Nikander. Certifying trust. In *Proc. First International Workshop on Practice and Theory in Public Key Cryptography PKC'98*, volume 1431 of *LNCS*, Yokohama, Japan, February 1998. Springer.
21. Nataraj Nagaratnam and Doug Lea. Secure delegation for distributed object environments. In *Proc. 4th USENIX Conference on Object-Oriented Technologies and Systems (COOTS)*, pages 101–115, Santa Fe, NM, April 1998. USENIX Association.
22. A guide to understanding discretionary access control in trusted systems. Technical Report NCSC-TG-003 version-1, National Computer Security Center, September 1987.
23. Pekka Nikander and Lea Viljanen. Storing and retrieving Internet certificates. In *Proc. 3rd Nordic Workshop on Secure IT Systems NORDSEC'98*, Trondheim, Norway, November 1998.
24. Ronald L. Rivest and Butler Lampson. SDSI — A simple distributed security infrastucture. Technical report, April 1996.
25. Edward P. Wobber, Martín Abadi, Michael Burrows, and Butler Lampson. Authentication in the Taos operating system. *ACM Transactions on Computer Systems*, 12(1):3–32, February 1994.
26. Philip Zimmermann. *The Official PGP User's Guide*. MIT Press, June 1995.

# A View–Based Access Control Model for CORBA

Gerald Brose

**Abstract.** Specifying and managing access control policies for large distributed systems is a non–trivial task. Commonly, access control policies are specified in natural language and later reformulated in terms of a particular access control model. This paper presents and discusses concepts for an object–oriented access model that is more suitable for describing access control policies for CORBA objects than the default access model specified in the OMG security service specification.

## 1 Introduction

Specifying and managing access control policies for large distributed systems is a non–trivial task. Commonly, access control policies are initially specified in natural language and later reformulated in terms of a particular access control model, e.g. a label–based or access matrix–based model. Because controlling the dynamic evolvement of policies and adjusting them by administrative operations, i.e. *managing* them, is highly sensitive and at the same time error–prone if done at too low a level of abstraction, language support for this kind of activity would be desirable.

As has been pointed out above, the language for specifying access control policies is defined by the underlying access model. If the concepts and abstractions of this model are not well designed, this has direct bearing on the quality of the policies that are to be written using that model.

In this paper, we take a software engineering or language–based approach to designing access policies and present an alternative access control model for CORBA [16] systems. We believe this model is better suited to express advanced policy concepts than the default access model specified in the OMG's *Security Service Specification* [17]. Also, it provides policy designers with more abstract concepts for specifying authorizations. This model is based on the concept of *views*, an object–oriented approach to specifying access rights.

The rest of this paper is organized as follows. Section 2 outlines the CORBA access control model and examines the default access control policy as defined in the *Security Service*. Section 3 introduces the concept of *views* and sketches how it can be used in implicit authorizations and for delegation. Section 4 mentions related work and Section 5 concludes the paper with a summary and an outlook on future work.

# 2 The default CORBA access model

The *Security Service* specification defines a reference model for access control which separates access control decisions from the actual access enforcement in a manner similar to the ISO authorization framework [9]. Access decisions may be made at both the client and the target side. Within this general framework, arbitrary access control models may be defined. Note that we use the term *access model* to denote a language for defining concrete access control policies. The security service defines a default access model but calls it the DomainAccessPolicy. Individual policies are indeed represented by DomainAccessPolicy objects, but the type DomainAccessPolicy at the same time defines the types of policies that can be expressed, i.e. the access model. Care should be taken not to confuse the OMG terminology with the terminology used in this paper.

This section examines the default CORBA access model and identifies some shortcomings in order to arrive at a set of requirements that a more suitable access model for CORBA would have to meet.

## 2.1 Concepts

We briefly explain and review the main concepts of the default access model.

**Access matrix.** The default authorization model in the *Security Service* is based on the access control matrix [14], which represents principals as rows, objects as columns and permissions or access rights in matrix entries. For a detailed description of the access matrix semantics of the default CORBA access control model see [12].

As CORBA is an open distributed architecture, an important requirement for a general CORBA access control model is scalability. The smallest unit of access control in object–oriented systems is a single operation on a single object, but in many cases this level of granularity would induce too much overhead in operation as well as in management. In order to reduce the number of entities that need to be dealt with, a number of grouping constructs are provided.

**Principals.** CORBA refers to both human users and system entities acting on their behalf a principals. Authorizations are granted to principals only indirectly on the basis of the security attributes they possess rather than directly using identities. Possible security attributes include (but are not limited to) access identifier, group and role names, clearance level and capabilities. If a number of principals share a common attribute value, they implicitly form a group to which access rights can be granted.

**Domains.** Objects are grouped into *security policy domains*, i.e. sets of objects to which the same security policies apply. For every domain, there is a DomainManager object that knows about the policies and the members of the domain. Access policies are represented by a `DomainAccessPolicy` object by default.

Domains can be nested, so a domain may contain subdomains and may itself be a member of an enclosing domain. The main purpose of forming hierarchies of policy domains is to reflect organizational hierarchies, so subdomains could have more specific security policies than enclosing domains. The precise meaning of hierarchically composed policies is, however, not specified. While the implication seems to be that subdomains have less authority over their members, it is not clear how conflicts between policies would be resolved.

Another way of composing policies is by forming federations of interoperating domains, where each domain has full authority but has some amount of trust in the other and agrees to give certain rights to the other side. As with domain hierarchies, the question of how this is done and what the semantics of such a federation would be is left unspecified.

**Rights and operations.** The security service defines individual rights in *rights families*. The default rights family is **corba** and contains four generic rights: **g, s, m, u** for *get, set, manage* and *use*. The definition of new rights families, albeit possible, is discouraged to keep policies simple.

Authorizations are checked per individual operation. The default access model defines no explicit grouping construct for operations. Operations are, however, grouped implicitly by the access rights they require. These *required rights* for an object access using a particular operation are to be defined by interface developers and specified per object type. Thus, the specification of required rights defines a mapping from generic access rights to actual operations. Required rights are defined as a *combination* of rights by stating whether the given rights are required in conjunction ("all"–combinator) or whether any of the listed rights is sufficient for the operation ("any"–combinator). They are stored in a global table and are not part of any individual access policy.

Using a domain's `DomainAccessPolicy` object, a particular access policy is defined by granting *effective rights* to principals identified by their security attributes. One implicit security attribute that is set by the ORB for every access is the *delegation state*. This attribute allows to identify for every request whether the principal is the initiator of the request or an intermediate in a call chain. It is thus possible to grant a different set of effective rights depending on the delegation state of the calling principal. Effective rights are registered in tables and compared to the required rights for an operation upon access. If a principal's effective rights match the required rights, the access is allowed.

## 2.2 An example policy

We will sketch a hypothetical access policy for naming context objects using the CORBA default access model. Naming contexts have the interface `CosNaming::NamingContext` from the OMG's name service specification [15]. The IDL for this interface is given in Figure 1. The policy is to distinguish between different uses

```
module CosNaming {
    interface NamingContext {
        void bind(in Name n, in Object obj);
        void rebind(in Name n, in Object obj);
        void bind_context(in Name n, in NamingContext nc);
        void rebind_context(in Name n, in NamingContext nc);
        Object resolve (in Name n);
        void unbind(in Name n);
        NamingContext new_context();
        NamingContext bind_new_context(in Name n);
        void destroy();
        void list (in unsigned long how_many,
            out BindingList bl, out BindingIterator bi);
    };
};
```

**Fig. 1.** Name server interface

of naming contexts with increasing sensitivity. It defines different authorizations for the following cases:

1. *name resolution*: only `resolve()` operations are allowed. Principals are neither permitted to learn about new objects by browsing the name context nor to alter the contents of the name space in any way.
2. additional *browsing*: allow `resolve()` and `list()`.
3. additional *binding of new names*: `list()`, `resolve()` and `bind()` are permitted. This case does not include the right to rebind a name, i.e. to bind a name that is already bound
4. additional *context creation*: `new_context()` and `bind_new_context()` operations are allowed. These operations return new context objects, the latter also binds this object to an argument name within the target context, i.e. the returned context is a subcontext. Note that it is not possible to bind other contexts as subcontexts than the ones created with `bind_new_context()`. The operations `bind_context()` and `rebind_context()` are explicitly prohibited to prevent "external" name spaces from being linked into local name space hierarchies.
5. *manage contexts*: in addition to allowing all the previous accesses, calling `destroy()` is permitted. This will remove a naming context if it is empty. Also, unbinding and rebinding names is permitted.

Please note that the hierarchical nature of these authorization types is incidental and simply a consequence of the example policy we chose to present here, it is not characteristic for our approach. While authorizations of the first two types would be considered "public", authorizations of type 3 and 4 are only granted to privileged users of two different groups. The last authorization is to be granted to a small group of administrators only.

**Defining Required Rights.** Before this policy can be expressed in the default CORBA access model and effective rights can be granted to holders of the appropriate security attributes, *required rights* for each operation of the NamingContext interface have to be defined. The rights combination for each operation can be specified using rights from

1. the default corba rights family exclusively.
2. another rights family, perhaps one that was introduced for exclusive use with the type NamingContext.
3. different rights families.

To keep management of rights simple, it would be desirable to refrain from defining new rights families and select the first of these options. However, it is not always straightforward how to model the intended semantics of authorization using the generic rights "get", "set", "manage" and "use". Note that these rights do not just describe distinct operation types $(g,s,u)$ but also the level of sensitivity for operations (the m right) [1].

A more serious limitation with using only the small set of rights from the corba family is that no more than 16 different combinations of rights can be distinguished. Thus, it is highly likely that a number of operations will require the same set of rights, especially if required rights are defined by individual interface designers and not by security administrators and the domain contains objects of a number of different types. If required rights are not unique, however, ensuring the principle of least privilege is very difficult if not impossible with this access model. Because rights are generic principals can invoke any operation on any object of any interface in the domain that happens to match the effective rights combination granted to them. As an example, imagine that the operation list() on naming contexts and the operation create() on some object of type JPEGFactory were to require corba:g and corba:u. Any principal that was granted this combination of required rights in a domain where objects of these types exist would be allowed both operations and possibly others as well. Determining which operations will be permitted with a given set of rights implies searching the whole *required rights* table because grouping operations by their required rights can only be done implicitly.

The second of the options outlined above would avoid this problem of interfering rights altogether. Also, defining a new rights family per IDL interface would allow policy designers to use access rights that directly correspond to the intended usages of these interfaces. However, introducing new rights families not only complicates management, it is also very cumbersome in practice as there are neither language support nor management interfaces for this task.

As a compromise, the basic corba rights could be used in conjunction with a minimal set of newly introduced, type–specific rights that help ensuring uniqueness of required rights. For our example, we introduce a new rights family naming with two rights n, m for *naming,* and *manage.* The right naming:n is used to make this required rights combination type–specific, the second is necessary to distinguish between the last two authorization types. These are AND–combined with the default corba rights to specify the required rights as in Figure 2.

| required rights | combinator | operation |
|---|---|---|
| corba :--u-<br>naming:n- | all | resolve |
| corba :g-u-<br>naming:n- | all | list |
| corba :gsu-<br>naming:n- | all | bind |
| corba :gsum<br>naming:n- | all | new_context<br>bind_new_context |
| corba :gsum<br>naming:nm | all | unbind<br>rebind<br>destroy |

**Fig. 2.** Required rights

Note that the rights required for, e.g., operation bind() include those required for list(). This is to model the policy feature that whoever has authority to invoke bind() can also invoke list(). Also note that to model this property of the policy, we had to give up using the four corba rights as a consistent classification of operation types: Operation bind() had to require corba:gsu- although it does not read the state of a naming context, as the presence of the right g would suggest. The example shows that this access model does not allow to reconcile the intended semantics with a descriptive and readable specification.

## 2.3 Limitations of the access model

The default CORBA access model is limited in a number of respects. First, the default domain access policy does not provide adequate support for very fine–grained policies. It is not possible to specify different *required rights* for individual object instances, nor is it possible to differentiate between domains by specifying different required rights. If a policy were to require that individual instances of a type be treated differently, different domains would have to be set up for each object. Obviously, this will lead to a proliferation of potentially very small domains when fine–grained access control is necessary, and would complicate management.

Second, the model will not scale up to systems with large numbers of objects and interfaces because the authorization requirements expressable using the CORBA rights concept will frequently coincide. Because rights are used as *generic* access types and can practically not be tied to particular IDL types, enforcing the principle of least privilege is not easily possible within domains. By granting a set of effective rights, principals will almost invariably gain more authorizations than they actually require if only the small set of rights defined in the corba rights family are used — many operations will happen to require the same rights combination.

Third, the default access model does not define any structural relations for its access control concepts, e.g. hierarchies of groups, rights or domains. Domain hierarchies are mentioned in the specification but not defined. Also note that the management interfaces to the default domain access control model are at a low level of abstraction and do not offer any language support for the sensitive and error–prone tasks of specifying and managing access rights. Other than domains, no abstractions are defined that would help structuring large specifications.

## 3 Views

To remedy the problems pointed out in the previous section we propose a new access model based on *views*. A view definition introduces an *authorization type* as a named subset of an object type's operations. Thus, individual access rights directly correspond to operations. Access policies can be described in terms of principals holding view–typed authorizations on objects. To allow for fine–grained access control, views can be granted either on a single object of that type or on all objects in the type's extension that belong to the domain. If a principal requests access to an object via one of its operations and this operation is contained in one of the views on that object held by the principal, the access is allowed.

Note that, although this access model appears to call for a capability–based implementation, this is not an inherent requirement of the model. While individual authorizations, i.e. view instances, are always related to either a single object or to an open set of objects (a type extension), they are typed, first–class objects in their own right. Thus, an implementation of this model is free to represent the relation between authorizations and objects in any way of its choosing.

Views, i.e. authorization types, help structuring access policies by defining different usages for object interfaces from the point of view of a security policy designer. Policy design will obviously benefit from existing use–case diagrams or role models that describe the intended object interactions from the application designer's point of view. In spite of this close relation between the design of object interfaces and views, it is desirable to keep them separate for two reasons. First, decoupling interface design from security aspects allows to reuse applications in contexts with different security requirements or, vice versa, to design a security policy for existing CORBA applications without having to rewrite their IDL specifications. Second, it enables us to provide specially tailored abstractions for describing access policies without having to integrate these with other, orthogonal language features. In particular, we do not want to extend CORBA IDL with security annotations.

### 3.1 NamingContext revisited

The authorization types for the example policy from the previous section can be described directly and conveniently as views as shown in Figure 3.

```
view CosNamingResolver controls CosNaming::NamingContext {
  allow:
     resolve;
};

view CosNamingBrowser : CosNamingResolver {
  allow:
     list;
};

view CosNamingBinder : CosNamingBrowser {
  allow:
     bind;
};

view CosNamingContextManager : CosNamingBinder {
  allow:
     new_context;
     bind_new_context;
};

view CosNamingOwner : CosNamingContextManager {
  allow:
     destroy;
     unbind;
     rebind;
};
```

**Fig. 3.** Views on name spaces

Views are defined as access controls for a particular IDL interface, which is referenced in the controls–clause of the view definition. In the example, the base view CosNamingResolver controls the IDL type CosNaming::NamingContext. As a consequence, authorizations granted to give access to objects of one type cannot interfere with other authorizations because of different types, even if operation names happened to be identical.

View definitions can be related through inheritance so that their specifications can be reused. This relation between views is expressed by listing parent views after the colon. In the example, all view definitions directly or indirectly extend CosNamingResolver, so they inherit the operation resolve allowed by CosNamingResolver and additionally permit the operations listed in their own definitions. View inheritance is monotonic in the sense that extending views may only *add* access permissions.

Apart from syntactic convenience, view definitions have the advantage that operations are *explicitly* grouped. It is thus always obvious which operations will be permitted if a particular view on an object is granted to a principal.

Being able to give names to sets of individual rights also adds descriptiveness as these names can refer to different usage aspects of a particular IDL type. Note that views can also be regarded as divisions of IDL interfaces according to the intended uses of these interfaces, or as retrospectively defined interfaces.

As in the original CORBA access model, authorizations can be granted to principals indirectly based on the value of some security attribute. The security service does not mandate any particular way of defining and managing a mapping of security attributes to users. For syntactic convenience, we suggest to introduce simple identifiers for predicates over security attributes or combinations thereof and use these predicate names to denote those principals for which the predicate holds true.

The view–based access model introduced in this section provides a structured way of defining rights that is better suited to express complex policies than the original concept of rights, which was not structurally related to object types. In the following, we will extend the expressiveness of the view language with concepts that address implicit authorizations and denials as well as the delegation of access rights.

## 3.2 Implicit authorizations and denials

An implicit authorization [18] is one that is implied by other authorizations. Authorizations are implied whenever a grouping construct is used for granting. If, e.g., a view $v$ on the extension of type T is granted to the principals with the security attribute *groupname = staff*, this implies granting individual access permissions for the operations in $v$ to every principal in group *staff* on every object in the extension of T.

While it is more convenient to specify general access rules this way than to grant each of the implied authorizations individually, there also needs to be a way of expressing exceptions to rules, e.g. that one particular principal in a group is not to be allowed one particular operation on objects of Type T. Consequently, it is necessary to define means by which negative authorizations [13] or denials can be explicitly specified. To this end, we introduce a keyword **deny** to the view definition language. Note that no extending view may contain denials because it can only extend the authorization defined in a parent view.

In some cases it may be necessary for denials to override permissions, but other cases may demand that permissions can be defined as the exception to a general rule and thus need to override denials. Hence, a general strategy of resolving conflicts between authorizations is called for. A number of strategies are possible, e.g. "denials take precedence", or bi–valued [18] or multi–level priorities [4]. Here, we will adopt the distinction between strong and weak authorizations from [18]: Assuming a partial order *is–more–specific* on authorizations, a weak authorization can be overridden by a more specific (strong or weak) authorization. A strong authorization, on the other hand, cannot be overridden by any other, more specific authorization, not even a strong one. The relation *is–more–specific* on authorizations is defined in terms of both view hierarchies and object hierarchies. Principal hierarchies are not explicitly supported in our model but may be defined ad hoc. They are not considered for resolving authorization conflicts.

First, an authorization is more specific than another if it is defined by a view that is more specific than the view used to define the other, i.e. if the first view extends the second. An example for such a case is given in Figure 4. Assuming an IDL definition for a type T with operations op_1 to op_5, we may specify a view BaseView that grants access to operations op_1 and op_2 while explicitly denying op_3 and op_4. Moreover, op_3 is declared as a strong authorization with the keyword final, so it cannot be overridden in refining views. A view definition that attempted to do so would be rejected. DerivedView refines BaseView and is thus more specific, so its authorizations will override the ones inherited from BaseView in case of conflicts. Such a conflict arises because DerivedView allows op_4, which was inherited from BaseView as denied. Additionally, DerivedView allows to access objects of type T using op_5.

```
view BaseView controls T {
   allow:
       op_1;
       op_2;
   deny:
       final op_3;
       op_4;
};

view DerivedView : BaseView {
   allow:
       op_4;
       op_5;
};
```

Fig. 4. Weak vs. strong authorizations

Second, an authorization $a_1$ is considered more specific than another authorization $a_2$ if $a_2$ is granted on the extension of some type $T$ and $a_1$ is granted on either the extension of a subtype S of T, one particular instance of S or a single instance of $T$. As *is-more-specific* is partial, there are cases where both the views and the involved objects of $a_1$ and $a_2$ are unrelated. The relation is also not defined if $a_1$ would be more specific than $a_2$ because of its more derived view while at the same time $a_2$ would be more specific than $a_1$ because of the type structure of the involved objects. In these cases, denials take precedence.

To decide whether an access request can be allowed it is necessary to search the initiator's views for both permissions and denials. The access is allowed if a permission but no denial for the operation is found. If both a permission and a denial are found, the access decision depends on the structural relation between the authorizations. If the permitting authorization is more specific than the denying authorization, the access is allowed. If the denying authorization is more specific or the authorizations are unrelated, the access is denied.

## 3.3 Delegation of authorizations

Some situations may require principals to delegate some or all of their own rights to other principals. This can be necessary, e.g., for cooperation purposes, for delegating authority or as part of other application protocols. The CORBA security reference model describes a number of different privilege delegation schemes to support *call chains*, i.e. delegation is necessary because calls may be delegated.

Principals pass their credentials with the access request. In the *no delegation* scheme, the target object uses these credentials for access checks but is not allowed to use them for accessing other objects. If calls are delegated and the target becomes an intermediate in a call chain, it has to use its own credentials (if any). In *simple delegation* — also called *impersonation* — the intermediate may use the received credentials in subsequent calls and may also delegate these further. Only these two schemes are required for compliant security service implementations. Two more delegation schemes, *composite delegation* and *traced delegation* are possible.

The effective delegation scheme to be used is selected by an administrator. This decision is taken for a *delegation policy domain* which need not be identical with the access policy domain. Security–aware applications can also set the delegation scheme according to application policy. The security service mentions but does not specify interfaces for achieving *controlled* delegation by limiting the validity period of delegated credentials or the number of invocations they may be used for. Restrictions on the target objects are also envisioned, but not currently defined.

In principle, this credentials–based delegation approach does not rule out implementations that pass authorizations directly, using capabilities [6] or authorization certificates, e.g. SPKI [5] or X.509 certificates. However, the CORBA delegation schemes actually aim at delegating *security attributes* (as indicated by calling simple delegation *impersonation*) and thus transfer authorizations only indirectly by changing the set of principals that possess these security attributes.

As a consequence, it is difficult for a principal to infer and control which of its own authorizations are actually delegated. Also, authorizations can only be delegated implicitly by calling other objects — there is no explicit "grant" operation that would simply transfer some authority to other principals. As a last observation, note that it is not possible to specify restrictions on delegation in an access control policy as delegating security attributes does not change the access rules defined in the policy.

For these reasons, we propose to add the meta–operation "grant" to our access model and mark view definitions as grantable if delegation of authorizations of this type is permitted. Delegating views on objects is an explicit operation, so applications wishing to delegate rights need to be security–aware. Note that there is no "revoke" right. Granting an authorization implies the right to revoke it any time.

A delegating principal might wish to restrict the delegated rights in a number of ways. First, it might want to ensure that the recipient may only invoke those operations that are necessary for a particular task. Second, it might want to disallow further delegation of its rights to other principals.

To allow controlled delegation of access rights, we introduce an additional **grant** operation for views. A view that lists this operation as allowed permits a principal to delegate authorizations of this type. If it does not allow **grant**, delegation is not permitted. The grant operation can optionally be parameterized with identifiers referring to principals or principal groups, thus restricting the range of recipients for a view to a specific subset of principals. An example of such a view definition is given in Figure 5.

```
view DelegatableView controls M::T {
    allow:
        grant {tech_staff,richards};
        op_1;
    deny:
        op_4;
};
```

**Fig. 5.** View delegation

In this example, a principal holding a `DelegatableView` authorization can delegate it only to the principals that are associated with either the identifier `tech_staff` or `richards`. If principals wish to impose further restrictions when delegating views, they can dynamically derive new, more limited authorizations from the ones they hold. Deriving new authorizations may only be done in a restricted manner by selecting a parent view as the type of the derived authorization. To prevent denial of service attacks, only authorizations without denials may be delegated, so delegation can only increase a receiving principal's access rights.

### 3.4 Combining access rights

Our access control model unifies the concepts of *operation* and *access right*: View definitions list operations, and holding a particular view on an object permits to access this object with precisely the operations listed in that view. Since operations are indivisible, so are access rights. While we believe this model to be more appropriate for object–oriented systems than approaches which separate access rights from operations, our model lacks the flexibility offered by the option of *combining* access rights to obtain a certain privilege.

As an example, consider an access control policy for a safe with multiple locks that states the safe can only be opened when a certain number of keyholders cooperate. Accessing the safe should require *multiple* rights which correspond to the keyholders' keys. Using the model outlined so far, however, we cannot express conditions on operations that require the caller to possess further authorizations than just the one that permits the operation.

To provide a flexible way of expressing access rights that depend on a combination of other rights, we introduce a new keyword **requires** as a modifier for a simple access right. In the example in Figure 6, holding a `SecuredSafeView` on an object is not sufficient to be allowed to access that object using **open**. Principals that want to do so need to hold other views that allow `key1`, `key2` and `key3`, such as `KeyholderOneView`. This view allows `key1` but lists it as `virtual`. By declaring an authorization as virtual, we allow to decouple actual operations in interfaces and access rights: a virtual right has no corresponding operation in an IDL interface and thus does not allow any direct object access. The sole purpose of having virtual authorizations is to avoid having to introduce unnecessary operations into IDL interfaces simply because combined access rights are needed.

```
view SecuredSafeView controls M::Safe {
   allow:
       close;
       open requires KeyholderOneView.key1,
                     KeyholderTwoView.key2,
                     KeyholderThreeView.key3;
};

view KeyholderOneView controls M::Safe {
   allow:
       grant{keyholder};
       virtual key1;
};
```

**Fig. 6.** Combined access rights

When a principal tries to open a `Safe` object, the access decision function checks not only that the principal holds a view that lists **open** as allowed, but also whether the principal possesses the additional authorizations `key1`, `key2` and `key3` for this object that are required by **open**. If it does not, the principal's access will be denied and it will have to obtain the missing rights, e.g. by having other principals grant them. In cases like this, where the cooperation between principals requires the exchange of access rights for a single operation invocation, the introduction of further delegation restrictions appears necessary so that granting principals could specify how often access rights may be used or for how long a granted view remains valid.

# 4 Related work

Using type information for specifying fine–grained object protection is, of course, not new. Language based–approaches such as [11, 19], typically rely on an extended notion of type that allows to selectively hide some of an abstract data type's operations for access control. We are not, however, aware of approaches that establish a separate type–concept for authorizations.

Views are a well–known concept in relational and object–oriented databases [20]. Their use for access control purposes resembles the use of type abstraction as a protection concept. Unlike database views that can span multiple types, a view in our model is restricted to objects of a single IDL type. Joining views on different IDL types $T_1, ..., T_n$ can, however, be modelled by specifying an additional IDL interface $T$ that extends $T_1, ..., T_n$ and defining a view on $T$. Another difference is that database views may define content–specific access controls, e.g. by stating that an attribute may only be read if its value is above a certain threshold. This is not possible in our model.

In [10], grouping concepts for objects, principals and access rights have been proposed in the context of downloadable code, but without proposing a language for the specification of access control policies. While this model also addresses implicit and negative authorizations, rights delegation and combination are not an issue.

In [8], views are lists of allowed operations that are used to define the access rights contained in capabilities. By recursively annotating parameters of view operations with other view names in interface definitions, protection requirements for arguments can be expressed. At run–time, access rights according to these views are passed implicitly. Structural relations between views and negative rights are not addressed.

# 5 Summary and future work

We have analyzed the CORBA default access model and identified a number of restrictions that make it desirable to replace this access model. We have presented and dicussed views as the basic concept of a new access control model that will allow policies to be expressed at a higher level of abstraction. We have also sketched how implicit authorizations and delegation could be expressed in access policies based on this model.

We are currently working on an implementation of the concepts presented in this paper as part of a partial security service implementation for our own Java implementation of the CORBA specification, JacORB [3]. In this implementation, view definitions are compiled into runtime representations that reside in a view repository. The function of such a view repository is similar to that of the CORBA interface repository. We are currently evaluating the possibility of representing authorizations in the form of SPKI certificates [5]. Future work includes formalizing the concepts presented in this paper and exploring how role models could be included.

Another question in this context that we intend to pursue is how interoperability between security policy domains can be supported. The security service specification does mention both hierarchies and federations of domains, but does not answer the question of how these federations are defined and what properties a resulting, composite policy would have to have. Moreover, in an open distributed architecture such as CORBA, it might not be possible to pre–define federations of policies for all possible situations, so it will be necessary to be able to establish interoperation dynamically in some cases.

In order to allow cross–domain accesses at all, a domain must be able to specify how much it trusts external principals and on what properties this trust is based. This determines what authorizations it is willing to grant to principals. Taking a pragmatic approach, the amount of trust a domain is prepared to invest in a principal can be directly identified with the authorizations it grants as in PolicyMaker [2] or SPKI [5].

This does not, however, address the issue on which grounds trust or authorization is granted. Granting certain authorizations to, e.g., a public key amounts to a certain level of trust being placed in the holder of that key *unconditionally*, simply on the basis of the existence of the key. Any supposed properties or characteristics of the entity holding that key are not expressed. One simple and straightforward way of specifying on which attributes of a principal trust is based is to grant authorizations to principals indirectly, i.e. on the basis of certain security attributes as mentioned in this paper. Security then depends on proving these properties, i.e. being able to do cross–domain authentication. The practical problem here is to define a mapping between external and internal security attributes. Other, theoretical problems include reasoning about properties of composite policies (cf. [7]).

## Acknowledgements

I would like to thank Peter Löhr and Richard Kemmerer for valuable discussions.

## References

1. Blakley, B., http://www.bhs.org/IT/Projects/cpr/security/CORBASEC-FAQ/, Section 4.3.2, April 1998.
2. Blaze, M., Feigenbaum, J., Strauss, M.: Distributed Trust Management. Proc. IEEE Symposium on Security and Privacy (1997) 143–154
3. Brose, G.: JacORB — design and implementation of a Java ORB. Proc. Distributed Applications and Interoperable Systems DAIS'97, Chapman & Hall (1997) 143–154
   http://www.inf.fu-berlin.de/~brose/jacorb/
4. Brüggemann, H. H.: *Spezifikation von objektorientierten Rechten*. DUD–Fachbeiträge. Vieweg (1997)
5. Ellison, C., Frantz, B., Lampson, B., Rivest, R., Thomas, B., Ylönen, T.: SPKI Certificate Theory. Internet Draft, draft-ietf-spki-cert-theory-02.txt (1998)

6. Gong, L.: A secure identity–based capability system. Proc. IEEE Symposium on Security and Privacy (1989) 156–83
7. Gong, L., Qian, X.: Computational issues in secure interoperation. IEEE Transactions on Software Engineering, Vol. 22(1), January 1996, 43–52
8. Hagimont, D., Huet, O., Mossière, J.: A protection scheme for a CORBA environment. Proc. ECOOP '97 Workshop, CORBA: Implementation, Use and Evaluation (1997)
9. ISO/IEC: Information Technology — Open Systems Interconnection — Security Frameworks for Open Systems: Access Control Framework. ISO (1996)
10. Jaeger, T., Rubin, A., Prakash, A.: Building systems that flexibly control downloaded executable content. Proc. 6th USENIX Security Symposium (1996) 131–148
11. Jones, A., Liskov, B.: A language extension for expressing constraints on data access. Communications of the ACM, Vol. 21(5), May 1978, 358–367
12. Karjoth, G.: Authorization in CORBA Security. Proc. ESORICS'98, LNCS 1485, Springer (1998) 143-158
13. Kowalski, O., Härtig, H.: Protection in the BirliX operating system. Proc. 10th Int. Conf. on Distributed Computing Systems (1990) 160–166
14. Lampson, B.: Protection. ACM Operating Systems Review, Vol. 8(1), January 1974, 18–24
15. OMG: CORBAservices: Common Object Services Specification. OMG document formal/97-12-02, Object Management Group (1997)
16. OMG: The Common Object Request Broker: Architecture and Specification, revision 2.2. Object Management Group (1998)
17. OMG: Security Service Revision 1.2. Object Management Group (1998)
18. Rabitti, F., Bertino, E., Kim, W., Woelk, D.: A model of authorization for next–generation database systems. ACM Transactions on Database Systems, Vol. 16(1), March 1991, 88–131
19. Richardson, J., Schwarz, P., Cabrera, L.-F.: CACL: Efficient fine–grained protection for objects, Proc. OOPSLA 1992, 263–275
20. Scholl, M., Laasch, C., Tresch, M.: Updatable views in object–oriented databases. Proc. 2. Int. Conf. on Deductive and Object–Oriented Databases, LNCS 566, Springer (1991) 189–207

# Apoptosis – the Programmed Death of Distributed Services

Christian Tschudin

**Abstract.** Active networks enable to deploy new services at run–time by using mobile code. While considerable effort is under way to build active network infrastructures and to understand how to *create* corresponding services, less is known about how to *end* them. A particular problem is the coordinated steering of mobile code based services, especially in the case of "strong" active networks where each data packet is replaced by a mobile program and where a distributed service can consists of a myriad of anonymous active packets. In this paper we introduce the concept of *apoptosis* for mobile code based services. This term is borrowed from cell biology and designates the programmed cell death. We discuss the need for a self–destruction mechanism inside a distributed mobile service and address the problem of securing such a mechanism against malicious activation, for which a simple solution is shown.

*Keywords:* Active networks, mobile code security, apoptosis.

## 1 From Mobile Servers to Highly Distributed Services

Most network services today are provided by stationary programs, either at the application level (e-mail) or at the network level (routing). Programmable networks enable to reconfigure the network's nodes and to bind servers to new physical locations at run-time. "Network-aware services" may choose different server locations for optimizing the quality of service [5]. Similarly, application level gateways were proposed that can perform transcoding or downgrading of multimedia data [1]. Within such proxy architectures, the thin clients – typically mobile devices with wireless links to the fixed network – can program the gateway by uploading servlets. In both cases we have rather large servers and services with a limited amount of mobility.

By reducing the granularity of mobility, we can think of distributed network services that consist of many tiny mobile programs going forth and back. Maintaining routing tables, for example, does not require large server programs sitting somewhere in the network: Small active packets can collect and propagate topology changes to all nodes, updating the routing tables directly. A natural form of mobility of such services consists in having them look around for "unserved" nodes to which the service will attempt to extend. Such services will self-deploy and form a floating, gas-like service cloud that reaches into every niche of the network [12]. It is also possible that such a service cloud retracts from selected nodes because offering the service is not viable anymore for some places due to increased resource competition or lack of clients. For the rest of this paper we will focus on such fine–granular mobile code based network services and call them highly distributed mobile services (HDMS).

## 1.1 Steering Distributed Mobile Services

In current distribute systems it is the duty of human operators to steer a service. This also includes the update of software because of changes in the protocol standards or bug fixes in the implementation. While this does not happen very frequently with todays large and non-mobile servers, we expect this to be a fairly common case in active networks simply because it is so easy to deploy new functionality. The question then is how to *steer* such a mobile service in an active network. One of the central steering functionalities will be the termination of a distributed service.

While it is possible to track the heavy weight servers and to establish special control channels to them, such an approach is useless in the HDMS case. The sheer number of tiny elements executing in the network, and the network's topology changes leading to a never-ending adaption process of HDMS services, makes it impossible to locate and address the single elements in a centralized way. Terminating a service in this case will rather be a question of using another HDMS service that will "spread the word". Because the targeted HDMS service knows best how and in which niches it extends, it is useful to build a self-destruction capability into the service. Once triggered by some external event, a termination signal will propagate along the same line as the HDMS service deployed itself. This enables to shut down a HDMS service in an ordered way such that we can speak about the *programmed death* of a mobile service. The overall effect is a joint service suicide.

The concept of programmed death is known in biology as *apoptosis*. This word, pronounced either as *APE-oh-TOE-sis* or *uh-POP-tuh-sis*, is Greek and stands for "to fall off". In section 2 we first describe apoptosis from a cell biology's point of view. In section 3 we link these observations to the problems of protecting the termination of HDMS services and present a simple way to weld together a specific death signal with the self-destruct routine. We close this paper by a brief discussion of related work and with an outlook.

## 2 Apoptosis

Research in biology has revealed that cells have a limited capacity to divide (mitosis). This is not due to physical limitations – like for example exploiting some resource beyond usability – but is a predetermined, intrinsic behavior of the cell. Mechanisms at the molecular level are in place that can trigger the *self–destruction* of a cell. Several reasons have been identified why it makes sense that a cell commits suicide (two recent publications that give an overview of this field are [9, 2]):

**Cell death is as important as mitosis:**
    During the growth of an organism and the specialization of cells it is necessary that some cells yield the place they occupy. Fingers, for example, are formed by apoptosis of the tissue between them. Another example is the formation of the connections between neurons in the brain that requires that surplus cells be eliminated by apoptosis.
**Combating cells infected with a virus:**
    Cytotoxic T lymphocytes (CTL) can kill virus–infected cells by inducing apoptosis i.e., killing the cell *and* the virus.

**Steering the response of the immune system:**
>   The immune system responds to a viral attack by creating CTLs. In order to reduce the immune response after the attack, CTLs induce apoptosis in each other and even in themselves. Defects in this machinery are associated with so called auto-immune diseases where CTLs continue their work and attack body constituents.

**Elimination of cells with damaged DNA:**
>   DNA damage leads to an increased cell–internal production of the p53 protein, which is a inducer of apoptosis. Apoptosis helps to eliminate cells with broken DNA before it can lead to birth defects. This process also aims at preventing that a cell becomes cancerous. In fact, many cancer cells have a mutation in the gene that encodes the p53 protein!

## 2.1 Apoptosis vs. Necrosis

The important aspect of apoptosis is that the cell's self-destruction proceeds in a programmed and controlled way. The cell starts to shrink, it decomposes internal structures and degrades all internal proteins. Then the cell breaks into small, membrane-wrapped fragments ("fall off") that later on will be engulfed by phagocytic cells for recycling (see figure 1). This process does not induce inflammation, no toxic substances are leaked to the cell's environment.

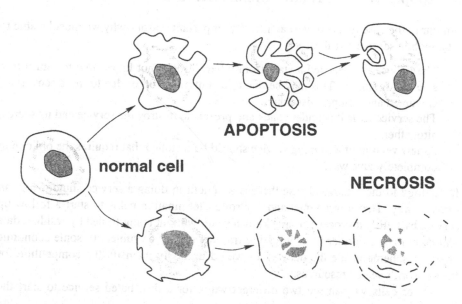

**Fig. 1.** Two forms of cell death: Programmed cell death (apoptosis) and necrosis due to injury.

The other form of cell death is necrosis, the *un*–programmed death of a cell. This happens if a cell is injured, either by mechanical damage or exposure to toxic chemicals. The response will be that the cell swells because the membrane's function is disrupted.

The cell contents leaks out which eventually leads to an inflammation of the surrounding tissue until phagocytic cells removed all cell debris.

In cell biology there are two ways known how to induce apoptosis. A cell can be led to commit suicide either by withdrawing specific *positive signals* i.e., signals needed for continued survival like grow factors. Or, apoptosis is triggered by *negative signals* like increased level of oxidants within the cell, UV light, X-rays, chemotherapeutic drugs as well as *death activators* specifically installed to induce apoptosis.

Surprisingly enough, the protection against an "unauthorized" triggering of a cell's self-destruction mechanism is not the major issue in biology. Because viruses as well as cancer genes require a cell to function for their own procreation, they will rather try to avoid destroying their host. This means that there is a natural selection of benign genes that are able to *block* apoptosis procedures. The battle between viruses and the immune system thus is rather a question of keeping the apoptosis mechanism intact.

In the context of active networks we have a different constellation. Active packets in general do not vitally depend on each other but execute independently of each other. Instead of a parasitic relationship there is competition between them, making the elimination of a rival mobile service a valuable goal: The apoptosis entry point of a mobile service would be an primary target for an attack. In the following section we will show a simple way to protect this deadly entry point.

## 3 Apoptosis of Distributed Mobile Services

Similar to the case of a cell, we can identify important reasons why we must be able to let a mobile service self-destruct:

- The service has reached a state from where it does not know how to return to a safe configuration. This may be due to a runtime error, or due to the discovery of corrupted and compromised data.
- The service feels it is under attack and prefers to destroy the service and its secrets altogether.
- A new version of a running service should be installed that requires the old one to completely give way.

In analogy to the biological case there is a benefit in doing a service shutdown in an *ordered* way. The programmed and controlled termination helps to start a follow-up service by letting it proceed from a known state, without being fooled by residual data and code traces. Furthermore, lingering fragments may be subject to some economic charging scheme inside the network or would uselessly intensify the competition for the network's scarce resources.

As for cells we can see two different ways for a distributed service to start the apoptosis process:

**Absence of positive signals:**
   A mobile service may depend on a continuous stream of credentials. For example, in an active network using economy inspired resource management, these signals would be a form of electronic money. Once a service realizes that it will soon run out of money, it can shut down partially or even completely.

**Presence of negative signals:**

A service that discovers modifications of its code base will probably decide to stop immediately. Some hardware systems even have this behavior built into them (e.g., the PC's memory parity check). We must also consider external sources of a negative signal, for example a network manager that wants to terminate the service that he created.

From a security point of view, positive signals are vulnerable to denial of service attacks. By the mere suppression of positive signals it is possible to bring a mobile code based service down, if it bases its apoptosis decision on the absence of positive signals. There is little that can be done against denial of service attacks at the level of active packets or with resource manipulations by a malicious host. We will not consider this case further in this paper.

Negative signals, on the other hand, have the problem that they can be faked. The executing host is in a particularly powerful position because it has access to the service's code and can figure out the decision logic that starts the "tear down" procedure as well as this procedure's code. But even in the case of a trustworthy host there is a need to protect the "negative signal" channel. Otherwise, attacks can be mounted by other nodes or mobile services that know the format of a negative signal message.

In the following we will look at the second problem. We show a code transformation technique that enables to securely use negative signals in an unsecured context such that arbitrary parties can try to induce the apoptosis and where malicious hosts may peek and poke the executing image of a mobile service at will.

## 3.1 Securing the Apoptosis Activator

In the context of active networks the "apoptosis activator" translates to the name and code of a self-destruction routine. A specific death signal shall be defined that activates this routine which starts the termination process, including the propagation of the signal to other parts of the distributed service. To this end, each element of a service has to provide its apoptosis activator. Three items need to be protected:

1. The activation signal:
   otherwise anybody can create a false apoptosis signal. The signal thus has to be encrypted or otherwise hidden.
2. The decision logic:
   otherwise a malicious host can override the conditional execution and make it unconditional. The apoptosis trigger code thus needs execution integrity.
3. The self-destruction routine:
   otherwise a malicious host can immediately access and execute the apoptosis routine. The code thus has to be encrypted.

We want to protect the following prototypical piece of code:

```
signal := read();
IF signal = secret_signal THEN
  self-destruct();
FI
```

We see that the execution of the self-destruction routine depends on "environmental data" requested by the read() instruction. How this data is gathered is usually outside the control of a mobile program. The only thing one can hope to secure is the way this data is processed. What we would like to do is to make this mobile code fragment a "clue-less mobile agent" in the terminology of Riordan and Schneier [7]. Although the agent's actions depend on data provided by the environment, it should not be be possible to infer which environmental value will trigger what action.

This goal can be achieved by transforming the previous code fragment into the following "wrapper" program:

```
key := read();
result := decrypt(key, ENCRYPTED_CODE);
IF is_valid(result) THEN
   execute(result);
FI
```

The ENCRYPTED_CODE constant is computed at the originator's site by encrypting the self-destruction code with the chosen signal. This constant byte array is then wrapped into the small program shown above. Note that neither the unencrypted code nor the signal's value appear in this program.

At the executing site, the now secured mobile program waits for a signal to be presented as environmental data. The received value becomes a key that the mobile program attempts to use for decryption. For each presented key we attempt to decrypt the ENCRYPTED_CODE. Looking at the result we can decide if this was a valid decryption or not.

Note that this final sanity test can be omitted if we do not care about having the host executing a nonsense program. The test, however, is simple and does not add any additional burden to the process. It suffices to include a message digest inside the encrypted code for comparison purposes.

### 3.2 An Implementation

The simple code transformation presented above was implemented in July 1997 for the M0 system [11]. M0 lends itself very well for this because of its interpreted nature and the easy with which code can be generated at runtime. A simple procedure was written that takes a pass–phrase together with the M0 code that is to be secured. The pass–phrase is hashed using the MD5 digest algorithm, the lower 64 bits are used as the DES key for encryption. The code, together with a nonce value and a message digest of the code, is then encrypted and emitted inside the "wrapper" code as described in section 3.1. The wrapper consists in a M0 procedure that takes an environmental data item, applies the hash function, decrypts the given string constant, checks for the correct digest value and, if correct, requests the execution of the decrypted code. The transformation procedure itself fits in 12 lines of M0 code.

# 4 Discussion

The presented welding together of an equality test with the conditional code is described in [7], as are further possible code transformations that enhance the "cluelessness" of mobile code. Note that the presented approach works for terminating a distributed service because we do not require the privacy of the apoptosis code to be maintained beyond the moment where we want the service to terminate. To obfuscate or completely hide the functionality of a piece of *executable* code for longer time spans is a much harder problem [3, 4, 8]. Our hope is that more simple building blocks as the one presented in this paper will be discovered, making security sensitive software fully mobile and deployable in unsecured environments. Active networks will be an important application domain for this.

## 4.1 Artificial Death

The programmed death topos is already present in computer science, namely in the domain of *artificial life*. These "alife" simulations have to deal with the problem of damping the procreation. For example, genetic algorithms have a selection step that imposes a limit on the individuals that can proceed to the next evaluation round. This leads to the "artificial death" of the less fit individuals. Or, in the Tierra system [6], an explicit reaper function eliminates the individual that made the most mistakes, while other artificial life systems introduced a suicide instruction. This topic is discussed in more general terms in [10]. Although artificial life experiments were carried out mostly in a non-distributed setting, today they start to enter the networked environment via distributed games.

# 5 Conclusions: Merging Control and Data

The analogy proposed in this paper between the programmed death of a cell and the self-termination of a distributed service points to the question on how active networks will be steered in the future. From an engineering point of view it makes sense that if we are required to firmly control the execution of mobile services, then we should built the support for this into the active network substrate. Thus, the approach would be to create privileged control channels that are different (or even separated) from the rest of the network infrastructure. However, it may be difficult, if not impossible, to come up with a universally applicable, reliable and scalable termination service. As an indication of the problems to be expected one can look at the related problem of finding *the* reliable broadcast protocol, or *the* effective support for distributed debugging. In our research we will continue to handle control and data at the same level, as the insights from biology suggest.

# References

1. Amir, E., McCanne, S. and Katz, R.: The Media Gateway Architecture: A Prototype for Active Services. Proc. SIGCOMM'98, Vancouver, Canada, 1998.
2. Bowen, I.D., Bowen, S.M. and Jones, A.H.: Mitosis and Apoptosis – Matters of Life and Death. Chapman & Hall, 1998.
3. Collberg, C., Thomborson, C. and Low, D.: Manufacturing Cheap, Resilient, and Stealthy Opaque Constructs. Proc. Principles of Programming Languages 1998 (POPL'98), San Diego, California, Jan 1998.
4. Hohl, F.: Time Limited Blackbox Security – Protecting Mobile Agents From Malicious Hosts. In Vigna, G. (Ed.): *Mobile Agents and Security*. LNCS 1419, Springer, April 1998.
5. Ranganathan, M., Acharya, A., Sharma, S., Saltz, J.: Network-Aware Mobile Programs. Proc. USENIX 97, Anaheim, California, USA, 1997.
6. Ray, T.: An Approach to the Synthesis of Life. In Langton, C., Taylor, C., Farmer, J. and Rasmussen, S. (Eds): *Artificial Life II*, Redwood City, CA, 1991.
7. Riordan, J. and Schneier, B.: Environmental Key Generation Towards Clueless Agents. In Vigna, G. (Ed.): *Mobile Agents and Security*. LNCS 1419, Springer, April 1998.
8. Sander, T. and Tschudin, C.: Towards Mobile Cryptography. Proc. IEEE Symposium on Security and Privacy, Oakland, May 1998.
9. Sluyser, M. (Ed): Apoptosis in Normal Development and Cancer. Taylor & Francis, London, 1996.
10. Todd, M.: Artificial Death. Proc. 2nd European Conference on Artificial Life (ECAL93), Brussels, Belgium, 1993.
11. Tschudin, C.: The Messenger Environment M0 – a Condensed Description. In Vitek, J. and Tschudin, C. (Eds): *Mobile Object Systems - Towards the Programmable Internet*. LNCS 1222, Springer, April 1997.
12. Tschudin, C.: A Self-Deploying Election Service for Active Networks. To appear in Proc. 3rd Int. Conference on Coordination Models and Languages, Amsterdam, April 1999. LNCS, Springer.

# A Sanctuary for Mobile Agents

Bennet S. Yee

## 1 Introduction

The Sanctuary project at UCSD is building a secure infrastructure for mobile agents, and examining the fundamental security limits of such an infrastructure.

First, what do we mean by "secure"?

An obvious issue is the privacy of computation. With standard approaches for agent-based systems, a malicious server has access to the complete internal state of an agent: software agents have no hopes of keeping cryptographic keys secret in a realistic, efficient setting. Distributed function evaluation approaches may seem to apply, but that requires an unrealistic fault model and is not likely to ever be practical. Approaches such as [1, 2, 27] are extremely expensive or have very restricted domains.

The privacy of computation is only one aspect of the security picture: the integrity of computation is perhaps more critical. In agent-based computing, most researchers have been concentrating on one side of the security issue: protecting the server from potentially malicious agents. Related work in downloadable executable content (Java [13], Software Fault Isolation [29], Proof-Carrying Code [24, 25], OS extension mechanisms such as packet filters [21], type safe languages [9, 16], etc) all focus on this problem. The converse side of the agent security problem, however, is largely neglected and needs to be addressed: how do we protect agents from potentially malicious servers? Why should we believe that the result returned by our software agents are actually correct and have not been tampered with?

## 2 Software Agents and Malicious Servers

In agent-based computing, not only do servers fear that agents bring in viruses or attempt to subvert the server, but the agent's user also needs to be able to trust that the agent was not subverted when visiting a series of servers, some of which may be malicious.

A simple example of how such a subversion might occur will make this problem clearer. Let's look at the standard air-fare agent scenario: I need to travel to Washington D.C. to attend a meeting, so I send a software agent to visit servers at all the airlines to query their databases to determine the least expensive airfare from San Diego to Washington D.C., subject to various trip timing, seat preference, and routing constraints. One of the airlines, Fly-By-Night Airlines, runs a server, www.flybynight.com, where my agent's code is automatically recognized and "brainwashed": its memory of what other airlines it has visited and what prices it had seen is modified, so that it ends up recommending a "red-eye" flight by Fly-By-Night Airlines, when a less expensive daytime flight offered by another airline would really have been preferred.

# 3 Partial Solutions

How can software agents be protected from malicious servers? This is a critical security problem to be solved if we are to have faith in agent-based computing. In the following sections, we will examine several approaches and discuss their limitations.

## 3.1 Legal Protection

One approach to the agent security problem is via legal/contractual means. Operators of the servers where agents run promise, via contractual guarantees, that they will keep their servers secure from external attackers and that they will not violate the privacy or integrity of the software agents' computation. No complex cryptographic protocols are required — there are no run-time overhead at all!

Such an approach, however, is not entirely satisfactory: for it to work the ability to detect breaches of contract is still critical. Furthermore, for that detection to be meaningful, tamper-proof logs must be available to serve as non-repudiable evidence of the breach of contract should lawsuits become necessary.

## 3.2 No Protection

For certain classes of computations, no protection is necessary, and if we are to carefully examine the cost/benefits of providing protection for software agents, this must be examined. What types of computations require no protection? Suppose the result of the computation is easily verifiable, e.g., the existence of an airfare that is below \$200. In this scenario, agents may simply replicate and flood-fill all airline servers to make sure that a copy of the agent has run on each server, and each agent copy can send the corresponding flight information if it finds one that costs less than \$200. No agent state needs to be transferred at all.

## 3.3 Fault Tolerance Approaches

In this section, we discuss fault-tolerance-style approaches to the agent security problem. First, we make some general observations on which aspects of agent state are vulnerable to attack, and which aspects may be systematically verified.

**Observations** First, note that uncorrupted servers can determine whether agent code and read-only state have been modified: the originator of the software agent can digitally sign the agent code and all read-only configuration variables before dispatching the agent to agent servers, and the agent servers can verify both the origin and the integrity of these aspects of the agent. (Message authentication codes are inappropriate, since potentially malicious agent servers should not share secrets with the originator of the agent.) Other than cryptographic techniques (if any) needed for the secure communication links, for now we will not require the servers to perform any cryptography.

It may seem that agent code signing could be circumvented by a malicious server, since the malicious server could tamper with the agent and then re-sign it with its own key. This approach, however, is thwarted by the following design: agents are constrained to send its results only to the entity that signed them. Thus, conceptually a server that re-signs an existing agent is simply performing two actions at once: denying service to the true originator of the agent, and sending out its own agent, possibly with initial data stolen from the "murdered" agent.

Next, note that the originator can specify the order in which the software agent will visit the airline servers. Abstractly, this is a circuit of the (complete) graph connecting the airline servers, and the originator may chose this circuit at the time of agent dispatch.

At any honest server, the agent code and its read-only state is checked when the agent arrives, so if the malicious server tries to tamper with the agent code or the read-only state the malicious server can not successfully pass the modified agent to an honest server. (Alternatively, the agent code and the read-only state may be considered to be reloaded from the originator by every server.) Furthermore, we assume that the variable agent state is transmitted among servers using authenticated and encrypted channels, so that only the server that is the intended migration target can receive the agent, as long as the agent is starting from an honest server. Thus, the malicious server can not intercept an agent as it migrates from an honest server to another server.

At any server, an agent may query the server's identity. At first glance, this identity could be authenticated via a public key certification chain, with the root certificate embedded as part of the read-only agent state. Note, however, that the use of cryptographic authentication does not really help a software agent to determine the hosting server's identity: since the server has control over the agent's computation, the malicious server may simply cause the program counter to bypass the cryptography-based identity query and force the program to take the conditional branch(es) which corresponds to the desired (falsified) server identity.

In addition to being able to ask for the identity of the current server, the agent may also ask from which server did the agent migrate. Because we assumed that server-to-server communications use authenticated and encrypted channels, servers will know from which server did an agent arrive. If the agent is running on an honest server, both these answers will be correct and they can be used to verify that the agent had migrated on an edge on the intended migration circuit; if the agent is running on the malicious server, these answers may be incorrect and the agent's state may be modified so that it believes it is running on a different server. In the special case where there is exactly one malicious server, this ruse will be discovered when the agent migrates off of this server to an honest server. If there are two or more malicious servers, the first malicious server encountered by an agent can hand it off to any of the other malicious servers in the route the agent is programmed to take. When the agent is passed on to the next (honest) server, the agent is brainwashed to believe it had visited all the servers in the original path between the two malicious servers, thus avoiding discovery. *If software agents are to depart from the route determined at agent dispatch time, such departures must start and end at a malicious server.*

Now, consider what visiting a malicious server can do to a software agent's memory. The read-write state variables of an agent may be completely altered by the malicious server; thus, an agent that has just left the malicious server can not trust any of its memory: All information collected prior to this point it time — including data from servers visited prior to visiting the malicious server — are suspect. Thus, only the results of computation done by those servers from the (maximal) *honest suffix* of the agent's route, assuming that the computation is independent of any input from previous servers, should be trusted.

**Server Replication** In [23], Minsky et. al. developed a general method for mobile agent computation security, marrying some ideas from the fields of fault tolerance and cryptography. They propose that servers should be replicated, and that replicated agents on these servers can use voting and secret sharing/resplitting to move from one phase of the computation to the next.

Unfortunately, the fault model assumed in the paper is completely unrealistic: it assumes that replicated servers fail independently. In our Fly-By-Night Airlines example, all replicated `www.flybynight.com` servers are under the administrative control of `flybynight.com`, and malicious attempts to brainwash software agents would occur on all of these servers. And while bribery of individual administrators of replicated servers by an outside adversary might be independent events, bribery of the software engineers responsible for the `www.flybynight.com` Web site is a much more likely scenario. Even if we assume that Fly-By-Night Airlines is trustworthy, replicated servers in the real world are likely to consist of identical hardware running copies of the same software: any security holes found by an external attacker that allows him/her to compromise one of the replicated servers is very likely to permit him/her to compromise all the servers.

**Agent Replication** While the general approach proposed by Minsky et. al. fails to be convincing, in certain special cases the fault tolerance style of approach can solve or at least ameliorate the mobile agent security problem. Because server replication does not help to reduce the risk of agent brainwashing, in the following we will assume that there is only one server per administrative/security domain, or when there are multiple servers in a domain, they are indistinguishable.

Consider the case where there is at most one malicious server in our airfare minimization example. Assume that secure communication links exists between the servers, and that the users possess individual certified public keys; servers may use these keys to verify the origin of the software agents. (Secure communication channels may be constructed cryptographically if servers also possess cryptographic keys to authenticated and encrypted data among the parties as needed.) Because we are assuming that there is only one dishonest server, we know that the agent must stay on the circuit prescribed during agent configuration.

Suppose we chose some sequence of servers $S = s_1, s_2, \ldots, s_n$. We configure two software agents $A_1$ and $A_2$, where $A_1$ will travel along $S$, and $A_2$ will travel over $S^{-1} = s_n, s_{n-1}, \ldots, s_1$.

Recall that we are assuming at most one malicious server. The all-honest servers case is trivial, so we can ignore that case; henceforth we will assume that there is exactly one bad server. Without loss of generality, assume that server $s_i$ is malicious, and that $s_j$ is run by the airline with the lowest fare ($j \leq i$). Furthermore, we assume that the malicious server will not attempt denial-of-service attacks — it may do so by killing the software agent or by implanting the belief that the lowest fare is offered by some third server which will later repudiate this idea.

First, consider the $j < i$ case. $A_1$ will encounter the lowest-fare server ($s_j$) first, and when it arrives at $s_i$, its memory of the lowest-fare seen-so-far may be altered. When $A_1$ returns with its result, it will report either $s_i$ as the server with the lowest fare, or some $s_k$ where $k > i$ if the malicious server did not declare a fare lower than one that the agent will see later in its travels.

$A_2$, on the other hand, will encounter the lowest-fare server after visiting the malicious server. It will report the correct minimum price — since we assume no denial-of-service attacks, the corrupt server will not have made this agent believe that a (false) lower price exists elsewhere — and when $A_2$ returns to the user, the user will be able to determine the true minimum airfare.

Next, consider the $j = i$ case. When this occurs, the malicious server can alter its price to be just below that of the second lowest price offered and still get business. This corresponds to a Vickery auction or second-price auction,[1] except the situation is upside-down: instead of the highest bidder paying the second highest bid price to obtain the goods being auctioned off, we have the lowest airfare offer selling tickets at the second lowest quoted price. Note that Vickery-style price determinations may be a desirable economic design choice anyway, since Vickery auctions are designed to maximize the flow of pricing information so bidders have no economic interest to hedge and not bid (and reveal) the true prices that they are willing to pay.

The above agent-replication approach provided a partial solution for a special case — at most one malicious server — the solution did not quite work "prop-

---

[1] We do not have sealed bids here since the minimization is done by the agent; an alternative design would be to gather bids encrypted using the public key of the agent originator, preventing servers from knowing each other's prices directly. Of course, servers could send out their own agents to discover such "commodity" prices; this may have to be done through anonymizing proxies if the pricing could depend on the consumer's identity.

erly" to compute the true minimum airfare: when $j = i$, we could only achieve second-best pricing, where what we obtain is the second-best airfare minus $\epsilon$. Arguably, since airline servers may also send out agents to determine pricing at other airlines — assuming price information can be obtained anonymously or in such a way that we are assured that it is independent of consumer identity (or race or age or ...) – Vickery pricing may be the end effect whenever there is great consumer price sensitivity in any case. Applying some basic cryptographic techniques, however, we can do a little better.

## 3.4 Cryptographic Approaches

There are three cryptographic techniques that apply or may apply. The first uses per-server digital signatures to vouchsafe partial results; the second is the use of state authentication codes to improve on the fault-tolerance solution above; and the third is the use of probabilistically checkable proofs (PCP) (a.k.a. "holographic proofs") or computationally sound proofs (CS proofs) to show that the computation at the servers ran correctly. Note that these techniques deal with the integrity of the result of computations at various servers — if the privacy of the result is needed, the result can simply be encrypted using the originator's public key.

**Digital Signatures** The application of digital signatures to mobile agents is to use the signatures to vouchsafe partial results from computation done while executing in a server. Going back to the airfare minimization example, what we will do is to have each airline server sign a message of the form "this is the best airfare found by your software agent at this server at this time".[2] The message signature is done using the airline's key, so it is non-repudiable and unforgeable. The message may optionally be encrypted by the originator's public key to ensure privacy.

The key observation is this: due to the unforgeability property, a malicious server can not completely brainwash the agent — at worse, it can make the agent forget the lowest airfare, which will be detected when an enumeration of the signatures show that one airline's quote is missing.

By using digital signatures, we will either obtain the true minimum airfare or be able to detect any tampering with the agent. The cost is that the agent state grows linearly with the number of servers visited, where the fault-tolerance approach required constant space (though the result was Vickery pricing rather than true minimum). This is an acceptable overhead for most applications. Like the fault-tolerance approach, however, the digital signature approach is not fully general: it only applies only certain classes of functions where there are intermediate results that can be "compressed" (e.g., in this case, the intermediate result is the best price found on the server — we don't care how much work was done

---

[2] It is important to note that the query as well as the answer is signed and times-tamped. Otherwise signed answers to the wrong question, asked by a different agent dispatched by the adversary, could be substituted in place of the expected answer.

in querying the airline's databases prior to finding this result, and we don't need to prove that it took place and that it ran correctly).

**Partial Result Authentication Codes** The idea of a Partial Result Authentication Code (PRAC) is very similar to that of a message authentication code (MAC)[4,5,17,19]. Instead of authenticating the origins of a message, we are demonstrating the authenticity of an intermediate agent state or partial result that resulted from running on a server. Similar to MACs, PRACs are cheaper than digital signatures to compute, and have slightly different security properties.

The property that PRACs ensure is *forward integrity*: if a mobile agent visits a sequence of servers $S = s_1, s_2, \ldots, s_n$, and the the first malicious server is $s_c$, then none of partial results generated at servers $s_i$, where $i < c$, can be forged. This contrasts with a simple digital signature, where if an attacker compromises the generating host where the signature key is stored, the authenticity of all messages signed with that key becomes questionable. The use of a digital timestamping service [14] can have similar properties, except that in that case a trusted third party (the timestamping service) is required and the granularity of the timestamps limits the maximum rate of travel for the agents — the agent must stay on a server until the next timestamping epoch before migrating to the next server.

The notion of forward integrity is a generalization of the notion of "forward secrecy", and have applications in other contexts [7]. The notion of forward secure cryptography applies to pseudo-random number generation as well as secrecy and integrity [6].

*Simple MAC-based PRACs* To have an agent use simple PRACs, we provide the agent with a list of secret PRAC keys at agent dispatch, with a key per server visited. Before leaving a server for the next, the agent summarizes its partial results from its stay at this server in a "message" back to the agent dispatcher. This message need not be sent back to the dispatcher immediately; instead, it may be carried with the agent as part of its migrating state for later transmission. This may be delayed so that it is "sent" to the dispatcher when the agent returns. Alternatively, these messages may be "batched" and sent when the networking bandwidth is cheap or available, e.g., when the dispatching mobile host has reconnected to the network. To provide integrity, a MAC is computed on this message, using the key associated with the current server; the message, along with its MAC, comprises the PRAC. The critical difference between MACs and PRACs is that after a PRAC is computed, the agent takes care to erase the PRAC key associated with the current server prior to migrating to the next server.

The erasure step provides a very important security property: the partial results from the *honest prefix* servers can not be modified. (This contrasts with the *honest suffix* property from section 3.3, where the partial results from honest servers visited after visiting the last malicious server are known to be unmodified.) Suppose an agent $A$ traverses a sequence of servers $S = s_1, s_2, \ldots, s_n$, where at each server $s_i$ a partial result $PR_i$ is computed using key $k_i$, and servers $s_1, \ldots s_j$ are honest and do not expose the internal state of the agent, then $\forall i, k : i \leq j < k, s_k$ can not forge $PR_i$, since $s_k$ must know $k_i$ to change $PR_i$.

*MAC-based PRACs with One-Way Functions* An obvious enhancement to simple PRACs is to use a single key instead of $n$ PRAC keys and use a $m$-bit to $m$-bit one-way function to generate the list of PRAC keys. When the agent is initially sent to server $s_1$, it contains key $k_1$. When the agent prepares to go from server $s_i$ to server $s_{i+1}$, it computes $k_{i+1} = f(k_i)$, where $f$ is a one-way function, and erases all knowledge of $k_i$. As before, a server $s_k$ can not forge PRACs from previous servers, since it would have to break the one-way assumption to determine the previous PRAC keys or break the MAC function.

More generally, instead of a $m$-to-$m$-bit function, an $m$ to $r$ bit one-way function may be used. (Typically $r < m$.) In this case, to obtain $k_{i+1}$ from $k_i$, we simply use some (perhaps pseudo-random) known $(m - r)$-bit string $t$ and set $k_{i+1} = f(k_i|t)$, where "|" denotes concatenation. If the probability that any algorithm, given $y$, will find a pre-image $x : f(x) = y$ is at most $2^{-m} + \epsilon$, knowing the last $(m - r)$ bits of the pre-image $x = k_i|t$ should not help: if knowing $t$ gives an algorithm a probability of finding a pre-image of $p > 2^{-r} + 2^{m-r}\epsilon$, then by guessing the value of $t$ values (probability $2^{r-m}$), we obtain an algorithm which will find a pre-image with probability $2^{r-m}p > 2^{-m} + \epsilon$, contradicting our one-way assumption.

*Publicly Verifiable PRACs* The MAC-based PRACs above required that the agent originator maintained a secret key or keys in order to detect tampering with the partial results. An obvious question is whether forward integrity can be provided such that the integrity verification may be public — so that an untrusted intermediate server not sharing the secret key with the originator may nonetheless help detect tampering.

Like MAC-based PRACs, publicly verifiable PRACs are implemented by relying on the destruction of information when agents migrate. Here, we use a digital signature system: when the agent is dispatched, it is given a list of secret signature functions $sig_1(m), \ldots, sig_n(m)$, along with usre-generated certificates for their corresponding verification functions $verif_1(m, s), \ldots, verif_n(m, s)$. The verification functions would be signed by the user's signature function $sig_{user}(m)$.[3] Like simple MAC-based PRACs, we use $sig_i(m)$ to sign the partial result computed on server $s_i$, and erase $sig_i(m)$ prior to migrating to server $s_{i+1}$.

Similar to one-way function MAC-based PRACs, we can also defer key generation, so that most of it is done on the servers, which presumably have greater resources. Here, the agent is given an initial secret signature function $sig_1(m)$ and a certified verification predicate $verif_1(m, s)$; the signature function is used both to sign partial results and to certify new verification functions.

---

[3] Signing a function $verif_i(.)$ simply consists of signing the parameters that specify the function; in RSA, it would be the two values $e_i, n_i$.

The verification predicate $verif_1(m, s)$ (and its certificate) is public, and the signature function $sig_1(m)$ is secret. When the agent is ready to leave server $s_1$, it signs the partial result $r_1$ by computing $sig_1(r_1)$. Next, it chooses (randomly) a new signature / verification function pair from the signature system, $sig_2(m)$ and $verif_2(m, s)$, and computes $sig_1(verif_2)$ to certify the new signature functions. Lastly, before the agent migrates to server $s_2$, $sig_1$ is destroyed.

To use publicly verifiable PRACs, the list of certified verification predicates must be either published and/or carried with the agent. When these predicates are available with the agent, publicly verifiable PRACs enjoy an important property not available with MAC-based PRACs: while at server $s_j$, the agent can itself verify the partial results obtained while at servers $s_i$, where $i < j$. In particular, this means that computations that depend on previous partial results can detect any integrity violation of those results — the agent's computation can abort early, instead of having to finish the computation and detecting integrity violation only when the agent results return to the agent originator.

**Proof Verification** We would like to get a guarantee that the agent's computation was done according to program specified in the agent. One possibility is to forward the entire execution trace — or a signature of it [28] — to the originator, who checks the trace if there is cause for suspicion. This however is too costly. Furthermore, if only a signature is sent to commit to a trace, it is unclear how to decide when to actually request the entire trace and then check it. We would like to explore the use of holographic proof checking techniques [3].

This is quite a speculative idea. The current approaches are very theoretical. In principle they do help, but the cost in practice of existing solutions is prohibitive. We are considering investigating ways to use the ideas in a more practical way. Let us describe the ideas and issues to see what it is about.

Call the program $x$. Let $y$ denote an execution trace. Define the predicate $\rho(x, y)$ to be 1 if this trace is correct (corresponding to running $x$) and 0 otherwise. The server does not want to send $y$. But it can encode $y$ as a holographic proof $y'$. This has the property that one needs to look at only a few bits of $y'$ to check that $\rho(x, y) = 1$. It is tempting from this to think that the server can just transmit a few bits. But this does not work. The model necessary for holographic proofs is that the verifier have available a fixed, "committed" proof string $y'$ that he can access at will. He will pick a few random positions here and check something. So there is no choice but to transmit $y'$ in entirety. We will not save bandwidth. We will gain something: the verification process is faster. (The verifier receiving $y'$ will perform some quick spot-checks).

A better approach is to use computationally sound (CS) proofs as in [20, 22]. Having constructed the holographic proof $y'$ as above, the server hashes it down via a tree hashing scheme using a collision-resistant hash function $h$. Only the root of the tree is sent to the originator. This is relatively short, so bandwidth is saved. In addition, certain challenges are implicitly specified by applying an ideal hash function to this root, and the server also provides answers to them. The total communication from server to originator is still small compared to the length of the original execution trace $y$, yet some confidence in the correctness of $y$ is transmitted!

The tree hashing is actually not impractical. What is prohibitive is constructing the holographic proof $y'$ to which it is applied. This currently calls for application of NP-completeness techniques, including the use of the construction underlying Cook's theorem. What we might hope instead is to find a direct holographic proof for the functions of interest, and then apply tree-hashing.

### 3.5 Trusted Environments (Secure Coprocessors)

An engineering solution to providing security for software agents is to build a trusted / trustworthy execution environment for the agents. The Sanctuary project is building such an environment to run within a secure coprocessor [18, 30, 32], allowing Java-based agents to run securely; designing and implementing the agent APIs needed to support mobile Java agents; and have developed the basic technology — analysis of code using "local continuations" — by which Java-based agents can migrate among unmodified Java interpreters running in an secure-coprocessor environment [15].

In addition to the basic support for agent execution, the Sanctuary project is developing the trust framework needed for inter-server communications. This necessarily implies having some basic public key infrastructure — we will leverage off of the existing work being done to support SSL [12], PCT [8], and TLS [11].[4]

A similar approach is found in [31]. Earlier work on analyzing the physical security assumptions for using tamper-detecting hardware, the trust model(s) involved, verification/inspection techniques, and the public key infrastructure needed to support such a system is found in [32]. The analysis there used a traditional operating system / application view instead of a more agent-centric view; in our opinion, an agent system is simply another application, a set of user-level servers which runs on top of a traditional security kernel within the secure coprocessor.

## 4 Trust Models

The issue of trust models is very important to agent-based computing. Agents do not just need a trusted computing base (TCB) — trust may not be so binary in nature. Instead, agents (or their deployers) may decide that it is okay to run in a software-only environment if such an environment is hosted by a well-known and trusted entity, but the use of physical protection to maintain the trustworthiness of a trusted third-party provided execution environment is needed when the environment is hosted by an entity with no reputation to protect and/or where no legal remedies may be obtained.

---

[4] The Internet Engineering Task Force's Transport Level Security group have developed a merged protocol based on SSL version 3 and features from PCT. These protocols require a merchant-side public key infrastructure.

In Sanctuary, we envision that the trust decision will be made by the agent's software itself. Thus, trust specification is simply an object in Java, and any effectively computable function may be used. This is similar in spirit with the work of Blaze and Feigenbaum [10], except that by unifying the agent language and the trust specification language, the programmer's work is simplified.

# 5 Mobile Java

Other approaches to providing mobility to Java programs [26] requires modifying the interpreter. In Sanctuary, we intend to provide a mechanism to migrate Java-based agents that can run on unmodified Java interpreters [15]. This strategy will enable wider acceptance of mobile agents, leveraging off of the work done by Sun/Javasoft and other companies. This means that just-in-time compilation as well as compilation of bytecode to native code are viable alternatives to bytecode interpretation for our system.

# 6 Future Work

The Sanctuary project group are examining important security issues in mobile agent computing. This paper has discussed some preliminary results and directions.

The primary goal is to build a secure agent environment insofar as it is theoretically feasible, including issues such as providing clean abstractions to make programming errors less likely as well as good cryptographic support. Currently, we are building a trusted Java agent environment to run within a secure coprocessor and designing APIs that permit agents to exist both in a hardware-based secure environment and in a software-only environment unchanged (but permitting security property queries). Next, we will build the necessary software tools to permit Java-based agents to be mobile. Our techniques, once implemented, will enable these agents to run on unmodified Java interpreters; this design approach permits greater acceptance of our work, since no complex installation process will be required, and it will allow our system to track new Java releases more easily. Additionally, we are examining alternative methods for providing security for software agents through fault tolerance and cryptographic approaches (e.g., distributed function evaluation, additional uses of digital signature techniques, etc).

# Acknowledgements

The author wishes to thank Mihir Bellare for his invaluable help in preparing this paper.

This research was funded in part by a National Science Foundation CAREER Award (CCR-9734243), a Faculty Development Award from National Semiconductor Corporation, and a gift from the Powell Foundataion.

# References

1. Martín Abadi and Joan Feigenbaum. Secure circuit evaluation. *Journal of Cryptography*, 2(1):1–12, 1990.
2. Martín Abadi, Joan Feigenbaum, and Joe Kilian. On hiding information from an oracle. *Journal of Computer and System Science*, 39(1):21–50, August 1989.
3. Laszlo Babai, Lance Fortnow, Leonid A. Levin, and Mario Szegedy. Checking computations in polylogarithmic time. In *Proceedings of the Twenty Third Annual ACM Symposium on Theory of Computing*, pages 21–31, New Orleans, Louisiana, May 1991.
4. Mihir Bellare, Ran Canetti, and Hugo Krawczyk. Keying hash functions for message authentication. In Neil Koblitz, editor, *Advances in Cryptology — Crypto '96*, volume 1109 of *Lecture Notes in Computer Science*. Springer-Verlag, 1996.
5. Mihir Bellare, Roch Guérin, and Phillip Rogaway. XOR MACs: New methods for message authentication using finite pseudo-random functions. In *Advances in Cryptology — Crypto '95*, volume 963 of *Lecture Notes in Computer Science*, pages 15–28. Springer-Verlag, 1995.
6. Mihir Bellare and Bennet Yee. Forward-secure cryptography: How to protect against key exposure. Work in progress.
7. Mihir Bellare and Bennet Yee. Forward integrity for secure audit logs. Technical report, Computer Science and Engineering Department, University of California at San Diego, November 1997.
8. Josh Benaloh, Butler Lampson, Terence Spies, Dan Simon, and Bennet S. Yee. The PCT protocol, October 1995.
9. Brian N. Bershad, Stefan Savage, Przemysław Pardyak, Emin Gün Sirer, Marc E. Fiuczynski, David Becker, Craig Chambers, and Susan Eggers. Extensibility, safety and performance in the spin operating system. In *Proceedings of the Fifteenth Symposium on Operating Systems Principles*, December 1995.
10. Matt Blaze, Joan Feigenbaum, and Jack Lacy. Decentralized trust management. In *Proceedings 1996 IEEE Symposium on Security and Privacy*, May 1996.
11. Tim Dierks and Christopher Allen. The TLS protocol, version 1.0, November 1998. Internet Engineering Task Force Internet Draft; see http://www.ietf.cnri.reston.va.us/internet-drafts/draft-ietf-tls-protocol-06.txt.
12. Alan Freier, Philip Karlton, and Paul Kocher. The SSL protocol version 3, December 1995.
13. J. Steven Fritzinger and Marianne Mueller. Java security, 1996. Published as http://www.javasoft.com/security/whitepaper.ps.
14. Stuart Haber and W. Scott Stornetta. How to time-stamp a digital document. *Journal of Cryptology*, 3(2), 1991.
15. Matthew Hohlfeld and Bennet S. Yee. How to migrate agents. Technical Report CS98-588, Computer Science and Engineering Department, University of California at San Diego, La Jolla, CA, August 1998.
16. Wilson C. Hsieh, Marc E. Fiuczynski, Charles Garrett, Stefan Savage, David Becker, and Brian N. Bershad. Language support for extensible operating systems. In *Proceedings of the Workshop on Compiler Support for System Software*, February 1996.
17. IBM Corporation. *Common Cryptographic Architecture: Cryptographic Application Programming Interface Reference*, SC40-1675-1 edition.
18. IBM 4758 PCI cryptographic coprocessor. Press Release, August 1997. http://www.ibm.com/Security/cryptocards/.

19. R. R. Jueneman, S. M. Matyas, and C. H. Meyer. Message authentication codes. *IEEE Communications Magazine*, 23(9):29–40, September 1985.

20. Joe Kilian. A note on efficient zero-knowledge proofs and arguments. In *Proceedings of the Twenty Fourth Annual ACM Symposium on Theory of Computing*, Victoria, British Columbia, Canada, May 1992.

21. Steven McCanne and Van Jacobson. The BSD packet filter: A new architecture for user-level packet capture. In *USENIX Technical Conference Proceedings*, pages 259–269, San Diego, CA, 1993. USENIX.

22. Silvio Micali. CS proofs. In *Proceedings of the 35th IEEE Symposium on Foundations of Computer Science*, pages 436–453, Santa Fe, New Mexico, November 1994.

23. Yaron Minsky, Robbert van Renesse, Fred B. Schneider, and Scott D. Stoller. Cryptographic support for fault-tolerant distributed computing. Technical Report TR96-1600, Department of Computer Science, Cornell University, July 1996.

24. George Necula. Proof carrying code. In *Proceedings of the Twenty Fourth Annual Symposium on Principles of Programming Languages*, 1997.

25. George Necula and Peter Lee. Safe kernel extensions without run-time checks. In *Proceedings of the Second Symposium on Operating Systems Design and Implementation*, Seattle, WA, October 1996.

26. Mudumbai Ranganathan, Anurag Acharya, Shamik D. Sharma, and Joel Saltz. Network-aware mobile programs. In *Proceedings of the Usenix 1997 Annual Technical Conference*. Usenix, 1997.

27. Tomas Sander and Christian F. Tschudin. Protecting mobile agents against malicious hosts. In Giovanni Vigna, editor, *Mobile Agents and Security*, volume 1419 of *Lecture Notes in Computer Science, Start-of-the-Art Survey*, pages 44–60. Springer-Verlag, 1998.

28. Giovanni Vigna. Cryptographic traces for mobile agents. In Giovanni Vigna, editor, *Mobile Agents and Security*, volume 1419 of *Lecture Notes in Computer Science, State-of-the-Art Survey*, pages 137–153. Springer-Verlag, 1998.

29. Robert Wahbe, Steve Lucco, T. E. Anderson, and Susan L. Graham. Efficient software-based fault isolation. In *Proceedings of the ACM SIGCOMM 96 Symposium*. ACM, 1996.

30. Steve R. White, Steve H. Weingart, William C. Arnold, and Elaine R. Palmer. Introduction to the Citadel architecture: Security in physically exposed environments. Technical Report RC16672, Distributed security systems group, IBM Thomas J. Watson Research Center, March 1991. Version 1.3.

31. U. Wilhelm, S. Staamann, and L. Buttyan. Introducing trusted third parties to the mobile agent paradigm. In *Secure Internet Programming*, Lecture Notes in Computer Science, Springer-Verlag Inc., New York, NY, USA, 1999.

32. Bennet S. Yee. *Using Secure Coprocessors*. PhD thesis, Carnegie Mellon University, 1994.

# Mutual Protection of Co-operating Agents

Volker Roth

**Abstract.** Security is a fundamental precondition for the acceptance of mobile agent systems. In this paper we discuss protocols to improve agent security by distributing critical data and operations on mutually supporting agents which migrate in disjunct host domains. In order to attack agents, hosts must collude/conspire across domains. Proper selection of itineraries can minimize the risk of such coalitions being formed.

**Keywords**: mobile agent security, malicious host, distributed applications, itinerary recording, agent cooperation, ecash

## 1 Introduction

Mobile agents are bundles of program and state, that move within a network to perform tasks on behalf of their owners. The benefits offered by mobile agents unfold in areas where it is advantageous to move the computation process over a network to the source of data instead vice versa; for instance if huge amounts of data must be processed, or the network is slow, expensive, or is not permanently available. Among the manifold uses for mobile agents, electronic commerce applications are noted most frequently. With good reason – electronic commerce provides perfect grounds to illustrate the benefits of mobile agents as well as the threats that keep us from using them in open networks, so far.

One example benefit of a mobile agent is its ability to carry out certain tedious or time–consuming tasks autonomously while its owner is offline. The goal of, for instance, a shopping agent might be finding the best offer for a given product description, thus optimising the benefit to its owner (which is legitimate). However, shops might be tempted to optimise for their own benefit, even if it means optimising at the expense of the agent in unfair ways (which is not legitimate). This includes manipulation of offers previously collected by the agent, as well as abusing agents as mediators of attacks on competitors. Hence, neither party trusts the other, and both share their distrust in the interconnecting network. As a consequence, the security requirements for mobile agent systems are manifold as well as demanding. Quoting from [2]:*"It is difficult to exaggerate the value and importance of security in an itinerant agent environment. While the availability of strong security features would not make itinerant agents immediately appealing, the absence of security would certainly make itinerant agents very unattractive."*

In general, the problem of *malicious hosts* is considered particularly challenging. The threats imposed by malicious hosts are immanent in the way mobile agent systems are built. Since agents are executed on their host, each instruction in the agent's code is observed by the controlling (virtual) machine which also maintaines the agent's state. This causes a number of security concerns of which the most prominent ones are:

1. The integrity of the agent, in particular the integrity of its mutable part, need to be protected. Agents might be abused as innocent carriers of illegal or offensive materials such as *warez* (pirated software). Hosts may also try to delete, replace, or invalidate commitments to the agent, such as terms negotiated in electronic commerce applications. This would enable the host repudiate said terms later.
2. Maintaining the secrecy of the agent's computations and data is a fundamental requirement for fair negotiations as well as for computations on confidential information such as the preferences (or *profile*) of the agent's owner, or secret keys.
3. Protecting the integrity of the agent's control flow is a precondition for any agent to trust its own decisions. Otherwise, malicious hosts might make agents believe that an offer is acceptable when it is actually not.

Notable advances were made with regard to items 1 and 2. Karjoth et al. [3] introduced the notion of *strong forward integrity* and proposed protocols for protecting the computation results of free–roaming agents. Their work is an extension of *partial result authentication codes* introduced by Yee [15]. Roth and Jalali proposed an agent structure that supports access control and authentication of mobile agents [5]. Agent authentication and state appraisal is covered by Berkovits et al. [8]. Sander and Tschudin [6] introduced the notion of *mobile cryptography* and devised approaches for non–interactive computing with encrypted functions using *homomorphic encrytion schemes*. Tschudin also proposes an approach for securing termination signals for mobile services [11] which incorporates ideas from Riordan and Schneier [4]. Regarding item 3, Vigna [12] proposed *cryptographic traces* to create verifiable execution traces of agents. Vigna also discusses a number of drawbacks with his approach such as limitation to single–threaded agents, extensive computational and memory overhead, as well as limitation to *a posteriori* detection. The notion of *trust*, its role in mobile code systems, as well as trust management is discussed for instance by Swarup et al. [10] and Blaze et al. [1].

The majority of risks stem from the fact that agents are deployed in open untrusted networks. However, even the hosts connected through this network do not know and do not necessarily trust each other. In the remainder of this paper we intend to exploit exactly this fact for improving the security of mobile agents against attacks by malicious hosts. The general idea is based on the co–operation of multiple agents with the goal of mutual protection (of the application built on them). Thus, co–operation of agents is used to establish a distributed "virtual shelter" inside the open network, in which agents can hide and to which they may retreat while assuring the security of their counterparts.

In Section 2 we motivate and formalise this idea, and give definitions and notations used in our paper. In Section 3 and Section 4 we devise two protocols, based on co–operating agents, suitable to protect different aspects of the general purchase agent against malicious hosts. One protocol is directed at recording the actual itinarary taken by a free–roaming agent; the second protocol addresses the delegation of electronic payments to mobile agents. Conclusions will be drawn in Section 5.

## 2 Co–operating Agents

With regard to mobile agent security, the most conservative approach is to assume that each host on a mobile agent's itinerary is hostile and willing to collaborate with other malicious hosts visited by the agent on its route. This assumption is as realistic as the assumption that hosts can be generally trusted, though. A more reasonable assumption is probably the following:

> Given a particular mobile agent, at any point in time, a certain percentage of hosts might be malicious.
> Not all malicious hosts are willing to collaborate with other hosts in attacking a mobile agent.

The percentage of malicious hosts likely depends on the gain which can be expected from successfully attacking mobile agents weighted against the costs of mounting the attack as well as the risk of detection and the consequences of being detected. Collaborations of multiple hosts on an agent's itinerary yields more power but it also requires close coordination and increases the danger of leaks which might lead to disclosure of the collaboration. Whether an agent will be attacked by a single malicious host or a collaboration of hosts on its itinerary depends on a sea of unpredictable parameters that are unique for each instantiation of an agent.

Still, we would like to model partitions of hosts based on their willingness to collaborate with regard to attacking a fixed agent. For this reason, let $\mathcal{H}$ be the set of hosts interconnected by a network. For a given instantiation of an agent let $\mathcal{R}$ be a relation defined as $\mathcal{R} \subseteq \mathcal{H} \times \mathcal{H}$ with the interpretation $(h_i, h_j) \in \mathcal{R} \Leftrightarrow h_i$ and $h_j$ collaborate in attacking the agent. Let $H_a, H_b$ be non–empty subsets of $\mathcal{H}$ with $(H_a \times H_b) \cap \mathcal{R} = \emptyset$. These two sets are denoted non–colluding. A special host is the first host (the origin) of an agent, since this needs to be a trusted host.

Two co–operating agents are defined to be agents $a$ and $b$ such that the itinerary of $a$ includes only hosts in $H_a$ and $b$'s itinerary only includes hosts in $H_b$. Let $h_a$ and $h_b$ be the computing environments currently executing agents $a$ and $b$ respectively. Occasionally, we will say that $h_a$ is "the host of" agent $a$, or "$h_a$ is agent $a$'s host".

Although agent $a$ might be attacked by host $h_a$, by definition this host may not attack the co–operating agent $b$ without breaking into host $h_b$. This can be exploited to design protocols for securing agents against attacks by single malicious hosts as well as hosts that collaborate with other hosts as long as the collaboration does not span the itineraries of both agents.

A number of strategies can be used as starting points for developing said protocols:

**Secret sharing:** Authorisation data is secretly shared by both agents. A single share conveys no information about the shared secret. Therefore, a malicious host must get the remaining share by asking a host on the co–operating agent's itinerary to steal it, or it must break into that host.

**Remote authorisation:** The decision whether the share of the authorisation data is passed to the host executing the agent is taken by the co–operating agent. The agent itself prefilters the data upon which the decision is based, and transfers it to its co–operating agent. Therefore, a malicious host must ask the remote host to manipulate the decision, or it must break into that host.

**Remote storage of commitments:** An agent transfers commitments of the host on which it runs, such as commercial offers, to its co–operating agent (probably in the course of remote authorisation), which verifies and stores it for future reference and non–repudiation. In order to undo or invalidate its commitment, a malicious hosts needs to break into a host on the co–operating agent's remaining itinerary.

In the remaining sections we illustrate the idea of mutual protection of co–operating agents by giving example protocols. For those protocols to work we need to make two additional assumptions:

- Hosts transport agents through authenticated channels.
- Hosts provide an authenticated communication channel to the two cooperating agents.
- The authenticated identity of the remote host, the authenticated identity of the host the agent came from as well as the local host's identity are provided to the hosted agent.

Yee already pointed out that "if an agent is running on an honest server, both these answers (for the peer identity and the local host's identity) will be correct..." [15]. We assume that a host is honest unless it may successfully attack an agent on its own, or with the help of other hosts on this agent's itinerary. In other words, we assume that hosts do not randomly introduce lies.

## 3 Tracing Loose Routes

A simple yet effective attack on a mobile agent is to not let the agent migrate to the servers of competitors. This particularly affects mobile agents with *loose itineraries* in comparison to agents whose itineraries are defined a–priori, because deviations from a fixed itinerary are easier to spot and prove.

We would like to record the actual loose route taken by a free–roaming agent without any possibility of manipulation by the hosts on its route.

Let $a$ and $b$ be two co–operating agents, and let $H_a, H_b \subseteq \mathcal{H}$ be two non-colluding sets of hosts. Both agents shall return to their origin upon completion of their tasks. Each agent $b$ records and verifies the route of its co–operating agent $a$ as described below.

**Definition:** Let $h_i \in H_a$ be the $i^{\text{th}}$ host being currently visited by agent $a$ and let $id(h_i)$ be the identity of host $h_i$. Let $prev_i$ be agent $a$'s idea of the identity $id(h_{i-1})$ of its previous hop. $next_i$ shall denote the identity of the next hop agent $a$ wants to take while being on host $h_i$. The agents start at host $h_0$, hence $h_n = h_0$ for a route with $n$ hops.

**Initialization:** Let $h_0$ be the origin of agents $a$ and $b$. $h_0$ has to be a trusted host with respect to $a$ and $b$. For agents $a$ and $b$, $next_0$ is set to the first hop of their respective itineraries. Both agents are subsequently sent to their first hop.

**Step $i, i \in \{1, \ldots, n\}$:** Agent $a$ sends a message containing the next hop $next_i$ and the previous hop $prev_i$ to agent $b$. The authenticated channel enables Agent $b$ to learn $id(h_i)$. Agent $b$ verifies that $id(h_i) = next_{i-1} \wedge prev_i = id(h_{i-1})$ and appends $next_i$ to the stored route.

**Security of the protocol:** It is straightforward to see that if host $h_i$ forwards agent $a$ to a host $h_{i+1}$ with $id(h_{i+1}) \neq next_i$ then host $h_{i+1}$ must either successfully masquerade as the host with id $next_i$ or it has to deny communication between the co–operating agents. On the other hand, if host $h_{i+1}$ permits the communication and properly authenticates itself (in other words, $h_{i+1}$ is honest regarding the protocol) then agent $b$ discovers that host $h_i$ sent agent $a$ to the wrong destination.

If $id(h_{i+1}) \neq next_i$ then host $h_{i+1}$ cannot put agent $a$ back on its route by sending $a$ to the host with identity $next_i$ because agent $b$ recorded $id(h_i)$ as $prev_{i+1}$. As a matter of fact, $h_{i+1}$ must either be honest (identifying $h_i$ as a cheater in the process) or $h_{i+1}$ has to collaborate with $h_i$ in putting the agent back on its expected route (more precisely, $h_i$ has to put back the agent on its route itself, or it must disclose its authentication keys to $h_{i+1}$). The last case reduces to either simply sharing a copy of the agent with $h_{i+1}$, or merging hosts $h_i$ and $h_{i+1}$ into a single host under the identity of $h_i$ – hardly something which can be prevented or detected at all.

A malicious host $h_{i+1}$ might incriminate a *honest* host $h_i$ by claiming to have received agent $a$ from some other host h', hence implicating that $h_i$ sent $a$ to h' instead of the host with identity $next_i = id(h_{i+1})$. The protocol is not able to decide which one of the two hosts is the culprit. However, if $h_{i+1}$ really received agent $a$ from h' then $h_{i+1}$ should be able to produce a copy of $a$ which is signed by h' given some additional agent protection mechanisms are implemented (see [5]).

If agent $a$ is killed, one of two hosts might be responsible and the protocol cannot decide which one. In addition to that, some host $h_{i+1}$ might take two agents $a_1$ and $a_2$ both being received by the same host $h_i$ and switch the recording of the route of $a_1$ to agent $b_2$ and vice versa. Therefore, co–operating agents should also exchange and verify (unique) identity information that is bound to the agent's static part by their owner's signature (see [5]). In that case, attempts to send fake ids are detected on the first honest host. The protocol must be enhanced accordingly.

## 4  Electronic Cash Payments

Current descriptions of mobile purchase agents primarily address collecting and filtering of offers. In this section, we would like to consider delegating payment authorisation to mobile agents as well. The risks in doing so are obvious. Digital representations of money may be copied, payment decision altered, and commitments erased after payment, by malicious hosts. However, modelling a complete purchase cycle with mobile agents, including payment authorisation, is an attractive thought. Cash–like systems are particularly well–suited because in contrast to for instance credit card based systems the possible loss is limited to the value of the digital coin.

Co–operating agents provide an approach to tackle security problems involved in payment authorisation. Protocols such as Chaum's digital electronic cash protocol (as described for instance in [7]) can be adapted to work with co–operating agents as described in the protocol given below. Chaum's protocol provides detection of double spending with cheater identification.

Let $a$ and $b$ be two co–operating agents, and let $H_a, H_b \subseteq \mathcal{H}$ be two non-colluding sets of hosts.

**Initialisation** The owner of the agents prepares a money order $m$ as described in [7]. The identity strings are prepared by randomly choosing keys $k_i^l$, $k_i^r$, $i = 1, \ldots, n$ and computing

$$\{I_i = (E_{k_i^l}(I_i^l, H(I_i^l)), E_{k_i^r}(I_i^r, H(I_i^r))) \mid i = 1 \ldots n\}$$

where $E$ is a suitable encryption function and $H$ is a strong cryptographic one–way hash function. The money order as well as the keys are secretly shared between agents $a$ and $b$. Both agents are sent on their respective itineraries.

**Step 1:** Agent $a$ locates a product or service on host $h_a$ (the one on which the agent runs) that it wishes to purchase, and requests a signed offer describing the subject and terms of the purchase.

**Step 2:** Host $h_a$ provides the requested offer as well as the *selector string* defined in the ecash protocol.

**Step 3:** Agent $a$ forwards the offer and the selector string to its co–operating agent $b$.

**Step 3:** Agent $b$ validates the offer's signature. In order to do so, it verifies that the identity of the offer's signer matches the one determined from the authenticated channel, and that the offer's signature is valid. It goes on to verify the terms of the offer. If the verification fails then $a$ is notified of the result and the protocol is aborted.

**Step 4:** Agent $b$ stores the offer (if $h_a$ later on repudiates having made that offer then its signature may be used as a proof), transfers its share of $m$ to $a$, and opens the selected halves of the identity strings by sending the appropriate key shares as well.

**Step 5:** Agent $a$ passes the data on to $h_a$.

**Step 6:** Host $h_a$ reconstructs the money order $m$, verifies the bank's signature and makes sure that agent $b$ properly opened the selected halves of the identity strings. The ecash protocol goes on as described in [7]. If the verification fails then the agents are notified, and the protocol is aborted.

**Step 7:** Host $h_a$ delivers the purchased goods.

**Security of the protocol:** Clearly, host $h_a$ cannot manipulate the payment *decision* in step 3 without collaborating with $h_b$. Neither of the hosts involved can steal the money order without the help of the other (or breaking into the remote host). Neither can host $h_a$ alter, invalidate or delete its offer after step 4. Of course, either the host or the co–operating agents may terminate the protocol at will. However, this is a general problem of electronic payment protocols.

However, any two hosts may profit from a joint attack on the cooperating agents by sharing the additional wealth gained from defrauding the agents compared to the profit gained from honest behavior. Therefore the domains of both agents' itineraries must be chosen with great care in order to assure $(H_a \times H_b) \cap \mathcal{R} = \emptyset$ holds with reasonable confidence.

Security can be improved by additional measures [5] which ensure that payment can only be made by $b$ while being on particular hosts.

## 5 Discussion and Conclusions

In this paper, we introduced the concept of co–operating agents as well as the basic principles on which protocols for mutual protection of such agents rest. These principles were illustrated by giving two example protocols, one for recording the actual itinerary taken by free–roaming agents, and one for protecting ecash payments with co–operating agents.

The ability to determine the actual route taken by an agent in principle allows further improvements of the security of agents against unauthorised and unnoticed manipulation. Hosts may commit to changes in the structure of an executed agent by digitally signing incremental logs of the agent's state upon its migration. According to the recorded route, the chain of signatures can be validated. Hence, in addition to *strong forward integrity* [3] co–operating agents may provide resistance against truncation and erasure with non–repudiation. Hosts which do not want to forward agents to the servers of certain competitors might still do so. However, the itinerary of the cooperating agent will always show this fact.

However, the ability of co–operating agents to mutually protect themselves relies crucially on the assumption that no pair of hosts chosen from both agent's itineraries collude. This precondition must be ensured with reasonable confidence. The most simple solution is to have one agent migrate to a trusted host while the other agent is free to roam the network. In this degenerate case, co–operating agents reduce to the trusted third party concept with the important difference, that *even the trusted third party need not be fully trusted*. Therefore, given a sufficient number of agent servers in the Internet, even a randomised strategy might be sufficient: One itinerary is randomly chosen and fixed while the second agent is free to choose its next hop at run time. The randomised strategy is based on the assumption that the sets of collaborating hosts are small compared to the number of available hosts. The overall security might be improved by complementing the approach taken in this paper with research in agent routing policies such as the one indicated by Swarup [9].

In particular, the ecash adaption protocol illustrates how distributed applications based on mobile agents may be securely deployed while preserving in particular the autonomy of mobile agents as well as their ability to perform useful tasks off–line, and maintain confidence in the delegation of authority as well.

In summary, protocols based on co–operating agents have merit since they are less susceptible to attacks by coalitions of hosts than single agents. The underlying principle is a generalization of the trusted third party concept which is less restrictive and easier to meet.

We plan to implement and evaluate the protocols described in this paper within the Java–based SeMoA platform (Secure Mobile Agents). SeMoA denotes an ongoing development project undertaken by the *Fraunhofer Institut für Graphische Datenverarbeitung*, with the goal of exploring and developing techniques and architectures allowing secure deployment of mobile agent technology in the area of multimedia and e–commerce applications.

# 6 Acknowledgements

I would like to thank the reviewers for their extensive comments on the initial manuscript, which were most valuable for improving the quality of this paper.

# References

1. BLAZE, M., FEIGENBAUM, J., IOANNIDIS, J., AND KEROMYTIS, A. he role of trust management in distributed systems security. In *Secure Internet Programming* [14].
2. CHESS, D., GROSOF, B., HARRISON, C., LEVINE, D., PARRIS, C., AND TSUDIK, G. Itinerant agents for mobile computing. *IEEE Personal Communications* (October 1995), 34–49.
3. KARJOTH, G., ASOKAN, N., AND GÜLCÜ, C. Protecting the computation results of free–roaming agents. In *Mobile Agents (MA'98)*, vol. 1477 of *Lecture Notes in Computer Science*. Springer Verlag, Berlin Heidelberg, September 1998, pp. 1–14.
4. RIORDAN, J., AND SCHNEIER, B. Environmental key generation towards clueless agents. In *Mobile Agents and Security* [13], pp. 15–24.
5. ROTH, V., AND JALALI, M. Access control and key management for mobile agents. *Computers & Graphics 22*, 3 (1998). Special issue *Data Security in Image Communication and Networks*.
6. SANDER, T., AND TSCHUDIN, C. F. Protecting mobile agents against malicious hosts. In *Mobile Agents and Security* [13], pp. 44–60.
7. SCHNEIER, B. *Applied Cryptography*, 1 ed. John Wiley & Sons, Inc., 1994, section 6.7, pp. 120–122. Digital Cash Protocol #4.
8. SHIMSHON BERKOVITS, JOSHUA D. GUTTMAN, V. S. Authentication for mobile agents. In *Mobile Agents and Security* [13], pp. 114–136.

9. SWARUP, V. Trust Appraisal and Secure Routing of Mobile Agents. DARPA Workshop on Foundations for Secure Mobile Code, Monterey, CA, USA, March 1997. Position Paper.

10. SWARUP, V., AND FABREGA, J. T. Understanding trust. In *Secure Internet Programming* [14].

11. TSCHUDIN, C. Apoptosis — the programmed death of distributed services. In *Secure Internet Programming* [14].

12. VIGNA, G. Cryptographic traces for mobile agents. In *Mobile Agents and Security* [13], pp. 137–153.

13. VIGNA, G. *Mobile Agents and Security*, vol. 1419 of *Lecture Notes in Computer Science*. Springer Verlag, Berlin Heidelberg, 1998.

14. VITEK, J., AND JENSEN, C. *Secure Internet Programming: Security Issues for Mobile and Distributed Objects*. Lecture Notes in Computer Science. Springer-Verlag Inc., New York, NY, USA, 1999.

15. YEE, B. S. A sanctuary for mobile agents. In *Secure Internet Programming* [14].

# Part III

# Implementations

# Access Control in Configurable Systems

Trent Jaeger

**Abstract.** In a configurable system, operating systems and applications are composed dynamically from executable modules. Since dynamically downloaded modules may not be entirely trusted, the system must be able to restrict their access rights. Current systems assign permissions to modules based on their executor, provider, and/or name. Since such modules may serve specific purposes in programs (i.e., services or applications), it should be possible to restrict their access rights based on the program for which they are used and the current state of that program. In this paper, we examine the access control infrastructure required to support the composition of systems and applications from modules. Access control infrastructure consists primarily of two functions: access control policy specification and enforcement of that policy. We survey representations for access control policy specification and mechanisms for access control policy enforcement to show the flexibility they provide and their limits. We then show how the Lava Security Architecture is designed to support flexible policy specification and enforcement.

## 1 Introduction

A hope afforded by the mass connectivity of the Internet is that it would enable users to engage in a variety of new applications regardless of their geographical distance. Thusfar, the most successful applications to be enabled by the Internet are client-server applications supported by the World-Wide Web. In these applications, clients simply request information from servers. Servers may use complex databases or dynamically determine the interface for processing the request, but almost all the computing is done at the server.

While a number of useful applications can be developed using the client-server paradigm, other computing approaches may be more appropriate for some applications. This is particularly true for applications where the movement of the computation is preferred over the movement of the data. In collaborative applications, often the computation is smaller than the application state, so each collaborator stores the application state and communicates their actions to the group [16, 26]. In this *peer-to-peer* approach, each collaborator may execute an action performed by any member of the group on their own copy of the shared state. Collaborative applications must be able to restrict the permissions of such actions based on the state of the application. For example, only the files currently being shared should be accessible to participants using a shared editor.

Second, research is underway to investigate how the modularity and extensibility of operating systems can be improved. A number of systems have been devised that can extend the operating system dynamically using *kernel extensions* [4, 12, 42]. Also, the OSKit project is investigating how operating systems can be composed from system service components [14]. This *module-on-demand* approach permits executable modules to be dynamically downloaded to support existing services or to compose services dynamically. The same argument also can apply for the composition of applications. The system must be able to restrict the permissions of such modules. This restriction may depend on the purpose for which they are used. For example, a memory system extension for an application should only obtain access to that application's memory objects.

Lastly, emerging applications, such as mobile agents, depend on the movement of the computation from clients to servers [46]. This *server-client* approach to computing permits a remote principal to act on server resources. In a commonly envisioned application, agents can perform complex queries on server data to gather information for decision-making. Thus, agents must be able to use server computing resources to read server data. Also, it may be permissible in some instances for such agents to modify server state. Servers must be able to restrict the permissions of its agents, particularly to system resources, but it must also be possible to enable applications to control the rights available to the agents they use.

The major impediment to the use of these computing approaches is an adequate framework to support the enforcement of system access control policies on dynamically loaded modules. At present, effective access control infrastructure for building such applications does not exist, so few applications use these computing approaches, regardless of their advantages. We consider that access control consists primarily of two functions: (1) access control policy specification and (2) enforcement of those access control policies. Access control models that support the specification of access control policies flexible enough to limit modules based on their purpose are not used in practice. The typical approach is to base permissions solely on the module author and name. Mechanisms for enforcement of limited rights for modules has been investigated primarily in language-specific systems [11, 18, 32, 35]. The effectiveness of these mechanisms are limited because they are depend on a large, complex trusted computing base (i.e., the virtual machine, byte code verifier, etc.), are language-specific, depend on unproven language separation features, do not control resource utilization, and focus solely on protection of the system from the components. The access control enforcement mechanisms need to be built into the operating system at the lowest levels to be generally effective, but they must not significantly degrade operating system performance.

In this paper, we survey representations for access control policy and mechanisms for access control policy enforcement that may be useful in building configurable systems. In Section 2, we outline the problems in enforcing access control on dynamically loaded modules. In Section 3, we examine the flexibility and limitations of different access control modeling features. The goal of this discussion is to identify the access control representation features necessary to express the access control policy for systems that use modules to compose applications and services. In Section 4, we examine the requirements of mechanisms that can enforce flexible access control policies. The goal of this discussion is to derive a enforcement mechanisms that can support flexible and efficient enforcement of access control policy. In Section 5, we describe the representations and mechanisms chosen for the Lava Security Architecture.

## 2 Security Requirements

We assume a computing model in which *principals* (e.g., users and services) consume *resources* (e.g., CPU and memory) to perform *operations* (e.g., read and write) on *objects* (e.g., files and channels). The ability to use resources to perform operations on objects are called the *access rights* of a principal. The fundamental problem posed by the computing approaches described above is to restrict the access rights of each dynamically downloaded module consistently with its service or application requirements. Since these requirements may vary with each use, the job of access control policy specification and management is daunting. Also, authorization mechanisms must be effectively and efficiently able to enforce these requirements. In this section, we specify the access control policy and authorization mechanism requirements for configurable systems.

### 2.1 Execution Model and Vulnerabilities

The execution model we envision for configurable systems is shown in Figure 1. Remote servers store executable modules that are downloaded as necessary to compose system services and applications. The modules may be written in any language and/or compiled into the binary language of that machine. A module may be loaded into an existing process with other modules or into a new process. The system's trust in individual modules may vary widely. Some may be trusted device drivers, but others may be untrusted to varying degrees. The system's security policy is enforced by its trusted computing base (TCB). The TCB must determine whether the module should be loaded, the process in which it is loaded, the permissions of that process, and the ability of that process to obtain other permissions.

Unfortunately, an untrusted binary module, unless controlled, can perform a wide variety of attacks. Below, we list a taxonomy of common attacks:

- **Unauthorized read**: Read secret host data
- **Unauthorized modification**: Change host data or modify host binaries (i.e., act as a virus)
- **Unauthorized execution**: Execute another program that gives the module greater privileges (e.g., starting a shell)
- **Unauthorized transmittal**: Forward secret data entrusted to a computation to a remote principal or to a place that another untrusted module can read
- **Abuse of system resources**: Consume RAM memory and disk space as well as CPU utilization

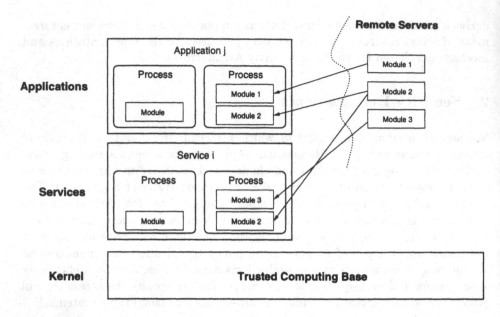

**Fig. 1. System Execution Model:** Services and applications are composed of processes containing one or more dynamically-loaded modules

- **Plant viruses and Trojan horses**: Add binaries to the host's system and modify the host's environment, so these malicious binaries are run by more privileged users

The first four types of attacks are what access control infrastructure is typically designed to prevent. For example, the second type of attack can occur if users do not adequately control discretionary access to their own executables (e.g., a program under development). A module could identify that a file is a binary executable, and infect the program with a virus or replace it with a Trojan horse.

The fifth type of attack is a denial-of-service of system resources. For example, a module that writes to the disk until it is full would deny other modules from writing to the disk. Operating systems typically do not prevent these attacks from occurring. However, it has been shown that proper management of system resources can enable control of the amount of service resources that a module may consume [30]. However, these mechanisms have not been demonstrated in practice, and it is non-trivial to determine reasonable resource limits.

In the sixth type of attack, the module leaves a trap that an unsuspecting user may be lured into. For example, a Trojan horse program may be written into a user's directory ostensibly used for application files, and the untrusted module may modify the path environment (e.g., due to lax user administration of their configuration files) resulting in the execution of the planted program with the user's full rights.

## 2.2 Access Control Requirements

To prevent the attacks described above, access control policy must enforce the following constraints (at a minimum):

- **Authorized object creation**: Objects may be created only with authorized names and with authorized permissions associated with them (e.g., limited delegation, see below). For example, few, if any, principals should be able to create executable files.
- **Immutable object identities**: Object names should be unique and immutable to prevent time-of-check-to-time-of-use (TOCTTOU) attacks [6].
- **Authorized read**: Only authorized objects may be read.
- **Authorized modification**: Only authorized objects may be modified.
- **Authorized execution**: Only modules that are trusted not to extend a principal's permissions may be executed by that principal.
- **Authorized transmission**: A principal may only communicate with authorized principals regardless of the available communication channel (e.g., sockets, files, etc.).
- **Authorized resource utilization**: Only authorized system resources may be used by these modules, and these resources must be revocable.
- **Authorized delegation**: A principal may be restricted in the rights that it may receive via delegation. For example, it cannot delegate a principal the right to communicate with it if a policy of separation exists between the two principals.
- **Maintain consistency with policy**: The system must be flexible enough to adjust to changes in permissions due to dynamic security policy changes.

The security requirements described above restrict the actions that a module may perform on any system or application objects. Fundamental to these requirements is the ability to create and name objects. In order for the system's access control policy to be enforced on dynamically composed services and applications, it must be possible for this policy to be mapped to dynamically-created object name spaces. These object names must be immutable to prevent renaming after authorization (time-of-check-to-time-of-use or TOCTTOU attacks). Then, basic access control on each operation on each object can prevent unauthorized operations from being performed. In addition, control of resource consumption may be desired to control some denial-of-service attacks. Next, it may be necessary to control the delegation of rights by dynamically loaded modules. For example, an application developer may not know that the delegation of a right may lead to the creation of an unauthorized communication channel. Lastly, this policy for controlling this delegation is determined outside the module, so it must be possible for the system to enforce its policy as it changes (e.g., due to a change in application state). Even though the system cannot prevent a principal who possesses a right (in this case, the application) from using it to circumvent security policy, it is often the case that the application wants to enforce security policy properly, but it cannot be completely aware of that policy. The system must be able to enforce its policy under these trust conditions.

Access control models must enable the specification of the desired security policies with a reasonable amount of effort. The key issue is that policies may be dependent on dynamic factors, such as application state. For example, the patient data available to a nursing application depends on the hospital, ward, etc. in which the nurse principal works. In these cases, the access control model must enable the association of application context and principals. Because policy may be context-specific, it may be desirable for both system administrators and other principals, such as application designers, to specify the rights available to a module. Thus, the access control model must enable the specification of policies by multiple principals, but these principals may not be completely trusted to administer rights, so permission management must be restricted based on a mandatory access control policy.

## 2.3 Authorization Mechanism Requirements

Once the security policy has been specified, the system must be able to enforce it. The system must be able to derive legal permissions for its principals and authorize their actions using these permissions.

A model for the derivation of a module's legal permissions is needed. As described above, this model must support the ability for multiple principals to delegate a limited set of rights. The set of rights that may be delegated may depend on the current state of the system or application. Therefore, there must a mechanism for keeping the access control policy of a module consistent with the factors it depends on (e.g., the state of the application in which it is being run). A problem is that such management itself can become ad hoc. The model needs a means for expressing when a modules permissions should be expanded or retracted within the mandatory limits.

Once the a module's permissions are determined, the authorization mechanism must be able to enforce these permissions. In general, authorization mechanisms must perform the following tasks [1]:

- Intercept all controlled operations
- Authorize each operation using the system's security requirements
- Protect the system from tampering

While the basic functions of the security mechanism remain the same as dynamically downloaded modules are introduced, the complexity of these tasks is increased. First, modules may be loaded into the same protection domain (i.e., address space) to improve performance. However, operations within a protection domain cannot be intercepted, so it is necessary for the security mechanisms to determine whether such a load is permissible. Next, a dynamically downloaded module may provide access to a resource that requires access control. For example, the file system may be a dynamically downloaded module. However, this module must be able to enforce system security constraints on the accesses to its objects. Therefore, the system security mechanisms and the module need to work together to enforce the system's access control policies properly.

# 3  Access Control Policies

In this section, we evaluate access control modeling concepts for their ability to describe the security policies outlined above. The requirements of these access control models are that they be able to express the security policy requirements and, as much as possible, ease the task of security policy specification. Role-based access control (RBAC) models are designed to ease the management of access control policy, so we center the discussion around these models. However, there is no standard RBAC model, but rather, several models containing various combinations of access control modeling features. We, therefore, examine these various features to determine the access control policy issues they address.

## 3.1  Role-based Access Control

Many systems associate principals directly with users or services. A user executes a program, and the program assumes the rights of the user principal. Unfortunately, when a user executes a downloaded module, the module cannot assume the full rights of the user without opening the user to the attacks described above.

In general, the permissions associated with a user executing a downloaded module would be those of that user assuming a role of executing that module. For example, Jaeger and Prakash show that the security policy in many collaborative situations is the intersection of the permissions of the collaborators [22]. In these cases, a user's permissions are those of the user acting on behalf of a collaborator.

This solution is specific to collaborative systems, but a more general approach has been known for many years: role-based access control (RBAC) [41]. In a basic RBAC model, called RBAC96 [38], the users are associated with the roles that they may assume. Permissions are then associated with the roles rather than the users. This enables users to execute programs with different (hopefully, least privilege [37]) access rights.

Many RBAC models utilize inheritance to ease the specification of access rights. For example, users may assume application-specific roles which have a subset of their rights as shown in Figure 2. In general, a role hierarchy represents a set-subset relation where the rights are inherited up the tree (which is the opposite of object-oriented inheritance). Thus, any descendant role has a subset of its ancestor's permissions.

Thus, roles can be created with the proper rights for each module, and users can switch to the appropriate role when they want to execute a module. In addition, RBAC models also prescribe the use of constraints to enforce more complex security requirements, such as separation of duty. For example, the roles of two modules can be evaluated to show that they share no access to common objects. Also, Chinese Wall requirements can be enforced to prevent a user from executing two mutually exclusive sets of privileges simultaneously [39]. Even denial-of-service requirements, such as memory usage limits, can be expressed as constraints on the use of permissions.

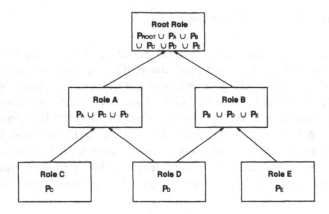

**Fig. 2. Role Hierarchy:** Note that permissions are inherited up the role hierarchy

Theoretically, RBAC models enable enforcement of a wide variety of security requirements and are intended to ease the task of security policy administration, but the specification of module access rights presents problems for the basic RBAC models. First, each module may define its own objects and operations, so we examine how some additional aggregations enable role specification. Second, a module's permissions may depend on a variety of factors, including its application, role in the application, and application state, so we discuss a generalization of the role concept, called *parameterized roles* that enables a single role definition to be applied to multiple contexts. Third, since any principal may compose an application or service from a set of modules, the number of potential administrators is increased, so we examine concepts that can describe role administration. Lastly, the use of parameterized roles and multiple administrators raises the importance of constraint enforcement, but this is not a well-developed area of RBAC. In the following subsections, we discuss these avenues for reducing the complexity of RBAC specification while still enabling the desired flexibility.

## 3.2 Aggregations

As we saw, RBAC models enable users to be aggregated into logical roles and permissions to be aggregated for use by those roles. However, access control models can support a number of other aggregations that may ease the specification of security policy. We examine the aggregations of objects and operations. Then, we propose an extended RBAC model in which these aggregations are included and assess what this extended model enables.

A number of systems enable objects with the same rights to be aggregated [19, 24, 7, 2, 49]. In the CORBA security model [19, 25], objects are aggregated into sets called *domains*. Permissions are specified per domain, and any principal can be given rights to access objects in a domain. That is, the assumption is that different principals have common object aggregations for specifying their rights. Of course, this may not always be the case, as different principals may

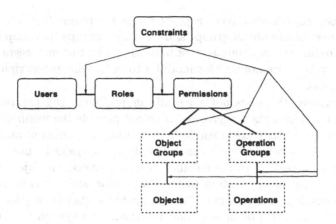

**Fig. 3. Extended Role-based Access Control Model:** Permissions are derived from object and operation groups

use their own objects to execute may have common rights over different object aggregations. In this case, multiple domains must be created.

Next, the operations of a specific type can be aggregated into a set of operations named by a type with common access control requirements. For example, certain operations may be designated as read operations and others as write operations for particular objects. This enables system administrators to specify the rights of principals to read and/or modify data given a definition of which operations perform those types of operations. In our work [23], application developers aggregate operations into *operation groups*, and system administrators define rights in terms of those groups. Similarly, CORBA enables the definition of *interfaces*, and administrators define the *required rights* needed to access those interfaces. For example, a principal needs read permission on a domain to access their read interface.

Therefore, the RBAC model presented in the previous subsection can be extended as shown in Figure 3. In this RBAC model, objects for which common rights may be expressed are aggregated into object groups. Operations which correspond to common operation types can be aggregated into operation groups. Then, the set of permissions is a relation between the sets of object groups and operation groups. Further, object groups and operation groups can themselves be aggregated, and these aggregations may be subject to constraints. For example, an object group can be created that contains the intersection of two object groups' members. Also, permissions can be constrained based on their constituent object and operation groups. For example, this would enable the specification of the intersection of two permission sets.

An obvious benefit of this extended RBAC model is that the task of expressing permissions is eased because it is possible to express permissions using fewer statements. An additional, less obvious benefit is that it enables a separation of labor between users/developers and system administrators. Because system administrators often do not know the semantics of application objects and operations, they cannot effectively express rights for them. Instead, application developers may create object groups and operation groups that map to semantically meaningful system administrator notions. While this may seem dangerous, it is generally not unreasonable for modules to define the access rights of others to their objects.

Unfortunately, this does not solve all our problems and creates some new ones. Object and operation aggregations do not provide the flexibility needed in some cases because they are static for all execution instances of an application. For example, in a collaborative context, only the objects in use in that context should be accessible to the collaborators. Therefore, an object aggregation should depend on the application state. Also, a new problem is created because application developers and users can assign rights to other principals. Every right that is delegated to a principal should be within the system's security policy. This does not preclude us from establishing that modules can enforce security policy on their objects – we must trust them to provide proper access to the objects they serve. However, module writers cannot be trusted to know the system security policy, so they cannot be allowed to delegate permissions arbitrarily. Constraints, such as separation of duty, may be violated. In the following two subsections, we address these two problems.

### 3.3 Context-Sensitive Roles

Context-sensitive RBAC models enable permissions to be specified relative to a context [15, 31]. Giuri and Iglio formalized this notion in terms of *parameterized roles*. A parameterized role consists of a role identifier and a set of parameters whose values determine the context. Object groups in the permissions are indexed by the parameters to indicate a particular set of objects.

Thus, by setting different parameter values, different permissions can be obtained. For collaborative applications, we use parameterized roles to represent the permissions of each collaborator [23]. Each collaborator is assigned a role that is parameterized by the user principal, module author (i.e., collaborator), application, module's role in the application, and the application's state. Thus, the rights associated with the role are dependent on the user's objects that are being used in this collaborative session. Therefore, least privilege rights are enforced on the collaborators because only the objects in use in this instance of the collaboration are accessible.

Context-sensitive roles can represent a set of roles using only one role specification. We also use context-sensitive roles to enable system administrators to specify the permissions which may be assigned to an application for any user, and for application developers to specify permissions for each execution of their applications. In this model, many principals may be able to specify roles, so the need for proper role administration becomes much more important. Also, the specification of roles must adhere to the system's security policy. Since constraints are used to enforce system security policy, the ability to specify and enforce constraints becomes more important.

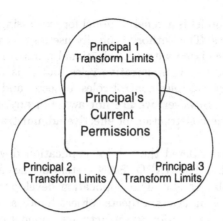

**Fig. 4. Transform Limits:** A principal's permissions are at most the union of the permissions that may be delegated by principals 1, 2, and 3.

Since a principal may obtain permissions based on a change in context, it may be necessary to restrict the permissions that may be delegated to adhere to system and application security policies. We envision that services will be composed from a set of modules where one distinguished module may be responsible for the correct behavior of the service. For example, consider a virtual memory system composed from several modules. The main virtual memory module enables the download of application-specific memory managers on the behalf of applications. Since memory manager modules may be requested to transfer pages among one another (e.g., to share memory), the virtual memory system must restrict this with respect to the system's security policy (or else it does not behave correctly. Thus, we make a distinction between the permissions that a principal possesses and a principal's *transform limits* [23]. A transform limit defines the set of permissions that a delegator may grant to a delegatee. The union of a principal's transform limits determine the maximal permissions that that principal may obtain (see Figure 4). In this example, the virtual memory system can restrict the permissions that its modules can distribute among one another. These restrictions depend on the context in which the module is used, so context-sensitive roles are necessary to describe such restrictions.

## 3.4 Administration

RBAC models have also been designed that support the administration of security policies. In the ARBAC 97 model [40], an administrative role hierarchy defines the administrative roles and their rights to modify the information in the basic role hierarchy: user-role assignment, permission-role assignment, and role-role assignment (i.e., construction of the role hierarchy itself). Based on the extensions described above, ARBAC 97 could likewise be extended to enforce object-object group assignment, operation-operation group assignment, and object-operation assignment (i.e., creation of permissions).

The ARBAC 97 model is a general model for expressing administrative roles and permissible duties. The authors typically use an example in which administrative roles are associated with organizational groups. No explicit semantics are associated with these administrative roles, but it is likely that the intent is that the administrative roles control roles, objects, and permissions in their organizational group. However, we are not aware of any use of administrative role hierarchies, so the construction of effective administrative hierarchies is an open issue.

Some work has considered the role of application developers and users in administration of roles. The NAPOLEAN system divides access control administration into seven layers [43]. The application developers are responsible for defining the bottom four layers: objects, object handles (operations), application constraints, and application keys (actually application roles). System administrators define the top three layers: enterprise constraints, enterprise keys (system roles), and key (role) chains. Despite the non-standard nomenclature, a number of important RBAC features are represented in NAPOLEAN: (1) application developers can define the object name spaces and application-specific roles and (2) system administrators associate users with these roles (or their aggregates, key chains) and restrict the rights that principals may be granted (using constraints). The enterprise constraints are not described in any detail, so we suspect that they are ad hoc.

In our access control model [23], role administrators (i.e., administrators of the role as specified by the role administration hierarchy) specify the transform limits of the role. There is a distinction made between the administrators of the role, who are trusted to grant all of their rights to the role, and the delegators of role, who are restricted in the rights that they may delegate by the transform limits. This distinction enables the role administrator to specify limits on the transfer of rights, so that their access control policy can be enforced. Such policies may be dynamic, however, so simply restricting the possible delegations may not be sufficient to enforce them. Consider the Chinese Wall policy [8] where one of disjoint subset of permissions is obtained based on an action. In this case, a single set of transform limits for a principal is insufficient because the transform limits that need to be enforced depend on which operations the principal has performed. It is envisioned that role constraints must be able to adjust the transform limits based on the current policy.

## 3.5 Constraints

The use of constraints in RBAC is the least-developed notion in RBAC models. Currently, research has identified two sub-satisfactory notions of constraints. In some systems, a general notion of constraints is included in the model, as is done in ARBAC 97 or NAPOLEAN, that does not include a language for specifying such constraints. In other systems, specific, limited constraints are supported. However, these constraint languages are not general purpose.

A security constraint language must enable enforcement of the variety of security constraints. For example, it must be possible to specify restrictions on the rights a principal may attain, that principals cannot modify executables, separation of duty between principals, Chinese Wall constraints, denial-of-service constraints, etc. However, some constraints are distinctly different, so entirely different constraint models may be appropriate. For example, enforcement of the Bell-LaPadula security policy is much different than the basic access control policy outlined here. While it has been shown that general RBAC models can enforce Bell-LaPadula [3], it is not clear whether a general constraint language should be exposed to the administrators who write the policies.

In our work, we take a two-pronged approach. First, we enable the specification of *transform limits*. A transform limit specifies the set of permissions that a delegatee can obtain from a specific delegator. The set of transform limits determine the maximal set of permissions that a principal can obtain. Second, the definition of such transform limits depend higher-level security constraints, such as Chinese Wall [8]. A Chinese Wall policy is a dynamic separation of duty policy in which only one of several disjoint sets of rights may be used depending on the actions of the principal. Constraints are written that determine the transform limits that may be active. The language for expressing such constraints is still under development.

Bertino *et al* propose a language for defining constraints on the assignment of users to roles and the creation of inheritance role hierarchies [5]. Their approach is designed to enforce constraints on the execution of workflow tasks. For example, a user may be restricted from executing a second task if he executes a previous task in a particular role. Therefore, constraints are specified in terms of tasks. Constraints specific to operations within a task cannot be expressed, however.

Our opinion is that a single general constraint language should be devised. This language should be general enough to express any constraint (on users, objects, operations, and their administration). However, such a language will likely be too abstract and complex for use by system administrators, so application specification languages must be built on this base constraint language for the individual applications.

## 4   Access Control Enforcement

In general, access control policy enforcement requires two mechanisms: (1) a mechanism to derive the access control policy associated with each principal (permission management mechanism) and (2) a mechanism to authorize controlled operations using this access control policy (authorization mechanism). We examine the functionality offered by traditional implementations of these two mechanisms and discuss how they must be altered to support our requirements. In the next section, we describe how the mechanisms provided in the Lava Security Architecture address these requirements.

## 4.1 Permission Management

Permission management mechanisms determine each principal's access rights at any time. Lampson has formalized the representation of access rights into an *access matrix* whose two practical variations are access control lists and capabilities [27]. An access control list associates an object with the principals and the operations they can perform on the object. A capability defines objects and the operations that can be performed upon them by any principal that holds the capability. Since our access control model involves the dynamic modification of principal rights, a capability approach is easier to maintain.

The early capability-based systems took the view that each invocation of a procedure may have its own access rights. Dennis and Van Horn formalized this notion into a concept called a *protected procedure call* [10]. A protected procedure call is designed to mutually protect the caller and the procedure from each other. The capabilities available to the procedure are the union of its own capabilities and the capabilities that the caller explicitly passed in the invocation. Thus, the procedure only gains access to the capabilities that the caller grants, and the caller does not obtain direct access to the capabilities of the procedure.

While many systems used the protected procedure call approach (e.g., [9, 48]), other system designers found its semantics of permission management inadequate. For example, the CAP system [47] derives a procedure's capabilities from a variety of inputs which, in addition to those of the procedure and those passed by the caller, include: (1) the capabilities of the process in which the procedure is run; and (2) the capabilities of all system procedures. Mungi protection domain extension enables capabilities not explicitly passed in the procedure call to also be provided to the procedure, but only for the duration of the procedure call [44].

Problems of confinement and revocation have made capability-based systems difficult to use to enforce system security policies. In general, the possession of a capability is sufficient to use it. Since a capability can be distributed in a procedure call, it is hard to prevent principals from being given unauthorized capabilities and it is hard to revoke capabilities once they have been granted. Enforcement of permission limits, such as transform limits, enable the system to restrict the set of capabilities that a process may obtain. Approaches that enable revocation involve some form of indirection. Redell's revoker capabilities enable invalidation of delegated capabilities. DTOS [33], MOSES [34], and Lava [21] cache capabilities in a trusted process, so immediate revocation is possible.

JDK 1.2 uses an approach to permission management that enables permissions to be determined based on run time factors, called *stack introspection* [17, 45]. Using stack introspection, the permissions of an executing thread are the intersection of the permissions of the classes whose methods have been executed. A class's permissions restrict the set of capabilities that the class's methods may ever obtain. In JDK 1.2, the permissions of a class depend on the class's provider and/or code base. In order for the class to execute properly in all reasonable contexts, the rights assigned to a class must be the union of all the rights that the class may ever need. Therefore, the intersection of these rights may still grant

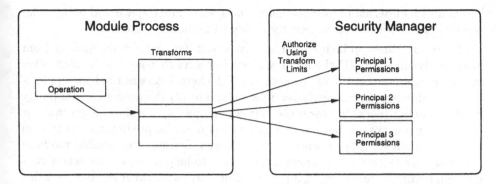

**Fig. 5. Transforms:** A module's operations may be associated with transforms that grant rights to or revoke rights to one or more principals, perhaps including the module's principal itself.

the thread many rights that are not necessary given the application in which the class is used, the purpose of the class in that application, and the application's current state.

Instead, we advocate an approach where a principal's permissions are always consistent with the current state of the application or service. Using our access control model, these delegations are restricted by the transform limits of the principal. The problem is to automate the process of delegation. For this purpose, we define the concept of a *transform* which associates an operation with a change in permissions of one or more principals [23] (see Figure 5). Thus, changes in application state can be correlated to changes in permissions. These permissions changes are authorized using the transform limits of the delegatees.

Once a principal obtains a permission, a capability can be obtained for it. For example, possession of a permission to read and write a file enables the principal to obtain a capability with those operations activated. When a transform revokes a principal's permission, the system may need to revoke some of its capabilities. However, multiple principals may grant the same permission, so any effected capabilities are only invalidated. They are authorized again upon the next use.

## 4.2 Authorization Mechanisms

Authorization mechanisms determine whether a principal is permitted to invoke an operation on an object. Logically, an authorizing agent retrieves the principal's access control policy and compares the request (perform an operation on an object) to the policy. If an entry in the policy grants the request and no policy precludes that request, then the authorizing agent permits the request.

Currently, most operating systems (e.g., UNIX and Windows NT) are monolithic, and they only enforce access control on system calls. Since the kernels store all objects to which access is controlled, they have access to the name spaces of the objects they need to protect (e.g., the file system). Therefore, the kernel uses its internal representation of the system name space and its internal representation of the system security policy to authorize system calls.

There are three problems with this approach for systems configured from modules dynamically: (1) the name spaces of objects that need to be controlled may be outside the control of the kernel; (2) the kernel does not aid the applications in enforcing their security requirements; and (3) the access control policy flexibility of our model increases the kernel's complexity. First, modules manage their own name spaces, but these name spaces must be predictable, so system and application security policies can be enforced. Second, downloaded modules may want the system's trusted computing base to help it enforce its access control requirements. For example, an application may use another module, but this module should only have a subset of the application's rights. Lastly, the addition of more flexibility to security policy means that the authorization mechanisms become more complex. In a configurable system, inter-process communication (IPC) must be very fast to support a reasonably fine granularity of processes, but the addition of a complex authorization mechanism into each IPC would add a mandatory cost to all IPCs (even those with few requirements to check).

Micro-kernel systems (e.g., Mach [36] and Spring [13]) avoid the name space problem by only controlling communication between processes. For a client process to invoke an operation on a server process, the client must have a capability to send a message to a port to which that server has a receive capability. The semantics of the operation are determined by the server and authorized by the server in its own way. Also, capabilities can be passed freely in messages, so no control on delegation is enforced. While this removes the complexity of the name space from the kernel, it prevents the kernel from being able to enforce the system's current security policy and requires each server to define its own authorization mechanism which may result in errors.

Reference monitors enable control of delegation. For example, the Distributed Trusted Operating System (DTOS) extends the Mach kernel by a mechanism that enables custom security policies to be enforced by security servers [33]. DTOS adds a capability cache to the kernel, so servers can call the kernel to authorize operations. If a capability is not present, a *security fault* is taken which results in a call to the appropriate security server. Security servers interpret the server's object name spaces. The administrators of the service that use this security server must know enough about the object name spaces of these servers to enforce the policy. Upon a successful authorization, the security server then updates the capability cache. Also, security servers can invalidate the entries in the capability cache which enables revocation. DTOS provides a flexible authorization mechanism, but it makes the kernel more complex (which has been found to degrade IPC performance [29]) and requires extra communication overhead to authorize the operation (1 round-trip IPC).

Our goal is to combine the kernel cache and security servers into one entity outside the kernel. The Clans & Chiefs mechanism is not explicitly an authorization mechanism, but it can be applied to authorization [28]. In this mechanism, a chief is a special process in a clan (i.e., set of processes). Any IPC between two processes in the same clan are forwarded directly to the destination by the kernel. However, any IPC either to a process outside the clan or from a process outside the clan is automatically redirected by the kernel to the chief. In a security scenario, the chief can authorize any communication between processes in its clan and the other processes in the system. In an early version of the Lava Security Architecture [21], we use a chief for every dynamically loaded module, so we could control its accesses to the trusted servers and other dynamically downloaded modules. The chief stores the access control policy of the process that it controls and authorizes all of this process's operations. Of course, if an IPC is between two different clans, then three system IPCs (client-chief, chief-chief, chief-server) are required for the communication to be complete. While we showed that the base cost could be as low as 4 $\mu$s and that we measured 9 $\mu$s, the extra IPC (chief-chief) performed no useful operations.

The problems with the Clans & Chiefs mechanism are: (1) that every process in a clan must be able to freely communicate with every other process in the clan and (2) at least two chiefs must be invoked for every inter-clan IPC. In order for two processes to belong to the same clan they must be able to freely communicate, freely distribute capabilities, and avoid revocation of the other's capabilities for their entire execution. To interpose a chief requires that the processes be deleted and re-created in the desired clans (i.e., clan relationships are static). Therefore, most of our clans have degenerated to a single clan member. Also, it has been shown that a single reference monitor is capable of enforcing very complex security requirements. The need to go through multiple chiefs, by default, is too expensive.

Therefore, we evolve the Clans & Chiefs mechanism to better satisfy these goals. In general, the notion of the IPC redirection is powerful: an IPC can either be sent to the destination process or redirected to another process. Therefore, we endow the kernel with the ability to maintain a mapping between destinations and redirections for each process [20]. For example, consider Figure 6. When the source sends an IPC to a destination, the kernel is invoked. The kernel examines the redirection cache to determine if there exists an entry for the destination. For example, a particular reference monitor may be assigned to this communication channel. In this case, a reference monitor receives the redirected IPC and can authorize it before sending it to the destination.

An effective reference monitor must be able to mediate all communication, but how the mediation is done can be controlled flexibly using this mechanism. In general, a reference monitor between a particular source and destination verifies that the source has the ability to invoke the requested operation on the destination (i.e., within the source's current permissions). Thus, the system's security policy can be enforced on each IPC. If the destination is trusted to enforce the system's security policy on a particular source, then the reference monitor may be removed from that communication channel (i.e., the redirection is changed from the reference monitor to the server). However, if the access control policy should change, then the IPC redirection mechanism enables the

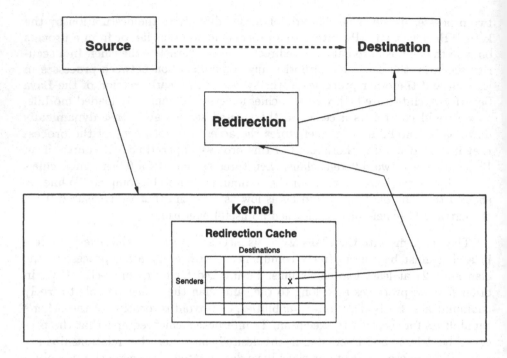

**Fig. 6. IPC Redirection:** An IPC from a source to a destination may be redirected if an entry is present in the redirection cache.

system to reactivate the reference monitor for this communication channel, so the more restrictive security requirements can be enforced.

A problem is to decide who is able to set the redirection policy for a process. We propose that this is where the notion of a chief appears. To avoid confusion, we rename the chief to *redirection coordinator*. A redirection coordinator is permitted to set the redirection entries for the processes that belong to its *redirection set*. Therefore, arbitrary configurations of reference monitors can be constructed dynamically to control the processes in a redirection set.

## 5 Lava Security Architecture

The Lava Security Architecture uses a role-based access control (RBAC) model to represent system access control policies and general mechanisms for permission management and authorization to enforce these policies. The architecture enables each module to be assigned access rights based on their purpose in an application, and to enforce those rights with a minimal communication overhead depending on the security policy. In this section, we outline how the architecture can achieve these goals.

The Lava Security Architecture consists of a system nucleus, security architecture interface (SAI) module, a set of reference monitors, a transform library,

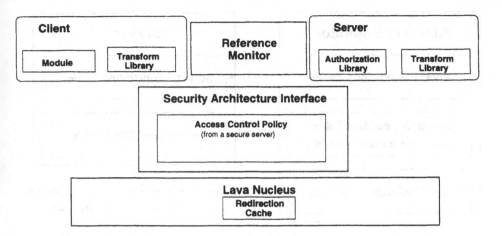

**Fig. 7. Lava Security Architecture:** Consists of the following components: (1) a Lava nucleus that provides fundamental O/S primitives and redirected IPC; (2) a Security Architecture Interface that enables modules to be loaded and the system access control policy to be enforced; (3) reference monitors that control module permissions; (3) an authorization library that manages and authorizes the use of server capabilities relative to system policy; and (5) a transform library that supports the execution of delegations, so permissions can be maintain consistently with application state.

and an authorization library (see Figure 7). The Lava nucleus provides operating system primitives upon which all applications and services are constructed: multi-threaded tasks, address spaces, and inter-process communication (IPC). The nucleus uses the system's hardware protection to separate individual tasks and IPC redirection to control communication. The SAI derives the access control policy for each module and loads the modules into tasks in such a way that this policy can be enforced. The SAI assigns reference monitors to enforce a task's access control policy. A reference monitor can mediate all IPCs on the communication links it has been assigned, so it can restrict communication between any two tasks, restrict delegation of permissions, restrict the operations its tasks can perform, and revoke permissions if the access control policy changes. The transform library supports the execution of transforms upon module operations, so that the access control policy can be maintained consistently with the application's state. The authorization library is provided to servers, so they may enforce system security policy on their objects without the need to build ad hoc security infrastructures.

The access control policy data must be distributed carefully between the servers and reference monitors to enable flexible and secure authorization as shown in Figure 8. Each reference monitor maintains its task's permissions. Permissions are stored per server in *server permission tables*. The reasons storing permissions per server are: (1) servers must be able to authorize the creation of capabilities to their objects, but we do not want them to have access to permissions for another server and (2) this reduces the memory fragmentation

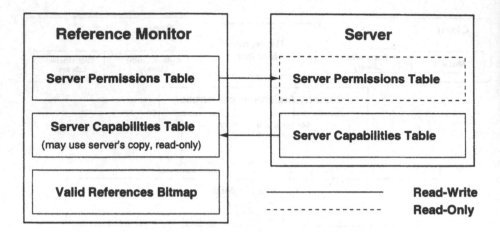

**Fig. 8. Access Control Data:** (1) *server permissions table* which holds the permissions of each task organized per server, so they may be mapped read-only to the server for authorizing capability creation; (2) *server capabilities table* which contains the capabilities the server has created for each task; and (3) *valid references table* which tells which server capabilities have been authorized for use by which tasks.

that would occur if the permissions were stored per task and server. However, the result is that all reference monitors have access to the same server permission table pages, so some concurrency control on update is required. Note that the servers have read-only copies of their permissions, so the reference monitors have control over what the system policy is.

Each server and reference monitor may maintain their own *server capabilities table* in which capabilities to the server's objects are stored. Obviously, the reference monitor's copy of a server's capabilities is redundant, but may be necessary because a server may not be trusted to maintain its own capability information securely (i.e., an authorization mechanism must ensure that the security data is tamperproof). For trusted servers, a single copy of its capabilities may be stored and used by reference monitors as well (read-only). When a capability is created, the servers return capability references to the holder of the capability. This reference refers to the index of the capability in the server's server capabilities table. The reference monitors may obtain read-only access to the server capabilities table which they use to authorize delegations and revoke capabilities to objects when permissions are removed.

The reference monitors must be able to revoke a capability reference at any time. For example, the principal's policy may change resulting in a removal of some of its permissions. The reference monitor must be able to revoke the associated capabilities immediately, but it cannot modify the server capabilities table. Instead, the reference monitors maintain *valid references bitmaps* which indicate which capability references are valid for a task.

## 5.1 Loading Modules

The security architecture interface (SAI) enables modules to be loaded into Lava tasks (see [23] for a detailed discussion). A task may request that a module be loaded into its own or a new task. Depending on the loading requirements (the specified task, application, and/or application role) the SAI retrieves the module's access control requirements from a secure server. The access control policy is represented using context-sensitive roles where the context parameters are defined to be: (1) the downloading principal; (2) the module's author; (3) the application in which the module is to be used; (4) the role the module assumes in the application; and (5) the specific application instance. Using this identity, the SAI derives the transform limits for the module. Thus, it is possible for a module to be a specific type of extension (i.e., role) to an instance of a system service or application. The module is then loaded into its task and transform limits are assigned to reference monitor for enforcement. If a module is loaded into an existing task the transform limits of that task are the intersected.

Also, module developers may specify information to keep the access control policy consistent with the application's state. First, they may specify mappings between their operations and known operation aggregations, such as read and write. Thus, module operations can be mapped to system security policy requirements. Also, module developers may specify transforms that describe how module operations trigger the delegation of permissions to individual delegatees.

The SAI is the redirection coordinator for the system. It assigns reference monitors to tasks by setting the redirection entries for those tasks. The Lava nucleus provides a system call that enables the SAI to set any redirection entry for any task in its redirection group (in this case, all tasks created by the SAI). The Lava nucleus then uses the redirection entries to forward the IPC to the task specified in the redirection entry.

Because the nucleus IPC mechanism performs redirection, the size of the redirection data might become important. If the amount of redirection data is large, then it is more likely that data cache misses will occur on examiniation of redirection data. In general, a redirection entry is needed for each possible combination of sender task and receiver task. Thus, the number of potential redirection entries grows by the square of the number of system tasks. In many cases, optimizations are possible. For example, we can assign a reference monitor to each task, but permit some exceptions to be created for which no or different redirections are possible. Therefore, we only need to store a task's redirection default (i.e., its reference monitor) and the exceptions. If the number of exception is small, then the data needed will be small. For some tasks this optimization may not apply, of course, so we are actively investigating useful compact representations.

## 5.2 Managing Permissions

The Lava Security Architecture implements the following model of permission management. Each task is assigned to a principal, and each principal has a reference monitor that stores its set of transform limits and current permissions.

A principal's current permissions at any time must be a subset of its transform limits. A principal may delegate permissions to another principal if the delegatee's transform limits allow it. Such delegations are automated by defining a transform that specifies a set of rights to be delegated and/or revoked. The module developer associates the transforms with the operations that trigger the change in rights.

Each task is provided with a transform library that enables transforms to be executed. The transform library forwards the transform to the delegatee's reference monitor. The reference monitor authorizes the transform using the delegatee's transform limits. If authorized, the reference monitor updates its current permissions for the principal. Multiple principals may delegate the same permissions independently, so each permission is associated with its delegator.

A task can obtain capabilities for any permission that it possesses. A capability consists of the following fields: (1) server id; (2) object type; (3) module instance id; (4) object id; (5) operations; and (6) server-specific data. Modules may define multiple interfaces, and each interface is an object type. Multiple instances of the same module may be loaded into a task, so the module instance id differentiates them. The server-specific data is used to express server-specific constraints, such as those pertaining to denial-of-service. To prevent modification, prevent forgery, and be able to revoke capabilities, the object id field actually stores an index to the capability in the server capability table (i.e., the capability reference).

## 5.3 Authorizing Operations

The reference monitors and the authorization library work together to authorize operations. An important goal is that the architecture enable the minimal authorization overhead given the security requirements that need to be enforced. Thus, the system supports the four monitoring configurations shown in Figure 9. In the first case, each task has a reference monitor that authorizes its operations. In the second case, the system's access control requirements permit direct communication between the client task and the server task. The third and fourth cases monitor the IPCs sent from one of the two tasks.

We now examine the authorization mechanism for case one. In this case, the task's operation request is intercepted by its reference monitor (step 1). The reference monitor uses the valid references bitmap for the task and server to determine if there is a valid capability that corresponds to that reference. There are three possibilities: (1) the reference is not valid, but there is a corresponding capability; (2) the reference is not valid, and there is no corresponding capability; and (3) the reference is valid. If the capability reference is not valid, the reference monitor determines if the capability associated with that reference is authorized by the task's permissions. If there is no capability associated with the reference, then the reference monitor takes a *reference fault* and obtains the reference's corresponding capability from the server. The reference monitor then authorizes the capability using the task's server permissions. If authorized, the capability is marked valid and the reference monitor allows the request. Note that if the

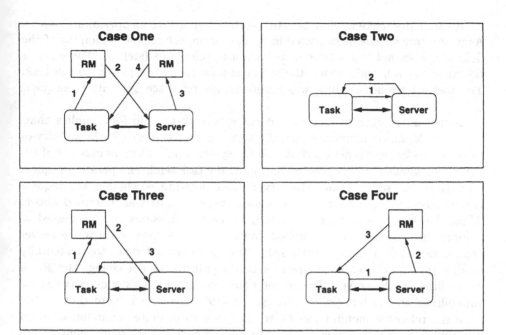

**Fig. 9. Authorization Configurations:** Using IPC redirection these four configurations of authorization can be supported on each communication channel.

server is trusted to maintain its capabilities, then no reference faults will occur because the reference monitor will have access to these capabilities.

If the operation is authorized by the reference monitor any capability references in the request are also passed to the server (step 2). This delegation is authorized by the server's reference monitor when the server tries to use them. Since the capability reference bitmap will indicate that the capability is invalid, the server must have a permission that enables it to use that capability. The server authorization library ensures that all capabilities for the same server object are stored at the same reference, so it is not possible to get a false positive.

The server uses the authorization library to authorize the operation requested using the system's security policy as well as its own. First, it checks its server capabilities table for the principal and capability. As described above, a capability may have been delegated to the requesting task by another task. In this case, the server authorizes the creation of a capability using the server permissions for the requesting task. The server may enforce additional security requirements on the client task which it specifies to the authorization library.

If the server generates a capability as a result of the operation, it uses the server authorization library to authorize the creation (using the server permissions) and to add it to the server capabilities table for the task. The server returns a capability reference which is an index to the capability in the server capabilities table.

A capability reference may be returned in a response to an operation (step 3). As in the case of references passed in an operation, the reference monitor of the delegator does not restrict the distribution of references (step 4). The server's reference monitor verifies that the server is able to send responses to the task. The task's reference monitor will authorize the reference upon its subsequent use.

Removal of reference monitors in cases two, three, and four implies that: (1) the task can communicate with the server and vice versa; (2) the validity of capability references is not checked; and (3) system policy changes may not affect current capabilities [1]. In cases two and four, the task sends an operation request directly to the server. Thus, the server alone determines whether the request is authorized using the server permissions and capabilities as described above. Thus, the server must track the system's server permissions and be trusted to enforce the system's security policy. Since the server may write to its server capabilities table, this trust implies that the server is trusted not to accidentally modify this data. Also, a change in security policy does not change the set of capabilities in the server. The server could maintain consistency between its capabilities and system policy, but this cannot be enforced. Note that at any time the reference monitor can be re-activated to mediate communication on any communication channel, so should policy change the reference monitor can enforce it.

## 6 Conclusions

A system that composes services and applications from modules that are dynamically downloaded must address the possibility that the modules used may not be fully trusted. However, these may be binary modules, so a wide variety of system compromises are possible. The fundamental means for controlling the operations that a module can perform is access control. Access control consists of two main functions: (1) access control policy specification and (2) access control policy enforcement. In this paper, we survey the representations for flexible access control policy specification and mechanisms for enforcing these policies to identify their useful features. We then describe how the Lava Security Architecture takes advantage of these useful features.

The main concern in the composition of applications and services from modules is that the permissions associated with a module are consistent with the module's purpose (i.e., *least privilege*). Current systems associate permissions either based on the executor of the module (e.g., in operating systems) or the provider and name of the module (e.g., in language-based systems). However, this information does not describe the permissions that are consistent with the application or service's state and the role of the module in the application or service. We develop a role-based access control model that enables permissions

---

[1] Some denial of service attacks may also be thwarted by reference monitors, so the removal of a reference monitor also implies that the server is not susceptible to these attack

to be maintained consistently with application state. The main features of this model are that: (1) context-sensitive principals can be defined that express a module's permissions based on its executor, provider, application, application role, and application state; (2) aggregations of objects and operations can be created to express the module's context; and (3) transform limits that restrict the rights that a principal may be granted due to context changes. Constraints ensure that the transform limits themselves are consistent with security policy as it evolves (e.g., due to dynamic policies, such as Chinese Wall). Work on constraint models for RBAC is fairly immature at present.

An access control mechanism must be able to manage permissions consistently with access control policy and enforce them efficiently. In current systems, permission management does not account for application state, and most authorization mechanisms do not address keeping the task permissions consistent with the system's security policy. We describe how transforms can be added to modules and how the system maintains task permissions relative to application state and within system policy. We define how a mechanism for IPC redirection enables minimal overhead in the enforcement of access control policy. At most, one reference monitor needs to be invoked to authorize communication, but, in under some conditions, even that reference monitor is not necessary. However, the IPC redirection mechanism enables a reference monitor to be interposed on any communication path dynamically.

## Acknowledgements

I would like to acknowledge the support of the Lava project team, particularly, Kevin Elphinstone, Jochen Liedtke, Seva Panteleenko, and Yoon Park. Other helpful direction has been provided by Ed Felten, Peter Honeyman, Li Gong, Atul Prakash, Avi Rubin, Jonathan Shapiro, Leendert van Doorn, and Dan Wallach.

## References

1. J. P. Anderson. Computer security technology planning study. Technical Report ESD-TR-73-51, James P. Anderson and Co., Fort Washington, PA, USA, 1972.
2. L. Badger, D. F. Sterne, D. L. Sherman, K. M. Walker, and S. A. Haghighat. Practical domain and type enforcement for UNIX. In *IEEE Symposium on Security and Privacy*, pages 66–77, 1995.
3. D. E. Bell and L. J. LaPadula. Secure computer system: Unified exposition and Multics interpretation. Technical Report MTR-2997, Mitre Corporation, January 1976.
4. B. N. Bershad, S. Savage, P. Pardyak, E. G. Sirer, M. E. Fiuczynski, D. Becker, C. Chambers, and S. Eggers. Extensibility, safety, and performance in the SPIN operating system. In *Proceedings of the 15th Symposium on Operating Systems Principles*, pages 267–284, 1995.

5. E. Bertino, E. Ferrari, and V. Atluri. A flexible model for the specification and enforcement of role-based authorizations in workflow management systems. In *Proceedings of the Second ACM Role-Based Access Control Workshop*, November 1997.

6. M. Bishop and M. Dilger. Checking for race conditions in file accesses. *Computing Systems*, 9(2):131–152, 1996.

7. W. E. Boebert and R. Y. Kain. A practical alternative to hierarchical integrity policies. In *Proceedings of the 8th National Computer Security Conference*, pages 18–27, 1985.

8. D. F. C. Brewer and M. J. Nash. The Chinese Wall security policy. In *Proceedings of IEEE Symposium on Security and Privacy*, pages 206–214, 1989.

9. J. S. Chase, H. M. Levy, M. J. Feeley, and E. D. Lazowska. Sharing and protection in a single-address-space operating system. *ACM Transactions on Computer Systems*, 12(4):271–307, November 1994.

10. J. B. Dennis and E. C. Van Horn. Programming semantics for multiprogrammed computations. *Communications of the ACM*, 9(3):143–155, March 1966.

11. S. Dorward, R. Pike, and P. Winterbottom. Inferno: la commedia interattiva, 1996. Available from inferno.bell-labs.com.

12. D. Engler, F. Kaashoek, and J. O'Toole. Exokernel: An operating system architecture for application level resource management. In *Proceedings of the 15th Symposium on Operating Systems Principles*, pages 251–266, December 1995.

13. J. G. Mitchell *et al.* An overview of the Spring system. In *Proceedings of Compcon*, February 1994.

14. B. Ford, G. Back, G. Benson, J. Lepreau, A. Lin, and O. Shivers. The Flux OSKit: A substrate for kernel and language research. In *Proceedings of the 16th Symposium on Operating Systems Principles*, pages 38–51, 1997.

15. L. Giuri and P. Iglio. Role templates for content-based access control. In *Proceedings of the Second ACM Role-Based Access Control Workshop*, November 1997.

16. Y. Goldberg, M. Safran, and E. Shapiro. Active Mail – a framework for implementing groupware. In *CSCW 92 Proceedings*, pages 75–83, 1992.

17. L. Gong. Java security: present and near future. *IEEE Micro*, 17(3):14–19, 1997.

18. L. Gong, M. Mueller, H. Prefullchandra, and R. Schemers. An overview of the new security architecture in the Java Development Kit 1.2. In *Proceedings of the USENIX Symposium on Internet Technologies and Systems*, pages 103–112, December 1997.

19. Object Management Group. Security service specification. In *CORBAservices: Common Object Services Specification*, chapter 15. November 1997. Available from http://www.omg.org.

20. T. Jaeger, K. Elphinstone, J. Liedtke, V. Panteleenko, and Y. Park. Flexible access control using IPC redirection. In *Proceedings of the 7th Workshop on Hot Topics in Operating Systems*, 1999. To appear.

21. T. Jaeger, J. Liedtke, and N. Islam. Operating system protection for fine-grained programs. In *Proceedings of the 7th USENIX Security Symposium*, pages 143–156, January 1998.

22. T. Jaeger and A. Prakash. Support for the file system security requirements of computational e-mail systems. In *Proceedings of the 2nd ACM Conference on Computer and Communications Security*, pages 1–9, 1994.

23. T. Jaeger, A. Prakash, J. Liedtke, and N. Islam. Flexible control of downloaded executable content. *ACM Transactions on Information System Security*, May 1999. To appear.

24. T. Jaeger, A. Rubin, and A. Prakash. Building systems that flexibly control downloaded executable content. In *Proceedings of the 6th USENIX Security Symposium*, pages 131–148, July 1996.

25. G. Karjoth. Authorization in CORBA security. In *Proceedings of ESORICS '98*, 1998.

26. M. Knister and A. Prakash. Issues in the design of a toolkit for supporting multiple group editors. *Computing Systems*, 6(2):135–166, 1993.

27. B. Lampson. Protection. *ACM Operating Systems Review*, 8(1):18–24, January 1974.

28. J. Liedtke. Clans & chiefs. In *Architektur von Rechensystemen*. Springer-Verlag, March 1992. In English.

29. J. Liedtke. Improving IPC by kernel design. In *Proceedings of the 14th Symposium on Operating Systems Principles*, pages 175–187, 1993.

30. J. Liedtke, N. Islam, and T. Jaeger. Preventing denial-of-service attacks on a $\mu$-kernel for WebOSes. In *Proceedings of the Sixth Workshop on Hot Topics in Operating Systems*, pages 73–79, May 1997.

31. E. C. Lupu and M. Sloman. Reconciling role-based management and role-based access control. In *Proceedings of the Second ACM Role-Based Access Control Workshop*, November 1997.

32. S. D. Majewski. Distributed programming: Agentware/ componentware/ distributed objects. Available at http:// minsky.med.virginia.edu/ sdm7g/ Projects/ Python/ SafePython.html.

33. S. E. Minear. Providing policy control over object operations in a Mach-based system. In *Proceedings of the 5th USENIX Security Symposium*, 1995.

34. N. H. Minsky and V. Ungureanu. Unified support for heterogenous security policies in distributed systems. In *Proceedings of the 7th USENIX Security Symposium*, pages 131–142, January 1998.

35. J. K. Ousterhout, J. Y. Levy, and B. B. Welch. The Safe-Tcl security model. In *Proceedings of the 23rd USENIX Annual Technical Conference*, 1998.

36. R. Rashid, A. Tevanian Jr., M. Young, D. Golub, D. Baron, D. Black, W. J. Bolosky, and J. Chew. Machine-independent virtual memory management for paged uniprocessor and multiprocessor architectures. *IEEE Transactions on Computers*, 37(8):896–908, August 1988.

37. J. H. Saltzer and M. D. Schroeder. The protection of information in computer systems. *Proceedings of the IEEE*, 63(9):1278–1308, September 1975.

38. R. Sandhu. Rationale for the RBAC96 family of access control models. In *Proceedings of the 1st Workshop on Role-Based Access Control*, 1995.

39. R. Sandhu. Role activation hierarchies. In *Proceedings of the Third Workshop on Role-Based Access Control*, 1998.

40. R. S. Sandhu, V. Bhamidipati, E. Coyne, S. Ganta, and C. Youman. The ARBAC97 model for role-based administration of roles: preliminary description and outline. In *Proceedings of the Second Workshop on Role-Based Access Control*, pages 41–50, 1997.

41. R. S. Sandhu, E. J. Coyne, H. L. Feinstein, and C. E. Youman. Role-based access control models. *IEEE Computer*, 29(2):38–47, February 1996.

42. M. I. Seltzer, Y. Endo, C. Small, and K. A. Smith. Dealing with disaster: Surviving misbehaved kernel extensions. In *Proceedings of the 2nd Conference on Operating Systems Design and Implementation*, pages 213–227, 1996.

43. D. Thomsen, D. O'Brien, and J. Bogle. Role based access control framework for network enterprises. In *Proceedings of the Fourteenth Computer Security Applications Conference*, 1998.

44. J. Vochteloo, K. Elphinstone, S. Russell, and G. Heiser. Protection domain extensions in Mungi. In *Proceedings of the Fifth International Workshop on Object Orientation in Operating Systems*, pages 161–165, October 1996.

45. D. S. Wallach and E. W. Felten. Understanding Java stack introspection. In *Proceedings of IEEE Symposium on Security and Privacy*, 1998.

46. P. Wayner. *Agents Unleashed*. AP Professional, 1995.

47. M. V. Wilkes and R. M. Needham. *The Cambridge CAP Computer and Its Operating System*. North Holland, 1979.

48. W. Wulf, E. Cohen, W. Corwin, A. Jones, R. Levin, C. Pierson, and F. Pollack. HYDRA: The kernel of a multiprocessor operating system. *Communications of the ACM*, 17(6):337–345, June 1974.

49. M. E. Zurko and R. Simon. User-centered security. In *Proceedings of the 1996 New Security Paradigms Workshop*, 1996.

# Providing Policy-Neutral and Transparent Access Control in Extensible Systems

Robert Grimm and Brian N. Bershad

**Abstract.** Extensible systems, such as Java or the SPIN extensible operating system, allow for units of code, or extensions, to be added to a running system in almost arbitrary fashion. Extensions closely interact through low-latency, but type-safe interfaces to form a tightly integrated system. As extensions can come from arbitrary sources, not all of whom can be trusted to conform to an organization's security policy, such structuring raises the question of how security constraints are enforced in an extensible system. In this paper, we present an access control mechanism for extensible systems to address this problem. Our access control mechanism decomposes access control into a policy-neutral enforcement manager and a security policy manager, and it is transparent to extensions in the absence of security violations. It structures the system into protection domains, enforces protection domains through access control checks, and performs auditing of system operations. The access control mechanism works by inspecting extensions for their types and operations to determine which abstractions require protection, and by redirecting procedure or method invocations to inject access control operations into the system. We describe the design of this access control mechanism, present an implementation within the SPIN extensible operating system, and provide a qualitative as well as quantitative evaluation of the mechanism.

## 1 Introduction

Extensible systems, such as Java [18, 25] or SPIN [6], promise more power and flexibility, and thus enable new applications such as smart clients [48] or active networks [44]. Extensible systems are best characterized by their support for dynamically composing units of code, called *extensions* in this paper. In these systems, extensions can be added to a running system in almost arbitrary fashion, and they interact through low-latency, but type-safe interfaces with each other. Extensions and the core system services are typically co-located within the same address space, and form a tightly integrated system. Consequently, extensible systems differ fundamentally from conventional systems, such as Unix [29], which rely on processes executing under the control of a privileged kernel.

As a result of this structuring, system security becomes an important challenge, and access control becomes a fundamental requirement for the success of extensible systems. As system security is customarily expressed through protection domains [22, 38], an access control mechanism must:

- structure the system into protection domains (which are an orthogonal concept to conventional address spaces),
- enforce these domains through access control checks,
- support auditing of system operations.

Furthermore, an access control mechanism must address the fact that extensions often originate from other networked computers and are untrusted, yet execute as an integral part of an extensible system and interact closely with other extensions.

In this paper, we present an access control mechanism for extensible systems that meets the above requisites. We build on the idea of separating policy and enforcement first explored by the DTOS effort [30, 34, 40, 39], and introduce a mechanism that not only separates policy from enforcement, but also access control from the actual functionality of the system. The access control mechanism is based on a simple, yet powerful model for the interaction between its policy-neutral enforcement manager and a given security policy, and is transparent to extensions and the core system services in the absence of security violations. It works by inspecting extensions for their types and operations to determine which abstractions require protection, and by redirecting procedure or method invocations to inject access control operations into the system.

The access control mechanism provides three types of access control operations. The operations are (1) explicit protection domain transfers to delineate the protection domains of an extensible system, (2) access checks to control which code can be executed and which arguments can be passed between protection domains, and (3) auditing to provide a trace of system operations. The access control mechanism works at the granularity of individual procedures (or, object methods), and provides precise control over extensions and the core system services alike.

Access control and its enforcement is but one aspect of the overall security of an extensible system. Other important issues, such as the specification of security policies, or the expression and transfer of credentials for extensions are only touched upon or not discussed at all in this paper. Furthermore, we assume the existence of some means, such as digital signatures, for authenticating both extensions and users. These issues are orthogonal to access control, and we believe that a simple, yet powerful access control mechanism, as presented in this paper, can serve as a solid foundation for future work on other aspects of security in extensible systems.

The remainder of this paper is structured as follows: Section 2 elaborates on the goals of our access control mechanism, and Sect. 3 describes its design. Section 4 presents the implementation of our access control mechanism within the SPIN extensible operating system. Section 5 reflects on our experiences with designing and implementing our access control mechanism, and Sect. 6 presents a detailed performance analysis of the implementation. Section 7 reviews related work, and Sect. 8 outlines future directions for our research into the security of extensible systems. Finally, Sect. 9 concludes this paper.

# 2  Goals

An access control mechanism for an extensible system must impose additional structure onto the system. But, at the same time, it should only impose as much structure as *strictly* necessary to preserve the advantages of an extensible system. Based on this realization, we identify four goals which inform the design of our system.

*Separate access control and functionality.* The access control mechanism should separate policy and enforcement from the actual code of the system and extensions. This separation of access control and functionality supports changing security policies without requiring access to source code. This is especially important for large computer networks, such as the Internet, where the same extension may execute on different systems with different security requirements, and where source code typically is not available. This goal does *not* prevent the programmer who writes an extension from defining (part of) the security policy for that extension. However, it calls for a separate specification of such policy, comparable to an interface specification which offers a distinct and concise description of the abstractions found in a unit of code. This policy specification may then be loaded into an extensible system as the extension is loaded.

*Separate policy and enforcement.* The mechanism should separate the security policy from its actual enforcement. This separation of policy and enforcement allows for changing security policies without requiring intrinsic changes to the core services of the extensible system itself. Rather, the security policy is provided by a (trusted) extension, and, as a result, the access control mechanism leverages the advantages of an extensible system and becomes extensible itself.

*Use a simple, yet expressive model.* The mechanism should rely on a simple model of protection that covers a wide range of possible security policies, including policies that change over time or depend on the history of the system. This goal ensures that the access control mechanism can strictly enforce a wide range of security policies, and that the security policy has control over all relevant aspects of access control. At the same time, it favors simplicity over complex interactions between security policy and its enforcement.

*Enforce transparently.* The mechanism should be transparent to extensions and the core system services, in that they should not need to interact with it as long as no violations of the security policy occur. This goal ensures that the mechanism actually provides a clean separation of security policy, enforcement, and functionality. Furthermore, it provides support for legacy code (to a degree), and enables aggressive, policy-specific optimizations that reduce the performance overhead of access control. At the same time, it guarantees that extensions *are* notified of security faults, and can implement their own failure model. Consequently, this goal attempts to reduce the access control interface, *as seen by extensions*, to handling a program fault such as division by zero or dereferencing a NIL reference.

The above four goals, taken together, call for a design that isolates functionality, security policy, and enforcement in an extensible system, and that provides a clear specification for their interaction. In other words, the goals call for an access control mechanism that combines the extension itself, the security constraints for the extension as specified by the programmer, and a site's security policy to produce a *secure* extension. At the same time, the mechanism is not limited to changing only the extension as a result of this combination process, but can impose security constraints on other parts of the extensible system as well. This process of combining functionality and security to provide access control in an extensible system is illustrated in Fig. 1.

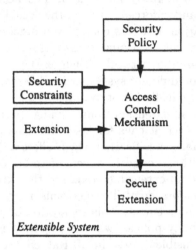

**Fig. 1.** Overview of access control in an extensible system. The access control mechanism combines the extension itself, the security constraints for the extension as specified by the programmer, and a site's security policy to place a secure version of the extension into the extensible system.

A design that addresses the four goals effectively defines the *protocol* by which the security policy and the access control mechanism interact, and by which, if necessary, extensions are notified of security-relevant events. As such, this protocol is an *internal* protocol. In other words, the abstractions used for expressing protection domains and access control checks need not be, and probably should not be, the same abstractions presented by the security policy. It is the responsibility of a security policy manager to provide users and system administrators with a high-level and user-friendly view of system security.

## 2.1 Examples

As long as extensions, such as Java applets in the sandbox model, use only a few, selected core services, providing protection in an extensible system reduces to isolating extensions from each other and performing access control checks in the core services. However, for many real-world applications of extensibility, such a protection scheme is clearly insufficient as extensions use some parts of the system and, in turn, are used by other parts. For example, an extension may provide a new file system implementation, such as a log-structured file system, offer additional functionality for existing file systems, such as compression or encryption, or support higher-level abstractions, such as transactions, on top of the storage services. An extension may also implement new networking protocols, such as multicast, or higher-level communication services, such as a remote procedure call package or an object request broker (ORB), on top of the existing networking stack.

From a security viewpoint, the programmer who writes such an extension will want to protect the resources used by that extension. So, for a transaction manager, she would like to ensure that the files or disk extents used for storing transaction data can only be accessed through the transaction manager. And, for an ORB, she would like to ensure that the network port used for communicating with other nodes can not be accessed by other extensions. A simple way to implement these security constraints is to place the transaction manager or ORB into its own protection domain and to use access checks in the storage services or networking stack to protect the resources they use. The security constraints in these examples thus not only affect the service provided by the extension itself, but also cover other services of an extensible system. At the same time, overall security in an extensible system requires coalescing the constraints for several extensions. Consequently, separating the specification of security constraints and functionality would clearly aid in providing security for an extensible system.

In addition to the programmer, the administrator of an extensible system may want to impose additional restrictions on an extension. For example, she may want to restrict how other extensions can call on the transaction manager in order to ensure that only a transaction's initiator can actually commit it. Or, she may require auditing of the transaction manager's operations to ensure that a log record is generated if the commit operation is not performed by a transaction's initiator. Alternatively, the administrator may want to impose a security policy that conflicts with the security constraints expressed by the programmer. For example, she may want to integrate the ORB into the same protection domain as the networking stack, since the ORB is the only means for remote communication in an installation (such as a corporate intranet), and providing access control on the ORB is adequate for security. As illustrated by these examples, the security policy for an extensible system varies according to the requirements of a specific installation, even if the functionality does not change. It is thus not sufficient to only separate access control from functionality, but also necessary to separate the security policy from its enforcement.

So far, we have argued for a clean separation of security policy, functionality, and enforcement, and for a system that transparently manages security. However, extensions need to be notified of failures so that they can implement their own failure model. For example, the transaction manager might decide to abort the offending transaction, or the ORB may need to clean up the internal state of the corresponding connection. It is thus important that access control is only transparent in the absence of failures, and that extensions are notified of security violations.

# 3   Design

The design of our access control mechanism divides access control in an extensible system into an enforcement manager and a security policy manager. The enforcement manager is part of the core services of the extensible system. It provides information on the types and operations of an extension, and redirects procedure or method invocations to perform access control operations. The security policy manager is provided by a trusted extension, and determines the actual security policy for the system. It decides which procedures require which access control operations, and performs the actual mediation for access control. This structure is illustrated in Fig. 2.

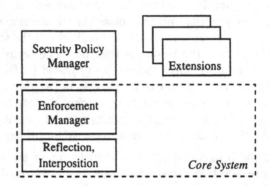

**Fig. 2.** Structure of the access control mechanism. The enforcement manager is part of the core system services, provides information on the types and operations of an extension (reflection), and redirects procedure or method invocations (interposition) to ensure that a given security policy is actually enforced onto the system. The security policy manager is a trusted extension, determines which abstractions require which access control operations, and performs the actual mediation.

The protocol that determines the interaction between the enforcement and the security policy manager relies on two abstractions, namely security identifiers and sets of permissions, or access modes. Security identifiers are associated with both subjects and objects, and represent privilege and access constraints. Permissions are associated with operations, and represent the right to perform an operation. The enforcement manager maintains the association of subjects and objects with security identifiers, and performs access control checks based on access modes. But, it does not interpret security identifiers and access modes, as their meaning is determined by the security policy manager which performs the actual mediation.

As extensible systems feature a considerably different structuring from traditional systems such as Unix, it is necessary to define the exact meaning of subjects and objects. We treat threads in an extensible system as subjects, as they are the only active entities, and all other entities, including extensions, as objects. This is not to say that subjects only represent the principal that created a thread. Rather, the rights of a subject depend on the current protection domain, i.e. the extension whose code the thread is currently executing, and, possibly, on previous protection domains, i.e. the history of extensions whose code the thread executed before entering the current extension. Furthermore, while we treat extensions as objects, they are subject to a somewhat different form of access control than other objects in an extensible system.

## 3.1 Access Control on Extensions

Conceptually, access control determines whether a subject can legally execute some operation on some object. Access control on extensions differs from this concept in that it is sometimes necessary to control how extensions interact with each other. Specifically, this is the case at link-time: The extension to be loaded into the system needs to be linked against other extensions, whose interfaces it will execute and extend. It is thus necessary, at link-time, to provide access control over which interfaces a given extension can link against for execution and extending [41, 35]. Enforcing this link-time control over extensions is important, since it presents a first line of defense against unauthorized access (after all, if an extension can not link against an interface, it can not directly use it), and since it may result in opportunities for optimizing away dynamic access control operations.

Link-time control over extensions *can*, however, be expressed through regular access control checks by enforcing checks on linkage operations, and by executing these operations within a protection domain appropriate for the extension to be linked. To impose access control checks on linkage operations, the enforcement manager injects the appropriate checks into the linking service during system start-up. To execute these operations within a protection domain appropriate for an extension, the loader spawns a new thread for each extension to be loaded into the system, which then performs the actual linkage operations as well as other necessary initialization. The initial security identifier of this thread represents the corresponding protection domain. It is determined by the security policy manager based on an extension's signature, and is associated with the thread and the procedures of the extension by the enforcement manager.

When loading an extension, the enforcement manager also determines the types and operations exported by that extension, and passes this information to the security policy manager. Based on this information and an extension's signature, the security policy manager determines which operations and types require which access control operations. The security policy manager, in turn, instructs the enforcement manager to provide security identifiers for an extension's types, and to inject access control operations into the extension and other parts of the system, if necessary. Once the actual linking of an extension is complete and the appropriate access control operations have been injected into the system, the extension is fully and securely integrated into the system and its code can now be executed.

## 3.2 Access Control Operations

The enforcement manager supports three types of access control operations. The operations are (1) protection domain transfers to structure the system into protection domains, (2) access control checks to enforce these protection domains, and (3) auditing to provide a trace of system operations. Protection domain transfers change the protection domain associated with a thread, based on the current protection domain of a thread and on the procedure that is about to be invoked. Access checks determine whether the current subject is allowed to execute a procedure at all, and control the passing of arguments and results. For each argument that is passed into a procedure, and for each result that is passed back from the procedure, access checks determine whether the subject has sufficient rights for the corresponding object. Finally, auditing generates a log-entry for each procedure invocation, and serves as an execution trace of the system.

When instructing the enforcement manager to perform access control operations on a given procedure, the security policy manager specifies the types of access control operations, i.e. any combination of protection domain transfer, access checks, and auditing. For access checks, it also specifies the required access modes, one for the procedure itself, one for each argument, and one for each result.

The access control operations are ordered as follows. Before a given procedure is executed, the enforcement manager first performs access checks, then a protection domain transfer, and, finally, auditing, which also records failed access checks. On return from the procedure, the enforcement manager first performs the reverse protection domain transfer, then access checks on the results, and, finally, auditing, which, again, also records failed access checks.

To perform the access control operations, the enforcement manager requires three mappings between security identifiers, types, and access modes. These mappings are used to communicate a site's security policy between security policy manager and enforcement manager. Using SID for security identifiers, TYPE for types as defined by the extensible system, and ACCESSMODE for access modes, the three mappings are:

$$
\begin{aligned}
&(1)\ \text{SID} \times \text{SID} &&\longrightarrow \text{SID} \\
&(2)\ \text{SID} \times \text{SID} &&\longrightarrow \text{ACCESSMODE} \\
&(3)\ \text{SID} \times \text{TYPE} &&\longrightarrow \text{SID}
\end{aligned}
$$

The first mapping is used for protection domain transfers. It maps the current security identifier of a thread and the security identifier of the procedure that is about to be called into the new security identifier of the thread. The enforcement manager associates the thread with the new security identifier before control passes into the actual procedure, and it restores the original security identifier upon completion of the procedure.

The second mapping is used for access checks. It maps the security identifier of a thread and the security identifier of an object into an access mode representing the maximum rights the subject has on the object. The enforcement manager verifies that the maximal access mode contains all permissions of the required access mode, as specified by the security policy manager when requesting the access check.

The third mapping is used for the creation of objects. It maps the security identifier of a thread that is about to create an object and the type of that object into the security identifier for the newly created object. The enforcement manager associates newly created objects with the resulting security identifier. A simplification of this mapping may omit the object type from the mapping, and simply map all objects created by a thread into the same security identifier.

Both variations of the third mapping provide relatively coarse-grained control over the security identifiers associated with objects, and are clearly insufficient for some services. For example, a file server typically executes threads within its own protection domain but may need to associate different files with different security identifiers. Thus, to support trusted services that provide finer-grained control over the security identifiers associated with objects, the enforcement manager provides an interface through which a trusted security service can change the security identifier of an object. In the example of a file server, this interface could be used to map files to security identifiers similar to the name-based security attributes in domain and type enforcement [3, 2].

New subjects, that is freshly spawned threads, are associated with the same security identifier as the spawning thread so that they possess the same privileges. An exception to this rule occurs for threads that are created to link and initialize extensions (as discussed above), and for threads that are created when a user logs into the system. In the latter case, an appropriate form of authentication (such as a password) establishes the identity of the user to the security policy manager, and the enforcement manager associates the thread with the corresponding security identifier.

Depending on the complexity of the security policy implemented by the security policy manager, lookup operations for the three mappings may incur a relatively high performance overhead. Consequently, the enforcement manager caches individual entries in the three mappings, which reduces the frequency with which the security policy manager needs to resolve entries and therefore the overall performance overhead of access control operations. The security policy manager has full control over this *mediation cache*. It sets the overall size of the cache, can remove any entry from the cache at any time, and also flush the entire cache. Furthermore, for any lookup operation on any of the mappings, it specifies whether that particular entry can be cached and, if so, for how long. For example, for multi-level policies [5, 12, 7], all mappings can be cached indefinitely since they never change. For access matrix based policies [22], mappings generally can be cached. But, if the access matrix is changed, the security policy manager must remove the corresponding entries from the mediation cache. And, for policies that depend on the mediation history, mappings may not be cached at all.

# 4 Implementation

We have implemented our access control mechanism in the SPIN extensible operating system [6]. Our access control mechanism does not depend on features that are unique to SPIN, and could be implemented in other systems. It requires support for dynamically loading and linking extensions, for multiple concurrent threads of execution, for determining an extension's types and operations, and for redirecting procedure or method invocations (for example, by patching object jump tables either statically or dynamically). Consequently, our access control mechanism can be implemented in other extensible systems that provide these features, such as Java.

Our implementation is guided by three constraints. First, it has to correctly enforce a given security policy as defined by the security policy manager. Second, it has to be simple and well-structured to allow for validation[1] and for easy transfer to other systems. Third, the implementation should be fast to impose as little performance overhead as possible.

In SPIN, a statically linked core provides most basic services, including hardware support, the Modula-3 runtime [42, 21], the linker/loader [41], threads, and the event dispatcher [35]. All other services, including networking and file system support, are provided by dynamically linked extensions. We have implemented the basic abstractions of our access control mechanism, such as security identifiers and access modes, as well as the enforcement manager as part of this static core.

Services in the static core are trusted in that, if they misbehave, the security of the system can be undermined, and the system may even crash. At the same time, the static core must be protected against dynamically linked extensions which usually are not trusted. Consequently, the enforcement manager imposes access control on the core services, including the linker/loader as described in Sect. 3.1, to protect itself and other core services, and to ensure that only a trusted extension can define the security policy. User-space applications in SPIN need not be written in Modula-3, are not guaranteed to be type-safe, and thus are generally untrusted. They can not access *any* kernel-level objects directly, but only through a narrowly defined system call interface, which automatically subjects them to our access control mechanism.

The implementation of our access control mechanism consists of 1000 lines of well-documented Modula-3 interfaces and 2400 lines of Modula-3 code, with an additional 50 lines of changes to other parts of the static SPIN core. The implementation uses the Modula-3 runtime to determine the types and operations of an extension, and the event dispatcher [35] to inject access control operations into the system. It defines the abstractions for security identifiers and access modes. Security identifiers are simply integers. Access modes are immutable objects, and are represented by a set of simple, pre-defined permissions in addition to a list of permission objects. The simple permissions provide 64 permissions at

---

[1] We have not validated the implementation. However, a critical characteristic for any security mechanism is that it be small and well-structured [38].

a low overhead. The list of permission objects lets the security policy manager define additional permissions (where each permission object can represent several permissions) by subtyping from an abstract base class, at some performance cost.

The functionality of the enforcement manager is visible through two separate interfaces. One interface lets extensions discover the state of system security in the presence of security faults. The other interface, together with the interface to the security policy manager, defines the trusted protocol between the security policy and the enforcement manager. The interface to the security policy manager is also defined as part of the static core, but an implementation of this interface must be provided by a trusted extension outside the static core. The enforcement manager operates as described in Sect. 3. It uses the simplified third mapping for assigning objects to security identifiers (see Sect. 3.2), and thus provides a default security identifier for all objects within a protection domain.

On object creation, the standard Modula-3 allocator, through a call-back into the enforcement manager, stores this default security identifier in the header of the newly allocated object. At the same time, only some types in an extensible system require access control. For example, an auxiliary object that is only used within an extension and never passed outside will never require access control. Thus, to limit the memory overhead of allocating an additional word in each object header, the security manager can dynamically activate and deactivate object security for each Modula-3 type individually. Access checks on objects that are not associated with a security identifier simply fail.

Storing an object's security identifier in the object header considerably simplifies the mapping from objects to security identifiers as the enforcement manager does not need to maintain a separate mapping. For example, when an unused object is freed by the garbage collector, the corresponding mapping is deleted with the object and no additional operation needs to be performed by the enforcement manager. Furthermore, as security identifiers are stored in the same location as the object itself, the performance overhead to access an object's security identifier is minimized.

To maintain a thread's security identifier and the corresponding default object security identifier, the enforcement manager associates each thread with a security identifier stack. Each record on this stack contains the two security identifiers for the subject and its objects. On a protection domain transfer, the enforcement manager pushes a new record onto the stack before the thread enters the corresponding procedure or method, and pops the record off the stack when the thread returns from the procedure or method. Records are pre-allocated in a global pool to avoid dynamic memory allocation overhead, and are pushed and popped using atomic enqueue and dequeue operations to avoid the overhead of locking the global pool.

# 5 Discussion

By using our access control mechanism, fine-grained security constraints can be imposed onto an extensible system. However, the expressiveness of our mechanism is limited in that it can not supplant prudent interface design. In particular, three issues arise, namely the use of abstract data types, the granularity of interfaces, and the effect of calling conventions.

Our access control mechanism provides protection on objects in that it provides control over which operations a subject can legally execute on an object, including control over which objects can be passed to and returned from an operation. To do so, it relies on abstract data types to hide the implementation of an object. In other words, if the type of an object does not hide its implementation, it is possible to directly access and modify an object without explicitly invoking any of the corresponding operations and thus without incurring access control.

The structure of an interface also influences the degree of control attainable over the operations on an object. In particular, the granularity of an interface, i.e. how an interface decomposes into individual operations on a type, determines the granularity of access control. So, an interface with only one operation, which, like `ioctl` in Unix, might use an integer argument to name the actual operation, allows for much less fine-grained control than an interface with several independent operations.

The calling convention used for passing arguments to a procedure or object method affects whether argument passing can be fully controlled. Notably, call-by-reference grants both caller and callee access to the same variable. As caller and callee may be in different protection domains, call-by-reference effectively creates (type-safe) shared memory. In a multi-threaded system, information can be passed through shared memory at any time, not just on procedure invocation and return. Consequently, caller and callee need to trust each other on the use of this shared memory, and access checks on call-by-reference arguments are not very meaningful. In SPIN, call-by-reference is almost always used to return additional results from a procedure, as Modula-3 only supports one result value. This unnecessary use of shared memory could clearly be avoided by supporting multiple results or thread-safe calling conventions such as call-by-value/result at the programming language level.

The three issues just discussed are directly related to our access control mechanism relying on an extension's interface, that is on the externally visible types and operations of an extension, to impose access constraints. A more powerful model could be used to express finer-grained security constraints. And, more aggressive techniques, such as binary rewriting [45, 43, 19, 37], could be used to enforce these constraints in an extensible system. But such a system would also require a considerably more complex design and implementation. At the same time, an extension's interface is a "natural" basis for access control, as it provides a concise and well-understood specification of what an extension exports to other extensions and how it interacts with them. Consequently, we believe that our access control mechanism strikes a reasonable balance between expressiveness and complexity.

As our access control mechanism relies on extensions' interfaces to provide protection for an extensible system, it also requires some means to ensure that these interfaces are, in fact, respected by the actual code. SPIN uses a type-safe programming language (Modula-3), and a trusted compiler to provide this guarantee. As a result, the compiler becomes part of the trusted computing base. Clearly, it is preferable to establish this guarantee in the extensible system that actually executes the code, especially for large computer networks. Considerable work has been devoted to this issue, and viable alternatives include typed byte-codes [25], proof-carrying code [33], as well as typed assembly language [31]. All of these efforts are complementary to our own.

## 6 Performance Evaluation

To determine the performance overhead of our implementation, we evaluate a set of micro-benchmarks that measure the performance of access control operations. We also present end-to-end performance results for a web server benchmark. We collected our measurements on a DEC Alpha AXP 133 MHz 3000/400 workstation, which is rated at 74 SPECint 92. The machine has 64 MByte of memory, a 512 KByte unified external cache, and an HP C2247-300 1 GByte disk-drive. In summary, the micro-benchmarks show that access control operations incur some latency on trivial operations, while the end-to-end experiment shows that the overall overhead of access control is in the noise.

### 6.1 Micro-Benchmarks

To evaluate the performance overhead of access control operations in our access control mechanism, we execute seven micro-benchmarks. All seven benchmarks measure the total time for a null procedure call (a procedure that returns immediately and does not perform any work), with and without access control operations. The first benchmark simply performs a null procedure call with no arguments. The other six benchmarks additionally perform a protection domain transfer, an access check on the procedure, and access checks on one, two, four and eight arguments, respectively.

The performance of the security policy manager is determined by a given security policy and its implementation. Consequently, for the micro-benchmarks, we fix the necessary entries in the mediation cache of the enforcement manager (see Sect. 3.2). The benchmarks thus measure common-case performance, where the security policy manager is not consulted because the necessary information is already available within the enforcement manager. Furthermore, benchmarks that perform access control checks use simple permissions instead of permission objects (see Sect. 4).

Table 1 shows the performance results for the seven micro-benchmarks. All numbers are in microseconds and the average of 1000 trials. To determine hot microprocessor cache performance, we execute one trial to pre-warm the processor's cache, and then execute it 1000 times in a tight loop, measuring the time

330

**Table 1.** Performance numbers for access control operations. All numbers are the mean of 1000 trials in microseconds. *Hot* represents hot microprocessor cache performance and *Cold* cold microprocessor cache performance.

|                                | Hot  | Cold |
| ------------------------------ | ---- | ---- |
| Null procedure call            | 0.1  | 0.5  |
| Protection domain transfer     | 4.4  | 7.8  |
| Access check on procedure      | 2.8  | 6.4  |
| Access check on 1 argument     | 4.0  | 9.7  |
| Access check on 2 arguments    | 6.7  | 12.0 |
| Access check on 4 arguments    | 12.1 | 17.7 |
| Access check on 8 arguments    | 24.0 | 29.5 |

at the beginning and at the end of the loop. To determine cold microprocessor cache performance, we measure the time before and after each trial separately, and flush both the instruction and data cache on each iteration.

Table 2 shows the instruction breakdown of the common path for protection domain transfers, excluding the overhead for the event dispatcher (which amounts to 31 or 48 instructions, depending on the optimizations used within the event dispatcher [35]). On a protection domain transfer, the enforcement manager establishes the new protection domain before control passes into the actual procedure, and restores the original protection domain upon completion of the procedure. Before entering the procedure, the enforcement manager first determines the security identifiers of the thread and of the procedure. Then, based on these security identifiers, it looks up the security identifiers for the thread and new objects created by the thread in the mediation cache, which requires obtaining a lock for the cache. Next, it sets up a new exception frame, so that the original protection domain can be restored on an exceptional procedure exit. Finally, it pushes a new record containing the security identifiers for the thread and new objects onto the thread's security identifier stack. After leaving the procedure, the enforcement manager pops the top from the thread's security identifier stack and removes the exception frame.

Additional experiments show that performing a protection domain transfer in addition to access checks adds 3.9 microseconds to hot cache performance and 5.6 microseconds to cold cache performance for those of the above benchmarks that perform access checks. Furthermore, using permission objects instead of simple permissions for access checks, where the required permission object matches the tenth object in the list of legal permission objects (which represents a pessimistic scenario as each permission object can stand for dozens of individual permissions), adds 6.8 microseconds for hot cache performance and 7.0 microseconds for cold cache performance per argument.

The performance results show that access control operations have noticeable overhead. They thus back our basic premise that access control for extensible systems should only impose as much structure as strictly necessary. Furthermore,

**Table 2.** Instruction breakdown of the common path for protection domain transfers, excluding the cost for the event dispatcher. "Overhead" is the overhead of performing both protection domain changes within their own procedure. The other operations are explained in the text.

| Operation | # Instr. |
|---|---|
| *Enter new protection domain* | |
| Get thread's security ID | 3 |
| Get procedure's security ID | 1 |
| Lookup in mediation cache | 52 |
| Locking overhead | 62 |
| Set up exception frame | 7 |
| Push security ID record | 26 |
| Overhead | 10 |
| *Total number of instructions* | 161 |
| *Restore old protection domain* | |
| Pop security ID record | 22 |
| Remove exception frame | 4 |
| Overhead | 4 |
| *Total number of instructions* | 30 |

they underline the need for a design that enables dynamic optimizations which avoid access control operations whenever possible.

## 6.2 End-to-End Performance

To evaluate the overall impact of access control on system performance, we present end-to-end results for a web server benchmark. The web server used for our experiments is implemented as an in-kernel extension. It uses an NFS client to read files from our group's file server, and locally caches the file data in a dedicated cache, backed by a simple, fast extent-based file system. As spawning new threads in SPIN incurs very little overhead, the web server forks a new thread for each incoming request. The thread first checks whether the requested file is available in the local cache, and, if so, sends the file data directly from the cache. Otherwise, it issues an NFS read request, stores the file in the local cache, and then sends the data.

Our security policy places the web server into its own protection domain. It performs access control checks on all NFS and local cache operations. Files in the local cache are automatically associated with a security identifier as described in Sect. 3.2. Files in NFS are associated with a security identifier by using a mapping from the file system name-space to security identifiers (similar to the one described in [3, 2]) to provide fine-grained control over which files are associated with which security identifier. Since the security policy imposes access control checks on both the NFS client and the local cache, and since the individual threads (spawned to serve requests) can only communicate through NFS and the local cache, the policy ensures that only authorized files are accessible through the web server. Furthermore, it makes it possible to securely change privileges on a per-request basis, either based on a remote login, or based on the machine from which the request originated.

Our performance benchmark sends http requests from one machine that is running the benchmark script to another that is running the web server. It reads the entire SPIN web tree, to a total of 79 files or 5035 KByte of data. We run the benchmark without access control, as a baseline, as well as with access control, to measure the end-to-end overhead of our access control mechanism. For each measurement, we first perform 15 runs of the benchmark to pre-warm the local cache, and then measure the latency for 20 runs. The average latency for one run of the benchmark both without and with access control is 16.9 seconds (including 5.4 seconds idle time on the machine running the web server), and the difference between the two is in the noise. Trials with access control incur a total of 1573 access checks, on average 20 for each file.

The end-to-end performance experiments show that the overhead of access control operations is negligible for a web server workload. We extrapolate from this result that other applications will see a very small overhead for other real-world applications. To better quantify this overhead, we plan to conduct further experiments in the future that use more complex security policies and require finer-grained access control operations.

# 7 Related Work

A considerable body of literature focuses on system protection [22, 38] and appropriate security policies. Starting from multi-level security [5, 12, 7], which has become part of the U.S. Department of Defense's standard for trusted computer systems [13], much attention has been directed towards mapping non-military policies onto multi-level security [26, 24], defining alternative policies more suitable for commercial applications [8, 10, 9, 3, 2, 1], and expanding multi-level security to be more flexible and powerful [27, 32].

Based on the realization that no single security policy is appropriate for all environments, the DTOS effort [30, 34, 40, 39] has the goal of providing a policy-neutral access control mechanism. As our mechanism builds on this work, we share with DTOS the same structuring of access control into a security policy manager and a policy-neutral enforcement manager as well as the same basic abstractions (security identifiers and permissions). However, as DTOS has been implemented on top of the Mach micro-kernel, it differs form our mechanism in that it relies on address-spaces for protection domains, resulting in a relatively high overhead for changing protection domains. Furthermore, as the DTOS effort does not separate security from functionality, it uses explicit access checks on pre-defined permissions for enforcing protection domains, making it impossible to change or remove access checks.

As reported in [40], adding explicit access checks to the micro-kernel presented a considerable challenge as it fixed part of the security policy within the system. Furthermore, as noted in [39], their choice of checking whether a subject can perform an operation on an object, where the object is the primary argument to an operation, does not provide sufficient flexibility, since the security decision may depend on other parameters to the operation as well. Our access control mechanism avoids these limitations, as access control operations are dynamically specified and injected into the system, and as they are strictly more expressive.

Due to Java's [18, 25] popularity for providing executable content on the Internet, and prompted by a string of security breaches [11, 28] in early versions of the system, research into protection for extensible systems has mostly focused on Java. In departure from the original sandbox model, which grants trusted code full access to the underlying system and untrusted code almost no access, the Java security architecture is currently being extended [15, 16] to allow for multiple protection domains, provide fine-grained access control primitives, and support cryptographic protocols.

The basic technique for performing dynamic access checks in Java, called extended stack introspection, is described in [46]. With this technique, each extension is implicitly associated with a protection domain, and access checks essentially take the intersection of all protection domains represented on the current call-stack to determine if an operation is legal. While extended stack introspection is sufficiently expressive to provide fine-grained access control [47], it is closely tied to the stack-based execution model of Java. Furthermore, it relies on explicit access checks, and thus fails to separate functionality from protection. Finally, as access checks need to walk the entire call-stack, they can incur considerable performance overhead [17].

Hagimont and Ismail [20] describe an alternative design for access control in Java which provides for a separate description of security constraints through an extended interface definition language. In their design, security constraints are expressed as part of the interface specification for each extension, and result in the creation of proxy objects which provide only limited functionality to their clients. The design essentially provides a form of type hiding [46] at the granularity of entire methods, as the visibility of object methods is controlled by the security constraints.

In its ability to provide access control at the granularity of object methods, Hagimont and Ismail's design is similar to CACL [36] which presents a general protection model for objects. At the same time, CACL offers a more complete model (which includes explicit representations of the owner of an object and its implementor) and a more efficient implementation (through object jump tables instead of proxy objects). The idea of using limited effective types to avoid repeated dynamic access checks that determine whether a subject can call on an object is complimentary to our design. We thus believe that it could be used to provide an efficient implementation of the enforcement manager in a pure object-oriented system.

# 8  Future Work

The access control mechanism described in this paper provides us with an ideal test-bed for future research on the security of extensible systems. Specifically, the policy-neutral and transparent enforcement manager, with its ability to arbitrarily inject protection domains and access checks into an extensible system, offers us considerable power and flexibility. We are particularly interested in three areas for future work: First, programmers and security administrators need to be able to specify security constraints for the code they write and use. We thus plan to investigate appropriate specification languages that are both user-friendly (i.e., present a high-level of abstraction) and sufficiently powerful to conveniently express detailed security policies (i.e., provide enough flexibility). Second, as extensions often execute in networked environments, a protocol for the secure expression and transfer of credentials is required. We thus intend to examine distributed authentication and authorization protocols, such as those described in [23, 4, 14], in the context of extensible systems. Finally, as illustrated by the micro-benchmarks in Sect. 6, the access control operations show a relatively high overhead when compared to a simple procedure invocation. We thus plan to explore aggressive optimizations that avoid dynamic access control operations whenever possible.

# 9  Conclusions

The access control mechanism for extensible systems described in this paper breaks up access control into a policy-neutral enforcement manager and a security policy manager, and is transparent to extensions in the absence of security violations. It structures the system into protection domains through protection domain transfers, enforces these protection domains through access control checks, and provides a trace of system operations through auditing. It works by inspecting extensions for their types and operations to determine what abstractions require protection, and by redirecting procedure or method invocations to inject access control operations into the system. The access control mechanism is based on a simple, yet powerful protocol by which the security policy and the enforcement manager interact, and by which, if necessary, extensions are notified of security-relevant events.

The implementation of our access control mechanism within the SPIN extensible operating system is simple, and, even though the latency of individual access control operations can be noticeable, shows good end-to-end performance. Based on our results, we predict that most systems will see a very small overhead for access control, and thus consider our access control mechanism an effective solution for access control in extensible systems.

# Acknowledgments

The research presented in this paper was sponsored by the Defense Advanced Research Projects Agency, the National Science Foundation and by an equipment grant from Digital Equipment Corporation. Grimm was partially supported by fellowships from the Microsoft Corporation and the IBM Corporation. Bershad was partially supported by a National Science Foundation Presidential Faculty Fellowship and an Office of Naval Research Young Investigator Award.

We thank Dennis Hollingworth and Timothy Redmond at Trusted Information Systems for their comments on our design. Marc Fiuczynski, Tian Lim, Yasushi Saito, Emin Gün Sirer and especially Przemysław Pardyak at the University of Washington were most helpful with various implementation issues and the integration of our access control mechanism into SPIN. Stefan Savage, Stephen Smalley, Ray Spencer, Amin Vahdat, and the anonymous reviewers for this volume provided valuable feedback on earlier versions of this paper.

# References

1. L. Badger, K. A. Oostendorp, W. G. Morrison, K. M. Walker, C. D. Vance, D. L. Sherman, and D. F. Sterne. DTE Firewalls—Initial Measurement and Evaluation Report. Technical Report 0632R, Trusted Information Systems, March 1997.
2. L. Badger, D. F. Sterne, D. L. Sherman, K. M. Walker, and S. A. Haghighat. A Domain and Type Enforcement UNIX Prototype. In *Proceedings of the Fifth USENIX UNIX Security Symposium*, pages 127–140, Salt Lake City, Utah, June 1995.
3. L. Badger, D. F. Sterne, D. L. Sherman, K. M. Walker, and S. A. Haghighat. Practical Domain and Type Enforcement for UNIX. In *Proceedings of the 1995 IEEE Symposium on Security and Privacy*, pages 66–77, Oakland, California, May 1995.
4. E. Belani, A. Vahdat, T. Anderson, and M. Dahlin. The CRISIS Wide Area Security Architecture. In *Proceedings of the 7th USENIX Security Symposium*, San Antonio, Texas, January 1998.
5. D. E. Bell and L. J. La Padula. Secure Computer System: Unified Exposition and Multics Interpretation. Technical Report MTR-2997 Rev. 1, The MITRE Corporation, Bedford, Massachusetts, March 1976. Also ADA023588, National Technical Information Service.
6. B. N. Bershad, S. Savage, P. Pardyak, E. G. Sirer, M. Fiuczynski, D. Becker, S. Eggers, and C. Chambers. Extensibility, Safety and Performance in the SPIN Operating System. In *Proceedings of the 15th Symposium on Operating Systems Principles*, pages 267–284, Copper Mountain, Colorado, December 1995.
7. K. J. Biba. Integrity Considerations for Secure Computer Systems. Technical Report MTR-3153 Rev. 1, The MITRE Corporation, Bedford, Massachusetts, April 1977. Also ADA039324, National Technical Information Service.
8. W. E. Boebert and R. Y. Kain. A Practical Alternative to Hierarchical Integrity Policies. In *Proceedings of the 17th National Computer Security Conference*, pages 18–27, Gaithersburg, Maryland, 1985.
9. D. F. C. Brewer and M. J. Nash. The Chinese Wall Security Policy. In *Proceedings of the 1989 IEEE Symposium on Security and Privacy*, pages 206–214, Oakland, California, May 1989.
10. D. D. Clark and D. R. Wilson. A Comparison of Commercial and Military Computer Security Policies. In *Proceedings of the 1987 IEEE Symposium on Security and Privacy*, pages 184–194, Oakland, California, April 1987.

11. D. Dean, E. W. Felten, and D. S. Wallach. Java Security: From HotJava to Netscape and Beyond. In *Proceedings of the 1996 IEEE Symposium on Security and Privacy*, pages 190–200, Oakland, California, May 1996.

12. D. E. Denning. A Lattice Model of Secure Information Flow. *Communications of the ACM*, 19(5):236–243, May 1976.

13. Department of Defense Computer Security Center. Department of Defense Trusted Computer System Evaluation Criteria, December 1985. Department of Defense Standard DoD 5200.28-STD.

14. C. M. Ellison, B. Frantz, B. Lampson, R. Rivest, B. M. Thomas, and T. Ylonen. SPKI Certificate Theory. Technical Report draft-ietf-spki-cert-theory-04.txt, Internet Engineering Task Force, November 1998.

15. L. Gong. Java Security: Present and Near Future. *IEEE Micro*, 17(3):14–19, May/June 1997.

16. L. Gong, M. Mueller, H. Prafullchandra, and R. Schemers. Going Beyond the Sandbox: An Overview of the New Security Architecture in the Java Development Kit 1.2. In *Proceedings of the USENIX Symposium on Internet Technologies and Systems*, pages 103–112, Monterey, California, December 1997.

17. L. Gong and R. Schemers. Implementing Protection Domains the Java Development Kit 1.2. In *Proceedings of the Internet Society Symposium on Network and Distributed System Security*, San Diego, California, March 1998.

18. J. Gosling, B. Joy, and G. Steele. *The Java Language Specification*. Addison-Wesley, Reading, Massachusetts, 1996.

19. S. L. Graham, S. Lucco, and R. Wahbe. Adaptable Binary Programs. In *Proceedings of the 1995 USENIX Technical Conference*, pages 315–325, New Orleans, Louisiana, January 1995.

20. D. Hagimont and L. Ismail. A Protection Scheme for Mobile Agents on Java. In *Proceedings of the Third Annual ACM/IEEE International Conference on Mobile Computing and Networking*, Budapest, Hungary, September 1997.

21. W. C. Hsieh, M. E. Fiuczynski, C. Garrett, S. Savage, D. Becker, and B. N. Bershad. Language Support for Extensible Operating Systems. In *Proceedings of the Workshop on Compiler Support for System Software*, pages 127–133, Tucson, Arizona, February 1996.

22. B. W. Lampson. Protection. In *Proceedings of the Fifth Princeton Symposium on Information Sciences and Systems*, pages 437–443, Princeton, New Jersey, March 1971. Reprinted in Operating Systems Review, 8(1):18–24, January 1974.

23. B. W. Lampson, M. Abadi, M. Burrows, and E. Wobber. Authentication in Distributed Systems: Theory and Practice. *ACM Transactions on Computer Systems*, 10(4):265–310, November 1992.

24. T. M. P. Lee. Using Mandatory Integrity to Enforce "Commercial" Security. In *Proceedings of the 1988 IEEE Symposium on Security and Privacy*, pages 140–146, Oakland, California, April 1988.

25. T. Lindholm and F. Yellin. *The Java Virtual Machine Specification*. Addison-Wesley, Reading, Massachusetts, 1996.

26. S. B. Lipner. Non-Discretionary Controls for Commercial Applications. In *Proceedings of the 1982 Symposium on Security and Privacy*, pages 2–10, Oakland, California, April 1982.

27. C. J. McCollum, J. R. Messing, and L. Notargiacomo. Beyond the Pale of MAC and DAC—Defining New Forms of Access Control. In *Proceedings of the 1990 IEEE Symposium on Research in Security and Privacy*, pages 190–200, Oakland, California, May 1990.

28. G. McGraw and E. W. Felten. *Java Security: Hostile Applets, Holes and Antidotes.* Wiley Computer Publishing, John Wiley & Sons, Inc., New York, New York, 1997.

29. M. K. McKusick, K. Bostic, M. J. Karels, and J. S. Quarterman. *The Design and Implementation of the 4.4BSD Operating System.* Addison-Wesley Publishing Company, Reading, Massachusetts, 1996.

30. S. E. Minear. Providing Policy Control Over Object Operations in a Mach Based System. In *Proceedings of the Fifth USENIX UNIX Security Symposium*, pages 141–156, Salt Lake City, Utah, June 1995.

31. G. Morrisett, D. Walker, K. Crary, and N. Glew. From System F to Typed Assembly Language. In *Proceedings of the 25th Symposium on Principles of Programming Languages*, San Diego, California, January 1998.

32. A. C. Myers and B. Liskov. A Decentralized Model for Information Flow Control. In *Proceedings of the 16th Symposium on Operating Systems Principles*, pages 129–142, Saint-Malo, France, October 1997.

33. G. C. Necula and P. Lee. Safe Kernel Extensions Without Run-Time Checking. In *Proceedings of the Second Symposium on Operating Systems Design and Implementation*, pages 229–243, Seattle, Washington, October 1996.

34. D. Olawsky, T. Fine, E. Schneider, and R. Spencer. Developing and Using a "Policy Neutral" Access Control Policy. In *Proceedings of the New Security Paradigms Workshop*, September 1996.

35. P. Pardyak and B. N. Bershad. Dynamic Binding for an Extensible System. In *Proceedings of the Second Symposium on Operating Systems Design and Implementation*, pages 201–212, Seattle, Washington, October 1996.

36. J. Richardson, P. Schwarz, and L.-F. Cabrera. CACL: Efficient Fine-Grained Protection for Objects. In *Proceedings of the Conference on Object-Oriented Programming Systems, Languages, and Applications '92*, pages 263–275, Vancouver, Canada, October 1992.

37. T. Romer, G. Voelker, D. Lee, A. Woman, W. Wong, H. Levy, B. N. Bershad, and B. Chen. Instrumentation and Optimization of Win32/Intel Executables Using Etch. In *Proceedings of the USENIX Windows NT Workshop*, pages 1–8, Seattle, Washington, August 1997.

38. J. H. Saltzer and M. D. Schroeder. The Protection of Information in Computer Systems. *Proceedings of the IEEE*, 63(9):1278–1308, September 1975.

39. Secure Computing Corporation. DTOS General System Security and Assurability Assessment Report. Technical Report DTOS CDRL A011, Secure Computing Corporation, Secure Computing Corporation, 2675 Long Lake Road, Roseville, Minnesota 55113-2536, June 1997.

40. Secure Computing Corporation. DTOS Lessons Learned Report. Technical Report DTOS CDRL A008, Secure Computing Corporation, Secure Computing Corporation, 2675 Long Lake Road, Roseville, Minnesota 55113-2536, June 1997.

41. E. G. Sirer, M. Fiuczynski, P. Pardyak, and B. N. Bershad. Safe Dynamic Linking in an Extensible Operating System. In *Proceedings of the Workshop on Compiler Support for System Software*, pages 134–140, Tucson, Arizona, February 1996.

42. E. G. Sirer, S. Savage, P. Pardyak, G. P. DeFouw, M. A. Alapat, and B. N. Bershad. Writing an Operating System with Modula-3. In *Proceedings of the Workshop on Compiler Support for System Software*, pages 141–148, Tucson, Arizona, February 1996.

43. A. Srivastava and A. Eustace. ATOM: A System for Building Customized Program Analysis Tools. In *Proceedings of the ACM SIGPLAN '94 Conference on Programming Language Design and Implementation*, pages 196–205, Orlando, Florida, June 1994.

44. D. L. Tennenhouse, J. M. Smith, W. D. Sincoskie, D. J. Wetherall, and G. J. Minden. A Survey of Active Network Research. *IEEE Communications Magazine*, 25(1):80–86, January 1997.
45. R. Wahbe, S. Lucco, T. E. Anderson, and S. L. Graham. Efficient Software-Based Fault Isolation. In *Proceedings of the 14th Symposium on Operating Systems Principles*, pages 203–216, Ashville, North Carolina, December 1993.
46. D. S. Wallach, D. Balfanz, D. Dean, and E. W. Felten. Extensible Security Architectures for Java. In *Proceedings of the 16th Symposium on Operating Systems Principles*, pages 116–128, Saint-Malo, France, October 1997.
47. D. S. Wallach and E. W. Felten. Understanding Java Stack Inspection. In *Proceedings of the 1998 IEEE Symposium on Security and Privacy*, pages 52–63, Oakland, California, May 1998.
48. C. Yoshikawa, B. Chun, P. Eastham, A. Vahdat, T. Anderson, and D. Culler. Using Smart Clients to Build Scalable Services. In *Proceedings of the 1997 USENIX Technical Conference*, pages 105–117, Anaheim, California, January 1997.

# Interposition Agents:
# Transparently Interposing User Code
# at the System Interface*

Michael B. Jones

**Abstract.** Many contemporary operating systems utilize a system call interface between the operating system and its clients. Increasing numbers of systems are providing low-level mechanisms for intercepting and handling system calls in user code. Nonetheless, they typically provide no higher-level tools or abstractions for effectively utilizing these mechanisms. Using them has typically required reimplementation of a substantial portion of the system interface from scratch, making the use of such facilities unwieldy at best.

This paper presents a toolkit that substantially increases the ease of interposing user code between clients and instances of the system interface by allowing such code to be written in terms of the high-level objects provided by this interface, rather than in terms of the intercepted system calls themselves. This toolkit helps enable new interposition agents to be written, many of which would not otherwise have been attempted. This toolkit has also been used to construct several agents including: system call tracing tools, file reference tracing tools, and customizable filesystem views. Examples of other agents that could be built include: protected environments for running untrusted binaries, logical devices implemented entirely in user space, transparent data compression and/or encryption agents, transactional software environments, and emulators for other operating system environments.

# 1   Introduction

## 1.1   Terminology

Many contemporary operating systems provide an interface between user code and the operating system services based on special "system calls". One can view the system interface as simply a special form of structured communication channel on which messages are sent, allowing such operations as interposing programs that record or modify the communications that take place on this channel. In this paper, such a program that both uses and provides the system interface will be referred to as a "system interface interposition agent" or simply as an "agent" for short.

\* This paper was originally printed in Proceedings of the 14th ACM Symposium on Operating Systems Principles, pages 80–93. Asheville, NC, December, 1993 ©1993 ACM

## 1.2 Overview

This paper presents a toolkit that substantially increases the ease of interposing user code between clients and instances of the system interface by allowing such code to be written in terms of the high-level objects provided by this interface, rather than in terms of the intercepted system calls themselves. Providing an object-oriented toolkit exposing the multiple layers of abstraction present in the system interface provides a useful set of tools and interfaces at each level. Different agents can thus exploit the toolkit objects best suited to their individual needs. Consequently, substantial amounts of toolkit code are able to be reused when constructing different agents. Furthermore, having such a toolkit enables new system interface implementations to be written, many of which would not otherwise have been attempted.

Just as interposition is successfully used today to extend operating system interfaces based on such communication-based facilities as pipes, sockets, and inter-process communication channels, interposition can also be successfully used to extend the system interface. In this way, the known benefits of interposition can also be extended to the domain of the system interface.

## 1.3 Examples

The following figures should help clarify both the system interface and interposition.

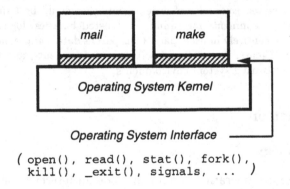

```
( open(), read(), stat(), fork(),
  kill(), _exit(), signals, ... )
```

**Fig. 1.** Kernel provides instances of system interface

Figure 1 depicts uses of the system interface without interposition. In this view, the kernel[1] provides all instances of the operating system interface.

---

[1] The term "kernel" is used throughout this paper to refer to the default or lowest-level implementation of the operating system in question. While this implementation is often run in processor kernel space, this need not be the case, as in the Mach 3.0 Unix Server/Emulator [16].

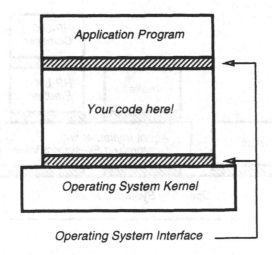

**Fig. 2.** User code interposed at system interface

Figure 2 depicts the ability to transparently interpose user code that both uses and implements the operating system interface between an unmodified application program and the operating system kernel.

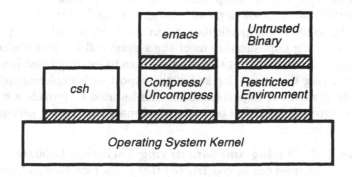

**Fig. 3.** Kernel and agents provide instances of system interface

Figure 3 depicts uses of the system interface with interposition. Here, both the kernel and interposition agents provide instances of the operating system interface.

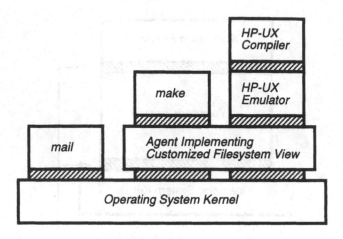

**Fig. 4.** Agents can share state and provide multiple instances of system interface

Figure 4 depicts more uses of the system interface with interposition. In this view agents, like the kernel, can share state and provide multiple instances of the operating system interface.

### 1.4 Motivation

Today, agents are regularly written to be interposed on simple communication–based interfaces such as pipes and sockets. Similarly, the toolkit makes it possible to easily write agents to be interposed on the system interface.

Interposition can be used to provide programming facilities that would otherwise not be available. In particular, it can allow for a multiplicity of simultaneously coexisting implementations of the system call services, which in turn may utilize one another without requiring changes to existing client binaries and without modifying the underlying kernel to support each implementation.

Alternate system call implementations can be used to provide a number of services not typically available on system call-based operating systems. Some examples include:

- **System Call Tracing and Monitoring Facilities:** Debuggers and program trace facilities can be constructed that allow monitoring of a program's use of system services in a easily customizable manner.
- **Emulation of Other Operating Systems:** Alternate system call implementations can be used to concurrently run binaries from variant operating systems on the same platform. For instance, it could be used to run ULTRIX [13], HP-UX [10], or UNIX System V [3] binaries in a Mach/BSD environment.
- **Protected Environments for Running Untrusted Binaries:** A wrapper environment can be constructed that allows untrusted, possibly malicious, binaries to be run within a restricted environment that monitors and

emulates the actions they take, possibly without actually performing them, and limits the resources they can use in such a way that the untrusted binaries are unaware of the restrictions. A wide variety of monitoring and emulating schemes are possible from simple automatic resource restriction environments to heuristic evaluations of the target program's behavior, possibly including interactive decisions made by human beings during the protected execution. This is particularly timely in today's environments of increased software sharing with the potential for viruses and Trojan horses.

– **Transactional Software Environments:** Applications can be constructed that provide an environment in which changes to persistent state made by unmodified programs can be emulated and performed transactionally. For instance, a simple "run transaction" command could be constructed that runs arbitrary unmodified programs (e.g., /bin/csh) such that all persistent execution side effects (e.g., filesystem writes) are remembered and appear within the transactional environment to have been performed normally, but where in actuality the user is presented with a "commit" or "abort" choice at the end of such a session. Indeed, one such transactional program invocation could occur within another, transparently providing nested transactions.

– **Alternate or Enhanced Semantics:** Environments can be constructed that provide alternate or enhanced semantics for unmodified binaries. One such enhancement in which people have expressed interest is the ability to "mount" a search list of directories in the filesystem name space such that the union of their contents appears to reside in a single directory. This could be used in a software development environment to allow distinct source and object directories to appear as a single directory when running make.

## 1.5 Problems with Existing Systems

Increasing numbers of operating systems are providing low-level mechanisms for intercepting system calls. Having these low-level mechanisms makes writing interposition agents possible. For instance, Mach [1, 16] provides the interception facilities used for this work, SunOS version 4 [44] provides new ptrace() operations used by the trace utility, and UNIX System V.4 [4] provides new /proc operations used by the truss utility. Nonetheless, they typically provide no higher-level tools or abstractions for effectively utilizing these mechanisms, making the use of such facilities unwieldy at best.

Part of the difficulty with writing system call interposition agents in the past has been that no one set of interfaces is appropriate across a range of such agents other than the lowest level system call interception services. Different agents interact with different subsets of the operating system interface in widely different ways to do different things. Building an agent often requires implementation of a substantial portion of the system interface. Yet, only the bare minimum interception facilities have been available, providing only the lowest common denominator that is minimally necessary. Consequently, each agent has typically been constructed completely from scratch. No leverage was gained from the work done on other agents.

## 1.6  Key Insight

The key insight that enabled me to gain leverage on the problem of writing system interface interposition agents for the 4.3BSD [25] interface is as follows: while the 4.3BSD system interface contains a large number of different system calls, it contains a relatively small number of abstractions (whose behavior is largely independent). (In 4.3BSD, the primary system interface abstractions are pathnames, descriptors, processes, process groups, files, directories, symbolic links, pipes, sockets, signals, devices, users, groups, permissions, and time.) Furthermore, most calls manipulate only a few of these abstractions.

Thus, it should be possible to construct a toolkit that presents these abstractions as objects in an object-oriented programming language. Such a toolkit would then be able to support the substantial commonalities present in different agents through code reuse, while also supporting the diversity of different kinds of agents through inheritance.

# 2  Research Overview

## 2.1  Design Goals

The four main goals of the toolkit were:

1. **Unmodified System:** Unmodified applications should be able to be run under agents. Similarly, the underlying kernel should not require changes to support each different agent (although the kernel may have to be modified once in order to provide support for system call interception, etc. so that agents can be written at all).
2. **Completeness:** Agents should be able to both use and provide the entire system interface. This includes not only the set of requests from applications to the system (i.e., the system calls) but also the set of upcalls that the system can make upon the applications (i.e., the signals).
3. **Appropriate Code Size:** The amount of new code necessary to implement an agent using the toolkit should only be proportional to the new functionality to be implemented by the agent — not to the size of the system interface. The toolkit should provide whatever boilerplate and tools are necessary to write agents at levels of abstraction that are appropriate for the agent functionality, rather than having to write each agent at the raw system call level.
4. **Performance:** The performance impact of running an application under an agent should be negligible.

## 2.2  Design and Structure of the Toolkit

I have designed and built a toolkit on top of the Mach 2.5 system call interception mechanism [1, 5, 16] that can be used to interpose user code on the 4.3BSD [25] system call interface. The toolkit currently runs on the Intel 386/486 and the VAX. The toolkit is implemented in C++ with small amounts of C and assembly language as necessary. Multi-threaded hybrid 4.3BSD/Mach 2.5 programs are not currently supported.

As a consequence of using the Mach 2.5 system call interception mechanism, which redirects system calls to handler routines in the same address space, interposition agents reside in the same address spaces as their client processes. The lowest layers of the toolkit hides this Mach-specific choice, allowing agents to be constructed that could be located either in the same or different addresses spaces as their clients.

This toolkit is structured in an object-oriented manner, allowing agents to be written in terms of several different layers of objects by utilizing inheritance. Abstractions exposed at different toolkit layers currently include the filesystem name space, pathnames, directories, file descriptors and the associated descriptor name space, open objects referenced by descriptors, and signals, as well as the system calls themselves. (These abstractions are discussed further in Section 2.3.) Support for additional abstractions can be incrementally added as needed by writing new toolkit objects that represent the new abstractions and by using derived versions of the existing toolkit objects that reference the new abstractions through the new objects. Indeed, the current toolkit was constructed via exactly this kind of stepwise refinement, with useful toolkit objects being produced at each step. The structure of the toolkit permits agents to be written in terms of whatever system interface abstractions are appropriate to the tasks they perform. Just as derived objects are used to introduce new toolkit functionality, interposition agents change the behavior of particular system abstractions by using agent-specific derived versions of the toolkit objects representing those abstractions.

Different interposition agents need to affect different components of the system call interface in substantially different ways and at different levels of abstraction. For instance, a system call monitoring/profiling agent needs to manipulate the system calls themselves, whereas an agent providing alternate user filesystem views needs to manipulate higher-level objects such as pathnames and possibly file descriptors. The agent writer decides what layers of toolkit objects are appropriate to the particular task and includes only those toolkit objects. Default implementations of the included objects provide the normal behavior of the abstractions they represent. This allows derived agent-specific versions of toolkit objects to inherit this behavior, while adding new behavior in the implementations of the derived objects. I believe that the failure to provide such multi-layer interfaces by past system call interception mechanisms has made them less useful than they might otherwise have been.

## 2.3 Toolkit Layers

Figure 5 presents a diagram of the primary classes currently provided with the interposition toolkit. Indented classes are subclasses of the classes above. Arrows indicate the use of one class by another. Many of these classes are explained in more detail in this section.

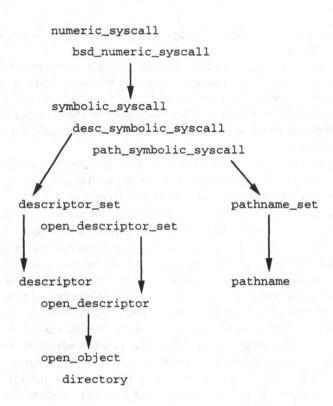

**Fig. 5.** Primary interposition toolkit classes

The lowest layers of the toolkit perform such functions as agent invocation, system call interception, incoming signal handling, performing system calls on behalf of the agent, and delivering signals to applications running under agent code. Unlike the higher levels of the toolkit, these layers are sometimes highly operating system specific and also contain machine specific code.

These layers hide the mechanisms used to intercept system calls and signals, those that are used to call down from an agent to the next level system interface, and those that are used to send a signal from an agent up to the application program. These layers also hide such details as whether the agent resides in the same address space as the application program or whether it resides in a separate address space. These layers are referred to as the *boilerplate* layers. These layers are not normally used directly by interposition agents.

The lowest (or zeroth) layer of the toolkit which is directly used by any interposition agents presents the system interface as a single entry point accepting vectors of untyped numeric arguments. It provides the ability to register for specific numeric system calls to be intercepted and for incoming signal handlers to be registered. This layer is referred to as the *numeric system call* layer.

Example interfaces provided by the numeric system call layer are as follows:

```
class numeric_syscall {
public:
  virtual int syscall(int number, int args[],
                      int rv[2], void *regs);
  virtual void init(char *agentargv[]);
  virtual void signal_handler(int sig, int code,
                              struct sigcontext *context);
  void register_interest(int number);
  void register_interest_range(int low, int high);
};
```

For instance, using just the numeric system call layer, by using a derived version of the numeric_syscall class with an agent-specific syscall() method, an agent writer could trivially write an agent that printed the arguments of a chosen set of system calls as uninterpreted numeric values. As another example, one range of system call numbers could be remapped to calls on a different range at this level.

The first layer of the toolkit intended for direct use by most interposition agents presents the system interface as a set of system call methods on a system interface object. When this layer is used by an agent, application system calls are mapped into invocations on the system call methods of this object. (This mapping is itself done by a toolkit-supplied derived version of the numeric_syscall object.) This layer is referred to as the *symbolic system call layer*.

Example interfaces provided by the symbolic system call layer are as follows:

```
class symbolic_syscall {
public:
  virtual void init(char *agentargv[]);
  virtual void init_child();

  virtual int sys_exit(int status, int rv[2]);
  virtual int sys_fork(int rv[2]);
  virtual int sys_read(int fd, void *buf, int cnt, int rv[2]);
  ... entries for all other 4.3BSD system calls ...

  virtual int unknown_syscall(int number, int *args, int rv[2],
                              struct emul_regs *regs);
  virtual void signal_handler(int sig, int code,
                              struct sigcontext *context);
};
```

Agents can interpose on individual system calls by using a derived version of the symbolic_syscall object with agent-specific methods corresponding to the system calls to be intercepted. For instance, the timex agent, which is described in Section 3.3, changes the apparent time of day by using a derived symbolic_syscall object with a new gettimeofday() method. Likewise, the trace agent, described in Section 3.3, prints the arguments to each executed system call in a human-readable from individual system call methods in a derived `symbolic_syscall` object.

The second layer of the toolkit is structured around the primary abstractions provided by the system call interface. In 4.3BSD, these include pathnames, file descriptors, processes, and process groups. This layer presents the system interface as sets of methods on objects representing these abstractions. Toolkit objects currently provided at this level are the filesystem name space (`pathname_set`), resolved pathnames (`pathname`), the file descriptor name space (`descriptor_set`), active file descriptors (`descriptor`), and reference counted open objects (`open_object`). Such operations as filesystem name space transformations and filesystem usage monitoring are done at this level.

For example, agents can interpose on pathname operations by using derived versions of two classes: `pathname_set` and `pathname`. The `pathname_set` class provides operations that affect the set of pathnames, i.e., those that create or remove pathnames. The `pathname` class provides operations on the objects referenced by the pathnames.

Example interfaces provided by the `pathname_set` class are as follows:

```
class pathname_set : public descriptor_set {
protected:
   virtual int getpn(char *path, int flags, pathname **pn);
public:
   virtual void init(char *agentargv[],
                     class PATH_SYMBOLIC_BASE *path_sym);

   // System calls with knowledge of pathnames
   virtual int open(char *path, int flags, int mode, int rv[2]);
   virtual int link(char *path, char *newpath, int rv[2]);
   virtual int unlink(char *path, int rv[2]);
   ... entries for other 4.3BSD system calls using pathnames ...
};
```

Example interfaces provided by the `pathname` class are as follows:

```
class pathname {
public:
   virtual int open(int flags, int mode, int rv[2],
                    OPEN_OBJECT_CLASS **oo);
   virtual int link(pathname *newpn, int rv[2]);
   virtual int unlink(int rv[2]);
   ... entries for other 4.3BSD system calls referencing objects
   via pathnames ...
};
```

The key to both of these interrelated classes is the getpn() operation, which looks up a pathname string and resolves it to a reference to a `pathname` object. The default implementation of all the `pathname_set` system call methods simply resolves their pathname strings to `pathname` objects using `getpn()` and then invokes the corresponding `pathname` method on the resulting object. The `pathname` method is responsible for actually performing the requested operation on the object referenced by the pathname.

With the `getpn()` operation to encapsulate pathname lookup, it is possible for agents to supply derived versions of the `pathname_set` object with a new `getpn()` implementation that modifies the treatment of all pathnames. For instance, this can be used to logically rearrange the pathname space, as was done by the `union` agent (described in Section 3.3). Likewise, it provides a central point for name reference data collection, as was done by the `dfs_trace` agent (described in Section 3.5).

A third set of toolkit layers focuses on secondary objects provided by the system call interface, which are normally accessed via primary objects. Such objects include files, directories, symbolic links, devices, pipes, and sockets. These layers present the system interface as sets of methods on objects, with specialized operations for particular classes of objects. The only toolkit object currently provided at this level is the open directory `directory` object. Operations that are specific to these secondary objects such as directory content transformations are done at this level.

For example, agents can interpose on directory operations by using derived versions of the `directory` class. The directory class is itself a derived version of the `open_object` class (one of the second layer classes for file descriptor operations), since directory operations are a special case of operations that can be performed on file descriptors.

Example interfaces provided by the `directory` class are as follows:

```
class directory : public OPEN_OBJECT_CLASS {
public:
  virtual int next_direntry();
  struct direct *direntry;  // Set by next_direntry()

public:
  virtual int read(void *buf, int cnt, int rv[2]);
  virtual int lseek(off_t offset, int whence, int rv[2]);
  virtual int getdirentries(void *buf, int cnt, long *basep,
                            int rv[2]);
};
```

Just as the `getpn()` method encapsulated pathname resolution, the `next_direntry()` method encapsulates the iteration of individual directory entries implicit in reading the contents of a directory. This allows the `union` agent (described in Section 3.3) to make it appear that the full contents of a set of directories is actually present in a single directory by providing a new `next_direntry()` function that iterates over the contents of each member directory. (And yes, that iteration itself is accomplished via the underlying `next_direntry` implementations.)

## 2.4  Using the Toolkit to Build Agents

As I built the toolkit, I also used it to implement several interposition agents. These agents provide:

- **System Call and Resource Usage Monitoring:** This demonstrates the ability to intercept the full system call interface.
- **User Configurable Filesystem Views:** This demonstrates the ability to transparently assign new interpretations to filesystem pathnames.
- **File Reference Tracing Tools:** that are compatible with existing tools [30] originally implemented for use by the Coda [38, 23] filesystem project: this provides a basis for comparing a best available equivalent implementation to a facility provided by an agent.

# 3  Results

## 3.1  Goal: Unmodified System

### Unmodified Applications

Agents constructed using the system interface interposition toolkit can load and run unmodified 4.3BSD binaries. No recompilation or relinking is necessary. Thus, agents can be used for all program binaries — not just those for which sources or object files are available.

Applications do not have to be adapted to or modified for particular agents. Indeed, the presence of agents should be transparent to applications.[2]

### Unmodified Kernel

Agents constructed using the system interface interposition toolkit do not require any agent-specific kernel modifications. Instead, they use general system call handling facilities that are provided by the kernel in order to implement all agent-specific system call behavior. Also, a general agent loader program is used to invoke arbitrary agents, which are compiled separately from the agent loader.

The Mach 2.5 kernel used for this work contains a primitive, `task_set_emulation()`, that allows 4.3BSD system calls to be redirected for execution in user space. Another primitive, `htg_unix_syscall()`, permits calls to be made on the underlying 4.3BSD system call implementation even though those calls are being redirected.

---

[2] Of course, an application that is intent on determining if it is running under an agent probably can, if only by probing memory or performing precise performance measurements.

## 3.2 Goal: Completeness

Agents constructed using the system interface interposition toolkit can both use and provide the entire 4.3BSD system interface. This includes not only the system calls, but also the signals. Thus, both the downward path (from applications to agents and from agents to the underlying system implementation) and the upward path (from the underlying implementation to agents and from agents to applications) are fully supported.

Completeness gives two desirable results:

1. All programs can potentially be run under agents. By contrast, if completeness did not hold, there would have been two classes of programs: those that used a restricted set of features that agents could handle, and those that used features that agents could not handle. The interposition toolkit avoids these problems.
2. Agents can potentially modify all aspects of the system interface. Agents are not restricted to modifying only subsets of the system behavior. For instance, it would have been easy to envision similar systems in which agents could modify the behavior of system calls, but not incoming signals.

## 3.3 Goal: Appropriate Code Size

Table 1 lists the source code sizes of three different agents, broken down into statements of toolkit code used, and statements of agent specific code.[3] These agents were chosen to provide a cross section of different interposition agents, ranging from the very simple to the fairly complex and using different portions of the interposition toolkit. Each of these agents is discussed in turn.

| Sizes of Agents | | | |
|---|---|---|---|
| Agent Name | Toolkit Statements | Agent Statements | Total Statements |
| timex | 2467 | 35 | 2502 |
| trace | 2467 | 1348 | 3815 |
| union | 3977 | 166 | 4143 |

**Table 1.** Sizes of agents, measured in semicolons

## Size of the Timex Agent

The timex agent changes the apparent time of day. It is built upon the symbolic system call and lower levels of the toolkit (see Section 2.3). The toolkit code used

---

[3] Note: The actual metric used was to count semicolons. For C and C++, this gives a better measure of the actual number of statements present in the code than counting lines in the source files.

for this agent contains 2467 statements. The code specific to this agent consists of only two routines: a new derived implementation of the gettimeofday() system call and an initialization routine to accept the desired effective time of day from the command line. This code contains only 35 statements.

The core of the timex agent is as follows:

```
class timex_symbolic_syscall : public symbolic_syscall {
public:
  virtual void init(char *agentargv[]);
  virtual int sys_gettimeofday(struct timeval *tp,
                               struct timezone *tzp, int rv[2]);
private:
  int offset;    // Difference between real and funky time
};

int timex_symbolic_syscall::sys_gettimeofday(
    struct timeval *tp, struct timezone *tzp, int rv[2])
{
  int ret;
  ret = symbolic_syscall::sys_gettimeofday(tp, tzp, rv);
  if (ret >= 0 && tp) {
    tp->tv_sec += offset;
  }
  return ret;
}
```

The new code necessary to construct the timex agent using the toolkit consists only of the implementation of the new functionality. Inheritance from toolkit objects is used to obtain implementations of all system interface behaviors that remain unchanged.

### Size of the Trace Agent

The trace agent traces the execution of client processes, printing each system call made and signal received. Like the timex agent, it is built upon the symbolic system call and lower levels of the toolkit, which contain 2467 statements. However, the code specific to this agent is much larger, containing 1348 statements. The reason for this is simple: unlike the timex agent, the new work of the trace agent is proportional to the size of the entire system interface. Derived versions of each of the 114 4.3BSD system calls plus the signal handler are needed to print each call name and arguments, since each call has a different name and typically takes different parameters. Even so, the new code contains less than 12 statements per
system call, 10 of which typically are of the form:

```
virtual int sys_read(int fd, void *buf, int cnt, int rv[2]);
```
*(line from TRACE_SYMBOLIC_CLASS class declaration)*

```
int TRACE_SYMBOLIC_CLASS::sys_read(int fd, void *buf, int cnt,
                                   int rv[2])
{
  register int ret;
  print_start();
  fprintf(f, "read(%d, 0x%x, 0x%x) ... ]
n", fd, buf, cnt);
  fflush(f);
  ret = TRACE_SYMBOLIC_BASE::sys_read(fd, buf, cnt, rv);
  print_start();
  fprintf(f, "... read(%d, 0x%x, 0x%x) ->", fd, buf, cnt);
  print_retx(ret, rv);
  return ret;
}
```

As with the timex agent, the new code necessary to construct the trace agent using the toolkit consists only of the implementation of the new functionality. Inheritance from toolkit objects is used to obtain implementations of all system interface behaviors that remain unchanged.

### Size of the Union Agent

The union agent implements union directories, which provide the ability to view the contents of lists of actual directories as if their contents were merged into single "union" directories. It is built using toolkit objects for pathnames, directories, and descriptors, as well as the symbolic system call and lower levels of the toolkit. The toolkit code used for this agent contains 3977 statements. The code specific to this agent consists of three things: a derived form of the toolkit pathname object that maps operations using names of union directories to operations on the underlying objects, a derived form of the toolkit directory object that makes it possible to list the logical contents of a union directory via getdirentries() and related calls, and an initialization routine that accepts specifications of the desired union directories from the command line. Yet, this new code contains only 166 statements.

The new code necessary to construct the union agent using the toolkit consists only of the implementation of the new functionality. As with the other agents, inheritance from toolkit objects is used to obtain implementations of all system interface behaviors that remain unchanged.

### Size Results

The above examples demonstrate several results pertaining the code size of agents written using the interposition toolkit. One result is that the size of the toolkit code dominates the size of agent code for simple agents. Using the toolkit, the amount of new code to perform useful modifications of the system interface semantics can be small.

Furthermore, the amount of agent specific code can be proportional to the new functionality being implemented by the agent, rather than proportional to the number of system calls affected. For instance, even though the union directory agent needs to change the behavior of all 30 calls that use pathnames, and all 48 calls that use descriptors, or 70 calls in all (eight of which use both), it is written in terms of toolkit objects that encapsulate the *behavior of these abstractions*, rather than in terms of the system calls that use them. Thus, the agent specific code need only implement the new functionality since the toolkit provides sufficient underpinnings to make this possible.

Finally, there can be substantial code reuse between different agents. All the agents listed above were able to use the symbolic system call and lower levels of the toolkit, consisting of 2467 statements. Both the union agent and dfs_trace agent[4] are also able to use the descriptor, open object, and pathname levels of the toolkit, reusing a total of 3977 statements. Rather than modifying an implementation of the system interface in order to augment its behavior, the toolkit makes it possible to implement derived versions of the base toolkit objects, allowing the base toolkit objects that implement the system interface to be reused.

## 3.4 Goal: Performance

### Application Performance Data

This section presents the performance of running two applications under several different agents. The two applications chosen differ both in their system call usage and their structure: One makes moderate use of system calls and is structured as a single process; the other makes heavy use of system calls and is structured as a collection of related processes. Likewise, the agents chosen range from very simple to fairly complex. The results are discussed in Section 3.4.

*Performance of Formatting a Document*
Table 2 presents the elapsed time that it takes to format a preliminary draft of my dissertation with Scribe [36] on a VAX 6250 both using no agent and when run under three different agents. In each case, the time presented is the average of nine successive runs done after an initial run from which the time was discarded.

This task requires 716 system calls. When run without any agents, it takes 131.5 seconds of elapsed time.

When run under the simplest agent, timex, an additional half second of overhead is added, giving an effective additional cost of under one half percent of the base run time. When run under trace, an extra 3.5 seconds of overhead are introduced. Furthermore, when run under union, the most complex agent

---

[4] The dfs_trace agent implements file reference tracing tools that are compatible with existing tools [30] originally implemented for use by the Coda [38, 23] filesystem project. This agent is discussed further in Section 3.5.

355

| Format my dissertation | | |
|---|---|---|
| agent Name | Seconds | Slowdown |
| None | 131.5 | — |
| timex | 132.0 | 0.5% |
| trace | 135.0 | 2.5% |
| union | 136.5 | 3.5% |

**Table 2.** Time to format my dissertation

considered, there is only an additional 5.0 seconds, giving an effective agent cost of 3.5% of the base run time.

It comes as no surprise that trace, while conceptually simple, incurs perceptible overheads. Each system call made by the application to the trace agent results in at least an additional two write() system calls in order to write the trace output.[5]

*Performance of Compiling C Programs*
Table 3 presents the elapsed time that it takes to compile eight small C programs using Make [15] and the GNU C compiler [40] on a 25MHz Intel 486. In each case, the time presented is the average of nine successive runs done after an initial run from which the time was discarded.

To do this, Make runs the GNU C compiler, which in turn runs the C preprocessor, the C code generator, the assembler, and the linker for each program. This task requires a total of 11877 system calls, including 64 fork()/execve() pairs. When run without any agents, it takes 16.0 seconds of elapsed time.

| Make 8 programs | | |
|---|---|---|
| Agent Name | Seconds | Slowdown |
| None | 16.0 | — |
| timex | 19.0 | 19% |
| trace | 33.0 | 107% |
| union | 29.0 | 82% |

**Table 3.** Time to make 8 programs

When run under the simplest agent, timex, an additional three seconds of overhead are added, giving an effective additional cost of 19% of the base runtime. When run under union, which interposes on most of the system calls and which uses several additional layers of toolkit abstractions, the additional overhead beyond the no agent case is 13.0 seconds, giving an effective additional cost

---

[5] Trace output is not buffered across system calls so it will not be lost if the process is killed.

of 82% of the base runtime. When run under trace, an additional 17.0 seconds of run time are incurred, yielding a slowdown of 107%.

Again, it comes as no surprise that union introduces more overhead than timex. It interposes on the vast majority of the system calls, unlike timex, which interposes on only the bare minimum plus gettimeofday(). Also, union uses several additional layers of implementation abstractions not used by timex.

As with the previous application, the larger slowdown for trace is unsurprising. Given the large number of system calls made by this application and the additional two write() operations performed per application system call for writing the trace log, the log output time constitutes a significant portion of the slowdown.

An analysis of low-level performance characteristics is presented in Sections 3.5 and 3.5.

## Application Performance Results

The application performance data demonstrates that the performance impact of running an application under an agent is very agent and application specific. The performance impact of the example agents upon formatting my dissertation was practically negligible, ranging from 0.5% for the timex agent to 2.5% for the trace agent. However, the performance impact of the example agents upon making the eight small C programs was significant, ranging 19% for timex to 107% for trace. Unsurprisingly, different programs place different demands upon the system interface, and different agents add different overheads.

The good news is that the additional overhead of using an agent can be small relative to the time spent by applications doing actual work. Even though no performance tuning has been done on the current toolkit implementation, the overheads already appear to be acceptable for certain classes of applications and agents.

Furthermore, the agent overheads are of a pay-per-use nature. Calls not intercepted by interposition agents go directly to the underlying system and result in no additional overhead.

Finally, even though some performance impact is clearly inevitable, presumedly the agent will have been used because it provides some benefit. For instance, agents may provide features not otherwise available, or they may provide a more cost-effective means of implementing a desired set of features than is otherwise available. The performance "lost" by using an interposition agent can bring other types of gains.[6]

## 3.5 Other Results

### Low-level Performance Measurements

*Micro Performance Data*
This section presents the performance of several low-level operations used to

---

[6] For a discussion on the tradeoffs of using interposition agents, see Section 5.3.

implement interposition and of several commonly used system calls both without and with interposition.

Table 4 presents the performance of several low-level operations used to implement interposition. All measurements were taken on a 25MHz Intel 486 running Mach 2.5 version X144. The code measured was compiled with gcc or g++ version 1.37 with debugging (-g) symbols present.

| Performance of Low Level operations | |
|---|---|
| Operation | $\mu sec$ |
| C procedure call with 1 arg, result | 1.22 |
| C++ virtual procedure call with 1 arg, result | 1.94 |
| Intercept and return from system call | 30 |
| htg_unix_syscall() overhead | 37 |

**Table 4.** Performance measurements of individual low-level operations

Table 5 presents the performance of several commonly used system calls both without interposition and when a simple interposition agent is used. The interposition agent, time_symbolic, intercepts each system call, decodes each call and arguments, and calls C++ virtual procedures corresponding to each system call. These procedures just take the default action for each system call; they make the same system call on the next level of the system (the instance of the system interface on which the agent is being run). This allows the minimum toolkit overhead for each intercepted system call to be easily measured. Measured pathnames are in a UFS [27] filesystem and contain 6 pathname components.

| Performance of System Calls | | | |
|---|---|---|---|
| Operation | $\mu sec$ without agent | $\mu sec$ with agent | $\mu sec$ toolkit overhead |
| getpid() | 25 | 170 | 145 |
| gettimeofday() | 47 | 214 | 167 |
| fstat() | 54 | 220 | 166 |
| read() 1K of data | 370 | 579 | 209 |
| stat() | 892 | 1101 | 209 |
| fork(), wait(), _exit() | 10350 | 22350 | 12000 |
| execve() | 9720 | 20000 | 10280 |

**Table 5.** Performance measurements of individual system calls

*Micro Performance Results*
Two times from Table 4 are particularly significant. First, it takes 30$\mu$secto

intercept a system call, save the register state, call a system call dispatching routine, return from the dispatching routine, load a new register state, and return from the intercepted system call. This provides a lower bound on the total cost of any system call implemented by an interposition agent.

Second, using htg_unix_syscall()[7] to make a system call adds $37\mu$sec of overhead beyond the normal cost of the system call. This provides a lower bound on the additional cost for an agent to make a system call that otherwise would be intercepted by the agent.

Thus, any system call intercepted by an agent that then makes the same system call as part of the intercepted system call's implementation will take at least $67\mu$sec longer than the same system call would have if made with no agent present. Comparing the $67\mu$sec overhead to the normal costs of some commonly used system calls (found in Table 5) helps puts this cost in perspective.

The $67\mu$sec overhead is quite significant when compared to the execution times of simple calls such as getpid() or gettimeofday(), which take $25\mu$sec and $47\mu$sec; respectively, without an agent. It becomes less so when compared to read() or stat(), which take $370\mu$sec and $892\mu$sec to execute in the cases measured without an agent.

Hence, the impact will always be significant on small calls that do very little work; it can at least potentially be insignificant for calls that do real work.

In practice, of course, the overheads of actual interposition agents are higher than the $67\mu$sec theoretical minimum. The actual overheads for most system calls implemented using the symbolic system call toolkit level (see Section 2.3) range from about 140 to $210\mu$sec; as per Table 5. Overheads for fork() and execve() are significantly greater, adding approximately 10 milliseconds to both, roughly doubling their costs.

The execve() call is more expensive than most because it must be completely reimplemented by the toolkit from lower-level primitives, unlike most calls where the version provided by the underlying implementation can be used. The underlying implementation's execve() call can not be used because it clears its caller's address space. While the application must be reloaded, the agent needs to be preserved. Thus, the extra expense of execve() is due to having to individually perform such operations as clearing the caller's address space, closing a subset of the descriptors, resetting signal handlers, reading the program file, loading the executable image into the address space, loading the arguments onto the stack, setting the registers, and transferring control into the loaded image, all of which are normally done by a single execve() call. Likewise, fork() and _exit() are more expensive due to the number of additional bookkeeping operations required.

While the current overheads certainly leave room for optimization (starting with compiling the agents with optimization on), they are already low enough to be unimportant for many applications and agents, as discussed in Section 3.4.

---

[7] The htg_unix_syscall() facility permits calls to be made on the underlying 4.3BSD system call implementation even though those calls are being intercepted.

Finally, it should be stressed that these performance numbers are highly dependent upon the specific interposition mechanism used. In particular, they are strongly shaped by agents residing in the address spaces of their clients.

## Portability

The interposition toolkit should port to similar systems such as SunOS and UNIX System V. Despite toolkit dependencies on such Mach facilities as the particular system call interception mechanism used, all such dependencies were carefully encapsulated within the lowest (boilerplate) layers of the toolkit. None of the toolkit layers above the boilerplate directly depends on Mach-specific services. Higher toolkit layers, while being intentionally 4.3BSD specific, contain no such dependencies. This 4.3BSD dependency imposes at most minor portability concerns to other UNIX-derived systems, given their common lineage and resulting substantial similarity. Thus, it should be possible to port the toolkit by replacing the Mach-dependent portions of the boilerplate layers with equivalent services provided by the target environment.

Likewise, interposition agents written for the toolkit should also readily port. Even if there are differences between the system interfaces, the toolkit port should be able to shield the agents from these differences, unless, of course, the agents are directly using the facilities which differ.

One caveat, however, is probably in order. While a port of the toolkit could shield interposition agents from low-level system interface differences, it certainly can not shield them from system performance differences. If the toolkit is ported to systems that provide significantly slower system call interception mechanisms (as, for instance, mechanisms based on UNIX signals are likely to be), then some agents which previously exhibited acceptable slowdown might exhibit unacceptable slowdown when ported.

## Comparison to a Best Available Implementation

As an element of this research, an interposition agent (`dfs_trace`) was constructed that implements file reference tracing tools that are compatible with the existing kernel-based DFSTrace [30] tracing tools originally implemented for use by the Coda [38, 23] filesystem project. This was done to provide a realistic basis for comparing a best available implementation of a task that was implemented without benefit of the toolkit with an equivalent interposition agent constructed using the toolkit.

While this comparison is not presented in detail here[8] several of the resulting conclusions are worth noting. Two key points made evident by the comparison are:

- Agents can be easy to construct. It appears that constructing an interposition agent that provides an enhanced implementation of the system interface can

---

[8] See [22] for a detailed presentation of this comparison.

be at least as easy and possibly easier than modifying an existing operating system implementation to perform the equivalent functions.

— Agents may not perform as well as monolithic implementations. Agents that need to access resources maintained by the underlying operating system implementation will be limited in their performance by the overhead involved in crossing the system interface boundary in order to access those resources. Hence, the best monolithic implementation of a given facility needing access to system resources will always perform better than the best interposition-based implementation of the same facility. For instance, the kernel-based DFSTrace tools in the default mode caused a 3.0% slowdown while executing the AFS filesystem performance benchmarks [19]. The agent-based implementation caused a 64% slowdown under the same workload.

Other points also made evident by the comparison are:

— Agents can be as small as the equivalent changes to a monolithic implementation. Interposition agents built using the interposition toolkit can contain no more new code than the amount of code changed or added to a monolithic system implementation to implement equivalent facilities. For instance, the original DFSTrace kernel and user data collection code contains 1627 statements, compared to 1584 statements for the agent-based implementation.

— Agents can be better structured than monolithic implementations. Interposition agents built using the interposition toolkit can be more logically structured and be more portable than a monolithic implementation of equivalent facilities.

— Agents require no system modifications. Unlike monolithic implementations, where providing an enhanced implementation of a system often requires modifying the code implementing the system, interposition agents can provide enhanced implementations as an independent layer requiring no modifications to the underlying system. For instance, the original DFSTrace implementation required the modification of 26 kernel files in order to insert data collection code under conditional compilation switches; the agent-based implementation required no modifications to existing code since inheritance was used to add functionality. Also, the kernel-based implementation uses four machine-dependent files per machine type; the agent-based implementation is machine independent.

In summary, the interposition agent was more logically structured, was probably simpler to write and modify, and required no system modifications to implement or run. The kernel-based tracing tools were more efficient.

## 4   Related Work

This section presents a brief survey of past work providing the ability to interpose user code at the system interface or to otherwise extend the functionality available through the system interface. This topic does not appear to be well described in the literature; despite intensive research into past systems I have been unable to find a comprehensive treatment of the subject.

In particular, no general techniques for building or structuring system interface interposition agents appear to have been in use, and so none are described. Even though a number of systems provided mechanisms by which interposition agents could be built, the agents that were built appear to have shared little or no common ground. No widely applicable techniques appear to have been developed; no literature appears to have been published describing those *ad hoc* techniques that were used.

Thus, the following treatment is necessarily somewhat anecdotal in nature, with some past interposition agents and other system extensions described only by personal communications. Nonetheless, this section attempts to provide a representative, if not comprehensive, overview of the related work.

## 4.1 Overview of Past Agents

A large number of systems have provided low-level facilities sufficient to interpose user code at the system interface. Both the number and types of interposition agents that have been built using these facilities have varied widely between the different systems. Those agents that have been built can be broken down into five somewhat overlapping categories:

1. Complete operating system emulations such as VM [33] emulating OS/360 or TSO, TENEX [7,48] emulating TOPS-10, and RSEXEC [47] emulating an Arpanet-wide TENEX.
2. Debuggers and debugging facilities, such as those for (CAL TSS) [43], DTSS [24], ITS [14], and SunOS [44].
3. System call trace facilities, such as the "SET TRAP JSYS" facility under the TENEX/Tops-20 [12] EXEC, the truss program under UNIX System V.4 [4], and the trace program under SunOS version 4.
4. Adding new facilities to the operating system interface, as was done in OS6 [41,42], CAL TSS, and the MS-DOS [29]/Windows [28] environment.
5. Providing enhanced implementations of the existing operating system interface (often enhanced filesystem implementations), as was done in CAL TSS, TENEX, the Newcastle Connection [8], NFS [50], ITOSS [34], Watchdogs [6], Taos [26], and particularly in the Macintosh [2] and MS-DOS.

Stackable interfaces are known to be useful in other domains as well. For instance, communication protocols are composed from stackable layers in the *x*-Kernel [20]. Streams are regularly stacked under UNIX System V [4]. Stackable layers are used for constructing flexible filesystems in Ficus [18,17] and with an enhanced Vnode interface [11].

Finally, interposition is certainly commonly used on communication channels in message-based systems. For instance, interposition was regularly used in the Accent [35] and V [9] systems.

## 4.2 Analysis of Past Agents

Each of these interposition agents was constructed by hand; almost no code was reused. In particular, whatever boilerplate code was necessary in order to intercept, decode and interpret calls made to the raw system interface typically had to be constructed for each agent. Whatever levels of abstraction that were necessary in order to build each agent were typically constructed from scratch.

Nonetheless, despite these difficulties, a number of applications of interposition have been built, taking advantage of the apparent flexibility and configurability provided by utilizing a layered approach to system implementation. In particular, the fact that today people pay real money for interposition agents that provide enhanced implementations of operating system interfaces (see [31, 37, 32, 46, 28, 39, 45, 49] to name just a few) appears to validate the claim that interposition can be a useful and effective system building paradigm.

# 5 Conclusions

## 5.1 Summary of Results

This research has demonstrated that the system interface can be added to the set of extensible operating system interfaces that can be extended through interposition. Just as interposition is successfully used today with such communication-based facilities as pipes, sockets, and inter-process communication channels, this work has demonstrated that interposition can be successfully applied to the system interface. This work extends the known benefits of interposition to a new domain.

It achieves this result through the use of an interposition toolkit that substantially increases the ease of interposing user code between clients and instances of the system interface. It does so by allowing such code to be written in terms of the high-level objects provided by this interface, rather than in terms of the intercepted system calls themselves.

The following achievements demonstrate this result:

- an implementation of a system call interposition toolkit for the 4.3BSD interface has been built under Mach,
- the toolkit has been used to construct the agents previously described,
- major portions of the toolkit have been reused in multiple agents,
- the agents have gained leverage by utilizing additional functionality provided by the toolkit, substantially simplifying their construction, and
- the performance cost of using the toolkit can be small relative to the cost of the system call interception mechanism and the operations being emulated.

A more detailed presentation of these results can be found in [22].

## 5.2 Contribution

This research has demonstrated both the feasibility and the appropriateness of extending the system interface via interposition. It has shown that while the 4.3BSD system interface is large, it actually contains a small number of abstractions whose behavior is largely independent. Furthermore, it has demonstrated that an interposition toolkit can exploit this property of the system interface. Interposition agents can both achieve acceptable performance and gain substantial implementation leverage through use of an interposition toolkit.

These results should be applicable beyond the initial scope of this research. The interposition toolkit should port to similar systems such as SunOS and UNIX System V. Agents written for the toolkit should also port. The lessons learned in building this interposition toolkit should be applicable to building similar toolkits for dissimilar systems, as explored in [21]. For instance, interposition toolkits could be constructed for such interfaces as the MS-DOS system interface, the Macintosh system interface, and the X Window System interface.

Today, agents are regularly written to be interposed on simple communication-based interfaces such as pipes and sockets. Similarly, the toolkit makes it possible to easily write agents to be interposed on the system interface. Indeed, it is anticipated that the existence of this toolkit will encourage the writing of such agents, many of which would not otherwise have been attempted.

## 5.3 Applicability and Tradeoffs

Interposition is one of many techniques available. As in other domains such as pipes, filters, IPC intermediaries, and network interposition agents, sometimes its use will yield a substantial benefit, while sometimes its use would be inappropriate. As with other layered techniques, peak achievable performance will usually not be achieved. Nonetheless, interposition provides a flexibility and ease of implementation that would not otherwise be available.

## 5.4 Vision and Potential

The potential opened up by interposition is enormous. Agents can be as easy to use as filters. They can be as easy to construct as normal application programs. The system interface can be dynamically customized. Interface changes can be selectively applied. Indeed, interposition provides a powerful addition to the suite of application and system building techniques.

## Acknowledgments

I'd like to extend special thanks to Rick Rashid, Eric Cooper, M. Satyanarayanan (Satya), Doug Tygar, Garret Swart, Brian Bershad, and Patricia Jones. Each of you have have offered helpful suggestions and criticisms which have helped shape and refine this research.

I'd also like to thank Mark Weiser for his valuable comments on ways to improve this paper.

# References

1. M. Accetta, R. Baron, D. Golub, R. Rashid, A. Tevanian, and M. Young. Mach: A new kernel foundation for UNIX development. In *Proc. Summer 1986 USENIX Technical Conference and Exhibition*, June 1986.

2. Apple Computer, Inc. *Macintosh System Software User's Guide Version 6.0*, 1988.

3. AT&T, Customer Information Center, P.O. Box 19901, Indianapolis, IN 46219. *System V Interface Definition, Issue 2*, 1986.

4. AT&T. *Unix System V Release 4.0 Programmer's Reference Manual*, 1989.

5. Robert V. Baron, David Black, William Bolosky, Jonathan Chew, Richard P. Draves, David B. Golub, Richard F. Rashid, Avadis Tevanian, Jr., and Michael Wayne Young. *Mach Kernel Interface Manual*. Carnegie Mellon University School of Computer Science, August 1990.

6. Brian N. Bershad and C. Brian Pinkerton. Watchdogs: Extending the unix filesystem. In *Winter Usenix Conference Proceedings*, Dallas, 1988.

7. D. G. Bobrow, J. D. Burchfiel, D. L. Murphy, and R. S. Tomlinson. TENEX, a paged time sharing system for the PDP-10. *Communications of the ACM*, 15(3):135–143, March 1972.

8. D. R. Brownbridge, L. F. Marshall, and B. Randell. The Newcastle Connection, or UNIXes of the world unite! *Software – Practice and Experience*, 12:1147–1162, 1982.

9. David R. Cheriton. The V distributed system. *Communications of the ACM*, 31(3):314–333, March 1988.

10. F. W. Clegg, G. S.-F. Ho, S. R. Kusmar, and J. R. Sontag. The HP-UX operating system on HP Precision Architecture computers. *Hewlett-Packard Journal*, 37(12):4–22, December 1986.

11. David S. H. Rosenthal. Evolving the vnode interface. In *USENIX Conference Proceedings*, pages 107–118. USENIX, June 1990.

12. Digital Equipment Corporation. *DECSYSTEM-20 Monitor Calls Reference Manual*, January 1978.

13. Digital Equipment Corporation. *ULTRIX Reference Pages, Section 2 System Calls*, 1989.

14. D. Eastlake, R. Greenblatt, J. Holloway, T. Knight, and S. Nelson. ITS 1.5 reference manual. Memorandum no. 161, M.I.T. Artificial Intelligence Laboratory, July 1969. Revised form of ITS 1.4 Reference Manual, June 1968.

15. S. I. Feldman. Make – a program for maintaining computer programs. *Software – Practice and Experience*, 9(4):255–265, 1979.

16. David Golub, Randall Dean, Alessandro Forin, and Richard Rashid. Unix as an application program. In *Summer Usenix Conference Proceedings*, Anaheim, June 1990.

17. Richard G. Guy, John S. Heidemann, Wai Mak, Thomas W. Page, Jr., Gerald J. Popek, and Dieter Rothmeier. Implementation of the Ficus replicated file system. In *USENIX Conference Proceedings*, pages 63–71. USENIX, June 1990.

18. John S. Heidemann. Stackable layers: an architecture for file system development. Master's thesis, University of California, Los Angeles, July 1991. Available as UCLA technical report CSD-910056.

19. J. H. Howard, M. L. Kazar, S. G. Menees, D. A. Nichols, M. Satyanarayanan, R. N. Sidebotham, and M. J. West. Scale and performance in a distributed file system. *ACM Transactions on Computer Systems*, 6(1), February 1988.

20. N. C. Hutchinson and L. L. Peterson. Design of the x-kernel. In *Proceedings of the SIGCOMM '88 Symposium*, pages 65–75, Stanford, CA, August 1988.

21. Michael B. Jones. Inheritance in unlikely places: Using objects to build derived implementations of flat interfaces. In *Proceedings of the Third International Workshop on Object Orientation in Operating Systems*, Paris, September 1992.

22. Michael B. Jones. *Transparently Interposing User Code at the System Interface*. PhD thesis, Carnegie Mellon University, September 1992. Available as Technical Report CMU-CS-92-170.

23. J.J. Kistler and M. Satyanarayanan. Disconnected operation in the coda file system. *ACM Transactions on Computer Systems*, 10(1), February 1992.

24. Philip Koch and David Gelhar. *DTSS System Programmer's Reference Manual*. Dartmouth College, Hanover, NH, November 1986. Kiewit Computation Center TM059.

25. Samuel J. Leffler, Marshall Kirk McKusick, Michael J. Karels, and John S. Quarterman. *The Design and Implementation of the 4.3BSD UNIX Operating System*. Addison-Wesley, October 1990.

26. Paul R. McJones and Garret F. Swart. Evolving the unix system interface to support multithreaded programs. Research Report 21, Digital Equipment Corporation, Systems Research Center, September 1987.

27. M. K. McKusick, W. N. Joy, S. J. Leffler, and R. S. Fabry. A fast file system for unix. *ACM Transactions on Computer Systems*, 2(3), August 1984.

28. Microsoft Corporation. *Microsoft Windows User's Guide*, 1987.

29. Microsoft Corporation. *Microsoft MS-DOS Operating System version 5.0 User's Guide and Reference*, 1991.

30. Lily B. Mummert and M. Satyanarayanan. Efficient and portable file reference tracing in a distributed workstation environment. To be published as a Carnegie Mellon University School of Computer Science technical report, June 1992.

31. Peter Norton Computing, Incorporated. *The Norton Utilities for the Macintosh*. 1990.

32. Now Software, Inc. *Now Utilities: File & Application Management, System Management, and System Extensions*, 1990.

33. R. P. Parmelee, T. I. Peterson, C. C. Tillman, and D. J. Hatfield. Virtual storage and virtual machine concepts. *IBM Systems Journal*, 11(2):99–130, 1972.

34. Michael O. Rabin and J. D. Tygar. An integrated toolkit for operating system security. Technical Report TR-05-87, Harvard University Center for Research in Computing Technology, Cambridge, MA, May 1987. Revised August 1988.

35. R. F. Rashid and G. Robertson. Accent: A communication oriented network operating system kernel. In *Proceedings of the 8th Symposium on Operating Systems Principles*, pages 64–75, December 1981.

36. Brian K. Reid and Janet H. Walker. *SCRIBE Introductory User's Manual*. UNILOGIC, Ltd., third edition, May 1980.

37. Salient Software, Inc. *DiskDoubler User's Manual*, 1991.

38. M. Satyanarayanan, J. J. Kistler, P. Kumar, M. E. Okasaki, E. H. Siegel, and D. C. Steere. Coda: A highly available file system for a distributed workstation environment. *IEEE Transactions on Computers*, 39(4), April 1990.

39. Stac Electronics, Inc. *Stacker 2.1 User Guide*, 1992.

40. Richard M. Stallman. *Using and Porting GNU CC, for version 1.37*. Free Software Foundatation, Inc., 1990.

41. J. E. Stoy and C. Strachey. OS6 – an experimental operating system for a small computer. Part 1: General principles and structure. *Computer Journal*, 15(2):117–124, May 1972.

42. J. E. Stoy and C. Strachey. OS6 – an experimental operating system for a small computer. Part 2: Input/output and filing system. *Computer Journal*, 15(3):195–203, August 1972.

43. Howard Ewing Sturgis. A postmortem for a time sharing system. Xerox Research Report CSL-74-1, Xerox Palo Alto Research Center, January 1974.

44. Sun Microsystems, Inc. *SunOS Reference Manual*, May 1988. Part No. 800-1751-10.

45. Symantec Corporation. *The Norton AntiVirus*, 1991.

46. Symantec Corporation. *Symantec AntiVirus for Macintosh*, 1991.

47. Robert H. Thomas. A resource sharing executive for the ARPANET. In *Proceedings of the AFIPS National Computer Conference*, volume 42, pages 155–163, June 1973.

48. Robert H. Thomas. JSYS traps – a Tenex mechanism for encapsulation of user processes. In *Proceedings of the AFIPS National Computer Conference*, volume 44, pages 351–360, 1975.

49. Trend Micro Devices, Incorporated. *PC-cillin Virus Immune System User's Manual*, 1990.

50. D. Walsh, B. Lyon, G. Sager, J. M. Chang, D. Goldberg, S. Kleiman, T. Lyon, R. Sandberg, and P. Weiss. Overview of the sun network filesystem. In *Winter Usenix Conference Proceedings*, Dallas, 1985.

# Interposition Agents: An Afterword

Interposition Agents were intended to make it easy to produce custom environments in which applications would execute. In 1991, when I first began the work on Interposition Agents, the idea of virtual machine environments was not new, although the idea that many of them could be easily constructed to provide different facilities to or to restrict the behavior of unmodified applications was new.

Computing has changed a lot in the almost eight years that have passed since I developed Interposition Agents. Much of this change is due to the Internet. In this time the Internet has gone from an obscure tool largely only known of and used by Computer Science researchers and those in the computer industry to a new mass communication medium.

One example of these changes is that the frequency with which individuals obtain and use new programs has increased by several orders of magnitude. Formerly most new programs were distributed as shrink-wrapped applications, explicitly downloaded shareware, or via copies on floppy disks passed from person to person (sometimes legally, sometimes not). All required a conscious purchase, download, or install step to be taken by the user.

Compare that to today's Internet. Web users may download and invoke several or even dozens of new programs a day without even being aware that they are doing so. Programs embedded in web pages may be in numerous languages, from Java to JavaScript to Visual Basic Script to native code for Intel, PowerPC, and other machine architectures. Execution environments also vary widely, from interpreted browser scripts to virtual machine environments with various execution restrictions, running both interpreted and Just-In-Time compiled code, to separate processes running with restricted rights, to full native access to the user's execution state and privileges.

The diversity of execution environments looks likely to continue increasing. For instance, software fault isolation allows safety properties of native code to be guaranteed even while executing at near native speeds. Even proof carrying code is at least a theoretical possibility.

This diversity of execution environments brings us back to Interposition Agents. The ability to easily construct a multiplicity of execution environments with different, custom tailored properties, was novel and of some practical use in 1991. But with the advent of routine transparent downloading and execution of code from untrusted sources, the need for building customized and secure environments in which that code executes seems much more compelling today. Interposition Agents are one technique for doing precisely this.

Providing instances of the system call interface with modified or restricted properties is one way of executing untrusted code in a safe manner. To be fair, I will point out that agents built with my particular toolkit, which supported building agents for Mach 2.5-based UNIX systems, could not enforce additional security restrictions since agents ran in the same address spaces as the applications whose execution environments they provided. Nonetheless, as described in the paper, if other system call interception techniques were used that can send system calls to distinct processes, such as those provided by Solaris, System V.4, and some versions of Mach 3.0, agents can make and enforce security guarantees. I believe the particular interception technique to be largely independent of the bulk of the techniques used in the Interposition Agents toolkit.

It is my hope that readers reviewing the Interposition Agents work will have a broadened understanding of the possibilities for easily building a multiplicity of coexisting custom execution environments for application code. With the rise of applets, controls, scripts and the other forms of executable content, the poignancy of the need for such environments seems ever more evident.

– Michael B. Jones, Redmond Washington, November 1998

# J-Kernel: A Capability-Based Operating System for Java

Thorsten von Eicken, Chi-Chao Chang, Grzegorz Czajkowski,
Chris Hawblitzel, Deyu Hu, and Dan Spoonhower

**Abstract.** Safe language technology can be used for protection within a single address space. This protection is enforced by the language's type system, which ensures that references to objects cannot be forged. A safe language alone, however, lacks many features taken for granted in more traditional operating systems, such as rights revocation, thread protection, resource management, and support for domain termination. This paper describes the J-Kernel, a portable Java-based protection system that addresses these issues. J-Kernel protection domains can communicate through revocable capabilities, but are prevented from directly sharing unrevocable object references. A number of micro-benchmarks characterize the costs of language-based protection, and an extensible web and telephony server based on the J-Kernel demonstrates the use of language-based protection in a large application.

## 1 Introduction

The notion of moving code across the network to the most appropriate host for execution has become commonplace. Most often code is moved for efficiency, but sometimes it is for privacy, for fault-tolerance, or simply for convenience. The major concern when moving code is security: the integrity of the host to which it is moved is at risk, as well as the integrity of the computation performed by the moved code itself.

A number of techniques have been used to place protection boundaries between so-called "untrusted code" moved to a host and the remainder of the software running on that host. Traditional operating systems use virtual memory to enforce protection between processes. A process cannot directly read and write other processes' memory, and communication between processes requires traps to the kernel. By limiting the traps an untrusted process can invoke, it can be isolated to varying degrees from other processes on the host. However, there's little point in sending a computation to a host if it cannot interact with other computations there; inter-process communication must be possible.

The major problems encountered when using traditional operating system facilities to isolate untrusted code are deciding whether a specific kernel trap is permissible or not and overcoming the cost of inter-process communication. The semantic level of kernel traps does not generally match the level at which protection policies are specified when hosting untrusted code. In addition, the objects on which the traps act are the ones managed by the kernel and not the ones provided by the hosting environment. Regarding performance, despite a decade of research leading to a large number of fast inter-process communication mechanisms [4, 9, 24], the cost of passing through the kernel and of switching address spaces remains orders of magnitude larger than that of calling a procedure.

In the context of mobile code, language-based protection is an attractive alternative to traditional operating system protection mechanisms. Language-based protection rests on the safety of a language's type system, which ensures that the abstractions provided by the language's types are enforced. A type system acts as a simple access control mechanism: it limits the objects that a computation can access (there is no way to "forge a pointer" to an object), and it limits the operations that code can perform on accessible objects.

The attraction of language-based protection is twofold: precision of protection and performance of communication across protection boundaries. Language-based protection mechanisms allow access rights to be specified with more precision than traditional virtual-memory based mechanisms: the data items to which access is permitted as well as the types of accesses permitted can be specified more finely. For example, in Java, access can be granted precisely to individual objects and even only to certain object fields using the `public` qualifier. In addition, with language-based protection, calls across protection boundaries could potentially be as cheap as simple function calls, enabling as much communication between components as desired without performance drawbacks.

But language-based protection alone does not make an operating system. Several projects [1, 2, 3, 8, 11, 14, 35] have recently described how to build protection domains around components in a safe language environment. The central idea is to use object references (i.e., pointers to objects) as capabilities for cross-domain communication. Object references in safe languages are unforgeable and can thus be used to confer certain rights to the holder(s). In an object-oriented language, the methods applicable to an object are in essence call gates. However, this approach, while both flexible and fast, suffers from two limitations: there is no way to revoke access to object references, and there is no way to track which domain owns which objects. This leads to severe problems with domain termination and resource accounting.

The J-Kernel [16] is an operating system layered on top of a Java Virtual Machine (JVM) that introduces additional mechanisms borrowed from traditional operating systems to provide the features missing at the language level. The goal of the J-Kernel is to define clear boundaries between protection domains, which are called *tasks* in the J-Kernel. This makes resource management and task termination tractable, and simplifies the analysis of inter-task communication. The boundaries are established by limiting the types of objects that can be shared between tasks. In the J-Kernel, only special objects called *capabilities* may be shared; all other objects are confined to single tasks. This allows the J-Kernel to equip capabilities with features like revocation, without adding any overheads to ordinary, non-capability objects.

The main benefits of the J-Kernel are a highly flexible protection model, low overheads for communication between software components, and operating system independence. The current J-Kernel implementation is written entirely in Java [13] and runs on standard Java Virtual Machines (JVMs). This implementation was chosen for practical reasons—Java is emerging as the most widely used general-purpose safe language, and dependable virtual machines are widespread and easy to work with. While Java in itself does allow for multiple protection domains within a single JVMs using the sandbox model for applets, that model is currently very restrictive. It lacks many of the characteristics that are taken for granted in more traditional systems and, in particular, does not provide a clear way for different protection domains to communicate with each other.

The J-Kernel also offers a simple form of resource management based on the JRes interface [7]. The interface allows accounting for resource consumption on per-thread and per-task basis. The resources accounted for are CPU time, heap memory, and network traffic. The implementation of JRes contains a small native component for interfacing to the threads package but is mostly based on Java bytecode rewriting.

Language-based protection does have drawbacks. First, code written in a safe language tends to run more slowly than code written in C or assembly language, and thus the improvement in cross-domain communication may be offset by an overall slowdown. Much of this slowdown is due to current Java just-in-time compilers optimized for fast compile times at the expense of runtime performance. However, even with sophisticated optimization it seems likely that Java programs will not run as fast as C programs. Second, all current language-based protection systems are designed around a single language, which limits developers and doesn't handle legacy code. Software fault isolation [34] and verification of assembly language [26, 27, 28, 32] may someday offer solutions, but are still an active area of research.

## 2   Language-Based Protection Background

In an unsafe language, any code running in an address space can potentially modify any memory location in that address space. While, in theory, it is possible to prove that certain pieces of code only modify a restricted set of memory locations, in practice this is very difficult for languages like C and arbitrary assembly language [5, 27], and cannot be fully automated. In contrast, the type system and the linker in a safe language restrict what operations a particular piece of code is allowed to perform on which memory locations.

The term *namespace* can be used to express this restriction: a namespace is a partial function mapping names of operations to the actions taken when the operations are executed. For example, the operation "read the field out from the class System" may perform different actions depending on what class the name System refers to.

Protection domains around software components can be constructed in a safe language system by providing a separate namespace for each component. Communication between components can then be enabled by introducing sharing among namespaces. Java provides three basic mechanisms for controlling namespaces: selective sharing of object references, static access controls, and selective class sharing.

**Selective Sharing of Object References** Two domains can selectively share references to objects by simply passing each other these references. In the example below, method1 of class A creates two objects of type A, and passes a reference to the first object to method2 of class B. Since method2 acquires a reference to a1, it can perform operations on it, such as incrementing the field j. However, method2 was not given a reference to a2 and thus has no way of performing any operations on it. Java's safety prevents method2 from forging a reference to a2, e.g., by casting an integer holding a2's address to a pointer.

```
class A {
    private int i;
    public int j;
    public static void method1() {
        A a1 = new A();
        A a2 = new A();
        B.method2(a1);
    }
}

class B {
    public static void method2(A arg) {
        arg.j++;
    }
}
```

**Static Access Control** The preceding example demonstrated a very dynamic form of protection—methods can only perform operations on objects to which they have been given a reference. Java also provides static protection mechanisms that limit what operations a method can perform on an object once the method has acquired a reference to that object. A small set of modifiers can change the scope of fields and methods of an object. The two most common modifiers, private and public, respectively limit access to methods in the same class or allow access to methods in any class. In the classes shown above, method2 can access the public field j of the object a1, but not the private field i.

**Selective Class Sharing** Domains can also protect themselves through control of their *class namespace*. To understand this, we need to look at Java's class loading mechanisms. To allow dynamic code loading, Java supports user-defined *class loaders* which load new classes into the virtual machine at run-time. A class loader fetches Java bytecode from some location, such as a file system or a URL, and submits the bytecode to the virtual machine. The virtual machine performs a verification check to make sure that the bytecode is legal, and then integrates the new class into the machine execution. If the bytecode contains references to other classes, the class loader is invoked recursively in order to load those classes as well.

Class loaders can enforce protection by making some classes visible to a domain, while hiding others. For instance, the example above assumed that classes A and B were visible to each other. However, if class A were hidden from class B (i.e. it did not appear in B's class namespace), then even if B obtains a reference to an object of type A, it will not be able to access the fields i and j, despite the fact that j is public.

## 2.1  Straight-Forward Protection Domains: The *Share Anything* Approach

The simple controls over the namespace provided in Java can be used to construct software components that communicate with each other but are still protected from one another. In essence, each component is launched in its own namespace, and can then share any class and any object with other components using the mechanisms described above. While we will continue to use the term *protection domain* informally to refer to these protected components, we will argue that it is impossible to precisely define protection domains when using this approach.

The example below shows a hypothetical file system component that gives objects of type `FileSystemInterface` to its clients to give them access to files. Client domains make cross-domain invocations on the file system by invoking the open method of a `FileSystemInterface` object. By specifying different values for `accessRights` and `rootDirectory` in different objects, the file system can enforce different protection policies for different clients. Static access control ensures that clients cannot modify the `accessRights` and `rootDirectory` fields directly, and one client cannot forge a reference to another client's `FileSystemInterface` object.

```
class FileSystemInterface {
    private int accessRights;
    private Directory rootDirectory;
    public File open(String fileName) {}
}
```

The filesystem example illustrates an approach to protection in Java that resembles a capability system. Several things should be noted about this approach. First, this approach does not require any extensions to the Java language—all the necessary mechanisms already exist. Second, there is very little overhead involved in making a call from one protection domain to another, since a cross-domain call is simply a method invocation, and large arguments can be passed by reference, rather than by copy. Third, references to any object may be shared between domains since the Java language has no way of restricting which references can be passed through a cross-domain method invocation and which cannot.

When we first began to explore protection in Java, this *share anything* approach seemed the natural basis for a protection system, and we began developing on this foundation. However, as we worked with this approach a number of problems became apparent.

**Revocation** The first problem is that access to an object reference cannot be revoked. Once a domain has a reference to an object, it can hold on to it forever. Revocation is important in enforcing the principle of least privilege: without revocation, a domain can hold onto a resource for much longer than it actually needs it.

The most straightforward implementation of revocation uses extra indirection. The example below shows how a revocable version of the earlier class A can be created. Each object of A is wrapped with an object of AWrapper, which permits access to the wrapped object only until the revoked flag is set.

```
class A {
  public int meth1(int a1, int a2) {}
}

class AWrapper {
  private A a;
  private boolean revoked;
  public int meth1(int a1, int a2) {
    if(!revoked) return a.meth1(a1, a2);
    else throw new RevokedException();
  }
  public void revoke() { revoked=true; }
  public AWrapper(A realA) {
    a = realA; revoked = false; }
}
```

In principle, this solves the revocation problem and is efficient enough for most purposes. However, our experience shows that programmers often forget to wrap an object when passing it to another domain. In particular, while it is easy to remember to wrap objects passed as arguments, it is common to forget to wrap other objects to which the first one points. In effect, the default programming model ends up being an unsafe model where objects cannot be revoked. This is the opposite of the desired model: safe by default and unsafe only in special cases.

**Inter-domain Dependencies and Side Effects** As more and more object references are shared between domains, the structure of the protection domains is blurred, because it is unclear from which domains a shared object can be accessed. For the programmer, it becomes difficult to track which objects are shared between protection domains and which are not, and the Java language provides no help as it makes no distinction between the two. Yet, the distinction is critical for reasoning about the behavior of a program running in a domain. Mutable shared objects can be modified at any time in by other domains that have access to the object, and a programmer needs to be aware of this possible activity. For example, a malicious user might try to pass a byte array holding legal bytecode to a class loader (byte arrays, like other objects, are passed by reference to method invocations), wait for the class loader to verify that the bytecode is legal, and then overwrite the legal bytecode with illegal bytecode which would subsequently be executed. The only way the class loader can protect itself from such an attack is to make its own private copy of the bytecode, which is not shared with the user and is therefore safe from malicious modification.

**Domain Termination** The problems associated with shared object references come to a head when we consider what happens when a domain must be terminated. Should all the objects that the domain allocated be released, so that the domain's memory is freed up? Or should objects allocated by the domain be kept alive as long as other domains still hold references to them? ¿From a traditional operating systems perspective, it seems natural that when a process terminates all of its objects disappear, because the address space holding those objects ceases to exist. On the other hand, from a Java perspective, objects can only be deallocated when there are no more reachable references to them.

Either solution to domain termination leads to problems. Deallocating objects when the domain terminates can be extremely disruptive if objects are shared at a fine-grained level and there is no explicit distinction between shared and non-shared objects. For example, consider a Java `String` object, which holds an internal reference to a character array object. Suppose domain 2 holds a `String` object whose internal character array belongs to domain 1. If domain 1 dies, then the `String` will suddenly stop working, and it may be beyond the programmer's ability to deal with disruptions at this level.

On the other hand, if a domain's objects do not disappear when the domain terminates, other problems can arise. First, if a server domain fails, its clients may continue to hold on to the server's objects and attempt to continue using them. In effect, the server's failure is not propagated correctly to the clients. Second, if a client domain holds on to a server's objects, it may indirectly also hold on to other resources, such as open network connections and files. A careful server implementation could explicitly relinquish important resources before exiting, but in the case of unexpected termination this may be impossible. Third, if one domain holds on to another domain's objects after the latter exits, then any memory leaks in the terminated domain may be unintentionally transferred to the remaining one. It is easy to imagine scenarios where recovery from this sort of shared memory leak requires a shutdown of the entire VM.

**Threads** By simply using method invocation for cross-domain calls, the caller and callee both execute in the same thread, which creates several potential hazards. First, the caller must block until the callee returns—there is no way for the caller to gracefully back out of the call without disrupting the callee's execution. Second, Java threads support methods such as `stop`, `suspend`, and `setPriority` that modify the state of a thread. A malicious domain could call another domain and then suspend the thread so that the callee's execution gets blocked, perhaps while holding a critical lock or other resource. Conversely, a malicious callee could hold on to a `Thread` object and modify the state of the thread after execution returns to the caller.

**Resource Accounting** A final problem with the simple protection domains is that object sharing makes it difficult to hold domains accountable for the resources that they use, such as processor time and memory. In particular, it is not clear how to define a domain's memory usage when domains share objects. One definition is that a domain is held accountable for all of the objects that it allocates, for as long as those objects remain alive. However, if shared objects aren't deallocated when the domain exits, a domain might continue to be charged for shared objects that it allocated, long after it has exited. Perhaps the cost of shared objects should be split between all the domains that have references to the object. However, because objects can contain references to other objects, a malicious domain could share an object that looks small, but actually contains pointers to other large objects, so that other domains end up being charged for most of the resources consumed by the malicious domain.

**Summary** The simple approach to protection in Java outlined in this section is both fast and flexible, but it runs into trouble because of its lack of structure. In particular, it fails to clearly distinguish between the ordinary, non-shared object references that constitute a domain's internal state, and the shared object references that are used for cross-domain communication. Nevertheless, this approach is useful to examine, because it illustrates how much protection is possible with the mechanisms provided by the Java language itself. It suggests that the most natural approach to building a protection system in Java is to make good use of the language's inherent protection mechanisms, but to introduce additional structure to fix the problems. The next section presents a system that retains the flavor of the simple approach, but makes a stronger distinction between non-shared and shared objects.

# 3 The J-Kernel

The J-Kernel is a capability-based system that supports multiple, cooperating protection domains, called tasks, which run inside a single Java virtual machine. Capabilities were chosen because they have several advantages over access control lists: (i) they can be implemented naturally in a safe language, (ii) they can enforce the principle of least privilege more easily, and (iii) by avoiding access list lookups, operations on capabilities can execute quickly.

The primary goals of the J-Kernel are:

- a precise definition of tasks, with a clear distinction between objects local to a task and *capability objects* that can be shared between tasks,
- well defined, flexible communication channels between tasks based on capabilities,
- support for revocation for all capabilities, and
- clean semantics of task termination.

To achieve these goals, we were willing to accept higher cross-task communication overheads when compared to the share anything approach. In order to ensure portability, the J-Kernel is implemented entirely as a Java library and requires no native code or modifications to the virtual machine. To accomplish this, the J-Kernel defines a class loader that examines and in some cases modifies user-submitted bytecode before passing it on to the virtual machine. This class loader also generates bytecode at run-time for stub classes used for cross-task communication. Finally, the J-Kernel's class loader substitutes safe versions for some problematic standard classes. With these implementation techniques, the J-Kernel builds a protection architecture that is radically different from the security manager based protection architecture that is the default model on most Java virtual machines.

Protection in the J-Kernel is based on three core concepts—capabilities, tasks, and cross-task calls:

- *Capabilities* are implemented as objects of the class `Capability` and represent handles onto resources in other tasks. A capability can be revoked at any time by the task that created it. All uses of a revoked capability throw an exception, ensuring the correct propagation of failure.
- *Tasks* are represented by the Java class `Task`. Each task has a namespace that it controls as well as a set of threads. When a task terminates, all of the capabilities that it created are revoked, so that all of its memory may be freed, thus avoiding the task termination problems that plagued the share anything approach.
- *Cross-task calls* are performed by invoking methods of capabilities obtained from other tasks. The J-Kernel's class loader interposes a special calling convention [1] for these calls: arguments and return values are passed by reference if they are also capabilities, but they are passed by copy if they are primitive types or non-capability objects. When an object is copied, these rules are applied recursively to the data in the object's fields, so that a deep copy of the object is made. The effect is that only capabilities can be shared between tasks and references to regular objects are confined to single tasks.

## 3.1   J-Kernel Implementation

The J-Kernel's implementation of capabilities and cross-task calls relies heavily on Java's *interface classes*. An interface class defines a set of method signa-

---

[1] The standard Java calling convention passes primitive data types (int, float, etc.) by copy and object data types by reference.

tures without providing their implementation. Other classes that provide corresponding implementations can then be declared to *implement* the interface. Normally interface classes are used to provide a limited form of multiple inheritance (properly called interface inheritance) in that a class can implement multiple interfaces. In addition, Sun's remote method invocation (RMI) specification [19] "pioneered" the use of interfaces as compiler annotations. Instead of using a separate interface definition language (IDL), the RMI specification simply uses interface classes that are flagged to the RMI system in that they extend the class Remote. Extending Remote has no effect other than directing the RMI system to generate appropriate stubs and marshalling code.

Because of the similarity of the J-Kernel's cross-task calls to remote method invocations, we have integrated much of Sun's RMI specification into the capability interface. The example below shows a simple *remote interface* and a class that implements this remote interface, both written in accordance with Sun's RMI specification.

```
// interface class shared with other tasks
interface ReadFile extends Remote {
   byte readByte() throws RemoteException;
   byte[] readBytes(int nBytes)
     throws RemoteException;
}

// implementation hidden from other tasks
class ReadFileImpl implements ReadFile {
   public byte readByte() {...}
   public byte[] readBytes(int nBytes) {...}
   ...
}
```

To create a capability in the J-Kernel, a task calls the create method of the class Capability, passing as an argument a target object that implements one or more remote interfaces. The create method returns a new capability, which extends the class Capability and implements all of the remote interfaces that the target object implements. The capability can then be passed to other tasks, which can cast it to one of its remote interfaces, and invoke the methods this interface declares. In the example below task 1 creates a capability and adds it to the system-wide repository (the repository is a name service allowing tasks to publish capabilities). Task 2 retrieves the capability from the repository, and makes a cross-task invocation on it.

```
// Task 1:
// instantiate new ReadFileImpl object
ReadFileImpl target = new ReadFileImpl();
// create a capability for the new object
Capability c = Capability.create(target);
// add it to repository under some name
Task.getRepository().bind(
    "Task1ReadFile", c);

// Task 2:
// extract capability
Capability c = Task.getRepository()
  .lookup("Task1ReadFile");
// cast it to ReadFile, and invoke remote method
byte b = ((ReadFile) c).readByte();
```

Essentially, a capability object is a wrapper object around the original target object. The code for each method in the wrapper switches to the task that created the capability, makes copies of all non-capability arguments according to the special calling convention, and then invokes the corresponding method in the target object. When the target object's method returns, the wrapper switches back to the caller task, makes a copy of the return value if it is not a capability, and returns.

**Local-RMI Stubs** The simple looking call to Capability.create in fact hides most of the complexity of traditional RPC systems. Internally, create automatically generates a stub class at run-time for each target class. This avoids off-line stub generators and IDL files, and it allows the J-Kernel to specialize the stubs to invoke the target methods with minimal overhead. Besides switching tasks, stubs have three roles: copying arguments, supporting revocation, and protecting threads.

By default, the J-Kernel uses Java's built-in serialization features [19] to copy an argument: the J-Kernel serializes an argument into an array of bytes, and then deserializes the byte array to produce a fresh copy of the argument. While this is convenient because many built-in Java classes are serializable, it involves a substantial overhead. Therefore, the J-Kernel also provides a fast copy mechanism, which makes direct copies of objects and their fields without using an intermediate byte array. The fast copy implementation automatically generates specialized copy code for each class that the user declares to be a fast copy class. For cyclic or directed graph data structures, a user can request that the fast copy code use a hash table to track object copying, so that objects in the data structure are not copied more than once (this slows down copying, though, so by default the copy code does not use a hash table).

Each generated stub contains a revoke method that sets the internal pointer to the target object to null. Thus all capabilities can be revoked and doing so makes the target object eligible for garbage collection, regardless of how many other tasks hold a reference to the capability. This prevents tasks from holding on to garbage in other tasks.

In order to protect the caller's and callee's threads from each other, the generated stubs provide the illusion of switching threads. Because most virtual machines map Java threads directly onto kernel threads it is not practical to actually switch threads: as shown in the next subsection this would slow down cross-task calls substantially. A fast user-level threads package might solve this problem, but would require modifications to the virtual machine, and would thus limit the J-Kernel's portability. The compromise struck in the current implementation uses a single Java thread for both the caller and callee but prevents direct access to that thread to avoid security problems.

Conceptually, the J-Kernel divides each Java thread into multiple segments, one for each side of a cross-task call. The J-Kernel class loader then hides the system Thread class that manipulates Java threads, and interposes its own with an identical interface but an implementation that only acts on the local thread segment. Thread modification methods such as stop and suspend act on thread segments rather than Java threads, which prevents the caller from modifying the callee's thread segment and vice-versa. This provides the illusion of thread-switching cross-task calls, without the overhead for actually switching threads. The illusion is not totally convincing, however—cross-task calls really do block, so there is no way for the caller to gracefully back out of one if the callee doesn't return.

**Class Name Resolvers** In the standard Java applet architecture, applets have very little access to Java's class loading facilities. In contrast, J-Kernel tasks are given considerable control over their own class loading. Each task has its own class namespace that maps names to classes. Classes may be local to a task, in which case they are only visible in that task's namespace or they may be shared between multiple tasks, in which case they are visible in many namespaces. A task's namespace is controlled by a user-defined *resolver*, which is queried by the J-Kernel whenever a new class name is encountered. A task can use a resolver to load new bytecode into the system, or it can make use of existing shared classes. After a task has loaded new classes into the system, it can share these classes with other tasks if it wants, by making a SharedClass capability available to other tasks [2].

Shared classes are the basis for cross-task communication: tasks must share remote interfaces and fast copy classes to establish common methods and argument types for cross-task calls. Allowing user-defined shared classes makes the cross-task communication architecture extensible; standard Java security architectures only allow pre-defined "system classes" to be shared between tasks, and thus limit the expressiveness of cross-task communication.

---

[2] Shared classes (and, transitively, the classes that shared classes refer to) are not allowed to have static fields, to prevent sharing of non-capability objects through static fields. In addition, to ensure consistency between domains, two domains that share a class must also share other classes referenced by that class.

Ironically, the J-Kernel needs to *prevent* the sharing of some system classes. For example, the file system and thread classes present security problems. Others contain resources that need to be defined on a per-task basis: the class System, for example, contains static fields holding the standard input/output streams. In other words, the "one size fits all" approach to class sharing in most Java security models is simply not adequate, and a more flexible model is essential to make the J-Kernel safe, extensible, and fast.

In general, the J-Kernel tries to minimize the number of system classes visible to tasks. Classes that would normally be loaded as system classes (such as classes containing native code) are usually loaded into a privileged task in the J-Kernel, and are accessed through cross-task communication, rather than through direct calls to system classes. For instance, we have developed a task for file system access that is called using cross-task communication. To keep compatibility with the standard Java file API, we have also written alternate versions of Java's standard file classes, which are just stubs that make the necessary cross-task calls. (This is similar to the interposition proposed by [35]).

The J-Kernel moves functionality out of the system classes and into tasks for the same reasons that micro-kernels move functionality out of the operating system kernel. It makes the system as a whole extensible, i.e., it is easy for any task to provide alternate implementations of most classes that would normally be system classes (such as file, network, and thread classes). It also means that each such service can implement its own security policy. In general, it leads to a cleaner overall system structure, by enforcing a clear separation between different modules. Java libraries installed as system classes often have undocumented and unpredictable dependencies on one another [3]. Richard Rashid warned that the UNIX kernel had "become a 'dumping ground' for every new feature or facility"[30]; it seems that the Java system classes are becoming a similar dumping ground.

## 3.2 J-Kernel Micro-Benchmarks

To evaluate the performance of the J-Kernel mechanisms we measured a number of micro-benchmarks on the J-Kernel as well as on a number of reference systems. Unless otherwise indicated, all micro-benchmarks were run on 200Mhz Pentium-Pro systems running Windows NT 4.0 and the Java virtual machines used were Microsoft's VM (MS-VM) and Sun's VM with Symantec's JIT compiler (Sun-VM). All numbers are averaged over a large number of iterations.

**Null LRMI** Table 1 dissects the cost of a null cross-task call (null LRMI) and compares it to the cost of a regular method invocation, which takes a few tens of nanoseconds. The J-Kernel null LRMI takes 60x to 180x longer than

---

[3] For instance, Microsoft's implementation of java.io.File depends on java.io.DataInputStream, which depends on com.ms.lang.SystemX, which depends on classes in the abstract windowing toolkit. Similarly, java.lang.Object depends transitively on almost every standard library class in the system.

a regular method invocation. With MS-VM, a significant fraction of the cost lies in the interface method invocation necessary to enter the stub. Additional overheads include the synchronization cost when changing thread segments (two lock acquire/release pairs per call) and the overhead of looking up the current thread. Overall, these three operations account for about 70% of the cross-task call on MS-VM and about 80% on Sun-VM. Given that the implementations of the three operations are independent, we expect better performance in a system that includes the best of both VMs.

| Operation | MS-VM | Sun-VM |
|---|---|---|
| Regular Method invocation | $0.04\mu s$ | $0.03\mu s$ |
| Interface method invocation | $0.54\mu s$ | $0.05\mu s$ |
| Thread info lookup | $0.55\mu s$ | $0.29\mu s$ |
| Acquire/release lock | $0.20\mu s$ | $1.91\mu s$ |
| J-Kernel LRMI | $2.22\mu s$ | $5.41\mu s$ |

**Table 1.** Cost of null method invocations

To provide a comparison of the J-Kernel LRMI to traditional OS cross-task calls, Table 2 shows the cost of several forms of local RPC available on NT. *NT-RPC* is the standard, user-level RPC facility. *COM out-of-proc* is the cost of a null interface invocation to a COM component located in a separate process on the same machine. The communication between two fully protected components is at least a factor of 3000 from a regular C++ invocation (shown as *COM in-proc*). For a comparison to the local RPC performance of research operating systems see the Related Work section.

| Form of RPC | Time |
|---|---|
| NT-RPC | $109\mu s$ |
| COM out-of-proc | $99\mu s$ |
| COM in-proc | $0.03\mu s$ |

**Table 2.** Local RPC costs using NT mechanisms

**Threads** Table 3 shows the cost of switching back and forth between two Java threads in MS-VM and Sun-VM. The base cost of two context switches between NT kernel threads (*NT-base*) is $8.6\mu s$, and Java introduces an additional 1-2$\mu s$ of overhead. This confirms that switching Java threads during cross-task calls would add a significant cost to J-Kernel LRMI.

**Argument Copying** Table 4 compares the cost of copying arguments during a J-Kernel LRMI using Java serialization and using the J-Kernel's fast-copy

| NT-base | MS-VM | Sun-VM |
|---------|-------|--------|
| 8.6μs | 9.8μs | 10.2μs |

**Table 3.** Cost of a double thread switch using regular Java threads

mechanism. By making direct copies of the objects and their fields without using an intermediate Java byte-array, the fast-copy mechanism improves the performance of LRMI substantially—more than an order of magnitude for large arguments. The performance difference between the second and third rows (both copy the same number of bytes) is due to the cost of object allocation and invocations of the copying routine for every object.

| Number x size | MS-VM | | Sun-VM | |
|---------------|-----------|-----------|-----------|-----------|
| of objects | Serializ. | Fast-copy | Serializ. | Fast-Copy |
| 1 x 10 bytes | 104μs | 4.8μs | 331μs | 13.7μs |
| 1 x 100 bytes | 158μs | 7.7μs | 509μs | 18.5μs |
| 10 x 10 bytes | 193μs | 23.3μs | 521μs | 79.3μs |
| 1 x 1000 bytes | 633μs | 19.2μs | 2105μs | 66.7μs |

**Table 4.** Cost of Argument Copying during LRMI

In summary, the micro-benchmark results are encouraging in that the cost of a cross-task call is 50x lower in the J-Kernel than in NT. However, the J-Kernel cross-task call still incurs a stiff penalty over a plain method invocation.

Inspection of the critical code paths shows that in the call path itself, the acquisition of a lock and the management of the thread state contribute most to the cost. While aggressive inlining could reduce that by perhaps a factor of 2x, the high cost of lock operations in modern processors will keep the cost significant. The largest cost of most cross-task calls is likely to be in the copying of the arguments. For small objects the allocation (and eventual garbage collection) dominates the cost and appears difficult to optimize by more than a small factor. A more promising avenue would be to optimize the passing of arrays of primitive (i.e., non-pointer) types by simply sharing the array. This clearly changes the semantics, but does not compromise the integrity of the J-Kernel.

## 4 An Extensible Web and Telephony Server

One of the driving applications for the J-Kernel is an extensible web and telephony server. The goal is to allow users to dynamically extend the functionality of the server by uploading Java programs, called *servlets* [21], that customize the processing of HTTP requests and telephone calls. Applications that integrate the two forms of communication are of particular interest.

The extensible web and telephony server is made possible by the ongoing merger of networking and telephony. The resulting new wave of commodity telephony equipment is designed to be controlled by a standard workstation. Examples are telephone interface cards with 2 to 24 analog telephone lines and the DSPs to handle real-time tasks, and full telephone switches (PBXs) that can be controlled over a LAN. On the software side, standard telephony APIs (e.g., Windows' TAPI or Java's JTAPI) allow programs to control the equipment in a relatively portable way.

The upshot of these developments is that today a single commodity PC can provide integrated communication services that use both the Internet and the telephone system. This section describes a prototype integrated web and telephony server called the J-Server, which uses the J-Kernel to support the extensibility necessary in this setting. The J-Server core manages a hierarchical namespace of resources where each resource can correspond either to a URL or to a telephone number. Users of the system can upload programs (called servlets) to the J-Server and attach each servlet to one or more resources. The servlets can then handle all HTTP requests and telephone calls that are sent to the resources. Furthermore, servlets may communicate with one another, so that one servlet may provide a service to another servlet. For example, a servlet that uses speech recognition to determine the nature of a call might need to dispatch the call to another servlet once it is clear whom the call is for.

In general, our experience with using these servers has shown that they place high demands on the extension mechanism:

- Protection is important because multiple users create their own independent webs.
- Failure isolation is important because webs are continuously expanded and new features must not disrupt old ones.
- Clean servlet termination is essential.
- Extensions must be able to call other extensions, and these cross-task calls should be cheap so that they can occur frequently.
- Resource management and accounting are necessary.

Our J-Server setup uses two off-the-shelf products: Lucent Technologies DEFINITY Enterprise Communications Server and the Dialogic Dialog/4 voice interface. At the core, the DEFINITY server is a Private Branch Exchange (PBX), i.e. a telephone switch, augmented by an Ethernet-based network controller. The network controller in this PBX allows the routing of telephone calls to be monitored and controlled from a PC over the LAN. Lucent provides a Java interface allowing the J-Server to communicate with the PBX using the Java Telephony API (JTAPI) [18].

The Dialog/4 Voice Processing Board, from Dialogic Corporation, provides four half-duplex, analog telephone interfaces and includes a digital signal processor (DSP) to play and record audio, and to detect and transmit DTMF (dual-tone multi-frequency) signals. Using two Dialog/4 boards, the J-Server is able to make eight simultaneous half-duplex voice connections to the telephone network.

## 4.1 Extensible Server Architecture

Each servlet in the J-Server runs as a separate task to isolate it from the J-Server core as well as from other servlets. This setup allows new servlets to be introduced into the system or crashed ones to be reloaded without disturbing the server operation. The J-Server core is also divided into several tasks. One task dispatches incoming HTTP requests to servlets. Three tasks handle telephony: the first is responsible for communicating with the PBX via JTAPI, the second deals with the Dialogic voice processing boards, and the third is in charge of dispatching telephony events to the appropriate servlets.

During operation, the J-Server performs a large number of cross-task calls to pass events and data around. This is best illustrated by looking at the handling of a telephone call by a simple voice-mail servlet. When a telephone call reaches the PBX, an event is sent to the J-Server via JTAPI and is handled by the task in charge of PBX events. This task then sends the event information to the telephony dispatch task, which in turn passes the information to the appropriate servlet. The servlet instructs the J-Server to route the call to one of the telephone lines connected to the Dialogic card. At this point, the voice processing task begins generating events, starting with a "ringing" event. These events are passed to the dispatching task, and then on to the appropriate servlet. The servlet proceeds to take the telephone off hook, and to start playing audio data. In this application, the data is passed from the servlet task to the dispatch task and then on to the voice task in one large chunk. When the voice channel has finished playing the audio sample, it alerts the servlet, which, in turn, responds by creating an appropriate response object. When the calling party hangs up, the servlet instructs the voice channel to stop recording. The servlet waits for all recorded data and then saves the sample as a Microsoft WAVE file for later playback.

## 4.2 Performance

We conducted a set of experiments on the J-Server to evaluate the performance of the J-Kernel in an application setting. The experiments were carried out on a 300MHz Pentium II, running Windows NT 4.0. The Java virtual machine used was Microsoft's VM version 1.1, with SDK 2.01.

Two tests measure the costs of cross-task calls and the frequency of such calls in the J-Server. The first test, *Half-Duplex Conversation*, mimics a 40-second telephone conversation between two people, each of whom is simulated by a servlet. The call initiator "speaks" for two seconds, then "listens" for two seconds, then "speaks" again, while the receiver is doing the opposite. "Speaking" involves sending uncompressed audio data in one kilobyte segments (which is equivalent to 1/8sec of conversation) to the voice processing task, where they are presented to the Dialogic driver, which plays the data over the phone line. "Listening" consists of recording data (in 512byte segments), collecting the data to accumulate two seconds worth of audio (16Kbytes) and writing it out to the disk in a standard, uncompressed WAVE file format.

The second test, *VoiceBox* Listing, measures the performance of the HTTP component of J-Server. Using a web browser, a user makes a request to the servlet, which displays the contents of a voice box directory, formatted as an HTML page. Cross-task calls are made from the HTTP dispatching task to the servlet task. In addition, a simple authentication servlet is used to verify the user's password, resulting in another cross-task call.

Table 5 summarizes the results. The *Initiator* and *Responder* columns correspond to two parties involved in *HalfDuplex Conversation*, while the *Listing* column corresponds to the servlet fetching and formatting information about voice messages. The first five rows present the actual measurement values; the remaining rows contain derived information.

| | Half-duplex conversation | | HTTP |
| | Initiator | Responder | Listing |
|---|---|---|---|
| Total CPU time | 1503 ms | 1062 ms | 18.5 ms |
| Total number of cross-task calls | 3085 | 2671 | 8 |
| Total cross-task data transfer | 962304 bytes | 984068 bytes | 3596 bytes |
| Total cross-task call overhead | 9.37 ms | 8.71 ms | 0.037 ms |
| Total cross-task data copy time | 2.91 ms | 2.58 ms | 0.01 ms |
| Average CPU time/cross-task call | 3.0 $\mu$s | 3.3 $\mu$s | 4.6 $\mu$s |
| Average bytes/call | 312 bytes | 368 bytes | 450 bytes |
| Average copy overhead/call | 31 % | 30 % | 27 % |
| Average copy bandwidth | 331 MB/s | 381 MB/s | 360 MB/s |
| Relative cross-task call overhead | 0.62 % | 0.82 % | 0.20 % |

**Table 5.** Selected performance measurements of *HalfDuplex Conversation* and *VoiceBox Listing*.

In all cases the overheads of crossing tasks (which include the cost of copying arguments and then return values) are below 1% of the total consumed CPU time. On the average, crossing tasks costs between 3$\mu$s-4.6$\mu$s and an average call transfers between 312 (*Initiator*) to 450 (*Listing*) bytes. The cost of copying data accounts for 27%-31% of an average cross-task call. This suggests that overheads of crossing tasks in real applications when no data transfer is involved are between 2.1$\mu$s-3.3$\mu$s. This is in contrast to the cost of a null cross-task call, measured in an isolated tight loop: 1.35$\mu$s.

The achieved bandwidth of copying data across tasks is sufficient for this application. About 85% of the data transferred across tasks in the two experiments is stored in byte arrays of 0.5Kbytes and 1Kbytes; the remaining data are either references to capabilities, primitive data types or data inside objects of the type java.lang.String. The average copying bandwidth is 330-380Mbytes/s, which is over 50% of the peak data copying bandwidth of 630Mbytes/s achieved in Java with a tight loop of calls to System.arraycopy().

With respect to scalability, our current hardware configuration supports at most eight simultaneous half-duplex connections. Every connection results in an additional 1.7%-2.3% increase in the CPU load. From this we estimate that, given enough physical lines, our system could support about 50 simultaneous half-duplex connections before reaching full CPU utilization. Since the J-Server demands modest amounts of physical memory, permanent storage and network resources, CPU is the bottleneck from the perspective of scaling the system, so the range of 50 simultaneous half-duplex connections is very likely to be achievable in practice.

While analyzing the performance, it is important to note that Java introduces non-obvious overheads. For instance, in the *Listing* experiment, a large part of the 18.5ms of CPU time can be accounted for as follows. About seven milliseconds are spent in the network and file system Java classes and native protocol stacks. Roughly eight milliseconds are spent performing string concatenations in one particular part of the *VoiceBox Listing* servlet (Java string processing is very slow under MS JVM). These overheads, which are introduced by Java and not easy to avoid, dwarf the relative costs of crossing task boundaries and lead to conclusions that may be not true if the JVM performance improves dramatically.

One conclusion, based on the current performance numbers, is that in large applications similar to J-Server, the task boundaries crossing overheads are very small relative to the total execution time and further optimizing them will bring barely noticeable performance improvements. Second, in applications where crossing tasks is frequent and optimizing cross-task calls actually matters, on the average 30% of task crossing overheads can be removed by wrapping data structures and arrays in capabilities. This avoids copying data between tasks but comes at the expense of increased programming effort. It is important to stress that the conclusions are drawn from observing several experiments based on a single, although complex and realistic, application. More study is needed to fully understand application behavior on top of Java in general and the J-Kernel in particular.

# 5   Related Work

The Alta and GVM systems [1] developed at the University of Utah are closely related to the J-Kernel. The motivation is to implement a process model in Java, which provides memory protection, control over scheduling, and resource management. Both systems are implemented by modifying a JVM (the free Kaffe JVM is used). In GVM each Java process receives separate threads, heap, and classes. Sharing is only allowed between a process and a special system heap. This invariant is enforced using a write barrier. Each heap is garbage collected separately and a simple reference counting mechanism is used for cross-heap references. Alta implements the nested process model used in the Fluke microkernel [10]. Child processes of the same parent process can share data structures directly: the resources used are attributed to the parent. While the inter-process communication costs of Alta and GVM are higher than in the J-Kernel (see [1]), the custom JVM modifications allow both GVM and Alta to take control of thread scheduling and to be more precise in resource management.

Several major vendors have proposed extensions to the basic Java sandbox security model for applets [20, 25, 29]. For instance, Sun's JDK 1.1 added a notion of authentication, based on code signing, while the JDK 1.2 adds a richer structure for authorization, including classes that represent permissions and methods that perform access control checks based on stack introspection [12]. JDK 1.2 "protection domains" are implicitly created based on the origin of the code, and on its signature. This definition of a protection domain is closer to a user in Unix, while the J-Kernel's task is more like a *process* in Unix. Balfanz et al. [2] define an extension to the JDK which associates domains with users running particular code, so that a domain becomes more like a process. However, if domains are able to share objects directly, revocation, resource management, and domain termination still need to be addressed in the JDK.

JDK 1.2 system classes are still lumped into a monolithic "system domain", but a new classpath facilitates loading local applications with class loaders rather than as system classes. However, only system classes may be shared between domains that have different class loaders, which limits the expressiveness of communication between domains. In contrast, the J-Kernel allows tasks to share classes without requiring these tasks to use the same class loader. In the future work section, Gong et al. [12] mentions separating current system classes (such as file classes) into separate tasks, in accordance with the principle of least privilege. The J-Kernel already moves facilities for files and networking out of the system classes and into separate tasks.

A number of related safe-language systems are based on the idea of using object references as capabilities. Wallach et. al. [35] describe three models of Java security: type hiding (making use of dynamic class loading to control a domain's namespace), stack introspection, and capabilities. They recommended a mix of these three techniques. The E language from Electric Communities [8] is an extension of Java targeted towards distributed systems. E's security architecture is capability based; programmers are encouraged to use object references as the fundamental building block for protection. Odyssey [11] is a system that supports mobile agents written in Java; agents may share Java objects directly. Hagimont et al. [14] describe a system to support capabilities defined with special IDL files. All three of these systems allow non-capability objects to be passed directly between domains, and generally correspond to the share anything approach described in Section 2. They do not address the issues of revocation, domain termination, thread protection, or resource accounting.

The SPIN project [3] allows safe Modula-3 code to be downloaded into the operating system kernel to extend the kernel's functionality. SPIN has a particularly nice model of dynamic linking to control the namespace of different extensions. Since it uses Modula-3 pointers directly as capabilities, the limitations of the share anything approach apply to it.

Several recent software-based protection techniques do not rely on a particular high level language like Java or Modula-3. Typed assembly language [26] pushes type safety down to the assembly language level, so that code written at the assembly language level can be statically type checked and verified as safe.

Software fault isolation [34] inserts run-time "sandboxing" checks into binary executables to restrict the range of memory that is accessible to the code. With suitable optimizations, sandboxed code can run nearly as fast as the original binary on RISC architectures. However, it is not clear how to extend optimized sandboxing techniques to CISC architectures, and sandboxing cannot enforce protection at as fine a granularity as a type system. Proof carrying code [27, 28] generalizes many different approaches to software protection—arbitrary binary code can be executed as long as it comes with a proof that it is safe. While this can potentially lead to safety without overhead, generating the proofs for a language as complex as Java is still a research topic.

The J-Kernel enforces a structure that is similar to traditional capability systems [22, 23]. Both the J-Kernel and traditional capability systems are founded on the notion of unforgeable capabilities. In both, capabilities name objects in a context-independent manner, so that capabilities can be passed from one domain to another. The main difference is that traditional capability systems used virtual memory or specialized hardware support to implement capabilities, while the J-Kernel uses language safety. The use of virtual memory or specialized hardware led either to slow cross-domain calls, to high hardware costs, or to portability limitations. Using Java as the basis for the J-Kernel simplifies many of the issues that plagued traditional capability systems. First, unlike systems based on capability lists, the J-Kernel can store capabilities in data structures, because capabilities are implemented as Java objects. Second, rights amplification [22] is implicit in the object-oriented nature of Java: invocations are made on methods, rather than functions, and methods automatically acquire rights to their *self* parameter. In addition, selective class sharing can be used to amplify other parameters. Although many capability systems did not support revocation, the idea of using indirection to implement revocation goes back to Redell [31]. The problems with resource accounting were also on the minds of implementers of capability systems—Wulf et. al. [36] point out that "No one 'owns' an object in the Hydra scheme of things; thus it's very hard to know to whom the cost of maintaining it should be charged".

Single-address operating systems, like Opal [6] and Mungi [17], remove the address space borders, allowing for cheaper and easy sharing of data between processes. Opal and Mungi were implemented on architectures offering large address spaces (64-bit) and used password capabilities as the protection mechanism. Password capabilities are protected from forgery by a combination of encryption and sparsity.

Several research operating systems support very fast inter-process communication. Recent projects, like L4, Exokernel, and Eros, provide fine-tuned implementations of selected IPC mechanisms, yielding an order of magnitude improvement over traditional operating systems. The systems are carefully tuned and aggressively exploit features of the underlying hardware.

The L4 $\mu$-kernel [15] rigorously aims for minimality and is designed from scratch, unlike first-generation $\mu$-kernels, which evolved from monolithic OS kernels. The system was successful at dispelling some common misconceptions about $\mu$-kernel performance limitations. Exokernel [9] shares L4's goal of being an ultra-fast "minimalist" kernel, but is also concerned with untrusted loadable modules (similar to the SPIN project). Untrusted code is given efficient control over hardware resources by separating management from protection. The focus of the EROS [33] project is to support orthogonal persistence and real-time computations. Despite quite different objectives, all three systems manage to provide very fast implementations of IPC with comparable performance, as shown in Table 6. A short explanation of the 'operation' column is needed. Round-trip IPC is the time taken for a call transferring one byte from one process to another and returning to the caller; Exokernel's protected control transfer installs the callee's processor context and starts execution at a specified location in the callee.

| System | Operation | Platform | Time |
|--------|-----------|----------|------|
| L4 | Round-trip IPC | P5-133 | $1.82\mu s$ |
| Exokernel | Protected control transfer (r/t) | DEC-5000 | $2.40\mu s$ |
| Eros | Round-trip IPC | P5-120 | $4.90\mu s$ |
| J-Kernel | Method invocation with 3 args | P5-133 | $3.77\mu s$ |

Table 6. Comparison with selected kernels.

The results are contrasted with a 3-argument method invocation in the J-Kernel. The J-Kernel's performance is comparable with the three very fast systems. It is important to note that L4, Exokernel and Eros are implemented as a mix of C and assembly language code, while J-Kernel consists of Java classes without native code support. Improved implementations of JVMs and JITs are likely to enhance the performance of the J-Kernel.

## 6 Conclusion

The J-Kernel project explores the use of safe language technology to construct robust protection domains. The advantages of using language-based protection are portability and good cross-domain performance. The most straightforward implementation of protection in a safe language environment is to use object references directly as capabilities. However, problems of revocation, domain termination, thread protection, and resource accounting arise when non-shared object references are not clearly distinguished from shared capabilities. We argue that a more structured approach is needed to solve these problems: only capabilities can be shared, and non-capability objects are confined to single domains.

We developed the J-Kernel system, which demonstrates how the issues of object sharing, class sharing, thread protection, and resource management can be addressed. As far as we know, the J-Kernel is the first Java-based system that integrates solutions to these issues into a single, coherent protection system. Our experience using the J-Kernel to extend the Microsoft IIS web server and to implement an extensible web and telephony server leads us to believe that a safe language system can achieve both robustness and high performance.

Because of its portability and flexibility, language-based protection is a natural choice for a variety of extensible applications and component-based systems. From a performance point of view, safe language techniques are competitive with fast microkernel systems, but do not yet achieve their promise of making cross-domain calls as cheap as function calls. Implementing a stronger model of protection than the straightforward share anything approach leads to thread management costs and copying costs, which increase the overhead to much more than a function call. Fortunately, there clearly is room for improvement. We found that many small operations in Java, such as allocating an object, invoking an interface method, and manipulating a lock were slower than necessary on current virtual machines. Java just-in-time compiler technology is still evolving. We expect that as virtual machine performance improves, the J-Kernel's cross-domain performance will also improve. In the meantime, we will continue to explore optimizations possible on top of current off-the-shelf virtual machines, as well as to examine the performance benefits that customizing the virtual machine could bring.

**Acknowledgments** Portions of this paper were originally published by the USENIX Association in *Proceedings of the USENIX 1998 Annual Technical Conference*, New Orleans, Louisiana, June 15-19, 1998.

The authors would like to thank Greg Morrisett, Fred Schneider, Fred Smith, Lidong Zhou, and the anonymous reviewers for their comments and suggestions. This research is funded by DARPA ITO Contract ONR-N00014-95-1-0977, NSF CAREER Award CCR-9702755, a Sloan Foundation fellowship, and Intel Corp. hardware donations. Chi-Chao Chang is supported in part by a doctoral fellowship (200812/94-7) from CNPq/Brazil.

# References

1. G. Back, P. Tullmann, L. Stoller, W. C. Hsieh, J. Lepreau. *Java Operating Systems: Design and Implementation*. Technical Report UUCS-98-015, Department of Computer Science, University of Utah, August, 1998.
2. D. Balfanz, and Gong, L. *Experience with Secure Multi-Processing in Java*. Technical Report 560-97, Department of Computer Science, Princeton University, September, 1997.
3. B. Bershad, S. Savage, P. Pardyak, E. Sirer, M. Fiuczynski, D. Becker, S. Eggers, and C. Chambers. *Extensibility, Safety and Performance in the SPIN Operating System*. 15th ACM Symposium on Operating Systems Principles, p.267-284, Copper Mountain, CO, December 1995.
4. B. Bershad, T. Anderson, E. Lazowska, and H. Levy. *Lightweight Remote Procedure Call*. 12th ACM Symposium on Operating Systems Principles, p. 102-113, Lichtfield Park, AZ, December 1989.
5. R. S. Boyer, and Y. Yu. *Automated proofs of object code for a widely used microprocessor*. J. ACM 43(1), p. 166-192, January 1996.
6. J. Chase, H. Levy, E. Lazowska, and M. Baker-Harvey. *Lightweight Shared Objects in a 64-Bit Operating System*. ACM Object-Oriented Programming Systems, Languages, and Applications (OOPSLA), October 1992.

7. G. Czajkowski and T. von Eicken. *JRes: A Resource Accounting Interface for Java*. To appear in proceedings of the 1998 Conference on Object-Oriented Programming Languages, Systems, and Applications.

8. Electric Communities. *The E White Paper*. http://www.communities.com/products/tools/e.

9. R. Engler, M. Kaashoek, and J. James O'Toole. *Exokernel: An Operating System Architecture for Application-Level Resource Management*. 15th ACM Symposium on Operating Systems Principles, p. 251266, Copper Mountain, CO, December 1995.

10. B. Ford, G. Back, G. Benson, J. Lepreau, A. Lin, and O. Shivers. *The Fluke OSKit: A substrate for OS and language research*. In Proc. Of the 16th SOSP, pp. 38-51, St. Malo, France, October 1997.

11. General Magic. *Odyssey*. http://www.genmagic.com/agents.

12. L. Gong, and Schemers, R. *Implementing Protection Domains in the Java Development Kit 1.2*. Internet Society Symposium on Network and Distributed System Security, San Diego, CA, March 1998.

13. J. Gosling, B. Joy, and G. Steele. *The Java language specification*. Addison-Wesley, 1996.

14. D. Hagimont, and L. Ismail. *A Protection Scheme for Mobile Agents on Java*. 3rd Annual ACM/IEEE Int'l Conference on Mobile Computing and Networking, Budapest, Hungary, September 2630, 1997.

15. H. Haertig, et. al. *The Performance of μ-Kernel-Based Systems*. 16th ACM Symposium on Operating Systems Principles, p. 6677, Saint-Malo, France, October 1997.

16. C. Hawblitzel, C. C. Chang, G. Czajkowski, D. Hu, and T. von Eicken. *Implementing Multiple Protection Domains in Java*. 1998 USENIX Annual Technical Conference, p. 259-270, New Orleans, LA, June 1998.

17. G. Heiser, et. al. *Implementation and Performance of the Mungi Single-Address-Space Operating System*. Technical Report UNSW-CSE-TR-9704, Univeristy of New South Wales, Sydney, Australia, June 1997.

18. JavaSoft. *Java Telephony API*. http://java.sun.com/products/jtapi/index.html.

19. JavaSoft. *Remote Method Invocation Specification*. http://java.sun.com.

20. JavaSoft. *New Security Model for JDK1.2*. http://java.sun.com

21. JavaSoft. *Java Servlet API*. http://java.sun.com.

22. A. K. Jones and W. A. Wulf. *Towards the Design of Secure Systems*. Software Practice and Experience, Volume 5, Number 4, p. 321336, 1975.

23. H. M. Levy. *Capability-Based Computer Systems*. Digital Press, Bedford, Massachusetts, 1984.

24. J. Liedtke, et. al. *Achieved IPC Performance*. 6th Workshop on Hot Topics in Operating Systems, Chatham, MA, May.

25. Microsoft Corporation. *Microsoft Security Management Architecture White Paper*. http://www.microsoft.com/ie/ security.

26. G. Morrisett, D. Walker, K. Crary, and N. Glew. *From System F to Typed Assembly Language*. 25th ACM Symposium on Principles of Programming Languages. San Diego, CA, January 1998.

27. G. Necula and P. Lee. *Safe Kernel Extensions Without Run-Time Checking*. 2nd USENIX Symposium on Operating Systems Design and Implementation, p. 229243, Seattle, WA, October 1996.

28. G. Necula. *Proof-carrying code*. 24th ACM Symposium on Principles of Programming Languages, p. 106119, Paris, 1997.

29. Netscape Corporation. *Java Capabilities API.* http://www.netscape.com.
30. Rashid, R. *Threads of a New System.* Unix Review, p. 3749, August 1986.
31. D. D. Redell. *Naming and Protection in Extendible Operating Systems.* Technical Report 140, Project MAC, MIT 1974.
32. Z. Shao. *Typed Common Intermediate Format.* 1997 USENIX Conference on Domain-Specific Languages, Santa Barbara, California, October 1997.
33. J. S. Shapiro, D. J. Farber, and J. M. Smith. *The Measured Performance of a Fast Local IPC.* 5th Int'l Workshop on Object-Orientation in Operating Systems, Seattle, WA. 1996
34. R. Wahbe, S. Lucco, T. E. Anderson, and S. L. Graham. *Efficient Software-Based Fault Isolation.* 14th ACM Symposium on Operating Systems Principles, p. 203216, Asheville, NC, December 1993.
35. D. S. Wallach, D. Balfanz, D. Dean, and E. W. Felten. *Extensible Security Architectures for Java.* 16th ACM Symposium on Operating Systems Principles, p. 116128, Saint-Malo, France, October 1997.
36. W. A. Wulf, R. Levin, and S.P. Harbison. *Hydra/C. mmp: An Experimental Computer System,* McGraw-Hill, New York, NY, 1981.

# Secure Network Objects*

Leendert van Doorn, Martín Abadi, Mike Burrows, and Edward Wobber

**Abstract.** We describe the design and implementation of *secure network objects*, which provide security for object-oriented network communication. The design takes advantage of objects and subtyping to present a simple but expressive programming interface for security, supporting both access control lists and capabilities. The implementation of this design fits nicely within the structure of the existing network objects system; we discuss its internal components, its performance, and its use in some applications.

## 1  Introduction

Object-oriented communication has become popular in distributed systems [2, 23, 19]. With objects or without them, distributed systems typically rely on networks with no low-level support for security; the vulnerability of distributed systems is by now evident and worrisome [24, 4]. Therefore, a need exists for secure object-oriented communication.

We describe the design and implementation of *secure network objects*. Secure network objects extend Modula-3 network objects [18, 2] with security guarantees. When a client invokes a method of a secure network object over the network, the main security properties are:

- The client must possess an unforgeable object reference.
- The client and the owner of the object can choose to authenticate each other.
- The arguments and results of the method invocation are protected against tampering and replay, and optionally against eavesdropping.

For high-speed bulk communication, the network objects system supports buffered streams called *readers* and *writers*. We make these streams secure also.

Our design accommodates both access control lists (ACLs) [11] and capabilities [6]. It seems natural to treat network object references as capabilities; moreover, these capabilities can be implemented efficiently. However, capabilities suffer from the well-known confinement problem: it is hard to keep them sufficiently secret (cf. [10]). The support for ACLs allows implementors to limit this problem, and to use identity-based security whenever that is appropriate, in particular for auditing. Systems with both ACLs and capabilities are not new; we include some comparisons in section 6.

* Based on "Secure Network Objects" by Leendert van Doorn, Martín Abadi, Mike Burrows, and Edward Wobber, which appeared in the Proceedings of the IEEE Symposium on Security & Privacy; Oakland, California, May 1996; 211–221. ©1996 IEEE.

The central goal of our work was the integration of security and network objects. We have obtained the following features:

- Applications can use security easily, with minimal code changes.
  * Security is mostly encapsulated within the network objects run-time system.
  * Objects and methods provide convenient units of protection.
  * Subtyping expresses security properties quite simply. Secure network objects are a subtype of regular network objects.
- Through the combination of ACLs and capabilities, the security model is rich enough to enable applications with sophisticated security requirements.
- The implementation of our design is reasonably straightforward. In this respect, we benefited from the structure of the existing network objects system. We also borrowed ideas from previous work on authentication [27]: each node runs an *authentication agent* that is responsible for managing keys and for identifying local users to other nodes. We feel that our experience partially validates those previous efforts.

The next section presents our programming interface. Sections 3 and 4 describe the two main components of our system: the authentication agent and the run-time system. Section 5 discusses experience with secure network objects, including performance measurements and some example applications. Section 6 discusses related work.

## 2 Programming Interface

In a world with fast CPUs, no government export controls, and pervasive use of cryptographic credentials, we would give uniform security guarantees for all objects, even for those that do not require them. This would make for a simpler system and a shorter paper.

As a compromise, we define network objects with three levels of security: (1) no security; (2) authenticity; (3) authenticity and secrecy. We call the last two kinds *secure network objects*. A *secure invocation* is the invocation of a method of a secure network object.

An important characteristic of our design is that it gives security guarantees for whole objects rather than for individual methods. This allows us to specify the properties of secure network objects through subtyping, rather than by inventing new language features. We have a type of objects with no security, a subtype with authenticity, and a further subtype that adds secrecy.

These types are explained in the following sections, along with a type to represent identities. We postpone the discussion of readers and writers to section 2.6.

### 2.1 Network Objects (Background)

A Modula-3 *object* is a reference (pointer) to a data record paired with a method suite. The method suite is a record of procedures that take the object as first parameter. A method invocation specifies a method name, an object, and additional arguments. It may yield results, consisting of a return value and values for any VAR parameters.

A *network object* is a reference meaningful throughout a network; its methods can be invoked from multiple address spaces, possibly on different nodes. A method invocation is *remote* if it crosses an address-space boundary. Method invocations have at-most-once semantics (at least in the absence of attackers). Each network object has one address space as *owner* (or *server*); the object always has the same owner. Other address spaces are *clients*. Typically, each host exports a well-known network object that acts as a local name server. To import an object, a client may contact the name server of the owner of the object, or it may receive the object as argument or result of a remote invocation.

Each client of a network object has a special object, the *surrogate*; passing a network object to a new client causes a corresponding surrogate to be created at the client. The client invokes the methods of the surrogate, which in turn invoke the methods of the object at the owner. The presence of a surrogate is invisible to the programmer.

An *object type* specifies a collection of methods. A new object type can be defined as a *subtype* of an existing object type; the new type may inherit some methods from the existing type, may override others, and may add some methods of its own. The type NetObj.T is the base type for the network object subtyping hierarchy: all types of network objects are subtypes of NetObj.T; the type NetObj.T does not specify any methods. In general, network objects of type NetObj.T are not secure.

## 2.2 Authenticity

We introduce a subtype AuthNetObj.T of NetObj.T. Network objects of type AuthNetObj.T are unforgeable references. When a client invokes a method of an object of type AuthNetObj.T, the following guarantees hold (even in the presence of attackers):

1. Integrity: The invocation that the server receives is exactly the one issued by the client. The results that the client receives are exactly the ones issued by the server as a response to this invocation.
2. At-most-once semantics: The server receives the invocation at most once. The client receives the response at most once.
3. Confinement: If the invocation or the response contains a secure network object, an eavesdropper does not learn enough to invoke a method of that object.

By (1), the server knows that the client has the method name, the object, and all additional arguments of the invocation; the client knows that the server has the results. In addition, since an object has a unique server, that same server responds to all invocations of methods of the object.

By (2), client and server are protected against replays.

By (3), a secure network object can be treated as a capability or protected name [17]. If a secure network object is passed only from the server to a single client in a secure invocation, the server knows that any later invocation using this object originates in this client. More generally, if the object is passed only in secure invocations between trusted parties, the server knows that any later invocation using this object originates in a trusted party.

One could imagine extending (3) to insecure invocations; one would protect secure network objects even when they are passed in insecure invocations. However, there is not much gain in doing this. For instance, the result of an insecure invocation may be a secure network object; there is little point in protecting this result against eavesdroppers because any address space could invoke the method that gives this result.

## 2.3 Secrecy

We introduce a subtype `SecNetObj.T` of `AuthNetObj.T` for secret communication. When a client invokes a method of an object of type `SecNetObj.T`, the following additional guarantee holds:

4. Secrecy: An eavesdropper does not obtain any part of the method name, the object, the additional arguments, or the results of the invocation.

However, we do not attempt to provide perfect anonymity. An eavesdropper may recognize that two method invocations are for the same object. As explained in the next section, an eavesdropper may also learn who is communicating.

## 2.4 Identity

An *identity* consists of a user name and a host name. For simplicity, we assume that each address space is running on behalf of one user on one host, and we associate with each address space the corresponding identity.

We introduce a type to represent identities:

```
INTERFACE Ident;

TYPE
  T <: OBJECT METHODS
        userName(): TEXT;
        hostName(): TEXT;
      END;

PROCEDURE Mine(): T;

END Ident.
```

This interface describes a type `Ident.T`, exposing the methods `userName` and `hostName`. (`Ident.T` is an object type, but not a network object type.) Each of userName and hostName takes no arguments and returns a string. An *identity object* is an object of type Ident.T. The interface also provides a procedure Ident.Mine; a call to Ident.Mine in an address space always returns the identity of the address space. Attempting to pass any identity other than Ident.Mine() in a remote invocation is a run-time error that raises an exception; this behavior is chosen for programmer convenience, but is not necessary for security.

The following guarantee is associated with the type Ident.T:

5. If an identity object is passed as argument or result of a secure remote invocation, the receiver is assured that calls on userName and hostName will return the identity of the sending address space.

In contrast, an identity object received in an insecure invocation may not identify its sender—the sender may have been dishonest.

Even if an invocation is secure, the anonymity of an address space that sends Ident.Mine() is not protected: an eavesdropper can obtain the corresponding user name and host name. In fact, an eavesdropper can deduce host names simply from the pattern of communication between address spaces, even when no identities are sent. On the other hand, if an interface does not require the exchange of identities, its users can remain anonymous; in principle, an address space discloses the name of its user only as a deliberate step.

Our treatment of identity suffices for our current applications and enables us to take advantage of existing mechanisms such as Kerberos [25] or Sun's secure RPC system [26]. However, it would be straightforward to elaborate our notion of identity and to allow each address space to have multiple identities. In particular, we could borrow from the work of Lampson, Wobber, et al. [12, 27]; our type Ident.T is a simplified version of the type Auth described in that work.

It is not hard to imagine other schemes for communicating identities. For example, identity objects could be passed explicitly or implicitly on every call. In choosing our scheme, we have been careful to avoid language changes, and have attempted to minimize overhead.

## 2.5 Discussion: Using Capabilities, Identities, and ACLs

One of the main applications of identity objects is in bootstrapping trust. A client typically obtains its first secure network object as result of an invocation on an insecure network object, often a name server. A priori, there is no trust between the owner of the secure network object and the client. This trust is established when client and server exchange and test identity objects. Once this has been done, they may choose to pass other secure network objects. Because these objects are obtained as part of secure invocations, further checks of identity may not be necessary.

For example, an insecure name server may export a secure network object fs of type FileServer.T providing access to a remote file server:

```
INTERFACE FileServer;

IMPORT AuthNetObj, Ident, Buffer;

TYPE
  T = AuthNetObj.T OBJECT METHODS
    owner(): Ident.T;
    open(id: Ident.T; name: TEXT): File;
  END;

  File = AuthNetObj.T OBJECT METHODS
    read(): Buffer.T;
    write(Buffer.T): INTEGER;
  END;

END FileServer.
```

By convention this object provides an **owner** method which returns the identity of the principal on whose behalf the file server is running. This result is used by a client to authenticate the file server.

Although **fs** is secure, anyone can obtain **fs** and invoke its methods. Therefore, it is reasonable for the file server to expect an identity as argument of any method invocation. When a client c issues the call **fs.open(Ident.Mine(), "/etc/motd")**, the **open** method should check the identity of c. If this check succeeds, the **open** method may return another secure network object **f**, which represents the open file "/etc/motd". Client c may then invoke **f.read()**. Because c and the file server have authenticated one another, c and the owner of **f** may choose not to authenticate one another further, even though the owner of **f** need not be the file server.

Identity objects have important applications beyond bootstrapping. They allow a server to confine the use of capabilities to particular clients. Additionally, identities can be logged to construct an audit trail.

In our example, c could pass its identity to the **read** method of **f**, which could check that c is a particular user, or belongs to a particular group. The identity check provides protection even if c publishes **f**. The **read** method could also record the names of all callers, for future inspection.

Another important application of the type **Ident.T** is the implementation of various authorization mechanisms, and particularly reference monitors with ACLs. Several designs are possible. For example, a secure network object may include a method **checkACL** for making access-control decisions; the arguments of **checkACL** are a mode m (such as **read** or **write**) and an identity i; the result is a boolean that indicates whether the user with identity i is allowed access with mode m to the object. In the intended implementation, **checkACL** compares i with names kept in lists (that is, in ACLs). Additional methods enable the modification of the ACLs. When group-membership checks are needed, **checkACL** can consult group registries across the network using secure invocations.

## 2.6  Readers and Writers

Modula-3 includes buffered streams, called readers and writers. For example, a reader might be the stream of data from a file or from a terminal. The network objects system allows readers and writers to be passed between address spaces, as follows: an address space creates a reader or writer, and passes it to one other address space, which reads from it or writes to it, but never passes it. The two address spaces can then use the reader or writer to transmit data directly on their underlying network connection, without the overhead of method invocations.

Readers and writers are treated specially when passed in secure invocations:

6. If a reader or writer rw is passed as argument or result of a secure invocation, operations on rw have the same security guarantees as the invocation.

For instance, if a reader rd is passed as argument in the invocation o.m(rd), and o is of type AuthNetObj.T, then operations on rd are secured in the same way as operations on an object of type AuthNetObj.T. Therefore, data read from rd is protected just as if it had been passed as an argument in the invocation. The example given in section 2.7 further illustrates the use of readers and writers.

An alternative treatment could be based on new types for readers and writers with security properties (analogous to AuthNetObj.T and SecNetObj.T). Modula-3 does not support multiple inheritance, so introducing these new types could have been troublesome. We have chosen our scheme in order to allow existing classes of readers and writers to be made secure without modification.

## 2.7  An Example

Let us consider a trivial terminal server that offers shells for remote users. Before a user gets a shell, the server obtains the user's identity, both to verify that the user is legitimate and to associate the identity with the shell. On the other hand, the user obtains the server's identity, and can check that the server is the expected one and not an impostor. Once the user has the shell, the user's commands and their results are protected against tampering, replay, and eavesdropping.

The terminal server exports the following interface:

```
INTERFACE STS;

IMPORT SecNetObj, Ident, Rd, Wr;

TYPE
  T = SecNetObj.T OBJECT METHODS
    owner(): Ident.T;
    create_shell(id: Ident.T; rd: Rd.T; wr: Wr.T);
  END

END STS.
```

This interface declares the object type STS.T as a subtype of SecNetObj.T with two new methods, owner and create_shell. The owner method returns the identity of the server (by calling Ident.Mine). The create_shell method creates a connection, starts a shell with the identity of the user, and connects the streams rd and wr as standard input and output, respectively.

A simple client program might be:

```
MODULE Client EXPORTS Main;

IMPORT NetObj, Ident, STS, Stdio;

CONST serverHost = "foo.bar.ladida";

VAR
  agent: NetObj.Address;
  sts: STS.T;
  server_ident: Ident.T;
BEGIN
  agent := NetObj.Locate(serverHost);
  sts := NetObj.Import("STS", agent);
  server_ident := sts.owner();
  IF  server_ident.userName() = "root"
  AND server_ident.hostName() = serverHost
  THEN
    sts.create_shell(Ident.Mine(),
        Stdio.stdin, Stdio.stdout);
  ELSE
    (* the server is an impostor *)
  END;
END Client.
```

The client program imports an object sts of type STS.T and verifies the identity server_ident of its owner. If this check succeeds, the client program starts a shell by calling sts.create_shell. Since STS.T is a subtype of SecNetObj.T, the shell's standard input and output benefit from the guarantees associated with SecNetObj.T.

## 3 Authentication Agents

So far we have focused on the design of a programming interface for security; in the remainder of the paper we describe our implementation for this programming interface. Our system has two main components, the authentication agent and the run-time system. We describe the first in this section and the second in the next.

In our system, each node runs an authentication agent. An authentication agent is a process that assists application address spaces for the purposes of security. It communicates with its local clients only via local secure channels. In our implementation, the authentication agent is a user-level process; as local secure channels we have used Unix domain sockets in one version of our implementation and System V streams in another. Each agent is responsible for managing identities and keys, as follows.

When an address space receives an identity object, it can ask the local agent for the corresponding user name and host name. The agent answers this question by communicating with its peers; each agent knows the name of its host and the user names associated with its clients.

The agent also provides *channel keys*. A channel key is an encryption key shared by two address spaces. The agent performs key exchange with its peers in order to generate these channel keys for its clients.

When the agent negotiates a new channel key, it also negotiates an expiry time for the key and a key identifier. A key identifier allows the sender of a message to tell the receiver which key was used for constructing the message. The key identifier can be transmitted in clear as part of the message, while the key itself should not be. The agent picks key identifiers so that they are unambiguous.

Our design encapsulates all of the key exchange machinery in the authentication agent. We have tried two implementations of key exchange, one based on our own protocol and another that relies on Sun's secure RPC authentication service. The change of implementation was transparent to user address spaces. In the second implementation, we wrote 1400 lines of C code for the agent.

We took the idea of using an authentication agent from the work of Wobber et al. [27]. The authentication agent described in that work is more elaborate than ours; for example, it deals with delegation and supports channel multiplexing. These features could be incorporated in our system, though they may preclude the use of off-the-shelf authentication software.

## 4 The Run-time System

In this section we describe the security-related code that runs in application address spaces. We adapted the original code of Modula-3 network objects, making a few changes:

- We defined secure network object references to be capabilities.
- We extended the protocol used by network objects with security information and with functions like message digesting and encryption.
- We modified the run-time system, adding marshaling code and cryptography.

The changes were relatively small. We added 2500 lines of Modula-3 code to the run-time system. We also integrated public-domain implementations of DES [16] and MD5 [22] in C. We did not modify the overall structure of network objects.

### 4.1 Capabilities

The wire representation of an insecure network object is a pair (*s*, *objid*), where:

- *s* is an address space identifier for the owner of the object,
- *objid* is an object identifier, which distinguishes this object from others with the same owner.

The wire representation of a secure network object is a tuple

$$(s, objid, capid, key, exp)$$

with the following additional components:

- *capid* is a capability identifier,
- *key* is a key associated with *capid*,
- *exp* is an expiration time.

The tuple $(s, objid, capid, key, exp)$ is a capability. The capability is created by the owner of the object. The key is the secret that is shared between the holders of the capability and the owner of the object. The key may never appear in clear on the network: it is encrypted using a channel key when transmitted between address spaces in secure invocations. The components *s*, *objid*, and *capid* determine *key* uniquely, and thus serve as key identifier.

The capability becomes invalid once its expiration time has passed. The use of an expiration time can be beneficial in revoking a capability; it also limits the use of the key. The client run-time system refreshes the capabilities it holds before they expire. This is transparent to the client application. Each secure network object has a hidden method that the client run-time system can call to obtain a fresh capability for the object.

In general, more than one capability may be in use for any given object. The owner of an object maintains a set of valid capabilities for the object, and is careful not to give out capabilities that are about to expire.

## 4.2 Protocol

If a client *c* holds a network object reference $(s, objid)$ for an object of type NetObj.T, an invocation of a method of the object consists of a request from *c* and a reply from the owner *s*. The request is $(\text{Request}: c, s, objid, reqdata)$, where *reqdata* includes the method name and arguments of the invocation. The reply is $(\text{Reply}: c, s, repdata)$, where *repdata* contains the results of the invocation.

If a client *c* holds a capability $(s, objid, capid, key, exp)$ for an object of type AuthNetObj.T, both the request and the reply are modified. We assume that the local authentication agents for *c* and *s* have authenticated one another, and that they make available a channel key *chankey* for communication between *c* and *s*. This key will be used for signing the request and the reply, and sometimes for encryption, as follows.

The request has two parts, a body and a signature. The body, *reqbody*, is:

$$(\text{Request}: c, s, objid, capid, mid, reqdata)$$

where *mid* is a message identifier that *c* has never before attached to a request signed using *chankey*. The signature is:

$$Hash(reqbody, chankey, key)$$

where *Hash* is a cryptographic hash function (a one-way message digest function such as MD5). Upon receipt of the request, *s* verifies that *mid* is not a duplicate and checks the signature.

Like the request, the reply has a body and a signature. The body, *repbody*, is:

$$(\text{Reply}: c, s, mid, repdata)$$

The signature is:

$$Hash(repbody, chankey, key)$$

Upon receipt of the reply, the client verifies that *c*, *s*, and *mid* match those of the request, and checks the signature.

Both *reqdata* or *repdata* may contain capabilities and identity objects. These are treated specially:

- On the wire, capability keys are encrypted under *chankey*.
- The wire representation of an identity object is simply a placeholder. When *c* (or *s*) receives such a placeholder, it replaces the placeholder with an identity object constructed locally; the methods of this identity object call the local authentication agent to obtain the user name and the host name associated with *s* (or *c*, respectively).

For an object of type SecNetObj.T, the protocol is the same, except that both the request and the reply are completely encrypted under the channel key *chankey*.

So far we have ignored readers and writers, because their discussion is independent of that of the protocol and because security for them is obtained by reducing them to secure network objects. In the existing implementation of network objects, passing a reader or writer rw amounts to passing a network object called a *voucher*. The voucher has a type with special marshaling routines; it mediates communication over rw. For security, we arrange that the type of the voucher be a subtype of AuthNetObj.T or SecNetObj.T.

We can now justify the guarantees listed in section 2:

1. The signatures provide integrity. Since only *c* and *s* have *chankey*, only they could have generated *Hash(reqbody, chankey, key)*. If *s* never generates a request of the form (Request: *c, s,* ...), which appears to come from *c*, then *s* knows that only *c* could have generated *Hash(reqbody, chankey, key)*, and hence that *c* must have endorsed *reqbody*. Similarly, *c* knows that *s* must have endorsed *repbody*. Moreover, the request and reply are matched because they both include *mid*.

2. At-most-once semantics is guaranteed because *s* checks that at most one request from *c* includes *mid* and is signed using *chankey*; and because *c* accepts replies only for outstanding calls.

3. $c$ and $s$ demonstrate knowledge of the capability key *key* by transmitting *Hash(reqbody, chankey, key)* and *Hash(repbody, chankey, key)*. Thus, *key* does not appear in clear on the wire. Any capability keys for other secure network objects are protected from eavesdroppers by encryption under *chankey*.

4. Since only $c$ and $s$ have *chankey*, encryption under *chankey* protects the secrecy of the invocation against eavesdroppers.

5. When an address space sends an identity object, the receiver constructs an identity object that reflects the true identity of the sender. An address space that runs our code will never pass an identity other than its own; but even if an address space runs other code and succeeds in passing an identity other than its own, it will not be believed.

6. When a reader or writer rw is passed in the invocation of a method of an object of type AuthNetObj.T (or SecNetObj.T), the voucher for rw has type AuthNetObj.T (or SecNetObj.T, respectively). Therefore, since operations on rw are mediated by the voucher, they have the same security guarantees as the invocation.

## 4.3   Implementation in the Run-time System

In order to implement our design, we made only a few changes to the existing network objects code. Most of these changes were in the implementation of StubLib, the interface that the network objects run-time system provides to stubs. (Stubs are machine-generated subroutines that are responsible for marshaling and unmarshaling arguments and results of remote invocations.) Some changes were also required in the StubLib interface itself, but they were minor; we added only two lines of code to the stub generator to accommodate them.

The network objects system allows the use of multiple transport protocols (such as TCP or X.25). Our security implementation is independent of the choice of transport protocol, so one can add support for new protocols without altering or writing security code.

In the network objects system, when two address spaces $a_1$ and $a_2$ communicate, each of them has a *connection object* consisting of a reader and a writer. Data written into $a_1$'s writer appears in $a_2$'s reader, and vice versa. We embed the cryptography necessary for the protocol of section 4.2 in our implementation of connection objects. We do so by defining readers and writers that apply cryptography to specified byte ranges in the data they transmit. These readers and writers have methods for computing cryptographic digests, for encryption, and for decryption.

As described in section 4.2, each message of our protocol includes an identifier *mid* for protection against replays. Were all address spaces single threaded, a simple sequence number would make a convenient message identifier. In order to accommodate multi-threaded address spaces, we associate each message with a *secure channel*, and let *mid* include a secure channel identifier. Next we explain secure channels and their use.

At each point in time, a secure channel from an address space $a_1$ to an address space $a_2$ determines a channel key and a sequence number. (Two secure channels

**Table 1.** Performance of secure network objects (in $\mu$s/call).

| Test | Old | Insecure | Authentic | Secret |
|------|-----|----------|-----------|--------|
| Null | 708 | 772 | 870 | 991 |
| Ten integer | 747 | 830 | 929 | 1244 |
| Existing surrogate | 751 | 822 | 973 | 1146 |
| New surrogate | 1896 | 2044 | 2263 | 2430 |

may have the same key.) Both $a_1$ and $a_2$ know the secure channel identifier and keep track of the key and the sequence number associated with the secure channel. With each method invocation from $a_1$ to $a_2$ that uses a secure channel, both $a_1$ and $a_2$ increment the corresponding sequence number. When the key for a secure channel is half way to its expiration, $a_1$ asks its authentication agent for a new key; on seeing a new key identifier, $a_2$ obtains the new key from its own agent.

In the normal case, a secure invocation from $a_1$ to $a_2$ proceeds as follows. First $a_1$ chooses a secure channel from $a_1$ to $a_2$ on which there is no outstanding invocation (and sets up a new secure channel if none is available). Then $a_1$ constructs the request using the channel key for the secure channel; *mid* is the concatenation of the sequence number and the secure channel identifier. When $a_2$ receives the request, it compares the sequence number in *mid* against its version of the sequence number. The reply uses the same key and message identifier as the request. When $a_1$ receives the reply, it verifies that the key is still current and checks *mid*.

In a more general scheme, the request and the reply may use different keys and message identifiers. This generality has some advantages; for example, it allows an invocation that returns after a long wait to use a fresh key. The changes in the definition of message identifiers are considerable, so we do not discuss them here.

# 5 Performance and Applications

Next, we describe our experiments with secure network objects. We discuss the performance of our system and two example applications.

## 5.1 Performance Measurements

We measured the performance of our system with the same tests used for the original implementation of network objects [2]. Table 1 presents a subset of our measurements that characterizes the performance of secure network objects in comparison with the performance of the original implementation.

We measured round-trip invocation latency for remote invocations. The first column of Table 1 (labelled *Old*) gives the performance of method invocations in the original implementation. The remaining three columns concern method invocations in our implementation, to objects of type `NetObj.T`, `AuthNetObj.T`, and `SecNetObj.T`, respectively. The rows of Table 1 indicate method invocations with different sorts of arguments and with no results. In the null test, the method has no arguments. In the ten integer test, the method takes ten 64-bit integers as arguments. In the existing surrogate test, a network object is marshaled to a receiver that already has a surrogate for it. The type of the argument matches the security level of the invocation, so for instance in the column *Authentic* the argument has type `AuthNetObj.T`. The new surrogate test is similar, except that the argument is unknown to the receiver; therefore, the receiver must create a new surrogate and register it at the owner (for garbage collection).

The tests do not include the establishment of a channel key. The cost of establishing a channel key depends on the implementation of the authentication agent; a typical cost may be in the order of tens of milliseconds. In most cases, this cost is insignificant when amortized over multiple secure invocations.

We performed all our measurements using DEC 3000/700 workstations, which contain DECchip 21064a processors at 225 MHz. On these workstations, our MD5 implementation runs at over 15 MBytes/sec; our DES implementation at 990 KBytes/sec. We used two workstations connected by an ATM network with a point-to-point bandwidth of over 16 MBytes/sec.

Our measurements show that our system adds a non-trivial cost to insecure invocations. This additional cost is largely due to the expanded size of the wire representation of network objects and of packet headers, and to the associated processing. Secure network objects require a 24-byte object representation that identifies both the host and address space of the object owner. The packet header format similarly requires a host and address space identifier as well as a message identifier.

Authentic invocations add a fixed minimum MD5 overhead of nearly 40 $\mu$s per invocation. Each call and return packet requires at least two 64-byte MD5 calculations, and both client and server must perform these. The remainder of the incremental cost can be attributed to the generation of a message identifier, and the checking of timestamps, message identifiers, and digests. The calls where an object is used as argument incur the additional overhead of encrypting each object capability under DES.

The difference between authentic and secret calls is primarily due to DES processing. Since the method identifier, return code, and MD5 digest are encrypted as well as all arguments and results, there is a minimum of 96 bytes of DES encryption/decryption ($\simeq$100 $\mu$s) per secret invocation. (The encryption of the MD5 digest is not necessary, and we could eliminate it for even better performance.) The ten integer test adds 80 bytes of arguments, to be encrypted and decrypted; this accounts for another 160 $\mu$s.

We have also measured the performance of readers and writers. Streams with authenticity are currently limited to about 8 MBytes/sec. We observed that 40% of the CPU cost is attributable to buffering and TCP overhead; this explains why the bandwidth of streams with authenticity is limited to around 55% of the raw MD5 bandwidth. Streams with both authenticity and secrecy are severely limited by the speed of DES. According to our measurements, such streams have a throughput of about 870 KBytes/sec; this implies that nearly 90% of the CPU is dedicated to DES computation.

As these measurements demonstrate, the performance of our system is acceptable for many applications. However, we believe that there remains much room for optimization.

## 5.2 Example Applications

To date, we have had two preliminary but encouraging experiences in the application of secure network objects.

In the first application, we have implemented a secure version of an answering service written by Rob DeLine. This service is part of a telecollaboration system and implements an answering machine for multi-media messages. The answering machine is a network object with methods create, retrieve, and delete. When a message is created, it is stored under a special name, called a *cookie*; the cookie is e-mailed to the intended recipient of the message. An e-mail reader can then present the cookie to retrieve or to delete the message.

The original answering service is not secure. In particular, cookies are essentially used as capabilities, yet they are communicated in clear and are easy to guess. Therefore, the service has neither authenticity nor secrecy.

Our version of the answering service addresses these problems. Because of the performance limitations of software encryption, we have not provided secrecy but only authenticity. In our version, the answering machine is a network object of type AuthNetObj.T; it would be easy to make it a network object of type SecNetObj.T instead. We store the names of both the sender and intended recipient with each message; appropriate identity objects must be passed as arguments of calls to the methods create, retrieve, and delete. For example, only the sender and intended recipient of a message can delete the message.

Our second application is a secure version of Obliq [3]. Roughly, Obliq is to Modula-3 as Tcl is to C. Obliq is an untyped, interpreted scripting language that supports distributed object-oriented computation. For example, it can be used to program computing agents that roam over a network.

In our version of Obliq, each object is implemented as a network object of type AuthNetObj.T. When an Obliq object o is exported, it is explicitly tagged with a list of the principals that may import it. The Obliq run-time system encapsulates o in a reference monitor of type AuthNetObj.T. This reference monitor provides two methods: a method for access to o and a method that returns the identity of the owner of the reference monitor. The former method is responsible for performing access control checks. The latter method allows a client that imports o to verify that the server is the expected one.

We have implemented the secure version of Obliq that we have just described. This implementation provides evidence that we can build useful security mechanisms for Obliq fairly easily. On the other hand, we do not yet have sufficient experience to decide which security mechanism is most appropriate.

# 6 Related Work

There has been much work on capabilities, in various contexts. Communication systems with a pure capability model, like that of Amoeba [15], suffer from the confinement problem. Several restrictions and variations of the capability model have been proposed. For example, Gong suggests adding identities to capabilities [7]; Bacon et al. suggest restricting their lifetime [1]. Karger's dissertation describes several others [9]. The ideas in our use of capabilities can be traced back through a vast literature.

There has also been substantial work in the area of security and network communication systems (e.g., [25, 14, 21]). However, to our knowledge, there is at present no object-oriented network communication system with support for security. Next we discuss two recent efforts in this area.

The Object Management Group has requested technology for integrating security in CORBA [19] and has received submissions [20]; security work is currently in progress in the Object Management Group. A general architecture for security in CORBA has also been proposed, and an implementation of the architecture was announced as future work [5]. In summary, there seems to be significant interest and activity on security in CORBA, but (at the time of the writing of this paper) not yet any resolution or experimental results.

The Spring object-oriented operating system [13] supports both ACLs and capabilities. An accurate comparison with secure network objects is difficult, as there has not been a complete description of security in Spring. Spring has more expressive capabilities than our system; for example, several capabilities for an object can give different privileges. Perhaps for this reason, the combination of identities and capabilities is less important in Spring, and has been explored less [8]. To date, Spring security has been implemented only on a single processor; all network communication is unprotected and capabilities are passed in clear.

# 7 Conclusions

Secure network objects behave like insecure network objects, but preserve the intended semantics even in the presence of an active attacker; optionally, secure network objects provide secrecy from eavesdroppers. In addition, identity objects form the basis for authentication in our system. The combination of secure network objects with identity objects leads to a simple programming model and a simple implementation, both in the spirit of the original network objects. Thus we have integrated security and network objects.

Overall, we felt that object-orientation was helpful. Not surprisingly, we found that objects give rise to natural units of protection. We also took advantage of the object type system to specify security properties, directly and economically.

In our description, we have tried to be precise, but not formal. We believe that a more formal study would be interesting. In particular, it would be worthwhile to give notations and rules for reasoning about secure network objects.

## Acknowledgments

We would like to thank Andrew Birrell, Greg Nelson, and Luca Cardelli for many helpful discussions; and Roger Needham, Cynthia Hibbard, Tim Mann, Rustan Leino, Andrew Tanenbaum, Philip Homburg, Raoul Bhoedjang, Tim Ruhl, and Greg Sharp for helpful comments on the paper.

# References

1. Jean Bacon, Richard Hayton, Sai Lai Lo, and Ken Moody. Extensible access control for a hierarchy of servers. *ACM Operating Systems Review*, 28(3):4–15, July 1994.
2. Andrew Birrell, Greg Nelson, Susan Owicki, and Edward Wobber. Network objects. *Software Practice and Experience*, S4(25):87–130, December 1995.
3. Luca Cardelli. A language with distributed scope. *Computing Systems*, 8(1):27–59, January 1995.
4. W.R. Cheswick. An evening with Berferd, in which a hacker is lured, endured, and studied. In *Proceedings of the Usenix Winter '92 Conference*, 1992.
5. R.H. Deng, S.K. Bhonsle, W. Wang, and A.A. Lazar. Integrating security in CORBA based object architectures. In *Proceedings of the 1995 IEEE Symposium on Security and Privacy*, pages 50–61, May 1995.
6. J.B. Dennis and E.C. van Horn. Programming semantics for multiprogrammed computation. *Communications of the ACM*, 9(3):143–155, March 1966.
7. Li Gong. A secure identity-based capability system. In *Proceedings of the 1989 IEEE Symposium on Security and Privacy*, pages 56–63, May 1989.
8. Graham Hamilton. Personal communication, 1994 and 1996.
9. Paul Ashley Karger. *Improving Security and Performance for Capability Systems*. PhD thesis, Cambridge University, October 1988.
10. Butler Lampson. A note on the confinement problem. *Communications of the ACM*, 16(10):613–615, October 1973.
11. Butler Lampson. Protection. *ACM Operating Systems Review*, 1(8):18–24, January 1974.
12. Butler Lampson, Martín Abadi, Mike Burrows, and Edward Wobber. Authentication in distributed systems: Theory and practice. *ACM Transactions on Computer Systems*, 10(4):265–310, November 1992.
13. J. Mitchell, J. Gibbons, G. Hamilton, P. Kessler, Y. Khalidi, P. Kougiouris, P. Madany, M. Nelson, M. Powell, and S. Radia. An overview of the Spring system. In *IEEE Compcon Spring 1994*, February 1994.
14. R. Molva, G. Tsudik, E. van Herreweghen, and S. Zatti. Kryptoknight authentication and key distribution system. In *Proceedings of the European Symposium on Research in Computer Security*, November 1992.
15. Sape J. Mullender, Andrew S. Tanenbaum, and Robbert van Renesse. Using sparse capabilities in a distributed operating system. In *Proceedings of the 6th IEEE conference on Distributed Computing Systems*, June 1986.
16. National Bureau of Standards. Data encryption standard. FIPS 47, 1977.
17. Roger Needham. Names. In Sape Mullender, editor, *Distributed Systems*, chapter 12, pages 315–327. Addison-Wesley, second edition, 1993.
18. Greg Nelson, editor. *Systems Programming with Modula-3*. Prentice Hall, 1991.
19. Object Management Group. Common object request broker architecture and specification. OMG Document number 91.12.1.

20. Object Management Group. OMG documents. See URL: http://www.omg.org/.
21. Open Software Foundation. Introduction to OSF DCE. Revision 1.0, 1992.
22. R.L. Rivest and S. Dusse. RFC 1321: The MD5 message-digest function. Internet Activities Board, 1992.
23. Marc Shapiro. Structure and encapsulation in distributed systems: The proxy principle. In *IEEE International Conference on Distributed Computer Systems*, May 1986.
24. Eugene H. Spafford. The Internet worm program: An analysis. *Computer Communication Review*, 19(1):17–57, January 1989.
25. J.G. Steiner, C. Neuman, and J.I. Schiller. Kerberos: An authentication service for open network systems. In *Usenix 1987 Winter Conference*, pages 191–202, January 1988.
26. Sun Microsystems. RFC 1057: RPC: Remote procedure call protocol specification: Version 2. Internet Activities Board, June 1988.
27. Edward Wobber, Martín Abadi, Michael Burrows, and Butler Lampson. Authentication in the Taos operating system. *ACM Transactions on Computer Systems*, 12(1):3–32, February 1994.

# History-Based Access Control for Mobile Code*

Guy Edjlali, Anurag Acharya, and Vipin Chaudhary

**Abstract.** In this chapter, we present a *history-based* access-control mechanism that is suitable for mediating accesses from mobile code. The key idea behind history-based access-control is to maintain a selective history of the access requests made by individual programs and to use this history to improve the differentiation between safe and potentially dangerous requests. What a program is allowed to do depends on its *own* behavior and identity in addition to currently used discriminators like the location it was loaded from or the identity of its author/provider. History-based access-control has the potential to significantly expand the set of programs that can be executed without compromising security or ease of use. We describe the design and implementation of *Deeds*, a history-based access-control mechanism for Java. Access-control policies for *Deeds* are written in Java, and can be updated while the programs whose accesses are being mediated are still executing.

## 1 Introduction

The integration of mobile code with web browsing creates an access-control dilemma. On one hand, it creates a social expectation that mobile code should be as easy to download and execute as fetching and viewing a web page. On the other hand, the popularity and ubiquity of mobile code increases the likelihood that malicious programs will mingle with benign ones.

To reassure users about the safety of their data and to keep the user interface simple and non-intrusive, systems supporting mobile code have chosen to err on the side of conservatism and simplicity. Depending on its *source*, mobile code is partitioned into *trusted* and *untrusted* code. Code is considered trusted if it is loaded from disk [9, 12] or if it is signed by an author/organization deemed trustworthy by the user [12, 30]. Untrusted code is confined to a severely restricted execution environment [9] (eg, it cannot open local files or sockets, cannot create a subprocess, cannot initiate print requests etc); trusted code is either given access to all available resources [30] or is given selective access based on user-specified access-control lists [12].

For the programs considered untrusted, these mechanisms can be overly restrictive. Many useful and safe programs, such as a well-behaved editor applet from a lesser-known software company, cannot be used since it cannot open local files. In addition, to implement new resource-sharing models such as *global computing* [6] all communication has to be routed through brokers. This significantly

---

* This paper is a reprint of a paper that appeared in the Fifth ACM Conference on Computer and Communications Security (November 3-5, 1998.)

limits the set of problems that can be efficiently handled by such models. For programs considered trusted, these models can be too lax. Errors, not just malice aforethought, can wipe out or leak important data. Combined with a suitable audit trail, *signed programs* [12] do provide the ability to take legal recourse if need be.

In this chapter, we present a *history-based* access-control mechanism that is suitable for mediating accesses from mobile code. The key idea behind history-based access-control is to maintain a selective history of the access requests made by individual programs and to use this history to improve the differentiation between safe and potentially dangerous requests. What a program is allowed to do depends on its *own* identity and behavior in addition to currently used discriminators like the location it was loaded from or the identity of its author/provider. History-based access-control has the potential to significantly expand the set of programs that can be executed without compromising security or ease of use. For example, consider an access-control policy that allows a program to open local files for reading as long as it has not opened a socket and allows it to open a socket as long as it has not opened a local file for reading. Irrespective of the source of the program, such a policy can ensure that no disk-resident data will be leaked. Strictly speaking, this is true iff it is possible to intercept *all* access requests being made on behalf of the program – the requests made by itself as well as the requests made on its behalf. The technique we present is able to intercept all requests.

We first present some examples of history-based access-control policies. Next, we discuss issues that have to be resolved for implementing history-based access-control mechanisms. In section 3, we describe *Deeds*,[1] an implementation of history-based access-control for Java programs. Access-control policies for *Deeds* are written in Java, and can be installed, removed or modified while the programs whose accesses are being mediated are still executing. *Deeds* requires policies to adhere to several constraints. These constraints are checked either at compile-time by the Java compiler or at runtime by the *Deeds* policy manager. We illustrate the operation of the *Deeds* user interface using snapshots. In section 4.4, we examine the additional overhead imposed by *Deeds* using micro-benchmarks as well as real programs. History-based access-control is not specific to Java or to mobile code. It can be used for any system that allows interposition of code between untrusted programs and protected resources. In section 5, we discuss how a system similar to *Deeds* can be used to mediate accesses to OS resources from native binaries. We conclude with a description of related work and the directions in which we plan to extend this effort.

## 2 Examples

**One-out-of-k:** Consider the situation when you want to allow only those programs that fall into well-marked equivalence classes based on their functionality

---

[1] Your deeds determine your destiny :)

and behavior. For example, you want to allow only programs that provide just the functionality of a browser or an editor or a shell. A browser can connect to remote sites, create temporary local files in a user-specified directory, read files that it has created and display them to the user. An editor can create local files in user-specified directories, read/modify files that it has created, and interact with the user. It is not allowed to open sockets. A shell can interact with the user and can create sub-processes. It cannot open local files, or connect to remote sites. This restriction can be enforced by a history-based access-control policy that:

- allows a program to connect to a remote site if and only if it has neither tried to open a local file that it has not created, nor tried to modify a file it has created, nor tried to create a sub-process;

- allows a program to open local files in user-specified directories for modification if and only if it has created them, and it has neither tried to connect to a remote site nor tried to create a sub-process.

- allows a program to create sub-processes if and only if it has neither tried to connect to a remote site nor tried to open a local file.

In effect, each program is dynamically classified into one of three equivalence classes (browser-like, editor-like or shell-like) based on the sequence of requests it makes. Once a program is placed in a class, it is allowed to access only the resources that are permitted to programs in that class.

**Keeping out rogues:** Consider the situation where you want to ensure that a program that you once killed due to inappropriate behavior is not allowed to execute on your machine. This restriction can be enforced, to some extent, by a history-based access-control policy that keeps track of previous termination events and the identity of the programs that were terminated.

**Frustrating peepers:** Consider the situation where you want to allow a program to access only one of two relations in a database but not both. One might wish to do this if accessing both the relations may allow a program to extract information that it cannot get from a single relation. For example, one might wish to allow programs to access either a relation that contains the date and the name of medical procedures performed in a hospital or a relation that contains the names of patients and the date they last came in. Individually, these relations do not allow a program to deduce information about treatment histories of individual patients. If, however, a program could access both relations, it could combine the relations to acquire (partial) information about treatment histories for individual patients. This example can be seen as an instance of the Chinese Wall Policy [4]. To block the possibility of a hostile *site* being able to deduce the same information from data provided by two different programs it provides, programs that have opened a socket are, thereafter, not allowed to access sensitive relations and programs that have accessed one of the sensitive relations are, thereafter, not allowed to open sockets.

**Slowing down hogs:** Consider the situation where you want to limit the rate at which a program connects to its home site. One might wish to do this, for example, to eliminate a form of denial of service where a program repeatedly connects to its home site without doing anything else. This can be enforced by a history-based access-control policy that keeps track of the timestamp of the last request. It allows only those requests that occur after a threshold period.

# 3 Issues for history-based access-control

**Identity of programs:** Associating a content-based, hard-to-spoof identity with a program is a key aspect of history-based access-control. That is, given any program, it should be hard to design a substitute program for whom the identity computation generates the same result. An important point to note is that the code for a mobile program can come from multiple sources (from local disk, from different servers on the network, etc). The identity mechanism should associate a single identity with *all the code* that is used by a program. This is important to ensure that a malicious program cannot assume the identity of another program by copying parts or all of the program being spoofed.

**Efficient maintenance of request-histories:** Wallach et al [40] mention that a collection of commonly used Java workloads require roughly 30000 crossings between protection domains per CPU-second of execution. Given this request-frequency, it is imperative that access-control checks on individual requests be fast. Simple logging-based techniques are likely to be too expensive. Fortunately, the request-history for many useful policies can be summarized. For example, the request-history for a policy that allows a program to open local files for reading if it has not opened a socket and allows it to open a socket if it has not opened a local file for reading can be summarized by a pair of booleans – one that records if the program has ever opened a socket and the other that records if it has ever opened a local file.

**Persistence of policies and histories:** Persistent request-histories are required to block attacks that consist of running a sequence of programs each of which makes requests that are allowed by the access-control policy but when taken as a whole, the complete sequence of requests violates the constraints the policy tries to enforce.

**Grouping privileges:** History-based mechanisms can provide extremely fine-grain access-control. Not only is it possible to control accesses to individual objects/resources, it is possible to differentiate between different patterns of accesses. While this allows us to expand the set of programs that can be executed safely, this level of flexibility can be hard to deal with. Requiring users to specify their preferences at this level of detail is likely to be considered intrusive and therefore ignored or avoided. This problem can alleviated to some extent by grouping acceptable patterns of program behavior and assign intuitive names to these patterns. For example, a policy that allows a program to open no sockets, open local files for reading, to create local files in a user-specified directory and to open a local file for modification only if it has been been created by itself. This set of restrictions allow a simple editor to be executed and can, jointly, be referred to as the *editor* policy.

**Composition and fail-safe defaults:** History-based access-control policies encode acceptable patterns of program behavior. Different classes of programs might have different behaviors all of which are acceptable to the user. It is, therefore, important to provide automatic composition of multiple policies. An important point to note here is that, by default, the access-control mechanism should be fail-safe [32] – potentially dangerous accesses should be denied unless explicitly granted.

# 4 Deeds: a history-based security manager for Java

In this section we describe the design and implementation of *Deeds*, a history-based access-control mechanism for Java. We first describe the architecture of *Deeds*. Next, we describe its current implementation and its user interface. In section 4.4, we examine the performance of the mechanisms provided by *Deeds*.

## 4.1 Architecture

In this subsection, we describe the architecture of *Deeds*. We focus on the central concepts of the *Deeds* architecture: secure program identity and security events.

**Program identity** The *Deeds* notion of the identity of a program is based on *all* the downloaded code reachable during its execution. To achieve this, *Deeds* performs static linking on downloaded programs, fetching all non-local code that might be referenced. Local libraries that are part of the language implementation (e.g java.lang for Java, libc for C) are linked in as shared libraries; a separate copy of non-system-library code is downloaded for every application that uses it.

*Deeds* concatenates all non-system-library code for a downloaded program and uses the SHA-1 algorithm [36] to compute a name for it. SHA-1 belongs to the group of algorithms known as secure hash functions [31, 36] which take an arbitrary sequence of bytes as input and generate a (relatively) short digest (160-bits for SHA-1). These functions are considered secure because it is computationally hard to construct two byte-sequences which produce the same digest. In addition, the requirement, in this case, that the byte-sequences being compared should represent valid programs increases the difficulty of constructing a malicious program with the same name as a benign one.

In addition to allowing a secure hash to be computed, static linking of down-loaded code has other advantages. First, having all the code available allows Just-in-Time compilers to perform better analysis and generate better code. Second, it removes potential covert channels which occur due to dynamic linking – the pattern of link requests can be used to pass information from a downloaded program to the server(s) that is (are) contacted for the code to be linked.

Note that Java allows programs to dynamically load classes. For such programs, it is not possible, in general, to statically determine the set of classes that might be referenced during the execution of the program. *Deeds* rejects such programs and does not allow them to execute.

**Security events and handlers** A *Deeds* security event occurs whenever a request is made to a protected resource. Examples of security events include request to open a socket, request to open a file for reading, request to create a file, request to open a file for modification etc. The set of security events in *Deeds* is not fixed. In particular, it is not limited to requests for operating-system resources. Programmers can associate a security event with any request they wish to keep track of or protect.

Handlers can be associated with security events. Handlers perform two tasks: they maintain an event-history and check whether it satisfies one or more user-specified constraints. If any of the constraint fails, the handler raises a security-related exception. For example, a handler for the security event associated with opening a socket can record whether the program currently being executed has ever opened a socket. Similarly, a handler for the security event associated with opening a file for reading can record whether the program has opened a file for reading.

Multiple handlers can be associated with each event. Handlers maintain separate event-histories. The checks they perform are, in effect, composed using a "consensus voting rule" – that is, one negative vote can veto a decision and at least one positive vote is needed to approve. In this context, a request is permitted to continue if and only if at least one handler is present and none of the handlers raises an exception.

Access-control policies consist of one or more handlers grouped together. The handlers belonging to a single policy maintain a common history and check common constraints. For example, the *editor* policy mentioned earlier would consist of four handlers:

- a handler for socket-creation that records if a socket was ever created by this program. It rejects the request if a file has been opened by this program (for reading or writing).
- a handler for file-creation that associates a creator with each file created by a downloaded program. If the file is to be created in a directory that is included in a list of user-specified directories, it allows the request to proceed. Else, it rejects the request.

- a handler for open-file-for-read that records if a file was ever opened for reading by this program. It rejects the request if a socket has been created by this program.
- a handler for open-file-for-modification that records if a file was ever opened for writing by this program. It rejects the request if a socket has been created by this program or if the file in question was not created by this program.

*Deeds* allows multiple access-control policies to be simultaneously active. Policies can be installed, removed, or modified during execution. A policy is added by attaching its constituent handlers to the corresponding events. For example, the *editor* policy would be added by attaching its handlers respectively to the socket-creation event, the file-creation event, the open-file-for-read event and the open-file-for-modification event. Policies can be removed in an analogous manner by detaching the constituents handlers from the associated events.

*Deeds* allows policies to be parameterized. For example, a policy that controls file creation can be parameterized by the directory within which file creation is allowed. Policies that are already installed can be modified by changing their parameters. This allows users to make on-the-fly changes to the environment within which mobile code executes.

*Deeds* provides a fail-safe default [32] for every security event. Unless overridden, the default handler for an event disallows all requests associated with that event from downloaded programs. The default handler can only be overridden by explicit user request – either by a dialog box or by a profile file containing a list of user preferences.

## 4.2  Implementation

In this subsection, we describe the implementation of *Deeds*. We focus on implementation of program identity, events, event-histories, policies (including conventions for writing them), and policy management.

**Program identity** We have implemented a new class-loader for downloading Java programs. A new instance of this class-loader is created for every downloaded program and is used to maintain information regarding its identity. This class-loader statically links a downloaded program by scanning its bytecode and extracting the set of classes that may be referred to during its execution. If the entire program is provided as a single `jar` file, this is straightforward. Else, the class-loader fetches and analyzes the non-local classes referred to and repeats this till transitive closure is achieved. If the scan of the bytecode indicates that the program explicitly loads classes, the linking operation is terminated and the program is not allowed to run.

After the linking operation is completed, the class-loader concatenates the code for all the non-system-library classes that are referenced by the program and uses the implementation of the SHA-1 algorithm provided in the `java.security` package to compute a secure hash. The result is used as the name of the program and is stored in the class-loader instance created for this program. This name can be used to maintain program-specific event-histories. It can also be stored in persistent storage and loaded as a part of the startup procedure.

**Events:** Two concerns guided our implementation of events: (1) the number of events is not fixed, and (2) the number of handlers associated with individual events could be large. We considered three alternatives. First, we could use a general-purpose mechanism (similar to Java Beans [8] and X [33]) to register events and handlers. The advantage of this approach is that it uses common code to manage all events and their associated handlers; the disadvantage is that all handlers must have the same type-signature which usually implies that the parameters need to be packed by the event manager and unpacked by each handler.

Second, we could dynamically modify the bytecode of the downloaded program to insert/delete calls to handlers at the points where the events are generated (as dynamic instrumentation programs [5, 15] do). To allow a user to modify an executing policy would require us to update the bytecode of running programs. We believe that the complexity of such an implementation is not commensurate with its advantages.

Finally, we could require that the handlers for each event be managed by a different event manager. This approach allows us to avoid the packing and unpacking of parameters as each event manager is aware of the parameters corresponding to its event. The disadvantage of this scheme is that a separate event manager has to be written for each event. However, event managers are highly stylized and can be automatically generated given a description of the event (see Figure 1 for an example).

We selected the third approach for implementing security events in *Deeds*. Combined with automatic generation of event managers, this allowed us to balance the needs of efficiency, implementation simplicity and ease of programming. Examples of *Deeds* security events include `checkRead()` and `checkConnect()`.[2]

**History:** Given the concern about the size of the log, we have chosen to avoid logging as a general technique for maintaining event-histories. Instead, we have left the decision about how to store histories to individual policies. All policies that we considered were able to summarize event-histories using simple data structures such as counters, booleans or lists. Note that this decision has the potential disadvantage that if policies do desire/need to log events, the lack of a common logging mechanism can result in the maintenance of duplicate logs. This can be fixed by using a selective logging mechanism that logs an event only if requested to do so by one or more handlers associated with the event.

**Access-control policies** A *Deeds* access-control policy consists of the data-structures to maintain event-histories, handlers for each of the events that are mediated by the policy, and auxiliary variables and operations to facilitate management of multiple policies. Concretely, an access-control policy is implemented

---

[2] Readers familiar with Java will recognize that all the `check*()` methods are security events.

```
public class checkReadManager implements EventManager {
  private static HandlerCheckRead hdlr = new HandlerCheckRead();

  public static void checkRead(FileDescriptor fd,DClassLoader cl)
  throws GeneralSecurityException {
    for (int i=0;i<hdlr.size;i++)
      hdlr.policy(i).checkRead(fd,cl);
  }

  public static void checkRead(String file,DClassLoader cl)
  throws GeneralSecurityException {
    for (int i=0;i<hdlr.size;i++)
      hdlr.policy(i).checkRead(file,cl);
  }

  public static void checkRead(String file,Object context,
                               DClassLoader cl)
  throws GeneralSecurityException {
    for (int i=0;i<hdlr.size;i++)
      hdlr.policy(i).checkRead(file,context,cl);
  }
}
```

**Fig. 1.** Example of an event manager class. Managers for other events would share the same structure but would replace checkRead by name the of the particular event. Some administrative details have been left out of the example; these details are common to all event managers.

as a Java class that extends the AccessPolicy class shown in Figure 2. Handlers are implemented as methods of this class and the event-history is implemented as variables of this class. For example, a handler for the open-file-for-reading event could check if a socket has yet been created by the program. If so, it could raise a GeneralSecurityException; else, it could set a boolean to indicate that a file has been opened for reading and return.

When a security event occurs (e.g., when checkRead is called), control is transferred to the Deeds Security Manager which determines the class-loader for the program that caused the event using the currentClassLoader() method provided by the Java Security Manager. This method returns the class-loader corresponding to the most recent occurrence on the stack of a method from a class loaded using a class-loader. Since a new instance of the class-loader is created for every downloaded program and since this instance loads all non-system-library classes for the program, currentClassLoader() always returns the same class-loader every time it is called during the execution of a program. This technique safely determines the identity of the program that caused the security event.

```
abstract synchronized public class AccessPolicy {
  public String name         ; // name of policy instance
  public Vector parameters   ; // policy parameters
  public Vector targetEvents ; //
  public String srcFileName  ; // source file location
  // these functions have to be provided by every policy
  public abstract String documentation();
  public abstract void    saveHistoryToDisk();
  public abstract void    restoreHistoryFromDisk();

  public Policy(String name) {
    ...
  }
}
```

**Fig. 2.** Skeleton of the AccessPolicy class. The **synchronized** keyword ensures that at most one handler is updating the event-history at any given time.

Once the class-loader corresponding to the currently executing program has been determined, the Deeds Security Manager invokes the event manager corresponding to event being processed (e.g., **checkReadManager** in Figure 1). The event manager maintains the set of handlers associated with the event and invokes the handlers in the order they were attached to the event. If any of the handlers throws an exception, it is propagated to the caller; the remaining handlers are not invoked.

*Deeds* policies are expected to adhere to several constraints. These constraints are checked either at compile-time by the Java compiler or at runtime by the *Deeds* policy manager. These constraints are:

- Handler methods must include a **throws GeneralSecurityException** clause and must have the same name as the security event that they are intended for. The type signature for a handler method must be the same as the type signature of the security event it handles except for one additional argument – the class-loader. See Figure 1 for an illustration.
- A handler method must have the same number of variants as the security event that it is intended for. For example, a checkRead event has three variants – **checkRead(FileDescriptor fd)**, **checkRead(String file)**, and **checkRead(String file, Object context)**. Handlers for this event must have three variants. See Figure 1 for an illustration.
- Parameters of a policy must be explicitly identified. Each parameter must have a default value and a documentation string.
- The vector **targetEvents** specifies which events the handlers in this policy are to be attached to. The specification is in the form of a regular expression which is matched against fully-qualified names. For example, the target events for a checkRead handler could be specified as ``FileIO.checkRead''

or ``*.checkRead''. The former expression specifies only the checkRead event defined in the FileIO package whereas the latter specifies all check-Read events irrespective of the package they have been defined in. This specification is needed as Java's hierarchical namespace allows multiple methods with the same name to exist in different regions of the namespace. Since a security event is implemented by a method in a subclass of EventManager and since every package can have its own security events, the possibility of name clashes is real. For example, a library to perform file I/O, and a library to interact with a database could both wish to create a checkRead event. Since packages are independently developed, extensible systems, such as *Deeds*, cannot assume uniqueness of event names.

– Each policy must be accompanied by its source code and the name of the file containing the source code should be available as a member of the class implementing the policy. We believe that availability of source code of a policy is important to instill confidence in its operation and its documentation.

**Policy manager** The *Deeds* policy manager makes extensive use of the Java reflection mechanism [17]. This mechanism allows Java code to inspect and browse the structure of other classes. The policy manager uses reflection to: (1) identify methods that are to be used as handlers (they are declared public void and throw the GeneralSecurityException); (2) identify parameters and their types; (3) initialize and update parameters; and (4) extract specification of the events that the handlers are to be attached to. In addition, it performs several administrative checks such as ensuring that all policy instances have unique names.

The policy manager is also responsible for ensuring that policies are persistent. It achieves this by storing the parameters for each policy instance on stable storage and using them to re-install the policy when the environment is reinitialized (on startup). It also periodically saves the event-history on stable storage.[3]

## 4.3   User interface

The *Deeds* user interface comes up only on user request and is used for infrequent operations such as browsing/loading/installing policies. In this section, we describe the functionality of the user interface and present snapshots.

**Browsing/viewing/loading policies:** The *Deeds* user interface allows users to browse the set of available policies, to view documentation and source code for these policies and to create instances of individual policies. Note that every policy is required to have documentation (via the documentation() method) and access to its own source code (via the srcFileName member). In addition, every parameter has associated documentation which can be viewed. To load a

---

[3] Note that individual policies are free to save the event-history as frequently as they wish.

parameterized policy, users need to specify values for all the parameters of the policy. Note that every parameter has a default value which is displayed. The *Deeds* policy manager uses the Java reflection mechanism to figure out the type of the parameters for display and parsing purposes. These functions of the user interface are illustrated in figures 3 and 4. In Figure 3, a policy is selected by clicking on its name and operations are selected using the buttons. Browsing and loading of individual policies is illustrated in Figure 4.

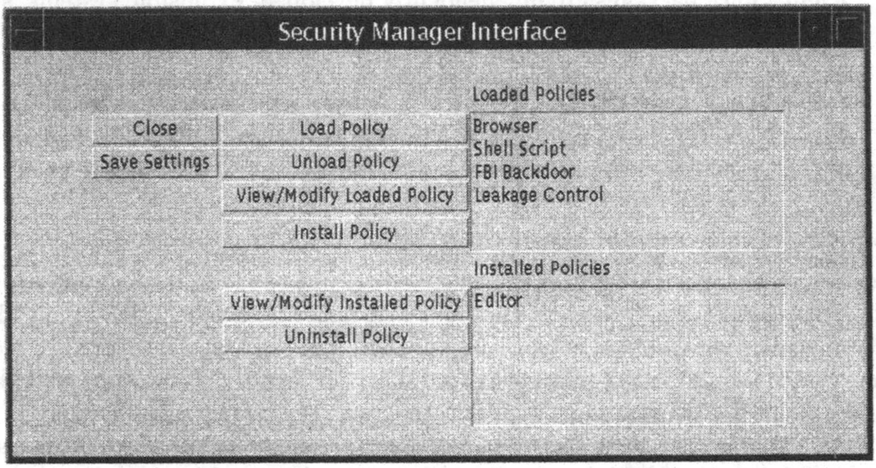

**Fig. 3.** Graphical interface to the Deeds Security Manager

**Fig. 4.** Graphical interface for loading a policy

**Installing/uninstalling policies:** The *Deeds* user interface allows users to install loaded policies as well as to remove currently installed policies. For an illustration, see Figure 3. A loaded policy can be installed using the Install

Policy button, and an installed policy can be removed using the Uninstall Policy button.

**Checkpointing event-histories:** *Deeds* allows user to checkpoint the current state of the event-histories for all policies using the Save Settings button (see Figure 3).

**Browsing/setting default handlers:** *Deeds* provides a fail-safe default for every security event. Unless overridden, the default handler for an event disallows all requests associated with that event from downloaded programs. The default handler can only be overridden by explicit user request – either by a dialog box or by a profile file containing a list of user preferences. The *Deeds* user interface allows users to browse and set default handlers for all security events.

### 4.4 Performance evaluation

There are two ways in which *Deeds* can impact the performance of downloaded code whose accesses it mediates. First, it can add an overhead to each request for protected resources. Second, it can increase the startup latency as it requires fetching, loading, linking and hashing of all non-system-library code before the program can start executing. In this section, we evaluate the performance impact of *Deeds*. All experiments were performed on a Sun E3000 with 266MHz UltraSparc processors and 512MB memory.

To determine the overhead of executing *Deeds* security-event handlers, we used a microbenchmark which repeatedly opened and closed files. A security event was triggered on the request to open a file. We varied the number of handlers from zero to ten. Each handler was identical (but distinct) and implemented the editor policy described earlier in this paper. It maintains two booleans, one that tracks if the program has ever tried to create a socket and the other that tracks if the program has ever tried to open a file. Each time it is invoked, it updates the file-opened boolean and checks the socket-opened boolean.

Table 1 presents the results. It shows that even with ten handlers, the overhead of *Deeds* security event handlers is less than 5%. Another point to note is that without any handlers, that is, when the infrastructure added to support security event handlers is not used, the overhead is less than 1%.

| Number of handlers | 0 | 1 | 2 | 3 | 4 | 5 | 6 | 7 | 8 | 9 | 10 |
|---|---|---|---|---|---|---|---|---|---|---|---|
| Percent overhead | 0.7 | 1.8 | 2.6 | 2.4 | 2.9 | 3.5 | 4.2 | 3.9 | 4.3 | 4.1 | 4.3 |

**Table 1.** Overhead of *Deeds* security event handlers. The overhead was measured using a microbenchmark which repeatedly opened and closed files. Each handler was identical (but distinct) and implemented the editor policy.

To evaluate the impact on startup latency, we compared the time it takes to load, analyze and link complete Java applications using the *Deeds* class-loader to the time it takes to load just the first file using existing class-loaders. In both cases, all the files were local and were in the operating-system file-cache. For this experiment, we selected seven complete Java applications available on the web. The applications we used were: (1) **news-server**, the Spaniel News Server [38] which manages and serves newsgroups local to an organization; (2) **jlex**, the JLex [23] lexical analyzer; (3) **dbase**, the Jeevan [22] platform-independent, object-oriented database; (4) **jawavedit**, the JaWavedit audio file editor [21] with multi-lingual voice synthesis, signal processing, and a graphical user interface; (5) **obfuscator**, the Hashjava [14] obfuscator for Java class files; (6) **javacc**, the JavaCC [20] parser generator; and (7) **editor**, the WingDis editor [42].

Table 2 presents results for the latency experiments. As expected, the additional startup latency increases with the number of files as well as the total size of the program. Note this does not represent an increase in end-to-end execution time. Existing class-loaders already parse the bytecodes of class files as a part of the Java verification process; signed applets require computation of a similar hash function. Instead, the increase in startup latency is caused by moving the processing for all the class files before the execution begins. We expect that, once downloaded, programs of this size and these types (lexer/parser generators, editors, news server, database etc) will be reused several times. In that case, the program can be cached as a whole (instead of individual files) and the additional startup latency has to be incurred only once.

| Application | newsserver | jlex | dbase | jawavedit | obfuscator | javacc | editor |
|---|---|---|---|---|---|---|---|
| Number of classes | 24 | 40 | 104 | 125 | 144 | 81 | 212 |
| Total code size (KB) | 120 | 289 | 514 | 508 | 483 | 578 | 979 |
| First class size (KB) | 5 | 1 | 11 | 2.5 | 4 | 7 | 1.5 |
| Loading classes | 0.2s | 0.3s | 0.5s | 0.9s | 1.0s | 0.8s | 1.3s |
| Parsing bytecodes | 0.1s | 0.1s | 0.2s | 0.5s | 0.5s | 0.4s | 1.2s |
| Hashing bytecodes | 0.1s | 0.5s | 0.7s | 1.1s | 1.4s | 2.6s | 2.9s |
| Additional latency | 0.4s | 0.9s | 1.4s | 2.5s | 2.9s | 3.8s | 5.6s |

**Table 2.** Breakdown of additional startup latency incurred by *Deeds*.

## 5 Discussion

**History-based access-control for native binaries:** History-based access-control is not specific to Java or to mobile code. It can be used for any system that allows interposition of code between untrusted programs and protected resources. Several operating systems (Solaris, Digital Unix, IRIX, Mach and Linux) allow users to interpose user-level code between an executing program and OS resources by intercepting system calls. This facility is usually used to implement debuggers and system call tracers. It has also been used to implement a general-purpose code interposition mechanism [24], a secure environment for helper applications used by browsers to display files with different formats [11] and a user-level file system [1]. It is also well-suited for implementing a *Deeds*-like history-based access-control mechanism to mediate access to OS resources from native binaries.

**Pre-classified program behaviors:** The *one-out-of-k* policy described in section 2 classifies program behaviors in an on-line manner. A program gets classified as a browser, an editor, or a shell depending on whether it has connected to a remote site, has opened local files for modification, or has created a sub-process. To be able to do this for a wide variety of program behaviors, the policy that does the classification and subsequent management of privileges has to contain code to handle all these behaviors. An alternative scheme would be to allow program-providers to label their programs with pre-classified behavior patterns and to allow the users to specify which behaviors they would like to permit. The policies governing individual behaviors could be added/deleted as need be. While this scheme would require agreement on the labeling scheme, it is no more complex than the MIME-types-based scheme that is already in use for displaying/processing different data formats. This scheme is similar to *program-ACLs* and related defenses proposed for trojan-horse attacks [25, 41].

**Joint-authorization:** Commercial applications, such as contracts and purchase orders, may require multiple authorizations since the organization may wish to reduce the risk of malfesance by dispersing trust over several individuals. History-based access-control policies can be used to implement joint-authorization [39] or *k-out-of-n-authorizations* [3]. For example, a policy may require that three out of five known individuals must make the same request within the last $T$ units of time for the request to be granted; else the request is denied. In this case, the history consists of the requests that have been made in the last $T$ units of time.

# 6 Related work

The primary problem for access-control mechanisms for mobile code is to be able to differentiate between different programs executing on behalf of the same user and to provide them with different privileges based on their expected behavior and/or potential to cause damage. A similar problem occurs in the context of trojan-horse programs and viruses. To deal with such programs, several researchers have developed mechanisms to limit the privileges of individual programs based on their expected behavior [10, 25–28, 35, 41]. Karger [25] uses information about file extensions and behavior of individual programs to determine the set of files that a program is allowed to access (eg. a compiler invoked on x.c is only allowed to create x.{o,u,out}). Lai [28] replaces the inference mechanism by an explicit list of files accessible by a program. Wichers et al [41] associate *program-ACLs* with each file thereby limiting the set of programs that can access each file. King [26] uses a regular-expression-based language to specify the set of objects each operation can access. Ko et al[27] use a language based on predicate logic and regular expressions to specify the security-relevant behavior of privileged programs and propose to use this specification for intrusion detection. All these approaches assume that the set of programs to be run are fixed and their behaviors are known. The mobile code environment is different as the set of programs that will execute is inherently unknown. History-based access-control is able to classify programs in an on-line manner and to thereafter execute them within an environment with appropriate privileges. For example, the *one-out-of-k* policy dynamically classifies downloaded programs into one of three classes: browsers, editors and shells.

Schneider proposes *EM* as the class of security enforcement mechanisms which work by monitoring the execution of a *target* (untrusted application in our terminology) and which terminates any execution that is about to violate the security policy being enforced [34]. Behavior-based confinement is a part of the *EM* class. Schneider also proposes a formalism (security automata) for specifying security policies. The finite-state nature of security automata implies that request-histories for policies specified using them can be summarized using a counter. This is similar to our experience with *Deeds* where we found that request-histories for policies of interest could be summarized using booleans/counters.

The use of secure hash functions to derive a content-based name for software has been proposed by Hollingsworth et al [16]. They propose to use these names for configuration and version management of large applications and application suites (such Microsoft Office).

An important feature of *Deeds* is its capability to install and compose multiple user-specified policies. Several researchers have proposed languages to allow users to specify access-control policies and frameworks to compose these policies [3, 13, 18, 19]. Three of them [13, 18, 19], propose logic-based declarative languages and use inference mechanisms of various sorts to compose policies. Blaze et al [3] propose a language that contains both assertions and procedural filters and use a mechanism similar of that used in *Deeds* to implement composition. Access-control policies for *Deeds* are entirely procedural. Furthermore, they can be updated while the programs whose accesses are being controlled are still executing.

Two research groups have recently proposed constraint languages for specifying security policies temporal aspects. Simon&Zurko [37] propose a language for specifying temporal constraints such as HasDone, NeverDid, NeverUsed and SomeoneFromEach for separation of duty in role-based environments. These predicates correspond to summaries of event-histories in *Deeds* terminology.

Mehta&Sollins [29] have independently proposed a constraint language for specifying simple history-based access-control policies for Java applets. This work was done in parallel with ours [7]. The approach presented in their paper has two major limitations. First, they use the domain name of the server that provides the applet as its identifier. This assigns the same identifier to all applets from the same host. In addition, it is vulnerable to DNS spoofing attacks. They suggest that this problem can be fixed by using the identity of the author/supplier of an applet as its name. This assigns the same identifier to all applets from a single author/supplier and results in a single merged history. It is not clear how such a merged history would be used as the predicates and variables in their language are applet-specific. Even if each supplier provides only one applet, this is a viable solution only if all the classes referenced by the applet are provided in a single jar file or are required to be signed by the same principal. Otherwise, it is possible for a malicious server that is able to spoof IP addresses to intercept intermediate requests for dynamically linked classes and provide malicious substitutes. The second limitation of their approach is that it provides a small and fixed number of events. This limits the variety and power of the policies that can be developed.

The event model used in *Deeds* is similar to that used in the SPIN extensible operating system [2]. An interesting feature of SPIN is the use of dynamic compilation to improve the performance of event dispatching [5]. If the performance of event dispatching becomes a problem for *Deeds* (eg. if individual events have a large number of handlers) we can use a similar technique.

## 7   Current status and future directions

*Deeds* is currently operational and can be used for stand-alone Java programs. We are in the process of identifying a variety of useful patterns of behaviors and evaluating the performance and usability of *Deeds* in the context of these behaviors.

In the near term, we plan to develop a history-based mechanism for mediating access to OS resources from native binaries. We also plan to explore the possibility of using program labels to indicate pre-classified behaviors and automatic loading/unloading of access-control policies to support this.

In the longer term, we plan to explore just-in-time binary rewriting to insert event generation and dispatching code into downloaded programs. This would allow users to create new kinds of events as and when they desire. Currently, new kinds of events are created only by system libraries.

## Acknowledgments

We would like to thank anonymous referees for their insightful comments which helped improve the presentation of this paper.

## References

1. A. Alexandrov, M. Ibel, K. Schauser, and C. Scheiman. Extending the operating system at the user level: the Ufo global file system. In *Proceedings of the 1997 USENIX Annual Technical Conference*, 1997.
2. B. Bershad, S. Savage, P. Pardyak, et al. Extensibility, safety and performance in the spin operating system. In *Proc of the 15th ACM Symposium on Operating System Principles*, pages 267–84, 1995.

3. M. Blaze, J. Feigenbaum, and J. Lacy. Decentralized trust management. In *Proc of the 17th Symposium on Security and Privacy*, pages 164–73, 1996.
4. D. Brewer and M. Nash. The Chinese Wall Security Policy. In *Proceedings of the 1989 IEEE Symposium on Security and Privacy*, 1989.
5. C. Chambers, S. Eggers, J. Auslander, M. Philipose, M. Mock, and P. Pardyak. Automatic dynamic compilation support for event dispatching in extensible systems. In *Workshop on Compiler Support for Systems Software*, 1996.
6. B. Christiansen, P. Cappello, M. Ionescu, M. Neary, K. Schauser, and D. Wu. Javelin: Internet-based parallel computing using Java. In *Proceedings of the 1997 ACM Workshop on Java for Science and Engineering Computation*, 1997.
7. G. Edjlali, A. Acharya, and V. Chaudhary. History-based access control for mobile code. Technical report, University of California, Santa Barbara, 1997.
8. R. Englander. *Developing Java Beans*. O'Reilly & Associates, 1997.
9. J. Fritzinger and M. Mueller. Java security. Technical report, Sun Microsystems, Inc, 1996.
10. T. Gamble. Implementing execution controls in Unix. In *Proceedings of the 7th System Administration Conference*, pages 237–42, 1993.
11. I. Goldberg, D. Wagner, R. Thomas, and E. Brewer. A secure environment for untrusted helper applications: confining the wily hacker. In *Proceedings of the 1996 USENIX Security Symposium*, 1996.
12. L. Gong. New security architectural directions for Java. In *Proceedings of IEEE COMPCON'97*, 1997.
13. C. Gunter and T. Jim. Design of an application-level security infrastructure. In *DIMACS Workshop on Design and Formal Verification of Security Protocols*, 1997.
14. The HashJava code obfuscator. Available from 4thPass Software, 810 32nd Avenue South, Seattle, WA 98144[4].
15. J. Hollingsworth, B. Miller, and J. Cargille. Dynamic program instrumentation for scalable performance tools. In *SHPCC*, 1994.
16. J. Hollingsworth and E. Miller. Using content-derived names for caching and software distribution. In *Proceedings of the 1997 ACm Symposium on Software Reusability*, 1997.
17. C. Horstmann and G. Cornell. *Core Java 1.1*, volume I - Fundamentals. Sun Microsystems Press, third edition, 1997.
18. T. Jaeger, A. Prakash, and A. Rubin. Building systems that flexibly control downloaded executable context. In *Proc of the 6th Usenix Security Symposium*, 1996.
19. S. Jajodia, P. Samarati, V. Subrahmanian, and E. Bertino. A unified framework for enforcing multiple access control policies. In *Proc. ACM SIGMOD Int'l. Conf. on Management of Data*, pages 474–85, 1997.
20. The JavaCC parser generator. Available from Sun Microsystems Inc. 901 San Antonio Road, Palo Alto, CA 94303 USA[5].
21. The JaWavedit Audio File Editor. Available from Florian Bomers' web site[6].
22. The Jeevan object-oriented database. Available from W3apps Inc., Ft. Lauderdale, Florida[7].
23. The JLex lexical analyzer generator. Available from the Department of Computer Science, Princeton University[8].

---

[4] *http://www.sbktech.org/hashjava.html*
[5] *http://www.suntest.com/JavaCC*
[6] *http://rummelplatz.uni-mannheim.de/ boemers/JaWavedit*
[7] *http://www.w3apps.com*
[8] *http://www.cs.princeton.edu/ appel/modern/java/JLex*

24. M. Jones. Interposition agents: Transparently interposing user code at the system interface. In *Proceedings of the 14th ACM Symposium on Operating System Principles*, 1993.

25. P. Karger. Limiting the damage potential of the discretionary trojan horse. In *Proceedings of the 1987 IEEE Syposium on Research in Security and Privacy*, 1987.

26. M. King. Identifying and controlling undesirable program behaviors. In *Proceedings of the 14th National Computer Security Conference*, 1992.

27. C. Ko, G. Fink, and K. Levitt. Automated detection of vulnerabilities in privileged programs by execution monitoring. In *Proceedings. 10th Annual Computer Security Applications Conference*, pages 134–44, 1994.

28. N. Lai and T. Gray. Strengthening discretionary access controls to inhibit trojan horses and computer viruses. In *Proceedings of the 1988 USENIX Summer Symposium*, 1988.

20. N. Mehta and K. Sollins. Extending and expanding the security features of Java. In *Proceedings of the 1998 USENIX Security Symposium*, 1998.

30. Microsoft Corporation. *Proposal for Authenticating Code Via the Internet*, Apr 1996. *http://www.microsoft.com/intdev/security/authcode*.

31. R. Rivest. The MD5 message-digest algorithm. RFC 1321, Network Working Group, 1992.

32. J. Saltzer and M. Schroeder. The protection of information in computer systems. *Proceedings of the IEEE*, 63(9):1278–1308, Sep 1975.

33. R. Scheifler and J. Gettys. *X Window System : The Complete Reference to Xlib, X Protocol, Icccm, Xlfd*. Butterworth-Heinemann, 1992.

34. F. Schneider. Enforceable security policies. Technical report, Dept of Computer Science, Cornell University, 1998.

35. C. Serban and B. McMillin. Run-time security evaluation (RTSE) for distributed applications. In *Proc. of the 1996 IEEE Symposium on Security and Privacy*, pages 222–32, 1996.

36. Secure hash standard. Federal Information Processing Standards Publication, FIPS, PUB 180-1, April 1995.

37. R. Simon and M. Zurko. Separation of duty in role-based environments. In *Proceedings of the IEEE Computer Security Foundations Workshop'97*, 1997.

38. The Spaniel News Server. Available from Spaniel Software[9].

39. V. Varadharajan and P. Allen. Joint actions based authorization schemes. *Operating Systems Review*, 30(3):32–45, 1996.

40. D. Wallach, D. Balfanz, D. Dean, and E. Felten. Extensible security architecture for Java. In *SOSP 16*, 1997.

41. D. Wichers, D. Cook, R. Olsson, J. Crossley, P. Kerchen, K. Levitt, and R. Lo. PACL's: an access control list approach to anti-viral security. In *USENIX Workshop Proceedings. UNIX SECURITY II*, pages 71–82, 1990.

42. The WingDis Editor. Available from WingSoft Corporation, P.O.Box 7554, Fremont, CA 94537[10].

---

[9] *http://www.searchspaniel.com/newsserver.html*
[10] *http://www.wingsoft.com/javaeditor.shtml*

# Security in Active Networks

D. Scott Alexander, William A. Arbaugh, Angelos D. Keromytis, and
Jonathan M. Smith

**Abstract.** The desire for flexible networking services has given rise to
the concept of "active networks." Active networks provide a general
framework for designing and implementing network-embedded services,
typically by means of a programmable network infrastructure. A programmable network infrastructure creates significant new challenges for
securing the network infrastructure.

This paper begins with an overview of active networking. It then moves
to security issues, beginning with a threat model for active networking,
moving through an enumeration of the challenges for system designers,
and ending with a survey of approaches for meeting those challenges.
The Secure Active Networking Environment (SANE) realizes many of
these approaches; an implementation exists and provides acceptable performance for even the most aggressive active networking proposals such
as active packets (sometimes called "capsules").

We close the paper with a discussion of open problems and an attempt
to prioritize them.

## 1   What is Active Networking?

In networking architectures a design choice can be made between:

1. Restricting the actions of the network infrastructure to transport, and
2. easing those restrictions to permit on-the-fly customization of the network
   infrastructure.

The data-transport model, which has been successfully applied in the IP Internet
and other networks, is called passive networking since the infrastructure (*e.g.*, IP
routers) is mostly indifferent to the packets passing through, and their actions
(forwarding and routing) cannot be directly influenced by users. This is not to
say that the switches do not perform complex computations as a result of receiving or forwarding a packet. Rather, the nature of these computations cannot
dynamically change beyond the fairly basic configuration options provided by
the manufacturer of the switch.

In contrast, *active* networking allows network-embedded functionality other
than transport. For current systems, this functionality ranges from WWW proxy
caches, multicasting [17] and RSVP [12] to firewalls. Since each of these independently designed and supported functions could be carried out as an application
of a more general infrastructure, the architecture of such *active* infrastructures
is now being investigated aggressively.

The basic principle employed is the use of *programmability*, as this allows many applications to be created, including those not foreseen by the designers of the switch. There are a number of forms this programmability can take, including treating each packet as a program (active packets or "capsules") and programming or reprogramming network elements on-the-fly with select packets. Note that the latter approach subsumes the former, as a program may be loaded that treats all subsequent packets as programs.

## 1.1 Why is Active Network Security Interesting?

From a security perspective, a large scale infrastructure with user access to programming capabilities, even if restricted, creates a wide variety of difficult challenges. Most directly, since the basis of security is controlled access to resources, the increased complexity of the managed resources makes securing them much more difficult. Since "security" is best thought of as a mapping between a policy and a set of predicates maintained through actions, the policy must be more complex than, in as much as they exist, equivalent policies of present-day networks, resulting in an explosion in the set of predicates.

For example, the ability to load a new queuing discipline may be attractive from a resource control perspective, but if the queuing discipline can replace that of an existing user, the replacement policy must be specified, and its implementation carefully controlled through one or more policy enforcement mechanisms.

Additionally, such a scenario forces the definition of *principals* and objects with which policies are associated. When compared with the policy at a basic IP router (no principals, datagram delivery guarantees, FIFO queuing, *etc.*) it can be seen why securing active networks is difficult.

## 1.2 Virtual and Real Resources

As the role of active networking elements is to store, compute and forward, the managed resources are those required to store packets, operate on them, and forward them to other elements. The resources provided to various principals at any instant cannot exceed the real resources (*e.g.*, output port bandwidth) available at that instant. This emphasis on real resources and time implies that a conventional <*object, principal, access*> 3-tuple for an access control list (ACL) is inadequate.

To provide controlled access to real resources, with real time constraints, a fourth element to represent duration (either absolute or periodic) must be added, giving <*object, principal, access, QoS guarantees*>. This remains an ACL, but is not "virtualized" by leaving time unspecified and making "eventual" access acceptable. We should point out that this new element in the ACL can be encoded as part of the *access* field. Similarly, we need not use an actual ACL, but we may use mechanisms that can be expressed in terms of ACLS and are better-suited for distributed systems.

# 2 Terminology

The term *trust* is used heavily in computer security. Unfortunately, the term has several definitions depending on who uses it and how the term is used. In fact, the U.S. Department of Defense's *Orange Book* [20], which defined several levels of security a computer host could provide, defines *trust* ambiguously. The definition of *trust* used herein is a slight modification of that by Neumann [46]. An object is defined as *trusted* when the object operates as expected according to design and policy. A stronger trust statement is when an object is *trustworthy*. A *trustworthy* object is one that has been shown in some convincing manner, *e.g.*, a formal code-review or formal mathematical analysis, to operate as expected. A *security-critical* object is one which the security — defined by a policy — of the system depends on the proper operation of the object. A security-critical object can be considered trusted, which is usually the case in most secure systems, but unfortunately this leads to an unnecessary profusion of such objects.

We note the distinction between *trust* and *integrity*: Trust is determined through the verification of components and the dependencies among them. Integrity demonstrates that components have not been modified. Thus integrity checking in a trustworthy system is about preserving an established trust or trust relationship.

## 2.1 Threat Model

An active network infrastructure is very different from the current Internet [3]. In the latter, the only resources consumed by a packet at a router are:

1. the memory needed to temporarily store it, and
2. the CPU cycles necessary to find the correct route.

Even if IP [53] option processing is needed, the CPU overhead is still quite small compared to the cost of executing an active packet. In such an environment, strict resource control in the intermediate routers was considered non-critical. Thus, security policies [8] are enforced end-to-end. While this approach has worked well in the past, there are several problems. First, denial-of-service attacks are relatively easy to mount, due to this simple resource model. Attacks to the infrastructure itself are possible, and result in major network connectivity loss. Finally, it is very difficult to provide enforceable quality-of-service guarantees. [12]

Active Networks, being more flexible, considerably expand the threat possibilities, because of the increased numbers of potential points of vulnerability. For example, when a packet containing code to execute arrives, the system typically must:

- Identify the sending network element.
- Identify the sending user.
- Grant access to appropriate resources based on these identifications.
- Allow execution based on the authorizations and security policy.

In networking terminology, the first three steps comprise a form of admission control, while the final step is a form of policing. Security violations occur when a policy is violated, *e.g.*, reading a private packet, or exceeding some specified resource usage. In the present-day Internet, intermediate network elements (*e.g.*, routers) very rarely have to perform any of these checks. This is a result of the best-effort resource allocation policies inherent in IP networking.

**Denial-of-Service Attacks.** Cryptographic mechanisms have proven remarkably successful for functions such as identification and authentication. These functions typically (although not necessarily) are used in protocols with a *virtual time* model, which is concerned with sequencing of events rather than more constrained sequencing of events with time limits (the *real time* model). The cases where time limits are observed are almost always for reasons of robustness, *e.g.*, to force eventual termination. Since such timeouts are intended for extreme circumstances, they are long enough so that they can cope with any reasonable delay.

In an environment where a considerable fraction (and perhaps eventually a majority) of the traffic will be continuous media traffic, security must include resource management and protection with an eye to preserving timing properties. In particular, a pernicious form of "attack" is the so-called "denial-of-service" attack. The basic principle applied in such an attack is that while wresting control of the service is desirable, the goal can be achieved if the opponent cannot use the service. This principle has been used in military communications strategies, *e.g.*, the use of radio "jamming" to frustrate an opponent's communications, and most recently in denying service to Internet Service Provider servers using a TCP *SYN* flood attack [50, 16]. Another very effective (even crippling) attack on a computer system can occur due to scheduling algorithms which implicitly embed design assumptions.

To look at an example in some detail, consider the so-called "recursive shell" shown in Figure 1.

The shell script invokes itself. This is in fact a natural programming style, except that the process of invoking a shell script consists mainly of executing two heavyweight system calls, fork() and exec(), which, respectively, create a new copy of the current process and replace the current process with a new process created from an executable file. Since the program spends the majority of its time executing system calls, which in UNIX cause the operating system to execute on behalf of the user (at high priority) the system's resources are typically consumed by this program (including CPU time and table space used for holding process control blocks).

With an active network element, it is easy to imagine situations where user programs (or errant system programs) run amok, and make the network elements useless for basic tasks. The solution, we believe, is to constrain *real* resources associated with active network programs. For example, if we limited the principal (*e.g.*, a "user") invoking the recursive shell script to 10% of the CPU time, or 10% of the system memory, the process would either limit its effects on the CPU to a 10% degradation, or fail to operate (since it could not invoke a new process) when it hit the table space limitation. Fortunately, a number of new operating systems [40, 35] have appeared which provide the services necessary to contain one or more executing threads within a single scheduling domain.

```
#!/bin/sh
$0 #invoke ourselves
```

**Fig. 1.** A recursive shell script for UNIX

## 2.2  Challenges for the System Designer

Independent of the specific network architecture, the designer of a network has a set of tradeoffs they must make which define a "design space." We consider five here:

1. *Flexibility.* Flexibility is a measure of the system to perform a variety of tasks.
2. *Usability.* Usability is a measure of the ease with which the system can be used for its intended task(s).
3. *Performance.* The system will have some quantitative measures by which it is evaluated, such as throughput, delay, delay variation.
4. *Cost.* A networking system will have quantifiable economic costs, such as costs for construction, operation, maintenance and continuing improvements.
5. *Security.* Since network systems are shared resources the designer must provide mechanisms to protect users from each other according to a *policy*.

It is our belief that, as in this list, security is often left until last in the design process, which results in not enough attention and emphasis being given to security. If security is *designed in*, it can simply be made part of the design space in which we search for attractive cost/performance tradeoffs. For example, if acceptable flexibility requires downloadable software, and acceptable security means that only trusted downloadable software will be loaded, our cost and performance optimizations will reflect ideas such as minimizing dynamic checks with static pre-checks or other means. If security is not an issue, there is no point in doing this.

The designer's major challenge is finding a point (or set of points) in the design space which is acceptable to a large enough market segment to influence the community of users. Sometimes this is not possible; the commercial emphasis on forwarding performance is so overwhelming that concessions to security slowing the transport plane are simply unacceptable. Fortunately, organizations have become sufficiently dependent on information networks that *security does sell.*

In the context of active networks, the major focus of security is the set of activities which provide flexibility; that is, the facility to inject new code "on-the-fly" into network elements. To build a secure infrastructure, first, the infrastructure itself (the "checker") must be unaltered. Second, the infrastructure must provide assurance that loaded modules (the dynamic checking) will not violate the security properties. In general, this is very hard. Some means currently under investigation include domain-specific languages which are easy to check (e.g., PLAN), proof-carrying code [45, 44], restricted interfaces (ALIEN), and distributed responsibility (SANE). Currently, the most attractive point in the design space appears to be a restricted domain-specific language coupled to an extension system with heavyweight checks. In this way, the frequent (per-packet) dynamic checks are inexpensive, while focusing expensive scrutiny on the extension process. This idea is manifest in the SwitchWare active network architecture [2].

## 2.3 Possible Approaches

Security of Active Networks is a broad evolving area. We will mention only some of the most directly relevant related work. In addition to the related works sections of the papers listed, we suggest Moore [41] as a source of additional information in this area.

Software fault isolation as a safety mechanism for mutually-suspicious modules running in the same address space was introduced in [62]. This technique involves inserting run-time checks in the application code. While it has been successfully demonstrated for RISC architectures, application of the same techniques to CISC architectures remains problematic.

Typed assembly language [42] propagates type safety information to the assembly language level, so assembly code can be verified. However, there are several security properties (e.g., resource usage, which is a dynamic measure) that do not easily map into the type-checking model because of the latter's static nature.

Proof-carrying code [44] permits arbitrary code to be executed as long as a valid proof of safety accompanies it. While this is a very promising technique, it is not clear that all desirable security properties and policies are expressible and provable in the logic used to publish the policy and encode the proof. Used in conjunction with other mechanisms, we believe that it will prove a very useful security tool.

PLAN [27, 28] is a part of the SwitchWare [2, 57] project at the University of Pennsylvania. The PLAN project is investigating the tradeoffs brought about by using a different language for active packets than is used for active extensions. They have designed a new language called PLAN (which is loosely based on ML [39]). PLAN is designed so that pure PLAN programs will not be able to violate the security policy. This policy is intended to be sufficiently restrictive that node administrators will be willing to allow PLAN programs to run without requiring authentication. Because this limits the operations that can be performed, PLAN programs can call *services* which can either be active extensions or facilities built into the system. These services may require authentication and authorization before allowing access to the resources they protect.

The Safetynet Project [63] at the University of Sussex has also designed a new language for active networking. They have explicitly enumerated what they feel are the important requirements for an active networking language and then set about designing a language to meet those requirements. In particular, they differ from PLAN in that they hope to use the type system to allow safe accumulation of state. They appear to be trying to avoid having any service layer at all.

Java [23] and ML [39, 34] (and the MMM [37] project) provide security through language mechanisms. More recent versions of Java provide protection domains [22]. Protection domains were first introduced in Multics [55, 56, 38, 54]. These solutions are not applicable to programs written in other languages (as may be the case with a heterogeneous active network with multiple execution environments), and are better suited for the applet model of execution than active networks. The need for a separate bytecode verifier is also considered by some a disadvantage, as it forces expensive (in the case of Java, at least) language-compliance checks prior to execution. In this area, there is some research in enhancing the understanding of the tradeoffs between compilation time/complexity, and bytecode size, verification time, and complexity.

It should be noted that language mechanisms can (and sometimes do) serve as the basis of security of an active network node. Other language-based protection schemes can be found in [9, 13, 26, 36, 33, 24].

## 3  SANE Architecture

Previous attempts at system security have not taken a holistic approach. The approaches typically focused on a major component of the system. For instance, operating system research has usually ignored the bootstrap process of the host. As a result, a *trustworthy* operating system is started by an *untrustworthy* bootstrap! This creates serious security problems since most Operating Systems require some lower level services, *e.g.*, firmware, for *trustworthy* initialization and operation. A major design goal of SANE [3] was to reduce the number and size of components that are assumed as *trustworthy*. A second major design goal of SANE was to provide a secure and reliable mechanism for establishing a security context for active networking. An application or node could then use that context in any manner it desired.

No practical system can avoid assumptions, however, and SANE is no different. Two assumptions are made by SANE. The first assumption is that the physical security of the host is maintained through strict enforcement of a physical security policy. The second assumption SANE makes is the existence of a Public Key Infrastructure (PKI). While a PKI is required, no assumptions are made as to the type of PKI, *e.g.*, hierarchical or "web of trust."[15, 31, 66, 10, 11]

The overall architecture of SANE for a three-node network is shown in Figure 2.

The initialization of each node begins with the bootstrap. Following the sucessful completion of the bootstrap, the operating system is started which loads a general purpose evaluator, *e.g.*, a Caml [34] or Java [23] runtime. The evaluator then starts an "Active Loader" which restricts the environment provided by the evaluator. Finally, the loader loads an "Active Network Evaluator" (ANE) which accepts and evaluates active packets, *e.g.*, PLAN [27], Switchlet, or ANTS [64]. The ANE then loads the SANE module to establish a security context with each network neighbor. Following the establishment of the security context, the node is ready for secure operation within the active network.

It should be noted that the services offered by SANE can be used by most active networking schemes. In our current system, SANE is used in conjunction with the ALIEN architecture [1]. ALIEN is built on top of the Caml runtime, and provides a network bytecode loader, a set of libraries, and other facilities necessary for active networking.

The following sections describe the three components of SANE. These include the AEGIS [5, 6] bootstrap system, the ALIEN [1] architecture, and SANE [2, 3] itself.

## 3.1 AEGIS Bootstrap

AEGIS [5] modifies the standard IBM PC process so that all executable code, except for a very small section of trustworthy code, is verified prior to execution by using a digital signature. This is accomplished through modifications and additions to the BIOS (Basic Input/Output System). In essence, the trustworthy software serves as the root of an authentication chain that extends to the evaluator and potentially beyond, to "active" packets. In the AEGIS boot process, either the Active Network element is started, or a recovery process is entered to repair any integrity failure detected. Once the repair is completed, the system is restarted to ensure that the system boots. This entire process occurs without user intervention. AEGIS can also be used to maintain the hardware and software configuration of a machine.

It should be noted that AEGIS does not verify the correctness of a software component. Such a component could contain an exploitable flaw. The goal of AEGIS is to prevent tampering of components that are considered trustworthy by the system administrator. AEGIS verifies the integrity of already trusted components. The nature of this trust is outside the scope of this paper.

Other work on the subject of secure bootstrapping includes [59, 65, 14, 32, 25]. A more extensive review of AEGIS and its differences with the above systems can be found in [5, 6].

**AEGIS Layered Boot and Recovery Process.** AEGIS divides the boot process into several levels to simplify and organize the BIOS modifications, as shown in Figure 3. Each increasing level adds functionality to the system, providing correspondingly higher levels of abstraction. The lowest level is Level 0. Level 0 contains the small section of trustworthy software, digital signatures,

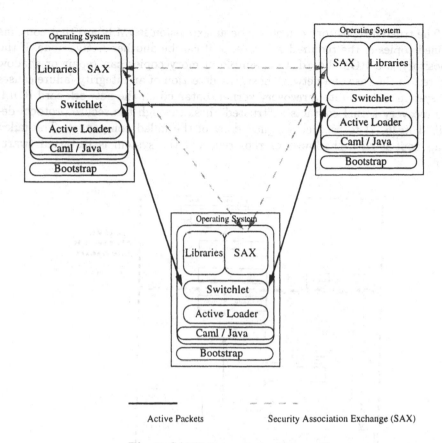

Active Packets                    Security Association Exchange (SAX)

**Fig. 2.** SANE Network Architecture

public key certificates, and recovery code. The integrity of this level is assumed as valid. We do, however, perform an initial checksum test to identify PROM failures. The first level contains the remainder of the usual BIOS code and the CMOS. The second level contains all of the expansion cards and their associated ROMs, if any. The third level contains the operating system boot sector. These are resident on the bootable device and are responsible for loading the operating system kernel. The fourth level contains the operating system, and the fifth and final level contains the ALIEN architecture and other active nodes..

The transition between levels in a traditional boot process is accomplished with a jump or a call instruction without any attempt at verifying the integrity of the next level. AEGIS, on the other hand, uses public key cryptography and cryptographic hashes to protect the transition from each lower level to the next higher one, and its recovery process through a trusted repository ensures the integrity of the next level in the event of failures [6].

The trusted repository can either be an expansion ROM board that contains verified copies of the required software, or it can be another Active node. If the repository is a ROM board, then simple memory copies can repair or shadow failures. In the case of a network host, the detection of an integrity failure causes the system to boot into a recovery kernel contained on the network card ROM. The recovery kernel contacts a "trusted" host through the secure protocol described in [6, 7] to recover a signed copy of the failed component. The failed component is then shadowed or repaired, and the system is restarted (warm boot).

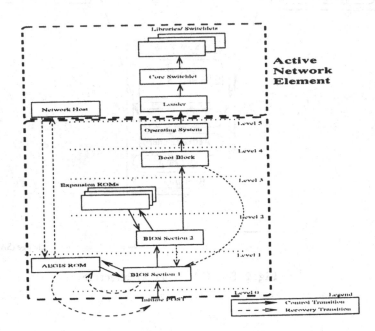

**Fig. 3.** AEGIS boot control flow

## 3.2 The ALIEN Architecture

The basis of the ALIEN approach is that we take a general model of computation and restrict it. Caml provides the general model and ALIEN provides the restrictions.

More precisely, Caml provides a model of computation equivalent to that of a Turing machine. By itself, this computation model is secure since it involves no shared resources. In practice, since we are running on a real machine, we have denial-of-service attacks that arise because our CPU and memory resources are finite. Additionally, the actual Caml environment also includes a runtime system that, among other features, provides access to operating system primitives, which, in turn, provide access to shared resources. Further, under this runtime, memory is a shared resource. The role of ALIEN is to control the access to these shared resources and thereby ensure that a loaded program (called *"switchlet"*) does not exceed its resource limits (ALIEN is not responsible for determining those limits).

ALIEN itself is built of three major components. The Loader provides the interface to the Objective Caml runtime system. The Core Switchlet builds on the Loader both by providing the security-related restrictions required and by providing more generally useful interfaces to low-level functions. Finally, the libraries are sets of utility routines. Each of these pieces will be briefly covered in turn in the following paragraphs.

**The Loader.** The Loader provides the core of ALIEN's functionality. It provides the interface to the operating system (through the language runtime) plus some essential functions to allow system startup and loading of switchlets, as shown in Table 1. Thus, it defines the "view of the world" for the rest of ALIEN. Moreover, since security involves interaction with either the external system or with other switchlets, the Loader provides the basis of security.

It should be noted that Loader provides mechanisms rather than policy; policies in the Core Switchlet can be changed by changing pieces of the Core Switchlet.

| startup routines | initialize system |
|---|---|
| switchlet loading | dynamically load switchlets consistent with ALIEN security |
| system console | console read loop |

**Table 1.** Loader functionality

**The Core Switchlet.** Above the Loader is the Core Switchlet. It is responsible for providing the interface that switchlets see. It relies upon the Loader for access to operating system resources, and then layers additional mechanisms to add security and, often, utility. In providing an interface to switchlets, it determines the security policies of the system. By including or excluding any function, it can determine what switchlets can or cannot do. Since it is loadable, the administrator can change or upgrade its pieces as necessary. This also allows for changes in the security policy.

The policies of the Core Switchlet are enforced through a combination of *module thinning* and *type safety*. Type safety ensures that a switchlet can only access data or call functions that it can name. This allows implementations of ALIEN that run in a single address space, thus avoiding the overheads normally associated with crossing hardware-enforced boundaries. [47].

Module thinning allows the Core Switchlet to present a limited interface to switchlets. Combining this with type safety, switchlets can be prevented from calling functions or accessing data even though they share an address space. It is even possible to differentiate switchlets so as to provide a rich interface to a trusted switchlet or to provide a very limited interface to an anonymous switchlet. Similar approaches have been taken in [33, 9, 61].

In many ways, the interface that the Core Switchlet presents to switchlets and libraries is like the system call interface that a kernel presents to applications. Through design of the interface the system can control access to underlying resources. With a well-designed interface, the caller can combine the functions provided to get useful work done. Table 2 shows the functionality provided by the Core Switchlet.

| language primitives | policy for access to the basic functions of the language |
|---|---|
| operating system access | policy for access to the operating system calls |
| network access | policy and mechanism for access to the network |
| thread access | policy for access to threads primitives |
| loading support | policy and mechanism to support loading of switchlets |
| message logging | policy and mechanism for adding messages to the log file |

**Table 2.** Core Switchlet functionality

Because we are implementing a network node, access to the network is particularly important. Generally this consists of allowing switchlets to discover information about the interfaces on the machines and the attached networks, receive packets, and send packets. One element of this task which is particularly important is the demultiplexing of incoming packets. The Core Switchlet must be able to determine whether zero, one, or more than one switchlet is interested in an arriving packet. If more than one switchlet is interested in the packet, policy should dictate which switchlet or switchlets receive a copy of the packet. Security is an important element of the decision as a switchlet should be able to be certain that it will get all packets that it should receive under the policy, and should not be able to get any packets that it should not receive under the policy. Without such security, denial-of-service attacks and information stealing are quite easy.

**The Library.** The library is a set of functions which provide useful routines that do not require privilege to run. The proper set of functions for the library is a continuing area of research. Some of the things that are in the library for the experiments we have performed include utility functions and implementations of IP and UDP [52].

**Locating Functionality.** When expanding our implementation, it is not always obvious in which layer the new functionality belongs. In this section, we present the principles we use to make this determination. Our first principle is that if the functionality can be implemented in a library, it should be. Said another way, if the functions exposed by the Core Switchlet or available from other libraries provide the infrastructure needed to implement the new functionality, a library is warranted.

If the new functionality relies on some element of the runtime not made available to unprivileged code, then either the Loader or the Core Switchlet must be expanded. Because these elements define the common, expected interface available at the switch, we attempt to keep them small to minimize the required resources. Therefore, our second principle is that we prefer to break off the smallest reasonable portion of the new functionality (consistent with security) that can be implemented in the privileged parts of the system. The remainder becomes a library. In our experience this also aids generality, as the privileged portion is often useful to other libraries developed later. For example, to implement IP, we built a small module inside the Core Switchlet which reads Ethernet frames from the operating system. It also demultiplexes the frames based on the Ethernet type field to increase generality. The remainder of IP, which processes headers, could then be made a non-privileged library.

Our third principle is that if this privileged functionality sets policy, it needs to go into the Core Switchlet. As discussed above, policy must be set in the Core Switchlet so that the loading mechanism can be used as needed to change policy. Our final principal is any functionality that provides pure mechanism is placed in the Core Switchlet unless it is needed before the Core Switchlet can be running.

## 3.3 SANE Services

SANE builds on AEGIS and ALIEN in order to provide security services for an active network. We believe that these services are required for the deployment of a robust active infrastructure. This is not to say that they contain all the security mechanisms one would ever want. Rather, they are basic building blocks needed for possibly more advanced mechanisms. These services include:

- Cryptographic primitives, provided as ALIEN libraries. A number of symmetric [43] and public-key [48] cryptosystems and hash [49] functions are made available for use by programmers and other system components. These are building blocks for cryptographic protocols and other mechanisms that provide higher-order security primitives.
- Packet authentication. This can be achieved through signing the packet with a public-key algorithm, or using some secret key method, like a MAC. Authentication can be used in a number of different contexts:
  - When dynamically loading switchlets over the network, to ensure code integrity and proper access authorization/resource allocation.
  - Similarly, when transmitting data over the network, to ensure data integrity, and packet-flow isolation. This latter may form the basis for economic traffic-management schemes, if the authentication mechanisms prove lightweight enough.

Public-key authentication allows for zero-roundtrip authentication, since no negotiation is required, but is relatively heavy-weight computationally and is subject to some replay attacks in the absence of node-persistent state or synchronized clocks [58, 21] in the network switches. This form of authentication is well-suited to mobile-agent types of applications, such as some active network management schemes [51], or where data generated on a switch needs to be securely combined with the code.

Secret-key based authentication is faster, and thus better suited for bulk transport. For scalability reasons however, it needs to be automated, and thus needs some public-key infrastructure to base the authentication on. The cost of the automated key establishment can be easily amortized after transmitting even a small amount of data.

- Packet confidentiality (encryption). The same issues with regards to public *vs.* secret key authentication are present here. The uses of this service are analogous to the packet authentication service.
- A key establishment protocol (KEP), which allows two principals in the network to establish secret keys and exchange certificates. The protocol is also used in bootstrap failure-recovery in AEGIS [6] and is based on the Station-to-Station [19] protocol, using Diffie-Hellman [18] key exchange and DSA [48] (or other) public-key signatures. This protocol is used in three different roles:
  1. Secure boostrap component recovery in AEGIS, as we discussed in Section 3.1.
  2. Secure neighbor discovery once the node boots. Similar to verifying the network cards and software components in AEGIS, at this stage the node verifies the immediate network topology and establishes trust between "adjacent" switches. The shared secret keys established in this manner can be used for hop-by-hop secure transmission of data or code, which is a requirement for some mobile-agent types of applications. Other critical infrastructure information can be secured by this mechanism as well, *e.g.*, routing updates.
  3. Session-key establishment, principal authentication and authorization. The shared secret keys can be used to secure the communications of any two principals in the network. Furthermore, principals can authenticate each other and exchange authorization credentials. For example, a user can verify the identity of a switch he needs to load a program on, while the switch can determine whether the user has permission to do so, and what other restrictions apply. We make use of KeyNote [10, 11] credentials to provide this functionality. These credentials specify the resource usage and access control policies that ALIEN enforces.
- Administrative domains allow a set of network elements under the same administrative control to restrict security requirements when communicating with each other. In such a configuration, "border" elements act as present-day firewalls and can require *e.g.*, a number of iterations of KEP to establish all the problem credentials. They can then mark the active packets such that further negotiation in order to determine credentials is not needed by the

"interior" switches. In essense, these "active firewalls" act as introducers of "outsiders" in a closed system. Administrative domains are built on top of secure packet exchange, in conjunction with the key management protocol.

- Naming services allow for unsupervised but collision-free[1] (secure) identification of programs. The basis of this approach is to combine hashes of the code, public keys (and signatures), and user-defined strings to generate "names" for pieces of code. Thus, a certain program can have different names, each with different semantics and trust dependencies. Such a service is necessary in an active network environment where different users' modules can explicitly interact with, or even depend on, each other. For more details, see [3].

## 4 Conclusions and Future Work

This paper has presented an overview of the programmable network architectures called "Active Networks" and illustrated the security issues facing the architects of such systems. While the goal of Active Networks is to increase the set of design options available in distributed systems, the flexibility of a programmable infrastructure introduces considerable burdens for control and management. We have outlined, and illustrated in some detail, strategies for coping with some of these issues. Many issues currently remain unresolved, and are thus important directions for future work.

First and foremost is the requirement that newly configured functionality not damage the network as an aggregate, in addition to not damaging the network element into which it is configured. The means for attacking such problems remains unclear, but two of the more promising approaches are the use of formal languages and methods for distributed concurrent systems (such as CSP [29, 30]), and the use of economic methods to deal with aggregate costs which accrue in a distributed fashion.

The second important direction is time-sensitive resource access, where Quality of Service (QoS) is part of the resource access model to which the security architecture applies. Much of the fundamental work of computer security has been based on a time-independent model of resource access, to which symbolic logic and formal methods can be applied. However, as any user of information, whether "secure" or "insecure" is well aware, if the information doesn't get there in time, it is useless. If the service is not provided, it has failed. Thus we have to push our security models to reflect time, so that service (or the attackers goal, "denial-of-service") is as first class as identification or access control in network security architectures.

Finally, we must worry about scale. Some of the solutions we have discussed here work well in the small but must be automated to permit scaling to large systems. For example, the SANE model of permitting resource access to trusted

---

[1] To the extent that the cryptographic hash functions employed are resistant to collisions.

entities presumes trust establishment and trust specification. In a (multi-) million node network, such trust management must be carried out automatically, and must be globally specified using human-comprehensible policies rather than node-node relationships.

## 5 Acknowledgements

Portions of this paper are updated from [3] and [4]. This work was supported by DARPA under Contract #N66001-96-C-852, with additional support from the Intel Corporation.

## References

[1] D. S. Alexander. *ALIEN: A Generalized Computing Model of Active Networks.* PhD thesis, University of Pennsylvania, September 1998.

[2] D. S. Alexander, W. A. Arbaugh, M. Hicks, P. Kakkar, A. D. Keromytis, J. T. Moore, C. A. Gunter, S. M. Nettles, and J. M. Smith. The SwitchWare Active Network Architecture. *IEEE Network Magazine, special issue on Active and Programmable Networks,* 12(3):29–36, 1998.

[3] D. S. Alexander, W. A. Arbaugh, A. D. Keromytis, and J. M. Smith. A Secure Active Network Environment Architecture: Realization in SwitchWare. *IEEE Network Magazine, special issue on Active and Programmable Networks,* 12(3):37–45, 1998.

[4] D. Scott Alexander, William A. Arbaugh, Angelos D. Keromytis, and Jonathan M. Smith. Safety and Security of Programmable Network Infrastructures. *IEEE Communications Magazine,* 36(10):84 – 92, 1998.

[5] W. A. Arbaugh, D. J. Farber, and J. M. Smith. A Secure and Reliable Bootstrap Architecture. In *Proceedings 1997 IEEE Symposium on Security and Privacy,* pages 65–71, May 1997.

[6] W. A. Arbaugh, A. D. Keromytis, D. J. Farber, and J. M. Smith. Automated Recovery in a Secure Bootstrap Process. In *Proceedings of Network and Distributed System Security Symposium,* pages 155–167. Internet Society, March 1998.

[7] W. A. Arbaugh, A. D. Keromytis, and J. M. Smith. DHCP++: Applying an efficient implementation method for fail-stop cryptographic protocols. In *Proceedings of Global Internet (GlobeCom) '98,* November 1998.

[8] R. Atkinson. Security Architecture for the Internet Protocol. RFC 1825, August 1995.

[9] B. Bershad, S. Savage, P. Pardyak, E. G. Sirer, M. Fiuczynski, D. Becker, S. Eggers, and C. Chambers. Extensibility, safety and performance in the spin operating system. In *Proc. 15th SOSP,* pages 267–284, December 1995.

[10] M. Blaze, J. Feigenbaum, J. Ioannidis, and A. Keromytis. The KeyNote Trust-Management System. Work in Progress, http://www.cis.upenn.edu/~angelos/keynote.html, June 1998.

[11] M. Blaze, J. Feigenbaum, J. Ioannidis, and A. Keromytis. The role of trust management in distributed systems security. In *Secure Internet Programming* [60].

[12] R. Braden, L. Zhang, S. Berson, S. Herzog, and S. Jamin. Resource ReSerVation Protocol (RSVP) – Version 1 Functional Specification. Internet RFC 2208, 1997.

[13] J. S. Chase, H. M. Levy, M. J. Feeley, and E. D. Lazowska. Sharing and Protection in a Single-Address-Space Operating System. In *ACM Transactions on Computer systems*, November 1994.

[14] Paul Christopher Clark. *BITS: A Smartcard Protected Operating System*. PhD thesis, George Washington University, 1994.

[15] Consultation Committee. *X.509: The Directory Authentication Framework*. International Telephone and Telegraph, International Telecommunications Union, Geneva, 1989.

[16] Daemon9, Route, and Infinity. Project neptune. *Phrack Magazine*, 7(48), 1996.

[17] S. E. Deering. Host extensions for IP multicasting. Internet RFC 1112, 1989.

[18] W. Diffie and M.E. Hellman. New Directions in Cryptography. *IEEE Transactions on Information Theory*, IT–22(6):644–654, Nov 1976.

[19] W. Diffie, P.C. van Oorschot, and M.J. Wiener. Authentication and Authenticated Key Exchanges. *Designs, Codes and Cryptography*, 2:107–125, 1992.

[20] DOD. Trusted Computer System Evaluation Criteria. Technical Report DOD 5200.28-STD, Department of Defense, December 1985.

[21] L. Gong. A Security Risk of Depending on Synchronized Clocks. *ACM Operating Systems Review*, 26(1), January 1992.

[22] L. Gong and R. Schemers. Implementing Protection Domains in the Java Development Kit 1.2. In *Proc. of Network and Distributed System Security Symposium (NDSS)*, pages 125–134, March 1998.

[23] James Gosling, Bill Joy, and Guy Steele. *The Java Language Specification*. Addison Wesley, Reading, 1996.

[24] R. Grimm and B. Bershad. Providing policy neutral and transparent access control in extensible systems. In *Secure Internet Programming* [60].

[25] Hermann Härtig, Oliver Kowalski, and Winfried Kühnhauser. The Birlix security architecture. *Journal of Computer Security*, 2(1):5–21, 1993.

[26] C. Hawblitzel, C. Chang, and G. Czajkowski. Implementing Multiple Protection Domains in Java. In *Proc. of the 1998 USENIX Annual Technical Conference*, pages 259–270, June 1998.

[27] M. Hicks, P. Kakkar, J. T. Moore, C. A. Gunter, and S. Nettles. PLAN: A Programming Language for Active Networks. Technical Report MS-CIS-98-25, Department of Computer and Information Science, University of Pennsylvania, February 1998.

[28] Mike W. Hicks and Jonathan T. Moore. PLAN Web Page. http://www.cis.upenn.edu/~switchware/PLAN/.

[29] C. A. R. Hoare. Communicating Sequential Processes. *Communications of the ACM*, 21(8):666–677, August 1978.

[30] C.A.R. Hoare. *Communicating Sequential Processes*. Prentice-Hall, 1984.

[31] B. Lampson and R. Rivest. Cryptography and Information Security Group Research Project: A Simple Distributed Security Infrastructure. Technical report, MIT, 1997.

[32] Butler Lampson, Martin Abadi, and Michael Burrows. Authentication in Distributed Systems: Theory and Practice. *ACM Transactions on Computer Systems*, v10:265–310, November 1992.

[33] X. Leroy and F. Rouaix. Security properties of typed applets. In *Secure Internet Programming* [60].

[34] Xavier Leroy. The Caml Special Light System (Release 1.10). http://pauillac.inria.fr/ocaml.

[35] I. M. Leslie, D. McAuley, R. Black, T. Roscoe, P. Barham, D. Evers, R. Fairbairns, and E. Hyden. The Design and Implementation of an Operating System to Support Distributed Multimedia Applications. *IEEE Journal on Selected Areas in Communications*, 14(7):1280–1297, September 1996.

[36] J. Y. Levy, J. K. Ousterhout, and B. B. Welch. The Safe-Tcl Security Model. In *Proc. of the 1998 USENIX Annual Technical Conference*, pages 271–282, June 1998.

[37] François Louaix. A Web Navigator with Applets in Caml. In *Fifth WWW Conference*, 1996.

[38] D.D. Clark M.D. Schroeder and J.H. Saltzer. The MULTICS Kernel Design Project. In *Sixth ACM Symposium on Operating Systems Principles*, pages 43–56, 1977.

[39] R. Milner, M. Tofte, and R. Harper. *The Definition of Standard ML*. MIT Press, 1990.

[40] A. B. Montz, D. Mosberger, S. W. O'Malley, L. L. Peterson, T. A. Proebsting, and J. H. Hartman. Scout: A communications-oriented operating system. Technical report, Department of Computer Science, University of Arizona, June 1994.

[41] J. Moore. Mobile Code Security Techniques. Technical Report MS-CIS-98-28, University of Pennsylvania, May 1998.

[42] G. Morrisett, D. Walker, K. Crary, and N. Glew. From System F to Typed Assembly Language. In *Proc. of the 25th ACM Symposium on Principles of Programming Languages*, January 1998.

[43] Data Encryption Standard, January 1977.

[44] George C. Necula. Proof-Carrying Code. In *Proceedings of the 24th Annual ACM SIGPLAN-SIGACT Symposium on Principles of Programming Languages (POPL)*, pages 106–119. ACM Press, New York, January 1997.

[45] George C. Necula and Peter Lee. Safe Kernel Extensions Without Run-Time Checking. In *Second Symposium on Operating System Design and Implementation (OSDI)*, pages 229–243. Usenix, Seattle, 1996.

[46] Peter G. Neumann. Architectures and Formal Representations for Secure Systems. Final Report. SRI Project 6401 A002, SRI International, October 1995.

[47] R. De Nicola, G. L. Ferrari, and R. Pugliese. Types as specifications of access policies. In *Secure Internet Programming* [60].

[48] Digital Signature Standard, May 1994.

[49] Secure Hash Standard, April 1995. Also known as: 59 Fed Reg 35317 (1994).

[50] Cracker Attack Paralyzes PANIX. RISKS Digest. Volume 18. Issue 45., September 1996.

[51] C. Partridge and A. Jackson. Smart Packets. Technical report, BBN, 1996. http://www.net-tech.bbn.com-/smtpkts/smtpkts-index.html.

[52] Jon Postel. User Datagram Protocol. Internet RFC 768, 1980.

[53] Jon Postel. Internet Protocol. Internet RFC 791, 1981.

[54] J. H. Saltzer. Protection and the Control of Information Sharing in Multics. In *Communications of the ACM*, pages 388–402, July 1974.

[55] M. D. Schroeder. *Cooperation of Mutually Suspicious Subsystems in a Computer Utility*. PhD thesis, MIT, September 1972.

[56] M.D. Schroeder. Engineering a Security Kernel for MULTICS. In *Fifth Symposium on Operating Systems Principles*, pages 125–132, November 1975.

[57] J. M. Smith, D. J. Farber, C. A. Gunter, S. M Nettles, D. C. Feldmeier, and W. D. Sincoskie. SwitchWare: Accelerating Network Evolution. Technical Report MS-CIS-96-38, CIS Dept. University of Pennsylvania, 1996.

[58] P. Syverson. A Taxonomy of Replay Attacks. In *Proceedings of the Computer Security Foundations Workshop VII (CSFW7)*, June 1994.

[59] J.D. Tygar and Bennet Yee. DYAD: A System for Using Physically Secure Coprocessors. Technical Report CMU–CS–91–140R, Carnegie Mellon University, May 1991.

[60] Jan Vitek and Christian Jensen. *Secure Internet Programming: Security Issues for Mobile and Distributed Objects*. Lecture Notes in Computer Science. Springer-Verlag Inc., New York, NY, USA, 1999.

[61] T. von Eicken. J-kernel a capability based operating system for java. In *Secure Internet Programming* [60].

[62] R. Wahbe, S. Lucco, T. E. Anderson, and S. L. Graham. Efficient Software-based Fault Isolation. In *Proc. of the 14th Symposium on Operating System Principles*, pages 203–216, December 1993.

[63] Ian Wakeman, Alan Jeffrey, Rory Graves, and Tim Owen. Designing a Programming Language for Active Networks. *submitted to Hipparch special issue of Network and ISDN Systems*, June 1998. http://www.cogs.susx.ac.uk/projects/-safetynet/papers/isdn.ps.gz.

[64] David J. Wetherall, John Guttag, and David L. Tennenhouse. Ants: A toolkit for building and dynamically deploying network protocols. In *IEEE OpenArch Proceedings*. IEEE Computer Society Press, Los Alamitos, April 1998.

[65] Bennet Yee. *Using Secure Coprocessors*. PhD thesis, Carnegie Mellon University, 1994.

[66] P. Zimmerman. PGP User's Manual, 1995.

# Using Interfaces to Specify Access Rights

J. Hulaas, A. Villazón and J. Harms

**Abstract.** Mobile agents are usually expected to execute in open environments. This openness implies that they should be able to dynamically learn how to interact with other agents and services which were not known at development time. The interlocutors therefore have to *publish* enough information about their functionality, while at the same time they have to *restrict* access rights in order to preserve their integrity. We describe in this paper a *messenger-based framework* which proposes run-time generated interfaces to address this duality.

## 1 Introduction

A mobile agent is an executing program which can migrate from machine to machine in a heterogeneous network under its own control. Its utility resides in the fact that, by enabling the movement of both code and data, it allows the programmer to reduce network load or to create application-specific communication protocols. Implementing reliable and secure agent systems is however a difficult task. The reason is that mobile agents are to execute autonomously in inherently open and dynamic environments, which moreover may be characterized as:

- *Vulnerable: Their openness makes them an easy target for direct attacks.*
  The security issues in mobile agent systems have been classified into five categories [1]: (1) transfer security, (2) authentication and authorization, (3) host system security, (4) computational environment security, and (5) mobile agent system security. We are interested in the second and especially the fifth aspects of security, which cover the problems related to initiating and maintaining secure interaction between mobile agents meeting or residing in the same computational environment on a given host.
- *Completely decentralized: There is no global management of user identities, and heterogeneity is common in offered services.*
  In our approach, we do not count on the availability of a unique user identification, because it does not scale well, and prefer to consider mobile agents as anonymous entities. By heterogeneity, we refer to the fact that available services may be implemented in different ways and may offer different interaction protocols from site to site. Mobile agents must therefore have the ability to adapt to each situation.

To address these two issues, we propose a single concept, the *interlocutor-specific interface*, that is both a view, i.e. a compound capability, describing what operations the actual client is authorized to use, and an extended interface, specifying, e.g. through the associated profiles, how to use the published operations. The advantage of this solution is that the interlocutor knows nothing more than what is contained in the granted interface. This entails, first, that the security policy is completely transparent to the client, since the presence of forbidden operations is never disclosed and always reported as non-existent, and second, that the process of learning how to interact with an interlocutor is greatly simplified by the fact that we prevent aquisition of information which is not relevant. More generally, a different semantics may be attached to each interface, according to the nature of each interlocutor. In this approach, the agent or service dynamically generates an interface corresponding to the client's specific role[1].

The idea of having several interfaces is now usual in object-oriented languages, such as Java, which is e.g. the language of the Aglets mobile agent system [18]. The first use is to provide a gradation in the levels of visibility on implementation details: direct instances, heirs and clients are not granted equal accessibility to the definition of a given class. The other use pertains to the frequent need to have several views of a single implementation, as attested by the inclusion of the interface construct of Java, which partly replaces the idiomatic uses of multiple inheritance. For instance, a client object may have to display a specific view of itself, independently of its true implementation provider, in order to be acceptable for a service which interacts with its clients through call-backs. In usual object-oriented languages this is all static, i.e. the number of interfaces and the contents of these interfaces are defined at compile-time, as well as who has the right to access them. Interfaces are not obtained by dynamic evaluation of access rights, they only depend on centralized and implementation-specific criteria such as class names. Moreover these languages generally do not directly provide support for building invocations dynamically with the appropriate arguments.

Our initial hypotheses result in a solution which is necessarily quite different from more static approaches. Contrarily to other mobile agent systems (e.g. based on Java[3]), in the *messenger paradigm* [12], that we have taken as basis for this work, (a) there is no semantic verification of an agent's code prior to its execution (as opposed to Java's *class loader* mechanism), and therefore we can take advantage of features like dynamic typing and run-time generation of executable code; (b) there are no predefined code libraries on the platform; this translates into a generally more adaptative behaviour, but also makes more difficult the implementation of infrastructure for checking digitally signed code; (c) there is no predefined equivalent of a direct *method call* to a mobile agent, because *communication* is rather performed through the platform's *shared memory*; the agent's protection domain is its private memory space, so that it has absolute control over the visibility of its data. These are the foundations of our approach and constitute the specificity of our proposal.

We try to provide a uniform answer to the design issues encountered when designing complex applications relying on secure cooperation between many mobile

---

[1] The interface can be seen as a meta-level [24] which performs the access right verifications.

agents from different origins. For instance, unlike objects in statically configured distributed applications, mobile agents cannot maintain permanent references to directly locate each other and communicate through access points known in advance. They need directories to find and to identify each other, as well as a uniform mechanism to initiate interaction, whether they belong to the same service or not. Moreover, mobile agents running under the same authority should not have the same rights if they implement different functionalities, and mobile agents implemented by different parties should be viewable as equivalent if they fulfill the same task. Therefore we promote an approach where each agent's access rights are determined according to its functionality, and not solely dependent on its implementation or authority.

## Overview of Inter-agent Interaction Mechanisms

Mobile agents do need to synchronize and communicate in order to collaborate to the accomplishment of higher-level operations. A mobile agent may interact with other mobile agents (e.g. to delegate the execution of sub-tasks) or with resident agents which implement local access points to distributed services. There exist numerous examples of distributed services for mobile agents in the literature: directory services as in Telescript *clouds* [15], distributed shared memory and distributed semaphore [4], resource monitoring [11], resource trading [13][14], service brokering and electronic cash validation [17], reliable communication [16]. Hence mobile agents do not only interact as peers, but there also clearly exists a necessity of layering services in order to build higher-level abstractions.

Inter-agent communication mechanisms may be classified into four categories [1]: shared memory (as in the Messenger paradigm [11] and sometimes in [3] ), generative communication (as in the *Secure Object Spaces* of [1]), datagrams (as in Agent Tcl [14]), and procedure/ method invocations (as in Telescript [15] and Java). The work described in this paper is based on the Messenger approach, and extends it to a system based on procedure calls and method invocations. We show a framework where mobile agent services protect their integrity by providing interfaces customized to their interlocutors. These interlocutors have to certify their rights, for instance through a public-key authentication scheme. Providing a multi-level interface structure is useful as a homogeneous approach to the management of security in both vertical (i.e. between client agents and agents furnishing a service) and horizontal (i.e. intra-service) mobile agent interactions. Other existing approaches, which only offer a fixed number of interfaces (usually two or three), do not allow an agent to modulate in a uniform and fine-grained way access rights between different kinds of clients (e.g. basic ones and privileged ones) or between different agents of the same service or organization (e.g. agents which transfer private data and maintenance agents whose role is to update the code of resident agents, or to shut down a distributed service in a coordinated manner). Moreover, interfaces may often not be obtained dynamically, although it is the most natural approach in changing environments. Also, access rights usually depend on static and language-dependent criteria such as types or implementation modules. The solution presented here allows anonymous

agents to interact synchronously and asynchronously, without relying on predefined meeting mechanisms, and is implemented efficiently since security checks
need to be performed only once, at the initiation of the interaction.

The rest of this paper is organized as follows. Section 2 presents the Messenger paradigm. Section 3 introduces the mechanisms and details the motivation
for integrating our extended interface structure. Section 4 shows typical situations where interlocutor-specific interfaces are needed. Section 5 discusses our
approach and compares it with related work. The paper is concluded by Section
6.

## 2   The Messenger Paradigm

In the *Messenger paradigm* [12], communication between computers is realized
through exchange of programs called *messengers*. Messengers are anonymous
and autonomous threads of control that are executed on *messenger platforms* in
a distributed environment, without any form of centralized control. Platforms
are connected by unreliable communication *channels*, and such an aggregation
of platforms is called a *platform system*.

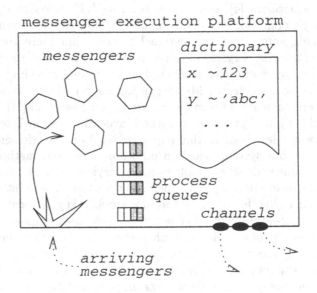

**Fig. 1.** Logical view of a messenger platform

Messenger platforms provide directory-like structures, called *dictionaries*,
which are the fundamental means for organizing storage and exchange of arbitrary data between messengers on a same platform. Dictionaries are constituted
as lists of tuples (key, value) and may be protected by Unix-like attributes
rwx telling respectively whether they are readable, writable and browsable. A

dictionary which is not browsable may not be listed: one can then only get the values for which one knows the corresponding key (Figure 1).

Messengers are basic mobile agent entities which execute in their own local context defined by a private address space. This constitutes the messengers' basic protection domain. Messengers do not directly provide any interface or callable procedures. They can however communicate through a platform-level *shared memory* (Figure 2) and coordinate their work by the means of *queues*. Data in the shared memory area (e.g. the string 'abc' of Figure 2) remains hidden as long as no reference to it is published by its creator, by insertion in a global browsable dictionary (the key y is here associated to the string 'abc').

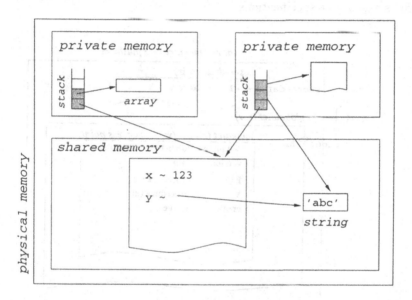

**Fig. 2.** Private and shared memory areas

The messenger platform supports an architecture for building distributed applications by composition of different services. This architecture makes possible the secure publication of services which are offered either by single transient messengers or by organized groups of messengers, which we call *families*. A family is composed of *"sedentary messengers"* [2] which fulfill a service locally and of helper messengers which migrate from platform to platform to convey information or to perform other auxiliary tasks on behalf of the sedentary ones. This corresponds to a vision of the network where agent services tend to aggressively people platforms as they become available.

---

[2] In principle a *resident* or *sedentary* messenger will not migrate after its arrival on a given platform, unless it is forced to (local resources too expensive, not enough clients, detection of threats to its security, etc.)

## 2.1 Service Publication Mechanism

Service publication is performed by creating in the shared memory area a dictionary which then functions as platform-level interface to the service. This data structure is called the *Service Access Point* (SAP). All interfaces are additionally described using the *Messenger Interface Description Language* (M-IDL) [4], which must be understood by the clients. *M-IDL* essentially is a grammar which specifies how to use the service through procedure profiles and rules for composing correct sequences of procedure calls. This already gives a good idea on how to use the service (*MIDL* does however not give a way to specify semantics). M-IDL specifications are intended to be interpreted at run-time; we can consider them as executable specifications.

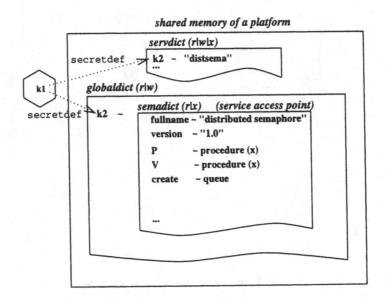

**Fig. 3.** Single-level secure service publication architecture

A messenger wishing to publish its service will choose a secret key k1 and generate a public key k2 (using a one-way function). The tuple (k2, SAP) is inserted into the global dictionary globaldict. Then the service provider has to add to the service dictionary servdict an entry (k2, explicit service name). Because servdict is a *browsable* dictionary, any messenger can search for the name of the service it is looking for; however only messengers possessing the original key k1 can remove the corresponding entry.

Clients will gain access to a service by the means of its name (e.g. distsema as in fig. 3). They will then use the corresponding key k2 to obtain the desired *SAP* from globaldict (which is not browsable). The latter operation will finally enable the client-furnisher interaction: in the *SAP*, each procedure name is associated with the corresponding code, which is not readable (and thus may not be copied), but only executable.

This first messenger service publication mechanism uses a uniform interface structure allowing for elementary interactions between messengers. In this model, a unique access policy is enforced for all service clients, with a single level of protection and no possibility of discrimination. Moreover, messengers of a same family must access internally shared information through ad-hoc strategies, involving e.g. predefined knowledge of hidden data structures, instead of resorting to homogeneous protected interfacing mechanisms. For higher-level abstractions, such as messenger families, more elaborated schemes providing multiple protection levels are needed. Our solution is described in the following section.

## 3 Interlocutor-Specific Interfaces

As an extension to the previously described publication mechanism, we designed a generic pattern for intra- and inter-family protection and elaborated a corresponding multi-level interface model. This model enables services to apply finer and more efficient protection schemes; we use it for instance to implement the visibility rules commonly found in object-oriented languages *(public, protected and private)*. In this approach, the service provider associates a customized interface to each client, i.e. the architecture allows the client to obtain the interface corresponding to its specific rights.

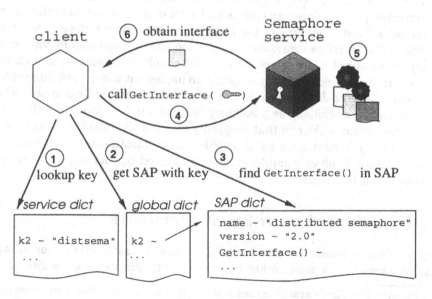

**Fig. 4.** Obtaining an interface

We have seen that the only criteria for accessing a service $SAP$ is the knowledge of the service name. Phases 1 and 2 of Figure 4 correspond to the single-level interface access to $SAP$. Phases 3, 4, 5 and 6 are related to the more elaborate protection scheme. Instead of obtaining directly a complete $SAP$, the `GetInterface()` procedure which is found in phase 3 must be called by the client, who also gives as argument a secret key for authentication. On the basis of this authentication, the service will decide to which level it wants to grant access to its own functionality, and return to the client a correspondingly generated interface. Note that the simplistic authentication scheme outlined here is just a conceptual view; in reality we may need symmetric keys or some ad-hoc infrastructure such as Kerberos [5].

The secret key described here determines how a client wants to identify itself. Several identities may therefore be adopted: this may be useful if a messenger is a composition of two services and must be viewable alternatively as belonging to the one or to the other. A family is thus characterized by the possession of a secret key which enables each messenger to authenticate itself w.r.t. other members of the family. For security reasons, a messenger's membership of one (or several) families is not a visible attribute. Similarly, messengers do not have identities (they are anonymous) and cannot be directly referenced either [3]. A family is not the same as a type, because small auxiliary messengers, which receive limited functionality for executing precise sub-tasks, such as to spread information within a distributed service, are also members of the family implementing this service.

The granted interface, with its (procedure name, procedure code) tuple set, is created in the receiver's private memory. The code associated to each procedure name is as usual accessible in *execute-only mode*, which prevents inspection or further copying (i.e. migration or transmission) of sensitive information to untrusted parties. This very code is just a set of stubs which hide the location of the actual code and data in the global memory. The interface is not transferable and is therefore equivalent to a session key. It could also be viewed as a proxy for an object which is not remote, but simply in another local protection domain. It must be noted that it is harder to implement non-transferable objects in systems such as Java, which do not provide separate address spaces within a single virtual machine. One possibility is to let the *interface stubs* check that the current client is the one that originally received the interface, which means that every agent must have an accessible unique identificator. The paper [25] describes the difficulties in implementing Java-based *capabilities*, a notion which is close to our interfaces.

## 4 Uses of Interlocutor-Specific Interfaces

The protection scheme we describe in this paper is usable every time an agent has to interact with many other kinds of agents and therefore wants to only

---

[3] Compare with Java's **synchronized** statement which allows anyone to *freeze* an object through a reference

partially reveal its functionality. Let us first consider a banking example. A bank has many kinds of clients: basic, private customers, VIPs, or international corporations, just to mention a few. Each category has its own set of burdens and privileges. The available operations are not the same (the international corporation may e.g. additionally discuss interest rates) and their usage are also specific (the VIP is not asked to check the balance before withdrawing money from a given account). The bank will therefore disclose to each client only those operations which are available to him, and provide together the simplest possible description. If you now consider the employees of the bank, the situation is the same, although they all belong to the same service and should have some kind of *"private"* access rights. They have different duties and prerogatives, according to their hierarchical rank and to which department they work in. Additionally, the rights of the basic employee, when he is acting as a client, do not even enclose those of the most important clients, as would be the case in a classical computer language.

We outline below two generic situations where one can make profitable use of the interlocutor-specific interfaces. The first we present is, in the frame of our notion of messenger family, the *Resident-Emissary pattern*. This description is performed following the model of [19]. The second use is demonstrated by a new object-oriented dialect of the MØ messenger programming language, and the protection mechanisms provided by the associated compiler.

## 4.1 The Resident-Emissary Pattern

**Intent:** The Resident-Emissary pattern allows collaboration between stationary agents over multiple hosts, as well as any form of intra-service critical interaction.

**Motivation:** When implementing distributed mobile agent services (i.e. distributed applications implemented with mobile agents), one can imagine distribution and installation phases in order to provide local service publication and support over multiple platforms (these phases are possible after the discovery of newly available resources for example). The local support is implemented by agents that remain on the platform to coordinate the service's distributed functionality. We qualify such agents as sedentary or resident.

The real functionality of the distributed service requires communication between resident agents. This might be e.g. to multicast new information, as when a member of an indexing service wants to propagate a new service or resource to be promoted.

The information which is exchanged should not be disclosed. Therefore a carrying agent, that we call the emissary agent, must have the necessary privileges to access the resident agents' updating input channels. These channels are visible only through a particular interface, the family's private interface.

It is preferable to use emissary agents, rather than resorting to direct interaction between residents, because the emissary contributes to the protection of sensitive information (stored in the family's hidden local repositories), by accepting to access the repositories only by the means of tailored interfaces.

**Applicability:** Use this pattern when:

- Distributed entities must interact to exchange data which ensure the service's coherency.
- Special "signals" between resident agents (that imply radical changes of behavior) must be delivered.

**Participants:**

**Resident:** Defines the stationary agent that performs the local service implementation and that has to exchange critical information with other stationary agents.

**Emissary:** Mobile agent which transports the information between resident agents.

**Interface:** Means by which selective access to vulnerable information is provided.

**Repository:** Location of information that must be only accessible through specific interfaces.

**Collaboration:** The *Resident* needs to communicate private data with other residents of the same family.

- On the local platform (say *Platform A*) *Resident A* creates an emissary agent with a specific itinerary in order to contact the remote resident (say on *Platform B*).
- The *Emissary* contacts its creator, asking for an interface that indirectly allows him to access data stored in the local repository (note that no direct access is allowed, all requests are processed through the interface).
- On arrival, the *Emissary* agent performs a similar interaction, contacting *Resident B* on the destination platform and requesting an interface.
- *Resident B* will provide a tailored interface according to its rights (allowing access to the family's update routines).
- Finally the *Emissary* will be able to update the information through the corresponding interface.

Tailored interfaces are only usable by the original requesting agent, and they are automatically discarded when this agent migrates or terminates. *Emissary agents* do not necessarily return to their origin.

**Consequences:** The *Resident-Emissary pattern* is useful for the design of families which need secure communication of critical data. The usage of emissary agents also eases, for example, incremental collection and update of information inside a service residing on several platforms. Indeed, an emissary can update its data each time it contacts another resident agent. Furthermore, even its itinerary can be dynamically adapted to new destinations (stored by residents as private data) leading to a globally more flexible and efficient approach than remote procedure calls.

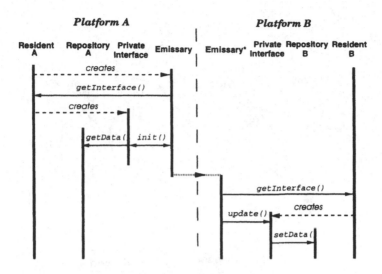

**Fig. 5.** Collaboration in the Resident-Emissary pattern. Agent migration is represented as dashed links with centered arrows. Names suffixed with a star, e.g. **AnAgent\***, denote agents *after* migration (i.e. arrived on a remote platform).

## 4.2 The Object-Oriented Compiler

Another situation where multiple interfaces and access levels are necessary is a messenger *on-the-fly* compiler service which makes possible the implementation of object-oriented systems. We have defined an object-oriented dialect for our messenger programming language MØ . The idea is then to allow messengers to carry with them the compiler for this dialect as well as the code of the programs to be compiled, so a messenger family can exploit its own class definitions for the collaboration between family members. A messenger will install the compiler code in the local platform's service dictionary making it available as a public utility (Step 1 in Figure 6). Other messengers (belonging or not to the same family) may then use it in order to compile and install new messenger services (Step 2). Finally, clients may perform requests resulting in the creation in their local memory of instances of those classes (Steps 3 and 4).

In the new object-oriented dialect we find the usual notions of *class, method, object, instance variable*, and *single inheritance*. Here we see the natural need for multi-level visibility, with messengers applying a three-level visibility to grant access according to family needs. Thus, members of the family have access to private data, while only public data is visible to clients. The protected keyword denotes a special inter-family mode, based on local criteria. In Java, the protected notion denotes visibility given to classes in the same *'package'*. The idea that we applied in our approach is that a messenger which wants to derive a subclass from a given library class, must obtain the right to do so. This is necessary because a class must expose part of its own internal structure to enable inheri-

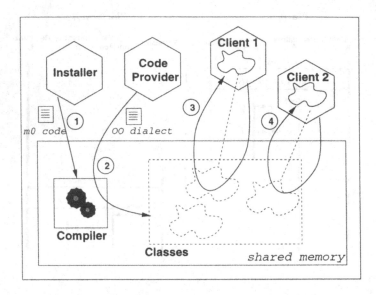

**Fig. 6.** The compiler as support for public services implemented as classes

tance. Practically, this is realized by adding a class method called inherit, which is available in its full form only through the protected interface of the class. Messengers which do not have enough privileges will only obtain a crippled version of the inherit method through the public interface, and thus they will not be able to inherit entities defined with the protected visibility mode. This approach partly solves the security holes of Java related to malicious sub-classing as described in [1]: now, if a client trusts a given root class, he can be more confident that the actual instances he deals with are not harmful to him, and that he will not receive harmful objects profiting from the sub-typing mechanism.

Another noteworthy characteristic of this compiler is that all instances generated by the classes it has compiled are systematically authenticated before any method call as part of the dynamic binding process. This is made possible by the insertion of a secret pattern (a kind of *"magic cookie"*) inside every instance created. This part of the instance cannot be explored by anyone, even the client, although it resides in a private memory area, since it is implemented as a nonbrowsable dictionary. If the instance must migrate, it must be authenticated and unmarshalled by a corresponding class on the destination platform in order to re-insert a new secret pattern. It is therefore not possible for malicious clients to forge instances which threaten the integrity of the service implemented by the class. This approach is reminiscent of Telescript's notion of *telename*, which is a unique and nonforgeable agent (or place) identifier; since a telename identifies a process, or a set of processes, it does however not provide the fine-grained, class-level protection described here.

# 5 Related Work

Some distributed systems include a notion of computational reflection which enables them to inspect and modify their own structure, in particular their interface. The HADAS system [21] for instance has mobile objects, called ambassadors, which provide an interface for remote applications and can be seen as an advanced form of proxy. Ambassadors are reflexive in the sense that they can change their interface according to local conditions, and can receive and even tailor part of the functionality of the remote application they represent. They however are not autonomous, since they cannot migrate any further, which is similar to the limitation of Java applets [3]. They do not either exploit their computational reflection with the objective of enhancing security.

In Dalang [20], reflection and code modification are used to adapt software components as they are downloaded into the executing environement. This work is based on Java and is not specific to the mobile agent domain. When the byte code is loaded, a specialized *class loader* analyzes it and modifies the behaviour by generating an interface with code to catch methods calls. This approach is thus based on a *meta-object protocol* that transparently enables security-related verifications. Interface generation in the sense of Dalang does not convey the same meaning as in our approach, because the single interface that is created is shared by all interlocutors. Another difference is that the associated code generation mechanism is not triggered at run-time, but at load-time.

An interface in the *Distributed Component Object Model* (DCOM) [6] is a set of functions bound to a certain object which implements them. Each object may introduce several interfaces and a user may query one of them using the QueryInterface function, which itself belongs to a default interface supported by every object. QueryInterface changes the semantics of the object as seen by its user. This approach is limited to traditional distributed systems and does not address mobile agents. Authentication is not performed by DCOM itself, but by the lower layers it is built upon (DCE RPC [7]). It is now unclear how well these two levels integrate, and whether the delivered interfaces can be customized on the basis of the results of the authentication in order to enhance security.

In the frame of CORBA [8], several current initiatives tend to answer issues described in this paper. The *Multiple Interfaces RFP* [9] deals with the resolution of conflicts between multiple interfaces on the same object, while the *Composition Facility* [9] provides the means for objects to be composed of logically distinct services by the use of multiple interface definitions. In CORBA in general, as well as in its draft *Mobile Agent System Interoperability Facility* (MASIF) [10], authentication for method invocations is performed on a *call-by-call* basis, and interface delivery is not under the control of the implementing objects, but of the Interface Repository mechanism.

In our approach, interfaces are not designed to be transmitted for remote usage. The stub routines they contain cannot be migrated because the corresponding code is execute-only and may not be copied. This is consistent with the mobile agent philosophy, which tries to limit the frequency of remote method invocations, and is indissociable from our security architecture. The granting of a dedicated interface is equivalent to a session key, which is more efficient than authentication on a call-by-call basis, and more secure than the publication of a single, big, public interface. Revocation of an interface by its creator is possible: the stub routines can check whether they should continue to service method calls, and if not, they can destroy themselves in order to eliminate any unwanted references. Any invocation will from there on result in an exception on the caller's side.

To our knowledge, the present paper presents the first approach to integrate the use and support for multiple interfaces in the mobile agent world. As already noted in [22], agents move towards the services they need, and then adapt to the interface they obtain. This enables a more flexible and efficient RISC-like interaction, as opposed to coarse-grained CISC-like remote method invocation protocols. This remark also strengthens the motivation for supporting multiple specialized interfaces.

This interaction mechanism is described for more clarity as happening between a service (implemented by a resident messenger) and an incoming messenger. It can however be generalized to the synchronization and communication between any pair of agents hosted by the same platform; to this end, they should locate each other not through the service dictionary, but through any other global dictionary.

Finally, we do not address in this work the problem of protecting messengers from malicious hosts. This issue remains largely unsolved by current research, although some encouraging results have been found lately [23]. In this paper we are only interested in inter-agent relationships, which makes possible the reliance on platform-provided mechanisms such as separate address spaces and the protection of code by an execute-only access mode.

# 6  Conclusion

We described in this paper a framework where anonymous mobile agents protect their integrity by providing interfaces customized to their interlocutors. By exploiting the characteristics of the Messenger platform, such as separate address spaces and execute-only code segments, it is possible for an agent to disclose only the information which is needed for other agents to securely interact with him. We showed that this customer-specific interface structure is useful in both vertical (i.e. *client-furnisher*) and horizontal (i.e. *intra-service*) relationships. It offers a level of flexibility and security which is unavailable in existing object-oriented or type-based approaches, but strongly needed for a wide deployment of mobile agents in open and dynamic environments. Our research was performed in the frame of the Messenger paradigm, which implies a rather low-level approach. In other words, we cannot force the programmer to write secure programs, but we give him the tools to ease his effort in that direction.

# Acknowledgements

The authors would like to thank the anonymous reviewers for their comments and useful suggestions. This work was funded by the Swiss National Science Foundation grant 20-47162.96.

# References

1. J. Vitek, M. Serrano and D. Thanos, Security and Communication in Mobile Object Systems, in Mobile Object Systems: Towards the Programmable Internet, Second International Workshop, MOS'96, Linz, Austria, Selected Presentations and Invited Papers, J. Vitek and C. Tschudin (eds), LNCS vol. 1222, July 1996.
2. C. F. Tschudin, An Introduction to the MØ Messenger Language, Technical Report 86, (Cahier du CUI), University of Geneva, 1994.
3. J. Gosling and H. McGilton. The Java Language Environment. A White Paper. Sun Microsystems, May 1995.
4. M. Muhugusa. Distributed Services in a Messenger Environment: The Case of Distributed Shared-Memory. Ph.D. Thesis no 2903, University of Geneva, 1997.
5. J. G. Steiner, B. Clifford Neuman, and J.I. Schiller, Kerberos: An Authentication Service for Open Network Systems, In Proceedings of the Winter 1988 Usenix Conference, February 1988.
6. N. Brown and C. Kindel, Distributed Component Object Model Protocol - DCOM/1.0, Internet draft, January 1998, http://www.microsoft.com/oledev/olecom/draft-brown-dcom-v1-spec-02.txt
7. CAE Specification, X/Open DCE: Remote Procedure Call, X/Open Company Limited, X/Open Document Number C309. ISBN 1-85912-041-5, Reading, Berkshire, UK, 1994.
8. Object Management Group, The Common Object Request Broker: Architecture and Specification (Revision 2.0), Object Management Group, Framingham, Mass., 1995.
9. Object Management Group, Multiple Interfaces and Composition, work in progress, April 1998, Web information page: http://www.omg.org/library/schedule/Multiple_Interfaces_and_Composition.htm
10. Object Management Group, The Mobile Agents Facility, work in progress, April 1998, Web information page: http://www.omg.org/library/schedule/Mobile_Agents_Facility_RFP.htm
11. A. Acharya, M. Ranganathan, J. Saltz, Sumatra: A Language for Resource-Aware Mobile Programs, in Mobile Object Systems: Towards the Programmable Internet, Second International Workshop, MOS'96, Linz, Austria, Selected Presentations and Invited Papers, J. Vitek and C. Tschudin (eds), LNCS vol. 1222, July 1996.
12. C. F. Tschudin, The Messenger Environment MØ - A Condensed Description, in Mobile Object Systems: Towards the Programmable Internet, Second International Workshop, MOS'96, Linz, Austria, Selected Presentations and Invited Papers, J. Vitek and C. Tschudin (eds), LNCS vol. 1222, July 1996.
13. C. F. Tschudin, Open Resource Allocation, First International Workshop on Mobile Agents (MA'97), Berlin, Germany, April 1997.
14. R. Gray, Agent TCL: A Flexible and Secure Mobile-Agent System, in Proceedings of the fourth annual Tcl/Tk Workshop (TCL 96), July 1996.

15. J. E. White, Telescript Technology: The Foundation for the Electronic Marketplace, General Magic White Paper, General Magic, Inc., 1994.

16. C. F. Tschudin, On the Structuring of Computer Communications, Ph.D. Thesis, University of Geneva, Switzerland, 1993.

17. D. Johansen, R. van Renesse and F. B. Schneider, Operating System Support for Mobile Agents, in Proceedings of the 5th IEEE Workshop on Hot Topics in Operating Systems, pages 42-45, Orcas Island, Wash., May 1994. Also available as Technical Report TR94-1468, Department of Computer Science, Cornell University.

18. D. Lange, M. Oshima, G. Karjoth and K. Kosaka, Aglets: Programming Mobile Agents in Java, in 1st International Conference on Worldwide Computing and its Applications (WWCA'97), T. Masuda, Y. Masunaga and M. Tsukamoto, Eds, LNCS vol. 1274, Springer, Berlin, Germany, pp. 253-266, 1997.

19. Y. Aridor, D. Lange, Agent Design Patterns: Elements of Agent Application Design. Second International Conference on Autonomous Agents (Agents'98). Minneapolis/St. Paul, May 10-13, 1998.

20. Ian Welch and Robert Stroud, Dynamic Adaptation of the Security Properties of Applications and Components., ECOOP Workshop on Distributed Object Security, Brussels, Belgium, July 1998.

21. O. Holder and I. Ben-Shaul, A Reflective Model of Mobile Software Objects, in Proceedings of the 17th IEEE International Conference on Distributed Computing Systems (ICDCS'97), Baltimore, Maryland, USA, May 27-30 1997.

22. F. B. Schneider, Towards Fault-tolerant and Secure Agentry, Invited paper, 11th International Workshop on Distributed Algorithms, Saarbrcken, Germany, Sept. 1997.

23. T. Sander and C. F. Tschudin, Towards Mobile Cryptography, In proceedings of Security&Privacy'98, May, 1998.

24. G. Kiczales, J. des Rivières and D. G. Bobrow, The Art of the Metaobject Protocol, MIT Press, 1991.

25. T. von Eicken, J-kernel a capability based operating system for java, In Secure Internet Programming, Lecture Notes in Computer Science, Springer-Verlag Inc., New York, NY, USA, 1999.

# Introducing Trusted Third Parties to the Mobile Agent Paradigm

Uwe G. Wilhelm, Sebastian Staamann, and Levente Buttyán

**Abstract.** The mobile agent paradigm gains ever more acceptance for the creation of distributed applications, particularly in the domain of electronic commerce. In such applications, a mobile agent roams the global Internet in search of services for its owner. One of the problems with this approach is that malicious service providers on the agent's itinerary can access confidential information contained in the agent or tamper with the agent.

In this article we identify trust as a major issue in this context and propose a pessimistic approach to trust that tries to prevent malicious behaviour rather than correcting it. The approach relies on a trusted and tamper-resistant hardware device that provides the mobile agent with the means to protect itself. Finally, we show that the approach is not limited to protecting the mobile agents of a user but can also be extended to protect the mobile agents of a trusted third party in order to take full advantage of the mobile agent paradigm.

## 1 Introduction

New approaches for distributed computing based on mobile agent technology, such as *Aglets*, *Telescript*, or *Voyager* become ever more pervasive and are considered as innovative new ideas to structure distributed applications. A particularly interesting and perhaps economically important class of applications, to which mobile agents seem well adapted, is electronic commerce.

A typical use of mobile agents in the domain of electronic commerce includes the scenario, in which an agent roams the global Internet in search of some service for a user (the owner of the agent). Such a service can have many different forms, for instance, the provision of a physical good, the execution of a search for an information item, or the notification of the occurrence of some event. The agent is configured by the user with all the relevant information about the desired service, the constraints that define under which conditions an offer from a service provider is acceptable, and a list of some potential providers of the service. It will then migrate to the sites of these service providers in order to locate the best offer for the service sought by the user and finalize the transaction with the chosen service provider.

Since an agent is vulnerable when it is executing on the execution platform of a service provider, it is necessary that the user obtains some guarantees concerning the protection of his agents. Consider a mobile agent that holds data for one or several payment methods, which it needs to finalize a purchase. These payment data should not be available to any principal other than the one that actually provides the service and, thus, is entitled to receive the payment. A malicious service provider might try to obtain the data of the payment method without providing the service or might otherwise tamper with the agent in order to trick it into accepting the malicious provider's offer (e.g., by removing some information about a better offer from the memory of the agent). The usual approach that is taken to provide a user with certain guarantees concerning the protection of his agents, is to assume that the service providers are *trusted* principals [13] or to create a mechanism that enables the user to detect which of the providers on the itinerary have misbehaved [21].

The notion of trust has long been recognized as being of paramount importance for the development of secure systems [6, 10, 28]. For instance, any conceivable system for authenticating users needs trusted functionality that holds the necessary authentication information (see e.g., [18, 26]). Yet, the meaning that is associated with trust or the notion of a trusted principal is hardly ever clearly defined in these approaches and the reader is left with his intuition.

In this article we address the question of how trust in a certain principal can be motivated based on technical reasoning and present a pessimistic approach to trust that tries to prevent malicious behaviour rather than correcting it after it has occurred. The approach relies on a trusted and tamper-resistant hardware device that can be used to enforce a policy. If this policy is properly chosen, an agent can take advantage of it in order to protect itself as well as the information it contains from possibly malicious service providers.

The mobile agent paradigm usually identifies two interacting principals: the owner of the agent who configures it and the executor of the agent, which may be identical to the service provider. However, many protocols for security related problems, especially those that are concerned with non-repudiation, require an additional third party that often has to be trusted by the other parties. This principal is called a *trusted third party* (TTP). Due to this trust requirement, the functionality of a TTP must be realized in a trustworthy environment, which is usually only available at the site of the TTP. Hence, the principals in the mobile agent paradigm have to interact with the TTP server using the classical client/server mechanisms. The approach described here, which provides protection for the mobile agents of regular users, can also be applied to mobile agents that are owned by a TTP. This allows us to take full advantage of the mobile agent paradigm and removes the need for remote messaging between the interacting principals.

In the following Section 2, we introduce our model for mobile agents and point out the problems related to trust within this model. Then, in Section 3, we discuss the notion of trust and define its relation to policy, which enables us to better assess the possible motivations for trust. In Section 4, we introduce a trusted and tamper-resistant hardware device and a protocol, which allow us to define certain guarantees for the execution of agents. In Section 5, we show how this approach can be used to protect the agents of a regular user as well as those of a TTP. In Section 6, we discuss why we consider this to be an adequate way to approach the problem and what effects this has on the notion of open systems. Finally, Section 7 concludes the paper with a summary of the main contributions.

# 2 The mobile agent paradigm

The mobile agent paradigm has been identified by many authors as a promising and innovative approach to structure problems in distributed computing [3, 4, 7, 8, 11, 23]. However, it is still under lively discussion and it has been shown in [9] that there is no single compelling reason to favour the mobile agent paradigm over classic client/server approaches. On the other hand, the same authors point out that the mobile agent paradigm provides interesting solutions to many real-life problems, for instance in the context of:

- *mobile users*, where an agent is sent out from a mobile computer in order to accomplish a well-defined task on behalf of the user while he is disconnected from the communication network. Once the user reconnects, the agent returns and reports the result of the task or the problems it encountered.
- *high-bandwidth interactions*, where an agent is sent to a database server that holds a large amount of unstructured data to search for some specific information for the user.
- *customizable services*, where a service provider can offer a small number of simple operations on its service interface that can be combined by an agent to obtain the desired functionality.
- *resident agents*, which are stationary agents that take residence at some service provider and handle simple routine actions for their owner (e.g., communication management for a mobile user, where the agent decides how to handle an incoming communication request).

## 2.1 Basic definitions

In this article, we do not focus on the underlying technology that is used to implement the paradigm, but we only require a simple model of agents for our discussion. Therefore, we identify the following major abstractions that we associate with mobile agents. A mobile agent consists of code, data, and its current execution state, which can be marshalled by the *agent owner* in a transport format and subsequently sent to the *agent executor*. The agent can be confidentiality and integrity protected during transit to prevent outside attacks through the use of cryptographic mechanisms. These mechanisms can also provide data origin authentication for the marshalled agent. The agent executor will then eventually unmarshall the agent and instantiate it on a special environment located at the agent executor, which is called *agent platform* (AP). Here, the mobile agent can interact with services of the local AP as well as other agents located at this AP and continue to accomplish the task it was given by its owner.

The literature on agents (e.g., [3, 13]) distinguishes between two different approaches to support agent mobility: *weak* mobility and *strong* mobility. The former does not automatically support the transfer of the current execution state of the agent. Thus, if an agent is supposed to visit more than a single AP (which is often referred to as multi-hop agent), the current execution state has to be explicitly encoded in the agent's data before it can migrate to another AP. The latter approach automatically supports the transfer of the current execution state and allows an agent to continue its execution exactly where it left off before initiating the migration. A mobile agent can thus easily visit as many APs as it deems necessary to accomplish the desired task. In both approaches, the result of the agent's remote execution can be sent directly to the agent owner in the form of a message or kept in the execution state of the agent and extracted by the agent owner when the agent returns.

The reason for only providing weak instead of strong mobility is that the execution environment in the AP and the agent transport format can be much simpler since the AP does not have to provide the current execution state (which is, for instance, not available from the Java virtual machine) and the transport format does not have to encode it. Also, if an agent visits only a single AP, which is supported by weak mobility, the trust model becomes much simpler. Any damage incurred by the agent to the AP (and thus to the agent executor) or by the AP to the agent (and thus to the agent owner) can easily be attributed to the other entity. If more than two principals are involved, the problem of accountability becomes much more difficult [13]. Each principal can defer any damage to actions by one of the other principals on the agent's itinerary.

In this article we will concentrate on the protection of a mobile agent on a particular AP. In our solution, a multi-hop agent that visits several sites only represents multiple instances of the same problem. Our main concern is how to protect the agent and especially the data it contains from undue manipulation by or undesired disclosure to the agent executor, which is mainly a question of trust in the agent executor.

## 2.2 The need for trust

There are many examples where an agent might need confidential information that should not be disclosed to the service provider, even though the agent needs the information to accomplish its task:

- a shopping agent in an electronic-commerce system might hold data that could give a bargaining advantage to the service provider if it were known to him (e.g., a maximum price that the service user is willing to pay or the lowest QoS that he is willing to accept before inquiring at another service provider).
- another agent for electronic commerce might hold a private key with which it can sign messages on behalf of its owner, for instance, to confirm an order placed by the agent. This key has to be kept secret to prevent that the service provider can also sign messages on behalf of the agent owner.
- an agent in a personalized information system might contain private data from the customization by its owner that is needed to find appropriate information. An agent searching for movies that are likely to interest its owner,

might contain some very personal information about the user's special interests, which the agent executor cannot infer from simply observing the agent's choice.

– finally, an agent that merely searches for some particular financial information (e.g., stock quotes) might, depending on the owner of the agent, convey some very sensitive information (the mere request already conveys the interest in the information).

## 2.3   Threats to a mobile agent

In a conventional mobile agent system, when the agent owner sends a mobile agent to an agent executor in order to use some service, the agent owner loses all control over the code and data of the agent. The agent executor can:

– reverse engineer the agent's code,
– analyze the agent's data,
– arbitrarily change the agent's code and data, or, if none of these direct attacks is feasible,
– experiment with the agent (e.g., by feeding it with arbitrary data and resetting it to its initial state, in order to observe the agent's reactions).

This constellation puts the agent executor in a much stronger position than the agent owner. The agent owner simply has to trust the agent executor not to use the methods described above to illicitly obtain confidential information from the agent that it has to carry in order to use the service. There is no way for the agent owner to control or even know about the behaviour of the agent executor.

The reason for the imbalance between agent executor and agent owner in the mobile agent model as compared to the principals in the client/server model is that in the former approach, the agent owner has no guarantees whatsoever concerning the execution of its agent. In the client/server approach, the client relies on many guarantees that are so basic that one hardly ever thinks of them. Nevertheless, these guarantees allow the implementation of certain types of behaviour in the client part of the distributed application that can not be implemented in conventional agent systems (e.g., code will be executed at most once, code will be executed correctly, or the code can rely on a reasonably accurate time service). This is due to the fact that the client implementation is under the physical control of the service user, who can can observe what is happening in the system and notice any irregularities. Thus, he is able to react accordingly, for instance, to interrupt an ongoing transaction or to log any irregularities at the client side so that they can be provided as evidence in the case of a dispute with some server. This is opposed to the mobile agent paradigm, where logged data can easily be deleted by the agent executor.

We intend to create an environment for mobile agents that allows them to base their execution on assumptions similar to the client/server approach, so that it becomes possible for a mobile agent to better protect itself from a malicious agent executor.

# 3 The notion of trust

We already mentioned the importance of trust for security in distributed systems and pointed out the lack of a clear definition of what is meant by the terms trust or trusted principal. In the following, we present our analysis of possible trust relations between different principals.

A reason for the lack of a clear definition of trust could be that trust is more a social than a technical issue and consequently quite difficult to tackle entirely in a technical approach. The major problem stems from the fact that the notion of trust mixes the goals of a principal with its behaviour to achieve these goals. In order to trust some principal, it is usually necessary to concur with or at least to approve of its goals (which are not always clearly stated) and to believe that it will behave accordingly. In our definition of trust, we will try to clearly separate these two issues by identifying a policy that is consistent with the goals of the principal. This policy is a set of rules that constrains the behaviour of the principal for all conceivable situations. It has to be written down and made available to all other principals that interact with the issuer of the policy. Then, we define *trust in another principal* as the belief that it will adhere to its published policy.

The question of whether a certain principal can be trusted now consists of (a) checking its published policy in order to decide if it is acceptable and (b) to establish a motivation for the belief that it will adhere to its published policy. The former is quite difficult but can be supported by a formal specification of the security policy (similar to the approach in [15]). The latter, however, is a problem that is quite difficult to formalize. Depending on how the belief in the adherence to the published policy is motivated, we have identified two fundamentally different approaches to the problem of trust:

- the optimistic approach and
- the pessimistic approach.

In the optimistic approach, we give an entity the benefit of the doubt, assume that it will behave properly, and try to punish any violation of the published policy afterwards. In the pessimistic approach we try to prevent any violation of the published policy in advance by effectively constraining the possible actions of a principal to those conforming to the policy. Both of these approaches have advantages and disadvantages.

## 3.1 The optimistic approach

This approach is easy to implement, since it does not require any special measures to make trusted interaction possible. This is probably the reason why it is the basis for most business conducted today. On the other hand, it requires some reliable mechanism to discover a policy violation after it has occurred. If such a mechanism does not exist, then the approach degenerates to *blind trust*, which indicates that there is no particular motivation to believe that a principal will adhere to its published policy other than its own assertion. Blind trust is obviously a very weak foundation for trust and not recommended for any important or financially valuable transaction. It is therefore important to make the probability that a policy violation is discovered as high as possible by improving controls and establishing checkpoints.

Once a policy violation is discovered and if it can further irrefutably be attributed to one of the participants in the corresponding transaction, this principal should be punished according to the appropriate laws and the damage caused by the policy violation. The primary goal of this punishment is to deter potential violators from committing a policy violation in the first place.

Depending on how this punishment is enacted, we identify the following two motivations for the belief that an entity will adhere to its published policy:

- trust based on (a good) reputation and
- trust based on explicit punishment.

Trust based on reputation stems from the fact that the principal in question is well known and has very little to gain through a violation of its own policy but a lot to lose in case a policy violation is discovered. This loss is supposed to transpire from the lost revenue due to customers taking their business to another provider. Reputation is an asset that is expensive to build up and that is invaluable for any company. Thus, we assume that a principal would not risk to lose its good reputation for a small gain and will consequently rather adhere to its policy.

Trust based on explicit punishment means that we do not trust the principal, but rather the underlying legal framework to ensure the principal's proper behaviour. Here, we explicitly introduce a similar tradeoff as in trust based on reputation by imposing disciplinary actions such as fines or imprisonment, depending on the severity of the offence. The short term gain that might be achieved through a policy violation is supposed to be negated by appropriate punishment.

Obviously, there are many problems with this approach, such as the enforcement of laws, which is usually expensive, quite slow, and sometimes very complex (in particular if the laws of different countries are applicable as can be expected for transactions on the Internet). The difficulty of very different perceptions of punishment, where a person who has not much to lose might readily risk some years of imprisonment for the possibility of a relatively large gain. Another problem in the optimistic approach stems from the fact that many abuses of confidential information are not necessarily conducted for the purposes of the company that holds this information, but rather by malicious insiders of such a company, who do it for strictly personal reasons or financial benefits [20, 25]. Such abuses are even more difficult to discover (there are less people involved) and to punish (it has to be decided if only the employee for malicious behaviour, only the company for negligence, or both have to be pursued).

The problem to reliably discover a policy violation could be resolved by requiring a high degree of transparency. However, this is difficult to achieve and it is quite likely that even trustworthy principals with a good reputation might not be eager to accept it in order to protect internal business processes. We therefore assume that complete transparency is not a very useful tool for supervision. A better approach would be to designate specialized appraisal companies that execute frequent in-depth controls of the conduct of companies.

Finally, by definition, the optimistic approach cannot prevent malicious behaviour, but it only tries to compensate for it after it has been discovered. For many situations in real-life, where a violation might have an irreparable effect or where a proper functioning of the system is absolutely essential, this guarantee might not be strong enough. A more detailed discussion of the notion of trust described above, can be found in the paper of Swarup and Fábrega [19].

We would like to remark that most of the described problems are also present in our every-day life and therefore quite well understood. However, the question stands if we can do better than that.

## 3.2 The pessimistic approach

The pessimistic approach removes all these disadvantages by simply preventing any violation of the published policy. This would clearly be the best foundation for trust since we can solely rely on a principal's policy to verify that its behaviour will be acceptable. The behaviour of the principal becomes completely transparent as far as it is constrained by its policy without the need to actually supervise any particular action. If the policy prescribes an action for some event and if the policy is enforced then it is guaranteed that the action will take place. Unfortunately, this policy enforcement can not be realized in its full generality, but is limited to those policies (or rules of a policy) that can effectively be enforced with some uncircumventable mechanism. For non-enforceable policies, we still have to rely on optimistic approaches to trust.

There is no simple way to conceive such an uncircumventable enforcement mechanism. Until recently it was considered impossible without relying on some piece of trusted and tamper-resistant hardware [4]. However, in [16] Sander and Tschudin describe a new approach that might eventually be capable to provide some protection for an agent without relying on such hardware. Unfortunately, in its current form the approach does not allow to create agents that encode arbitrary programs, but it only supports polynomial and rational functions. Thus, the only viable way that can be implemented with current knowledge has to rely on trusted and tamper-resistant hardware. In the following section, we will describe such a piece of hardware and the requirements that have to be met so that it can be used to enforce certain rules of a policy. This hardware is comparable to the *Secure Coprocessor* described by Yee in [27].

## 4 Tamper-resistant hardware and the CryPO protocol

We will first present the execution environment that we rely on and then describe the protocol that uses it. Figure 1 gives an overview of the principals in the system.

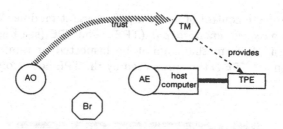

**Fig. 1.** Overview of the Principals in the CryPO protocol

A manufacturer (TM) produces the execution environment(TPE), which can be bought by any agent executor (AE). An agent owner (AO) has to trust the manufacturer to design and produce its execution environments properly (see Section 6). The broker (Br) is basically a directory service to locate other principals and to obtain their credentials.

### 4.1 Notation

The described approach relies on public key cryptography [5] (such as RSA [14]). A detailed description of cryptography and the corresponding notations is not within the scope of this presentation. For information on this topic see e.g., [12, 17]. The notation we will use is as follows.

A principal $P$ has a pair (or several pairs[1]) of keys $(K_P, K_P^{-1})$ where $K_P$ is $P$'s public key and $K_P^{-1}$ its private key. Given these keys and the corresponding algorithm, it is possible to encrypt a message $m$ using the receiver $P$'s public key $K_P$, denoted $\{m\}_{K_P}$, so that only $P$ can decrypt it with its private key. A signed message, including a digital signature on the message $m$, generated by $P$ using its private key $K_P^{-1}$ and verifiable by anybody using the respective public key $K_P$, is denoted $\{m\}_{S_P}$.

In the following we assume the usage of optimization schemes such as encrypting a large message with a symmetric session key, which in turn is encrypted using public key cryptography and prepended to the message as well as the use of hash algorithms to reduce the computational complexity of signing. However, for ease of presentation, we will not make this explicit.

### 4.2 The processing environment

As we have noted above, there is no way to enforce any particular behaviour from another principal without a piece of trusted and tamper-resistant hardware. The concept of tamper-resistance usually applies to a well-defined module, sometimes called black-box, that executes a given task. The outside environment cannot interfere with the task of this module other than through a restricted interface that

---

[1] It is advisable to have at least two pairs of keys, one for encryption/decryption and one for digital signatures.

is under the complete control of the tamper-resistant module. We will call this device *trusted processing environment* (TPE). The TPE (see Figure 2) provides a complete agent platform that cannot be inspected or tampered with. Any agent residing on the TPE is thus protected by the TPE both from disclosure and manipulation.

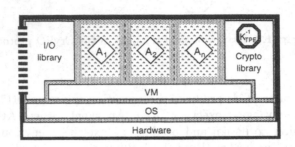

**Fig. 2.** The trusted processing environment (TPE)

The TPE is a complete computer that consists of a CPU, RAM, ROM, and non-volatile storage (e.g. hard-disk or flash RAM). It runs a virtual machine (VM) that provides the platform for the execution of agents and guarantees the correct execution of the agent's code according to the definition of the used language (e.g., Java byte-code). Below the VM is the operating system that provides the external interface to the TPE and controls the VM (e.g., protection of agents from each other). Furthermore, the TPE contains a private key $K_{TPE}^{-1}$ that is known to no principal other than the TPE – also the physical owner of the TPE does not know the private key. This can, for instance, be achieved by generating the private key on the TPE[2]. Using this approach, the private key is never available outside of the TPE and, thus, protected by the operating system and the tamper-resistance of the TPE. The secrecy of the private key is a crucial requirement for the usage of the TPE to enforce a particular behaviour.

The TPE is connected to a host computer that is under the control of the TPE's owner. This host computer can access the TPE exclusively through a well defined interface that allows, for instance, the following operations on the TPE:

– upload, migrate, or remove agents;
– facilitate interactions between host and agent or between agents on the TPE;
– verify certain properties of the TPE (such as which agents are currently executing).

Due to its implementation as a tamper-resistant module and the restricted access via the I/O interface, it is impossible to directly access the information

---

[2] Other, more sophisticated approaches to create the pair of keys could be envisaged, which could also incorporate key recovery mechanisms (e.g., escrowed key shares).

that is contained in the TPE. This property is ensured by the TPE manufacturer
($TM$), which also provides the agent executor ($AE$) with a certificate (signed
by TM). The certificate contains information about the TPE, such as its manufacturer, its type, the guarantees provided, and its public key. The agent owner
($AO$) has to trust the TM (see Section 6) that the TPE actually does provide
the protection that is claimed in the certificate.

## 4.3  CryPO protocol

The CryPO (cryptographically protected objects[3]) protocol transfers agents exclusively in encrypted form over the network to a TPE, using the TPE's public
key. Therefore, it is impossible for anyone who does not know the private key to
obtain the code or data of such a protected agent.

The protocol is divided into two distinct phases. The first phase consists of an
initialization, which has to be executed once before the execution of the second
phase of the protocol. This second phase is concerned with the usage of the TPE
and the actual transfer of the agent. The protocol is based on the interactions
given in Figures 3 and 4.

**Initialization**  In the initialization phase, the participants exchange the required
key information:

- we assume that the AO holds an authentic copy of the TM's certification
  key $K_{TM}$.
- the TM sends the certificate $Cert_{TPE} = \{K_{TPE}, ...\}_{S_{TM}}$ to the AE.
- the AE registers its reference $Ref_{AE}$[4] with one or several brokers.

**Usage**  After the participants have finished the initialization, they can execute
the usage part of the CryPO protocol:

- the AO queries the broker for the reference to the AE with which it wants
  to interact (or it already holds this reference from a previous interaction).
- the AO verifies the policy of the AE whether it is acceptable as well as the
  certificate $Cert_{TPE}$ to check the manufacturer and the type of the TPE, in
  order to decide if it satisfies the security requirements of the AO. If any of
  these checks fail, the AO will abort the protocol.
- the AO sends the agent encrypted with the public key of the TPE, $\{A\}_{K_{TPE}}$,
  to the AE.

---

[3] We had originally chosen the term object since it is more general than the term
agent.

[4] A reference to an AE consists of its name, its physical address in the network, its
policy, and the certificate $Cert_{TPE}$ for its TPE. The broker can also verify that the AE
actually controls the corresponding TPE by executing a challenge-response protocol
with the TPE via the AE.

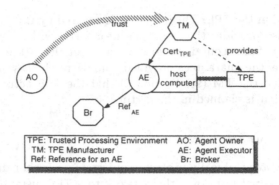

**Fig. 3.** Initialization of the CryPO protocol

- the AE cannot decrypt $\{A\}_{K_{TPE}}$ nor can it do anything other than upload the agent to its TPE.
- the TPE decrypts $\{A\}_{K_{TPE}}$ using its private key $K_{TPE}^{-1}$ and obtains the executable agent $A$, which it will eventually start. The agent can then interact with the local environment of the AE or with other agents on the TPE.
- the agent can, after it has finished its task, migrate back to its owner ($\{A\}_{K_{AO}}$) or to another AE to which it holds a reference.

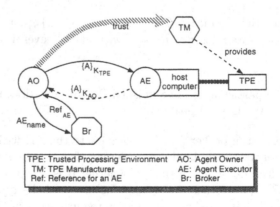

**Fig. 4.** Usage of the CryPO protocol

The obvious problem of protecting the TPE from malicious agents is independent of the described approach and has to be tackled with additional mechanisms, such as code signing and sandboxing. The problem of protecting the TPE from tampered agents can easily be solved by concatenating the agent with a hash of the entire agent $h(A)$, including its execution state, before encrypting it $\{A, h(A)\}_{K_{TPE}}$. The TPE simply has to verify the correct hash before starting the agent.

## 4.4 Notes on feasibility

The actual construction of a tamper-resistant module in the real world is difficult; nevertheless, there are many applications that rely on them (e.g., payphones, debit cards, or SIM cards for GSM). Given sufficient time and resources, it becomes very probable that an attacker can violate the protection of such a module (see e.g., [1]). We believe that the actual realization of the presented TPE with reasonably strong guarantees in real-world settings is also quite difficult, but nonetheless feasible. Especially, since we do not require the prevention but only the detection of tampering with the TPE for most envisioned applications.

We imagine the TPE as a regular computer with a special operating system. It is physically protected with a special hardware that can effectively be sealed to detect tampering, is under continuous video surveillance similar to the systems used to supervise automatic teller machines, and is subject to challenge inspections by the TM or an independent appraisal and inspection organization. As explained in [1], such an installation is conceivable and can even resist massive attacks. A thorough analysis of the remaining risks has to be undertaken, but this is not within the scope of this presentation.

## 5 Usage of the TPE

The CryPO protocol together with the concept of a TPE guarantee the integrity of the agent platform to the AO and protect the code and data of an agent against manipulation and disclosure, both in transit and during execution. These guarantees are based on the trust relation between the AO and the TM, in which the AO trusts the TM to properly manufacture its TPEs and to control them regularly (if necessary) so that the claimed guarantees hold. The certificate enables the AO to ensure that it really deals with a TPE from a certain manufacturer.

The above guarantees can be extended by additional properties, formulated as rules of a policy, that can effectively be enforced by a TPE. In [24], we have discussed how this approach can be used to allow an agent to base its execution on results of possible previous executions on the same TPE. This can, for instance, be used to limit the number of times an agent can be executed on a given TPE. To achieve this, it is necessary to identify a policy that provides sufficient support for the agent and to ensure that this policy is enforced on the TPE on which the agent executes. With this approach, the AO does not need to trust the AE on the proper protection of his agent, but it suffices to trust the TM. The question why the AO should trust the TM rather than the AE is discussed in section 6.

Now we want to address a problem that requires the cooperation with a *trusted third party* (TTP). Many security related protocols, in particular those that deal with non-repudiation, rely on such a cooperation [12]. The role of the TTP is to provide a well defined functionality (e.g., timestamping or logging of messages) to create non-repudiable evidence that can later be used to resolve a dispute. The special character of this functionality requires that it is provided on a trustworthy environment, which can be guaranteed in the administrative domain of the TTP. Thus, a user of this functionality has to interact with the TTP server via a remote interaction, which suffers from the usual problems of limited bandwidth, high latency, and inflexibility of the interface. In order to get rid of this remote message exchange we propose to encapsulate the functionality of the TTP in a *TTP agent* that can be executed on a TPE, which is also a trustworthy environment. This allows us to gather all interacting parties on a single platform and to take full advantage of the mobile agent paradigm (see Section 5.4).

We will first introduce a policy for a TPE and discuss its effect on the agent of a regular user at the example of a shopping agent. Then we will show how the same concepts can be applied to a TTP agent and discuss the implications of the approach.

## 5.1 The policy of the TPE

We assume that the TPE of the service provider enforces the following set of rules, detailed in its policy:

a) the code of an agent will never be disclosed or altered by the TPE.

b) any invocation of the agent's methods will be executed exactly according to the code in the agent.

c) the data of an agent can exclusively be accessed and manipulated through the interface of the agent. If the agent does not provide methods to directly access a particular data item, its value can at most be inferred from the responses to other method invocations.

d) an agent is protected against interference from other agents executing on the same TPE (other than calls on its public interface).

e) prior to a migration, an agent will obtain the certificate of the designated receiver's TPE that also contains the policy. The agent can decide whether it wants to be transferred and the current TPE will honour the agent's decision. The actual transfer follows the CryPO protocol.

f) the TPE provides an internal clock with reasonable accuracy (on the order of several seconds). It will try to synchronize this clock with a trusted time service and will inform the agent if this synchronization did not succeed.

The first rules a) and b) guarantee the basic protection of the agent's code as well as its proper execution, while c) guarantees the protection of the agent's data from undesired disclosure and manipulation. Rule d) requires the protection of agents from one another, which is a regular operating system functionality. The next rule e) ensures that the agent knows the policy of the TPE to which it is transferred. Thus, the agent can ensure that it will not be sent to a TPE that provides insufficient protection. Finally, rule f) can be used for several purposes. For instance, it allows an agent that contains an expiration date to implement a limited lifetime (on the order of a few days or hours). Upon its arrival the agent requests the current time and checks if this time is still within its attributed lifetime. If its expiration date has passed or if the TPE did not succeed to synchronize its clock, the agent can simply abort. An AE can not prevent this if the code of the agent is protected and if it will be executed correctly.

## 5.2 The shopping agent

Consider a shopping agent that searches for a particular service for its owner. Once it has found a suitable offer, it will negotiate the details of the service provision, such as exact price and various QoS parameters, with the service provider. As a special requirement, we specify that the shopping agent has to create a log entry with a TTP server[5] that contains the details of the negotiated contract before providing the payment data. This allows the AO to reconstruct the activities of his agent in the case of a dispute or if the agent is lost.

In order for the shopping agent to effectively conduct a negotiation it needs to conceal some of its configuration information from the service provider, such as the highest acceptable price or the lowest acceptable QoS parameters. Furthermore, the shopping agent holds the public key of the TTP, which it needs to verify the acknowledgement from the TTP server, as well as the payment data, which should only be provided to the selected service provider after the successful creation of a log entry.

If the shopping agent executes only on TPEs that enforce the policy discussed in Section 5.1, it is clear that it is protected from any interference. Provided that the agent is correct, no other entity will be able to access or manipulate any data contained in the agent other than what is accessible via the methods of its public interface. Thus, the agent can effectively negotiate with a service provider, request the logging of the contract with a TTP server, and delay any further actions until it has received a signed acknowledgement from the TTP server.

## 5.3 The TTP agent

The interaction described above allows for an efficient negotiation between the agent and the service provider exploiting all the performance advantages of the mobile agent paradigm. However, due to the special requirements of the AO, the agent has to interact with a TTP server via a remote interaction. Apart from the performance penalties of this remote interaction, the TTP server can also become a bottleneck if its resources are consumed by a large number of clients. Therefore, we propose to encapsulate the functionality of the TTP in a TTP

---

[5] The agent could send the corresponding information directly to the AO, but since it needs an acknowledgement for the receipt of the log message and since the AO might not have a permanent connection to the network, it is preferable to delegate this task to a TTP.

agent (*TA*) that can be executed on the TPE, relying on the same protection mechanisms as the shopping agent[6].

In the case of message logging, the functionality of the TTP consists of accepting arbitrary messages, storing them up to a well defined point in time $t$, and responding with an acknowledgement asserting that the message has been logged. This acknowledgement has to be signed by the TTP and must clearly identify the message that was supposed to be logged, either by including the message itself or, preferably, a hash of the message. Furthermore, the TTP must be capable to reproduce a logged message up to the time $t$ and to provide it (exclusively to authorized principals) upon request. If necessary, a log message can be confidentiality protected with regular encryption methods.

The task of the *TA* is to act as the proxy for the actual TTP on the TPE. It will accept messages that have to be logged from agents on the TPE, store them in a local cache, and respond with an acknowledgement in which it guarantees that it will forward the message to the TTP server unless the TPE is destroyed (see below). Once a log message arrives at the TTP server, it will be handled like a normal message. In order for the *TA* to provide such a guarantee, it needs access to a sufficient amount of non-volatile storage on the TPE, in which it can safely store the log messages. Since this non-volatile storage is a limited resource of the TPE, the *TA* needs a special authorization to use it. If the TPE owner does not grant this authorization, the *TA* will abort.

Apart from the access to the non-volatile storage of the TPE, the requirements of the *TA* are very similar to those of the shopping agent. It has to be protected against manipulation of its code and data and it also has to conceal certain data items from the agent executor such as two different cryptographic keys. The first key is necessary as a means to securely forward the logged messages to the TTP server. Since the *TA* is configured by the TTP, this can simply be a secret key of a symmetric key cryptosystem. The second key is needed as a signature key to sign the acknowledgements for logged messages. This does not necessarily have to be the long-term signature key of the TTP, but can be a temporary key that is validated by a certificate signed with the TTP's long-term signature key.

Again, if the TTP ensures that the *TA* only executes on TPEs that enforce the policy discussed in Section 5.1 with sufficiently high assurance, it is clear that the keys are protected and that the proper execution of the *TA* is guaranteed. The remaining problem is how the *TA* can guarantee that logged messages that are stored in the non-volatile storage of the TPE will eventually be forwarded to the TTP server. The TPE owner could simply intercept all the messages of the *TA* to the TTP server or, ultimately, request the TPE to terminate the *TA*. This functionality has to be offered by the TPE to protect its owner from malicious or simply buggy agents that refuse to terminate.

This problem can be solved with a supervision of the *TA* by the TTP and with the help of the internal clock provided by the TPE. The TTP has to keep

---

[6] A TTP might require a higher level of assurance in the protection of the TPE than a regular user. This could be a differentiating feature of TPEs from different manufacturers.

track of all the *TA*s it sent to the various service providers and of an expiration date that is associated with each *TA*. A *TA* will accept log messages only until its expiration date. After this date it will refuse to accept and acknowledge any further messages. Thus, the TTP has to receive a final message from the *TA* after its expiration date (there should be an additional delay to accommodate for clock skew) indicating that no further messages for the TTP are stored in the non-volatile storage of the TPE. Provided that the *TA* only deletes messages from this non-volatile storage after sending them to the TTP server and obtaining an acknowledgement, the TTP knows that all the messages that the *TA* acknowledged have been forwarded to the TTP server. If this final message is not received, the TTP will request the TPE owner to restart the *TA* and to forward any messages it sends to the TTP server. Under the assumption that the TTP has a possibility to enforce the access to the TPE by legal means, the only possibility of the TPE owner to avoid the provision of missing messages is to destroy the TPE. Thus, the approach cannot guarantee that all logged messages will be delivered to the TTP server. But it can guarantee that a TPE owner can not cheat without being discovered. Furthermore, if it can be proven that the TPE owner intentionally destroyed the TPE, he can be punished with adequate fines.

The problem of destruction of storage media is not new and also applies to a regular TTP. However, it is assumed that the TTP operator implements adequate measures to avoid this problem.

## 5.4 Discussion

The relocation of the TTP functionality from a remote site to the locally managed TPE allows us to prevent it from becoming a bottleneck that slows down other components. This is possible since the TPE owner can allocate as many resources as necessary to the *TA* without having to coordinate this with the TTP. Also, since the *TA* can collect and merge several log messages from interactions of different agents with the service provider, it can accumulate several log messages and forward them in a single remote interaction. Another major advantage of the described approach is that the remote interaction with the TTP server is taken off the critical communication path between the agent and the service provider. They can continue their interaction as soon as the *TA* has stored the log message and sent the acknowledgement. Moreover, the entire interaction can exploit the locally available communication links with higher bandwidth and lower latency. This enables not only a better overall performance of the system, but allows interactions that were not possible before due to an unreasonable overhead. For instance, a *TA* could be used by two interacting parties as an intermediate through which all messages are exchanged. The *TA* could, thus, easily log the entire interaction and forward it to the TTP.

The concept of the *TA* is suitable for any TTP functionality that can be wrapped up in a reasonably small object and that does not have to rely on a large centrally managed database. Other interesting examples are timestamping or fair-exchange. The former consists of a *TA* that adds a timestamp to a message and signs the resulting message with its signature key. The latter is a classical security problem, for which several solutions relying on a TTP have been proposed [2]. The problem of fair-exchange is that of principals $A$ and $B$ who want to exchange the data items $D_A$ and $D_B$, but neither of them wants to provide its data item before receiving that of the other principal. A $TA$ can facilitate the exchange by accepting the data items as well as a description of the data items expected by the designated receivers. It will verify if the descriptions match the actual data items (e.g., in the case of payment, it verifies if the paid amount corresponds with the amount expected by the receiver) and, if this is the case, deliver the data items to the designated receiver.

## 6 Trust in the TPE manufacturer

We have introduced the mechanism, with which an agent can take advantage of the policy enforced by a TPE. However, as we have mentioned above, in order for a principal to trust in the proper enforcement of this policy, it is necessary that he also trusts the TPE manufacturer to properly design, implement, and produce its TPEs. Since there is no way (to the knowledge of the authors) to enforce a correct behaviour of the TPE manufacturer, it seems that the presented approach simply replaces one required trust relationship with another one. This is a correct observation from a theoretical point of view. Nevertheless, we believe that the replacement of trust in an arbitrary service provider with trust in a TPE manufacturer has several more subtle implications. We will briefly discuss the following advantages that we identified:

- better understanding of security and privacy problems
- centralized control
- resources to build reputation
- separation of concern

The TPE manufacturer is a specialized service provider, which primarily deals in the field of the provision of security devices. Therefore it has a better understanding of security and privacy problems, which makes it a much more capable entity to ensure this service since it is more aware of the potential problems and pitfalls.

We assume that there will be relatively few TPE manufacturers (on the order of several hundreds) compared to the number of possible operators of the TPE (on the order of several millions). This makes the control of their behaviour much easier for expert appraisal organizations. Also, it is quite conceivable that a TPE manufacturer might invite external experts to control its internal operation, in order to obtain a better position in the market (similar to the approach for quality assurance in the ISO-9000).

The production of TPEs is considered to be a difficult task (see Section 4.4). Therefore, we assume that it will be undertaken by major corporations, which have the necessary resources to build a good reputation and which have an incentive to protect this reputation. This allows us to rely on good reputation as foundation for trust in the TPE manufacturer.

The TPE manufacturer that is responsible for the enforcement of the proper policy rules on the TPE, has nothing to gain by not accomplishing its task. Since the TPE will be operated independent from the TPE manufacturer by a completely different principal and since the TPE manufacturer has no means to access the data that is processed on the TPE (no physical connection), there is no possibility for the TPE manufacturer to draw a direct benefit from a TPE that does not properly enforce its policy[7].

We assume that the above arguments of high expertise, effective controllability, good reputation, and lack of incentive are sound reasons to trust a TPE manufacturer to build reliable and powerful TPEs. The main advantage of the approach lies in the possibility to leverage this trust in the TPE manufacturer onto a completely different principal in the role of the service provider, which

- might not have the proper expertise to ensure a secure operation of its hardware and to guarantee the protection of the processed data.
- is quite difficult to control, due to the sheer number of such service providers.
- might have no particular reputation (and therefore none to lose).
- might have short term goals that (in its point of view) justify a policy violation.

With the presented approach, such a service provider can easily define the policy rules that it would like its TPE to enforce (by selecting from the options offered by the TPE manufacturer) and buy the appropriate TPE from a reputable TPE manufacturer. The service provider can then immediately benefit from the trust that users have in the manufacturer of its TPE to convince them that it will not maliciously abuse an agent sent by a user.

With this, the approach favours the open systems philosophy, where any principal can possibly become a provider of services. Such a service provider simply has to obtain a TPE from some reputable manufacturer and can then easily convince a client that the client's confidential information is sufficiently well protected. Thus, it becomes much easier for a new service provider to establish itself in the market.

# 7 Conclusion

In this paper, we have discussed the notion of trust in the context of mobile agent systems and introduced a structuring for this problem domain. Starting from this structure, we have proposed an approach that relies on a trusted and tamper-resistant hardware device, which allows the prevention of malicious behaviour rather than its correction. We believe this to be the better form of protection for

---

[7] There is the possibility that a TPE operator bribes a TPE manufacturer to provide an incorrect TPE. We assume that such a behaviour is a severe offence that is subject to criminal investigation and not within the scope of this discussion.

confidential data. We have shown how the approach can be used to effectively protect the confidential data contained in the shopping agent of a user and how it can be extended to protect specialized agents from TTPs that provide facilitation services.

In real-life, there are limitations to the approach. Given sufficient time and resources, a TPE operator might succeed in breaking the system and it would thus be possible for him to violate the policy that should be enforced by the TPE. Our goal is to make this attack so costly that it would negate a possible gain (there may be many different implementations that provide different levels of assurance in the protection of a TPE). As further deterrent, we assume that a non-repudiable proof for a policy violation of an enforced policy or for an attempted or successful breaking of a TPE might be punished much more severely than a mere policy violation since it proves a much larger determination to commit a criminal offence.

## Acknowledgements

This research was supported by a grant from the EPFL ("Privacy" project) and by the Swiss National Science Foundation as part of the Swiss Priority Programme Information and Communications Structures (SPP-ICS) under project number 5003-045364.

## References

1. R. Anderson and M. Kuhn. Tamper resistance — a cautionary note. In *The Second USENIX Workshop on Electronic Commerce Proceedings*, pages 1–11, Oakland, California, November 1996.
2. H. Bürk and A. Pfitzmann. Value exchange systems enabling security and unobservability. *Computers & Security*, 9(8):715–721, 1990.
3. A. Carzaniga, G. P. Picco, and G. Vigna. Designing distributed applications with mobile code paradigms. In R.Taylor, editor, *Proceedings of the 19th International Conference on Software Engineering (ICSE'97)*, pages 22–32. ACM Press, 1997.
4. D. M. Chess, B. Grosof, C. G. Harrison, D. Levine, C. Parris, and G. Tsudik. Itinerant agents for mobile computing. *IEEE Personal Communications*, 2(3):34–49, October 1995.
5. W. Diffie and M. E. Hellman. New directions in cryptography. *IEEE Transactions on Information Theory*, IT-22(6), November 1976.
6. DoD. Trusted Computer System Evaluation Criteria (TCSEC). Technical Report DoD 5200.28-STD, Department of Defense, December 1985.
7. J. Gosling and H. McGilton. The java language environment. White paper, Sun Microsystems, Inc., 1996.
8. R.S. Gray. Agent Tcl: A transportable agent system. In *Proceedings of the CIKM Workshop on Intelligent Information Agents*, Baltimore, MD, December 1995.
9. C. G. Harrison, D. M. Chess, and A. Kershenbaum. Mobile agents: Are they a good idea? In *Mobile Object Systems: Towards the Programmable Internet*, volume 1222 of *Lecture Notes in Computer Science*, pages 25–47. Springer Verlag, 1997.

10. ITU. *ITU-T Recommendation X.509: The Directory – Authentication Framework*. International Telecommunication Union, 1993.

11. D. B. Lange and M. Ishima. *Program and Deploying Java Mobile Agents with Aglets*. Addison-Wesley, 1998.

12. A. J. Menezes, P. C. van Oorschot, and S. A. Vanstone. *Handbook of applied cryptography*. CRC Press, Inc., 1997.

13. J. Ordille. When agents roam, who can you trust? Technical Report Technical Report, Computing Science Research Center, Bell Labs, 1996.

14. RSA Data Security, Inc. *PKCS #1: RSA Encryption Standard*. RSA Data Security, Inc., November 1993.

15. R. A. Rueppel. A formal approach to security architectures. In *EuroCrypt*, pages 387–398, Brighton, England, 1991.

16. T. Sander and C. Tschudin. Towards mobile cryptography. In *IEEE Symposium on Security and Privacy*, May 1998.

17. B. Schneier. *Applied cryptography*. Wiley, New York, 1994.

18. J. G. Steiner, C. Neuman, and J. I. Schiller. Kerberos: An authentication service for open network systems. In *Proceedings of the USENIX Winter 1988 Technical Conference*, pages 191–202. USENIX Association, Berkeley, USA, February 1988.

19. V. Swarup and J. T. Fabrega. Understanding trust. In *Secure Internet Programming* [22].

20. New York Times. U.S. workers stole data on 11,000, agency says, April 6, 1996.

21. G. Vigna. Protecting mobile agents through tracing. In *Proceedings of the Third Workshop on Mobile Object Systems*, Finland, June 1997.

22. Jan Vitek and Christian Jensen. *Secure Internet Programming: Security Issues for Mobile and Distributed Objects*. Lecture Notes in Computer Science. Springer-Verlag Inc., New York, NY, USA, 1999.

23. J. E. White. Telescript technology: The foundation for the electronic market place. White paper, General Magic, Inc., 1994.

24. U. G. Wilhelm, L. Buttyàn, and S. Staamann. On the problem of trust in mobile agent systems. In *Symposium on Network and Distributed System Security*, pages 114–124. Internet Society, March 1998.

25. I. S. Winkler. The non-technical threat to computing systems. *Computing Systems, USENIX Association*, 9(1):3–14, Winter 1996.

26. T. Y. C. Woo and S. S. Lam. Authentication for distributed systems. *IEEE Computer*, 25(1):39–52, January 1992.

27. B. Yee. A sancturary for mobile agents. In *Secure Internet Programming* [22].

28. P. Zimmermann. *PGP User's Guide*. MIT Press, Cambridge, 1994.

# Part IV

# Appendix

# List of Authors (Feb 1999)

---

## Foundations

---

**Martín Abadi**
Systems Research Center
Compaq
130 Lytton Avenue
Palo Alto, CA 94301
U.S.A.

**Massimo Ancona**
DISI - University of Genova
Via Dodecaneso 35, 16146 Genova
Italy
ancona@disi.unige.it
http://www.disi.unige.it/person/AnconaM/

**Luca Cardelli**
Microsoft Research
1 Guildhall St, Cambridge CB2-3NH
United Kingdom
luca@luca.demon.co.uk
http://www.luca.demon.co.uk

**Walter Cazzola** (DSI - University of Milano)
C/O DISI - University of Genova,
Via Dodecaneso 35, 16146 Genova
Italy
cazzola@dsi.unimi.it
http://www.disi.unige.it/person/CazzolaW/

**Rocco De Nicola**
Dipartimento de Sistemi e Informatica
Università di Firenze
Via Lombroso 6/17, I-50134 Firenze
Italy
denicola@dsi.unifi.it
http://dsi2.dsi.unifi.it/~denicola

**Eduardo B. Fernandez**
Department of Computer Science and Engineering
Florida Atlantic University
777 Glades Road, Boca Raton, Florida 33431 U.S.A.
ed@cse.fau.edu
http://www.cse.fau.edu/~ed/

**GianLuigi Ferrari**
Dipartimento di Informatica
Università di Pisa
Corso Italia 40, I-56125 Pisa
Italy
giangi@di.unipi.it
http://www.di.unipi.it/~giangi

**Matthew Hennessy**
School of Cognitive and Computer Science
University of Sussex
Falmer, Brighton BN1 9QH
United Kingdom
matthewh@cogs.susx.ac.uk
http://www.cogs.susx.ac.uk/users/matthewh/

**Xavier Leroy**
INRIA Rocquencourt
Domaine de Voluceau, 78153 Le Chesnay
France
Xavier.Leroy@inria.fr

**Rosario Pugliese**
Dipartimento de Sistemi e Informatica
Università di Firenze
Via Lombroso 6/17, I-50134 Firenze
Italy
pugliese@dsi.unifi.it
http://dsi2.dsi.unifi.it/~pugliese

**James Riely**
Department of Computer Science
North Carolina State University
Raleigh, NC 27695-7534
U.S.A.
riely@csc.ncsu.edu
http://www.csc.ncsu.edu/faculty/riely

**François Rouaix**
Liquid Market Inc
5757 West Century Bld
Los Angeles CA 90045
U.S.A.

**Vipin Swarup**
The MITRE Corporation
202 Burlington Road
Bedford, MA 01730
U.S.A.

**Javier Thayer**
The MITRE Corporation
202 Burlington Road
Bedford, MA 01730
U.S.A.

---

# Concepts

---

**Tuomas Aura**
Helsinki University of Technology
Laboratory for Theoretical Computer Science
P.O. Box 1100, FIN-02015 HUT
Finland
Tuomas.Aura@hut.fi
http://www.tcs.hut.fi/

**Matt Blaze**
AT&T Labs – research
180 Park Avenue
Florham Park, NJ 07932
U.S.A.
mab@research.att.com

**Gerald Brose**
Institut für Informatik
Freie Universität Berlin
Takustraße 9, D–14195 Berlin
Germany
brose@inf.fu-berlin.de
http://www.inf.fu-berlin.de/~brose

**Joan Feigenbaum**
AT&T Labs – research
180 Park Avenue
Florham Park, NJ 07932
U.S.A.
jf@research.att.com

**John Ioannidis**
AT&T Labs – research
180 Park Avenue
Florham Park, NJ 07932
U.S.A.
ji@research.att.com

**Angelos D. Keromytis**
Distributed Systems Lab
CIS Department University of Pennsylvania
200 S. 33rd Str.
Philadelphia, PA 19104
U.S.A.
angelos@dsl.cis.upenn.edu

**Christian F. Tschudin**
Department of Computer Systems
Uppsala University
Box 325, SE – 751 05 Uppsala
Sweden
tschudin@docs.uu.se
http://www.docs.uu.se/ tschudin/

**Bennet S. Yee**
Department Computer Science and Engineering, 0114
University of California San Diego
9500 Gilman Dr
La Jolla, CA 92093-0114
U.S.A.
bsy@cs.ucsd.edu
http://www.cse.ucsd.edu/~bsy/

**Volker Roth**
Fraunhofer Institut für Graphische Datenverarbeitung
Rundeturmstraße 6, D-64283
Germany
vroth@igd.fhg.de
http://www.igd.fhg.de/~vroth

# Implementations

**Martín Abadi**
*See contact information above.*

**Anurag Acharya**
Department of Computer Science
University of California
Santa Barbara, CA 93106
U.S.A.
acha@cs.ucsb.edu

**D. Scott Alexander**
Bell Labs, Lucent Technologies
600 Mountain Avenue
Murray Hill, NJ 07974
U.S.A.
salex@research.bell-labs.com

**William A. Arbaugh**
Distributed Systems Lab
CIS Department University of Pennsylvania
200 S. 33rd Str.
Philadelphia, PA 19104
U.S.A.
waa@dsl.cis.upenn.edu

**Brian N. Bershad**
Department of Computer Science and Engineering
University of Washington
Box 352350
Seattle, WA 98195
U.S.A.
bershad@cs.washington.edu
http://www.cs.washington.edu/homes/bershad

**Mike Burrows**
Systems Research Center
Compaq
130 Lytton Avenue
Palo Alto, CA 94301
U.S.A.

**Levente Buttyán**
Institute for computer Communications and Applications
Swiss Federal Institute of Technology (EPFL)
1015 Lausanne
Switzerland
Levente.Buttyan@epfl.ch
http://icawww.epfl.ch/buttyan


**Chi–Chao Chang**
Department of Computer Science
Cornell University
Ithaca, NY 14850
U.S.A.
chichao@cs.cornell.edu
http://simon.cs.cornell.edu/Info/People/chichao/chichao.html


**Vipin Chaudhary**
Depeartment of ECE
Wayne State University
Detroit, MI 48202
U.S.A.
vipin@ece.eng.wayne.edu


**Grzegorz Czajkowski**
Department of Computer Science
Cornell University
Ithaca, NY 14850
U.S.A.
grzes@cs.cornell.edu
http://simon.cs.cornell.edu/home/grzes/


**Leendert van Doorn**
IBM Thomas J. Watson Research Center
30 Saw Mill River Rd.
Hawthorne, NY 10532
U.S.A.
leendert@watson.ibm.com


**Guy Edjlali**
Depeartment of ECE
Wayne State University
Detroit, MI 48202
U.S.A.
edjlali@ece.eng.wayne.edu

**Thorsten von Eicken**
Department of Computer Science
Cornell University
Ithaca, NY 14850
U.S.A.
tve@cs.cornell.edu
http://www.cs.cornell.edu/tve/


**Robert Grimm**
Department of Computer Science and Engineering
University of Washington
Box 98195
Seattle, WA 98195
U.S.A.
rgrimm@cs.washington.edu
http://www.cs.washington.edu/homes/rgrimm


**Jürgen Harms**
Centre Universitaire d'Informatique
University of Geneva
Rue Général Dufour 24
1211 Genève 4
Switzerland
Juergen.Harms@cui.unige.ch


**Chris Hawblitzel**
Department of Computer Science
Cornell University
Ithaca, NY 14850
U.S.A.
hawblitz@cs.cornell.edu
http://simon.cs.cornell.edu/Info/People/hawblitz/hawblitz.html


**Deyu Hu**
Department of Computer Science
Cornell University
Ithaca, NY 14850
U.S.A.
hu@cs.cornell.edu
http://simon.cs.cornell.edu/Info/People/hu/hu.html

**Jarle G. Hulaas**
Centre Universitaire d'Informatique
University of Geneva
Rue Général Dufour 24
1211 Genève 4
Switzerland
Jarle.Hulaas@cui.unige.ch


**Trent Jaeger**
IBM Thomas J. Watson Research Center
30 Saw Mill River Rd.
Hawthorne, NY 10532
U.S.A.
jaegert@watson.ibm.com


**Michael B. Jones**
Microsoft Research, Microsoft Corporation
One Microsoft Way, Building 31/2260
Redmond, WA 98052
U.S.A.
mbj@microsoft.com
http://www.research.microsoft.com/~mbj


**Angelos D. Keromytis**
*See contact information above.*


**Jonathan M. Smith**
Distributed Systems Lab
CIS Department University of Pennsylvania
200 S. 33rd Str.
Philadelphia, PA 19104
U.S.A.
jms@dsl.cis.upenn.edu


**Dan Spoonhower**
Department of Computer Science
Cornell University
Ithaca, NY 14850
U.S.A.
spoons@cs.cornell.edu

**Sebastian Staamann**
Operating Systems Laboratory (LSE)
Swiss Federal Institute of Technology (EPFL)
1015 Lausanne
Switzerland
Sebastian.Staamann@epfl.ch
http://lsewww.epfl.ch/~staa

**Alex Villazón**
Centre Universitaire d'Informatique
University of Geneva
Rue Général Dufour 24
1211 Genève 4
Switzerland
Alex.Villazon@cui.unige.ch

**Uwe G. Wilhelm**
Operating Systems Laboratory (LSE)
Swiss Federal Institute of Technology (EPFL)
1015 Lausanne
Switzerland
Uwe.Wilhelm@epfl.ch
http://lsewww.epfl.ch/~wilhelm

**Edward Wobber**
Systems Research Center
Compaq
130 Lytton Avenue
Palo Alto, CA 94301
U.S.A.

# Springer
## and the
# environment

# Lecture Notes in Computer Science

For information about Vols. 1–1537
please contact your bookseller or Springer-Verlag

Vol. 1578: W. Thomas (Ed.), Foundations of Software Science and Computation Structures. Proceedings, 1999. X, 323 pages. 1999.

Vol. 1579: W.R. Cleaveland (Ed.), Tools and Algorithms for the Construction and Analysis of Systems. Proceedings, 1999. XI, 445 pages. 1999.

Vol. 1580: A. Včkovski, K.E. Brassel, H.-J. Schek (Eds.), Interoperating Geographic Information Systems. Proceedings, 1999. XI, 329 pages. 1999.

Vol. 1581: J.-Y. Girard (Ed.), Typed Lambda Calculi and Applications. Proceedings, 1999. VIII, 397 pages. 1999.

Vol. 1582: A. Lecomte, F. Lamarche, G. Perrier (Eds.), Logical Aspects of Computational Linguistics. Proceedings, 1997. XI, 251 pages. 1999. (Subseries LNAI).

Vol. 1583: D. Scharstein, View Synthesis Using Stereo Vision. XV, 163 pages. 1999.

Vol. 1584: G. Gottlob, E. Grandjean, K. Seyr (Eds.), Computer Science Logic. Proceedings, 1998. X, 431 pages. 1999.

Vol. 1585: B. McKay, X. Yao, C.S. Newton, J.-H. Kim, T. Furuhashi (Eds.), Simulated Evolution and Learning. Proceedings, 1998. XIII, 472 pages. 1999. (Subseries LNAI).

Vol. 1586: J. Rolim et al. (Eds.), Parallel and Distributed Processing. Proceedings, 1999. XVII, 1443 pages. 1999.

Vol. 1587: J. Pieprzyk, R. Safavi-Naini, J. Seberry (Eds.), Information Security and Privacy. Proceedings, 1999. XI, 327 pages. 1999.

Vol. 1590: P. Atzeni, A. Mendelzon, G. Mecca (Eds.), The World Wide Web and Databases. Proceedings, 1998. VIII, 213 pages. 1999.

Vol. 1592: J. Stern (Ed.), Advances in Cryptology – EUROCRYPT '99. Proceedings, 1999. XII, 475 pages. 1999.

Vol. 1593: P. Sloot, M. Bubak, A. Hoekstra, B. Hertzberger (Eds.), High-Performance Computing and Networking. Proceedings, 1999. XXIII, 1318 pages. 1999.

Vol. 1594: P. Ciancarini, A.L. Wolf (Eds.), Coordination Languages and Models. Proceedings, 1999. IX, 420 pages. 1999.

Vol. 1596: R. Poli, H.-M. Voigt, S. Cagnoni, D. Corne, G.D. Smith, T.C. Fogarty (Eds.), Evolutionary Image Analysis, Signal Processing and Telecommunications. Proceedings, 1999. X, 225 pages. 1999.

Vol. 1597: H. Zuidweg, M. Campolargo, J. Delgado, A. Mullery (Eds.), Intelligence in Services and Networks. Proceedings, 1999. XII, 552 pages. 1999.

Vol. 1598: R. Poli, P. Nordin, W.B. Langdon, T.C. Fogarty (Eds.), Genetic Programming. Proceedings, 1999. X, 283 pages. 1999.

Vol. 1599: T. Ishida (Ed.), Multiagent Platforms. Proceedings, 1998. VIII, 187 pages. 1999. (Subseries LNAI).

Vol. 1601: J.-P. Katoen (Ed.), Formal Methods for Real-Time and Probabilistic Systems. Proceedings, 1999. X, 355 pages. 1999.

Vol. 1602: A. Sivasubramaniam, M. Lauria (Eds.), Network-Based Parallel Computing. Proceedings, 1999. VIII, 225 pages. 1999.

Vol. 1603: J. Vitek, C.D. Jensen (Eds.), Secure Internet Programming. X, 501 pages. 1999.

Vol. 1605: J. Billington, M. Diaz, G. Rozenberg (Eds.), Application of Petri Nets to Communication Networks. IX, 303 pages. 1999.

Vol. 1606: J. Mira, J.V. Sánchez-Andrés (Eds.), Foundations and Tools for Neural Modeling. Proceedings, Vol. I, 1999. XXIII, 865 pages. 1999.

Vol. 1607: J. Mira, J.V. Sánchez-Andrés (Eds.), Engineering Applications of Bio-Inspired Artificial Neural Networks. Proceedings, Vol. II, 1999. XXIII, 907 pages. 1999.

Vol. 1609: Z. W. Raś, A. Skowron (Eds.), Foundations of Intelligent Systems. Proceedings, 1999. XII, 676 pages. 1999. (Subseries LNAI).

Vol. 1610: G. Cornuéjols, R.E. Burkard, G.J. Woeginger (Eds.), Integer Programming and Combinatorial Optimization. Proceedings, 1999. IX, 453 pages. 1999.

Vol. 1611: I. Imam, Y. Kodratoff, A. El-Dessouki, M. Ali (Eds.), Multiple Approaches to Intelligent Systems. Proceedings, 1999. XIX, 899 pages. 1999. (Subseries LNAI).

Vol. 1612: R. Bergmann, S. Breen, M. Göker, M. Manago, S. Wess, Developing Industrial Case-Based Reasoning Applications. XX, 188 pages. 1999. (Subseries LNAI).

Vol. 1614: D.P. Huijsmans, A.W.M. Smeulders (Eds.), Visual Information and Information Systems. Proceedings, 1999. XVII, 827 pages. 1999.

Vol. 1615: C. Polychronopoulos, K. Joe, A. Fukuda, S. Tomita (Eds.), High Performance Computing. Proceedings, 1999. XIV, 408 pages. 1999.

Vol. 1617: N.V. Murray (Ed.), Automated Reasoning with Analytic Tableaux and Related Methods. Proceedings, 1999. X, 325 pages. 1999. (Subseries LNAI).

Vol. 1620: W. Horn, Y. Shahar, G. Lindberg, S. Andreassen, J. Wyatt (Eds.), Artificial Intelligence in Medicine. Proceedings, 1999. XIII, 454 pages. 1999. (Subseries LNAI).

Vol. 1621: D. Fensel, R. Studer (Eds.), Knowledge Acquisition Modeling and Management. Proceedings, 1999. XI, 404 pages. 1999. (Subseries LNAI).

Vol. 1622: M. González Harbour, J.A. de la Puente (Eds.), Reliable Software Technologies – Ada-Europe'99. Proceedings, 1999. XIII, 451 pages. 1999.

Vol. 1625: B. Reusch (Ed.), Computational Intelligence. Proceedings, 1999. XIV, 710 pages. 1999.

Vol. 1626: M. Jarke, A. Oberweis (Eds.), Advanced Information Systems Engineering. Proceedings, 1999. XIV, 478 pages. 1999.

Col. 1628: R. Guerraoui (Ed.), ECOOP'99 - Object-Oriented Programming. Proceedings, 1999. XIII, 529 pages. 1999.

Vol. 1629: H. Leopold, N. García (Eds.), Multimedia Applications, Services and Techniques - ECMAST'99. Proceedings, 1999. XV, 574 pages. 1999.

Vol. 1634: S. Džeroski, P. Flach (Eds.), Inductive Logic Programming. Proceedings, 1999. VIII, 303 pages. 1999. (Subseries LNAI).

Vol. 1639: S. Donatelli, J. Kleijn (Eds.), Application and Theory of Petri Nets 1999. Proceedings, 1999. VIII, 425 pages. 1999.